PRAISE FOR
The Road to the Dark Tower

"Vincent proves himself a master of the Dark Tower world."

—*Publishers Weekly*

"There's much . . . literature on Stephen King's work, but most of it can be skipped. Not so with Vincent's *The Road to the Dark Tower*, the first full-length study of King's thirty-year opus, a book-by-book summary with explanations and commentary." —Charles N. Brown, *Locus*

"Vincent has done yeoman's work here. While *The Road to the Dark Tower* will not be the last word on Roland's quest and the Stephen King Universe, it will undoubtedly be the standard by which all future works on the subject will be judged." —Joe Hartlaub, Bookreporter.com

"An excellent and maybe even vital guide to King's grand opus."

—Faren C. Miller, *Locus*

THE
DARK TOWER
COMPANION

A Guide to Stephen King's Epic Fantasy

BEV VINCENT

NEW AMERICAN LIBRARY
Published by the Penguin Group
Penguin Group (USA) Inc., 375 Hudson Street,
New York, New York 10014, USA

USA / Canada / UK / Ireland / Australia / New Zealand / India / South Africa / China

Penguin Books Ltd., Registered Offices: 80 Strand, London WC2R 0RL, England
For more information about the Penguin Group visit penguin.com.

First published by New American Library,
a division of Penguin Group (USA) Inc.

First Printing, April 2013
10   9   8   7   6   5   4   3   2   1

 REGISTERED TRADEMARK—MARCA REGISTRADA

LIBRARY OF CONGRESS CATALOGING-IN-PUBLICATION DATA:

Vincent, Bev.
    The Dark Tower companion: a guide to Stephen King's epic fantasy/Bev Vincent.
        p. cm.
    ISBN 978-0-451-23799-6
    1. King, Stephen, 1947– Dark tower.   2. Fantasy fiction, American—History and
criticism.   3. Roland (Fictitious character: King)   I. Title.
    PS3561.I483D3757 2013
    813'.54—dc23   2012036847

Set in Times New Roman
Designed by Spring Hoteling

Printed in the United States of America

PUBLISHER'S NOTE
While the author has made every effort to provide accurate telephone numbers, Internet addresses
and other contact information at the time of publication, neither the publisher nor the author assumes
any responsibility for errors, or for changes that occur after publication. Further, publisher does not
have any control over and does not assume any responsibility for author or third-party Web sites or
their content.

For Virginia

TABLE OF CONTENTS

THE
DARK TOWER
COMPANION

INTRODUCTION

In my first book, *The Road to the Dark Tower*, published a month after the final installment in Stephen King's Dark Tower series in 2004, I wrote for an audience who had already read to the end of book seven. The only way to discuss the significance of certain events in the first book as they related to the way the series ended was to talk about how the series ended. For that reason, the introduction to that book warned readers to set it aside until they reached the final page of *The Dark Tower*.

This book is aimed at a different audience. My assumption is that you haven't necessarily read the entire series, or that you are currently reading it. Perhaps you became interested because of the Marvel graphic novel adaptations and want to learn more about certain characters, events or locations. Maybe the concept of *ka* has you a little mystified and you'd like to find out what it really means. Perhaps you took a break between reading *The Waste Lands* and *Wizard and Glass* and you'd like to refresh your memory of the earlier books. Maybe you're planning a trip to Manhattan and would like to visit some of the real or imaginary locations mentioned in the series. The Dark Tower really does stand at the corner of Second Avenue and 46th Street in Turtle Bay—and Maturin dwells nearby, too. Or maybe you've read the entire series but you can't remember who Theresa Maria Dolores O'Shyven is. If any of these apply, this book is for you.

The spoilers come sequentially. At the end of each chapter about one of the individual books, you'll find a labeled, easily avoided section where I mention a few things that the book foreshadows about the rest of the series. The glossary is a different matter—each entry there contains a summary of everything known about the person, place or thing, so if you read the entry about the Dark Tower itself, you will see things you might not want to know until you're done with the series.

A few things have changed in the Dark Tower universe since 2004. First, there is the Marvel graphic novel series that tells Roland Deschain's story between his coming of age and the end of *The Gunslinger*. Though these comics adapt existing material from the Dark Tower novels, they also expand upon it. Some incidents that are mentioned in passing in King's books are developed into full scenes. For example, *The Long Road Home* turns a few pages from *Wizard and Glass* detailing Roland, Cuthbert and Alain's journey back to Gilead after their adventures in Mejis into a five-issue adventure. The story of the fall of Gilead has never been told before, so the Marvel graphic novels venture into uncharted territory there. At the helm is Robin Furth, King's research assistant when he was working on the latter volumes in the original series, so the graphic novel series is in hands that respect the Dark Tower mythos; however, these stories diverge from King's at times because of the nature of the graphic format. You'll hear from many of the writers and artists involved about their contributions to the series.

There have been developments at King's Web site, too. The Dark Tower section has undergone a couple of redesigns since the series ended, the most recent in 2012. In 2009, the site debuted an interactive game called Discordia, in which players play the part of Tet Corporation's Op19, who explores the Dixie Pig, the "mind-trap" tunnel leading to Fedic and, ultimately, Mid-World and the rotunda at the Fedic Dogan. Discordia represents another component of the expanded universe of the Dark Tower, one that is also directed by Robin Furth, who, together with a team of collaborators, developed an intricate mythos around the battle between Tet Corporation and Sombra/North Central Positronics and how this conflict opened the way for a mobster with a Dark Tower fascination to make her way to Mid-World. Phase II of this game—the Mid-World section—launched in early 2013, and Phase III is in development.

Attempts to adapt the series for film have come and gone. Ron Howard currently owns the rights and seems eager to adapt the series in his unique hybrid vision of film and TV miniseries. Hear what he and screenwriter Akiva Goldsman have to say about their plans.

And, finally, we have an eighth novel in the Dark Tower series: *The Wind Through the Keyhole*, which King has dubbed "The Dark Tower 4.5." The Voice of the Turtle spoke once again and King found himself revisiting Roland, Eddie, Jake, Susannah and Oy, filling in a gap in the "contemporary" story of the *ka-tet*'s quest, adding another incident from the young gunslinger's adventures and introducing readers to a "fairy tale" from the olden days of Mid-World.

This companion contains a list of all the characters, places and things from the eight Dark Tower novels and the Marvel graphic novel series. You'd be *ka-mai* not to check it out.

Finally, King talks about the series and reveals a few secrets. For the first time ever, he reveals the name of Roland's sister. Did you even know Roland had a sister? You do now!

WHAT'S IT ALL ABOUT?

The Dark Tower is a series of eight novels written by Stephen King between 1970 and 2011, set (mostly) in an alternate reality called Mid-World. The books detail a gunslinger's quest to save the Dark Tower, which is the linchpin of reality. The series combines the feel of a Clint Eastwood Western with the epic scope of *The Lord of the Rings* and the horrors of, well, a Stephen King novel.

The gunslinger's name is Roland Deschain. He was born into one of the noble families of Gilead in the Barony of New Canaan, the hub of "In-World." He is the equivalent of one of King Arthur's Knights of the Round Table, except he carries revolvers instead of a sword. The other big difference is that, in his universe, Arthur Eld died many generations before. The other gunslingers of Roland's time were mostly descendants of Arthur Eld, but they too are dead, and Gilead was destroyed in a civil war. Roland is the last of his kind, and he has been wandering Mid-World for hundreds of years in search of his destination.

Technically, Mid-World is just one region of Roland's universe, which consists of In-World, Mid-World and End-World, territories that become decreasingly civilized the farther one gets from Gilead, the home base of Arthur Eld's gunslingers. However, Mid-World has become synonymous with Roland's world.

The name calls to mind Middle Earth from J. R. R. Tolkien's saga. There are similarities and differences. For the most part, Mid-World is populated by humans. There *are* nonhuman creatures, and even monsters, but except for one or two groups, they don't have cultures like the elves, dwarves, orcs and hobbits of Tolkien.

Mid-World exists in a universe parallel to our own. Some geographic locations can be seen as analogs of ones from Earth. The River Whye is like the Mississippi and the Clean Sea is akin to the Gulf of Mexico, for example. Lud is located geographically near St. Louis but is physically similar to Manhattan. Discordia is apparently west of the White Mountains in New Hampshire.

In most ways, Mid-World is medieval. However, traces of technology date back to a once-thriving ultramodern civilization known as the Old People or the Great Old Ones. Most of this technology is broken. Other modern contraptions may appear in Mid-World because they were brought from another world—including our own—because some people still know the secret of how to travel between universes. It is conceivable that the Great Old Ones were people from our modern Earth who traveled to Mid-World in its distant past.

Mid-World is falling apart. People call this process "moving on." Civilization has, for the most part, collapsed. Gilead, once the center of a feudal realm akin to King Arthur's—or to the Roman Empire—has been gone for centuries, defeated by insurrection and hubris. The great cities have fallen, technology has failed, and mutations run rampant among animals and even some humans.

Worse still, the once reliable physical constants of time, distance and direction are adrift. What was southeast one day may be south-southeast the next. The distance from Gilead to the Western (Pacific) Sea was once only a thousand miles, but it took Roland hundreds of years to cross it. And during those hundreds of years, Roland glanced off the surface of time the way a flat rock skips off the surface of water. He appears to be middle-aged, but he's far, far older.

The reason everything is falling apart can be traced to the Dark Tower. In one respect, the Tower is simply a building located in End-World. Imagine a black lighthouse that has a varicolored oriel window at the top and a series of balconies that follow a helical pattern around its exterior, corresponding to the windows found in rooms that extend off the spiral staircase inside. There are spires at the top, and it sits in the middle of a field of roses.

However, the Dark Tower is also the axis around which all of the (presumably) infinite versions of reality rotate. It is the sun in the solar system of reality. Each level (or floor) of the Tower corresponds to a different world. Many worlds are nearly identical, differing only in subtle details. The dollar bill has a different president on it in one parallel world. New York's Co-Op City is in Brooklyn in one reality and in the Bronx in another. The town at the end of the George Washington Bridge is Fort Lee in one world and Leabrook in another. Other worlds, though, are vastly different from ours—Mid-World is one example. In each of these parallel universes, there is something that represents the Dark Tower. In the most important version of our world (known as Keystone Earth), it is represented by a pink rose that grows in a vacant lot in Manhattan.

The Dark Tower arose out of the magical primordial soup of creation in Mid-World. It is supported by six magical Beams that extend from one end of the known universe to the other, all intersecting above the Tower. Left alone, there was enough magic to hold the Tower up forever. However, the Great Old Ones, slaves to technology, mistrusted magic and replaced the Beams with artificial, scientific equivalents. After they died off—or killed one another off in a great war—there was no one left to tend to them, so they have been failing ever since.

Even so, the Beams should have lasted for many centuries. Their decline is accelerated by the work of an evil being known as the Crimson King. He hates creation and wants to destroy it, returning the world to chaos, where he will be the king in more than just name. He has minions (one of them travels under various guises, including the man in black, Walter o'Dim, Marten Broadcloak and Randall Flagg) and kidnappers who round up psychics and force them to weaken the Beams, bringing about the premature collapse of the Tower. If the Tower falls in Mid-World, all of reality will collapse. Roland's quest, then, is about more than saving one world. It is a mission to save all of creation.

Roland doesn't know all of this when he sets out as a young man. He knows only that the Tower is in trouble and that he needs to reach it to save it. Part of him isn't even sure the Tower exists, because a lot of what he thinks he knows about his world is myth and legend. However, during his quest he learns more and more details that tell him where he needs to go and what he needs to do when he gets there.

The term "*ka-tet*" describes a group of people united in a common mission. Roland sets out alone in search of the Dark Tower after his original *ka-tet* (a group that included Cuthbert Allgood, Alain Johns and Jamie De-Curry) is killed during the last great battle between the gunslingers of Gilead and their adversaries. He has no direction to guide him—directions aren't reliable anymore, even if he did.

In the beginning, he's not very likable. Solitude has turned him cold and ruthless. Saving the universe is a serious mission, and he takes it so seriously that he's willing to sacrifice anything and anyone to accomplish it. This is one reason why some readers have found *The Gunslinger* a difficult book.

Gradually, though, starting with *The Drawing of the Three*, Roland assembles a new *ka-tet*. He doesn't simply pluck people from thin air, nor do they start following him of their own volition, like children trailing after the pied piper. In Egyptian mythology, the word "*ka*" represents the life force that is imparted from the gods. In the Dark Tower series, it is a force in the universe that wants Roland's mission to succeed. In one sense, *ka* is personified by Stephen King who is, after all, Roland's creator and has the power to give him the tools he needs to accomplish his goal. Primary among Roland's requirements—especially after *ka* delivers a serious setback at the beginning of the second book in the series—is a set of people with special, though unexpected, characteristics. *Ka* puts these people in Roland's path and he plucks them out of their ordinary lives and drags them along kicking and screaming.

Eddie Dean, Odetta Holmes and Jake Chambers all come from our world, specifically from New York City. At first they seem like an unlikely group of heroes: a junkie, a legless kleptomaniac with multiple personality disorder and a preteen boy, combined with a doglike creature that can bark in words. None of them volunteers for this assignment but, though they resist at first, ultimately they adopt the mission as their own.

As the quest develops, it expands to include both Mid-World and our world, with frequent trips back and forth between the two. Similarly, King's Dark Tower saga jumps back and forth between the books in the series and other novels published between installments in the series. Characters and concepts are often introduced in nonseries books before they show up in the main series itself. Just about everything King has ever written is about the Dark Tower in one way or another.

Where did the idea for this sprawling series come from?

INSPIRATION AND INFLUENCES

King has discussed the primary influences that inspired him to begin a series that has been a major part of his writing career. Initially, a number of disparate things came together. One of these is fairly abstract: King acquired a ream of oddly shaped and garishly colored paper. This green paper seemed to demand something special, and parts of the opening sections of *The Gunslinger* were typed on it.

Then there was the compulsion to write a quest. As a university student in the late sixties, he couldn't help but be aware of *The Lord of the Rings*, Tolkien's epic saga. King was young and ambitious—so much so that he entertained the idea of writing the longest popular novel in history.

Two years before he graduated from the University of Maine, King studied "Childe Roland to the Dark Tower Came," a romantic poem by Robert Browning about a knight-errant on a quest to find a mysterious Dark Tower. The poem's influence is readily apparent—not only did King name his protagonist after the poem's lead character and utilize the goal of reaching the Dark Tower, but he used other elements from the poem as well. Cuthbert's name comes from the text. Touch points appear throughout the series—from a picture of Browning on the calendar in Calvin Tower's storage room office, to the subtle use of the phrase "not-see" as a soundalike for Nazi in the story of David Quick and the water-rats Mia consumes, to the more literal appearance of a photocopy of the poem in the final book.

King was also fascinated by spaghetti Westerns such as *The Good, the Bad and the Ugly* and *The Magnificent Seven*. Some of these films starred Clint Eastwood as a taciturn and violence-prone cowboy with a well-defined (though sometimes morally skewed) code of conduct. For many years, readers of the series saw Eastwood as Roland Deschain. Even Roland's companions make the comparison, and many of the artists who have depicted Roland were inspired by Eastwood as well. While there's no chance Clint will ever play Roland in a film adaptation, the comparison will always exist.

King was intrigued by the possibility of blending the epic fantasy novel with the Western. He underscored the influence of these films in *Wolves of the Calla*, the fifth book in the series. The novel is a variation on the story of *The Magnificent Seven* (itself a remake of the Japanese film *Seven Samurai*), and the name of the town that seeks the gunslinger's help—Calla Bryn Sturgis— alludes to John Sturges, who directed *The Magnificent Seven*. Eddie Dean, who saw many of these spaghetti Westerns when he was a teenager, eventually realizes the similarity between their adventure and the film—an important discovery about the nature of their reality.

The Dark Tower series follows Joseph Campbell's hero's journey in some aspects and diverges from it in others. At its heart, though, it is a quest wherein one man has a monumental goal that causes him to embark on a great journey. *The Lord of the Rings*, though it spawned many imitators, is an unusual quest story. In most, the hero and his followers set out to find something. In *The Lord of the Rings*, Frodo and Sam are tasked with destroying something they already possess. The quest element comes in their need to get to the only location in Middle Earth where the ring can be destroyed.

The archetype for the quest is the story of King Arthur's knights, who are dispatched to locate the Holy Grail. Arthur senses that his empire is falling apart and comes up with a mission to unify his followers under a common goal. Similarly, Roland Deschain's Mid-World is falling apart, for some of the same reasons. The gunslingers of Gilead, analogs to King Arthur's knights, have become so obsessed with the problem of the Dark Tower that they neglect to take care of the immediate issues facing their empire. Those they are meant to govern are growing disenchanted because they are paying taxes without receiving anything in return. Rebels are organizing against them. It's understandable that the gunslingers might dismiss anything that isn't as important as the end of reality, but the rebellion destroys their ability to do anything about the problem of the Dark Tower.

Getting back to King Arthur—the inspiration here is, again, obvious. The first leader to unify the various Baronies and kingdoms of All-World was Arthur Eld. He had a sword called Excalibur. His chief adviser was a magician named Maerlyn. One of his ill-begotten descendants is named Mordred. Though the reign of Arthur Eld takes place long before even the earliest stories in the Dark Tower mythos, his presence is felt throughout. Roland of Gilead is also Roland of the Eld. Most gunslingers are directly descended from Arthur. Roland's gun barrels are made from the metal of Excalibur's blade.

Finally, one of the most intriguing inspirations for the Dark Tower series is Stephen King himself. One of Michael Whelan's early illustrations of Roland, used for the cover of the Plume trade paperback of *The Gunslinger* in 1988, was based on a profile shot of the author. Over the years, the series began to extend tentacles into many of King's other works. Were the Territories that Jack Sawyer visited in *The Talisman* a part of Mid-World? Ultimately, we discover that they were. Did Mrs. Todd's shortcut take her through a thinny? Perhaps. Though some of these crossovers are subtle, the influence of the Dark Tower became more pervasive. King's 1994 novel *Insomnia* is for all intents and purposes a Dark Tower novel, although Roland appears only in a brief cameo. In the 1990s, he used his nonseries books as "proving grounds" in which he introduced concepts and characters that would become crucial to the series. Low men, the Crimson King, Breakers, Ted Brautigan, Dinky Earnshaw—all of these appeared first in nonseries books and stories.

And then the books themselves became part of the series, as did their author. When King was nearly killed in a car-pedestrian accident in 1999, he realized that there was a possibility that if the creator were killed—or died of natural causes, even—the series would remain incomplete. Roland's quest would never succeed. So he wrote that into the story. The Crimson King is aware that Stephen King is the creative force driving Roland and his friends from the Western Sea to Lud to the Callas and onward. If he can stop Stephen King, he can stop Roland. Stephen King scholars pore over his works looking for clues that will help Roland. Other characters discover that they are characters from a Stephen King novel—a cause of great existential angst.

So King became his own inspiration and influence, along with all of the other factors mentioned above. No wonder the series is often considered to be his magnum opus. It consists not only of the seven—now eight—books, but everything he has ever written, because he is a character in the story.

"The Little Sisters of Eluria"

The novella "The Little Sisters of Eluria," first published in Robert Silverberg's anthology *Legends* in 1998, relates an incident that takes place after the battle of Jericho Hill and before Roland Deschain ends up in the Mohaine Desert on the trail of the man in black. As such, it is the earliest appearance of Roland outside of the stories of his youth in *Wizard and Glass* and *The Wind Through the Keyhole*.

The idea behind *Legends* was that it would feature self-contained stories set in each author's respective fictional universe. People unfamiliar with a particular ongoing epic fantasy could sample it and perhaps be inspired to tackle the series. As a stand-alone, "The Little Sisters of Eluria" could be read before, during or after the Dark Tower books. However, *The Gunslinger* is a difficult book. This novella is a more accessible introduction to Roland, since it shows him during a transitional phase. He's alone, but he doesn't shun companionship. His skills are still developing, and he's prone to making potentially lethal mistakes, but he is growing to understand that *ka* may want him to succeed at his quest.

King said that he accepted Silverberg's invitation to write about Roland in a moment of weakness. It took him a while to come up with a story. He started with a series of images: the pavilion from *The Talisman* in ruins. Whispering women who were ghosts or vampires. Nurses of death instead of life. Once he got started, though, he had trouble keeping it down to novella length. "Everything about Roland and his friends wants to be not just long but sort of *epic*," he wrote in the story's introduction when it was reprinted in *Everything's Eventual* in 2002.

It is impossible to pinpoint exactly when this story takes place in Roland's time line. In the Marvel adaptation, Robin Furth places it a year after the battle of Jericho Hill. According to the text, Roland looks at least twenty years older than the teenager he encounters.

Roland is wandering around in Mid-World, trying to find a clue that will lead him to the Tower. The world is moving on, so he isn't surprised to arrive at a ghost town. Eluria isn't completely abandoned—there are mutants in the area, the product of something toxic in the mines beneath the Desatoya Mountains—but there are also signs of recent habitation, including a fresh body in a horse trough. The mutants pose a threat, but Roland won't shoot them without provocation. He pays for this error in judgment when they overwhelm him, almost ending his quest for the Dark Tower before it really gets started.

He wakes up in a hospital tent, suspended in a harness, in pain. The female voices he hears make him remember Susan Delgado, the first woman he ever loved, though he was only fourteen at the time and she was just sixteen. He's in the care of the Little Sisters and, while they appear human, he soon discovers that they are terrible creatures who are attended by scuttling black bugs known as little doctors. The bugs heal their patients so the Little Sisters, who are vampires, can feed on them. The only thing saving Roland is the religious medallion hanging around his neck, which he took from the dead body in Eluria.

The boy in the bed next to Roland is John Norman of Delain. Roland pretends to be John's brother—it is James Norman's medallion he's wearing. The Normans were part of a caravan that was waylaid by slow mutants as they passed near Eluria. The mutants have an uneasy alliance with the Little Sisters. The mutants supply the Little Sisters with their living victims, but they get to keep the provisions they steal from them. The Little Sisters have no need for material goods.

The Little Sisters drug Roland's food but are thwarted by the gold charm. The youngest of them, Jenna, befriends Roland. She wears the Dark Bells that give her the power to summon the little doctor bugs, acquired through lineage. The eldest of the group, Sister Mary, resents that Jenna has this honor, which she feels is rightfully hers.

The Little Sisters enlist the help of one of the smarter slow mutants to remove John's medallion, leaving Roland as the only remaining food. Because Roland is kind to Jenna, she decides to help him. She gives him a stimulant to counter the sedative, returns his guns and decides to leave with him. She no longer wishes to partake of a blood diet, but she is damned already.

She summons the little doctors to destroy one of the other Little Sisters who tries to intervene, and they make good on their escape. When Sister Mary catches up with them, Roland has no weapons to use against her. However, *ka*, the indomitable force that wants Roland to succeed on his quest, sends a dog bearing a cross-shaped patch of fur to kill Sister Mary. The dog doesn't exactly come out of nowhere—Roland first saw it in the town square in Eluria—but almost. Later, in a dream, the dog leads him to the Dark Tower.

Jenna collapses into a swarm of the little doctor bugs when she tries to leave with Roland. The other Little Sisters will pull up stakes and go on. They have survived for a long, long time and will presumably continue in a new setting. Roland heads west. He has no tangible destination in mind yet—he has not yet found the trail of the man in black or one of the Beams that will guide him to the Tower. All he can do is search.

> **Characters (in order of mention):** Roland, Cuthbert, Chas. Freeborn, James Norman, slow mutants, Jamie DeCurry, Susan, Cort, Rhea, Sister Mary, Sister Louise, Sister Michela, Sister Coquina, Sister Tamra, Sister Jenna, John Norman, Barons, Ralph, Smasher.
>
> **Places:** Gilead, Desatoya Mountains, the Bustling Pig, Mid-World, Eluria, Lexingworth, Dark Tower, Mejis, Thoughtful House, Tejuas, End-World, Delain, Great House, Kambero.
>
> **Things:** Full Earth, Topsy, pube, *sigul*, cully, *ka-tet*, Dark Bells, pop-kin, Kissing Moon, *can-tam*, *ka*.
>
> **Crossovers to Other Works:** Eluria is near the Desatoya Mountains, which is also the site of the Nevada mine in *Desperation*. The Little Sisters speak the same language of the unformed as Tak. The great pavilion where Jack Sawyer first saw the Queen of the Territories in *The Talisman* inspired the story. The pavilion where he later meets Sophie in *Black House* once belonged to the Little Sisters. After telling Jack about the vampire nurses whose patients never heal who once used it, Sophie says that they also serve the Beam. The tent, she says, is perhaps the last one of the dozen or more that once existed in the Territories, On-World, and Mid-World. Jack Norman is from Delain, the realm of King Roland in *The Eyes of the Dragon*.
>
> **Foreshadowing and Spoilers:** One might wonder whether the Sisters of Serenity in *The Wind Through the Keyhole* were corrupted after the fall of Gilead and became the Little Sisters.

THE GUNSLINGER: RESUMPTION

S tephen King was only twenty-one years old when he wrote the most famous and memorable opening line of any of his books: "The man in black
fled across the desert, and the gunslinger followed." In a dozen words, he introduces readers to two characters and the setting, and creates a sense of action and conflict. One man is fleeing, another is pursuing. Because the story
and the book are titled *The Gunslinger*, readers will assume (correctly) that
the unnamed gunslinger is the protagonist.

Though King began writing the Dark Tower series in late 1970, none of
it was published for the better part of a decade, when the five stories that make
up *The Gunslinger* appeared in *The Magazine of Fantasy and Science Fiction*
(*F&SF*) between October 1978 and November 1981.

Because the tale was incomplete and set in an unfamiliar world, King had
no plans to collect the stories until Donald M. Grant asked whether he had
anything that might be suitable for his small press. *The Dark Tower: The
Gunslinger* was issued in 1982 as a signed, limited-edition and limited-trade
hardcover without much fanfare outside of the fantasy community. The book,
illustrated by Michael Whelan, was dedicated to Ed Ferman, the editor at
F&SF, thanking him for taking a chance on the stories.

When King listed *The Gunslinger* (as *The Dark Tower*) along with his
other publications at the front of *Pet Sematary* in 1983, he set off an avalanche
of inquiries about the book, which led to a second printing of the limited-
trade hardcover, though in numbers too small to satisfy demand. *The Gunslinger* wasn't available to the general public until it was released as a trade
paperback and an audiobook (narrated by King) in 1988.

Many years later, when he was preparing the final books in the series for
publication, King admitted that about half of his readership hadn't read the
Dark Tower. This was in part due to the fact that the series was long and—at

that point—incomplete, but could also be attributed to the fact that a lot of readers had problems with the first volume. It is very different in style and mood than the rest of King's work. The protagonist is sullen, dark, moody and driven. Some of the things he does in the name of his quest are hard to accept. King came to believe that the original version of *The Gunslinger* demonstrated the work of a pretentious young man exposed to far too many writing seminars. Its language and tone do not sound at all like the later books.

Because the book had never been copyedited and contained a number of continuity errors (Farson is a town in the first book, but a man in later volumes, for example), and because it was written long before he understood the entire scope of the series, King decided to revise *The Gunslinger* during a hiatus between editing *Wolves of the Calla* and *Song of Susannah*. If the Dark Tower series had been written in the same manner as his other novels, this would have been a natural part of the process. He would have gone back to the beginning to weave in elements of the story and its themes that weren't revealed to him until the series was complete. Readers can see how King's thinking about the story evolved early on by reading the notes that accompany the original publications of the short stories that make up *The Gunslinger*. In particular, he grapples with the man in black and his relationship to Walter and Marten.

The added material consists of about nine thousand words, or thirty-five pages of text. He reworked sentences and paragraphs and inserted foreshadowing, a prevailing sense of déjà vu and other details that hadn't occurred to him when he set the story down thirty years earlier. Gilead is never mentioned in the original version, nor are Arthur Eld, the Crimson King, Sheemie, the Manni, taheen, Algul Siento, bumblers or the commala dance.

Though the overall plot remains the same, some scenes have been expanded. The importance of certain characters changes. He follows his own advice from *On Writing* and removes most of the adverbs. These revisions, he says in the book's new foreword, were designed to give newcomers a slightly easier entry into the series.

Since the revised and expanded edition of *The Gunslinger* contains King's preferred text, for the purposes of this book, the original edition will be treated as a first draft and the differences between the two versions will be mentioned only when they are illuminating.

When the four existing Dark Tower novels were repackaged in 2003, they all bore new subtitles, each consisting of single word beginning with "re." For *The Gunslinger*, the subtitle was "Resumption," a word that is a vague clue, though its significance won't be revealed until much later in the series.

The linear story line of *The Gunslinger* is fairly simple. Roland Deschain buys a mule in Pricetown and arrives in Tull, where the man in black has set a trap for him after raising a man from the dead. Roland is forced to kill everyone in town, including a woman who became his lover. He follows the old stagecoach road southwest toward the desert and stops at a hut owned by a hermit named Brown, where he recounts his recent adventures. He follows the man in black's spoor, confident that he is getting closer, though he is still several weeks behind.

Almost out of water, he reaches a Way Station, where he mistakes the sole occupant of the abandoned inn for the man in black. However, it turns out to be a young boy named Jake Chambers, who was pushed in front of a car while on his way to school in Manhattan, died, and woke up in Roland's world. Jake joins Roland on a trek toward the mountains, where the gunslinger believes he will finally catch up with his prey. Roland seeks counsel from a succubus in a Speaking Circle and learns that Jake will need to be sacrificed if he is to attain his goal.

When they reach the mountains, they discover a tunnel that will take them through, following an old rail line. A group of slow mutants attacks, but Roland fends them off, rescuing Jake from their grasp. The farther they go, the more certain Jake becomes that he will die soon. He begs Roland to turn away and, for a moment, Roland almost agrees to do so. However, they see the light at the end of the tunnel, and Jake falls to his death on a decrepit trestle when Roland is forced to choose between rescuing him and speaking with the man in black.

The man in black and Roland hold palaver in a golgotha on the far side of the mountains, where much is revealed about Roland's quest and the nature of the universe. After they talk, Roland loses ten years of his life, but ends up on the coast of the sea.

Whereas most of King's novels tend to be about ordinary people thrust into extraordinary circumstances, Roland is no ordinary man. By the time *The Gunslinger* begins, he has been through major hardships. He's a desperate man on a demanding mission, traveling across a harsh environment. He is the last of his people. The world has moved on, people say, but it's not clear what that means. It might be a natural progression or it could have more ominous implications. King is stingy with the details about the cause of Mid-World's malaise—perhaps because he didn't understand them fully himself at the time.

The story is told in a nonlinear fashion, starting in the middle and backtracking to Pricetown. Mid-World is not the Earth, but it isn't entirely alien, either. Roland knows the song "Hey Jude" and certain brand names like Amoco. The setting feels like something from a Western movie, yet there are indications that the story might take place in the future, after some cataclysm has destroyed civilization. During Roland's travels, he encounters relics of an old but advanced society: atomic pumps and talking pushcarts that advertise unknown product brands, for example. The man in black says that the people of Roland's world once walked on the moon. There are references to the Great Old Ones, the mythic creators of the world whose wars may have led to their downfall and whose relics may still be lethal.

The language is littered with unknown, almost archaic words like "bucka." There is a stilted formality in their greeting: "Long days and pleasant nights." Roland grew up in an environment that is almost Arthurian. He lived in a castle, and a group of gunslingers ruled not only the local Barony (province), but also the surrounding Baronies as well. The alliance of these provinces is reminiscent of the Roman Empire, and it suffered from many of the same problems. Ultimately, the Affiliation fell.

Roland wasn't always solitary or hard, but even as a boy he was different from his peers. His father, Steven Deschain, was in line to become the *dinh* (leader) of the gunslingers who ruled In-World, the collection of Baronies that made up the Affiliation. Their domain is Gilead, the capital of the Barony of New Canaan, which is analogous to Camelot.

As a descendant of the great Arthur Eld, the first gunslinger, it was always Roland's destiny to train to be a gunslinger. Once he became an apprentice, his life changed. He no longer lived at home with his parents. He rarely saw his mother, Gabrielle Deschain, and when he did there was a distance between them caused by the formality and stringent requirements of his studies. His life seemed idyllic, with balls in the Great Hall of Gilead and all the associated pomp and circumstance. If all went according to plan, he would become a gunslinger, marry a young woman selected by his parents and become a member of the court, one of the prestigious and revered ruling class and in line to be the *dinh* himself someday.

Apprentice gunslingers attended classes taught by Abel Vannay and were trained in the arts of battle by Cort, a harsh taskmaster. He harangued and punished his young charges for any perceived lapse or failure. Ultimately, he decided if a student became a gunslinger. The final test came when an apprentice felt ready to challenge Cort in combat, using the weapon of his choice. Generally this challenge took place when the apprentice was between eighteen and twenty-four. Any older and the apprentice was deemed a failure and was forced to step away from the path. Roland's father was the youngest ever to take the coming-of-age test, sixteen.

Roland's childhood friends include Cuthbert Allgood, Alain Johns, Jamie DeCurry and Thomas Whitman, all gunslingers-in-training. By the time *The Gunslinger* opens, his friends are all dead, many of them killed at the battle of Jericho Hill, the last confrontation between the forces of Gilead and their enemies.

Roland is slow and methodical. Not imaginative or creative, but diligent and skilled. He doesn't think about matters deeply, but is troubled when he overhears a favorite cook named Hax plotting to send poisoned meat to a nearby town. Hax has aligned himself with John Farson, the so-called Good Man and leader of the rebellion against Gilead. This is part of his coming-of-age story, the realization that people are plotting against them. He is further dismayed when he realizes that some of the people who witness Hax's execution don't hide their support for the traitor. His eyes are opened to the condition of his world, though there is little he can do about it.

Corruption strikes close to home. Roland has been suspicious of the way Marten, the court magician and chief adviser to the gunslingers, has insinuated himself into the Deschain family. During one of the spring balls, Roland and his friends spy on the gunslingers and see Marten dancing with his mother, Gabrielle Deschain. Roland's father knows about the affair and is either unwilling to or incapable of doing anything about it. Perhaps he thinks he has the upper hand on Marten by not revealing what he knows, or maybe he has bigger problems to deal with, not realizing that this domestic discord has larger implications for Gilead.

Marten, who is constantly plotting the downfall of Gilead while pretending to be one of its great supporters, recognizes Roland as a future threat. He deliberately reveals to him that he is sleeping with his mother. He believes this will goad Roland into launching his challenge against Cort before he is ready.

Roland is two years younger than his father was when he became a gunslinger. If he fails, he will be sent west into exile, never to see his family or friends again. However, Marten underestimates Roland's cunning and his willingness to sacrifice a longtime friend—his hawk, David—in the name of his goal. It is a side of Roland that will become more obvious during his quest to reach the Dark Tower. Many friends will fall by the wayside or be left behind because he believes his goal is more important than any one person. This story has particular resonance for Jake, who believes—correctly—that he will be another of these sacrifices. Another hawk to be thrown in the face of an adversary.

After Roland defeats him, Cort counsels the new gunslinger to let the news of his victory spread instead of going after Marten straightaway. Cort knows that Roland might not win against the sorcerer, who is more devious than Roland will ever be. Though Roland doesn't tell Jake what happened next, he does reveal that Gilead fell within five years and that Roland's parents were both killed. Ominously, Roland says that he killed his mother, an event that—regardless of the circumstances—must weigh heavily on his conscience.

The other revelation from Roland's past comes from his dreams of Susan Delgado, whom he loved and lost. The details of their romance and how she ended up dying in a fire form a major part of the fourth book in the series, *Wizard and Glass*.

All of this serves to explain to the reader some of the reasons why Roland is the way he is: determined, driven and oblivious to the rest of humanity. In his solitude, he has honed his skills as a gunslinger. When he springs the trap that the man in black left for him in Tull, he is capable of taking care of himself, even when beset by dozens of people armed with rocks and sticks. Almost every bullet he fires finds its target, and he can reload on the fly without missing a beat. He has no compunctions about slaughtering men, women and children, including a woman whose bed he recently occupied. He must succeed; hence they must die. He believes—and he may be correct in this, but there's no concrete evidence to support it—that only he can save the Dark Tower.

Walter, the man in black, is a man of many faces and names, whose path will cross Roland's several more times before the quest reaches its conclusion. He taunts Roland, though his purposes are veiled. There's no indication that he truly believes any of the traps he lays for the gunslinger will succeed. He appears to be enjoying their game of cat and mouse. The ideograms left behind in his campfire ashes could be messages, but if they are, Roland doesn't understand them. There are also signs during their palaver that he isn't omniscient or infallible.

One question that arises in *The Gunslinger* is the matter of Roland's age. He appears to be an ordinary man, but Gilead fell in the distant past—perhaps centuries or millennia ago. Roland claims that he has skipped entire generations, without explaining what that means, and says that he has spent a thousand years learning the skills of a gunslinger. After his palaver with the man in black, he ages ten years overnight. Is he slipping through time, or is time slipping past him? Stephen King addresses that issue in the interview found later in this book.

At the heart of the story is the Dark Tower, though its nature is not explained in this book. Roland needs to reach it, and it is in some kind of danger, but King did not yet understand what all of this meant to Roland's world when he wrote the novel.

Though *The Gunslinger* focuses primarily on Roland and his pursuit of the man in black, Jake Chambers is also important. Though he dies twice over the course of the book—once offstage, before he arrives at the Way Station—this is not the last that readers will see of the boy. One of the subtle changes King made to the book when revising it in 2003 was to strengthen Jake's character, given his future importance to Roland's quest. In the first version, he was docile and weaker, whereas in the revised version, he speaks up for himself. Though he understands his fate and is powerless to change it, he does not go gently.

King must have sensed that Jake would be important to the story, given how much time he spends exploring the boy's past life. Jake is a latchkey kid whose father is an executive at a major television network and whose mother neglects him. That's not to say he isn't loved—the housekeeper, Greta Shaw, is tender toward him, and even Roland comes to love the boy soon after they meet. Jake's introduction into the story reveals the fact that there is a connection between Roland's world and ours, and that there are ways of getting from one to the other. Roland has always heard this was possible—a religious order called the Manni were said to be able to travel between worlds—but he had believed it to be a myth, like many stories about his world.

One major difference between Roland's world and ours is the presence of magic. The clearest example of this is when Walter raises Nort the Weedeater from the dead, but there are other signs of the supernatural as well. Demons live in Roland's world, including the Speaking Demon he encounters in the basement of the Way Station and the succubus he consults in the Speaking Ring shortly before they reach the mountains. These are not unexpected encounters. Roland knows the rules of dealing with demons. He is not amazed to discover that the man in black can perform magic tricks. In fact, he relies on magic constantly. He carries a "grow bag," in which things miraculously appear when he needs them.

Though the Oracle's message and the details revealed by the man in black when he reads the tarot cards for Roland lay out some of what will transpire in *The Drawing of the Three*, an argument could be made that Roland does not gain much assistance from these insights. He is told what will happen, and it happens. He doesn't even remember a lot of what the man in black tells him, shrugging it off as if it doesn't matter.

However, he sacrificed a lot—much more than is apparent at this point in his story—to gain this information. Given the fact that the man in black is a habitual liar, he cannot place much faith in what he is told during their palaver at the golgotha. Walter is, after all, a minion of the Crimson King, who wants nothing more than to see Roland fail. He may claim that Jake must die before they can palaver, or that he has to talk if Roland catches him, but that doesn't mean he's speaking the truth. By encouraging Roland to sacrifice the boy, he adds significantly to the moral imbalance of the gunslinger's soul.

The tarot reading ends with Death, the Tower and Life. Walter doesn't add the final card to the spread but instead throws it into the fire. It is a card— and a gesture—that readers are not meant to understand yet, but the implications will become known later in the series.

Through their discussion, readers gain a bit of insight into Roland's ultimate motivation: he intends to find the Tower and mount its stairs to the top, where all universes meet. An element of hubris is associated with this mission: Roland believes that God has dared to enter this room, so why should he not? Assuming that there is a god.

The first book ends when Roland reaches the Western Sea, which is ironic. The punishment for failing the challenge to become a gunslinger is to be sent west, and that's where Roland ends up. Once this sea was only a thousand miles from Gilead, but the world is expanding and his journey has taken him many times farther than that. Time, distance and direction have been set adrift and Roland is still casting about, seeking direction.

Things are about to change for him, and fast.

> **Characters (in order of mention):** The man in black (Walter o'Dim), Roland Deschain, Manni, taheen, Cort, Brown, Sheemie, Sheb, Nort the Weedeater, Jubal Kennerly, Alice (Allie), Zachary, Amy Feldon, Aunt Mill, Soobie Kennerly, Susan Delgado, Eldred Jonas, Coffin Hunters, Castner, Sylvia Pittston, Jonson, John (Jake) Chambers, Greta Shaw, Cuthbert Allgood, Alain Johns, Jamie DeCurry, Merlin, Arthur Eld, Hax, slow mutants, Maggie, Farson, Robeson, Steven Deschain, Vannay, Oracle, Rhea, Charles (son of Charles), Aileen Ritter, Gabrielle Deschain, Thomas Whitman, Mark, Ageless Stranger.

Places: Mohaine Desert, Jericho Hill, Algul Siento (Blue Heaven), In-World, Tull, Mid-World, Garlan, Pricetown, Sheb's, Gilead, Mejis, Clean Sea, Way Station, Piper School, Manhattan, Lud, South Islands, Taunton, Hendrickson, Gallows Hill, Forest o'Barony, New Canaan, King's Town, Na'ar, the Western Sea.

Things: Zoltan, billy-bumblers, Watch Me, High Speech, devil-grass, nineteen, LaMerk, the Dark Tower, North Central Positronics, Old Mother, Horn o'Deschain, David, charyou tree, Amoco, Crisp-A-La, Larchies, not-man.

Foreshadowing and Spoilers: The revised version of *The Gunslinger* has numerous elements that allude to the ending of the series, including the subtitle, Roland's sense of disorientation at the beginning, the pervasive sense of déjà vu, Walter's veiled comments to past iterations of his quest and the recurring motif of wheels and circles. Walter tells Roland he stands close to the Tower in time, but what he is really referring to is the past—Roland has just come from the Tower. Roland is oblivious to most of this, just as he fails to appreciate the significance of the pattern of the clouds that Allie points out in Tull, which is a clear indicator that he is near a Path of the Beam. If he had noticed that fact, he might have given up his pursuit and headed straight for the Tower. Also in Tull, Roland encounters— or thinks of—characters who played an important part in his past shortly after he became a gunslinger. Roland's vision of a bullet exploding in his hand while hypnotizing Jake foreshadows the injury he will suffer in the next book. When Jake and Roland leave the Way Station, Jake feels like someone is watching them. This is Father Callahan, who will report having watched two people in the distance after he was drawn to the Way Station after his death. The Oracle predicts the arrival of Eddie Dean, Susannah and Jack Mort in the next book.

THE DRAWING OF THE THREE: RENEWAL

King had already written sections of the next cycle of stories, originally titled *Roland Draws Three*, when *The Gunslinger* appeared in 1982. The first forty handwritten pages of the book vanished, however, and he still doesn't know what happened to them.

The first chapter of *The Drawing of the Three* was published in the April/May 1987 issue of *Castle Rock: The Stephen King Newsletter,* and Donald M. Grant published the limited and limited-trade editions, illustrated by Phil Hale, shortly thereafter. King dedicated the book to Grant for taking a chance on the novels one by one.

Like *The Gunslinger*, *The Drawing of the Three* was not copyedited prior to publication. It contains more mistakes than any other book in the series. Character names change from one page to the next, and several geographical details are wrong. King will subsequently use these errors as part of the story. Some will become cues that let readers know whether something is taking place in one version of reality or another. Many of them, though, are simply mistakes and no meaning should be read into them.

The second book in the series opens on the beach by the Western Sea seven hours after the end of *The Gunslinger* and relates events that take place over about a month. During this period, Roland makes no forward progress toward the Dark Tower. He probably gets farther from it as he makes his way up the coastline.

He is dealt a major setback within the first few pages. Though he has just slept for an unknown length of time after his palaver with the man in black, he is dead tired. He falls asleep on the beach. The incoming tide awakens him and, to his horror, he discovers that some of his limited supply of ammunition has gotten wet. He doesn't know if any given bullet will work when needed.

Worse, though, is the grievous injury delivered to him by a lobsterlike monster that emerges from the ocean and clips off two fingers on his right hand and one of his big toes. Until now, it seemed as though Roland could accomplish his goal without any assistance. Losing a toe is inconvenient. Losing two fingers, though, is a crushing blow for a man who lives and dies by the gun. He also loses a boot to the lobstrosities, which will make walking to the Dark Tower difficult. However, none of that matters if he is poisoned by the infection that sets in afterward. His quest might have come to an end in those few moments of uncharacteristic inattention.

One of the issues people had with *The Gunslinger* is that Roland is a loner, and not a very nice man. He is the kind of person who would sacrifice a young boy in the name of some abstract goal. He isn't exactly hero material, and some readers found it difficult to spend time with him.

All of that changes in this book. For the first time since the fall of Gilead, Roland assembles a *ka-tet*—a group of people bound together with a common goal. In the past, the members of his *ka-tet*, which included Cuthbert Allgood, Alain Johns and Jamie DeCurry, joined him willingly. On his quest for the Dark Tower, some force that wants him to succeed delivers his allies to him. He has no say in the selection process—nor do they. Roland essentially conscripts them into duty. Because of his injuries—and because *ka* demands it—he is forced to embrace these new companions. Without help, he will never make it to the Dark Tower. He needs them; therefore, they must come.

At first glance, they seem like unlikely candidates: a heroin junkie and a woman who lost her legs after being pushed in front of a train and who suffers from multiple personality disorder. And yet Roland understands that these people can become gunslingers. The structure of the book parallels the man in black's tarot reading, with sections named for each of the three cards/doors and interludes where the deck gets shuffled.

In addition to expanding the cast, King also broadens the story's scope. In *The Gunslinger*, Jake Chambers tells Roland about New York City. In *The Drawing of the Three*, Roland experiences that universe, both vicariously and in person, thanks to three magical doors that appear along the beach. They're one-dimensional: visible from only one side. Their hinges aren't connected to anything. Only Roland can open them and, when he does, he can enter the minds of the people they represent, leaving his body inert and defenseless on the beach. If he so chooses, he can step through into the alternate location—or locations, since each door opens into a different time: 1987, 1964 and 1977 respectively.

Another aspect of *The Gunslinger* that presented problems for some readers was the fact that a lot of it was told in flashback, which can impede forward momentum. Not so with *The Drawing of the Three*. From the opening salvo in which Roland is injured, the novel advances at breakneck pace from one crisis to the next to the next.

Roland's experiences with the three doors are quite different from one another. His first glimpse through the door marked THE PRISONER shows him a world he's never seen before from a perspective he's never had before: out the window of an airplane. When he enters the world of THE LADY OF SHADOWS, he finds himself inside a divided mind. The door marked THE PUSHER gives him access to a sociopath who represents death.

When Roland enters Eddie Dean's mind, he spends some time figuring out the rules of doorway travel and learning what he can about this new universe. He discovers that he can bring things from one world to the other, in both directions. This is important, because he needs medicine, and for it to do any good, he has to get it back to the beach. He also learns that he can remain in the background and observe what's happening around him or he can step forward and take full control.

Eddie, a heroin addict who has been somewhat clean for a while, is the most accepting of the three people Roland enters. They quickly establish détente. Roland needs Eddie and, as it turns out, Eddie needs Roland. He's carrying cocaine back from the Bahamas and the flight attendants have grown suspicious of him. If he doesn't find a way to ditch the drugs, he'll go to prison. However, if he loses the drugs, he'll be in serious trouble with the mobsters who sent him on this junket. Roland offers a solution. Before the plane lands, they take the drugs through the door to the beach, where they can retrieve them later.

Roland will always be a fish out of water in New York. He understands some letters and words, but many things elude him. However, his training allows him to detect danger before it happens. He is the one who notices that the flight attendants are suspicious of Eddie, even if he doesn't understand exactly what they are. He senses that Eddie will have problems with the ritual of Customs, without knowing what it is. He isn't protecting Eddie out of goodwill, though. If Eddie ends up in jail, he won't be able to provide the antibiotics Roland badly needs. Eddie is a means to an end, like most other people Roland encounters.

Their intimate connection, however, gives Roland a chance to size Eddie up. He is weak, primarily because of his drug addiction, but Roland sees strength in him, too. He reminds Roland of his old friend Cuthbert. With Roland providing moral support, Eddie stands up to the customs officials in a way he couldn't have managed on his own. He's also ready to confront Enrico

Balazar and a dozen of his henchmen who are holding his older brother, Henry, hostage until he delivers the drugs.

Henry is Eddie's true weakness, the source of most of his problems and destroyer of his self-esteem. Their single mother relied on Henry to "look after" Eddie after a drunk driver killed their sister, to make sure something similar didn't happen again. Henry used this obligation to excuse his own shortcomings, especially when it turned out that Eddie was better than his brother at just about everything. Henry was wounded in Vietnam and came back addicted to painkillers, the first step in his downward spiral into drug addiction. He pulled Eddie in after him, but Eddie was smart enough and resourceful enough to keep at least a partially clear head, which meant that he ended up looking after his brother instead of the other way around.

For the first time, readers are given an independent assessment of Roland. Though Roland is in bad shape, Eddie can see the strength within him. He respects Roland and develops a nascent love for him, even though he knows this is a man who will likely cause him harm.

Eddie pulls off a bravura performance at Balazar's headquarters. Roland's faith in his inner steel makes him almost unrecognizable to the drug kingpin. He's assertive and self-confident, taking part in a gunfight while naked. He is driven by the discovery that Henry died from a drug overdose shortly before he got there. He willingly goes to war with Roland, who steps through the doorway to join in the fray. For the first time ever, Roland gives up one of his guns—he can no longer use both at once, thanks to his maimed hand—and they reduce the population of the Leaning Tower to zero, just as Roland did back in Tull.

Being thrust into such a dangerous situation together is a bonding experience. Eddie's need for payback is satisfied and Roland gets his antibiotics, though not a large enough dose to cure him. Roland had planned to wrest Eddie back to Mid-World, but in the aftermath of the battle, he offers Eddie the choice to join him on his quest without guaranteeing that he'll survive. The only thing he can promise is that if they make it to the Tower, Eddie will see something remarkable.

Even though he's battling withdrawal, Eddie looks after Roland in the days following the gunfight, providing food—in the form of lobstrosity meat, much to Roland's horror—and making sure the gunslinger takes his medication. He even builds a serviceable travois and drags Roland up the beach. He's not cured of his addiction, though. He needs Roland so he can get back to his own world to score drugs.

Roland knows better than to trust an addict—advice, like most, usually delivered to him in Cort's chiding voice. He's also reluctant to get too close to Eddie because he might have to sacrifice him, too. Eddie believes that he is unlikely to survive in Roland's world, even if they make it to the Dark Tower. He recognizes the addiction in Roland's personality, too: Roland is a Tower junkie.

When they reach the second doorway, marked THE LADY OF SHADOWS, Eddie is so determined to go with Roland that he threatens to kill the gunslinger's defenseless body if he's left behind. Roland puts his trust in *ka* and plows ahead, ditching Eddie and throwing himself into another strange place. He had warned Eddie that the doorway might take them to a completely alien destination. In a way it does. Roland ends up in Macy's in New York City, nearly a quarter of a century earlier than the time from which he drew Eddie.

The second person destined to become part of Roland's *ka-tet* is Odetta Holmes, a black woman who is in a wheelchair because her legs are missing below the knees. She is a strong, independent woman who is active in the civil rights movement. Inspired by Rosa Parks, she has become nearly as famous as Martin Luther King and has appeared on the cover of *Time* magazine. She has recently returned from a trip to Oxford, Mississippi, where she was jailed and humiliated after attending a protest.

However, it is not Odetta's mind Roland enters but that of Detta Walker, a personality of which Odetta is unaware. Detta first materialized after Odetta was hit in the head by a brick when she was five years old, but her appearances were rare until 1958, when Odetta was pushed in front of a subway train, the incident that cost her her legs. Odetta is still the dominant personality, and Detta's adventures are sufficiently infrequent that Odetta can fill in the blanks the way a person with an eye injury learns to compensate for the missing part of their field of vision. Detta is more aware that something is wrong, but she doesn't know what.

Where Odetta is refined and genteel, Detta is rage personified. She talks like a caricature, spouting vile and illiterate jargon that even Eddie will have a hard time understanding. She doesn't shoplift because she needs things, but out of spite. The things she takes are of little value, which reflects how she sees herself, and she usually throws them away. She is promiscuous and crude and completely amoral. Her greatest desire, Eddie comes to believe, is to be killed by a white person.

Roland is only vaguely aware of any of this when he opens the door. Detta is on a shoplifting spree when he enters her mind. Detta and Odetta become briefly aware of each other and are equally horrified by what they see. Detta fights back against the invading white man. With the house detectives closing in, Roland sends her through the doorway to the beach.

When they arrive, she is Odetta. Yanked out of her world and disoriented, she denies her new surroundings. She has no memory of going to Macy's. The last thing she remembers is watching the news on television. She is either dreaming, has suffered another brain injury or has gone crazy, she decides. Even when presented with contradictions in her story—the costume jewelry she's wearing, for instance—she refuses to believe what Roland and Eddie tell her.

She won't eat, but allows herself to be pushed along the beach. Roland thinks that Eddie will be okay now because he has someone to look after—a surrogate for his brother—and he sees the early signs that Eddie is falling in love.

Eddie is taken completely by surprise when Detta emerges that night. Whereas Odetta refuses to acknowledge the truth, Detta fervently believes things that never happened, most of them terrible. She accuses Eddie and Roland of raping her and trying to poison her.

Roland is getting sick again—the antibiotics only knocked back the infection without eliminating it—but he is alert enough to warn Eddie that Odetta is two women in one body. Because Roland believes that Eddie needs a lesson in how dangerous Detta can be, he allows Detta to steal his unloaded gun while they sleep. She tries to shoot Eddie and hits him in the head with the gun when that fails. This is the way Cort taught Roland important lessons.

Detta remains in control of the body as they struggle toward the third doorway. She does everything possible to impede their progress, just to be contrary. Even strapped to the chair, she manages to throw the hand brake and upset herself. She tries to bite any fingers that get within reach. At night she screams if Roland and Eddie fall asleep. Eddie is getting sick, too, from malnourishment caused by a constant diet of lobstrosity meat. Roland is too weak to push the chair and finally grows too weak to even walk. Fortunately, Odetta reasserts control. Since she is more cooperative, Eddie can take her ahead to the next door and come back with the chair for Roland.

They have a dilemma, though. In addition to the lobstrosities, there are wild creatures in the nearby hills. Roland has a gun to defend himself while Eddie and Odetta are gone, but Odetta will need to stay by herself for a couple of days while Eddie comes back for Roland. Roland tells Eddie not to leave his gun with her, but Eddie is in love and ignores Roland's advice. When they arrive at the doorway marked THE PUSHER, Odetta is missing. Eddie worries that an animal might have killed her, but Roland knows that she is lurking in the hills, a creature more dangerous than any wildcat or lobstrosity. And armed.

This time, Roland wants Eddie to come with him through the doorway, where he'll be safe, but Eddie refuses to abandon Odetta. Roland enters the mind of sociopath Jack Mort, a CPA who amuses himself by dropping bricks on people and pushing them in front of cars. He was responsible for both of Odetta's traumas, even though they took place years apart in different cities. Mort isn't interested in Roland, and Roland can't take being inside the killer's head for any longer than necessary. Fortunately, Mort's consciousness faints, allowing Roland free rein of his body and complete access to his mind and all the information it contains.

His objective in New York is twofold: get ammunition and antibiotics to fight his infection. He has a third item on his checklist, too, though that one requires Detta to emerge from the hills and to look through the door at the right moment.

To his horror, Roland realizes that Mort's next target is Jake Chambers. He wonders if this is a form of punishment: to witness Jake's first death without being able to stop it. Regardless of what it means for his quest, he won't stand aside and let Jake be sacrificed a second time. He steps forward long enough to make Mort miss his chance. Roland is improving. His brief exposure to Eddie and Odetta has made him more aware of the way his quest impacts the lives of others.

Throughout his adventures during this trip to New York, Roland has to worry about Eddie, who fell asleep while watching for Odetta and was captured by Detta. She hog-ties him and leaves him at the high-water line for the lobstrosities, hoping that this will draw Roland back so she can shoot him. Roland can't let her see what he sees when he looks through the door until he's ready, though, so he proceeds with his mission and resists the temptation to check up on the situation on the beach.

Nothing goes smoothly. At the gun shop, he is stymied by the fact that, though he has enough money to buy more bullets than he could imagine ever needing, he requires a carry permit to purchase them, and Jack Mort doesn't have one. He has to concoct an elaborate plan involving two rather stupid police officers who are keeping an eye on the gun shop in hopes of catching the owner selling weapons to criminals. Roland tells them the clerk robbed him. Once they are inside the shop, he disarms the police officers and "robs" the store, taking all the bullets he needs, but paying for them.

He proceeds around the corner to the pharmacy, where he pulls off the first penicillin heist in history, leaving behind Mort's gold Rolex as payment for the Keflex. To maintain order, he has to shoot one of the guns he confiscated from the cops, which attracts the attention of more police officers.

For the final part of his plan, Roland has Jack Mort lead him to the subway station where he pushed Odetta. A patrol officer shoots Mort, but his cigarette lighter saves him—an unlikely happenstance, but the sort of thing that occurs frequently when the Dark Tower is involved. Roland forces Mort to jump in front of the oncoming train and yells for Detta and Odetta to look at the moment the train cuts Mort's body in half at the waist.

The traumatic experience causes the woman to split into two factions that fight for control of her body. Odetta offers love and forgiveness and, as a result, a new entity is born: Susannah, who has Detta's "fight until you drop" stamina tempered by Odetta's calm humanity. She demonstrates her abilities as a gunslinger by taking Roland's guns to the beach to rescue Eddie from the lobstrosities.

Roland now has two companions. Though he was meant to draw three, he now believes that Susannah, who is three people in one, represents the three. Eddie still doesn't trust Roland completely. He knows that he and Susannah could still be sacrificed, and Roland doesn't deny this. He's already damned for letting Jake fall, but would sacrifice someone else if it meant he could save everything—not just his own world, but all worlds.

Though it would be several years before he returned to the Dark Tower series, King lays out the general shape of the next two books in the afterword to *The Drawing of the Three*. He even gives the titles of the books. *The Waste Lands*, he says, would detail half of their quest to reach the Dark Tower, and *Wizard and Glass* would be mostly about Roland's past, an enchantment and a seduction. He even raises the possibility that Roland won't make it to the Tower.

He doesn't mention Jake Chambers.

Characters (in order of mention): Roland Deschain, the man in black, Jake Chambers, Cort, Eddie Dean, Cuthbert Allgood, Henry Dean, Enrico Balazar, Jane Dorning, Paula, William Wilson, Susy Douglas, Captain McDonald, Selina Dean, Deere, Marten, Hax, Colin Vincent, Jack Andolini, Claudio Andolini, Carlocimi Dretto, George Biondi, Tricks Postino, Truman Alexander, Desmond, Jimmy Haspio, Kevin Blake, Farson, Dario, Rudy Vechhio, Mrs. Dean, Detta Walker, Odetta Holmes, Andrew Feeny, Lee Harvey Oswald, John Kennedy, Poppa Doc Duvalier, Fidel Castro, the Diem brothers, Howard, Aunt Sophia, Rosa Parks, Martin Luther King, Medgar Evers, Alice Holmes, Dan Holmes, Julio Estevez, George Shavers, Miguel Basale, Jimmy Halvorsen, Miss Hathaway, Jack Mort, Dorfman, Carl Delevan, George

O'Mearah, Justin Clements, Fat Johnny Holden, Alain Johns, Flagg, Dennis, Thomas, Mrs. Rathbun, Katz, Ralph Lennox, Andrew Staunton, Norris Weaver, Mr. Framingham, Susannah Dean, Susan Delgado.

Places: Western Sea; Regency Tower; Nassau; Kennedy International Airport; Aquinas Hotel; Garlan; Co-Op City; the Dark Tower; the Leaning Tower; Tull; Vietnam; Oxford, Mississippi; Manhattan; Greenwich Village; Montgomery, Alabama; Odetta, Arkansas; Greymarl Apartments; Sisters of Mercy Hospital; the Hungry i; Macy's; Elizabeth, New Jersey; the Pushing Place; Mort's office; Clements Guns and Sporting Goods; Mort's apartment; Katz's Drug Store; Christopher Street Station.

Things: Lobstrosities, the Honor Stance, David the hawk, popkins, the Grand Featherex, Presentation Ceremonies, Holmes Dental, A train, forspecial plate, Shipmate's Disease, the Shooter's Bible, docker's clutch, devil-weed, jawbone.

Continuity Errors and Mistakes: When Roland travels north, the sea should be on his left, not his right. Eddie comes from Co-Op City, Brooklyn; however, in our reality, Co-Op City is in the Bronx. Balazar's first name changes from Emilio to Enrico. The gun shop owner is either Justin or Arnold Clements. Odetta's mother is Alice here but changes to Sarah in the next book. Patrol officer Norris Weaver is called Norris Wheaton twice. The handgrips on Roland's guns are said to be ironwood instead of sandalwood.

Foreshadowing and Spoilers: Though killed in this book, Enrico Balazar, Jack Andolini and the rest of the gang will show up in future adventures once Roland and his *ka-tet* start traveling back to New York via other doorways. Enrico Balazar's car is the one that killed Jake Chambers. Detta Walker's fascination with china plates will serve Susannah Dean well when she is introduced to a weapon called an Oriza in *Wolves of the Calla*. The fact that Roland stopped Mort from killing Jake Chambers sets up a paradox in their minds in *The Waste Lands*.

THE WASTE LANDS: REDEMPTION

By the end of the 1980s, the Dark Tower series was generally available to Stephen King's fans. *The Gunslinger* was issued in trade paperback in 1988 and *The Drawing of the Three* in 1989. King also recorded audio versions of these two books, the first he had ever narrated. As the years went by, he mentioned his intention to write *The Waste Lands*, but he didn't finish the book until 1991. In the book's afterword, he admitted that he had problems getting back to the series, using a metaphor drawn from *The Waste Lands* to explain: the key Eddie shapes to open the doorway between Mid-World and Earth. "It seems to take more and more whittling to make each successive key fit each successive lock."

An excerpt from *The Waste Lands* called "The Bear" appeared in the December 1990 issue of *The Magazine of Fantasy and Science Fiction*. The limited edition and limited-trade hardcover came out in August 1991, and a trade paperback edition was issued in January 1992.

The title of the book is a literary allusion to the poem "The Waste Land" by T. S. Eliot. The titles of the two halves of the novel are quotes from that poem: "Fear in a Handful of Dust" and "A Heap of Broken Images." Several characters quote from the poem as well. Another meaning of the title is a reference to Detta Walker's "Drawers," the place where she destroyed her aunt's special plate. Roland generalizes the word to mean any place of self-destruction. Lost places that are spoiled, useless or desolate. However, he also thinks these are powerful places where people can reinvent themselves.

The novel covers about twenty-five days in Mid-World, leading up to the beginning of autumn. In the first half, Roland finishes assembling his *ka-tet*. He has Eddie Dean and Susannah (who has adopted Eddie's last name), both of whom are proving to have all the characteristics of gunslingers, but he needs one more person: Jake Chambers. He feels the need to atone for letting him fall in the chasm beneath the mountains so he could catch up with the man in black, but he is also suffering from a mental schism brought about by killing Jack Mort. He has two sets of memories: one in which he found Jake in the Way Station and allowed him to die and another in which the Way Station was empty and the boy was never part of his life. He believes this is another trap the man in black set for him. Bringing Jake back to Mid-World is the only way to keep from going insane.

Soon after the *ka-tet* is assembled, they face the first test of their mettle. They must pass through a city where an ages-old civil war still rages. The group is split up for one very long day and, as will happen on a number of occasions in the future, each person in the *ka-tet* will have an important part to play in resolving the crisis and getting everyone back together again alive and well. Though the conflict has little to do with Roland's quest to save the Dark Tower, it is important for the group's morale. They are forced to realize that, though Roland is their *dinh* (leader), they are more than just children to a symbolic father. They are warriors, individually vital to the completion of the mission, which by now has become their own. As Eddie Dean tells Roland, if the gunslinger should die in his sleep, they would mourn him, but then they would pick up and carry on in his stead, even if they don't have much chance of succeeding without him.

Then, after the *ka-tet* completes their mission, King leaves them stranded on a train rocketing across Mid-World at more than eight hundred miles per hour, trying their best to outwit the insane computer intelligence controlling their fate in a battle of riddles.

The book opens a few months after the ending of *The Drawing of the Three*. Roland, Eddie and Susannah, the latter two now living as husband and wife, have moved sixty miles inland from the Western Sea and have set up camp in a place they call the shooting gallery while Roland teaches them the skills they need to become gunslingers. In addition to teaching them to shoot, he shows them how to navigate by the stars, how to hunt and how to get every possible use from what they kill, including tanning and curing hides for clothing and other provisions.

Most important, he needs to teach them how to kill. Eddie was forced to learn this lesson in Balazar's headquarters, but Susannah—the first-ever female gunslinger (Aileen Ritter from the Marvel comics notwithstanding)—has fired only at inanimate objects. Like Cort, Roland is a harsh teacher. He belittles and berates his charges until they are so angry with him they're almost ready to kill him. He needs to get them riled up to see how they will perform under pressure.

Their training comes in handy the day they encounter Shardik, the Guardian of one of the twelve Beams that hold up the Dark Tower. Shardik is a seventy-foot-tall robot, built by North Central Positronics in the days of the Great Old Ones. Though a lot of what Roland heard about the Tower and the nature of his world was thought to be a myth, he is beginning to realize there was a lot of truth in those stories.

If there's a Guardian around, that means there's a portal nearby. If he can find it, he will have his trajectory. All he needs to do is put his back to the portal and follow the Path of the Beam and he will end up at the Dark Tower. He has no idea how far that is—the distance could be great since Mid-World seems to be expanding—but for the first time in his long life, he no longer has to cast about. These Beams have been flowing along the same paths for so long that they leave a clear sign of their presence in the herringbone pattern of the clouds, the direction needles on trees grow and the pattern of shadows on the ground.

First, though, they have to deal with Shardik. He has had an innate hatred of people ever since the Great Old Ones tried to destroy him. His batteries are running down, he is infected by parasites and he is going insane. He is on a rampage when he stumbles upon Eddie Dean, who has recently become compelled to whittle. He goes off by himself to do this because his brother always made fun of him when he carved as a boy and he's afraid that his new friends might treat his hobby the same way. Eddie scrambles up a tree, but the bear is immense.

When Susannah shoots the satellite dish atop Shardik's head, the Guardian is disabled and begins his final process of dying. Roland, Eddie and Susannah follow the bear's trail back to the portal, where they dispatch a number of other robotic animals, one of which almost kills Susannah.

The time for training is over. Now that they have a direction, they must move on. However, Roland has a confession to make: he thinks he's going insane. He's in worse condition than when he was suffering from infection on the beach. He hears voices chattering so loudly that he can't think straight. He considers himself so dangerous to his friends that he surrenders his gun and his knife. Susannah and Eddie are dismayed by this development. Their chances of surviving alone in Roland's world are slim.

Eddie's compulsion to whittle settles in on a single object: a key that he sees in the fire (along with a rose) after Roland casts off the jawbone he took from the golgotha after his palaver with the man in black. He believes this is Walter's jawbone. Something external and powerful is guiding Eddie so that he will be prepared when the time is right. This is one of the fundamental and ongoing mysteries of Roland's quest for the Dark Tower. Something or someone—in a word, *ka*—wants him to succeed and regularly presents him with tools—including people—that will help him.

Dreams play an important part in the Dark Tower series and in *The Waste Lands*. Eddie begins to dream of New York—specifically the part of Manhattan known as Turtle Bay. He sees people from his past—Jack Andolini and Enrico Balazar—and places laden with Tower symbolism. His dream takes him to Second Avenue and 46th Street, which is occupied by a deli. When he goes through the door, he finds himself standing before an enormous field of roses and, in the distance, the Dark Tower. He is the first among his group to see their objective, even if only in a dream. He also gets the sense that something is wrong with the Tower and that they have an adversary. This dream is enough to inspire Eddie to adopt the quest as his own. He's no longer a prisoner in Mid-World.

Jake Chambers is suffering from the same condition as Roland, only for him it's more personal. The eleven-year-old boy, an all-A student at a prestigious private school, is living with the knowledge that he was supposed to die on May 9, 1977. He awoke that morning with the foreknowledge of when and where it would happen and, up until the moment passes, he's sure it will happen. When it doesn't, he's cast adrift. He becomes a walking dead person, as far as he's concerned. The conflict raging inside his head prevents him from concentrating on his schoolwork, and he becomes obsessed with doorways, convinced that one of them will lead him back to Mid-World, which is where he thinks he's supposed to be.

His subconscious mind generates a term paper called "My Understanding of Truth" for his English comp class that is full of symbolism he doesn't understand, though his teacher claims she does. It contains references to his experiences in the desert with the gunslinger and to people who he has never met, including Eddie and Susannah. It talks about doors and towers, has quotes from T. S. Eliot and Robert Browning, and contains clues about what will happen after he rejoins Roland, including references to riddles, Blaine and a train.

He is mortified when he reads the essay, which he does not remember writing. He runs away from school and ends up on Second Avenue at the Manhattan Restaurant of the Mind bookstore, where he meets the owner, Calvin Tower, and his only friend, Aaron Deepneau. A children's book called *Charlie the Choo-Choo* catches his attention, as does a raggedy book of riddles titled *Riddle-De-Dum!* He buys the first and is given the other because of its poor condition. The answers section has been removed.

Charlie the Choo-Choo seems to be an ordinary book about an anthropomorphic train with a friendly engineer. After Charlie is replaced by a faster, sleeker model, he comes to the rescue when the newer train breaks down. However, Jake finds the story ominous. He doesn't trust Charlie. He thinks he looks downright evil. Other things in the book strike him—a girl named Susannah and a character named Martin (i.e., Marten). He will subsequently learn that both Eddie and Susannah owned and lost copies of this book when they were young. The implication is that *ka* has been trying to put the book into their hands and some other force is trying to keep it away from them.

He continues down the street, following Eddie's dream route, and ends up at the same address, the corner of Second Avenue and 46th. He expected to find the doorway to Mid-World here, but the deli is gone and the lot is empty, a construction site. The fence around the lot is covered with graffiti that references Beams and the Turtle (one of the Guardians of the Beam). In the empty lot, he hears sweet sounds, millions of voices, and finds a key that is the same shape as the one Eddie is trying to carve. He also sees the rose from Eddie's dream and understands that it is in danger—there's a worm and a shadow over it. Once he has the key, the nagging voices inside his head are silenced.

Jake and Eddie have never met each other and Eddie has no proof of Jake's existence. When Roland ranted in his fever delirium while on the beach, Eddie remembers him saying that he was alone under the mountains. However, because they are destined to be *ka-tet*, they form a connection, passing messages back and forth across the dimensions. Jake tells Eddie that the key he's carving should calm Roland's voices. When it does, the gunslinger weeps with relief. Until then, he had thought that only death would grant him peace.

In Jake's dreams, Eddie is about the same age as he is, which makes sense given that they're from different decades. He sees Eddie shooting baskets and understands intuitively that this is where he is supposed to go, though he knows only that it is in Co-Op City in Brooklyn. Eddie assures Jake that he will find his destination the same way he found the key. *Ka* will provide. He awakens to find his knees scraped the way they were when he fell in the dream.

The next morning, when he sets out, he knows he will probably never see his parents again. Reuniting with Roland is more important. He takes a few belongings and steals his father's gun and ammunition. He wanders Manhattan, unconsciously following the Path of the Beam southeast, killing time until his appointment in Brooklyn and trying to keep from getting picked up for being truant.

He makes his way to Brooklyn and finds Markey Avenue, an address that popped into his head unbidden. There he sees Eddie and Henry shooting hoops. He studies the two boys long enough to understand their dynamics. Eddie is smarter and more skilled than Henry, but he knows that his older brother is insecure and knows how to handle him to keep him from lashing out. The two boys set out on an adventure to go see the Mansion in Dutch Hill, an abandoned house several blocks away that is supposedly haunted.

Jake follows. Henry and Eddie can't make themselves get close to the house, but Jake knows it is where he needs to be. There's a demon inside—a doorkeeper who wants to prevent anyone from crossing over. The house is a physical manifestation of this doorkeeper and once Jake is inside, it turns on him, seeking to devour him.

Eddie senses that Jake is getting ready to cross over, so he redoubles his effort to finish the key. Years of insecurity caused by Henry's constant put-downs have him doubting his ability to get it right, but Roland has faith in him and both encourages and chides him. Susannah isn't happy with the way Roland treats her husband, but they are growing to accept his coldness and single-mindedness.

Their route along the Path of the Beam gradually becomes a coach road and then one of the Great Roads. They see signs of past civilization and en-counter a number of billy-bumblers. The designated place for Jake's return is a Stonehenge-like circle of stones where a demon dwells. Roland knows these places are "thin," a common theme in King's books. Eddie finalizes his key and draws a door in the ground, labeling it THE BOY like the doors on the beach and the one in the Mansion are marked.

Roland and Susannah have to distract the demon to keep it from going after Eddie. The only way to do this is with sex, and which one of them gets called into action will depend on the demon's gender. When it proves to be male, Susannah relies on the Detta aspect of her personality to get her through this ordeal. Roland gets his chance to atone for letting Jake fall by jumping through the doorway once it is open on both sides. He seizes the Speaking Demon and crams it into the mouth of the doorkeeper, thus taking care of both threats, and pulls Jake upward to safety. He promises he will never let Jake fall again, though he's not entirely sure he believes himself. The success of this mission is a personal victory for Eddie. He thinks he's defeated the voice in his head, too—that of his nagging older brother.

The *ka-tet* is complete—in human form, that is. The quartet acquires a fifth member with the arrival of a billy-bumbler—a doglike animal that has been cast out from its herd, probably for being too smart. It is a rare example of its kind that remembers when bumblers were friends of men. Jake dubs him Oy after the bumbler's efforts to mimic the word "boy." He and Jake become fast friends. Oy tolerates the others but is nervous around them—especially Roland.

They are now in the geographic region called Mid-World. Roland remembers hearing about a huge city at the edge of Mid-World when he was young. That city, Lud, is 160 wheels (approximately 175 miles) down the Great Road. They see its skyline from the top of a ridge, and Eddie hopes they will find someone there who will tell them what they're supposed to do. The ominous drumbeats they hear in the distance aren't encouraging.

Before they get there, they arrive in River Crossing, a humble town consisting of a few dozen buildings, a church and a jail—the closest thing to civilization Roland has seen since he passed through, and eradicated, Tull. The town's residents, when they decide to emerge from hiding, prove to be a handful of very old people—well beyond being octogenarians. They invite the gunslinger and his companions to dinner and tell them what they know about the conditions in Lud, where a civil war that spread from a distant Barony has been raging for more than a century.

The Great Old Ones built Lud many centuries ago, but most of the technology has failed. What little might remain is beyond the abilities of the residents to operate. The two factions, the Grays and the Pubes, don't even remember what they're fighting over. The Grays were harriers who besieged the city and the Pubes are Lud's former residents, who used the weapons of the Great Old Ones to fend the Grays off until they ran out of ammunition. The matriarch of River Crossing, Aunt Talitha, recommends that the *ka-tet* go around Lud rather than through it, because Jake will be an attractive prize for the people of Lud, since there are few children born there anymore.

Roland ignores this advice for two reasons. He doesn't want to get in the habit of making detours, prolonging his journey and taking him off the Path of the Beam. He also believes that they are meant to go to Lud and if they try to go around it, *ka* will push them back on track. He believes they will find a train that will take them closer to their final destination. Jake thinks that this train will be called Blaine, whose name he included in his term paper.

Aunt Talitha tries to discourage Roland from seeking the Dark Tower. For generations, anyone who pursued that goal never came back, she says. When she sees he won't be dissuaded, she gives Roland her silver cross and asks him to lay it at the foot of the Tower should he ever get there.

During their visit, Susannah exhibits signs that she may be pregnant. Whether this is because of her relationship with Eddie or because of what happened with the demon in the Speaking Circle won't be known for some time.

Though the *ka-tet* is invited to spend the night, Roland knows that leaving won't get any easier if they stay. Tull was a trap and he doesn't want River Crossing to be another, even if it is more benevolent. When Jake says he doesn't think it's right to leave without helping, Roland says that if you look too hard at the small rights close at hand, you lose sight of the bigger ones that stand farther off. This is a lesson Roland will have to unlearn someday.

To get to Lud, they first have to cross the Send Bridge. The three-quarter-mile span is a thousand years old and on the verge of collapse. Another bridge farther up the Mississippi-like river has already fallen. They pick a pedestrian walkway as the safest route, but even that has gaps and the wind makes the crossing risky. A strong gust threatens to sweep Oy away. Jake leaps after him, and Eddie, who is afraid of heights, comes to their rescue. Roland assists, too. Seeing Jake dangling from another bridge strikes a sensitive chord.

When they recover from this near miss, a man is standing nearby with a live grenade. Though Roland could shoot it from the man's hand, it's too big a risk. The explosion might bring the bridge down, and the man who calls himself Gasher seems ready to die. He offers a deal: he will let the others go free if they give him Jake. Eddie can't believe Roland is seriously considering this, but the gunslinger knows a standoff when he sees one and he quietly promises Jake that he will find him. Jake, who now trusts the gunslinger with his life, steps forward and allows himself to be taken.

The *ka-tet* now has two missions in Lud. They have to get Jake back and find the train that will carry them out of the city. Roland divides the group—in part out of necessity. Susannah can't navigate the rubble-filled (and booby-trapped) streets of Lud fast enough to keep up with Jake and Gasher. Eddie and Susannah are dispatched to find the train station while Roland goes after Jake. He's not alone. He has Oy, who can follow Jake's scent in dark places where Roland's tracking skills fail.

The streets of Lud are lined with thousands of bodies hanging from the speaker poles that broadcast war drums. The Pubes believe this sound comes from ghosts in the machine, a kind of dark god that demands sacrifice. When they hear them, they conduct a lottery to decide which of them will die next to appease the gods. This is a terrible trick perpetrated by the Grays, who have figured out how to make the Great Old Ones' machinery play the drums.

Eddie and Susannah have a showdown with a group of Pubes. Susannah kills for the first time. The mob is relentless at first, akin to the people of Tull, but it dissipates after Eddie and Susannah shoot several more. One of their victims even apologizes to them once he discovers they are gunslingers and not Grays. Eddie and Susannah force two of the survivors to take them to the Cradle of Lud, the train station housing Blaine the Mono. The Pubes are terrified of Blaine, whom they consider a vengeful god, but Eddie and Susannah's guns carry more weight. They enter a street guarded by a statue of a turtle and reach the immense square where the Cradle of Lud is situated. Statues of the Guardians of the Beam parade around the top of the structure, along with a sixty-foot golden statue of Arthur Eld.

Inside, they find Blaine the Mono and discover that he is as insane as Shardik was. He is suffering from a split personality—something Susannah identifies with. One voice is the original voice of the train: Little Blaine. The real intelligence controlling Blaine exists in the collection of computers under Lud. Blaine is simply the last operating machine that can manifest the personality of these computers, which used to run all of the city's systems. Centuries of solitude and boredom have driven this artificial sentience mad. He is delighted to find people who might play a game of riddles with him. After he accepts the possibility that one last gunslinger might exist and learns about Roland, who knows many riddles from the Fair-Day contests in the days of Gilead, he is intrigued.

Gasher brings Jake to the inner sanctum of the Grays and their leader, the Tick-Tock Man, the great-grandson of the famed warrior David Quick. Quick led the last great army of the Grays against Lud and was successful in breaching their defenses. However, he died in a plane crash outside the city. The Tick-Tock Man rules his people with an iron fist, dispatching any who defy him.

Oy leads Roland to the inner sanctum and demonstrates his intelligence by going on reconnaissance missions through the ventilation shafts. The gunslinger tries to send a mental message to Jake but isn't convinced it will work because he isn't completely in *ka-tet* with them. Jake receives enough to know that Roland is nearby and wants him to create a distraction, which he does by turning some of Tick-Tock Man's henchmen against one another.

Jake is supposed to open the door for Roland, but in the chaos that follows, he is prevented from doing so. However, the door opens anyway—Blaine opens it because he wants to meet Roland and his remembered riddles and Jake with his book of riddles.

Oy leads the charge. Other than one woman, whom Roland allows to escape, the only survivor is the Tick-Tock Man. Jake shoots him in the head, but his skull deflects the bullet. After Jake and Roland leave the Grays' headquarters, guided by Blaine, a wizard who calls himself Richard Fannin appears before the Tick-Tock Man and converts him from a strong, essential leader into a sniveling minion. Fannin is determined that the *ka-tet* not get any closer to the Dark Tower than they are now.

Reunited, the *ka-tet* solves Blaine's first puzzle, which permits them to board the train. Blaine agrees to take them to Topeka, where Mid-World ends and End-World begins. However, he decides to kill everyone remaining in Lud with poison and nerve gas. Since he was created to serve, he argues that he is doing what the people wanted. They turned him into a god through their desires, and he is acting as one now, deciding when they live and die. Susannah is forced to abandon her wheelchair in the rush to leave before the gas attack obliterates everyone.

Jake realizes that Blaine intends to commit suicide. Blaine is bored and his circuits are failing in ways that he can no longer repair. He has already talked his only companion, Patricia the Mono, into killing herself. He accelerates to a speed that is in the red zone for the tracks and switches off the sensors that would tell him if there are any breaches. It's been a decade since he last ran this route, and there's a good chance the track has failed since then. He uses computer-generated images to make himself invisible as he speeds up. His route takes them through postapocalyptic landscapes, some of which are the result of the Great Poisoning, places where the world is trying to heal, and some of which are so alien that they may not be in Mid-World at all. In a dream, Eddie was told that Blaine could travel across all universes.

Blaine demands riddles from the *ka-tet*, but Roland refuses, enraging the petulant train. It turns into a classic Western showdown, with Roland adopting the stance of a gunslinger ready to draw. Blaine comes to see reason. He isn't offering anything in return. He agrees to save their lives if they can stump him with a riddle before they cover the eight thousand miles to Topeka, which should take eight hours. He even apologizes when Roland accuses him of being rude.

Though King knew something of what came next, he ended the book on that cliffhanger. It would be several years before he returned to his *ka-tet*.

> **Characters (in order of mention):** Susannah Dean, Roland Deschain, Eddie Dean, Cort, Sarah Holmes, Jack Mort, Enrico Balazar, the Great Old Ones, Henry Dean, Gloria Dean, Jake Chambers, Alain Johns, Cuthbert Allgood, Hax, Jamie DeCurry, Marten

Broadcloak, Zoltan, Susan Delgado, Sheb, Allie, Nort, Sylvia Pittston, Jack Andolini, John Farson, Laurie Chambers, Elmer Chambers, Greta Shaw, Leonard Bissette, Joanne Franks, Mr. Harley, Bonita Avery, Mr. Knopf, Stan Dorfman, Calvin Tower, Wayne D. Overholser, Aaron Deepneau, Bango Skank, Mr. Hotchkiss, Engineer Bob Brooks, Raymond Martin, Mr. Briggs, Susannah Martin, Oy, Tom Denby, Si, Mercy, Bill Tudbury, Till Tudbury, Aunt Talitha Unwin, Blaine the Mono, David Quick (Lord Perth), Ageless Stranger, Maerlyn, King Arthur, Jack Mort, Vannay, Uncle Reg, Gasher, Tick-Tock Man (Andrew Quick), Copperhead, Spankerman, Luster, Winston, Frank, Jeeves, Ardis, Maud, Arthur Eld, Hoots, Patricia the Mono, Little Blaine, Steven Deschain, Tilly, Brandon, Deidre the Mad, Dewlap, Richard Fannin, Gabrielle Deschain.

Places: The Shooting Gallery; Oxford, Mississippi; the Great West Woods; Out-World; Mystic, Connecticut; Granite City; Pricetown; Tull; Dragon's Grave; House of Cards; Tom and Gerry's Artistic Deli; the Dark Tower; the Portal of the Bear; Gilead; Downland Baronies; Western Sea; Dutch Hill; the Mansion; Reflections of You; Piper School; 70 Rockefeller Plaza; Sunnyvale Sanitarium; the Way Station; the Pushing Place; Mid-Town Lanes; Vassar; Manhattan Restaurant of the Mind; Chew Chew Mama's; Tower of Power Records; the Paper Patch; Turtle Bay; United Nations Building; St. Louis, Missouri; Topeka, Kansas; Mid-World Amusement Park; Oz; Brooklyn; Co-Op City; Bleecker Street; Markey Avenue; Mid-World; Metropolitan Museum of Art; Times Square; Denby's Discount Drug; Send River; Brooklyn Vocational Institute; Lud; Jimtown; River Road; Garlan; River Crossing; Porla; the Church of the Blood Everlasting; the Big Empty; Elizabeth, New Jersey; Send Bridge; Fifth Avenue (Lud); Street of the Turtle; Cradle of Lud; the Plaza of the Cradle; Kashmin; Send Basin Nuclear Plant; West River Barony; Candleton; Rilea; the Falls of the Hounds; Dasherville; End-World; the Hall of the Grandfathers.

Things: Old Star (Apon), Old Mother (Lydia), Great Book, docker's clutch, gunslinger's catechism, Mir, Shardik, Guardians of the Beam, slow mutants, North Central Positronics, portals, Watch Me, Speaking Demon, the Drawers, *ka-tet*, *tet*, Beams, *Charlie the Choo-Choo*, *Riddle-De-Dum!*, Sombra Real Estate, the rose, Mid-World Railway

Company, Charlie (train), lobstrosities, *khef,* billy-bumblers, gunslinger burritos, the Oracle, David, Keflex, wheel, the White, *graf,* dockey, Sellian, *Watership Down, khef-mate,* char, younkers, Fair-Day Riddling, Winter, Wide Earth, Sowing, Mid-Summer, Full Earth, Reaping, Year's End, wenberry, Old War, Great Fire, Cataclysm, Great Poisoning, LaMerk Foundry, mandrus, grenado, cradle, *sigul,* dipolar circuits, unipolar circuits, firedim tubes, transitive circuits, the Imperium, slo-trans engines, way-gog.

Continuity Errors and Mistakes: Susannah's mother's name is Sarah in this book, whereas it was Alice before. Eddie's sister was Selena in *The Drawing of the Three,* but now it's Gloria. Co-Op City is really in the Bronx, not in Brooklyn. The Metropolitan Museum of Art is on the east side of Central Park, not near Times Square.

Crossovers to Other Works: *Rose Madder,* the book published immediately after *The Waste Lands,* refers to the bodies hanging from poles in Lud. Richard Fannin is another aspect of Randall Flagg from *The Stand.* He forces the Tick-Tock Man to adulate him in the words of Trashcan Man: My life for you.

Foreshadowing and Spoilers: The fact that the knees Jake scraped in his dream were scraped when he awoke is a sign that he went todash. Susannah's sexual encounter with the demon in the Speaking Circle will have far-reaching implications for the future of the *ka-tet.* Jake's key has the same hypnotic power as a certain turtle figurine that will appear later in the series. Aunt Talitha's cross will play a part in the story, too, and might even end up where she intended. The array of colored lights inside the Tick-Tock Man's lair is reminiscent of the oriel window atop the Dark Tower. "The wheel which turns our lives is remorseless; always it comes around to the same place again" is as close to a thematic statement as there is in the series. When Eddie asks Roland to tell them how he learned about the Dark Tower in the first place, Roland responds that it's a very long story that he will tell only once. This sets the stage for *Wizard and Glass.* Calvin Tower and Aaron Deepneau will become important secondary characters in the series starting with *Wolves of the Calla.*

WIZARD AND GLASS: REGARD

Though King promised in the afterword to *The Waste Lands* that the fourth volume in the series would appear in the not-too-distant future, years passed with no sign that he had returned to the series. Many of his other novels had Dark Tower tie-ins, though, so the series was clearly on his mind. As early as 1994, he expressed a plan to write the final four books back-to-back to finish the series.

The fans grew increasingly demanding. Every week, his assistants put on his desk all the angry letters he received demanding the next book in the series. One of the more creative pleas had a Polaroid of a teddy bear in chains, threatening to execute the bear unless King released the next Dark Tower book. At once. In 1996, he promised fans they would have to wait only another year or so. He simply had to summon his courage to start. Plus he had to review the first three novels, armed with a highlighter and sticky notes.

He started writing in motel rooms while driving from Colorado to Maine after finishing work on *The Shining* miniseries. Ads announcing the book's upcoming publication appeared in the back of the final four installments of his serial novel, *The Green Mile*.

The first two chapters of *Wizard and Glass* were released as a promotional booklet that accompanied bundles of his twin novels, *Desperation* and *The Regulators*. Though this delighted fans, there was some complaining, too, as many people had already purchased the books. King chastised the complainers in a harshly worded message posted by his publisher on the Usenet newsgroup alt.books.stephen-king. Penguin released the chapters on their Web site two months later.

King read from the novel at a conference in October, stating that the first draft was more than fourteen hundred pages long. *Wizard and Glass*, dedicated to his personal assistants and published in August 1997, proved to be the longest book of the series. The Donald M. Grant limited-trade edition was the first book from a small press publisher to ever appear on the *New York Times* hardcover bestseller list. The trade paperback appeared a few months later.

The novel picks up where *The Waste Lands* left off, repeating the final section of the earlier book to bring readers up to speed. In terms of the contemporary action, the book covers a four- or five-day period, although there is some uncertainty due to the slippage of time when Roland is telling his story and because of an adventure inside a magical orb. The backstory set in Mejis spans a period of several months, from the day after Roland's test of manhood until he and his friends return from Mejis.

The first part of *Wizard and Glass* resolves the cliffhanger involving the suicidal Blaine the Mono. The second part finds Roland and his followers in Topeka, Kansas, in a version of America that is similar to the ones the New Yorkers came from, except in this reality a superflu virus has killed almost everyone. Before they visit a mysterious green palace that has materialized across the interstate, Roland needs to tell his companions a story from his youth. Then the *ka-tet* enters the palace and has a showdown with a wizard who goes by many names, including Marten and Randall Flagg.

As the monorail hurtles across Mid-World at breakneck speed, Blaine behaves like a petulant child. He hates being corrected or contradicted and demands to be entertained. When crossed, he metes out punishment, as when he amplifies the sound of the Falls of the Hounds.

Ka has provided Roland and his followers with a couple of clues about how to handle Blaine. The book of riddles Jake got at the Manhattan Restaurant of the Mind is a red herring—a fact hinted at by the missing answers section at the back. The real clue to cracking Blaine is in *Charlie the Choo-Choo*, and it is Eddie who figures it out. After watching Roland spend hours exhausting all the riddles from Fair-Day contests and after Jake tests Blaine with the hardest entries in *Riddle-De-Dum!*, Eddie starts zinging Blaine with stupid, illogical joke-riddles, shooting with his mind like a gunslinger firing bullets. Though Blaine knows the answers to many of them, it pains him to be forced to respond to these unworthy riddles. His circuits blow, his engines cease and the train coasts into Topeka instead of crashing into the barrier at the terminus. The train derails, but at a slow enough speed that the *ka-tet* survives uninjured.

They emerge into a version of Topeka, Kansas, that is different from the one known to the New Yorkers. They see unfamiliar automobile models, soft drink brands and sports franchises. A superflu has decimated the population of America. They find a newspaper dated 1986, a year before Roland drew Eddie from New York, so they can't be in his Earth, but perhaps in a universe that is next door. They also find Gage Park, which has a train that must have inspired Beryl Evans to write *Charlie the Choo-Choo.*

They're no longer on the Path of the Beam. Equipped with a new, light, high-tech wheelchair found in the train station parking lot to replace the one Susannah abandoned in Lud, they head east on Interstate 70, where they encounter a thinny, a place where the fabric of existence is almost entirely worn away. It emits a sound that disturbs the *ka-tet* on a fundamental level. It also brings back a flood of memories for Roland, who first encountered a thinny shortly after he passed his test of manhood in Gilead. Thinnies have been increasing in number since the Dark Tower began its decline. Blaine may have passed through one to get them into this version of America.

In the distance, they see a shimmering green palace that seems to be floating above the lanes of the interstate. Roland knows it means trouble for them. As they draw near, he feels compelled to tell them the story of what happened after his father confronted him the day he beat Cort and won his guns, though the story is going to be difficult for him to face. To reach the Tower, he needs a whole heart and must put the past to rest as much as possible. Finally, he summons the courage to do so and, over the course of a night that seems to last far longer than a handful of hours, he tells his story.

Though young Roland is now a gunslinger, he is no match for the sly Marten. Certain that the wizard will try to kill Roland, Steven Deschain sends his son east to the Barony of Mejis on the Clean Sea, a place that resembles the American Southwest or Mexico both in geography and in lingo. Roland chooses two friends to join him, Cuthbert Allgood and Alain Johns. Their cover story is that they're counting things that the Affiliation might need in a battle with John Farson. As a subtext, they are to imply that this is a punishment for rowdy teenage behavior. Little does Steven Deschain know that he is sending three fourteen-year-olds to a place where Farson has corrupted most of the town's politicians and landowners. Mejis has oil, which Farson needs to run the machinery of the Great Old Ones he discovered in the West. He plans to get this equipment running and lure the Affiliation forces into an ambush.

Before they even officially check into Mejis, Roland meets a beautiful girl two years his senior and soon falls in love with her. Susan Delgado's position is delicate, though. Her father used to be in charge of the Barony's horses, but he stood up against the other landowners and was murdered to keep him quiet. Susan thinks his death was an accident but, regardless of the cause, the outcome is the same: she has no parents and is at risk of becoming destitute and homeless after their papers of ownership go missing.

Susan's greedy spinster aunt, Cordelia Delgado, coerces her into accepting an arrangement with the mayor, Hart Thorin, whereby she will become his "gilly." According to the old laws, if a man's wife cannot bear an heir, he can take a woman on the side to serve this purpose. Susan rationalizes that she can still get married once she has given Thorin a son. Thorin is more interested in bedding a beautiful young woman than in fathering an heir, but Susan doesn't realize this until it's too late. Not until after the deal is finalized and she can't turn back does she consider the effect of this arrangement on Thorin's wife, Olive.

Meeting Roland—traveling under the alias Will Dearborn—complicates her situation. She is attracted to him, too, but she can't go back on her word. She feels bound to honor the memory of her father. The book's subtitle, "Regard," comes from a look Susan gives Roland at the reception party at Thorin's mansion. It's all he needs for encouragement, even though he is furious when he discovers what she has agreed to do. He empathizes with Olive Thorin, who reminds him of his alienated mother.

The temptation of young love is strong, and the two eventually begin a torrid romance loosely modeled on *Romeo and Juliet*. They keep their affair secret from everyone except Alain and Cuthbert, who are dismayed by the way Roland is distracted. The boys (the locals dub them the Affiliation Brats) know that something is amiss in Mejis. The locals are too ready to declare their undying loyalty for the Affiliation when even Roland knows that the Affiliation is coming apart. The Outer Baronies don't see much benefit from the taxes they pay to Gilead. It is left to Alain and Cuthbert to keep up the pretense of counting things while they try to get to the bottom of whatever is going on, a daunting task for boys so young, even prospective gunslingers.

Cuthbert is especially vexed with his friend, comparing him to wet ammunition that might not fire when needed. He's jealous that Roland is always first at everything: first to get his guns, first to fall in love. He tries to browbeat Roland into waking up and conveying their findings to Gilead, but Roland ignores him.

Three mercenary "regulators" called the Big Coffin Hunters, led by failed gunslinger Eldred Jonas, are in Mejis on Farson's behalf. Farson needs horses, of which Mejis has many, and oil. Jonas, who was sent west after losing to

Cort's father, is savvy and skilled, but he underestimates the Affiliation Brats, even after they prove their mettle in a confrontation at the local saloon (where the piano player is Sheb, whom Roland will encounter in Tull) involving a mentally challenged boy named Sheemie. Jonas worries that the "Little Coffin Hunters" have been sent to disrupt their plans, but he thinks that keeping them out of the way while they complete their mission is sufficient.

Thus begins a game of Castles that lasts the rest of the summer. In Castles, each player begins with an army hidden behind a hillock, which prevents him from seeing how his opponent is arranging his men. The crucial point in the game comes when one player emerges from behind the hillock, leaving him vulnerable and exposed if he hasn't planned wisely. Roland and his *ka-tet* and the Big Coffin Hunters are all aware that the other side is up to something, but neither group wants to show its hand too early. Jonas tries to provoke the boys by vandalizing their living quarters. Cuthbert thinks Roland isn't playing the game at all, which leads to a showdown between the two boys and an awakening for Roland, who believed that his falling in love had nothing to do with the game they were playing. That it would somehow lift him above *ka*.

Jonas and his henchmen make the first major move, framing Roland, Cuthbert and Alain for the murders of the mayor and his chancellor. With the boys out of the way, Jonas gets ready to deliver the oil to Farson. He doesn't count on the resourcefulness and strength of Susan Delgado, who, with the help of slow-witted but faithful Sheemie, frees Roland and the others from jail. Susan and Sheemie become full-fledged members of the *ka-tet*, and Susan becomes a de facto gunslinger after being forced to use Roland's guns during the breakout.

Now that Jonas's intentions are exposed, the game of Castles turns deadly. The *ka-tet* destroys the oil field, thus cutting off Farson's source, and attacks the convoy, killing many corrupt local ranchers and scattering the rest. Then they attack and destroy the tankers. They lead the rest of Farson's men into the thinny to their deaths. This will be a major setback to Farson's plans—though ultimately it only delays his victory over the Affiliation.

The wild card in Mejis is a pink glass ball that is part of Maerlyn's Rainbow. Farson uses this glass to monitor the Affiliation's movements. It has allowed him to launch surprise attacks and to avoid capture. There is danger associated with using the glass, though, so he sends it away when he doesn't need it. The Big Coffin Hunters assign it to a local witch named Rhea Dubativo, who uses it to spy on the people of Mejis. She knows about Susan's affair with Roland and is enraged when Susan thwarts her plan to play a prank on Mayor Thorin. Roland also attracts her ire when he warns her to stay out of their business and kills her pet snake.

Rhea becomes addicted to the orb and to the idea of getting back at Susan. When the Big Coffin Hunters take the orb away from her to return it to Farson, Susan—who is pregnant with Roland's child and a captive in the mayor's mansion—is the only person available for her to get back at, so she exposes Susan's infidelity and raises the townspeople against her during the Reaping Night festivities, a time when, historically, a person was burned in ritual sacrifice to appease the gods and seek blessings for their crops. After the terrible losses the town suffered, the people are ready for blood, and Susan pays the price.

Roland learns of her fate through the Wizard's Glass, which he took from Jonas during the battle. The glass shows him many things, most of them hurtful. It reveals how foolish he was, exposing his teenage bravado as stupidity. This explains how he is able to tell parts of the story that happened when he wasn't present to Eddie, Jake and Susannah. The glass misled him into thinking Susan was safe after she was captured by Jonas.

From it, Roland also learns about the Dark Tower and its peril. By the time he returns from his journey inside the glass, he has adopted the quest to find the Tower and save it as his mission in life. While he had once believed he could live a quiet family life with Susan after Farson was defeated, he now realizes he will have to sacrifice any happiness in his life for this cause. He also understands why the gunslingers of Gilead are ignoring the imminent threat to the Affiliation: none of it matters if the Tower falls. He inherits their fatal flaw, sacrificing all short-term concerns in the name of the long-term goal of saving reality. Even if Susan hadn't been killed in Mejis, he wouldn't have stayed with her.

Roland ends his story with the boys' return to Gilead, where they are feted as heroes. Alain and Cuthbert are elevated to gunslingers based on their performance against Farson's troops. Roland doesn't immediately tell his father that he has the Wizard's Glass, though. It reveals a murder plot against his father, which he thwarts, though he doesn't provide details to his new *ka-tet* before they reach the Green Palace.

Eddie, Jake and Susannah tell Roland the story of *The Wizard of Oz* after they find red shoes tailored to their individual needs. The Green Palace may be their way back home—which to the New Yorkers now means Mid-World, not Manhattan.

Inside the building, over which the Crimson King's standard flies, they discover the Tick-Tock Man, who is playing the part of the wizard from the Baum novel, and a real wizard, whom Roland recognizes as Marten Broadcloak from Gilead but who is now calling himself Randall Flagg. Flagg has the pink Wizard's Glass. He tries to convince Roland to give up his quest with promises of an easier life and warns Roland's followers that everyone he has ever loved has been killed, including all the members of his original *ka-tet*.

After Flagg flees from the palace, Roland picks up the Wizard's Glass and uses it to show his friends the end of his story. The conspiracy against his father involved his mother, Gabrielle, who was Marten's lover, a fact Steven Deschain has known for years. While Roland was in Mejis, Gabrielle was at a woman's retreat in Debaria. Upon her return, she was to beg Steven for forgiveness and take him into bed, where she would kill him with a poisoned knife provided by Marten. After intercepting the knife, Roland thinks he can convince his mother to see the error of her ways and swear off the affair. However, Gabrielle stole the pink Wizard's Glass from Steven as a consolation prize for her lover. When Roland visits her chambers, the glass shows him a false vision. He thinks the person sneaking up on him from behind is the witch, Rhea, carrying a poison snake, when it is really his mother bearing the belt she made for him as a peace offering while in Debaria.

Roland kills his mother with his father's guns, a sin that he carries with him all his life. He blames himself for Susan's death, and now he has this burden to bear as well. He needed to show this part of the story to his new followers so they would understand what kind of man was leading them. It is a crucial point in their relationship. He has brought them into his world against their will and infected them with his passion for the Tower. They need to know what being a part of his team means. He offers them the chance to cry off the quest, but it is now their quest, too.

When they leave the Green Palace, they find themselves back in Mid-World on the Path of the Beam. They continue toward the Dark Tower with a new sense of understanding and commitment.

The train trip across Mid-World carried the *ka-tet* farther in several hours than Roland has covered in his entire life. After that, though, the forward momentum of Roland's quest screeches to a halt for hundreds of pages, which frustrated some fans of the series. However, *Wizard and Glass*, coming as it does at the midpoint of the series, is crucial for a number of reasons. It explains how Roland learned of the Tower's plight and when he made it his quest, and it reveals how the wide-eyed and innocent boy seen in flashbacks in *The Gunslinger* becomes the hardened loner who has spent his life in search of the Tower. Since meeting up with the New Yorkers, Roland has learned to love again. Readers come away with a richer understanding of the man and, perhaps, much more sympathy for him.

By the time King finished *Wizard and Glass*, he knew how the series would end. In the book's afterword, he outlines the general shape of the final three books. He intended to start work on the fifth book the following year and carry through to the end because he wanted to finish before he died—a concern shared by the series' fans—or became senile.

Fate intervened in a number of ways. The following year King switched publishers, signing a contract for three books that didn't allow much room for work on the series. However, the Dark Tower was clearly still on his mind. He wrote "The Little Sisters of Eluria" in response to a request for a Dark Tower novella from Robert Silverberg and the short story "Everything's Eventual," which would later reveal itself as a Dark Tower story. His second book for Scribner, *Hearts in Atlantis*, contained the novella "Low Men in Yellow Coats," which introduced the concept of Breakers working on behalf of the Crimson King.

On July 19, 1999, King was struck by a van and almost killed. The Dark Tower was in grave peril. The accident significantly changed King's life, but it also provided inspiration for his writing and became an important plot element in the finale of the Dark Tower series.

> **Characters (in order of mention):** Roland Deschain, Blaine the Mono, Eddie Dean, Jake Chambers, Susannah Dean, Oy, Henry Dean, Aunt Talitha, Elmer Chambers, Cort, the Manni, the doorkeeper, Scheherazade, Cuthbert Allgood, Jimmie Polino, Skipper Brannigan, Tommy Fredericks, John Parelli, Georgie Pratt, Csaba Drabnik, Frank Duganelli, Larry McCain, Marten/Walter, Big Coffin Hunters, Eldred Jonas, Clay Reynolds, Roy Depape, Rhea Dubativo, Susan Delgado, Beryl Evans, Omaha, John Corcoran, Luster, Winston, Jeeves, Maud, Spanker, Gasher, Ronald Reagan, Lord Perth, Walkin' Dude, Crimson King, Engineer Bob, Gabrielle Deschain, Steven Deschain, John Farson, Old People, Hart Thorin, Cordelia Delgado, Pat Delgado, Kimba Rimer, Will Dearborn, Stanley Ruiz, Mrs. Beech, Richard Stockworth, Arthur Heath, Hax, Barons, Alain Johns, Barkie Callahan, Arthur Eld, Pettie the Trotter, Coral Thorin, Sheb McCurdy, Sheemie, Deborah, Herk Avery, Dave Hollis, James Reed, Piet

Ravenhead, Lucas Rivers, Francis Lengyll, John Croydon, Hank
Wertner, Hash Renfrew, Judy Hollis, Olive Thorin, Jake White, John
Haverty, Countess Jillian of Up'ard Killian, Gert Moggins, Dolores
Sheemer, George Latigo, George Riggins, Affiliation Brats, Little
Coffin Hunters, Garbers, Jolene, Miguel Torres, Brian Hookey, Jamie
McCann, Maria Tomas, Conchetta, Laslo Rimer, Vannay, Amy, Mil-
licent Ortega, Frank Claypool, Sylvia Pittston, Old Pa, Flagg, Fardo,
Robert, Francesca, Robert Allgood, Christopher Johns, Hiram Quint,
Alvarez, Todd Bridger, Theresa Maria Dolores O'Shyven, Rufus
Hookey, Soony, the Turtle, Total Hogs, Rodney Hendricks, Raines,
Misha Alvarez, John Farson's nephew, Mother Abigail, Dorothy Gale,
Tick-Tock Man, Andrew Quick, Jamie DeCurry, Megan Chambers.

Places: Candleton; Rilea; Falls of the Hounds; River Crossing; To-
peka, Kansas; Lud; Hambry; Mejis; Tom and Gerry's Artistic Deli;
Cradle of Lud; Gage Park; Clements; Dutch Hill; Gilead; River
Send; New Canaan; Eyebolt Canyon; Cöos Hill; Inner Baronies;
Outer Arc; Western Drop; Seafront (Mayor's House); Travellers' Rest;
Clean Sea; Citgo; Hemphill; Pennilton; Northern Baronies; West'rd
Baronies; Great Hall of Gilead; Desoy; Garlan; Cressia; Indrie;
Southwest Edge; Bar K Ranch; Old Quarter; Rocking B Ranch; Mill-
bank; Rocking H Ranch; Ritzy; Vi Castis Mountains; Wind; Hatti-
gans; Tepachi; Barony Sea Road; Bad Grass; Hanging Rock; Hookey's
Stable and Fancy Livery; Town Lookout; Onnie's Ford; Green Heart;
Seven-Mile Orchard; Shavéd Mountains; Craven's Undertaking Par-
lor; Glencove; Pass o' the River; Dis; Bayview Hotel; Thunderclap;
the Dark Tower; Lake Saroni; Il Bosque; Debaria; Oakley; Nebraska;
Las Vegas; Piper School; Green Palace; Kashamin.

Things: Threaded stock, DEP3, slo-trans engines, Demon Moon,
Riddle-De-Dum!, Watch Me, hile, *dinh*, *khef*, *ka*, Barony Class,
hand-scan spectrum magnifier, *graf*, Wide Earth, Full Earth, *ka-mai*,
astin, Path of the Beam, thinny, shake-loop, saligs, *Charlie the
Choo-Choo*, *Topeka Capital-Journal*, docker's clutch, Captain Trips,
superflu, fottergraf, Takuro Spirit, Kansas City Monarchs, Boing
Boing Burger, I-70, gunslinger burritos, cozening, LaMerk Foundry,
gunna, wot, *ka-tel*, fuzer, Kissing Moon, glam, Musty, Ermot, High
Speech, Maerlyn's grapefruit, Wizard's Rainbow, cully, werewolves,
Great Road, trig, Fair-Night, Rusher, sai, the Affiliation, wheels,

sparklights, Grand Featherex, Reap Morn, rook's skull, Buckskin, Glue Boy, Castles, the Romp, Chancellors' Patience, gilly, iced tea, earth-gas, Honda, Glowing Day, firedims, Dance of Easterling, Excalibur, *sheevin*, camel bucket, Satan's First Law of Malignity, clouts, Peddler's Moon, Pylon, pettibone, bumblers, Ocean Foam, ken/kennit, oxen, Vi Castis Company, Sanday, corvette, Huntress Moon, wolf, fash, Reaping Bonfire, Reaping Day Fair, parey, mingo, sharproot, helio-graph, jewels of Eld, Year's End Fair, water-stool, stuffy-guys, Caprichoso, *Homilies and Meditations*, carvers, the touch, Casa Fuerte, the White, Maerlyn's Rainbow, Black Thirteen, *an-tet*, charyou tree, cotton-gillies, Conversational, coozey, Horsemen's Association, drogue, Zoltan, *The Wizard of Oz*, Nozz-A-La.

Continuity Errors and Mistakes: A Barony famous for rugs changes from Kashmin in *The Waste Lands* to Kashamin in this one. Jake Chambers's mother's name was Laurie in *The Waste Lands*, but here it is Megan. In *The Gunslinger*, Cort's predecessor is named Mark, but in *Wizard and Glass* we learn that Cort's father, Fardo, sent Eldred Jonas West.

Crossover to Other Works: The superflu, Abigail and Randall Flagg will be familiar to readers of *The Stand*.

Foreshadowing and Spoilers: Sheemie Ruiz's part in the quest for the Dark Tower is far from over. In *The Wind Through the Keyhole*, Roland visits the retreat where his mother stayed in Debaria and learns more about her involvement with Marten. Father Callahan will visit Gage Park in Topeka during his travels. The number of oil wells still working in Mejis is nineteen, soon to become "the magic number." However, this is probably just a coincidence, as the inspiration for this number, King's accident, had not yet happened. There are more hints about Susannah's pregnancy, which will become increasingly impor-tant in subsequent books. Oy's fate is also foreshadowed in Roland's vision in the grapefruit. In the afterword, King hints at the upcoming appearance in the series of Father Callahan from *'Salem's Lot*.

THE WIND THROUGH THE KEYHOLE

While Stephen King was reviewing the copyedited manuscript of *11/22/63* in 2011, he heard the Song of the Turtle again, right on schedule, a half dozen years after the "final" book in the Dark Tower series was published. He realized there was at least one hole in the narrative progression—the roughly seven-week period after Roland's *ka-tet* left the Green Palace and before they reached Calla Bryn Sturgis.

The Wind Through the Keyhole is dedicated to Robin Furth and the gang at Marvel. Jae Lee, who did the artwork for *The Gunslinger Born* from Marvel, illustrated the Donald M. Grant limited edition. It could be read as a stand-alone novel. However, anyone familiar with the adventures of Roland and his friends will definitely get more out of the book.

In the interview found in this book, King says that three ideas came together to inspire *The Wind Through the Keyhole*. At the core was a plan to write a fairy tale—perhaps a book of them. He wanted to write about a little boy who had an evil stepfather and needed to go on a journey. Then Roland stepped in and said that this was his story. The skin-man tale was going to be something else. As he posted on his Web site, he then saw a vicious storm and a line of riders in a dusty wind, a severed head on a fencepost and a dangerous swamp. Though the book doesn't reveal much new about the *ka-tet*'s quest, it does show Roland growing into himself as a young gunslinger on a mission, representing Gilead in a world that is moving on.

The novel contains three distinct parts and time periods: the "contemporary" story, Roland's reminiscences of his trip to Debaria after he returned from Mejis and the fable of Tim Ross that young Roland tells to comfort a traumatized boy.

In the contemporary story, the *ka-tet* is continuing along the Path of the

Beam, heading toward Thunderclap. They are on a road, though only barely, and do see occasional signs of life, but these people—some of them mutants—don't approach the gunslingers; nor do they seem dangerous. The number nineteen hasn't yet intrigued them. Oy is behaving strangely, which should have been a clue to Roland, but his childhood is so far behind him—perhaps as much as a thousand years—that he can be forgiven for not picking up on it right away.

When they reach the western branch of the Whye (the eastern branch or Devar-Tete Whye flows past Calla Bryn Sturgis), they meet an old man named Bix who runs a ferry service, though he hasn't had much custom for many years. Bix is friendly and welcomes company, feeding them fish popkins. He knows what Oy's behavior is all about: a starkblast—a freezing tornado—is coming, so the *ka-tet* needs to find cover. Bix directs them toward the abandoned town of Gook, where they hole up in the stone meeting hall for a few days after gathering wood and blocking the windows.

While the storm rages, killing trees, destroying buildings and freezing birds in flight, the *ka-tet* grows restless. To pass the time, they huddle in front of the fire and ask Roland to tell them a story of his youth. He says that he will tell them two stories, one nested inside the other. One is true and the other is a story his mother read to him when he was small.

The story of "The Skin-Man" is split into two parts, interrupted when Roland recounts "The Wind Through the Keyhole." One of the interesting aspects of the skin-man story is that it is told in first person from Roland's point of view. When he told his *ka-tet* about his adventures in Mejis, that story was told in third person, in part because Roland learned much of it from the pink Wizard's Glass.

Shortly after Roland returns from Mejis, his father sends him on another mission, this time with Jamie DeCurry. The High Sheriff of Debaria, a town west of Gilead, reported that a creature has killed and maimed dozens of people in his district. The attacker is said to resemble a wolf, a lion, a tiger or a bear, and its tracks change from enormous to man-sized when followed. Roland's teacher, Vannay, has assembled all of the available information, along with the legends of the skin-man.

Sending Roland to Debaria will prove to the people that the gunslingers of Gilead still care about what is happening in their realm. However, it's more than a token gesture—Steven Deschain expects Roland and Jamie to solve the mystery and put an end to this scourge. It's also a way of getting Roland out of his funk. He's depressed after killing his mother and punishing himself by acting as Cort's nursemaid.

Debaria has resonance for Roland—it's where his mother, Gabrielle, went on retreat while he was in Mejis. After being dumped off the little train that carried them from Gilead when it derails, and observing during their journey how many people outside of Gilead appear to be for the revolutionary John Farson, their first stop is at the Serenity retreat, where the skin-walker attacked two women, one of whom survived but was disfigured. There they meet the prioress, Everlynne, who recognizes Roland by his resemblance to his mother. She invites Roland to return to the retreat when his work is done, for she has something to give him.

Two boys representing Gilead don't impress the locals, though their weapons do. Sheriff Peavy is cooperative, though. He has Steven Deschain to thank for his position. The gunslinger gave him credit for capturing the Crow Gang twenty years ago, when Peavy was a deputy. The then-sheriff and the rest of the posse were killed when they ignored Deschain's advice. Peavy removed a bullet from Deschain's arm—Roland's father sent the bullet as a gift via Roland.

Jamie sees a pattern in the attacks and the course of the tracks that leads him to believe that the skin-walker is one of the miners in nearby Little Debaria. Their problem becomes reducing the field of two hundred potential suspects to something manageable and breaching the creature's defenses—if he even knows what he is.

They bunk out at the jailhouse and are awakened by a call the next morning reporting another attack. Almost everyone at the Jefferson Ranch— eighteen people, including the owner, his family, the staff and hands—has been slaughtered. The only survivors are three hands who were out gathering strays and the son of the cook, who was camping.

The boy, Young Bill Streeter, saw the creature and provides two helpful clues when Roland hypnotizes him. After transforming back into a man, the killer rode away on a horse. He had a tattoo on his ankle. Few miners are likely to know how to ride, and the tattoo—which turns out to be a sign the man spent time in Beelie Stockade—will further reduce the suspect pool. Roland sends Jamie with a team to Little Debaria to round up possible suspects and spread word that they have a witness who can identify the man. Only a cold person like Roland could conceive of and execute a plan that uses a young boy as bait.

While Jamie is away, Roland hires a blacksmith to make a silver bullet, on Vannay's advice. He spends the rest of the time at the jailhouse with Young Bill, bringing him food and candy, helping him to be brave. Finally, as the hours grow long, he tells the boy the story of "The Wind Through the Keyhole," one that Gabrielle Deschain used to read to him when he was younger.

Soon after he finishes, Jamie returns with wagons containing twenty-one miners, one of whom may be the skin-man. Roland screens out those who don't have the Beelie Stockade tattoo and parades the remaining ten in front of Young Bill, who is safely behind bars. If Bill can't identify the skin-man, Roland plans to lock them all up until one changes.

The oldest miner in the group, Steg Luka, tells Roland they discovered a crack with a pulsing light at the bottom of a mine. A voice from the crack invites men to enter it. Luka thinks it's a voice from the Old People. The foreman ordered the crack plugged, but someone has been at the rocks. He believes that person went to the other side and was changed.

On the second pass, Billy sees something in one of the tattoos that registers in his mind. The culprit also carries a watch, which Luka thinks must have come from inside the crack. The miner quickly changes shape, becoming a poisonous snake like the one in Roland's story. He kills two more people before Roland slays him with the silver bullet, mirroring his ancestor, Arthur Eld, who once killed a monstrous snake called Saita. In death, the skin-man reverts to human form, passing through a number of creatures along the way.

One of the responsibilities of being a gunslinger is to take part in the celebrations that follow a victory. Roland and Jamie fulfill their duty and, as a bonus, Jamie loses his virginity that night after they dispose of the skin-man's body. Roland visits with Prioress Everlynne to see if she will take in the orphaned Bill Streeter. She agrees and then gives Roland a message his mother left for him. He learns that Gabrielle Deschain knew that she would die by her son's hand if she returned to Gilead and went back anyway, believing it was the role *ka* had cast for her. She'd still been in Marten's thrall. The wizard had tried to see her at Serenity, but Everlynne had sent him packing. He may have been able to communicate with her anyway. Gabrielle's message reveals her tenuous grasp on sanity, but it offers Roland something he may have needed: her forgiveness.

The centerpiece of the novel is the story of another gunslinger, a young boy named Tim Ross who lived in Tree Village on the edge of the Endless Forest. People in that region of Mid-World earned a living by chopping down the ironwood trees at the edge of the forest and selling them to Gilead.

Tim's father, Jack Ross, and his partner, Bern Kells, were lifelong friends who worked a patch of the forest. As the story begins, Tim finds himself in a plight similar to that of Susan Delgado in *Wizard and Glass*. Jack Ross is killed—by a dragon, according to Kells—which means Tim and his mother, Nell, are in danger of losing their home to the greedy Barony Covenanter when he comes to collect the annual taxes in a few months. Susan Delgado's solution to her problem was to become Mayor Hart Thorin's jilly. Nell Ross's solution is to accept Bern Kells's marriage proposal. She doesn't love him, but she thinks she can put up with him, especially if it means she and Tim won't end up homeless. After they marry, Kells sells his house and moves in with Nell and Tim.

Kells is an alcoholic who becomes violent when he drinks. He's been on the wagon for some time, convinced to get sober by his wife, who died in childbirth. Tim takes it as a bad sign that Kells can't find a new woodcutting partner and that many of the other woodsmen didn't attend the wedding. Things go from bad to worse after the wedding. He returns to his old ways, abuses Nell and forces Tim to give up his schooling and go to work at the sawmill.

The Barony Covenanter is more than a taxman—he's a wizard who doesn't seem to age. He enjoys squeezing money out of people, but he also likes using the truth to hurt them. He identifies Tim as a likely victim, but also sees the potential to use him in a grander scheme. He gives Tim a magic key that will open Kells's trunk, in which the boy finds his father's lucky coin, which should have been destroyed by the dragon.

When Tim accepts the Covenant Man's invitation to visit his camp, he discovers the truth about his father's death. There was no dragon. Bern Kells murdered him and secreted the body in a cold stream. One reason his drinking has resumed is that he's worried the woodcutters who work that patch will return to it and discover the body, revealing his crime. The Covenant Man shows Tim a vision in a basin of water: Bern Kells flying into a rage when he finds his trunk unlocked. He beats Nell so badly she goes blind. The Covenant Man gives Tim a gift: Jack Ross's ax, which Kells threw across the stream after the murder. This is how he works: he winds Tim into a frenzy, identifies his enemy, arms him and sends him homeward.

However, Kells runs away, so Tim can't kill his evil stepfather. His teacher, Widow Smack, knows who the Covenant Man is—an enchanter from the court of Gilead. Marten Broadcloak, in other words, though she doesn't know his name. Tim raises a posse against Bern Kells and sees to the return of his father's body for burial. Then the Covenant Man sends another vision. If Tim goes into the Endless Forest and finds Maerlyn, he will be rewarded with a cure for his mother's blindness. Widow Smack can't talk Tim out of acting on this vision, so she provides him with food, a light and a gun that had once belonged to her brother. The Covenant Man won't anticipate that Tim will go on his mission armed.

King said he wanted to write a fairy tale, though one that didn't necessarily contain a real fairy. "The Wind Through the Keyhole" does feature a fairy, a naked, flying green woman only four inches tall who will doubtless conjure mental images of Tinker Bell. The *sighe*, named Armaneeta, is beautiful, delightful, seductive—and malign. Like a siren, she leads Tim through the Endless Forest into the Fagonard Swamp, where she strands him on a tussock surrounded by all manner of dangerous creatures, including a dragon.

Tim is determined to die fighting. In that moment, he is transformed into a gunslinger. Like Roland, his mouth becomes a rictus grin as he shoots for the first time, killing a creature that emerges from the swamp. The gunshot draws the attention of the closest thing to human residents Fagonard has. At first Tim thinks of them as mudmen but later he realizes they are closer to plants. Living in the swamp for so long has made them take on its appearance. They are slow mutants, but benevolent ones, and probably doomed to extinction.

They respect Tim as a gunslinger and hile him. Tim uses their reaction to his advantage, asking for their service as bondsmen. They can understand him, and, though they can't speak, they communicate in sign language. They try to warn him of a pending starkblast, but he doesn't understand. He gets the sense, though, that something is going to happen that will kill them.

Using a makeshift boat, they transport him from the tussock to the end of the swamp, depositing him on solid ground. They give Tim food and water and a device (produced by North Central Positronics) that will lead him north, to where he hopes to find Maerlyn in a magic house where time stands still.

For the next few days, Tim heads north through the forest, following the Beam of the Lion. The direction finder, Daria, Tim discovers, can talk, providing helpful information, though some of its data is protected by Directive Nineteen.

The appearance of six billy-bumblers (throcken) and their behavior is another clue to the mudmen's unsolved pantomime. There's a starkblast coming that will likely destroy the swamp. Tim needs to find cover. His course is leading him toward North Forest Kinnock Dogan, which Daria advises is offline due to the presence of magic. She keeps offering to show him a detour around it, but magic is what Tim is after, so he proceeds.

Like Roland's *ka-tet*, Tim must cross a hazardous bridge near his destination. This one is narrow and crumbly, but the biggest danger comes from tentacled plants that live in the chasm below. Once across and past the skeleton of a man, he climbs a stone staircase and sees the Dogan in the distance. A metal tower with a blinking red light stands beside it.

Beyond the Dogan is the Great Canyon, which seems at least one hundred wheels wide. At the edge of the chasm is an enormous tyger in a cage. Tim also sees the tin bucket the Covenant Man gave him in Tree Village. The tyger has a metal key and a card key hanging from its collar. Daria identifies the tyger as the source of the magic she detected, but in doing so she violates Directive Nineteen and self-destructs.

Tim can hear the starkblast in the distance, but the Dogan is locked. Under the pail he finds a message from the Covenant Man signed with the initials "RF" and "MB"—Randall Flagg and Marten Broadcloak. Tim has two choices: he can shoot the tyger, or he can negotiate with it. Is the tyger a trap for him, or is he a trap for the tyger? He thinks the Covenant Man expects him to use the gun, so he opens the cage instead. If he and the tyger remain outdoors, they'll both die. If the tyger will allow him to take the keys from his neck, they can find shelter from the storm.

The card key doesn't work because the Dogan is offline, but the other key opens a box beside the door. It contains a feather, a bottle and a napkin. The tyger shows Tim that the napkin will unfold, becoming magically bigger each time until it's the size of a blanket that is resistant to the cold. Tim and the tyger climb underneath. Tim shares the last of his food with the tyger and they ride out the storm. "The Wind Through the Keyhole" takes its title from a passage that compares time to a keyhole and the breath of the living universe to the wind we feel on our cheeks when we peer through it.

Afterward, the tyger shows an interest in the bottle Tim found in the box. He opens his mouth and Tim administers a few drops with an eyedropper. The tyger transforms—like a skin-man—into Maerlyn, the magician of Eld. The remaining drops, Maerlyn tells him, are meant for his mother as a reward for freeing the magician from captivity. Tim questions Maerlyn about many of the legends surrounding him, but the magician thinks no one is interested in the banal truth—that he's retired to a cave with only the bare necessities. He doesn't confirm that he lives backward in time, either, but it's clear from his instructions that he knows about the future. He orders Tim to give his father's ax to his mother, but he won't say why.

Maerlyn reveals that he was trapped in this form by one of the Red King's servants, who tricked him when he was drunk. The Great One won't be happy that the Covenant Man's unauthorized high jinks ended up freeing Maerlyn. His days collecting taxes for Gilead are likely over. Maerlyn then tells Tim that he is destined to be a gunslinger and that he will be buried with his father's lucky coin around his neck.

He shows Tim how to turn the magic napkin into a flying carpet that will take him home. The feather, which is from the tail of Garuda, the Guardian of the Beam of the Bird, helps him navigate. On the way, he sees the destruction caused by the starkblast. Fagonard is ruined and the dragon—which spared his life—is dead.

In Tree, the damage is minor, except for the sawmill, which has been destroyed. Tim rushes home to administer the eyedrops to his mother and give her his father's ax. Then he discovers that Widow Smack, who sat with his mother during the storm, has been killed. Bern Kells erupts into the room in a murderous rage. The reason for Maerlyn's instructions becomes apparent. Nell buries Jack Ross's ax in Kells's head, killing him.

Young Roland finishes his tale by saying that Tim carried the gun Widow Smack gave him for the next ten years and later carried bigger ones, six-shooters. When he was twenty-three, three gunslingers passed through Tree, hoping to raise a posse. Tim was the only one who joined them. They called him the "left-handed gun" because of how he drew. He eventually became one of the few gunslingers not from the proven line of Eld, though Roland admits that Arthur Eld had many children from three wives and many more illegitimate children. He eventually became known as Tim Stoutheart and took his mother to Gilead.

Tim promises himself he will go to the Dark Tower someday. He saw Maerlyn once more, when he was an old man—but that, like so many incidents Roland mentions, is a story for another day.

When Roland and his *ka-tet* emerge from the stone meeting hall, Gook is gone. Susannah asks Roland about the final two lines in his mother's note—a note he carried with him until the wind carried it away, as the wind eventually takes all things. One line offered Gabrielle Deschain's forgiveness and the other asked for Roland's. With a rare smile on his face, Roland says that, yes, he was able to forgive his mother.

The next morning, the *ka-tet* returns to the Path of the Beam heading toward Calla Bryn Sturgis and the Dark Tower beyond.

Characters (in order of mention): Arthur Eld, Roland, Tick-Tock Man, Jake Chambers, Eddie Dean, Susannah Dean, Oy, Gasher, Randall Flagg, Detta Walker, Bix, Blaine the Mono, Patricia the Mono, Andy the Messenger Robot, Elmer Chambers, Jamie De-Curry, Steven Deschain, Henry the Tall, Gabrielle Deschain, Cort,

John Farson, Vannay, Marten Broadcloak, Rhea, Cuthbert Allgood, Alain Johns, Hugh Peavy, Manni, Tim Stoutheart Ross, David Quick, Lord Perth, Everlynne, Ellen, Clemmie, Brianna, Fortuna, Dolores, Peter McVries, Crow Gang, Belinda Doolin, Pea Anderson, Allan "Pa" Crow, Salty Sam, Kellin Frye, Vikka Frye, Yon Curry, Great Old Ones, Bill Canfield, Travis, Snip, Arn, Young Bill Streeter, Bill Streeter, Elrod Nutter, Susan Delgado, Strother, Pickens, Nell Ross, Big Jack Ross, Big Bern Kells, Hodiak, Barony Covenanter, Ardelia "Widow" Smack, Destry, Millicent Redhouse, Baldy Anderson, Straw Willem Destry, Randy Destry, Rupert Venn, the Crimson King, Haggerty the Nail, Square Peter Cosington, Slow Ernest Marchly, Howard Tasley, Maerlyn of the Eld, Dustin Stokes, Ada Cosington, Hunter Destry, Joshua, Gan, Armaneeta, Splinter Harry, Helmsman, Headman, Deaf Rincon, Will Wegg, Puck De-Long, Man Jesus, Sam Shunt, Steg Luka, Banderly, Bobby Frane, Jake Marsh, Ollie Ang, Gary Cooper.

Places: Green Palace, Oz, Thunderclap, the Dark Tower, Took's Outland Mercantile, Gilead, Whye River, Callas, Lud, In-World, Calla Bryn Sturgis, Great Woods, New Canaan, Gook, Cressia, Mejis, Debaria, Serenity, Mohaine Desert, Out-World, Beesford-on-Arten, Cheery Fellows Saloon & Café, Sallywood, Little Debaria, Low Pure, Ambush Arroyo, High Pure, Nis, Salt Rocks, Delightful View, Endless Forest, Racey's Café, Salt Village, Beelie Stockade, Beelie, Tree, Ironwood Trail, North'rd Barony, Goodview, West'rd Baronies, Gitty's Saloon, Tree Sawmill, Fagonard, Garlan, Na'ar, Tavares, Stape Brook, Waypoint Nine, North Forest Kinnock, Great Canyon, Lake Cawn, Busted Luck, Kuna.

Things: Billy-bumblers, Path of the Beam, slinkum, popkins, throcken, *The Throcken and the Dragon*, gunslinger burritos, sandalwood, shannies, harriers, shume, ironwood, North Central Positronics, Dogan, *Magic Tales of the Eld*, "The Wind Through the Keyhole," bright, starkblast, limbits, gook, bin-rusties, *ka-mate*, David, *dinh*, clouts, jakes, moit, Maerlyn's grapefruit, ammies, wheels, *sigul*, Western Line, Sma' Toot, specie, bah, Watch Me, bill of circulation, Deep Cracks, the White, Peddler's Moon, chary, trig, salt-houses, Efday, Ethday, Reaptide, pokie, proddie, salties, shaddie, simoom, Old Mother, Old Star, blossie, wervels, Wide Earth, vurt,

Full Earth, *graf*, Huntress Moon, gormless, fashed, jilly, bitsy, pooky, glam, nen, chary, Wizard's Rainbow, *ka*, dragons, Points, cully, hile, delah, Daria, jippa, Directive Nineteen, New Earth, North Forest Kinnock Dogan, tyger, Aslan, bull-squirter, dibbin, Garuda, Sunshine, *tet-fa*, *ka-tet*, Debaria Salt Combyne, clobbers, skiddums, snick, slowkins, *ka-essen*.

Continuity Errors and Mistakes: Bix mentions Andy and his horoscopes, and Roland's story mentions Dogans, Directive Nineteen and North Central Positronics, but the *ka-tet* remembers none of these things when they encounter them in Calla Bryn Sturgis.

Crossovers to Other Works: The Covenant Man's lips are as red as if they'd been colored with madder—the color that gives rise to Rose Madder in the book of the same name. The creature the miners discover at the bottom of the mine in Little Debaria is reminiscent of Tak from *Desperation*.

Foreshadowing and Spoilers: Bix mentions Andy the Messenger Robot, who will feature prominently in *Wolves of the Calla*, as will the rice farmers. Daria's Directive Nineteen also prevents Andy from revealing certain critical information. The *ka-tet* will encounter other Dogans in their journeys. Susannah is still grappling with her pregnancy, which will also become increasingly important in the final books in the series. The fact that the skin-man has a pocket watch foreshadows the identity of the spy in Calla Bryn Sturgis, who is the only person in town who owns something of the old technology.

WOLVES OF THE CALLA: RESISTANCE

When they heard of King's near-fatal accident in 1999, Dark Tower fans despaired that he would ever finish the series. King, too, worried that he might not write again, but before long he was back at it, writing in longhand during his rehabilitation. Then he and Peter Straub decided to work on a sequel to *The Talisman*. King eagerly accepted Straub's suggestion that they lace the book with Dark Tower mythos.

Shortly before *Black House* was published in September 2001, King announced that he had returned to the land of the gunslinger and intended to publish the remaining three books all at once. He felt like if he didn't push through to the finish then, he might never be able to. He listened to Frank Muller's audio versions of the first four books and hired Robin Furth as a research assistant to document every important person, place and thing from the earlier books.

He toyed with different titles for the fifth book. His first idea was *The Crawling Shadow*, but he decided that was corny. According to *Song of Susannah*, he also considered calling it *The Werewolves of End-World*.

True to his word, he wrote the final three books back-to-back-to-back before any of them appeared. Two excerpts from *Wolves of the Calla* came out prior to publication. King posted the prologue on his Web site and "The Tale of Grey Dick" appeared in *McSweeney's Mammoth Treasury of Thrilling Tales*, edited by Michael Chabon, in February 2003. The prologue also appeared in the Viking reprint of *Wizard and Glass*, a rare case of publisher cross-promotion.

Wolves of the Calla came out in November 2003. The six-year gap between the appearance of the fourth and fifth installments of the series equaled the longest interval between books. It is dedicated to audiobook narrator

Frank Muller, who'd suffered a debilitating accident. King calls him the man who hears the voices in his head.

King returns to one of the influences for the Dark Tower series, *The Magnificent Seven*. In the John Sturges Western, a small Mexican village is raided regularly by a group of bandits led by Calvera. The citizens decide to arm themselves against their return but are instead advised to hire gunslingers to defend the village.

Wolves of the Calla uses this concept as the story's launching point. In the film, some townspeople who disagree with the plan betray the seven gunmen, leading to their capture. The hired guns never anticipated waging a full-out war against the bandits—they believed their presence would be enough to discourage Calvera and his men. But Calvera is desperate, so a battle ensues during which many of the hired guns are killed. The townspeople take up arms in their own defense and rout the bandits. The surviving gunslingers ride off into the sunset, feeling like the town has won but they've lost.

The "bandits" who raid Calla Bryn Sturgis once a generation aren't hungry, desperate men but are instead fearsome Wolves who ride in on horseback. They aren't after crops—they're after twins, which are the rule rather than the exception in the Callas that are spread along the Whye River, a kind of fertile crescent similar to the Mississippi region. They take one of every twin from as young as three to late adolescence.

Taking the children is torment enough. However, the stolen children are returned via train in a condition described as "roont" (ruined). Something has been extracted from them, causing a permanent mental handicap. Some can function better than others, but even the best require full-time care. Eventually they will undergo a painful growth spurt that turns them into oversized galoots, unable even to control their bodily functions. They age and die prematurely. It's almost insult to injury—the Calla-folken might have been better off without the added burden of having to look after their roont offspring. Some come up with creative solutions. Tian Jaffords uses his sister as a mule for his plow when trying to reclaim a rocky patch of farmland.

News of the pending arrival of the Wolves is delivered by Andy the Messenger Robot, a seven-foot-tall Asimov robot built by North Central Positronics who is good for little other than casting horoscopes, singing and spreading gossip. On the subject of the Wolves, though, he is never wrong. The Calla-folken have a month to prepare for their coming.

There is dissension among the townspeople about whether to hire the gunslingers who are reportedly passing by on the Path of the Beam northeast of town—mostly among the richest citizens who have the most to lose financially if the strategy fails and the Wolves destroy the town and farms. However, they are also the ones with the least to lose in terms of children, as most of them don't have any vulnerable twins.

Tian Jaffords is the unlikely hero of the piece. Most people in the Calla are resigned to their fate. The Wolves have been coming for five or six generations, and any attempts to fend them off have been disastrous. The Wolves are heavily armed, with light sabers and self-guided grenades (sneetches), whereas the Calla-folken have nothing more than a few rusty old guns. As in *The Magnificent Seven*, the idea Tian proposes at a town meeting is not to defend themselves but to enlist the aid of professionals.

He's on the verge of losing control of the meeting when an old man steps up to support his proposal—Father Callahan, the exiled priest from 'Salem's Lot, Maine. Callahan ended up on the borders of Thunderclap after he left the vampire-ridden town and has been in Calla Bryn Sturgis long enough to build a church and convert half the folken to his religion. He plays the part of the wise old man who lives outside town in *The Magnificent Seven*. He has an ulterior motive for contacting the gunslingers, though. He has a terrible object hidden beneath the floorboards of his church and he hopes they will take it off his hands.

Several people ride out to meet the travelers to see if they can offer any help. No one believes they're gunslingers, for the line of Eld had all been dead for a thousand years.

Roland is forced to take his eyes away from his quest for the Tower, compelled by the code of the gunslingers. If people ask for his help and he deems them to be on the side of the White, he must assist. He has other problems to worry about, too. He's suffering from arthritis that hasn't yet afflicted his hands but might soon. Also, he knows that Susannah is pregnant and that her child is probably the product of the demon from the Speaking Circle where Jake reentered Mid-World from Dutch Hill. At night, Susannah is venturing naked into swamps and eating frogs and bugs. Roland believes a new personality has emerged, one who calls herself Mia, which is the word for "mother" in High Speech. She shares some of Detta's memories, but Susannah has no awareness of her presence.

The *ka-tet* is distracted by the mystery number nineteen. They see it in everything, though Roland isn't impressed. They have also started traveling to New York in 1977 in their dreams, a process called going todash. Some of their essence is left behind in Mid-World, and people step around them in New York as if they can sense their presence without actually seeing them. Eddie and Jake go to the Manhattan Restaurant of the Mind in time to see Jake leave with *Charlie the Choo-Choo* and the riddle book. Then they observe what happened afterward: Enrico Balazar and two bodyguards—all familiar to Eddie Dean—show up to remind Tower that he has a signed agreement with them to keep the vacant lot at the corner of Second Avenue and 42nd Street until July 15, at which point they expect him to sell it to Sombra Corporation.

There are enough differences between this day and the one Jake remembers to indicate that this is a different version of reality. *Charlie the Choo-Choo* has a different author (whose name has nineteen characters) and Stephen King's name shows up on the deli board in the bookstore window. Eddie knows that if Balazar is coming to a meeting, he means business.

Eddie tells the *ka-tet* that they have to protect the rose in the vacant lot, which is the Dark Tower's representation in that universe. He wants to buy the property from Calvin Tower, but they have no money. Also, they would need to find targeted doorways to take them to Manhattan at the right times because they can't transact business while todash. Susannah figures she has enough money from Odetta's inheritance to buy the lot, but they'd have to go back to 1964 to acquire the funds since she's probably been declared dead by 1977. Roland says they are taking magic doors for granted. Until the Western Sea, he'd never seen one in all his years of travel.

This is where Father Callahan steps in, believing he might have the solution to their problem. Roland guesses correctly that Father Callahan has Black Thirteen, the most dangerous of the glass balls from the Wizard's Rainbow. Some of these glasses have the power to send people todash—Black Thirteen has done this to Callahan twice—and they may be able to wrest its power and bend it to their will.

Roland and his *ka-tet* do an impromptu demonstration of their abilities, sufficient to convince even the most reluctant among the group that it is worthwhile to explore the possibility of hiring the gunslingers. Roland displays his skills as a diplomat when discussing the matter with Overholser, the Calla's biggest farmer.

Another todash trip that night takes the entire *ka-tet* to the vacant lot. Susannah's new personality, Mia, is afraid to go near the rose, so she makes excuses to stay on the sidewalk. Whenever Mia asserts her presence during these todash trips, Susannah has legs—white legs—and when she steps back,

Susannah loses her legs. As they are about to leave, Jake picks up a bowling bag provided by *ka* to contain Black Thirteen and shield the *ka-tet* from the worst of its powers. When they return to Mid-World, the bag goes todash with them.

The *ka-tet* accompanies Callahan, Overholser and the others back to Calla Bryn Sturgis, where they are treated like celebrities. The town throws a huge party to welcome them. This gives the *ka-tet* time to get to know some people. Jake makes friends with Benny Slightman, the son of Overholser's foreman, and accepts an invitation to stay at their ranch. Eddie is forced to speak before the assembled audience, Susannah sings and Roland surprises his friends by dancing the commala during "The Rice Song." In doing so, he wins over the hearts of the Calla-folken, and the outcome of the pending decision seems like a foregone conclusion.

Roland leaves nothing to chance, though. They have the better part of a month to gather intelligence about the Wolves and to see what local resources they might rely upon. He's counting things again, like he did in Mejis. They talk to anyone who will spare the time, and the effort proves worthwhile. They learn that the Wolves are vulnerable. One of them was killed in the past, and when Eddie finally gets Jamie Jaffords—Tian's grandfather—to recount that story, they discover a crucial detail that may turn the tide of the battle in their favor.

Though there are few usable guns in the Calla, there is another weapon that intrigues Roland. A number of the women throw sharpened titanium dishes called Orizas. They're like lethal Frisbees and some of the best throwers are deadly. He sends Susannah to train with them and to identify the best markswomen among the Sisters of Oriza.

It's not all work, though. Roland finds time to befriend Rosalita Muñoz, Father Callahan's assistant. She has a balm that soothes his aching joints, and she takes him to bed—his first lover since Allie in Tull.

Father Callahan tells the story of how he got from Maine to Calla Bryn Sturgis. After being tainted by Barlow's blood, he took a bus to New York, went to work at a homeless shelter and discovered that he could detect vampires. When one infects his friend Lupe Delgado with AIDS, he makes it his mission to kill the ones he encounters, which brings him to the attention of the low men, who begin to hunt him. He travels across the country to evade them and, to his surprise, travels between different versions of America where certain details are different. The name of a city, for example, or who appears on the twenty-dollar bill.

His alcoholism worsens, and he hits bottom in Topeka. He dries out and continues to travel. In California, he sees an article about another friend, Rowan Magruder, who was attacked by the Hitler Brothers in New York. The assault was meant to lure him back to Manhattan, and it works. After he visits Magruder in the hospital, the Hitler Brothers attack him, too. Though they usually only maim their victims with swastikas carved into their foreheads, they mean to kill Callahan on behalf of the low men. However, two men interrupt the attack—Calvin Tower and Aaron Deepneau from the Manhattan Restaurant of the Mind. Callahan is left with a cross-shaped scar on his forehead, but he survives.

He ends up working at another shelter in Detroit, thinking that he's fallen off the low men's radar. However, they lure him to a meeting at Sombra Corporation's local offices with promises of a grant. It's another trap, set by Richard Sayre, the name Eddie saw on the memorandum of agreement Balazar was showing to Calvin Tower. Callahan commits suicide rather than fall victim to the vampires.

Like Jake Chambers, though, for Callahan death isn't the end. He wakes up in the same Way Station where Jake arrived, greeted by Walter o'Dim, who circled back from leading Roland into the mountains. Walter doesn't think Roland will survive their encounter, but in case he does, he plans to use Callahan as a trap. He gives the priest Black Thirteen and sends him through the Unfound Door. This magic door goes with him, ending up in the former Cave of Voices north of Calla Bryn Sturgis. The Manni find Callahan and nurse him back to health.

After Roland finishes sharing *khef* with his *ka-tet*, he thinks Callahan will be joining them when they leave Calla Bryn Sturgis. Callahan takes Roland to his church to see Black Thirteen, which sleeps beneath the floorboards except when it sent him todash to see Ben Mears's funeral and, another time, to the Castle of the Crimson King.

Because the *ka-tet* splits up for maximum efficiency, they need to meet often to share information. Roland finally tells Eddie about Susannah's pregnancy. His main concern is to make sure she isn't distracted during the battle. Jake learns the secret on his own because of his strong sense of touch. Roland broaches the possibility of abortion to Father Callahan, who promptly threatens to raise the town against the *ka-tet* if Roland moves forward with that idea and if he doesn't do everything in his power to prevent Susannah from doing it on her own.

Jake also suspects that his new friend's father is lying, suspicions that are confirmed when he follows Ben Slightman and Andy on a late-night sojourn across the Whye to a North Central Positronics monitoring station (Dogan). Andy coerced Slightman into betraying his friends because Benny's twin sister is dead, which makes him uniquely vulnerable to the Wolves. Jake also learns that the Calla is bugged with cameras, which is why the Wolves are always a few steps ahead of any planned resistance. Slightman and Andy make their reports to someone named Finli o'Tego in Algul Siento.

Time is moving faster in New York, and each time they cross over it will be later, because the version of reality containing the rose is special. They can't afford to miss the July 15 deadline. Eddie comes up with a simplified version of their plan—rather than messing around with Susannah's money, he thinks they can convince Tower to sell them the lot for a dollar. That means they have to return only to 1977.

Henchick of the Manni takes Roland to the Doorway Cave, where anyone who enters is tormented by voices from the past. The doorway is exactly like the ones on the Western Sea except it is labeled UNFOUND. Using Black Thirteen, Roland is sure they can open the door to any place or time they want. Once again, Walter's trap fails—this time it actually proves helpful, perhaps further evidence that all things serve the Beam.

Roland and Eddie use the Unfound Door and Black Thirteen to send Eddie to New York. As long as the box containing Black Thirteen is open, the door remains open, so Roland stays behind to make sure it doesn't snap shut on its own. The cave's voices and the seductive voice of the ball are difficult to withstand.

Eddie shows up in time for another meeting at Tower's store. This time it's his old nemesis, Jack Andolini, and George Biondi, though it will be a decade before the two men know him. He catches them by surprise, disables Biondi and frightens Andolini sufficiently that he believes he will carry a message back to Balazar: Tower is off-limits. Once the men are gone, Eddie convinces Tower that he is representing the line of Eld and gets the man to agree to sell the lot to the ad hoc company, Tet Corporation, for a dollar.

Balazar's men have already threatened to burn Tower's books. Eddie knows Tower won't be safe in Manhattan, so he convinces him to take a trip out of town until the deadline passes. Deepneau will leave the zip code of their destination on the fence outside the vacant lot. Before Eddie leaves, Tower makes him move a shelf containing his most valuable books through the Unfound Door. Later, when Father Callahan goes to New York to retrieve the zip code, Roland discovers a copy of *'Salem's Lot* in Tower's collection.

He can't read much of the book, but he understands its importance. When Callahan goes to Stoneham, Maine, to deliver a message to Tower, the voices in the cave almost convince Eddie to jump off the mountain.

As the day of the Wolves approaches, Roland has Tian assemble the Calla-folken once more. He asks them the three prerequisite questions for hiring gunslingers and gets a resounding yes to each. He then lays out their plan, though much of what he says is a lie. It's part of a disinformation campaign meant to mislead the Wolves. The night before the battle, Eddie tricks Andy and convinces the robot to shut himself down. For generations, he has been coercing someone local into betraying his own people. Those days are done, at least.

Roland's first clue to Ben Slightman's complicity was his glasses. Like the pocket watch worn by the salt miner in Debaria, this example of Old People technology gave him away. Even before Andy's destruction, Slightman believed Jake knew what he was doing because the boy's attitude toward his son changed. Roland tells him he won't expose him to his son if he fights hard to save the children. Slightman reveals the reason behind the raids: the twins' brains contain a special chemical used to enhance the powers of the Breakers, who are working to destroy the Tower.

Susannah's water breaks moments before the Wolves arrive, but she makes a deal with Mia: allow her to take part in the battle and she will help Mia with the baby. Mia agrees.

The battle is brief. The children are hidden in the rice fields—not the caves, as Roland had led everyone to believe—and the best of the Sisters of Oriza join the *ka-tet* (forming a Magnificent Seven) in an ambush. From Jamie Jaffords's story, they know that the Wolves are robots like the ones they dealt with near Shardik's Portal of the Bear. The hoods cover their vulnerable satellite dishes. There is a momentary crisis when one of the children Roland sends out with Jake to leave a false trail breaks his ankle in a hole. Jake blames him for what happens after. The gunslingers and the Oriza flingers prevail, killing all the Wolves in short order, but Jake's friend Benny Slightman and one of the Sisters of Oriza are killed.

Even if there are more Wolves back in Thunderclap, the people of the Calla know the secret to destroying them, but Roland believes they'll never see them again. Despite the deaths, the Calla-folken believe they got off easy and begin a celebration. During the confusion, Mia takes charge of Susannah and leads her up to the Doorway Cave. She passes through, taking Black Thirteen with her, closing the door.

Thwarted in their efforts to pursue Susannah, Roland picks *'Salem's Lot* from the shelf and shows it to the others. Father Callahan is understandably mystified to learn that he's a character in a novel written by Stephen King, a name Jake recognizes from the deli board at Tower's bookstore.

Wolves of the Calla ends with twin dilemmas. The *ka-tet* needs to rescue Susannah, and they need to protect the rose, but their gateway to Keystone Earth is now firmly closed against them. And, of course, there's the ever-present issue of the Breakers and the failing Tower.

For once, though, readers didn't have to wait for years to see what happened next. The sixth book in the Dark Tower series was already written and scheduled to be published in just seven months.

Characters (in order of mention): Tian Jaffords, Andy the Messenger Robot, Jamie Jaffords, Tia Jaffords, Father Callahan, Manni, Zalia Jaffords, Heddon Jaffords, Hedda Jaffords, Lyman Jaffords, Lia Jaffords, Aaron Jaffords, Zalman Hoonik, Vaughn Eisenhart, Reuben Caverra, Benito Cash, Henchick, Jorge Estrada, Garret Strong, Diego Adams, Bucky Javier, Eben Took, Neil Faraday, Georgina Faraday, George Faraday, Ben Slightman, Benny Slightman, Louis Haycox, Wayne Overholser, Rossiter, Farren Posella, Freddy Rosario, George Telford, Jake Chambers, Arthur Eld, Susan Delgado, Blaine the Mono, Eddie Dean, Susannah Dean, Roland Deschain, Oy, Tick-Tock Man, Flagg, Marten, Maerlyn, Shardik, Lord Perth, Rhea, Greta Shaw, Moses Carver, Gasher, Hoots, Elmer Chambers, Ms. Avery, Calvin Tower, Stephen King, Aaron Deepneau, Claudia y Inez Bachman, Alain Johns, Cuthbert Allgood, Enrico Balazar, Kevin Blake, Henry Dean, Jack Andolini, George Biondi, Mia, Odetta Holmes, Detta Walker, Aunt Blue, Vannay, Wallace, Jamie DeCurry, Cort, Engineer Bob, Richard Patrick Sayre, Big Coffin Hunters, Old People, Jack Mort, Dan Holmes, Jessica Beasley, Officer Bosconi, Welland Overholser, Roberta Javier, Bully Javier, Miguel Torres, Grissom, DeMullet, John Farson, Eldred Jonas, Roy Depape, Clay Reynolds, Jimmie Polino, Tommy Fredericks, Skipper Brannigan, Csaba Drabnik, Dora Bertollo, Talitha Unwin, vagrant dead, Chris Johns, Timmy, Dahlie Lundgren, Frank, Luster, Topsy the Sailor, Maud, Winston, Rosalita Muñoz, Frank Tavery, Francine Tavery, Nort the Weedeater, Ben Mears, Matthew Burke, Daniel Glick, Susan Norton, Kurt Barlow, Straker,

Mark Petrie, doorkeeper, Loretta Coogan, Hitler Brothers, Lupe Delgado, Rowan Magruder, low men, Crimson King, Dicky Rudebacher, Walter o'Dim, Verna Eisenhart, Margaret Eisenhart, Gray Dick, Lady Oriza, Marian, Lord Grenfall, Tom Eisenhart, Tessa Eisenhart, Sisters of Oriza, Sarey Adams, Hugh Anselm, Pokey Slidell, Eamon Doolin, Molly Doolin, Minni, Gabrielle Deschain, Steven Deschain, Jemmin, Rowena Magruder Rawlings, Norton Randolph, William Garton, slow mutants, Diane Caverra, Cantab, Deelie Estrada, Mr. Tubther, Cimi Dretto, Tricks Postino, Claudio Andolini, Tommy Graham, Benjamin Slightman, Jr., Stefan Toren, Finli o'Tego, Latigo, Bernardo, Haggengood, Bango Skank, Lucas Hanson, Petra Jesserling, Lord Seminon, Breakers, taheen, Annabelle Javier, Krella Anselm, Ara.

Places: Calla Bryn Sturgis; Thunderclap; Borderlands; Out-World; Our Lady of Serenity; Took's General Store; Mid-World; In-World; Rocking B Ranch; Ayjip; Green Palace; River Whye; Devar-Tete Whye; Calla Lockwood; Gilead; Jerusalem's Lot; Mejis; I-70; Topeka, Kansas; Dark Tower; Cradle of Lud; Kansas City Blues; Barcelona Luggage Store; Dutch Hill; Piper School; Tom and Gerry's Artistic Deli; Manhattan Restaurant of the Mind; River Crossing; Chew Chew Mama's; Tower of Power Records; Calla Fundy; Castle Discordia; Western Sea; Morehouse; Outer Arc; Mansion; Inner Baronies; Turtle Bay Luxury Condominiums; Detroit, Michigan; Callas; Lud; Calla Amity; Calla Bryn Bouse; Calla Staffel; Calla Sen Pinder; Calla Sen Chre; South Seas; Grand Crescent; Eastern Plains; Jericho Hill; Seven Mile Farm; Bleecker Street; Rimrocks; Salt Sea; Clean Sea; Macy's; Dixie Pig; United Nations; Mid-Town Lanes; Co-Op City; Travelers' Rest; Silk Ranch Road; Great Road; Middle Crescent; West Road; North Field; Majestic Theater; Marsten House; St. Andrew's; Washington Square Park; Home; Lighthouse Shelter; Plaza Hotel; Marine Midland Bank; New York General Hospital; Americano Bar; Battery Park; City Lights; Gage Park; Leabrook, New Jersey; Fort Lee, New Jersey; Waydon; River Send; Calla Divine; Doorway Cave; Eyebolt Canyon; Calla Redpath; Na'ar; Turtle Bay Washeteria; Riverside Hospital; Tishman Building; Way Station; Los Zapatos; All-World; Keystone Earth; Blimpie's; Dogan; Buckhead Ranch; Algul Siento; Gloria; Redbird Two; Station Shoes & Boots; U.N. Plaza Hotel; New York Public Library; East Stoneham, Maine.

Things: *seppe-sai,* madrigal, threaded stock, roont, Full Earth, Huntress Moon, New Earth, Wolves, jilly, Path of the Beam, Out-World, North Central Positronics, LaMerk Industries, *killin,* Reaping Night, stuffy-guys, bucka, *khef, Book of the Manni,* opopanax, Year-End Gathering, sneetches, *dinh, ka,* todash, Kansas City Monarchs, Nozz-A-La, Takuro Spirit, thinny, Peddler's Moon, Wizard's Glass, mystery number, nineteen, gunslinger burritos, muffin-balls, slew-feet, wheels, kammen, rose, *Charlie the Choo-Choo,* Sergio, Sombra Corporation, mia, slo-trans engines, dipolar computers, forspecial plates, lobstrosities, Seven Dials of Magic, binnie-bugs, Voice of the Turtle, Holmes Dental, the White, rustie, *Riddle-De-Dum!,* Guardians of the Beam, gunna, *Tales of Arthur,* trig, Black Thirteen, *an-tet,* sh'veen, docker's clutch, charyou tree, sharproot, harriers, *graf,* Great Letters, High Speech, kennit, Grays, Pubes, Goat Moon, Directive Nineteen, delah, soh, Shardik, *The Wizard of Oz,* Horn of Eld, tack-see, Castles, cradle-amah, popkin, commala, "The Rice Song," Reap Fair, folken, Maid of Constant Sorrow, Old Star, Old Mother, Points, Wickets, clouts, moit, dry twist, spriggum, rock-cats, pokeberries, *Air Dance,* ironwood, *Leabrook Register,* ghostwood, Unfound Door, *Look Homeward, Angel,* dead-letter, pulls, bolt and bah, Orizas, trum, slaggit, throg, cosy, drotta stick, Zn, Saita, "My Understanding of the Truth," *dan-dinh,* telamei, *dash-dinh,* alleyo, grow bag, devil-grass, the Over, *ka-tel, sigul, kai-mai,* kra, Buffalo Star, *fan-gon,* Tet Corporation*, ka-me,* Dogan, Watch Me, Snuggle-butt, boom-flurry, *'Salem's Lot,* mortata, blossiewood, skölpadda, language of the unformed, seminon, oggan, Beams.

Crossovers to Other Works: The basic idea behind King's novel *11/22/63* is outlined by Father Callahan. Callahan, of course, appears in *'Salem's Lot.*

Foreshadowing and Spoilers: Eddie's ultimate fate is foreshadowed during his meeting with Jamie Jaffords. Finli o'Tego is the head of security at Algul Siento, where the Breakers do their work.

SONG OF SUSANNAH: REPRODUCTION

Song of Susannah, one of the series' shortest installments, was published in
June 2004. The novel, which is dedicated to Tabitha King, focuses on the
twenty-four hours after Susannah and Mia leave Calla Bryn Sturgis following the battle with the Wolves, though the action takes place in two different
decades.

Once again, the *ka-tet* is split up. The fact that Mia took Black Thirteen
with her stymies Roland's plan of using the Unfound Door. The urgency of
his need to solve the problem of the Breakers is underscored the morning after Mia leaves, when Calla Bryn Sturgis is rocked by seismic activity that
Roland attributes to a Beamquake. One of the few remaining Beams supporting the Dark Tower yields to the Breakers' efforts. It's not the Beam the *ka-tet*
has been following—the effects would have been much more dramatic if it
were—but that's of little comfort to anyone.

Roland believes that two Beams remain, though he can't be sure. If one
more goes, that may be enough to topple the Tower. However, he also believes
they need Susannah to save the Dark Tower, so rescuing her is a priority, as is
closing the deal with Calvin Tower for the vacant lot. They might even need
Susannah's child, demon-spawn though it may be. They have to get to East
Stoneham, Maine, in 1977 to find Tower, and they need to go to wherever—
and whenever—Susannah is. Because of the linear nature of time in Keystone Earth, they have to get things done right the first time. There are no do
overs and no doubling back.

The big question is: how can they achieve any of these goals?

Roland knows the Manni have traveled to other worlds without benefit of
magic doors and glasses from the Wizard's Rainbow. He consults with Henchick, the Manni elder, to see what can be done. Although a large number of

Manni were too shaken by the Beamquake to come, Henchick assembles a large contingent of his followers in the Doorway Cave. Sensing Jake is strong with the touch, Henchick appoints him chief sender. Roland has his plan all mapped out: Jake and Callahan will go after Tower while he and Eddie follow Susannah. Oy is to stay behind with Cantab of the Manni. *Ka* has a different plan. It sends Roland and Eddie to 1977 and Callahan, Jake and Oy to June 1, 1999.

The Unfound Door delivered Mia to the corner of Second Avenue and 46th Street. Where Tom and Gerry's Artistic Deli once stood, where once there was a vacant lot containing a rose, now there is a black skyscraper, 2 Dag Hammarskjöld Plaza. The people who work there call it the Black Tower. Mia is in the early stages of labor and barefoot. Her first order of business is to get shoes, which she does by accosting a hapless accountant named Trudy Damascus, who is returning to work after lunch. The Black Tower is still a magical place. The barely perceptible singing draws people to it, but it's not as strong as it once was.

Susannah and Mia are forced to cooperate if they're to survive. New York is completely alien to Mia, but 1999 is almost as foreign to Susannah, who comes from 1964. Susannah constructs a mental Dogan based on Jake's description of the North Central Positronics monitoring station outside Calla Bryn Sturgis, using it to control her pregnancy as much as possible. Certain operations result in unbearable pain. She adds a microphone that she uses to try to communicate with Eddie, but gets no response.

During one of Father Callahan's trips through the Unfound Door, Eddie noticed something in the bowling bag containing Black Thirteen, but he'd had no time to investigate. Susannah sees it and discovers a scrimshaw turtle: Maturin, the Guardian of the Beam of the Turtle. She finds another turtle in a pocket park near the Black Tower—a life-sized statue identical to the ivory carving.

Using the turtle's magical powers of persuasion, she talks a Swedish diplomat into reserving her a room at a nearby hotel, where she goes to wait for a phone call. She stores Black Thirteen and Susannah's remaining Orizas in the room safe. With time to kill, Susannah convinces Mia to take her somewhere so they can talk face-to-face. They go to the Castle on the Abyss, once known as Castle Discordia, deep in End-World. The dead town of Fedic, outside the main walls of the castle keep, was where the Wolves brought the kidnapped twins from the Callas. The Discordia side of the castle is a wasteland like the one outside Lud, with an abyss filled with monsters.

Mia has decided to call her baby Mordred, a name she plucks from Susannah's mind. It is appropriate, because she believes her child will fulfill a legend and slay Roland, his father, just as Mordred did in the tales of King Arthur that Susannah studied. This is all news to Susannah—she has no idea how Roland could be the baby's father. Mia traces the baby's conception back to the Speaking Ring of the Oracle, where Roland traded sex for information. Instead of an Oracle, though, he was consorting with a demon elemental, one of six that represent the Beams. These demons have both sexual aspects. This one inverted itself to become male and transmitted Roland's semen to Susannah in the Speaking Circle where Jake returned to Mid-World.

Mia gives Susannah a lesson in Mid-World history, going back to the time of creation. Roland, she says, cannot prevent the Tower from falling. The best he can hope to do is to delay the inevitable. The Crimson King seeks to hasten its decline, believing he will be the lord of the resulting chaos.

In a subsequent tête-à-tête, Mia tells Susannah how she was a disincorporated spirit, wandering Fedic and coveting a rare healthy human child born to a young couple in the then-vibrant town. Centuries after the Red Death killed most and drove the rest away, Walter o'Dim saw her and perceived her need, making her an offer she was created to accept. She gave up her immortality as a demon so she could bear a child.

The transformation took place in the Fedic Dogan—the same place where the twins from the Callas were ruined. However, she was sterile, so the only way she could bear a child was to steal Susannah's, which is being slowly transmitted to her throughout the pregnancy. Mia knows that Mordred will grow quickly and believes she may get to raise him for only five or seven years, but that will be enough to fulfill her imperative.

Their palaver is interrupted when Richard Sayre, the man whose name Eddie saw representing Sombra Corporation on the memorandum of understanding with Calvin Tower and who presided over the meeting where Father Callahan died, calls Mia to supply her destination: the Dixie Pig, a name the *ka-tet* saw while todash in the vacant lot.

On the way to the restaurant, Susannah exposes Mia to some details from her life to show her what she's given up. She will be a mother without ever getting to experience all the things that make motherhood wonderful. While Mia is distracted, she tosses the scrimshaw turtle aside so that someone else might find and use it. Her mental Dogan can no longer hold the pregnancy back. She goes into full labor.

The scene inside the Dixie Pig is something out of Hieronymus Bosch. Waiting for them are vampires, low men and taheen. The restaurant has been catering to flesh-eaters for centuries, and the meat cooking in the kitchen is baby meat, not pig. Richard Sayre presides over the scene. Susannah's Detta personality tries to assert itself, but Mia is in charge now—of the body, at least. Sayre has no respect for her at all and humiliates her in front of his minions.

Mia and Susannah have one more hasty meeting on the ramparts of Castle Discordia. Mia finally accepts that she's been misled. She wants Susannah to help her escape with her son. Failing that, she wants Susannah to kill them both.

Sayre and his henchmen drag Mia beneath the Dixie Pig to a doorway that crosses over to the Fedic Dogan, the place where Mia was made mortal. Susannah and Mia separate physically but are connected by headsets to final-ize the transfer of the fetus to Mia. This part of the story ends with Mordred about to be born.

Sayre told Mia that Eddie and Roland had been killed in an ambush. Mia had supplied him with information about their intended destination, so he had Jack Andolini and a small army of thugs waiting.

It was a good thing that Jake and Father Callahan didn't arrive in 1977 as planned. A gunslinger apprentice and a priest would have been no match for Andolini's men. Roland was built for this kind of situation, though, so he drags Eddie out of the line of fire into the general store, where they meet an unlikely ally—an old-timer named John Cullum who can handle himself in a dangerous situation. Roland and Eddie kill almost all of Andolini's men (many of them for the second time, though this is a decade earlier than the shoot-out at Balazar's headquarters) and escape in Cullum's boat.

Cullum is a cottage caretaker, so he knows the locals and outsiders. He knows where Calvin Tower and Aaron Deepneau are staying and agrees to take them there. After some tense negotiations during which Eddie feels like killing the stubborn bookseller, the deal is struck. They tell Cullum to leave town for his own safety and seek out Tower.

Eddie asks about Stephen King and learns that the author moved to the area recently, at about the same time as walk-ins—mutants and other strange creatures—started appearing. While Roland is removing a bullet from Ed-die's leg, Eddie starts to get a sense of the true nature of their existence. He realizes the similarity between their adventure in Calla Bryn Sturgis and *The Magnificent Seven*. This, combined with Father Callahan turning out to be a character in a Stephen King novel, makes him eager to meet the author, who may be his and Roland's creator.

The closer they get to King's house, the stronger their sense that they are approaching something profoundly important. Eddie theorizes that King and the rose are twins—that each of them represents one of the two surviving Beams supporting the Tower.

In 1977, Stephen King hasn't thought up Eddie yet, but he recognizes Roland for what he is. He's dumbstruck. Eddie and Roland are less awed by King. For one thing, if he's their god and creator, he's been responsible for the deaths of a lot of people they knew and loved. For another, he's marked by a black aura. Under hypnosis, King reveals that the Crimson King has been trying to kill him or stop him from writing the Dark Tower story for decades. Among those who stepped in to help him at an early age were Cuthbert and Eddie.

The Dark Tower stories are moldering in a box in the basement. Fear of the Crimson King, who seems to see him every time he works on Roland's story, coupled with a growing dislike for Roland as a character, has kept him from writing more or from publishing what he's already written. At first he says he caused Roland to drop Jake, but then he recants and says it was Roland's decision.

For Roland, King is Gan, the creative force, channeling *ka* through himself but not creating it. The story blows into him (like the wind through the keyhole, perhaps). He doesn't always like what he is inspired to write, but he has no choice. It is crucial for Roland that King resume the story, but they have to keep him safe from the Crimson King and the low men. He plants a post-hypnotic suggestion that will allow the author to pick up the story from time to time but put it aside for long periods, too. Under hypnosis, King knows much more of the story. He tells Roland that Susannah's baby is dangerous to her, and that Black Thirteen must be destroyed. He also allows himself to send a message to Jake in 1999—this is *ka* in action at its most basic level.

Jake and Father Callahan arrive in New York half an hour after Susannah left for the Dixie Pig in a taxi. Their sudden appearance on a busy street causes a momentary stir and a confrontation between Jake and a taxi driver who narrowly avoids running over Oy.

They meet Reverend Earl Harrigan—Henchick of the Manni's twin—who tells them that Susannah left a message with him, instructing Jake and Callahan to go to the hotel. Black Thirteen is still in the safe, and if the low men get it there's no telling what will happen. Before they go to the hotel, they check out the rose in the lobby of the Black Tower and see its subliminal effect on people.

Stephen King's message to Jake is in the form of a room key. Black Thirteen, probably sensing what Callahan has in store for it, tries to exert its power against them, but they are able to resist, which restores Callahan's faith in God. He thinks he's finally getting his chance to redeem himself for the loss of faith that tarnished him in 'Salem's Lot. They leave Black Thirteen in a coin-op locker in the basement of the World Trade Center with enough money to last three years and then follow Susannah's trail to the Dixie Pig.

Both of them think they may die at the restaurant. Callahan gives Jake the last rites. Their unexpected weapon comes in the form of the scrimshaw turtle that Oy finds in the gutter where Susannah threw it.

The coda section of the book presents Stephen King's journal from the time of Eddie and Roland's visit until the date of his accident a couple of weeks after Susannah arrives in 1999. In these entries, he discusses returning to the Dark Tower series, getting the first installments published, and how the story comes back to him time and time again over the years.

He also discusses fan reaction to the series—their demands for the next installment, how they howl at the way some of the books end as cliffhangers, and pleas from dying people to know how it's going to end.

Writing Roland's story feels good, but it also feels dangerous. He worries that he may die of a heart attack while writing and leave behind an unfinished series. His wife worries about his daily walks on the country road near their new house on Turtleback Lane. The journal ends with a clipping about King's accident on June 19, 1999. In this version of reality, he dies.

Characters (in order of mention): Roland Deschain, Henchick of the Manni, Cantab, Manni, Eddie Dean, Jake Chambers, Oy, Benny Slightman, Margaret Eisenhart, Susannah Dean, Rosalita Muñoz, Father Callahan, Mia, Vaughn Eisenhart, Wayne Overholser, Sisters of Oriza, forgetful folk, Frank Tavery, Crimson King, Maturin, Cuthbert Allgood, Alain Johns, Jamie DeCurry, Ben Slightman, Henry Dean, Enrico Balazar, Lewis, Thonnie, Elmer Chambers, Calvin Tower, Aaron Deepneau, Hedron, Trudy Damascus, Paul Antassi, Mitch Guttenberg, low men, vampires, Andy the Messenger Robot, Mordred Deschain, Detta Walker, Odetta Holmes, Beryl Evans, Claudia y Inez Bachman, *Ka-tet* of Nineteen, Mathiessen van Wyck, *can toi,* Blaine the Mono, Maerlyn, Breakers, Arthur Eld, Guardians of the Beam, demon elementals, Talitha Unwin, Topsy the Sailor, Richard Sayre, John Cullum, harriers, Chip McAvoy, Jack Andolini, Tricks Postino, George Biondi, walk-ins, slow mutants, Sylvia Goldover, Henry Dean, Jane Sargus, Stephen King, Teddy Wilson, Donnie Russert, Stefan Toren, Alaric, Roland of Delain, Hitler Brothers, Cort, John Sturges, Andrew Feeny, Jack Mort, Bango Skank, Walter o'Dim, Amos Depape, Roy Depape, Eldred Jonas, Michael, Earl Harrigan, Moses Carver, Gasher, Hoots, Tick-Tock Man, Susan Delgado, Tabitha King, Dave King, Owen King,

Joe King, Brown, Nort the Weedeater, Richard Bachman, Allie, Hax, Gan, Steven Deschain, Wayne D. Overholser, Ray Hogan, Officer Benzyck, Kurt Barlow, Mark Petrie, Rowan Magruder, taheen, little doctors, Jey, Meiman, Queen Rowena, Tian Jaffords, Zalia Jaffords, Haber, Dr. Scowther, Alia, Aunt Ethelyn, Uncle Oren, Naomi King, Charles McCausland, Bobby Garfield, Ted Brautigan.

Places: Calla Bryn Sturgis; 'Salem's Lot; East Road; Redpath Kraten; Tempa; Mid-World; Borderlands; the Dark Tower; Thunderclap; End-World; Devar-Tete Whye; Topeka, Kansas; Dogan; Doorway Cave; Dennis's Waffles and Pancakes; Chew Chew Mama's; 2 Dag Hammarskjöld Plaza; U.N. Plaza Hotel; Castle Discordia; Discordia; Fedic; Morehouse; Dutch Hill; River Crossing; Dixie Pig; Took's General Store; Western Sea; Keystone Earth; Jericho Hill; East Stoneham General Store; Manhattan Restaurant of the Mind; Leaning Tower; Keywadin Pond; Dimity Road; Bridgton, Maine; Turtleback Lane; Lovell; Kezar Lake; Garlan; Turtle Bay Washateria; Co-Op City; Bahamas; Oxford, Mississippi; Columbia University; Christopher Street; Eluria; East Downe; Fedic Station; Arc 16 Experimental Station; Mejis; Fedic Good-Time Saloon; In-World; Gilead; Tull; World Trade Center; Blackstrap Molasses Café; the Hungry i.

Things: *ka*; Black Thirteen; *'Salem's Lot*; kaven; glammer; *khef*; lobstrosities; North Central Positronics; docker's clutch; todash; Beamquake; *sigul*; Beams; Watch Me; Wands; Unfound Door; molly; *ka-tet*; seminon; oggan; sneetches; the Over; the Prim; kra; *can-tah*; coffs; *dinh*; commala; twim; rose; Guttenburg, Furth, and Patel; Orizas; skölpadda; *Charlie the Choo-Choo*; Sombra; Forge of the King; pokeberries; slo-trans engines; dipolar engines; High Speech; dry twist; *ka-daddy*; roont; gunna; *dan-tete*; *The Dogan*; Jaffords Rentals; dead-letter; Holmes Dental; Tet Corporation; Takuro Spirit; *The Magnificent Seven*; astin; Path of the Beam; Microsoft; Nozz-A-La; charyou tree; *collum-ka*; Red Death; Devil's Arse; magic doors; todash darkness; Old Star; Old Mother; stem; scrip; Fair-Day Goose; Zoltan; lobstrosities; Voice/Song of the Turtle; Guardians of the Beam; todana; "Man of Constant Sorrow"; *ka-mai*; cozened.

Crossovers to Other Works: The scrimshaw turtle is reminiscent of the *can-tah* found near the mine in *Desperation*. Susannah's mental Dogan is similar to Jonesy's storage room in *Dreamcatcher*.

THE DARK TOWER: RESUMPTION

The Dark Tower was published three months after *Song of Susannah*, on September 21, 2004, Stephen King's birthday. It is dedicated to the Constant Readers who have listened to the Song of the Turtle as channeled by King.

The book covers an impressive amount of time and distance, both in Mid-World and in Keystone Earth. So many things happen that it's sometimes hard to believe they all took place in one book. It is also the most brutal book in the series. Several major characters don't make it to the end.

In brief, the novel relates the story of Jake and Father Callahan's battle at the Dixie Pig and Jake's return to Mid-World; the birth of Mordred Deschain and its aftermath in the Fedic Dogan; Eddie and Roland convincing John Cullum to help form Tet Corporation; Roland and Eddie's return to Mid-World; the showdown between Mordred and Walter o'Dim; the battle of Algul Siento; the trip to 1999 to save Stephen King; Roland's meeting with Tet Corporation; the harrowing passage under Castle Discordia; the long trek through the Badlands; the encounter at Le Casse Roi Russe; the long trek across Empathica; the encounter with Joe Collins; Susannah's return to Earth; the showdown between Roland and Mordred; the showdown with the Crimson King and what happens when Roland reaches the Dark Tower.

The battle at the Dixie Pig is mostly about Father Callahan's redemption. When Barlow challenged his faith in 'Salem's Lot, Callahan faltered. He's had a lot of time to consider his actions and their repercussions. Now that he is a member of Roland's *ka-tet*, he is prepared to retake that test. Armed with Jake's Ruger and the scrimshaw turtle, he confronts a room full of low men and vampires. His life is disposable by now—he's already died once. Callahan is to serve as a distraction so Jake can escape—as he and Jake learn through the voices of Roland and Eddie—and he relishes the role.

This time, when challenged to throw away his cross, Callahan is prepared. He won't throw it away, but he does put it away. His faith is renewed and the power of the White runs through him. When the smell of blood draws the vampires, he shoots himself, satisfied that he has done his job and fulfilled his duty. Jake slips into the kitchen and through a secret door in the pantry into a tunnel that runs beneath the restaurant, past a mind-trap, to a North Central Positronics door to the Fedic Dogan, where he and Oy are reunited with Susannah.

Roland and Eddie need a way to get the title to the vacant lot to Moses Carver. Aaron Deepneau is too susceptible to Calvin Tower's wishy-washy behavior. Their go-to guy is John Cullum, who didn't leave town like he was supposed to and is ready to answer their call. He believes their story and takes Aunt Talitha's cross with an embedded message containing a secret Susannah revealed to Eddie to convince Moses Carver to join up. The newly established Tet Corporation, financed by Holmes Dental's assets, will have three purposes: protect King, guard the rose in the vacant lot, and thwart North Central Positronics in every way possible. Eddie and Roland travel to the Fedic door beneath the Dixie Pig via a magic door that opened up over Kezar Lake near Stephen King's house, kill the posse that followed Jake, and reunite with Susannah, Jake and Oy, the first time they've all been together since the battle in Calla Bryn Sturgis.

Susannah has her own story to tell. No one—not even Richard Sayre—is prepared for the creature that Mia births in the Fedic Dogan. Moments after Mordred is born, he turns into a were-spider and sucks the life out of his mother. Susannah is sufficiently startled that she misses the opportunity to kill the creature, though she does wound it. She kills almost everyone else in the Dogan, including Sayre. She also blinds the Asimov robot, Nigel the Domestic, who reminds her of Andy, though Nigel is mostly harmless.

Mordred gets away, though he can stay in spider form for only a short period because of the amount of energy it requires. As a human, though, he's only a baby, so he forces Nigel to bring him food. Walter o'Dim shows up in the Dogan's control room, intending to kill Mordred and take his foot, which bears the mark of the Eld that provides access to the Dark Tower. Throughout his long existence, Walter has underestimated people—especially Roland—but none so much as he underestimates the babe in diapers, who literally has Walter for lunch.

The *ka-tet* turns their attention to freeing the Breakers, which will save the Dark Tower. They pass through the same failing scientific door the Wolves used to raid the Callas and end up in Thunderclap Station, where a trio of Breakers led by Ted Brautigan waits. These renegades now know what they are breaking at the prison camp, Algul Siento, and they've decided to assist the *ka-tet* in ending this destructive work. They also suspect that the Calla raids had something to do with them.

One member of the trio is Roland's old friend from Mejis, Sheemie Ruiz, whose special talent is creating doorways—another way of describing tele-portation. Ted, Dinky Earnshaw and Sheemie used this power to amass an arsenal in a cave outside Algul Siento and explain the compound's security features. It's up to Roland to come up with a plan of attack.

Their time line is complicated by one fact Ted reveals: *ka* is fed up with Stephen King because he has decided to stop working on Roland's story. The *Ka* of Nineteen and the *Ka* of Ninety-nine will collide on a country road in western Maine. They have to save the Beams first, but as soon as that's done they have to get to Maine in time to save King. Roland's aches aren't from arthritis—they're sympathetic pains that mirror the injuries King will suffer in a fatal accident.

The battle of Algul Siento—and the lead-up to it—forms the novel's cen-terpiece. The battle—like most—is over in minutes, but it has a profound effect on everything that comes after. The *ka-tet* had a sense that something bad was going to happen to their tight-knit group and something does—the first of their core group ends up on the wrong end of a gun barrel. Though the battle is a success—the work of the Breakers is ended, the Beams are saved and can begin to renew themselves, and the prison camp is dismantled—the cost is high. Gran-pere Jaffords's prediction about Eddie Dean's fate was proved correct. Worse, it's not a quick death, but a long, drawn-out affair that delays Roland and Jake from their appointment with King.

Once they finally get away, thanks to Sheemie's talent, they find another helpful person in the East Stoneham General Store: Irene Tassenbaum. She knows how to get to Turtleback Lane, where King lives. Roland is determined to change *ka*, though he knows there will be a price. He intends to pay that price with his life—he won't sacrifice Jake again—but *ka* has other plans. They reach King just as a minivan is about to hit him. Roland attempts to fling himself in front of the oncoming vehicle, but his weak hip fails and Jake leaps into action. King is saved—though seriously injured (as he was in real life)—but Jake succumbs to his injuries while Roland is dealing with the van driver. Within a few hours, nearly half of Roland's *ka-tet* is killed.

Roland buries Jake, convinces King to return to his story, and gets Irene to drive him to New York so he can take the door under the Dixie Pig back to Fedic, where Susannah should be waiting for him. Oy decides to come along, too, rather than perishing at Jake's grave. Irene is revitalized by her part in saving the world and does her best to console and comfort Roland in the two days it takes them to get to Manhattan.

Roland's first stop is 2 Dag Hammarskjöld Plaza, which Tet Corporation built to protect the rose and where they have their headquarters. Moses Carver, who is now one hundred, is the only surviving member of the Founding Fathers. Aaron Deepneau's cancer returned—though he lived a good many years longer than anyone might have expected—and John Cullum was shot, probably by an agent working for North Central Positronics. Marian Carver, Moses's daughter, is now the company's president. Roland learns about their work over the past two decades and is given information and several gifts. The most important of these is Aunt Talitha's cross, which he promised to lay before the Dark Tower. The least important is a copy of *Insomnia*, which he later gives to Irene Tassenbaum because he thinks it might contain too many mind-traps.

The people of Tet tell Roland that his job is done. He has saved the Beams and Stephen King. He need go no farther. If he does, he will be going beyond *ka*. They are shocked to discover that saving the Tower is only a means to an end for Roland. If the Tower fell, he couldn't confront whoever is at the top. He wants that entity to undo all the harm that has befallen Mid-World—and all of the terrible things Roland has had to do during his quest.

Roland and Oy rejoin Susannah in Fedic. She tells him that Sheemie died on the train from Algul Siento from an infection, and how a handful of Breakers, including Ted and Dinky, went on toward the Callas in hopes of finding a way back home. While gathering provisions for the continuation of their journey, they find two paintings bearing the signature of Patrick Danville, someone the Calvin researchers who work for Tet Corporation advised he should look out for. One of the paintings depicts the Dark Tower from the perspective of someone who must have seen it.

They outrun a creature from the abyss in the dark passage under Castle Discordia and emerge on the Badlands leading to Le Casse Roi Russe. They have plenty of food and water but little warm clothing, so they are miserably cold as they trudge down the rutted road. When they reach the Crimson King's castle, they encounter another trap: the promise of food and warm garments. This ruse is meant to draw them across the dead-line the Crimson King set around the castle before he killed his staff and fled for the Tower.

Three men resembling Stephen King—presenting themselves as King's id, ego and superego—tell Roland and Susannah of the last days the Crimson King spent here and try to encourage Roland to give up his mission. If he goes on, he runs the risk that the Crimson King will capture him and use his weapons to regain access to the Tower, undoing everything Roland has accomplished.

Roland leaves Rando Thoughtful, the Crimson King's former minister of state, behind in the hopes that he will be able to lure Mordred into the same trap or warn him off. Mordred is terribly hungry, but he is too smart to be tricked and too angry to be diverted from his mission. He dines on Thoughtful and continues his pursuit.

The Badlands give way to the White Lands of Empathica in the heart of winter. Roland and Susannah spend a few days killing deer and preparing the meat for meals and the hides for clothing. Their days of discomfort are over. Susannah even makes Roland snowshoes to speed up their journey. She's pleased to contribute in this way, even though she's dreaming of Eddie and uncertain that she'll make it to the Tower.

They might have passed by the occupied house on Odd's Lane except Roland felt duty bound to warn the resident about Mordred. Joe Collins was waiting outside to greet them anyway, so they decide to accept his hospitality. He claims he was a stand-up comic from America who was badly beaten after one of his performances and woke up in a deserted town in Mid-World nearly two decades ago. He seems old and harmless—and is of particular interest to Roland because he has a Polaroid photograph of the Dark Tower pinned to his wall—but is in fact Dandelo, someone Eddie and Jake tried to warn Roland about: a vampire who feeds on emotions rather than blood. Roland is caught in Dandelo's trap, but Susannah comes to the rescue, with the help of Stephen King, who passes her a couple of overt clues about their predicament, including a photocopy of the Browning poem "Childe Roland to the Dark Tower Came."

In the basement, they find the artist, Patrick Danville, a severely damaged man of indeterminate age who has been Dandelo's victim for untold years. Dandelo fed him just enough to keep him alive and stole his emotions time and time again. He also stole Patrick's tongue.

With assistance from Stuttering Bill, a friendly Asimov robot, Roland, Susannah, Oy and Patrick set off down Tower Road. Susannah is still dreaming of Eddie but unable to interpret his message. She finally realizes that Patrick is the solution to her dilemma. When he draws, he changes reality.

Dandelo realized this and removed the erasers from his pencils to prevent him from undoing reality. After he successfully deletes the cancerous sore from Susannah's face—caused by exposure to the toxic atmosphere of the Badlands—she gets him to re-create the Unfound Door so she can go to Central Park and join Eddie. She knows it won't be her Eddie, nor will it be the Keystone World, but it will be better than what might lie ahead for her if she stays with Roland.

The version of Eddie she meets has a brother, but it isn't the great sage and eminent junkie Henry Dean, but rather Jake, and their last name is Toren. Eddie and Jake have been dreaming of her, too, and Eddie is already in love with her. They will join up with Tet Corporation and live long and mostly happy lives together.

Oy and Patrick choose to stay with Roland. With his tongueless mouth, Patrick feels he would be an outcast in America, and Oy still has a part to play. When Roland tries to get some much-needed sleep the night before they reach the Tower and Patrick falls asleep while standing watch, Oy is the only one on guard when Mordred finally launches his attack. Mordred is near death, poisoned from eating Dandelo's horse, and is prepared to sacrifice himself if it means he can thwart the gunslinger, especially when he is so close to his goal. Oy keeps Mordred at bay long enough for Roland to awaken and draw his gun.

Mordred's hatred prevents him from accepting Roland's offer to let him live. He fulfills Roland's vision from the pink Wizard's Glass and impales Oy on a tree branch. Roland kills his son and hears the distant howl of the Crimson King, who is also Mordred's father.

That leaves only Patrick to accompany him to the Tower. It's an unusual choice, to have Roland attain his goal with someone who is so new to the story but, as it turns out, Patrick is exactly the person Roland needs at the end. Susannah wouldn't have been of any help. *Ka* knows best.

When Roland is within five miles of the Tower, the Crimson King—who is armed with sneetches—launches an attack from the balcony where he is imprisoned on the Tower's second floor. Roland and Patrick take cover behind a steel pyramid. Roland can handle the sneetches, even when they come two and three at a time, but the Voice of the Tower is summoning him, and he won't be able to resist it for long. If he emerges from cover, he'll be killed.

Roland wanted to kill the Crimson King himself, but he can't. He gets Patrick to draw him instead. The final detail he adds is two drops of color for his eyes, using paint derived from rose petals, saliva and Roland's blood. He then erases the drawing, leaving behind only the red eyes, which will remain on the balcony outside the Tower for eternity. Roland sends Patrick back the way they came, telling him to get Stuttering Bill to lead him to a doorway back to America.

Roland then turns to face the Tower, calling out the names of all those who have died during his quest and announcing his presence. He discovers that the Tower is the living body of Gan. The script on the doorway says UN-FOUND at first, but when he presents his gun and Aunt Talitha's cross, it changes to FOUND and opens to him.

Inside, he finds . . . well, if you've read all the way to the end, you know what he finds. And if you haven't, the best way to find out is to read it! Stephen King gave readers a chance to turn away before Roland went inside, after all. In a way, there's nothing inside that you haven't seen already . . .

> **Characters (in order of mention):** Father Callahan, Jake Chambers, Susannah Dean, Mia, harriers, Gan, Oy, Roland Deschain, low men (fayen folken/*can toi*), vampires, Elmer Chambers, Meiman (Tweety Bird/Canary Man), Richard P. Sayre, Mark Petrie, Kurt Barlow, Walter o'Dim, the Crimson King (Los' the Red), Andrew Feeny, Detta Walker, Tirana, Eddie Dean, Stephen King, John Cullum, Aaron Deepneau, Calvin Tower, Blaine the Mono, Vannay (the Wise), Cort, Steven Deschain, Gabrielle Deschain, taheen, slow mutants, Arthur Eld, Cuthbert Allgood, Alain Johns, Jamie DeCurry, Moses Carver, Odetta Holmes, Jack Andolini, Wolves, Charlie Beemer, walk-ins, Child of Roderick, Aunt Talitha, Chevin of Chayven, Scowther, Haber, Jey (Gee), Alia, Daniel Holmes, Straw, Breakers, Mordred Deschain, Andy the Messenger Robot, Nigel, Mech Foreman, Chef Warthog, Margaret Eisenhart, Sisters of the Plate, Jochabim, Sheemie Ruiz, Greta Shaw, Patricia the Mono, Bango Skank, Reverend Earl Harrigan, Mrs. Chambers, the Old People, Mrs. Mislaburski, Henry Dean, Conor Flaherty, Lamla, Dick Beckhardt, Rosalita Muñoz, Chip McAvoy, Albrecht, John Farson, Susan Delgado, Mathiessen van Wyck, the doorkeeper, Ted Brautigan, Eldred Jonas, Rhea, Walter Hodji, Walter Padick, Sam Padick, Ben Slightman, Bobby Garfield, Finli o'Tego, Dinky Earnshaw, Pimli (Paul) Prentiss, senders, Will Dearborn, Arthur Heath, Richard Stockworth, Coral Thorin, Roy Depape, Pettie the Trotter, Gangli Tristum, the Manni, Tanya Leeds, Joey Rostosovich, Carol Gerber,

Beeman, Trelawney, Jakli, Conroy, David Burke, Dani Rostov, Timothy Atwood, Rowan Magruder, Frank Armitage, Dave Ittaway, Sully-John, Phil, Trampas, Humma o'Tego, Tassa, Gaskie o'Tego, Haylis of Chayven, Sheb, Stanley Ruiz, Cordelia Delgado, Cameron, Jenkins, Tammy Kelly, Garma, James Cagney, Jack London, Birdie McCann, Ben Alexander, Waverly, Baj, Sej, Belle O'Rourke, Granpere Jaffords, Grace Rumbelow, Sharpton, Dandelo, Fred Worthington, Irene Tassenbaum, Rhoda Beemer, Ruth Beemer, Bryan Smith, David Tassenbaum, Justine Anderson, Elvira Toothaker, Garrett McKeen, Richard Bachman, Chuck Verrill, Morphia, Selena, George Biondi, Nancy Deepneau, Marian Carver, *Ka-tet* of the Rose, Gasher, Tick-Tock Man, Calvins, Ed Deepneau, Ralph Roberts, Patrick Danville, Fred Towne, Hax, Candor the Tall, Henchick of the Manni, Robert Browning, Jack Mort, gunslingers, uffis, Feemalo, Fumalo, Fimalo, Rando Thoughtful, Austin Cornwell, Brass, Compson, Joe Collins, Stuttering Bill, Shantz, Eddie Toren, Jake Toren.

Places: 'Salem's Lot; Dixie Pig; Calla Bryn Sturgis; Gilead; Fedic; Bridgton; Co-Op City; Turtleback Lane; Lovell, Maine; East Stoneham, Maine; Kansas Road; Callas; Keystone Earth; All-A-Glow; Cave of Voices (Doorway Cave); Mid-World; Garlan; Keywadin Pond; Kennedy International Airport; River Crossing; South Plains; Castle Discordia; Thunderclap; Oxford, Mississippi; Plaza-Park Hyatt; Derva; Rotunda; Cradle of Lud; Ludweg; Lud; Piper School; Dogan; Castle Avenue Market; Bleecker Street; Kezar Lake; Cara Laughs; Discordia; Nassau, Bahamas; East Road; Mid-Town Lanes; Dutch Hill; the Mansion; Jericho Hill; World Trade Center; Le Casse Roi Russe; River Whye; Devar-Toi (Blue Heaven/Algul Siento); Green Palace; Mejis; Mohaine Desert; French Landing, Wisconsin; Delain; East'ard Barony; Pleasantville; Damli House (Heartbreak House); the Study; Thunderclap Station; Can Steek-Tete; In-World; Travellers' Rest; The Mall; Shapleigh House; Gingerbread House; Corbett Hall; Xay River; Hartford, Connecticut; Akron, Ohio; Keystone Earth; Arc of the Callas; Court of the Crimson King; the Dark Tower; Gage Park; Markey Avenue; Western Sea; Feveral Hall; Na'ar; East Stoneham General Store; Took's General Store; Warrington's; Sunset Cottage; Sir Speedy-Park; 2 Dag Hammarskjöld Plaza; the pocket park; Manhattan Restaurant of the Mind; Taos, New Mexico; Bangor, Maine; Fedic Station; Gin-Puppy Saloon;

Arc 16 Experimental Station; the Hungry i; Central Park; Devil's Arse; Badlands; Badlands Avenue; Great Hall; Audience Chamber; Nis; Empathica; Tower Keystone; Castle-town; Hide Camp; Odd's Lane; Tower Road; Stone's Warp; Westring; Jango's; Times Square; Federal Outpost 19; the Drawers; the Drop; White Plains, New York.

Things: Maturin, the White, Orizas, *ka-mai, ka-hume, dinh, ka,* Cross of Malta, hile, Path of the Beam, todash, *aven kal, aven kas,* Voice (Song) of the Turtle/Bear, *chassit* (nineteen), Voice of the Beam/Gan, *ka-tet, an-tet,* Bends o' the Rainbow, *canda, can-tah,* the Prim, doctor bugs/Grandfather-fleas, waseau, Beamquake, Unfound Door, Shardik, magic doors, Holmes Dental, Tet Corporation, Sombra Corporation, North Central Positronics, *dan-tete,* level of the Tower, fottergraf, astin, popkin, Cullum Caretaking and Camp Checking, delah, can Discordia, commala, Wide Earth, docker's clutch, pubes, clouts, *ka-dinh,* mind-trap, the rose, dry twist, Aunt Talitha's cross, Pimsy, *sigul,* Microsoft, gunna, sandalwood, *chary-ka,* blackmouth disease, devar-tete, Black Thirteen, tooter-fish, Nozz-A-La, Asimov robots, throcken, Peddler's Moon, the Am, gadosh, godosh, bah-bo, ironwood, ghostwood, ki'dam, ki'box, rustie, sneetches, the Romp, jakes, *graf,* Reap Moon, Beams, the Bleeding Lion, teleportation, good mind, *ka-shume,* Wollensak, Takuro Spirit, ma'sun, *can-toi-tete, khef,* coffah, *anti-ka,* hume, *Hansel and Gretel,* Caprichoso (Capi), *Sacramento Bee,* ki'cans, kammen, Gan's Beam, darks, *Ka* of Nineteen, *Ka* of Ninety-nine, Keystone Year, *dan-dinh,* "Hey Jude," kes, *Charlie the Choo-Choo,* Dobbie, Fire-Response Team Bravo, *ki'come,* chary man, Ves'-ka Gan, Can'-Ka No Rey, Pistol, Bullet, kas-ka Gan, Urs-A-Ka-Gan, Cujo, Spathiphyllum, Mills Construction, Garden of the Beam, Great Letters of Gilead, Excalibur, George Washington Bridge, *The Hogan, Insomnia,* folken, Royal Court of Gilead, slinkum, oggan, Spirit of Topeka, hot-enj, todash darkness, todash monsters, Marlowe, Llamrei, Ho Fat's Luxury Taxi, devil-grass, Gan's blackbirds, Forge of the King, dead-line, Nis, glammer, hobs, cheflet, chert, Lippy, thiddles, Demon Moon, Rossco, Honda, wheels, childe, pokeberries, Old Star, Old Mother, Lydia's Dipper, bannock, Gan's gateway, houken, bougie, Speaking Rings/circles, pyramid, Mim, Song of the Tower, Horn of Eld, *tet-ka can Gan,* clouts, Ring-a-Levio (Ringo), Full Earth.

Continuity Errors and Mistakes: Is the GWB visible from Turtle Bay? Rowan Magruder is called George.

Crossovers to Other Works: French Landing (*Black House*), Warrington's and Cara Laughs (*Bag of Bones*), Ed Deepneau, Ralph Roberts and Patrick Danville (*Insomnia*), Dinky Earnshaw ("Everything's Eventual"), Ted Brautigan, Carol Gerber, Bobby Garfield, and Sully-John ("Low Men in Yellow Coats").

BOOKS AND STORIES
RELATED TO THE DARK TOWER

When the final three Dark Tower novels were published in 2003 and 2004, the author's ad card at the front of the book listed a number of Stephen King's nonseries books in bold, indicating that they were related to the Dark Tower mythos. Some of the titles were obvious, but a few provoked lively discussions as to the nature of the Dark Tower connection. In subsequent years, other books and stories have had ties to the series.

Avid readers often go to great lengths coming up with connections to the Dark Tower series. One of the most frequent is the presence of the number nineteen or numbers that add up to nineteen. Many of these are purely coincidental—especially those that appear in books that were written long before that number had any significance to King. It can be safely assumed that any occurrence of the number nineteen appearing in a book written prior to June 19, 1999 isn't a true Dark Tower connection.

Made-up brand names, such as the Takuro Spirit car and Nozz-A-La soda, sometimes appear in King's nonseries books. In the altered time line in *11/22/63*, for example, Jake Epping sees a Honda Zephyr and a Takuro Spirit. However, as King states in the interview he gave for this book, he made a special effort not to have *11/22/63* turn into a Dark Tower book because it is so firmly rooted in real history. Appearances of these brand names, which are associated by many with the Dark Tower series, should probably be treated as indicators of a parallel or altered time line rather than as a strong connection to the series.

The following books are associated with the Dark Tower series.

'SALEM'S LOT
Father Frank Callahan, the priest who flees the Maine town of 'Salem's Lot after it is overrun by vampires, ends up in Calla Bryn Sturgis, a community

on the edge of Thunderclap. Over the course of the final three books, Callahan tells the story of what happened to him after he got on a bus shortly after being forced to drink vampire Barlow's blood and being rejected by his church. In a sense, *Wolves of the Calla* is the sequel to *'Salem's Lot* that King sometimes said he'd like to write.

The book itself shows up on a shelf of rare collectibles in the Manhattan Restaurant of the Mind in *Wolves of the Calla*. It is one of the first signs that Stephen King's fictional universe is somehow connected to Roland's reality. The fact that Father Callahan, a living person, is a character in a novel confounds everyone involved. Especially Father Callahan.

THE STAND

When Roland and his *ka-tet* end up in Topeka, Kansas, after defeating Blaine the Mono, they find themselves in a different universe, one that has been overrun by a superflu known as Captain Trips. This is the name given to the virus in *The Stand*. They see graffiti that mentions "the Walkin' Dude" and ultimately meet up with Randall Flagg, the villain of *The Stand*, who also turns out to be Marten Broadcloak, Roland's nemesis. Mother Abigail, the leader of the "good" faction, is mentioned, as is her home in Nebraska.

THE TALISMAN

Ties between *The Talisman* and the Dark Tower series are tenuous. They arise mostly out of the much stronger connection to the series of the book's sequel, where the Territories, the parallel universe where Jack Sawyer travels when he isn't in America, are revealed to be a borderland near Mid-World. The Agincourt Hotel in California that contains the Talisman might be the Dark Tower's representation in Jack's reality. It is an axis of all universes.

King drew inspiration from *The Talisman* for the novella "The Little Sisters of Eluria." He began by imagining the great pavilion where Jack first saw the Queen of the Territories and then saw it in ruins and filled with vampire nurses.

SKELETON CREW

King included this collection in the list of books connected to the Dark Tower without specifying which story or stories elevated it to this status. Several fit the bill. The title character in "Mrs. Todd's Shortcut" is probably saving time by veering through a portal or a thinny into another reality where distances are shorter than in the real world. The creatures that end up on her bumper and under her tires as roadkill are reminiscent of those that emerge through the trunk of the strange car in *From a Buick 8*. Scientists build technological doorways that allow travel across vast distances in "The Jaunt," reminiscent of the ones built by the Great Old Ones in the Dark Tower series.

It is also possible that the Arrowhead Project in "The Mist" ripped a hole between universes, allowing todash creatures to emerge into the world. They might also have inadvertently created a thinny. Mrs. Carmody's sermons bear a remarkable similarity to the one delivered by Sylvia Pittston in *The Gunslinger*.

IT

Derry, Maine, is one of those places where the border between neighboring universes is very thin. As seen later in *Insomnia*, the Crimson King has business in this city. The tangible connections between this novel and the Dark Tower series, though, are slight. When Jake Chambers enters the Mansion on Dutch Hill while returning to Mid-World, he notices that the wallpaper features capering elves wearing green caps. The same is true of the house on Neibolt Street in Derry, which implies that both houses may be doorways to alternate realities.

The robot who fills Joe Collins's propane tanks in the White Lands of Empathica is called Stuttering Bill, which is also the nickname of Bill Denbrough in *It*. Collins is revealed to be a shape-shifting clown who feeds on emotions, which puts him in the same category as Pennywise from *It*, although King has stated definitively on his message board that Dandelo is not Pennywise.

One other connection between *It* and the Dark Tower series is the Turtle. In Mid-World, the turtle Maturin is one of the Guardians of the Beams. In Derry, the group of kids—and, later, adults—who form a *ka-tet* to fight off Pennywise is supported by a Turtle, though this entity is somewhat different from a Guardian.

THE EYES OF THE DRAGON

The Eyes of the Dragon takes place in the Mid-World kingdom of Delain, which is mentioned several times in the Dark Tower series. The fact that the ruler of that realm is named Roland is not significant. However, the king's chief adviser is a wizard named Flagg, which is another guise of Randall Flagg, aka the man in black, the Covenant Man and Marten Broadcloak. Before coming to Delain, Flagg was in Garlan, another kingdom that is mentioned in the series. Flagg is an agent of chaos, stirring up mischief and looking for something good to destroy for no reason other than the fact that he can. He always manages to escape before he is called to accounts for his misdeeds.

As recounted in *The Drawing of the Three*, in the final days of Gilead, Roland encountered a demon that pretended to be a man who called himself Flagg. In pursuit of this creature were two young men named Dennis and Thomas. Thomas was one of King Roland's sons, and Dennis was the son of the butler to Thomas's brother Peter. Roland saw Flagg change a man who had irritated him into a howling dog. Thomas and Dennis left Delain heading south in pursuit of Flagg at the end of *The Eyes of the Dragon* and apparently caught up with him at some point, but that story has never been told.

INSOMNIA

Stephen King described *Insomnia* as a Dark Tower novel while touring to promote the book in 1994, saying that it cast a light on what he had to do with the series. At the time, a few years after the publication of *The Waste Lands*, he was considering writing the last four books in the series back-to-back, though that plan didn't come to fruition for the better part of a decade.

The book itself shows up in *The Dark Tower*. A copy is given to Roland when he visits the Tet Corporation's headquarters at 2 Dag Hammarskjöld Plaza. The Calvins, a group of researchers scrutinizing King's novels for clues, believe it is the keystone book relating to the Dark Tower series, containing veiled clues to help Roland save the Tower. Its red-and-white dust jacket symbolizes the fight between good (the White) and evil (the Crimson King).

Some of the clues are subtle. A character named Ed Deepneau falls under the power of the Crimson King, an evil being from another level of reality. In the Dark Tower series, Aaron Deepneau has a distant cousin named Ed who died the year Stephen King was born. The character's name might have been a flag for Roland to pay attention to Aaron Deepneau when he meets him.

Insomnia contains the first-ever mention of the Crimson King. When Roland sees a reference to the Crimson King in *Wizard and Glass*, he claims to have no idea who that is. However, King inserted references to the Crimson King in the revised and edited version of *The Gunslinger* in 2003.

The book explains in detail the nature of the multiverse as it relates to levels of the Tower. On one hand, each level of the Tower is a different universe, one of a near-infinite multitude of realities. Levels that are higher up are more elevated in a developmental sense. The lowest levels are occupied by "short-timers" like protagonist Ralph Roberts. In another sense, each level of the Tower represents a year or a phase in a person's life, which is how it reveals itself to Roland.

Clotho, one of the agents of Purpose, tells Ralph that there are elevators in the Tower that short-timers are not ordinarily allowed to use. Ralph says that he has seen a vision of the Tower, and it doesn't have an elevator but rather "a narrow staircase festooned with cobwebs and doorways leading to God knows what." Perhaps to God himself, he speculates.

The Crimson King sent his minions to Derry to kill Patrick Danville, a four-year-old boy who is a skilled crayon artist. The Crimson King understands that Patrick will play an important part in his downfall, so he wants to prevent that from happening. This is in keeping with some of the Crimson King's efforts to kill Stephen King before he could finish writing Roland's journey. If Patrick dies before his fate is fulfilled, the Dark Tower will fall.

Ralph becomes an instrument of *ka*, called into action by agents of Purpose (the White) in a battle against the Random (the Red) where he doesn't understand what's at stake. Ralph becomes part of a *ka-tet* that includes his friend Lois and a man named Dorrance Marsteller, who provides Ralph with things he needs before he needs them.

Atropos, an agent of Random, is one of the Crimson King's servants. Events in Derry are of such import that everything at the levels of Higher Purpose and Higher Random in the Tower has come to a stop. Ralph acquires some of the touch, a power that Alain Johns and Jake Chambers both developed. When he first meets Patrick, he senses a pink aura that may tie him to the rose. Patrick is also attuned to the larger multiverse. One of his crayon drawings is a picture of the Dark Tower in a field of roses. At the top, he puts a Red King who glares down at Roland with hatred and fear. Patrick says that Roland is a king, too.

When Ralph saves Patrick's life, Roland, who is still in the desert on the trail of the man in black, senses something. He rolls over in his bedroll and sleeps more easily.

In *Insomnia*, King implies that Patrick Danville will save two people. This isn't exactly how things play out in the Dark Tower series; nor is it ever revealed how or when he ended up in the basement of Dandelo's cabin on Odd Lane.

There are a number of other contradictions between *Insomnia* and what transpires in the series. The Crimson King who battles Ralph Roberts seems less daunting than the mad king who dominates End-World. One way of resolving this is to regard the book the same way the Calvins do—symbolic rather than literal. It contains subconscious messages from Stephen King to Roland. References to the Dark Tower are masked, and sometimes mean nothing at all.

ROSE MADDER

In *Rose Madder*, a woman buys a painting that provides access to another world. In the coda to *Song of Susannah*, the fictional version of Stephen King wonders if this world is Mid-World and whether she might meet Roland. Instead she meets a woman named Dorcas, who knows about the people who were hanged from the light poles in Lud and is conversant with *ka*. There is also a passing reference to a weedy vacant lot that calls to mind a similar lot in Manhattan containing a pink rose. The novel also shares the character of Cynthia Smith with *Desperation*, which has Dark Tower connections, and a framed picture of Susan Day from *Insomnia*.

DESPERATION

One connection between *Desperation* and the Dark Tower series is geography. The China Pit Mines in Desperation, Nevada, are located in the Desatoya Mountains, which is also the location of the dead town of Eluria from the novella "The Little Sisters of Eluria."

The creature Tak who inhabits the bowels of the mine could be one of the creatures that dwell in the todash spaces between universes. He is freed when miners break through a wall, which is also how the skin-man is unleashed in *The Wind Through the Keyhole*. He speaks the same language of the unformed used by the Little Sisters.

The book also features powerful little figures called *can-tah*, translated as "little gods." The turtle Jake finds in the bowling bag he picked up in the vacant lot has similar powers, although it is more aligned with good than evil. Tak is *"can-tak,"* or "big god." He mentions the *"can toi,"* which is another name for the low men.

THE REGULATORS

Though *The Regulators* is not set in Desperation, Nevada, it features Tak, who originated from there. The book is connected to *Desperation* in a topsy-turvy manner, with characters bearing the same names having completely different relationships to one another. The book was published under King's pen name, Richard Bachman. His alter ego's fictitious wife is Claudia Inez Bachman, the author of *Charlie the Choo-Choo* in Keystone Earth, where she is known as Claudia y Inez Bachman to give her name nineteen letters. The Big Coffin Hunters in Mejis are also called "regulators," and Ted Brautigan shows Bobby Garfield a (fictional) Western movie called *The Regulators* in "Low Men in Yellow Coats."

BAG OF BONES

Bag of Bones is set in Derry and in western Maine, both thin places. Mike Noonan's summer home, Sara Laughs, becomes Cara Laughs, Stephen King's summer home at 19 Turtleback Lane, in *Song of Susannah* and *The Dark Tower*. The novel features a cameo appearance by Ralph Roberts from *Insomnia*, a book with very strong connections to the series. The number nineteen plays a part in the book, but this is probably just a coincidence since *Bag of Bones* was published before King's accident. Mike's journeys to the Fryeburg Fair are reminiscent of the todash journeys the *ka-tet* takes to New York.

HEARTS IN ATLANTIS

In several books, King introduces Dark Tower concepts before they become part of the series. In *Insomnia*, he debuted the Crimson King and elucidated the nature of the levels of the Tower. In "Low Men in Yellow Coats," the opening section of *Hearts in Atlantis*, King introduces Breakers, people with psychic powers sought by the Crimson King.

The Dark Tower subsequently fills in Ted Brautigan's backstory before he showed up at Bobby Garfield's boardinghouse in Connecticut, trying to evade the mysterious and menacing low men. He has just escaped from Algul Siento with the help of Sheemie from Mejis. Ted has extraordinarily strong precognitive powers that make him attractive to the low men, who scour the country looking for people with such talents. According to Ted, he is the best of the Breakers.

The low men wear gaudy clothes and hats lined with wire to protect them against psychic assault. They communicate with astrological symbols—including a red eye—chalked on sidewalks. Their cars look normal, but they aren't—they're alive, too, like the cars in *From a Buick 8* and "Mile 81." They wear the Crimson King's red eye on their lapels like badges. Ultimately they will be revealed to be disguised *can toi*, a cross between the taheen and humans.

One of the books Ted introduces to Bobby is *Ring Around the Sun* by Clifford D. Simak, which King once said was probably his inspiration for the concept of multiple universes. Ted knows that a gunslinger has reached the Borderlands of End-World. On one occasion, while in a trance, Ted says, "All things serve the Beam," a phrase that appears often in the Dark Tower series. The low men talk about their boss, the Crimson King.

The low men drag Ted back to his duties as a Breaker—though readers still don't know what this means. In the closing section of *Hearts in Atlantis*,

"Heavenly Shades of Night Are Falling," Bobby gets a message from Ted. The envelope contains rose petals, and Bobby senses the multiverse all spinning on the axis of the Tower. He understands that Ted has once again escaped from the low men.

Another connection between *Hearts in Atlantis* and the Dark Tower series is a man named Raymond Fiegler, another name for Randall Flagg. Fiegler was the leader of a fringe group that Bobby's childhood girlfriend, Carol Gerber, joined. Fiegler had the power of becoming dim or not being seen.

THE PLANT

There are a few tenuous ties between this unfinished novel and the Dark Tower series. Carlos Detweiller prays to the god Abbalah, which is another name for the Crimson King. He also utters words from the language of the unformed and mentions opopanax, the name of the feather used to call meetings in Calla Bryn Sturgis and a word that haunts Jack Sawyer in *Black House*.

BLACK HOUSE

Black House represents the first time that Stephen King allowed another writer to contribute to the Dark Tower mythos: Peter Straub. Though *The Talisman* has tenuous ties to the series, there is no question that *Black House* is a Dark Tower novel.

It was Straub's suggestion that he and King use elements from the Dark Tower. He was curious about what Breakers were and who the Crimson King was, and writing this book with King was one way to find those things out. Via the character Parkus, the nature of Breakers is spelled out. For the past two hundred years (a period those at the upper levels call the Age of Poisoned Thought and roughly the same amount of time the Wolves have been raiding the Callas), the Crimson King (aka Ram Abbalah) has been gathering people with psychic powers from the Earth and the Territories. He is using them to speed up the destruction of the Beams. One of the six Beams collapsed on its own thousands of years ago, part of the ordinary course of decay. Since starting their work, the Breakers have destroyed two Beams and weakened two others. Only one (Gan's Beam) still has its original strength.

Parkus calls the gunslingers an ancient war guild of Gilead and says that it is their job to protect the Beams. As a *ka-tet*, they are capable of countering the Breakers, but they are mostly gone now. He knows of one gunslinger who has created at least three more of his kind. This last group of gunslingers is the final hope for the Tower to stand until the end of its natural days. If the Crimson King can break the Beams before Roland and his *ka-tet* reach the Tower, he will never have to confront them, which is why he has stepped up his search for Breakers.

Only a small percentage of the children he captures are sufficiently talented to become Breakers. Those who don't qualify are sent as slave labor to power the Big Combination, An-tak, the Forge of the King, his energy source located in End-World, from which he powers evil in many different universes. An End-World demon called Mr. Munshun possesses Charles Burnside, an aging serial killer, using him to kidnap children. Any the Crimson King can't use, Mr. Munshun is allowed to eat.

Jack Sawyer, now a police officer in Wisconsin, has forgotten his adventure retrieving the Talisman. After seeing it in a newspaper article, he is haunted by the word "opopanax," the name of the feather used to call meetings in Calla Bryn Sturgis. He is responsible for finding the latest kidnap victim, Tyler Marshall, who has the potential to be as powerful a Breaker as Ted Brautigan, who Munshun calls the Chief Breaker. If Jack can't save Tyler, he has to kill him before Munshun can take him through the Black House, a portal to Mid-World, where he will be swept off to End-World on a monorail much like Blaine and Patricia, both of which are now gone. One more Breaker like Tyler might be all the Crimson King needs to bring down the Tower. His mother collapses after he is taken, rambling about the Crimson King. She also dreams of the Dark Tower in a field of roses.

Jack meets Sophie, the Queen of the Territories, in a tent that once belonged to the Little Sisters of Eluria. It may be the last such tent of a dozen or more that once existed in the Territories, On-World and Mid-World. Sophie tells Jack that even the Little Sisters serve the Beam, though Jack has no idea what that means.

Speedy's twin in the Territories explains the nature of the multiverse to Jack after leading him to an abandoned Speaking Circle like the ones encountered by Roland and his *ka-tet*. He says that there are "da fan" worlds—a number beyond telling, all bound together by the Dark Tower, the axle upon which many wheels spin. Ram Aballah, the Crimson King, wants to bring down the Tower. His physical being is trapped there, but he thinks his other manifestation will be freed from his court, Can-tah Abbalah, if the Tower falls.

With the rescue of Ty Marshall, the Crimson King feels a deep pain in his gut. Something fundamental has changed in his plans. Parkus thinks Jack

Sawyer might end up having some part to play in the "business of the Tower" but he did not.

FROM A BUICK 8

The mysterious driver of the unusual Buick that is abandoned in Pennsylvania was probably a low man, one of the *can toi*. The car itself is a portal to another universe. An even more tenuous connection is the fact that one of the characters in the book, Sandy Dearborn, shares a name with the alias Roland assumes in *Wizard and Glass*, Will Dearborn. Dearborn was Western novelist Louis L'Amour's middle name.

EVERYTHING'S EVENTUAL

This collection contains two stories with strong ties to the Dark Tower series. The first is the novella "The Little Sisters of Eluria," which is discussed earlier in this book. It is a stand-alone Dark Tower story that relates one of Roland's adventures after the fall of Gilead but before he finds the man in black's trail.

When the short story "Everything's Eventual" was published in *The Magazine of Fantasy and Science Fiction* in 1997, there was no reason to suspect that it had anything to do with the Dark Tower. However, as King developed the concept of Breakers in *Hearts in Atlantis* and *Black House*, he came to realize that the protagonist of "Everything's Eventual," Dinky Earnshaw, was a Breaker. A subtler crossover between the story and the series is the fact that Dinky knew Skipper Brannigan, who was a friend of a friend of Eddie Dean's brother, Henry. His name comes up when Henry and his friends are discussing who they'd want on their side in a fight. Skipper Brannigan was Dinky's tormentor at the grocery store where he gathered shopping carts, and Dinky was responsible for Skipper's death.

Dinky is hired to become an e-mail assassin by Trans Corporation, which turns out to be a subsidiary of North Central Positronics. His setup is reminiscent of Algul Siento. He is provided with accommodations and anything he wants if he performs mysterious work on behalf of this shady organization. Dinky's employer, a man named Sharpton, employs people who look for those with powers like Dinky has. Low men, in other words.

At the end of the story, Dinky writes a lethal e-mail message that contains the word "Excalibur," which is the name of Arthur Eld's sword, the metal from which was used to make Roland's guns. Dinky runs away from his safe house but, as revealed in *The Dark Tower*, low men caught him and took him to Thunderclap.

THE COLORADO KID

At first glance, King's short crime novel *The Colorado Kid* has no obvious connection to the Dark Tower series. However, readers pointed out what seemed to be an error in the story: there were no Starbucks franchises in Denver in 1980. In response, King wrote the following on his official Web site in October 2005: "Don't assume that's a mistake on my part. The Constant Readers of the Dark Tower series may realize that that is not necessarily a continuity error, but a clue." In other words, King is implying that the novel takes place in the same kind of universe where there are Takuro Spirit cars and Nozz-A-La soft drinks.

One of the story's biggest mysteries is how the Colorado Kid made it from Colorado to Maine in an impossibly short period of time. The answer could be that he went through a magic or scientific portal. Or, like Jack Sawyer, he may have crossed into another reality where distances are shorter and time moves at a different pace.

UR

This novella was published as a Kindle-only eBook in 2009. It has subsequently been made available for other eBook devices and has been released on audio. The story involves a college English professor named Wesley Smith who is shamed into buying a Kindle. However, the one that arrives is pink (the color of a rose?) and has a special feature that allows him to access books and newspapers from parallel universes. When Wesley uses these features, the screen shows an ominous black tower instead of the typical author caricature.

In the alternate realities, famous authors were born and died on different dates and produced works beyond those that are known in our "ur," the name the device gives to each possible time line or level of the Tower. Wesley is also able to access newspapers from the future.

After he changes the future, two "low men in yellow coats" chastise him for causing unfixable damage to the time line. Wesley understands that they aren't really men and that underneath they are reptiles or birds—or both. They wear badges featuring the Crimson King's red eye on their lapels, only these eyes are alive and watching him. The low men tell him that he has no idea what he did. "The Tower trembles; the worlds shudder in their courses. The rose feels a chill, as of winter."

When Wesley mentions the Tower he saw on the screen, the low men say that all things serve the Tower. Wesley responds that that means he also serves the Tower, to which they have no answer. The story's unanswered question is who sent the Kindle to him. Was it, perhaps, *ka*?

MILE 81

The mud-covered station wagon that materializes at a closed rest stop along the Maine Turnpike is a "low men" vehicle that is actually alive and hungry, like the car in *From a Buick 8*.

11/22/63

Though King took measures to keep *11/22/63* from being an overt Dark Tower novel, many of its concepts are familiar to readers of the series. Most obvious is the use of a portal to travel to a different time. It is a North Central Positronics kind of door, always arriving at the same place and time, rather than a magic door, which can be aimed. The lead character, Jake Epping, spends a few months in Derry, which is a significant location in the Dark Tower universe.

The entire concept for *11/22/63* is laid out in *Wolves of the Calla*. Using Black Thirteen and the Unfound Door, a person could go back to Dallas on November 22, 1963, and see whether Oswald acted alone or was part of a larger conspiracy, Father Callahan says. "And perhaps you could change what happened that day. If there was ever a watershed moment in American life, that was it. Change that, change everything that came after. Vietnam . . . the race riots . . . everything." Eddie replies, "But, Pere . . . what if you did it and changed things for the worse? I think it takes a great man to make a great mistake. And besides, someone who came after him might have been a really bad guy. Some Big Coffin Hunter who never got a chance because of Lee Harvey Oswald, or whoever it was."

There are other more incidental connections. Eddie Dean saw Kubrick film *The Shining* (though he's never heard of Stephen King). Nigel the robot is reading *The Dead Zone* and has an extensive collection of King books, including *Hearts in Atlantis*. The word *"cujo"* means "sweet one" in Mejis. For an extensive look at the myriad crossovers found in King's work, including those in books not directly connected to the Dark Tower series, see *The Complete Stephen King Universe* by Stanley Wiater, Christopher Golden and Hank Wagner.

An Interview with
Stephen King

The following interview was conducted by telephone on January 9, 2012, a few months before the publication of *The Wind Through the Keyhole*.

Q: **To what extent are you involved with the Marvel graphic novel adaptations of the Dark Tower series?**

    A: I monitored them really closely at the beginning. I wanted to make sure everything was on track and going the right way. I know Robin [Furth] does a really great job. After they went off on their own, I didn't want to junk up my head with their story lines. That's Robin's take on all this, and she's fine with it and she can do whatever she wants because I'm more or less done. I've got this one book coming out, *The Wind Through the Keyhole*, and there might be more after that, but if there are, they won't be influenced at all by whatever's going on in the comics and indeed might run contradictory to what's in the comics. You know what Roland always says: There are other worlds than these.

Q: **Do you have any idea why you find yourself going back to the Dark Tower series every five or six years?**

    A: No. I really don't. What happened after *Wizard and Glass*, Marsha and Julie in the office started to bug me about all these letters they were getting. "When is he going to finish this?" So finally I said to myself: "I'm going to sit down and I'm going to write these things—the whole thing—as one novel." By then I had a good starting place with *Wolves of the Calla*, because I knew what I wanted to do with it, which was kind of like *Seven Samurai* and *The Magnificent Seven*, the Western, the John Sturges thing. Once

I started there, the whole thing just sort of spun itself out and I thought I was done with it.

I started to think about fairy tales. It even crossed my mind for a while that maybe what I really wanted to do was to write a book of fairy tales—not about fairies, necessarily—but make-believe stories. Then Roland just kind of walked in and said, "This is my story." The story originally was the story of Tim Stoutheart, and all I knew was that it had to be a little boy and he had to have an evil stepfather—or stepmother, but I picked stepfather in this case. He had to go on a journey. The skin-man story was going to be something else in that same vein and ultimately the three stories just folded one into the other.

Q: Tim Ross grows up to be a gunslinger. Do you think we'll see him again?

A: I don't know. I never know. I know that I sort of left the door open to go back to Mid-World. I guess the one story that I might want to tell, that Robin and her gang [at Marvel] have already told—is Jericho Hill. I don't know how they did that. I *really* didn't want to read that, because if I went back to Roland at all, that would have to be the story.

Q: Would there be another meeting up with Rhea?

A: I don't know. I don't know anything about this stuff. I just know that when this thing comes up, every time I've gone into one of these things, I've gone in with a feeling of . . . this will never work. And every time it does. From the time you sit down, you know you're in the right place. And it was great to be with Roland and his friends again and to see Eddie alive and Susannah, Oy. It was great. I really do think the book has the feel of some of those old stories.

Q: One thing that has always confused me about Roland is his age. He meets up with people over the course of his travels who knew him when he was a child, like Sheb in Tull, but he talks about being a thousand years old.

A: Sheb knows him from when he came to Mejis, not exactly as a child but as an adolescent. I don't know any of these things. Your guess is as good as mine, really. My assumption is that something happened to Roland after Gilead fell and it has to do with the Beams and time getting funny and that he really has lived a more or less normal life, that it's time itself that's gone off the rails. That's all I know. The only other thing that I can say is that my concept of the book when I started, when I was very young, like twenty-two years old, probably mutated to something that was a little less mythic as time went by.

Q: **There was a period during the nineties when the Dark Tower came up in just about everything you wrote. Do you still feel that happening these days?**

A: I certainly felt it happening in *11/22/63,* partly because it was Derry again. The guy shows up in Derry. But also because of the very idea of the yellow card man saying, "You guys think that you haven't been changing anything when in fact you've been changing everything and the whole structure of the universe is getting ready to topple." At that point I thought to myself, I can very easily reference the Dark Tower here, but in a way I didn't want to do that. I wanted the book to kind of stand apart, I think because of the historical basis—the whole idea of the Kennedy assassination. I wanted to make it as least fantastical as I could. So I think that people who have read the Dark Tower books and who read *11/22/63* will say that this is certainly a Tower-ish situation at the end of the book.

Q: **Marten Broadcloak is a guy who has come up in many guises over the years, including in *The Wind Through the Keyhole* again as the tax collector.**

A: You're right. It is Marten Broadcloak, but Chuck Verrill edited the book and said, Why don't you take out references to him until the very end when you talk about Roland's mother, so that's what I did. But, sure. That guy is undoubtedly Marten Broadcloak. Who's also lived a very long life.

Q: **Another character that seems to be one of his aspects is Farson.**

A: Farson has nothing to do with Marten Broadcloak. Farson is a guy, and there could be stories about him, except I've never known how to write them, except maybe for Jericho Hill, because he never figures in. Roland is never sent to palaver with Farson or to have anything to do with him. I'm sure that Farson is a minion of the Crimson King, and Marten Broadcloak is as well, and I think there's a reference to the two of them actually being in contact in *Wizard and Glass*. What I could never figure out was whether Marten Broadcloak was Flagg.

Q: You can sort of see in the early days, when the stories were first published in *The Magazine of Fantasy and Science Fiction*, how your thoughts about Marten and Walter and the man in black evolved.

A: These stories all want to cohere. The Dark Tower books are always trying to get back to some kind of central myth core, but I could never define it and I never tried to, because I'm not that kind of writer. I'm very instinctive. It's not anything that I'm really thinking of ahead of time.

Q: Do you still plan to go back and revise the other books to bring them all into line?

A: I don't know if it's a project that anyone would care about and I'm a little bit leery about doing it. The first book really had to be done because it had to be brought in line with the way book seven ends. If I went and rewrote the rest of them, I know that I could do work that would please me as the author, but I think that a lot of people might pick up the books and pay the money and say, geez, I don't know why I bought this. He sold me the same book. The changes would be there, but they would be subtle. The real Dark Tower junkies would know but, for the general reader, I don't think so.

Q: The character of Maerlyn interested me in *The Wind Through the Keyhole* because he's sort of a tired, cranky old man. He was reminiscent of the Turtle from *It*, who was also world-weary.

A: Yeah, he is. It's nothing that I ever thought of consciously. I think that if I drew from anything there, I might have drawn from T. H. White's *The Sword in the Stone*. His Merlin is sort of cranky, too. I may have drawn a little bit from that. But basically I wanted to play against type. I didn't want any big, magnificent Disney-animated Merlin. I wanted somebody who seemed like he could be a real person. I love it when the kid says to him, "Was his magic stronger than yours?" And Maerlyn says, "No, but I was drunk." That's a very human thing.

Q: At what point did you know how the Dark Tower series was going to end?

A: I knew how things were going to end from probably *Wolves of the Calla* or *Wizard and Glass*. There was always a question of what was going to happen when Roland got to the Tower. One possibility was that we would never know. That he would blow his horn and go to the Tower and that would be the end of the series. I've never had a lot of patience for that kind of thing. I feel like you have to give people everything and if they like it they like it, and if they don't, they don't. A lot of people didn't like the way the thing ended, but after all the things that I'd written about how *ka* is a wheel and it always comes back to where it started, I don't see how anybody could have expected anything different, really. That's the way it works. The same idea exists in *Ghost Brothers of Darkland County*, that until you get things right, you have to do them over and over and over again. That's human nature, as I understand it. That's how we do what we do. If you want to quit smoking, for instance, if you fail, then you're smoking again. You're back where you were. Maybe you try again, and sooner or later something changes, but only through that process of repetition and incremental learning.

I used to get crazy and I stopped finally by the time that I got into those last three books—the Internet was a growing concern, and people were sending all these posts and everything. There were all these theories about how the Dark Tower was going to end. There were Web sites that were dedicated to it, and all these physicists would write in and say all these things about wormholes and everything, and I'm thinking, Jesus Christ, you guys, I'm an English major. I flunked fucking physics. Give me a break. I did what I did. That's it.

Q: Do you have an idea of what changes Roland needs to make to re-deem himself?

A: Sure. I do. I know exactly what he's got to do. You have to go back to the first book and look at that and then you'll know the answer.

Q: Did you always plan to include yourself in the series?

A: No. But after the accident, I was thinking if I had died in that accident it would have been like *The Mystery of Edwin Drood*. There would have been this whole setup with no conclusion, and to me that was kind of an awful thought—that I would not have a chance to finish what I started. I began to think, well, I am the god of these people's world. I'm sort of the over-soul that they don't know anything about, and if all things serve the Beam, then I'm a part of that because I've written all these books with the Dark Tower in it and everything, and I thought it was really a neat thing to do. The idea that if they saved me, then the story continued. You know, that's kind of an old idea, too, the idea of saving the creator so the story continues.

Q: When I was working on *The Road to the Dark Tower*, you mentioned in passing that Roland had a brother and a sister. Would you like to elaborate on that?

A: Nope.

Q: Robin Furth speculated at the time that if there was some hidden tragedy in Gabrielle and Steven's past, it might explain their cold relationship.

A: Everlynne at Serenity knows everything that there is about Roland's sister, whose name is Clarissa Deschain. Everlynne knows a lot about that family. It would be kind of good to go back and talk about her a little bit. She's a good character. That's all I know. I don't know a lot about these things.

Q: Do you have any sense of what's going to happen with the movie adaptation?

A: I think something is going to happen with it at Warner Bros., but I haven't heard anything from Ron [Howard] in a while, and I let them go their own course. I can just say that if the movie does get made from the script that I read, I think that the people who read the books will be in equal parts delighted and infuriated by what they see, but I also think that they'll keep coming back because, to me, they got a brilliant take on the whole thing. My lips are sealed. I can't say. But I can tell you that the character of Jake Chambers is very important, and Akiva Goldsman did a brilliant job of integrating the fantasy world of Mid-World with the real world of New York City, and the two things interchange in a way—I was just delighted by it and by the way that they use Blaine the Mono. I hope it happens, but I'm not counting the days or anything. Ron's very determined to make it, and I think in the end he will.

DISCORDIA

———— 🐦 ————

Stephen King's official Web site, stephenking.com, has a section devoted to the Dark Tower series. It covers the books, the graphic novels, the artwork, connections to other books, has a glossary, and features a section called Discordia, which is the name for the chaos out of which Mid-World arose and to which the Crimson King wants all realities to return.

> Note: *Discordia* players are advised that it contains a parental advisory due to graphic text and imagery. It is intended for adults. Discordia—and the discussion below—also contains numerous spoilers for the Dark Tower series.

When King's Web site was revamped in 2007, designer Brian Stark came up with a concept that focused on North Central Positronics, the company built by the Great Old Ones to meld magic and technology in Mid-World. Imprints of NCP and its various subsidies, including Sombra Corporation and LaMerk Industries, are seen throughout the Dark Tower series. Stark thought that he could design the Dark Tower section of the Web site using a "retrotech" theme derived using NCP concepts. The ultimate goal of the redesign was to sharpen the Dark Tower brand and present a better understanding of the story to the uninitiated.

The North Central Positronics concept gradually evolved into an online game—a progressive storytelling platform—called Discordia. It is inspired by the Dark Tower series, though it gradually developed its own mythology. The idea of an interactive experience appealed to King's personal assistant, Marsha DeFilippo, who had fielded many requests over the years for a video game based on the Dark Tower mythos. While the concept is firmly rooted in the ongoing war between Sombra Corporation and Tet Corporation, the company founded to protect the rose and Stephen King in the real world, the Discordia story line reaches far beyond the day-to-day conflict between the two companies.

Phase I of the project took two years to develop and execute. King's former research assistant, Robin Furth, became the project's director. As Stark rendered the artwork, designs and animations using high-powered custom computers, he sought feedback from a focus group called the Secret Window that consisted of ten people who were regular visitors to the message board on King's site (including the author of this book). As executive producer, King approved all artwork and concepts and made decisions great and small, helping to keep the development team grounded in the world of the Dark Tower.

In Chapter I, which launched in late 2009, players are given a verbal mission briefing by Stephen King. In the role of Op19, a highly trained rookie agent working for the Tet Corporation's Investigation and Surveillance Unit, players are to search the Dixie Pig for magical objects created by North Central Positronics. Op19 is then to travel beneath the restaurant to the Fedic Dogan. If mutants or robots or Sombra Operatives are encountered, they are to be neutralized. Once the mission is complete, players will need to find a doorway back to the present, where they are to provide a full report.

Chapter I (now considered to be the prequel to Discordia) begins with a shooting range tutorial, where players acquire skills they will use in Chapter II. Then Op19 enters the filthy, disgusting Dixie Pig, fully rendered in 3D graphics that are utterly faithful to the way the restaurant is described in *The Dark Tower*. Alert players will observe details and items that reference the series as they explore. The exquisitely lit and incredibly detailed set features the main dining room, the kitchen, pantry, bathroom and VIP room. Players can explore these rooms by moving the mouse—a perspective that can be as dizzying as the one Roland experienced when he went through the doorway into Eddie Dean's body—and by clicking on numbered viewpoint icons that change Op19's location in the room.

To complete Chapter I, Op19 must find five magical items (an Oriza, for example) and seven orbs that depict major characters from the series, designed by Michael Whelan, the artist who illustrated the first and final novels. The model Whelan used for Father Callahan was David Williamson, the current proprietor of Betts Bookstore, an online store that deals exclusively in Stephen King books, many of them signed or rare. DeFilippo interviewed Williamson about the experience for King's official Web site.

As each orb is located, players are given the chance to download a high-resolution image as computer wallpaper. Printable high-resolution versions of these definitive character depictions are awarded to players who find all the orbs. Whelan also contributed art used in the opening-credit animation and made other conceptual and art direction contributions for Discordia.

A secret passage provides access to a lobby that gives way to the mind-trap tunnel that leads up to the doorway that allows travel between New York and Fedic. Players who know the magic word that opens the door are rewarded with the closing credits.

Every time a player enters a new room, his journal is updated with a discussion of the room's significance to the story narrated from the point of view of Op19, who is investigating the Dixie Pig as a crime scene ten years after the fact. These entries contain hints about what players might expect to find in that room. Players can also access descriptions of the magical items and lengthy biographies of the characters associated with the orbs, all written by Dark Tower expert Robin Furth.

With Chapter II, which launched in 2013, the story branches out into completely new territory. Going down the rabbit hole, in the words of Brian Stark. New characters are introduced, and the war between the two powerful corporations veers off from King's story line. Roland and his *ka-tet* are not part of the plot except for their appearance in the orbs. However, members of the development team were mindful of "the faces of their fathers," seeking to honor the original series while mapping new territory.

One of the interesting aspects of Discordia is the fact that it plays out in real time. Between Chapter I in 2009 and Chapter II in 2013, the world did not stand still. Op19 spent the intervening years in Mid-World, engaging in battles with opposing forces, monsters, demons and todash creatures. Op19 can't return to the Keystone World because he hasn't been able to find a working doorway out of Mid-World. Worse, the doorway to the Fedic Dogan malfunctioned after Op19 passed through, which means Tet Corporation can't send backup forces to assist him.

The real-time aspect goes a step further. Roland returned to the Mohaine Desert at the end of *The Dark Tower*. Time has been moving forward for him since then, so, by 2013, nearly a decade has passed. Roland has repeated the events of *The Gunslinger* and is asleep after his meeting with the man in black. He doesn't play a part in the interactive adventure, but the designers imagine that Op19 could conceivably venture off to the golgotha and find Roland asleep there.

There is a three-way struggle going on within the Fedic Dogan. The three sides are represented by Op19, Richard Sayre—who is working on behalf of the Crimson King to gather Breakers and bring down the Tower—and a new character named Arina Yokova, a Russian mobster with a Mid-World fixation. Arina and her mercenaries are headquartered in Castle Discordia, which is protected by skilled marksmen and armed sentries. Sayre's operations are disrupted somewhat by the arrival of Op19 and Arina. He and his team are using isolated parts of the Dogan and the tunnels beneath as their base of operation.

Who is Arina Yokova? She is the daughter of Pasha Yokova, the boss of the Crimson Crescent, a multigenerational crime family, one of the oldest and most dangerous in the world. As a child, Arina was sheltered from her family's business. She was educated in Russian boarding schools and obtained a degree in mechanical engineering from Brown University.

While in graduate school, Arina's father dies and she inherits leadership of the Crimson Crescent from him. She has no choice but to accept the position, but she becomes a figurehead, delegating the day-to-day operations to other family members.

Arina is a huge fan of the works of Stephen King and, in particular, the Dark Tower series. Her studies in metaphysics and science lead her to believe that Mid-World and the Dark Tower really exist. She holds Roland Deschain in high regard and engages in online debates about the science of the Dark Tower. This attracts the attention of Sombra Corporation, who make her an offer she can't refuse. They tell her that her theories about the existence of the Dark Tower are true and that Roland really does exist. Once they offer to take her to Mid-World, she agrees to become the CEO of Sombra while maintaining a close connection with the Crimson Crescent.

In 2002, Sombra is looting the Fedic Dogan of the ultra-advanced weapons stored there, including weapons of mass destruction. Sombra reverse engineers and sells these weapons to private and government organizations connected to the Crimson Crescent in the Keystone World.

Arina is shocked, enraged and perplexed when, in 2004, she reads *The Dark Tower*. She interprets Roland's situation as being analogous to a software programming glitch that causes an infinite loop, and she becomes determined to free Roland from this loop, by any means necessary, an endeavor she code-names "The End Game." Her advantage is this: she knows every detail of Roland's life from the Mohaine Desert forward.

To fund her operations in Mid-World, she embezzles billions of dollars of profits that Sombra's arms operation garnered, using the Crimson Crescent's money-laundering network. Once her crimes become known to intelligence and investigative organizations in the Keystone World, Arina becomes a hunted woman, but she is safe from arrest in Mid-World. She takes advantage of the hundreds of magical and scientific doorways in the rotunda to gather as much information about the Dark Tower as she can.

This is the situation Op19 encounters on the other side of the Fedic door and forms the basis for Chapter II of Discordia.

AN INTERVIEW WITH BRIAN STARK

Brian Stark is the producer and art director responsible for more than one hundred interactive and branding projects. He created the Streetwise.com portal and co-owned a production boutique in New York, building a catalog of well-known and highly respected clients.

He became a specialist in interactive culture and admits to an obsession with culture, motion pictures, music and technology. A filmmaker at heart, he attended the School of Visual Arts in Manhattan but, during orientation, discovered that digital video editing was poised to make what he was being taught in the classroom obsolete.

He took a job as a digital video editor for a CD-ROM developer that exposed him to programs like Adobe Premier and Macromedia Director. Then he began to experiment with digital music and sound. He and his partner created a Web site for their Vertigo Studios in 1996. Vertigo produced dozens of songs for companies around the country. Stark then switched gears, building Web sites for other companies, which is where he discovered Macromedia (now Adobe) Flash, a product that brought new freedom to Web designers with motion graphics and integrated sound.

His obsession with Flash developed into an asset. He worked on projects for companies like PricewaterhouseCoopers and Harvest Consulting. He then created Streetwise.com, which was an immediate success, drawing the attention of *Time*, *Billboard*, the *Wall Street Journal* and the *New York Times*. He created and maintained interactive content for bands like Linkin Park, Marilyn Manson, Rob Zombie and Papa Roach, and the attendant publicity got him side gigs with Ozzfest and others. He also produced the official Web site for the movie *Almost Famous* for DreamWorks.

He and his partner reinvented themselves as Metro Digital Media Artists. One of their first big jobs was building the official Web site for *La Bohème* on Broadway. They followed up with sites for *Les Misérables* and *Man of La Mancha*.

In 2004, he was hired by Stephen King to work on the Dark Tower section of his Web site. The following interview was conducted by phone in February 2012, prior to the launch of the second phase of Discordia.

Q: How did the connection with King come along? Did he approach your company?

A: This goes back to 2003. Another Web developer was hired by Stephen to build a new official Web site. That developer placed a call for designers on a popular job board. Judy [Hahn] responded to the ad and we were hired a few weeks later. In a strange twist of fate, the original developer was forced to abandon the job. We then took over as webmaster and have been with the team ever since.

Q: What was your familiarity with King at that point? Were you a fan?

A: I have a picture of me on Christmas morning opening *Nightmares & Dreamscapes*. I had read *The Gunslinger* when it was a couple of years old. Stephen King was my idol all through any of my creative efforts. I loved *The Gunslinger* and *The Dark Half* and all the movies that were out at the time like *Stand By Me* and *Misery*. All of that stuff really captured my imagination. Then I got the opportunity to work for Steve. It was really strange that it came to that.

I took *The Gunslinger* out of the library because I was so fascinated with Whelan's art and fell in love with the story. The whole cowboy thing that you would get from looking at the cover wasn't that appealing to me. I had no idea that it was all such cool sci-fi/ *Matrix*-like content.

Q: At some point you decided to do a Dark Tower section of the Web site. Was that Steve's suggestion?

A: We did a design for the official site and we were also tasked with doing the old Flash Dark Tower site that had a Tower that moved when you clicked buttons. I think that was the first thing I ever did for Steve, a Dark Tower site, so they wanted to do that before I was ever in the mix.

Q: That would be around the time when the final books were headed toward publication.

A: It was. We were representing the existing books and then adding them for, I guess, a year or so.

Q: You had a concept inspired by North Central Positronics.

A: We were going to design a new Dark Tower Web site to get away from it being a Flash vehicle. We took this concept of a site that looked like it was made by North Central Positronics. I can't believe this is actually the inception point for Discordia. It's so far and completely removed—technologically, the way the execution is and everything else—compared to what Discordia is. That's the first time that the development team that's on it kind of fell in love with doing something about North Central Positronics and Tet. It goes back that far.

Q: How did it get from there to Discordia?

A: We did The Office [an interactive tour of Stephen King's office], saw it was cool, and then we wanted to apply that to the Dark Tower. That was when we went back to the North Central Positronics concepts and the war between Tet and Sombra. We saw the potential of using 3-D to do very cool things. We wanted a special-feature project for the Dark Tower just like The Office.

Q: When Robin Furth came on as director, had you already developed this concept?

A: Robin came on as a director from the very beginning. We had a meeting in the city at this crazy vegan restaurant. Robin was immediately up for Discordia, even though it's kind of expanded universe and it's minimizing the ultra-importance of some of the sacred aspects of the Dark Tower. Discordia said that expanded universe is okay. If you want to think of it as canon, think of it as canon. If you want to think of it as expanded universe, think of it as expanded universe, which is what I do. I believe it gives us much more creativity and freedom to do things. It's a separate thing.

Q: The fact that Stephen King recorded the mission plan at the beginning for Discordia is his stamp of approval.

A: Absolutely. And we really needed that with some of the outlandish things that we brought to the table with the Discordia concept. That really helped.

Q: The Marvel graphic novels were already in the works, so the idea of branching out from King's stuff into new territory had already been accepted.

A: Other than the fact that we were creating a couple of characters, most of the time we would be doing representations of things that were specifically mentioned in the books. Early concepts for Discordia revolved around more espionage-type things going on in

New York City between the two companies. Those ideas were scrapped, and then we moved on to the more creative concepts of the Dixie Pig and going to Mid-World, which was a huge step for us. Representing an adventure to Mid-World is huge, and a big responsibility for me creatively. Getting that changed from a simpler game that took place in New York City to a Mid-World adventure was huge for me. That's the stuff that we spoke about at that initial meeting on one of the hottest days of the summer that I can ever remember in New York. That Op19 would exist. The war between Tet and Sombra is really a great angle to tell a lot of other things, and I think that's the way we all saw it. To tell more about the Dark Tower universe in almost a promotional sense. Discordia continues to grow and evolve, whether you're talking about creative or technology or 3-D.

The development team is quoted as saying we honor the face of our fathers, but we also look at the Dark Tower series as part of an übernovel the same way that Steve does. It's not even close to done. Discordia is just another piece. Everything that we're doing is based on the first seven books, but we don't hold anything that sacred. We're not afraid to get nasty and do crazy things. That freedom allows us to come up with some very cool ideas. Discordia does not honor the Dark Tower series in such a deep sense that we're afraid to do things, which I think was one of the things that we struggled with all the way up to the part where we pitched Arina Yokova, this Mafia character, and all the things that go along with it. Steve said he really liked it.

The game itself is that you arrive at the Fedic Dogan and have to investigate. You're going to have a gunfight. All the principles of the first game will be there, only probably modified and different technology by the time it comes out later this year. Sayre's setting up shop to do the extractions. Arina is fighting with them trying to use the rotunda. For the most part, Arina and her thugs are controlling the whole area. She's living in the castle. She controls the tunnel. She controls the rotunda, and Sayre's low men hold down parts of the Fedic Dogan. That sets the stage for that three-man kind of trifecta, which I always love, when there are three opposing sides. The cool factor about Discordia is that, yeah, it's this game, and that's definitely its primary thing, but it also details this very cool character Arina, who is obsessed with the Dark Tower, and not only the Dark Tower, but Steve King, too.

While working for Sombra, Arina reads the final Dark Tower book. For several reasons, she is outraged and perplexed by the open ending. Perhaps most important, Arina believes that the Tower is malfunctioning and should not restart its time line at the year that it does, trapping Roland in the time loop. By the mid-2000s, Arina is completely obsessed with Roland's cycle and begins to formulate a plan to liberate her hero.

Q: There are people on the message boards who aren't fond of the way the series ends.

A: That's the thing. I've read essays about how people hate the way that the series ended. Personally, I'm okay with most of it. I think there should have been some kind of crazy epic battle, which is one of the things that I want Discordia to satisfy. But for the most part, I'm reasonably satisfied. I think a lot of people don't like that open-ended thing, and for somebody like Arina, it became a serious problem. She just didn't like it, but she also then is dead set on ending it and bringing peace to the cycle.

This is why she killed everybody and took over in the rotunda and the tunnels—to use this recently discovered ancient device that North Central Positronics engineered. It's the "offer you can't refuse" thing that they show her when they got her to work for them. It's called a snapper. It allowed maintenance crews to test the functionality of doors. They could go through any door, one-way or not, and return at the click of a button. The base of the snapper is a brasslike disc about the size of a large pizza. It stands about four inches tall and hovers above the ground, with dim green light emanating beneath it. The base houses a removable device similar to a pocket watch and chain named a clicker. This has the button that returns the user to the base, as well as basic controls for the snapper's cloaking features.

Once Arina figures out how to use the snapper, she realizes that she can pretty much do anything that she wants. She travels through time and space to countless "wheres and whens" while performing dangerous interdimensional field research and espionage, all in an effort to gain as much knowledge about the Tower as she can. She can travel to the farthest reaches of time and space and always return to Mid-World at the same time as when she left.

She's used the money from the heist to fund this effort, to lure men to work for her as protection, or people to go through doors using the snapper to test it and see where it goes. She's funding a rather extensive venture. The ghost town of Fedic is being held by Arina's thugs and mercenaries. That's where a lot of that money goes. At the end of it, we learn through journal entries and some clue that 1) Arina has been going through the doors for what is technically hundreds of years; and 2) that she is dead set on ending Roland's perpetual journey and she has figured out how to do it. She is basically on the loose somewhere in time, is the way we leave it.

A FEW WORDS WITH ROBIN FURTH

When Stephen King was preparing to work on the final three books in the Dark Tower series, he hired Robin Furth to be his research assistant. He wanted her to index the first four books and make notes of the major characters, places and events so he could refer back to them for continuity. That project led to her book *Stephen King's The Dark Tower: A Concordance*. As an acknowledged expert in the Dark Tower, she went on to write the scripts for the Marvel graphic novel adaptations (see interview later in this book), which was her first step in expanding the Dark Tower universe beyond what King had written.

She became the director of the Discordia project for King's official Web site, writing the text content associated with found items and making sure the details in this interactive experience remained consistent with the overall mythos. The following interview was conducted by e-mail in March 2012, prior to the launch of Phase II of Discordia.

Q: Brian Stark mentioned a dinner at a vegan restaurant in New York on a very hot summer day, where the basic concepts of Discordia were hashed out. What are your memories of that day?

A: I remember that dinner very well! Marsha [DeFilippo] and I met Brian, Judy [Hahn], and Judy's son, Jordan, at a vegan restaurant. At that point Brian and Judy were still trying to decide the best approach for Discordia. Brian really wanted to make his espionage tale work within the context of the novels so that he could stay true to the Dark Tower universe. Inevitably, the conversation drifted to

"Tet versus Sombra," since that is such a big part of the final Dark Tower novel. After that, the project really grew wings. In retrospect, I attribute that dinner to *ka*.

Q: Did the fact that you were already involved with the Marvel adaptation make the decision to move into an expanded world experience easier?

A: The fact that I was already involved with the Marvel adaptation really made a difference when it came to working with Discordia. For that first thirty-issue comic book run, I had to fill out Roland's backstory (the "lost years" between the end of Roland's Hambry adventure and the battle of Jericho Hill), so I'd already been involved with adding detail to the Dark Tower universe. (As you know, for any Dark Tower fan, that is an incredibly exciting but incredibly daunting prospect.) Hence, when we started talking about Arina's tale, it felt like we were doing something very similar, but in a different time stream, if that makes sense! In both cases, we had the backing of Steve, which is always the most important thing.

Brian is always really modest and makes sure that credit for Discordia is evenly distributed, but he is really the brains behind this operation. He and Judy have put untold hours into the project. It's amazing.

Q: What is your role as director?

A: I make sure the details are right, and I write the journal entries and item descriptions. Brian and I went over the floor plan for the Dixie Pig, the mind-trap tunnel, and for the rotunda many times, making certain that all the details were right on the money. We even swapped sketches, just to make sure. Writing the journal entries was an amazing experience, because on one level, I actually became Op19. I wandered through the Pig as if I were actually journeying there. It even affected my dream life. I'm not great with technology (you should see my dinosaur of a computer), but Brian was incredibly patient and has really educated me about computer games. It's been great.

Q: Listening to Brian talk about Arina, it was like he knew this woman. Like she was real.

A: In the Dark Tower universe, Arina *is* real!

THE DARK TOWER: THE MOVIE

As long as there's been an Internet—even back in the days when people communicated on bulletin boards using dial-up modems—there have been ongoing discussions about who should be cast in a movie version of the Dark Tower. Series fans seem to assume that it will happen eventually, especially after the highly successful adaptation of *The Lord of the Rings*. If that complex fantasy series could be turned into a movie, then why not the Dark Tower?

Clint Eastwood was an early favorite to play Roland, but as the decades passed, it was clear that the actor on whom Roland was modeled had become too old to play the thousand-year-old gunslinger. These discussions continue, however, with each new generation of reader suggesting the latest and greatest actors to fill this fantasy cast.

At New York Comic Con in February 2007, King sat on a panel with many of the creative people involved with the Marvel Dark Tower graphic novels. King told the audience that he'd refused offers for the film rights to the series because he didn't think much of the chances of it being a good movie. Though he usually doesn't care much about what happens with many of the movies made from his works—beyond hoping they're good because he is a fan of movies—the Dark Tower is important to him. He regards it as his life's work.

He saw the Marvel graphic novels as the best of all possibilities. They would adapt the series visually the way it was supposed to look, in his opinion. However, they also rekindled interest in a film adaptation. Frank Darabont approached King, but King thought Darabont already had too many other works optioned (including *The Mist*, which hadn't yet been filmed). Darabont underscored his enthusiasm for the Dark Tower by turning David Drayton in *The Mist* into an artist working on a poster for a Dark Tower film.

Real-life movie poster artist Drew Struzan created the painting as a prop for the film. It eventually ended up in Stephen King's office.

The first proposal King considered seriously came from J. J. Abrams and Damon Lindelof, who had come to his attention through the TV series *Lost*. The series creators were King fans, using many references to his work during the show's six-year run. They said that *The Stand* was a major influence on how the series was structured. The Others read *Carrie* at their book club. A lab rabbit with the number eight on its back was drawn from *On Writing*. After King wrote about his admiration for the show, they flew up to Maine to meet with him.

Damon Lindelof, in particular, was a huge fan of the Dark Tower. For nineteen dollars, King gave them a period of exclusivity to see what they could come up with. By late 2009, though, the team had decided they wouldn't be doing an adaptation. In interviews, Abrams said he thought the series was tricky and Lindelof admitted to being intimidated. He was such a big fan of King and the series that he was terrified of screwing the movie up. His reverence for the author got in the way of taking creative license to change things in the series.

It didn't take long for someone else to snap up the film rights. Ron Howard's Imagine Entertainment and Akiva Goldsman's Weed Road presented a novel idea for how to adapt the series. Their plan consisted of a trilogy of movies with TV miniseries bridging the films, all featuring the same cast. The TV series would focus on characterization and the films would be action and adventure. They also talked about using elements of the story that wouldn't appear in either the film or the TV series in narrative video games, drawing from both King's books and the graphic novels.

Akiva Goldsman secured the rights and brought the package to Ron Howard and Brian Grazer at Imagine Entertainment. Howard plans to direct. Grazer, King and Goldsman will produce. Their first studio of choice was Universal, where Imagine is based, although Warner Bros. also vied for the project.

King said that he'd never considered this multimedia format for an adaptation before, but he liked it. He was also complimentary of Howard as director, saying that he told honest stories with style and substance without showing off.

The first movie was optimistically scheduled to launch on May 17, 2013. Then came the announcement that Javier Bardem was their pick to play Roland. Bardem didn't accept the role for a while, but indicated that he was favorably inclined to do so. Howard spent a lot of time with him and reported that Bardem was fascinated by the character and had great instincts for Roland.

Filming was tentatively set to begin in September 2011. However, the deal with Universal started to unravel once the studio reviewed the script. They asked Goldsman for a rewrite to lower the projected budget. Filming was pushed back to February 2012. Howard said in an interview that Goldsman's cuts weren't deep or radical. Producer Brian Grazer was quoted as saying that the revised budget dropped from approximately $140 million to something in the vicinity of $100 million.

In July 2011, Universal decided the project was too costly and risky for them to go forward. This was a blow to the adaptation, but not a fatal one, as Universal's decision allowed Howard and his partners to seek alternate financing.

In March 2012, Warner Bros. confirmed that they were in ongoing discussions to revive the project. The studio bought Goldsman's script and hired him to polish it. In August 2012, they decided not to move forward with the adaptation; however, the very next day reports emerged that Media Rights Capital was in talks to take on the series. There has been no news of any developments since then.

AN INTERVIEW WITH RON HOWARD

The following interview was conducted by phone in March 2012.

Q: When did you first discover the Dark Tower series?

A: Akiva Goldsman began talking to me about the gunslinger as a character—he didn't call him Roland in those days—and the Dark Tower series when we were doing *A Beautiful Mind*. At that point, he said that he had always dreamed of these books becoming movies. I was working hard on *A Beautiful Mind*. I didn't have a chance to pick up the books, but when I eventually did, J.J. [Abrams] was already engaged in developing the project. I continued reading. I read the first three. I really enjoyed them and was kicking myself the entire time that I'd let it get away.

So then, J.J. got so busy and he moved on, and Akiva came back to me and said, "I think there's a possibility of meeting with Stephen King and talking about doing it again." I said, "Well, I can't be glib about this or fake it. I've got to go ahead and read the other four." I was in the middle of something, so it took some time. I revisited the first three, went ahead and read the other four, and I was enthralled and challenged, but also a little frustrated by what I could immediately see we were going to have to leave out. Particularly in the backstory of Eddie and Odetta, that period of her life.

I knew that one of the challenges was going to be making movies for the big screen that would be great broad-appeal action movies that would deal with the journey with the kind of momentum that movies on the big-screen cinema need. I was worried that we would lose the intensity, the coolness, the texture and the humanity of much of the backstory.

One day, I literally was on an elliptical trainer, and I was now reviewing the books by listening to them on audio. It just struck me that so much of that would be great TV. I love what has happened with TV in the last six, seven, eight years. The notion struck me that we could do the biggest ideas in the series on the big screen and we could bundle the more intimate ideas and do that for television. Not only was I excited about the world, the universe and what it had to offer for audiences and for me as a filmmaker, but I also felt that this was a really interesting opportunity to use both mediums to their fullest.

And then it went further. We also began to explore—we were *still* realizing how much we were going to have to leave out. I said, instead of creating games that just sort of piggyback on or sort of regurgitate whatever the movie or TV show was, why don't we devise games that actually deal with the narrative threads and some of the twists and turns that we know we're never going to be able to get to, even in three movies and a miniseries. That got to be an exciting idea. It really ultimately is this sort of attempt to try to take advantage of as much of what Stephen created as possible and for fans to know that we love and respect the entire universe. We're going to do everything we can to dramatize that using all the mediums at our disposal.

That's what we presented to Stephen eighteen months ago. Nearly two years. That was the eureka moment for Akiva Goldsman and I when, one day, at Akiva's house, we sat down with all the key narrative points in all the books and even the graphic novels. We put them all out in index cards on the floor and started moving things around and bundling certain ideas into what we thought could be used for television. Certain ideas which could be collected into movies. We began to believe that it was cohesive and compelling and an interesting approach—and sort of an unexpected approach, but very true to the spirit of the characters and the narrative. When Stephen agreed with that, it was thrilling. It was a great creative day when we landed on the approach and really gratifying that Stephen concurred a hundred percent. And whenever we talk to fans who know the books and we sit and explain our approach, they are across the board excited about it, and very, very supportive of it, even though it departs in certain ways from what you'd call a rigid adaptation. They're novels, and novels are not movies. They're great novels. And, again, Stephen has been fantastic in acknowledging that and being excited about empowering us with his belief that we could go out there and make strong adaptations. Movies, television and even games.

Q: **King said he thought the way the script integrated Mid-World with New York City was brilliant.**

A: We looked at all of the novels and we're working with it as one giant narrative. We're moving certain ideas from novel six and seven up into the first movie. Ultimately, over the course of what we hope is three or four movies and a miniseries—and possibly an ongoing series as well—and the games, to navigate our way around and delve into as many of these areas as we possibly can. He understands—and is thrilled by the fact—that we're not really necessarily dealing with it all chronologically.

Q: **Plus he keeps writing more. The eighth book will be coming out in April.**

A: He loves it. He just loves the world. And with good reason. It's fascinating. He feels so comfortable when he's working with those characters in that world, for some reason. And that's why he keeps going back there. There is something very human and relatable to the attitudes of those characters. And it's also kind of comprehensive. You can delve into almost every corner of the human psyche or every emotion of the human heart through what those characters are going through, past and present.

Q: Is there room in your concept to go all the way back to the Mejis days?

A: We haven't talked about that. We certainly hope to suggest that in some way. But, no, that we haven't done. We have hopes that, if we're good enough, down the road, there's great material there. We could go even further. We really didn't go beyond Roland and the *ka-tet*. The first *ka-tet* is part of what we would be dealing with, but we even hope that would all be an origin story television series. Our *Smallville*.

Q: Has anybody ever tried to tie TV and the big screen together like this before?

A: I don't believe anybody really has in a planned way. I think that some version of *Star Wars* has existed in all the mediums. I'm sure that *Star Trek*'s that way now, too. I'm not really a gamer, so I don't know what the *Star Trek* games are, but I'm sure they've got them. But to really say, look, here's an epic saga that exists. We don't have to invent, stretch, extrapolate to try to create material for these other mediums. All we're doing is trying to say: where would this best live? It's thrilling and it's also satisfying. And, by the way, we still won't get it all in. It's fascinating and sprawling, and Stephen is the first one to give us license to make creative choices, although, clearly, he has his pets. If we do get down to making it, there are some things that he really wants to see, but he doesn't have to argue—they're all the ideas that we really want to pack into the films.

Q: There's been a lot of chatter this past week about Warner Bros. Is that all hype, or is there something behind it?

A: There's been something going on for a while, but I'm afraid it was premature to declare it a done deal. There've been serious conversations. I think there are very real intentions, but still some steps to take before we have a start date. The media is so interested in the subject, along with the fans. Every time it gets mentioned, it seems like somebody wants to put a start date on it—or, hell, they want a release date. We got caught with that before a little bit. I think in all our minds we want to do it, but we want to do it the right way, with the right partners. I think we're moving in a really positive direction. All along I've just felt it would happen. My sense is that I think we're onto something that's too rich and interesting to not ultimately find its way to the audience. I believe that the support will ultimately be there for it.

The project means a lot to Akiva and myself, and a handful of people who put in close to a year focusing on it. I really hope we get to do it, and I have a very good feeling about it.

Q: **When you go to a new studio, do you start from the revised script or do you go back to an earlier version before the rewrites you did for Universal?**

A: It continues to evolve. He's just beginning to write, so it's hard for me to comment on it much right now. It's not just a matter of reverting. There are some new ideas that we're going to be exploring.

Q: **Is Javier Bardem still under consideration? A lot of people were concerned about the color of his eyes and his accent.**

A: That was pretty controversial, I know. Now, with scheduling and so forth, it will be starting over. Javier wanted to wear contacts. He's a great actor, and I actually thought the accent was fine because who knows quite what Roland sounds like? What is the accent?

Q: **I think King is angling to do the voice of Blaine the Mono.**

A: He has mentioned that, and I said I think you'd be a helluva Blaine. I don't think we'll have to audition him. I think we know he'd be a good Blaine.

AN INTERVIEW WITH AKIVA GOLDSMAN

The following interview was conducted by phone in late March 2012.

Q: **What's your history with the Dark Tower series?**

A: I was in Boston when *The Gunslinger* came out. There was a specialty bookstore where I got that first edition. Just fell in love, as everybody who's a fan of the series has. Then I read them as they came out. I'm an old King fan. I was lucky enough to meet him a couple of times in this process, and he remains the only person I'm speechless around. It's because he's really one of the great writers of our time. He's today's Charles Dickens. For those of us who read him when we were younger, he was a "genre writer" who finally proved that genre writing was actually literature. The Dark Tower, from a more scholarly standpoint, is unique in that it is trans-genre, which is extraordinary and remarkable. For me, it's just wildly inviting and always has been. Stephen seems to have an ability to replicate or access what I think of as the child's imagination in all of us. There's an intuitive correctness to the worlds that he paints. Dark Tower has evolved obviously into a nexus of all those worlds. Whether one is a fan of *The Stand* or *'Salem's Lot* or *Hearts in Atlantis* and comes to the Dark Tower that way or directly on through *The Gunslinger*, it allows you a really remarkable path to travel throughout King's universe or multiverse.

Q: When did you say, "This should be a movie"?

A: I—as anybody who reads King and writes for the screen—always hoped for some version of the Dark Tower on the screen. When J.J. and Damon bought it, I felt both thrilled and envious because I love those guys, and I think they're super-talented. Very early on, J.J., who's an old friend of mind, invited me, along with a bunch of really smart people—a lot of them smarter than me—to sit in a room with him and Damon and Jeff Pinkner and Drew Goddard. A bunch of folks. They were putting *Lost* together. It was a brainstorming session about mythology. Damon was very clear about his admiration for the Dark Tower, and we ended up talking a lot about it. It was definitely part of the fabric of the ideas that inspired the more super-ordinary parts of *Lost*. You can see the influences in it, and Damon has always been very open about that. At the end of that brainstorming session, which was the beginning and end of my involvement with that TV show, Damon sent me a framed print of the cover of *The Gunslinger* as a thank-you. I knew of his admiration for the work and I had my own. When he and J.J. decided that this was not something they were going to end up undertaking, I grabbed hold of the idea and called Ron [Howard]. I had been pitching Ron the Dark Tower in various forms since we were making *A Beautiful Mind* together. I think he confessed, too, to some envy when J.J. and Damon and Stephen had agreed to do it. So when it became free, Ron and I started conspiring to figure out how it could be ours.

I started rereading the books and realized that it is tricky. The access points are harder if you're not familiar with the mythology. At the same time, the tone of *The Gunslinger* is not necessarily the tone of the rest of the books. *Wolves of the Calla* is action-adventure

Western, *Wizard and Glass* is almost *Romeo and Juliet*, but *The Gunslinger* is surrealist. It's literary musing and is probably the least muscular when it comes to plot, which is typically required for access to movie. I was wrestling with the order of the material, and I thought, What if you come in around the third book. At which point, Ron looked at me and said, "Why don't we mix it up? Why don't we start with the third book, and then we can go backward, but let's do it on TV." And so began this construct of movie-TV-movie-TV, etc., which is our fantasy. Whether it comes to pass, who knows? It was born of trying to find an access point for the uninitiated while also being inclusive of all the material that the initiates want and love.

Q: Do you have the whole thing mapped out?

A: We have the whole thing mapped out in the grossest possible sense, and I have a script for the first movie, which I'm currently revising, and a script for the pilot of what would be an interstitial component, which is actually material that in literary continuity would predate the third book. It's really material from the first two books.

Q: Do you go all the way back to Mejis?

A: We go all the way back and we go all the way forward. Without tipping too much, our Roland begins this turn of the wheel with the Horn of Eld. It is the next iteration of the cyclical journey, which affords us the opportunity to maintain fidelity to what Stephen has done and also to what Stephen has spoken of in his own introductions to the more recent editions, which is a little bit of retcon work—some retroactive continuity in order to stitch backward that which came later. One thing we did try to do was play with the idea of what it would be like to be Jake and to be alive—just as Stephen was dealing with a contemporary New York when he was writing, we moved that into today. That makes for a lot of fun. As the books have gone on, we've discovered—through Callahan or other characters—very interesting things about New York, which we can now bring back into the beginning of the narrative.

Q: Are you including material from the Marvel comics?

A: The original plan was to go with the first movie, then do interstitial material, six or seven episodes that were flashbacks to the material of the first two books. Then two episodes that were flashbacks to Roland and the young gang, which would be precursors to *Wizard and Glass*. Then go do *Wolves of the Calla* as a stand-alone feature. Then do *Wizard and Glass* as a season. Then do—let's just call it *The Dark Tower*. Close out the series as a stand-alone feature. Then go back and continue on post–*Wizard and Glass* into the Marvel material.

Q: Do you still plan to use some of the unused material for video games?

A: What we were going to do is use video game material to link movies one and two because there would be a section of narrative where the character results were going to be the same but things could have happened differently. We really did have the whole thing mapped out. It was clever—maybe too clever by half. Even then we couldn't get all of it in. You look at that Father Callahan material from *Wolves of the Calla* and you want that to be a stand-alone movie. You want to go back and redo *Hearts in Atlantis* using the Dark Tower connectivity rather than excising it. If you resource television, movies and gaming, it seems like you could do a lot of the material.

Q: You also worked on a possible *Black House* adaptation, which has Dark Tower connections.

A: *Black House* becomes complicated because it is inexorably linked with *The Talisman*. Those two objects have been trying for a long time to find their own way independently. Ultimately, I hope somebody bundles the two. I think that's its best chance for success.

Part of what's happening now—and I do think *Lost* was a precursor to this and I think people are doing it much more commonly, and I say that with some pleasure—is that people are attending to serialized storytelling. The idea that you can use filmed entertainment to continue stories rather than sticking strictly to episodes. Sticking strictly to that old "they can't know anything when they come in and they have to not need to know anything when they go out," which was the model for such a long time. And still is. That was based on the idea of syndication. Things shouldn't really live in a world of "to be continued . . ." The conventional model for syndication doesn't exist anymore. Now anybody can watch anything at any point, mostly. The idea of serialized storytelling is getting a real shot in the arm. As such, something like Dark Tower, despite our ambitions to jump back and forth between features and TV, is a perfect candidate for a long serialized arc, as is *Talisman/Black House*. You could easily see that stretching on HBO beautifully for several seasons. *Game of Thrones* has shown us that really rich cinematic storytelling is available on television and is available in a way that asks the audience to bring to it a knowledge base. If that's true of *Game of Thrones,* it can certainly be true of Dark Tower or *The Talisman* or any of King's other longer works.

Q: Would you consider doing Dark Tower strictly as a cable series?

A: We really want to tell this story, so the answer is: certainly, but the ambitions of the series—visually in scope and scale—one would think of them as being better suited to the kind of funds available to features. Now, having said that, you sit there and watch *Game of Thrones* and you can't do anything but admire the production value. It feels like a movie. More and more, the scope that is required for Dark Tower is available on television, but our initial ambition is still our ambition, which is to bring it out in feature form and then cross over to television and cross back over to features. What's interesting about Dark Tower is that the material can be organized—and sort of does naturally organize itself—in a way that is scale-specific. There are things that feel movielike. Then there are things—if you think about Eddie and his brother, that stuff almost feels like it wants to be gritty television. It speaks to both platforms in a way that we found unique.

THE ARTWORK OF THE DARK TOWER

Not all fantasy series are illustrated and certainly not all of Stephen King's novels come with artwork inside and out. The fact that the Dark Tower novels are all illustrated can be traced back to Donald M. Grant. When *The Gunslinger* was published in 1982, it was intended only as a limited edition. Grant was well known and respected for his lavish books, all of which featured artwork from some of the best in the business.

The Gunslinger wasn't King's first limited edition. Phantasia Press published a limited edition of *Firestarter* in 1980 with wraparound cover art by Michael Whelan. Even before *The Gunslinger* was published, volume 5 of *Whispers* magazine (August 1982) featured artwork by John Stewart inspired by the book. The cover illustration was called *Old Nort the Weedeater* and five other Dark Tower illustrations appear in the magazine featuring a zombielike gunslinger, Brown at his cabin, the man in black, Sylvia Pittston and Zoltan plucking out the eyes of Roland's mule.

Michael Whelan, who illustrated *The Gunslinger*, wasn't available when it came time to publish *The Drawing of the Three*. This started a trend whereby each subsequent book featured the work of a different artist—all the way up to the final book, where Whelan was once again called into action, forming a kind of bookend to the series.

The first mass-market publications of the Dark Tower books were trade paperbacks, oversized volumes like the one you are now holding. Publishing at this size meant that the interior artwork from the Grant editions could be reproduced without shrinking it down to a point where detail would be lost. In a few cases over the years, some of the art from the Grant books has been omitted from the trade publication.

With the final three books in the series, the publication paradigm changed.

Scribner became a copublisher with Grant. However, the interior artwork continued to be shared between the publishers. In addition to the signed/limited edition, Grant published a new state of these books, the artist's edition, which was limited but unnumbered and signed by only the artist and had a slightly different dust jacket design. *The Wind Through the Keyhole* is the only Dark Tower book where the Scribner edition doesn't contain any of the artwork.

The styles of the various artists are radically different from book to book, ranging from Whelan's naturalistic depictions to Dave McKean's abstract works to Jae Lee's illustrations, which are reminiscent of the work he did in the Marvel graphic novel adaptations of the series.

Here is a summary of the interior art produced for the Grant editions of the eight Dark Tower novels:

THE GUNSLINGER

Artist: Michael Whelan

Michael Whelan was the first person to illustrate Stephen King for the small press. King thought of Whelan when considering who should illustrate *The Gunslinger* based on his work for *Firestarter*. Though Whelan generally does only cover art, he made an exception for the Dark Tower books. He found *The Gunslinger* bleak and depressing, but he got into the project once he started doing some sketches. In retrospect, he chides himself for not watching any of the Clint Eastwood spaghetti Westerns, but his depictions of Roland and the Tower are legendary.

For the first edition of *The Gunslinger*, Whelan produced several pen-and-ink spot illustrations, along with six acrylic or watercolor board paintings.

1. *Silence Came Back in, Filling Jagged Spaces . . .*—Roland after the battle of Tull
2. *They Paused . . . Looking up at the Dangling, Twisting Body.*—Roland and Cuthbert at Hax's hanging
3. *The Way Station*—Roland and Jake leaving the Way Station
4. *He Could See His Own Reflection . . .*—Roland looking in the spring near the Speaking Circle
5. *The Boy Shrieked Aloud . . .*—Roland and Jake fending off the slow mutants (also used for the cover)
6. *There the Gunslinger Sat, his face turned up into the fading light*—Roland on the beach with the Dark Tower on the horizon

He also drew black-and-white illustrations, which appeared at the beginning of each chapter:

1. The Gunslinger—Brown with Zoltan on his shoulder
2. The Way Station—Jake sitting in the shadow of the Way Station
3. The Oracle and the Mountain—Roland using the jawbone to fend off the demon in the Speaking Circle to save Jake
4. The Slow Mutants—young Roland with his hawk, David
5. The Gunslinger and the Dark Man—the man in black's skeleton after the palaver at the golgotha

The third Donald M. Grant printing of *The Gunslinger* features a new cover, based on the battle of Tull painting. Whelan produced another painting of Roland for the cover of the Plume trade paperback of *The Gunslinger* (based, presciently, on a profile shot of Stephen King). The final artwork used for that cover is an amalgam of the new painting coupled with the sky extracted from another of his works. He illustrated Grant's book that combines the revised and expanded version of *The Gunslinger* with "The Little Sisters of Eluria," and he profusely illustrated *The Dark Tower*, the final book in the series (see below). He also contributed the definitive depictions of the main characters for the character orbs in the Discordia interactive game at King's official Web site. Because King's description of Roland and the Dark Tower evolved over the two decades between the times Whelan worked on *The Gunslinger* and when he illustrated *The Dark Tower*, Whelan thought of himself as something of a weathervane, responding to these changes.

"THE LITTLE SISTERS OF ELURIA"
Artists: Michael Whelan and Erik Wilson

For the novella's appearance in *Legends*, edited by Robert Silverberg, two artists contributed illustrations. Michael Whelan created a painting of Roland standing before an open magic door with the Dark Tower in the background and a pencil drawing of Roland with crossed guns standing in a cemetery. Erik Wilson's drawing is a montage of scenes from the story that features the sisters, the mutants, the dog with the cross-shaped patch of fur, the doctor bugs, the Tower, and Roland in bandages.

For the Grant edition of *The Gunslinger* combined with "The Little Sisters of Eluria," Whelan produced another set of color paintings and black-and-white illustrations. The original artwork from *The Gunslinger* is also included in this edition.

1. *Quest* (frontis)—Roland crossing a desert. His very long shadow extends in front of him.
2. *The Gunslinger Stood in His Dusty Boots*—Roland, wearing a hat, with his guns crossed at his shoulders and a decrepit signpost in the background
3. *Time Belongs to the Tower*—A hatless Roland with the moon in the background and vultures circling
4. *Sister Mary Came from the Shadows*—A ghastly figure in a robe enters a tent, bearing a candle, skeletons at her feet
5. *The Gunslinger Moved on West*—A two-page spread featuring Roland and his horse standing before a Western scene. Behind him, mesas and Eluria on the horizon.
6. *The Man in Black Fled across the Desert*—A two-page spread. Walter, in his black robe, grinning fiendishly as he crosses the desert. He's carrying tarot cards, one of which features the Tower.
7. *The Gunslinger Followed*—Roland stands in the swirling desert with the demonic Walter in the background. There's a rotting signpost near him
8. *Roland and the Dark Tower*—Roland stands astride an Unfound Door with the Dark Tower in the background (from *Legends*).

THE DRAWING OF THE THREE
Artist: Phil Hale

Phil Hale is part of a group of artists who have illustrated multiple Stephen King books. He contributed one plate to the 1984 Donald M. Grant limited edition of *The Talisman* and illustrated *Insomnia*.

He was not happy with his artwork for the first edition of *The Drawing of the Three* so, given the opportunity twelve years later, he replaced all of it. The illustrations bear the same names as the originals, but the style and composition is markedly different. The new illustrations are less cartoonish, more subdued in color and more photorealistic.

His 1989 illustration of Roland standing in front of a door with his hand bandaged and his clothing ripped, done for the NAL audio version of *The Drawing of the Three*, represents an intermediate stage in his evolution. The painting is colorful but less gaudy than the work for the original Grant edition, but not as realistic or dark as those in the second edition.

In addition to small, symbolic black-and-white illustrations for the beginning of each chapter, Hale produced ten oil-on-linen color prints. They are:

1. *Did-a-Chick*—Roland stomps on one of the lobstrosities
2. *Roland*—The wounded gunslinger
3. *On the Beach*—Jack Andolini gets a surprise
4. *Souvenir*—Eddie, naked, in Balazar's hideout, and Henry Dean's head
5. *Waiting for Roland*—Eddie with a knife to Roland's throat while Roland is with Odetta
6. *Detta*—Detta Walker strapped into her wheelchair
7. *Waiting for the Pusher*—Eddie trying to stay awake next to Roland's body and the doorway
8. *Nothing but the Hilt*—During Roland's robbery at Katz's Drug Store
9. *Jack Mort*—the Pusher, after the lighter stops a police officer's bullet
10. *The Gunslinger*—cover art. Roland with a fiendish rictus on his face.

THE WASTE LANDS

Artist: Ned Dameron

Ned Dameron was an artist exhibitor at Necon, the Northeast Writer's Conference, which was cofounded by Donald M. Grant, where Stephen King saw some of his work—much of it from Grant editions of Robert E. Howard books—in the art room. Grant suggested Dameron as the illustrator for *The Waste Lands* and, after seeing some of his non-Howard work, King agreed.

Dameron produced twelve full-color paintings (oil on acetate) for *The Waste Lands*, spot illustrations for the book's sections, and a gouache and watercolor on scratchboard drawing of Jake and Oy for the endpapers. Several of his illustrations are two-page spreads. They are:

1. *Mir Embraced the Tree*
2. *Hold Me Still, Roland*—Susannah on Roland's shoulders, firing at Shardik

3. *The Dark Tower*
4. *The Rose*—Jake in the vacant lot
5. *Charlie the Choo-Choo*—reproducing a page from the book
6. *The Plaster Man Roared*—featuring the doorkeeper
7. *Roland Knelt before Her*—Aunt Talitha from River Crossing
8. *Better Duck, Dearie*—Gasher with Jake in Lud
9. *He Fired*—Roland, wearing Aunt Talitha's cross
10. *Blaine the Mono*—after they left Lud
11. *Leather Wings*—pterodactyl-like creatures outside Lud
12. *The Waste Lands*.

Dameron also contributed artwork to the Donald M. Grant limited edition of *The Talisman*. He sells his artwork—oil paintings and sculptures—in galleries in Louisiana under his given name, Edward Palfrey Dameron, using Ned Dameron for his commercial illustrations.

WIZARD AND GLASS
Artist: Dave McKean

Dave McKean became well known as the cover artist for the Sandman graphic novels. He uses Photoshop to combine a variety of images to create pieces that resemble dioramas. One gets the impression that these abstract photomontages have a third dimension, as with found objects affixed to a canvas.

McKean produced fourteen color plates. He also did full-page black-and-white sketches for the prologue, afterword and each of the four major sections. The color plates are:

1. *Rose*
2. *God Help Us*—the *ka-tet* in Topeka with the last page of the *Topeka Capital-Journal* showing the crucifixion*
3. *All Hail the Crimson King*—Eddie's dream of the bulldozer in the vacant lot
4. *Two Drops of Poison*—Rhea extracting poison from Ermot*
5. *Her Arms and Belly and Breasts Breaking Out in Gooseflesh*—Susan Delgado being tested for purity
6. *And at the Bar, a Whole Line of Assorted Toughs*—inside the Travellers' Rest, featuring "The Romp"*
7. *Cuthbert, Meanwhile, Had Reloaded*—the showdown in the Travellers' Rest with the Big Coffin Hunters

8. *But He and His Love Were No Longer Children*—Roland and Susan and their clandestine meetings in Hambry

9. *Pinch and Jilly*—a puppet show for the Reap Fair*

10. *Smiling Lips Revealed Cunning Little Teeth*—Randall Flagg

11. *There They Died Together-o*—the story of Robert and Francesca, the Hambry version of *Romeo and Juliet*

12. *Of the Three of Them, Only Roland Saw Her*—Roland, Alain and Cuthbert on horseback, with Susan, the girl in the window, waving

13. *The Firelight Made Baleful Streaks on her Face*—Cordelia Delgado*

14. *It cut the old man's throat efficiently enough*—Roy Depape murdering Mayor Hart Thorin

15. *The Dark Tower Rearing to the Sky*—part of Roland's vision in the pink Wizard's Glass

16. *A Flash as the Big Bang Exploded*—Roland, Alain and Cuthbert attacking the tankers at Hanging Rock

17. *The Wicked Witch of the East*—part of the *ka-tet*'s vision in the pink Wizard's Glass

18. *And Then That Strange Albino Leaf Caught His Eye*—Eddie finds Randall Flagg's message after they leave the Green Palace*

* omitted from Plume paperback

THE WIND THROUGH THE KEYHOLE

Artist: Jae Lee with coloring by June Chung

Jae Lee produced a series of black-and-white and color illustrations. See the interview concerning his work on *The Wind Through the Keyhole* and on *The Gunslinger Born* elsewhere in this book.

Color:

1. *They Regard Each Other*—Tim Ross and the tyger, used as both the cover and the frontispiece

2. *I Turned to Run . . . It Caught Me*—Sister Fortuna from Serenity and the skin-man

3. *He Kneed His Mount in a Circle*—The Covenant Man with Tim Ross on his horse

4. *She Was Looking at Him from Beady, Red-Veined Eyes*—Tim Ross and the dragon

5. *Ancient Tumblers Turned*—Tim Ross frees the tyger from its cage

6. *It Lunged, Fangs Flashing*—The skin-man as a pooky

B&W:

1. *Jake Snatched Him Up*—Jake with Oy as the starkblast approached
2. *Scales Instead of Skin*—the skin-man as described by Sister Fortuna
3. *Those Were Good Years*—Tim Ross on his father's shoulders
4. *Perhaps it Would Work*—young Roland looking at a bullet
5. *Storm's over, Sugar*—a bin-rustie on a limb with icicles

In addition, there are black-and-white drawings on the section pages.

1. Starkblast—a billy-bumbler
2. The Skin-Man—the shape-shifter in one of its many guises
3. The Wind Through the Keyhole—Armaneeta, the *sighe*
4. The Skin-Man—the miners from Little Debaria
5. Storm's Over—Roland

Bin-rusties appear throughout, and what appears to be a cave drawing forms the book's endpapers.

WOLVES OF THE CALLA
Artist: Bernie Wrightson

Like Michael Whelan, Bernie Wrightson is another artist with a long and varied history of illustrating Stephen King projects. He produced the movie poster and the comic book associated with the anthology movie *Creepshow* and illustrated the limited editions of *Cycle of the Werewolf, The Stand* and *From a Buick 8.*

Wrightson was on the set of *The Green Mile* with his friend, director Frank Darabont, to celebrate King's birthday in 1998. Someone made a cake that reproduced the cover of the final installment of the serialized novel, and King played around with the cast, agreeing to take his place in the electric chair. During that party, King asked Wrightson if he would illustrate the fifth book in the Dark Tower series. He agreed and reread the previous four books before tackling the new manuscript. Wrightson contributed twelve acrylic-on-board paintings, plus black-and-white spot illustrations and endpaper artwork featuring Susannah as Mia. They are:

1. *Time to Be Men*—Father Callahan speaks up in Calla Bryn Sturgis
2. *She Lifted It to Her Mouth*—Susannah on her nightly foraging expedition

3. *Gunslingers, to Me!*—The battle at Jericho Hill

4. *Do You See Him?*—Eddie and Susannah confront one of the vagrant dead

5. *Come-Come-Commala*—Roland dances for the people of Calla Bryn Sturgis

6. *Its Blade Gleams Brightly*—Father Callahan prepares to kill a vampire attacking Lupe Delgado

7. *She Throws It Hard*—Molly Doolin kills one of the Wolves

8. *The Searchlight Goes on Again*—Calvin Tower saves Father Callahan from the Hitler Brothers

9. *Riza*—Susannah Dean demonstrates her skills with the Oriza

10. *The Reclining Skeleton Grinned at Him*—Jake and Oy in the Dogan

11. *You Stainless-steel Bastard*—Eddie shoots Andy

12. *For Gilead and the Calla*—Roland takes the first shot in the battle with the Wolves

SONG OF SUSANNAH

Artist: Darrell Anderson

Like Dave McKean, Anderson's artwork stands apart from the rest because of its abstract composition. He deliberately made the color paintings suggestive and abstract so that there would be room for interpretation by the viewer, though they are, in general, more accessible than McKean's. He contributed ten color paintings, along with endpaper artwork and spot illustrations for the beginnings of each of the thirteen "stanzas" and the coda.

The color prints are:

1. *Bursts of Green Lightning*—the Beamquake

2. *He Sees the Doors, at Least a Thousand of Them*—Jake's vision of a multitude of doors as he works with the Manni to open the Unfound Door

3. *Huge Rock Formations Sawed at the Sky*—Discordia as seen from the Castle on the Abyss

4. *"Down!" Roland Bellowed*—the gunfight in Bridgton, Maine

5. *. . . Signed His Name in a Quick Scrawl*—Calvin Tower signs over the vacant lot to Tet Corporation

6. *Susannah Closes Her Eyes*—Susannah enters her mental Dogan (also the cover art)

7. *Into a Forest of Watching Faces*—Roland and Eddie approach Stephen King's house

8. ... Ka *Comes to Me*—Stephen King
9. *Two Hammarskjöld Plaza*—the Black Tower in Manhattan, with the rose overlaid
10. *Emerging from the Shirt's Collar Was the Head of a Bird*—A taheen in the Dixie Pig

THE DARK TOWER

Artist: Michael Whelan

In an interview printed in *Knowing Darkness: Artists Inspired by Stephen King*, Whelan admits that he was "stoked" when he was asked to illustrate the final book in the series. In addition to the wraparound painting for the dust jacket that shows Roland standing at the base of the Tower among roses, with a Beam in the background—which is also included as an interior two-page illustration—Whelan contributed eleven paintings to the final book in the series. He also designed the endpapers and full-page black-and-white illustrations for the book's major sections and contributed nearly three dozen black-and-white drawings, one for the end of each of the novel's chapters.

The color illustrations are:

1. *The White Commands You*—Father Callahan in the Dixie Pig
2. *Come on Then, You Bastards*—Jake (armed with Orizas) and Oy at the New York–Fedic door
3. *Will You?*—Randall Flagg
4. *He Reached for It Again*—Walter and Mordred
5. *Below Them in the Seeping Light Was the Village*—Roland, Jake and Oy above Blue Heaven
6. *He Moved in Between Jake and Eddie*—Susannah, Jake, Eddie, Oy and Roland after the battle in Blue Heaven, with dead humes and taheen scattered around them
7. *The Place Where Roland Finally Stopped Felt More Like a Church Than a Clearing*—Roland carries Jake into the woods
8. *He Sat on His Throne, Which Is Made of Skulls*—the Crimson King
9. *Woe to Whoever Happened to Be in His Path*—Mordred Deschain in Empathica
10. *It Would Never Open Again*—Roland in front of the doorway marked THE ARTIST
11. *His Face Went Slack with a Peculiar Sort of Ecstasy*—Patrick Danville
12. *The Dark Tower*—a two-page spread reproducing the cover art

OTHER ARTISTS

Other artists have tackled the subject of the Dark Tower over the years. These include Alan M. Clark, who chose Roland at the Tower for his subject matter for the cover of *The Stephen King Universe* by Stanley Wiater, Christopher Golden and Hank Wagner. Movie poster artist Drew Struzan created a painting of Roland and the Tower to be used in the movie *The Mist*.

Though much of this artwork can be found online in various forms, the ideal place to see it is in a book called *Knowing Darkness: Artists Inspired by Stephen King* from Centipede Press. Though the book is rare and quite expensive, it is enormous, which means the artwork is displayed in a format even bigger than the "originals" in the Grant books.

Illustrating the Dark Tower series went in a completely different direction in 2007 with the launch of Marvel's graphic novel adaptation of the early parts of Roland Deschain's life and quest.

MARVEL GRAPHIC NOVELS:
THE GUNSLINGER BORN

INTRODUCTION

In 2006, two years after the final book in the Dark Tower series was published, Marvel announced plans to release a series of Dark Tower graphic novels. From Marvel's perspective, it was a chance to open up the world of comics to a whole new audience, and from King's perspective it was an opportunity to introduce the Dark Tower series to a new generation of readers, people who might migrate from the graphic novels to the books themselves.

King said that one reason he agreed to the plan was that he felt there probably would never be a Dark Tower movie and that this adaptation would be the next best thing.

Before the deal was announced, King visited the Marvel offices to discuss what kind of Dark Tower stories he could tell in this format. According to Joe Quesada, Marvel's editor in chief, within ten minutes King reeled off a number of complete stories about Roland's adventures, enough to fill several paperbacks.

While some fans of the series hoped that these monthly installments would pick up with the story where it ends at the conclusion of *The Dark Tower*, King wanted the story to begin with Roland's coming of age, moving on to the Mejis story that is told in *Wizard and Glass*. He wanted to explore events that were important in Roland's development as the last gunslinger.

From that point, it expands on things that are not mentioned or only briefly alluded to in the novels. The journey back to Gilead is greatly expanded. For the first time, readers learn how Farson's forces regroup after their defeat in Hamby and rise against Gilead, eventually sacking it. The climax of the series was to be the battle of Jericho Hill, where the gunslingers made their last stand. King went into a lot of detail about what happened during that final battle.

His research assistant, Robin Furth, was listening in on the phone and transcribing these stories. It would be her job to write the scripts for the graphic novels. As the author of *Stephen King's The Dark Tower: A Concordance*, she had access to the fruits of her vast research into the mythos and was able to bring in and develop characters who were only briefly mentioned in the novels.

The adaptation was conceived as thirty issues broken up into five self-contained arcs or miniseries. These were titled The Gunslinger Born, The Long Road Home, Treachery, Fall of Gilead and Battle of Jericho Hill, each with between five and seven issues. The Gunslinger Born was released in February 2007, with new issues appearing at one-month intervals. Originally, Marvel planned a five-to-six-week break between each miniseries to allow the artists to get a head start on the next installment. However, they discovered they were losing readers during those breaks, so they were shortened.

Though a passing familiarity with the Dark Tower books will no doubt enhance a reader's enjoyment of these graphic novels, the creators intended for them to stand by themselves and to be accessible to people who have never read the books or, for that matter, comics.

A press release from Diamond stated, "King is directly involved in the creative aspects of this project, supervising all editorial and visual content. Robin Furth . . . is outlining the Dark Tower comic book series, providing scene-by-scene plotting and maintaining the continuity and consistency of each story arc." In other words, as executive editor and creative director of the series, King didn't write the scripts from which the graphic novels are created, but the stories have his stamp of approval.

Should the incidents within them be treated as part of the Dark Tower canon? There is some debate among Dark Tower fans on this matter. Many consider this, like Discordia, to be part of an expanded universe and thus not canon. Since this visual medium is different from prose, the creators have taken some liberty with the known "facts" and there are times when the graphic novels contradict King's books. King said that he wanted to give a lot of creative control to other imaginations that he had come to respect. See also his comments about the graphic novels in his interview in this book.

In addition to the story arcs, Marvel ordered a number of single-issue references (*Gunslinger's Guidebook*, *Guide to Gilead* and *End-World Almanac*), along with some single- or two-issue stories: *The Sorcerer* and *Sheemie's Tale*, for example.

Robin Furth also writes essays in each issue that elaborate on the Dark Tower mythology, covering such diverse topics as the geography of

Mid-World, the Guardians of the Beam and the magic number nineteen. She often seeks King's input and approval when writing these essays, but they are her own creations and not King's.

Marvel promoted the series heavily, producing a trailer, screensavers, a free promotional volume that was given out at comic book stores a few months before the launch date and midnight launches for the different series with artists and writers on hand. Collectible issues with variant covers by noted comic book artists were released. The issues were among the most popular titles from Marvel throughout their five-year run.

THE GUNSLINGER BORN

Original release dates: February 2007 through August 2007 (7 issues)
Credits:

- **Creative Director and Executive Director:** Stephen King
- **Plotting and Consultation:** Robin Furth
- **Script:** Peter David
- **Art:** Jae Lee and Richard Isanove
- **Lettering:** Chris Eliopoulos

As with *The Gunslinger*, issue one of The Gunslinger Born introduces the man in black before Roland and delivers the iconic opening sentence of the first novel among some rather chaotic visuals. Then Roland is introduced in all his glory in a two-page spread that also drops in the concepts of *ka* and the Dark Tower.

Turning the page, readers see a new image of Roland in a similar stance. His face, which aligns neatly with the one on the previous page, is younger. Fourteen-year-old Roland has his hawk on his outstretched arm and his fellow gunslingers-in-training are with him. In rapid succession, readers are introduced to Roland Deschain, Cuthbert Allgood, Alain Johns, Thomas Whitman (mentioned only in passing in *The Gunslinger*) and their fighting instructor, Cort.

The story picks up with Marten Broadcloak exposing Roland to his mother's infidelity, which goads him into his test of manhood, presumably before he's ready. The story of Roland using his hawk, David, against Cort follows the tale Roland told Jake Chambers in *The Gunslinger*, except for a scene that shows Marten's reaction to Roland's victory.

While Roland's father is chastising him for acting rashly and allowing Marten to manipulate him so easily, Marten shifts into the guise of Walter o'Dim and communes with his master, the Crimson King, at his infernal castle via Black Thirteen, which isn't introduced in King's novels until *Wolves of the Calla.*

This scene introduces the pink orb from the Wizard's Rainbow that will play an important part in Roland's adventure in Mejis, The appearance of the Crimson King here is also unique, in that the Lord of the Spiders is offstage for most of the Dark Tower series, appearing in person only at the end of *The Dark Tower.* They discuss John Farson's planned ambush at the Shavéd Mountains, which Roland learns about only near the end of his stay in Mejis.

The Crimson King knows of a prophecy that says Roland will one day be the end of him and his minions. Steven sends men to arrest Marten, but the wizard turns them into dogs and vanishes through a magic door that he draws on the wall with chalk.

The elder gunslingers send Roland, Cuthbert and Alain to Mejis to count horses, but also to see if the oil fields there can supply Farson with fuel for the machines of the Great Old Ones. This is another way the graphic novels diverge subtly from King's text. Roland learns of the Citgo field and Farson's plan only after he arrives in Hambry.

The Big Coffin Hunters—all of them deputies instead of just Eldred Jonas—are introduced in a scene of wanton violence, and Sheemie Ruiz is left to clean up their mess, though he isn't named. The young *ka-tet*'s stopover in Ritzy, which Roy Depape will discover after he backtracks their trail, is shown chronologically. This is where Roland learns that Pat Delgado is dead, which is never explained in the novel.

The Big Coffin Hunters deliver the grapefruit to Rhea as Susan Delgado arrives for her inspection and she meets Roland (Will Dearborn) in the aftermath. This part of the story is a direct—if abbreviated—translation of the scenes from *Wizard and Glass.*

A dramatic difference from the novels, though, is the physical appearance of John Farson, who is never seen directly in King's text. He is depicted as a grotesque figure, reminiscent of Vlad the Impaler. Walter arrives through his magic door and consults with Farson, which confirms that the two are distinct beings and that Walter appears to be in Farson's service.

The welcome dinner at Mayor Thorin's is much as it is in *Wizard and Glass,* but the showdown between the Affiliation Brats and the Big Coffin Hunters has a different onset. In the novel, Sheemie simply trips and spills camel piss on Roy Depape. Here, Clay Reynolds kicks a loudmouth drunk, who stumbles into Sheemie, causing the camel piss to spill on Depape. Roland and Susan's relationship proceeds apace, and he enlists her help to reconnoiter the oil field and the thinny. A new scene shows Walter meeting with Farson's lieutenant, George Latigo, who is using expendable slow mutants to prepare the oil-refining equipment.

Roland and Susan consummate their relationship without as much dithering as in the novel, and the comics have less time to spend on Cuthbert's anger over Roland's distraction, too, though it does culminate in Cuthbert punching Roland after he intercepts Rhea's note sent via Sheemie. The rest of The Gunslinger Born plays out as in *Wizard and Glass*, though in abbreviated form. The seventh and final issue ends with Susan Delgado's death and Roland's fascination with the pink Wizard's Glass.

> **Characters (in order of mention):** The man in black (Walter o'Dim, Marten Broadcloak), John Farson, Roland Deschain (Will Dearborn), Cuthbert Allgood (Arthur Heath), Alain Johns (Richard Stockworth), Thomas Whitman, Jamie DeCurry, Cort, Gabrielle Deschain, Steven Deschain, the Crimson King, Robert Allgood, Clay Reynolds, Eldred Jonas, Roy Depape, Rhea Dubativo (Rhea of the Cöos), Susan Delgado, Mayor Thorin, Fran Lengyll, Sheriff Avery, Mr. Renfrew, Olive Thorin, Coral Thorin, Sheemie Ruiz, George Latigo, Maria Tomas, Deputy Dave Hollis, Cordelia Delgado.

> **Places:** The Mohaine Desert, Gilead (New Canaan, In-World), Le Casse Roi Russe (End-World), Hambry, the Citgo oil patch, Eyebolt Canyon, Indrie (Cressia).

> **Things:** Black 13, the Pink One (the grapefruit), thinny, slow mutants.

EXTRA FEATURES:

ISSUE 1:
MAP OF THE BARONY OF NEW CANAAN

In this map, the walled city of Gilead is shown at the center of New Canaan, with the Baby Forest to the west, the larger Blosswood Forest to the east, and orchards and fields outside the northern and southern walls. There are Baronies in all directions, and the easterly direction leads to Mejis and the Outer Arc. Other towns in the Barony include Kingstown to the northeast, beyond the Blosswood Forest, Hemphill to the north, Taunton and Debaria to the southwest (in *The Wind Through the Keyhole*, it is more westerly and distant) and Pennilton to the southeast. The Shavéd Mountains lie to the west; the Barony Forest forms an arc from the southeast to the east. Beyond this forest, farther south, is the desert. Lake Saroni occupies most of the northeastern sector.

THE SACRED GEOGRAPHY OF MID-WORLD

In this vignette, Abel Vannay, the gunslingers' philosophy tutor, takes Roland, Alain and Cuthbert on a field trip, during which he explains to them the fundamental geography of Mid-World: the Dark Tower at the center of six intersecting Beams, one of which passes through Gilead's Great Hall. With Vannay's prompting, the boys name the twelve Guardians and explain the nature of the Tower as a manifestation of Gan. The portals are not only the source of the Beams that support the Tower, but they are also doorways to other worlds. Vannay tells them about how the Manni perfected another method of traveling between worlds using a form of magic. Ultimately, Vannay explains why people were forbidden from entering the Tower.

ISSUE 2:
MAP OF THE BARONY OF MEJIS

This map shows Hambry, the seat of the Barony of Mejis, located at the edge of the Clean Sea. Mejis is east of New Canaan; farther to the east is the Barony of Tepachi. The Vi Castis Mountains form a boundary to the west, and Eyebolt Canyon, site of a thinny, lies to the north, beyond which is the desert. The towns of Oakley and Tavares are to the northeast. There is a Dogan to the west, near Xay River. The Clean Sea surrounds the Barony on the southern side.

MAERLYN'S RAINBOW

This essay tells of Maerlyn's rise from the Prim, his desire to wreak havoc on Mid-World for his own amusement, and how he created thirteen magical orbs to present to Arthur Eld upon his coronation. Each orb contained a different kind of magic, and one of them entranced Arthur during the debauchery that followed his coronation. He was seduced by one of the Great Ones who attended the festivities in the guise of a Crimson Queen, and this union gave rise to a creature that was half man, half spider, who would become the Crimson King. Though Arthur Eld tried to have the orbs destroyed, they were beyond his power to unmake, so they were buried. However, their magic summoned thieves, and the components of Maerlyn's Rainbow found their way back into the world again.

AN OPEN LETTER FROM STEPHEN KING

King talks about how the Dark Tower project ended up with Marvel. He mentions other ideas for graphic novel adaptations featuring zombies and witches, including one that is the basis for his 2011 novel *11/22/63*.

ISSUE 3:

THE GUNS OF DESCHAIN

This essay covers Arthur Eld's rise to power and how he used his two pistols to defeat his enemies, along with his sword, Excalibur. Jealous of his advantage, he refused to allow others to inspect or replicate his weapons. However, during his battle with the monster serpent Saita, the guns were damaged and many of his knights were lost because they had inferior weapons. In the aftermath, Arthur Eld allowed his court wizard to forge new guns from the blade of Excalibur and to use Mid-World steel to create new guns for his knights.

STEPHEN KING PANEL, PART 1

A transcript of the New York Comic Con panel held on February 24, 2007, featuring Joe Quesada, Jae Lee, Robin Furth, Peter David, Ralph Macchio, Richard Isanove, Chris Eliopoulos, and Stephen King. Panelists respond to answers from the audience about the Dark Tower series.

ISSUE 4:

THE LAUGHING MIRROR, PART I

The story of how Maerlyn captured drops of Gan's creative water and turned them into a mirror, the backing of which came from gobs of Maerlyn's spit in layers of accusation, vanity and self-deception. He used the mirror to claim his place as king over the other demons from the Outer Dark. Though its original intent, which was to fool Gan through its distortion, failed and the mirror was destroyed, its shards penetrated the Tower, spreading corruption throughout the multiverse.

MAKING A PAGE

A four-page illustrated feature explaining how a page of the graphic novel is created, starting from Robin Furth's outline. Jae Lee breaks the plot down into pages and panels and pencils the pages, which he scans and sends to the editorial team, who forward it to Peter David. Peter reviews the pages, Robin's outline and any notes from Jae Lee before writing the script. He indicates the location of word balloons on the pencil art printouts. At the same time, Richard Isanove formats the scanned pencil art to the right size. Chris Eliopoulos uses the script and the placement notes to do the lettering. The pages go to the editors and back to Jae Lee, who sometimes revises his illustrations to strengthen the storytelling. Finally, Richard Isanove paints the page and the final PDFs are assembled with ads and special features, inside and outside covers and sent to the printer.

STEPHEN KING PANEL, PART 2
More of the transcript of the New York Comic Con panel held on February 24, 2007.

ISSUE 5:
THE LAUGHING MIRROR, PART II:
THE SEDUCTION OF RHEA
The story tells about a clever and spiteful little girl named Rhea, from the southern edge of the Barony of Delain, who terrorized her community and grew into an arrogant and selfish young woman. One day, while pretending to hand out punishments in her self-appointed role as princess of the world, she was struck in the eye by a sliver from the shattered mirror fashioned by Maerlyn, an object concocted from concentrated evil and cruelty. In Rhea, it increased her awareness of magic, but because of her nature, it was corrupt. The spells she provided as a service always had unexpected and unpleasant repercussions. She was forced to wander from village to village to ply her trade as her reputation soured. Her physical being was also corrupted by her evil magic. In return for longer life, she pledged her service to the Outer Dark. The demon who granted her request sent her to Hambry, where she was to await the arrival of a descendant of Arthur Eld. It was her task to prevent that young man from fathering any children.

STEPHEN KING PANEL, PART 3
Last installment of the transcript of the New York Comic Con panel held on February 24, 2007.

THE LAUGHING MIRROR, PART III:
THE CORRUPTION OF JONAS

The story of Eldred Jonas, a yeoman's son and failed gunslinger from Gilead. He was not a descendant of the knights of Eld, but Fardo Andrus saw potential in him and adopted him as a son, alongside Cort. While wrestling with Cort, he stepped on a sliver of Maerlyn's evil mirror. When Eldred recovered from the infection, he was a changed boy—impatient, brash, cruel and willing to lie or cheat to win. Given one last chance to rehabilitate his behavior, Eldred instead challenged Fardo to the all-or-nothing battle to become a gunslinger. Eldred's laziness and inexperience revealed itself during the battle. Fardo dealt him a blow to the leg that left him with a permanent limp. Eldred was exiled from that moment forward, but he vowed vengeance against the gunslingers and promised to align himself with the enemies of Gilead.

ISSUE 6:
CHARYOU TREE, PART I:
THE HISTORY OF THE CHARYOU TREE

Even though Arthur Eld had unified All-World, many people suffered from the mutations, famine and lack of fertility that followed the Great Poisoning. One group who lived in Brockest, in the toxic borderlands near the shores of the Prim, gave up worshipping Gan and gathered to discuss their need for a new religion. Maerlyn saw this as an opportunity to foment the seeds of discontent among these forgotten and forsaken people. He demanded a blood sacrifice in return for relief from their misery. At first the people refused, continuing their animal sacrifices to the traditional deities, to no avail. After four years, they accepted Maerlyn's offer. They planted a dying ghostwood tree in the middle of the village and turned it into a funeral pyre: the first charyou tree. They selected a boy as their sacrifice and discovered in the spring that their tribute had worked. The tradition spread throughout the kingdom and continued for many years.

A GUNSLINGER'S GUNS

This pictorial essay describes the three basic types of guns in Gilead's armory: the old and slightly awkward practice weapons used by apprentices that remain locked in the armory between training sessions, the somewhat better ironwood-handled nickel-plated guns used by yearling novices and the heavy sandalwood-handled six-shooters used by full-fledged gunslingers, heirlooms passed down from father to son for generations, which take bullets similar to those of a Winchester .45.

ISSUE 7:
CHARYOU TREE, PART II: COME REAP

The story of how Arthur Eld attempted to stop the annual human sacrifices across Mid-World but was unable to do so. His solution was to institute a lottery system where one random person would be selected for sacrifice in a public celebration in Gilead. However, agents of the Prim capitalized on Queen Rowena's jealousy over the fact that Emmanuelle Deschain had given birth to Arthur's only male heir, manipulating her into surrendering her soul in exchange for having Emmanuelle selected as the sacrifice and the promise of becoming pregnant by Arthur. Instead, her pregnancy was like that of Susannah Dean's (or Mia's), and the child that she ultimately gives birth to is a creature similar to Mordred Deschain. The palace guards kill the monster after it sucks the life from Queen Rowena. Enraged, Arthur thrusts the carcass into the crowd waiting below and uses this abomination to put an end to the Reaptide tradition of the charyou tree.

THE LONG ROAD HOME

Original release dates: February 2008 through June 2008 (5 issues)
Credits:
- **Creative Director and Executive Director:** Stephen King
- **Plotting and Consultation:** Robin Furth
- **Script:** Peter David
- **Art:** Jae Lee and Richard Isanove
- **Lettering:** Chris Eliopoulos

The Long Road Home begins exactly where The Gunslinger Born left off, after Susan Delgado's death. Though the story of the boys' return to Gilead and Roland's obsession with the pink orb from the Wizard's Rainbow was told briefly in *Wizard and Glass*, this series greatly expands on the tale and introduces elements absent from King's novels.

Roland insists on burying Susan. He blames the grapefruit for her death and shoots it. The glass does not shatter—it turns into something alive that rebuilds itself. It then wraps itself around Roland's face and sucks his essence inside.

The gunshot attracts the attention of the Hambry posse, led by Clay Reynolds, the only surviving Big Coffin Hunter. Cuthbert and Alain slow him down by shooting his horse. They drag Roland's limp body with them until they reach a dilapidated bridge with missing slats. In *The Dark Tower*, Roland told his *ka-tet* about cutting a bridge that would have inconvenienced Sheemie Ruiz, who was following them, though they didn't know it. In this story, Alain and Cuthbert cut the bridge to prevent the posse from catching up with them—after one of their horses breaks a leg during the crossing and must be put down.

Sheemie Ruiz is distraught over his failure to save Susan. When he gets lost, he ends up at one of North Central Positronics' Dogans, where his presence activates a long-dormant robot. The robot experiments on Sheemie, giving him new powers that will come into play shortly and again much later in Roland's adventures.

Roland's trapped mind travels to Thunderclap, where he encounters Marten. He sees a vision of Oy and one of himself alone as an older man. Marten tells him he killed his friends one by one. When Alain attempts to use his touch to rescue Roland, the orb sends him todash and Cuthbert is left behind to handle the mutant wolves that kill their remaining horses. Marten has no use for Alain, so he sends him back. More mutant wolves attack. Roland emerges from his trance long enough to kill one of the wolves with his bare hands.

Alain is injured and perhaps poisoned by another of the beasts. Cuthbert fires into the woods, thinking more wolves are coming, but shoots Sheemie instead. Sheemie accepts the wounds as punishment for failing Susan. However, the wounds aren't fatal and Sheemie's new powers give him the ability to heal himself and Alain.

Marten carries Roland to the Castle of the Crimson King. He presents himself in a nearly human form, but he has the avatar of the third eye of his minions in his forehead. Roland is totally irreverent in the face of this evil figure. The Crimson King calls Roland his cousin, explaining that Arthur Eld had affairs after Queen Rowena went barren. One of Arthur's jillies was one of the Great Old Ones of the Prim. While Steven and Roland are direct descendants of the line of Eld, Arthur Eld is the Crimson King's father. He is the rightful sovereign because he was born first.

The Crimson King explains his motives: he wants the kingdom restored to the chaos that existed before the Dark Tower came to be. Steven Deschain's guns, the ones Roland will inherit, are the keys to the Tower since they originated from within it. The Crimson King wants Roland to help him claim the throne at the top of the Tower and destroy all the universes so the Prim will once again run rampant. Marten knows that Roland will never go along and advises the Crimson King to kill and eat Roland and steal Steven's guns when Gilead falls to Farson.

Sheemie enters the grapefruit and arrives in time to snatch Roland from the Crimson King's clutches just as he is about to be killed. Sheemie uses his power of teleportation to spirit them away and escape from the grapefruit. Roland awakens, but has little recollection of what transpired inside the glass. Yet he remains fascinated by it.

The boys walk the rest of the way home only to discover that everyone thinks they're dead. Farson spread rumors of their demise to demoralize the people of Gilead. Roland is reunited with his father and learns that his mother is at a woman's retreat in Debaria. He does not turn over the pink orb to his father. Alain and Cuthbert keep his secret.

> **Characters (in order of mention):** Roland Deschain, Susan Delgado, Alain Johns, Cuthbert Allgood, John Farson, Rhea Dubativo, Big Coffin Hunters (Clay Reynolds, Eldred Jonas, Roy Depape), Taylor (posse member), Sheemie Ruiz, Great Old Ones, Steven Deschain, Marten Broadcloak, Oy, Roland Deschain (adult), the Crimson King, the Manni, Queen Rowena, Arthur Eld.
>
> **Places:** Hambry, In-World, Thunderclap, End-World, Gilead, Le Casse Roi Russe, All-World, Debaria.
>
> **Things:** Maerlyn's grapefruit, Dogan, billy-bumbler, todash, taheen, kennit, Prim.

EXTRA FEATURES:

ISSUE 1:

WELCOME TO THE DOGAN, PART I: THE GHOSTLY QUEEN

After reporting on the development of a new territory that arose from the Prim in the Borderlands region called Thunderclap, a land of nightmares, where the Great Ones were rumored to have built a fortress from which they hoped to launch an attack on Gan—the Dark Tower, in other words—this essay picks up the story of Arthur Eld after the deaths of Emmanuelle Deschain (mother of his heir), Queen Rowena, and the monstrous spawn. Arthur descends into a paranoid period of mourning, distraught over the loss of the woman he loved (Emmanuelle, not Rowena) and fearing an attack from his enemies in the Prim. He blames himself for Rowena's restless spirit when he hears reports of her ghost wandering the halls and grounds of the castle, cradling the bloody pieces of her spider child in her arms. Arthur encounters her for the first time in the center of a forest clearing while hunting deer. He dismounts from his horse, Llamrei, and follows the specter into the forest to a Druit circle where he finds an ironwood door labeled THE KING, reminiscent of the ones Roland found on the beach. Following Rowena, he opens the door and finds himself in an alternate world where the Great Poisoning had obliterated everything. She leads him to a Dogan, where he is ambushed by a legion of robots.

ISSUE 2:
WELCOME TO THE DOGAN, PART II: THE EVIL UFFI

Arthur's knights follow his tracks through the forest to try to discover why he didn't return from his hunting trip. They are unable to find any trace of him or his horse, and the ghost of Queen Rowena stops haunting the halls of the castle at the same time. The people of Gilead wonder if the ghost dragged him off to the punishment pits of Na'ar and pray for his safe return. Reports of sightings of his animated corpse start coming in, and a young woman accuses the reanimated king of accosting her, spearing her in the stomach and making off with her young child. The corpse of the baby was found on her hearth two days later. Arthur is joined in terrorizing the countryside by the reanimated spirits of any of his knights who had fallen in battle. Gunslingers sent out to stop the terror were killed and drained of their blood. Some people believed that these creatures were evil uffis—shape-shifters in the guise of the king and his men—and that the intent was to destroy the peace and unity of All-World.

Two of Arthur's knights, Bertrand Allgood (ancestor to Cuthbert) and Alfred Johns (ancestor to Alain) believe the Great Ones from the Prim are behind this scheme. They return to the place where their king had last been seen and find the freestanding door, though it is locked. They wait until the posse of vampire riders in the guise of their fallen friends returns. The two gunslingers follow them through the door just before it closes again. They follow the horses to the Dogan, where they discover the golems in stasis chambers under the supervision of a tall robot. The droid wheels in a gurney bearing Arthur Eld, who was sedated but alive. The helmet it places on Arthur's head creates a link to the golems in their chambers, drawing upon his memories to create two more uffis—that resemble Allgood and Johns.

Q&A: PETER DAVID WITH MARC STROM

The man responsible for the scripts of the Dark Tower graphic novels answers questions about The Long Road Home.

Q&A: ROBIN FURTH WITH FRANK DEANGELO IV

Stephen King's research assistant discusses The Long Road Home and how the story this series tells arises out of the existing material in the Dark Tower novels.

THE LONG ROAD HOME MIDNIGHT LAUNCH

A one-page report on the midnight launch of The Long Road Home at Midtown Comics in Manhattan, attended by Jae Lee and Peter David.

ISSUE 3:
WELCOME TO THE DOGAN, PART III: CITY OF THE DEAD

Arthur Eld, who has been missing from Gilead for three months, awakens in the Dogan to find two entities hovering over him—a droid and Arthur Eld's ghoulish double. He doesn't know that his kingdom has fallen into anarchy. His citizens have fled to safer havens and harriers once again prey on travelers. His only hope for salvation comes in the form of Sir Alfred Johns and Sir Bertrand Allgood, who have tracked their *dinh* to the Dogan in time to see a droid produce their uffis (evil twins), designed to join the terror campaign being waged against New Canaan. The vampiric versions of Eld, Allgood and Johns arrive at Gilead, impervious against all efforts to stop them from entering the castle, where the false king takes his place at the banquet table. The real Arthur Eld, however, is in possession of a Manni plumb bob, one of the arcane devices they use to travel between worlds. They have no control over where the plumb bob will take them but *ka* exerts its hand, sending them to Can'-Ka No Rey, the rose-filled fields around the Dark Tower. The Tower's twelve Guardians arrive in answer to Gan's summons to bear Arthur and his two knights back to Gilead, where they exile the uffi to their proper level of the Tower.

THE MAKING OF A COVER

A two-page illustrated essay showing each stage of Jae Lee and Richard Isanove's work in creating a cover for this issue of The Long Road Home.

DARK TOWER ON THE ROAD BY FRANK DEANGELO IV
Peter David discusses (and sometimes refuses to discuss) the story that remains to be told in The Long Road Home.

ISSUE 4:
MID-WORLD MUTANTS
A pictorial essay detailing the major kinds of animal and human mutations that developed as a result of the Great Poisoning. Animals covered include deer, dogs, horses, insects, rats and wolves. Human mutations include the slow mutants, the Children of Roderick and the Wasteland Mutants.

ISSUE 5:
INVOKING THE GUARDIANS
A scholarly discourse on the Guardians of the Beam, whose exact nature and origins are unknown. Some see them as magical or spiritual forces. Other speculate that they are no more than cyborgs created by the Old People to atone for the great evil their culture perpetrated against the Earth and use as evidence blueprints discovered in North Central Positronics Dogans in the Borderlands. The true believers explain this apparent discrepancy by arguing that the cyborgs are mechanical avatars that focus the sacred powers of the true Guardians, akin to the *can-tah* stones that represent the Beams. The Guardians oversee the White aspect of the portals, and their opposites, the hermaphroditic demon elementals, represent the Outer Dark at these gateways to other worlds. Instead of being baptized, each child born in Mid-World undergoes a ceremony known as the Invocation of the Guardians. At the conclusion of this ritual, one of the parents may dream of a particular Guardian that will give the child a second, secret, powerful name.

MAP OF END-WORLD
This map starts at the Mid-Forest bog in the northwest corner and shows the wedge of Mid-World along Shardik's Beam between the Elephant Beam and the Horse Beam, ending in the fields of Can'-Ka No Rey and the Dark Tower. The regions represented are the Borderlands; the Grand Crescent containing the Callas, which are distributed along the River Whye; Thunderclap, home

to Devar-Toi, Fedic and Castle Discordia; the Discordia Badlands, home to Le Casse Roi Russe and the White Lands of Empathica.

NORTH CENTRAL POSITRONICS

North Central Positronics (NCP) was a corporation at the center of the advanced knowledge amassed by the Great Old Ones, who mastered every scientific field and used this knowledge to manipulate the fabric of the multiverse and reality itself. One of the corporation's goals was to replace magical elements of their reality (the Dark Tower and its supporting Beams, for example) with scientific analogs. Their experiments fusing magic and technology were conducted in research stations known as Dogans. Among the creations of NCP that continued to function long after the Great Old Ones and their Imperium vanished are the robots designed to maintain and manage the Dogans.

DOGANS

The Great Old Ones constructed the Dogans following Maerlyn's specifications. While most are research labs, many are surveillance outposts located in strategic places throughout Mid-World. The weapons of the Great Old Ones that led to the Great Poisoning were built here and survived whereas their creators did not.

LE CASSE ROI RUSSE

This is the Castle of the Crimson King, a fortress located in End-World on the edge of the White Lands of Empathica. Its red glow (known as the Forge) can be seen from a great distance.

A NOTE FROM ROBIN FURTH

Plot writer Robin Furth discusses how she was able to turn her dreams of Cuthbert and Alain into a coherent tale.

COMMENTS FROM PETER DAVID

Scriptwriter Peter David talks about the daunting process of adapting the Dark Tower, especially in parts of the graphic novel that do not appear in the original novels—a process he likens to pedaling the Dark Tower bicycle without the aid of training wheels. An audience of one, he reassures readers, stands between him and them: Stephen King, who continually approves of their work.

TREACHERY

Original release dates: September 2008 through February 2009 (6 issues)
Credits:
- **Creative Director and Executive Director:** Stephen King
- **Plotting and Consultation:** Robin Furth
- **Script:** Peter David
- **Art:** Jae Lee and Richard Isanove
- **Lettering:** Chris Eliopoulos

Though the focal event of this miniseries—the death of Gabrielle Deschain—was related in *Wizard and Glass*, events leading up to it are revealed for the first time. Treachery is aptly titled, for it deals with several forms of deceit that are occurring simultaneously in Gilead and are symptomatic of the empire's impending collapse.

By failing to give the pink orb from Maerlyn's Rainbow to his father, the *dinh* of Gilead, Roland's treachery is nearly treason. Alain and Cuthbert are frustrated by his obsession with the grapefruit. He isn't eating or sleeping or bathing. If it traps Roland again, they don't have Sheemie around to free him. Roland rationalizes his deceit by telling himself he is protecting his father. Alain and Cuthbert worry they will need to take the orb from him.

The ball reveals the Tower to Roland. The roses around its base are dying. The Voice of the Tower bids him to look up—he sees the Crimson King. Then the orb shows him a spidery Rhea of the Cöos soaring across the desert, on the way to Gilead as an agent of Farson. He sees her decapitating his father with a garrote. In a trance, he shoots, thinking he is attacking Rhea but instead narrowly misses Cuthbert. Alain and Cuthbert finally make Roland see reason and he delivers the pink orb to his father. A spy—a supposed scout—named Justus sends word to Farson's men that Steven has the Wizard's Glass.

A grand party is planned to celebrate the coming of age of Alain, Cuthbert and Roland. Alain and Cuthbert are becoming gunslingers based on their performances in Hambry, which doesn't sit well with some of the other apprentices. They think the two boys are getting special treatment. Roland is okay—he faced Cort, unlike his friends. There are ugly confrontations and hateful graffiti of the type Eldred Jonas left for the boys in Mejis.

Traitors and spies are infiltrating Gilead at every level. The gunslingers unwittingly rely on Justus, who promises to lead them to one of Farson's camps, but it's a trap. Steven Deschain is nearly killed. Justus's treachery goes unsuspected, and he convinces the gunslingers to consider attacking Farson's camp in the Shavéd Mountains, where Farson is planning an ambush.

Not even the gunslingers of Gilead are immune to turning into traitors. John Farson captures Charles Champignon, who threw himself in front of a hand grenade to save Steven Deschain's life. His wife is raped and their unborn child is ripped from her womb before his eyes. He is forced to recommend Kingson, John Farson's nephew, for a position as court minstrel. (This story is told in greater detail in the one-shot issue *The Sorcerer.*)

Kingson also delivers the poisoned knife that Gabrielle Deschain is supposed to use to kill her husband after the coming-of-age feast. Cort catches Kingson cheating at the riddling contest and kills him. In his pocket he finds a signet ring marking him as one of Farson's men. Roland told this story to his *ka-tet* in *The Waste Lands*, although he didn't say when this took place.

A new character enters the story, Aileen Ritter. Her mother's brother, Cort, is her only living relative and guardian. She is only mentioned in *The Gunslinger* as the girl his parents wanted him to marry. She plays a much larger part in The Gunslinger Born series. Cort is the one who wants Aileen to marry Roland, the future *dinh* of Gilead. She would rather be a gunslinger at Roland's side than his wife. She "borrows" weapons from her uncle's armory and practices alone, sharpening her skills, even though by tradition she can never be a gunslinger. Cort promises to speak to Steven on her behalf, though.

Roland invites Aileen to dance at the banquet and tells her of the tragedy that occurred in Mejis and about his vision of the Dark Tower. Aileen thinks the Tower is a myth, but Roland assures her it is real. He wants to reach the Tower, climb to its top and confront whatever dwells behind the varicolored oriel window to force it to erase the plague rotting Mid-World's soul. Aileen pledges herself to the mission and kisses Roland. At first Roland resists; then he relaxes into the kiss.

The final acts of treachery involve Gabrielle Deschain. When Roland was in Mejis, she was exiled in Debaria, where she was expected to confess her sins and pay penance. However, her confessor turns out to be Marten Broadcloak. She confesses her love for him, and he convinces her it's better to take the fight to the gunslingers than flee. She knows that he wants her to kill her husband and deliver the Wizard's Glass to him. With fingers crossed, he promises that Roland won't be harmed.

At the feast, Steven promises both the guns of Eld and the Horn of Eld to

Roland upon his eventual demise, along with the title of *dinh*. Steven accepts Gabrielle back into his arms and asks Roland to forgive her. However, Roland is wary of her, especially when he sees her with the musician who Cort later kills. During a dance, Gabrielle steals the key to her husband's safe.

Roland hurries to his father's chambers, where he discovers the safe open and the grapefruit gone. His suspicions are confirmed when he finds the orb in his mother's room. Once again it captivates him, showing him Rhea of the Cöos sneaking up behind him with a garrote. He turns and fires without looking, shooting his mother in the chest. Instead of a garrote, she holds a belt she had made for Roland while in Debaria.

The Wind Through the Keyhole, published three years after Treachery, contradicts details in this graphic novel, which is an indication of how King considers them spin-offs rather than part of the mythos. In the novel, Cort was so badly injured during his battle with Roland that he is permanently incapacitated. Before he goes to Debaria to stop the skin-man, Roland is acting as his nursemaid. While Marten did attempt to see Gabrielle at Serenity (not Our Lady of the Rose) in Debaria, they never met face-to-face. Roland told his friends that he learned of Gabrielle's plot to kill her husband and intercepted the knife before it ever reached her. In *Wizard and Glass*, the *ka-tet* left Mejis after Reap, so the Fair-Day riddling contest would have taken place recently. However, it is possible that riddling contests were also held during coming-of-age feasts. In one of the essays in the Fall of Gilead series, Robin Furth talks about how she tempted the wrath of Dark Tower fans by changing details like these.

> **Characters (in order of mention):** Steven Deschain, Roland Deschain, Alain Johns, Cuthbert Allgood, Jamie DeCurry, Thomas Whitman, Cort, the Crimson King, John Farson, Justus, Wells, Aileen Ritter, Charles Champignon, Chris Johns, Robert Allgood, Gabrielle Deschain, Gan, Marten Broadcloak, Rhea of the Cöos, Susan Delgado, Abel Vannay, Kingson (James Farson), Arra.
>
> **Places:** Gilead, Great Hall, the Dark Tower, Our Lady of the Rose, Debaria, Hambry, Xay River Canyon, New Canaan, Cressia, Indrie.
>
> **Things:** *ka-tet*, pink Wizard's Glass, *dinh*, Guardians of the Beam, Affiliation, Horn of Eld, charyou tree, *ka*, Roland's belt.

EXTRA FEATURES:

ISSUE 1:
INJURED HAWKS AND FAILED GUNSLINGERS

A discussion of the process by which boys become gunslingers, using hawks as an analogy for these trained fighters. Candidates are selected at the age of six and sent to live in communal barracks. Their training nominally lasts until the age of eighteen, at which point they are expected to take the all-or-nothing test to become a gunslinger. If they feel unprepared, they may defer the test for up to seven years. If a boy fails at the challenge, he will be banished forever, but if he fails to take the challenge by the age of twenty-five, he will become a laughingstock and fade into obscurity. Many of the candidates are children of gunslingers, but gunslingers also adopt the sons of merchants and farmers in the area, basing their selections on open contests for boys held during the Fair-Day festival. Those who fail the test ("injured hawks") often became violent, vicious or addicted to alcohol or weed. Many join the ranks of John Farson, Gilead's deadliest enemy. Cuthbert and Alain are the only two boys to be promoted to gunslingers without facing the solitary challenge against their teacher in Gilead's Square Yard. Because they avoided the possibility of public humiliation and failure, the other trainees resented them.

ISSUE 2:
WOMEN OF MID-WORLD AND THE CULT OF ORIZA

Father figures are fundamental to the belief system of Mid-World. Forgetting the face of one's father is the ultimate shame. The system is eminently patriarchal, with daughters of gunslingers having fewer opportunities than their brothers. The most basic difference is that daughters are never allowed to take up guns. However, Mid-World scholars tell of a time before the Imperium of the Old People when mothers were as honored as fathers. The ancient Druit circles were the realms of female spirits with the gift of prophecy. These scholars are willing to go so far as to suggest that the word *dinh* does not apply to a father but instead to a respected elder of either gender. There are also a number of female deities worshiped in the Baronies, one of which, Lady Oriza, patron of rice and corn and protector of small children, was a warrior who took up arms against her enemies. In some creation stories, it was she who created human beings after Gan created the world. The weapons used by Lady Oriza and her followers, the Sisters of Oriza, were discuslike plates with razor-sharp edges. She rose to fame after using her weapons to kill the harrier Gray Dick, who murdered her father, Lord Grenfall.

INTERVIEW: TALKING WITH ROBIN FURTH, PART 1

Robin Furth discusses how her journey to the Dark Tower began, whether she has always wanted to be a writer, the challenges she faced in writing *The Dark Tower: A Complete Concordance*, whether there are any "rules" she needs to follow when working on The Dark Tower, how she handles the language and vocabulary of the series and how she reacted to the sample pages produced by Marvel when the series was pitched.

ISSUE 3: _____
THE SHADOW OF THE ROSE

The Little Sisters of the Rose is one of many Mid-World religious sects. Its members devote themselves to charity, chastity and to the *khef,* the liquid element that represents life to all things. *Khef* is also the force that binds *ka-tets* together and is the blood that runs through everyone's veins. They act as nurses, erecting tents as portable clinics where they tend to the wounded. Since they follow in the wake of John Farson's destruction, their path is a dangerous one and many have been killed, tortured or raped.

The Little Sisters of the Rose have a retreat called Our Lady in Debaria, where disgraced women go to pay penance for their sins. (Gabrielle Deschain was one of their guests, and young Roland Deschain visited the retreat—where it was called Serenity—when investigating the shape-shifter in *The Wind Through the Keyhole*.) The retreat has a rose garden that is modeled after the fields of Can'-Ka No Rey, in the middle of which stands a temple in the shape of the Dark Tower. Legend has it that the roses are all descended from one that was plucked from the field surrounding the real Tower. The sister who spent ten years traveling to and from the Tower brought back an invisible affliction, too, that laid waste to her fellow Sisters, though they were resuscitated from death with amazing healing powers. Not everyone who entered their healing tent emerged, however. Many men disappeared. Big Sister discovered that the reborn Sisters were vampires and that they were led by another who feasted on the *khef* of the dying men in their care. The vampires were staked and the convent reconsecrated with the twelve Guardians of the Beam.

THE LONG ROAD TO TREACHERY

A summary of the characters who have appeared in the series so far, featuring biographies of Roland Deschain, Cuthbert Allgood, Alain Johns, Steven Deschain, Marten Broadcloak, John Farson, Clay Reynolds, Sheemie Ruiz, Cort Andrus and the Crimson King.

ISSUE 4:
THE MANNI, THE TOUCH, THE TOWER AND THE ROSE

The touch is the Mid-World term for psychic powers. Most people who belong to the religious order known as the Manni possess this extrasensory perception as well, and it is fundamental to their central religious rite, which is traveling "todash"—moving between worlds without using portals. In the olden days, gunslingers were encouraged to take Manni wives to introduce this power into the gunslingers' repertoire of abilities. The Manni are somewhat akin to the Amish in our world, wearing cloaks and hats, growing beards, and allowing polygamous relationships. In some places they are persecuted because of their unusual abilities. The Manni believe their powers are a gift from the Prim and the Over, which is another term for Gan. Their todash travels are undertaken in the pursuit of knowledge and not for personal gain. Such travels are dangerous, for if their preparations are flawed, they could end up traveling to one of the voids between universes that are filled with todash creatures. Their travels have revealed to them that Roland's version of Mid-World is the Keystone Tower, in which time travels in only one direction and events can never be undone. Its counterpart is an Earthlike reality called Keystone Earth, where the Tower has the form of a pink rose that protects the heart of reality. While the Crimson King threatens the Dark Tower in Keystone Tower, the rose is under threat from other enemies in Keystone Earth. These agents have isolated it from those who would seek comfort from it.

INTERVIEW: TALKING WITH ROBIN FURTH, PART 2

Robin Furth discusses how long it took to get the process of creating the Dark Tower comics started, whether there were any hard-and-fast rules about crafting stories that had never been told before, how much description she included in her plots and how much of the information included in the essays in each issue comes from her concordance and how much is brand-new.

ISSUE 5:
REGICIDE: POISON GARDENS AND THE TRAINING OF APPRENTICE GUNSLINGERS

Though many of Arthur Eld's personal tasters sacrificed themselves to assure the safety of their king and *dinh*, many of those who followed in his footsteps were not so lucky. Most of the poisons that ended up in the kitchens at Gilead were derived from plants grown in a garden in a walled courtyard of Le Casse Roi Russe in the heart of End-World—the Castle of the Crimson King. These poisons are complicated, disguising their natures and symptoms until it is too late. Arthur Eld had a well-protected, secret apothecary where prophylactic medicines and antidotes were conjured with the same diligence that the Red King devoted to his toxins. The essay concludes with a list of poisons that a gunslinger needed to be familiar with before he could take his final test.

INTERVIEW: TALKING WITH ROBIN FURTH, PART 3

Robin Furth discusses world building, which Dark Tower characters haunt her, which other Marvel comics she would like to work on and her feelings about being in the spotlight at fan conventions.

ISSUE 6:
MID-WORLD FAIR-DAYS AND MID-WORLD RIDDLING

The essay explores the popular pastime of riddling, which was serious business in Gilead, considered a sacred art form. The Fair-Days scattered throughout the Mid-World calendar were the times when riddles were played for amusement and competition. A group of judges sifted through a barrel filled with riddles—some new, some ancient—to select those that were deemed fair. A good riddle described familiar things in a way that made them seem unfamiliar, often from the perspective of an animal or an element of nature. Losing early in a riddling contest was a form of public disgrace. The essay concludes with a description of the various Fair-Days in New Canaan and some typical riddles.

THE SORCERER

Original release date: April 15, 2009
Credits:
- **Creative Director and Executive Director:** Stephen King
- **Plotting and Script:** Robin Furth

- **Art:** Richard Isanove
- **Lettering:** Chris Eliopoulos

The Sorcerer, released between Treachery and Fall of Gilead, is devoted to Marten Broadcloak. The creative team for this book was pared back, with Robin Furth providing the script for the first time. To allow Jae Lee the time needed to give the final installment, the epic Battle of Jericho Hill, the attention everyone thought it deserved, Richard Isanove took over the artwork for both *The Sorcerer* and the fourth arc, Fall of Gilead.

Furth starts by defining what magic means in Mid-World, calling it a willful alteration of the spin of *ka*'s wheel. She then introduces us to Marten and his various aliases. He claims to be the bastard child of Maerlyn, the "evil" sorcerer who created the Wizard's Rainbow. His mother was Selena, goddess of the black moon (an idea supplied by Stephen King). He was abandoned at the home of a mill owner in Delain (kingdom of Roland in *The Eyes of the Dragon*). This rationalizes the source of his magic, given his seemingly human upbringing.

Marten calls the Crimson King his cousin, which would make Roland his cousin, too. This would be the case only if Maerlyn were part of the line of Eld, too, and not just Arthur Eld's court magician.

At the age of thirteen, he left home to find his real parents. He encounters a Medusa-like jinni whom he regards as his sister—a creation of Maerlyn, the personification of the pink orb. "She" becomes his consort and ally. The House of Deschain stands between him and his ultimate goal: the Dark Tower.

The story jumps ahead to his plot to manipulate Gabrielle into murdering Steven. His connection to the grapefruit allows him to observe what the orb tells Steven about Roland's adventures in Hambry. Marten sees much of Steven's life in the orb, including the birth of Roland.

Walter's real motivation behind the murder of gunslinger Charles Champignon is the fact that his son would be a gunslinger with the Manni power of the sight. Steven tries to persuade Arra to remain in the castle, but she vowed to her mother that she would give birth in her Manni village. Marten's men ambush the family at Gallows Hill. They coerce Charles into writing a letter of introduction for Kingson, the minstrel, who is really Farson's nephew James. Charles thinks he can save his wife's life—and that of his unborn son—if he complies.

As told in *Wizard and Glass*, Clay Reynolds and Coral Thorin became lovers after leaving Hambry, but John Farson is displeased with the last remaining Big Coffin Hunter for failing to bring him the pink orb. Marten knows where the orb is and explains his plans to use it. He gives Farson's nephew the poisoned blade that Gabrielle is to use as a weapon. As a backup, he has a magic book that will fascinate any reader before killing them with its poisoned pages.

After Cort kills Kingson, Marten reanimates James Farson's body because he promised to bring Farson's nephew back alive.

The pink grapefruit still has Roland in its thrall. They are almost lovers, in the same way that Marten has taken the orb as his consort. The grapefruit is jealous of Marten's love for Gabrielle and uses her influence over Roland to trick him into killing his mother. Marten is outraged and exiles the manifestation of his sister back into the sphere like a genie in a bottle.

> **Characters (in order of mention):** Arthur Eld, Marten Broadcloak (Walter o'Dim, the man in black, Randall Flagg, Rudin Filaro, the Walkin' Dude, the Magician, Necromancer), Maerlyn, Selena, Gabrielle Deschain, Steven Deschain, Roland Deschain, John Farson, Susan Delgado, Crimson King, Charles Champignon, Arra Champignon, Robert Allgood, Manni, Coral Thorin, Clay Reynolds, Kingson (James Farson), Cuthbert Allgood, Alain Johns, Aileen Ritter.
>
> **Places:** Gilead, All-World, Delain, the Dark Tower, Shavéd Mountains, Hambry, Gallows Hill, Travellers' Rest, In-World, Na'ar.
>
> **Things:** *ka*, Wizard's Rainbow, grapefruit, kra-ten, kra.

EXTRA FEATURES:

BEHIND THE SCENES OF *THE SORCERER*

Robin Furth discusses how, for the first time, she both plotted and scripted an issue of the Dark Tower graphic novel adaptations. She wanted to use the issue to explore Marten Broadcloak, the shape-shifting magician who is Roland's most visible enemy in the Dark Tower series and a source of chaos in many of King's other books. Through her conversations with King, she learned things about Marten's past that King had never written down before. Her collaborator, Richard Isanove, came up with the visual representation of the jinni that was the human aspect of the pink orb, which further inspired Furth. She decided to script the issue in Walter o'Dim's voice, as well as using the poetry of William Blake, Milton's *Paradise Lost,* The Song of Solomon from the Bible and the writings of twentieth-century Satanist Aleister Crowley.

Fall of Gilead

Original release dates: May 2009 through October 2009 (6 issues)
Credits:

- **Creative Director and Executive Director:** Stephen King
- **Plotting and Consultation:** Robin Furth
- **Script:** Peter David
- **Art:** Richard Isanove
- **Color Assists:** Dean White (Issue 1)
- **Lettering:** Chris Eliopoulos

Fall of Gilead uses a few details from the Dark Tower series as guide-posts, but for the most part the story told here is completely original. Cort's death, as well as that of Steven Deschain, is drawn from details Roland told his *ka-tet* on the road to the Dark Tower, but the fates of the other characters were never revealed.

In *The Wind Through the Keyhole*, Roland tells his friends that Gabrielle's death was attributed to suicide and that there was a period of mourning in Gilead following her death. It was during this time that Roland was sent to Debaria to handle the skin-man, putting the chronology of Fall of Gilead at odds with King's novels. Cort's death, Roland says, took place two years before the civil war began, which is also out of sync with this time line.

Fall of Gilead is mostly a story of death. Over the course of six issues, Robert Allgood, Cort, Dr. DeCurry, Abel Vannay, Chris Johns and Steven Deschain are all murdered—as well as just about every resident of Gilead. The only survivors are Roland's first *ka-tet*, including Aileen Ritter.

Steven Deschain discovers Roland with his mother's body. Though Roland could have professed his innocence, he immediately explains what happens. Ever the diplomat and considerate of the court of public opinion, Steven has his son arrested and jailed so that his innocence can be demonstrated. The fact that Gabrielle was in possession of a knife with the *sigul* of John Farson will prove that Roland's actions were justified.

Cort finds a book beneath the floorboards of Farson's nephew's room. It's a trap—the pages are poisoned. Against Vannay's warnings, Cort reads the book, which shows a reader whatever he desires to see (like psychic paper from *Doctor Who*). Thinking he's uncovered Farson's master plans, Cort poisons himself, though his death is slow and painful.

Jamie DeCurry's father, a doctor, attends him in his final days. Abel

Vannay suggests that the young gunslingers pay Cort their final respects and see what their enemy is capable of. Cort tells his young charges not to blubber at his bedside. He saves his final lesson for his niece, Aileen, telling her that women deserve to be gunslingers and expressing his pride in her by comparing her to Lady Oriza, slayer of Gray Dick (a story told in *Wolves of the Calla*).

Roland thinks that he is bound for the gallows like Hax. After Cort dies, Aileen disguises herself as a man so she will be taken seriously as a gunslinger. She frees Roland from his cell so he can pay his respects to his teacher. When they arrive in the morgue, they discover Vannay's body, too. The once-trusted guards of Gilead have all gone over to Farson's side and, over the next few hours, execute many of the city's most prominent men.

To explain how the pink Wizard's Glass ended up back in Flagg's possession, one scene shows Marten, transformed into a raven, flying from the castle carrying the orb in its velvet sack. He and Kingson—whose reanimation is shown in *The Sorcerer*—flee Gilead. When the gunslingers follow Marten's trail, they are ambushed by slow mutants armed with blowguns. Robert Allgood dies protecting his *dinh*.

Farson's spy, Justus, leads the gunslingers to Farson's camp, which, he says, is protected by only a skeleton crew. However, the twenty gunslingers find it fully guarded and armed with the weapons of the Old People. Justus's duplicity is revealed and the gunslingers are surrounded. Steven tries to use Justus as a prisoner to negotiate their way out of the predicament, but the spy is just another tool to be used and discarded, so the gunslingers are forced to try to shoot their way out, though vastly outnumbered. Steven sounds the Horn of Eld. When Roland hears it from the castle, he knows it is the beginning of the end for Gilead.

Steven and Christopher are the only survivors of the ambush. Steven Deschain prepares to bring the castle's defenses online. The city's founder, Arthur Eld, installed them and they have never been used or maintained, so there's some doubt about whether they still work. Corrupt castle guards stab Christopher and Steven shortly after their return. Steven manages to kill his attacker, safeguarding the castle's plans. His assailant falls out a window into the moat, which explains why no one ever knew who killed Steven. The *dinh* of Gilead lives long enough to leave a message for Roland in his own blood: open the pits.

The council of gunslingers that meets to consider options is considerably younger than the one that recently gathered in the same chambers. Roland takes possession of his birthright, his father's guns and the Horn of Eld. He is now the *dinh* of Gilead.

After reviewing the castle's defenses, Roland and his friends stand on the ramparts and watch Farson's army approach the castle. The defenses include spears buried in the grass, blades embedded in the castle walls, an impressive supply of spiders, and fake guards to make it seem like they have more defenders than they actually do. Guns are handed out to any man or boy tall enough to see over the parapet. When the first of the slow mutants reaches the traps, the gunslingers get their first proof that the defenses will work. Hundreds of attackers fall into the pits and are impaled on centuries-old spikes.

Farson plows ahead, riding over this cannon fodder. Gilead's walls are quickly breached. The traitors who remained inside the castle descend to the keep where the women and children are hiding. The gunslingers arrive too late to protect their people. Everyone in the city is dead except for them, a handful of young fighters.

The final insult: Marten removes the flag of Gilead and replaces it with the eye of Farson.

> **Characters (in order of mention):** Roland Deschain, Gabrielle Deschain, John Farson, Rhea of the Cöos, Cuthbert Allgood, Alain Johns, Kingson, Aileen Ritter, Susan Delgado, Cort, Steven Deschain, Abel Vannay, Marten Broadcloak, Dr. DeCurry, Sheemie Ruiz, not-men, Marguerite, Hax, slow mutants, Chris Johns, Robert Allgood, Lady Oriza, Gray Dick, Marietta, Justus, Liam, Arthur Eld, Randolph, Thomas Whitman, General Grissom.
>
> **Places:** Gilead, New Canaan.
>
> **Things:** Maerlyn's grapefruit, Roland's belt, *ka-mai*, Dragon's Blood, Capi, the Imperium, *dinh*, Saita, the White, Horn of Eld.

Extra features:

Issue 1:
Poisoned Pen, Poisoned Book: The Fall of Cortland Andrus
Robin Furth writes about the havoc she had to wreak on Gilead as *ka*'s Grim Reaper in this miniseries. Though she had some cues from things Roland said in the Dark Tower novels, often it was up to her to flesh out the details—and, she says, Stephen King sometimes left her to figure things out for herself.

MATRICIDE
Robin Furth discusses how her family connections to pathologists have served her by allowing her to withstand some of the more gruesome aspects of horror and how she has made use of this knowledge as Stephen King's research assistant. Her compassion for Roland's secret pain is what has drawn her to him more than his skills with a gun. The first thirty issues of the Dark Tower adaptation, though in one sense a prequel, were necessary to show how Roland transformed from a wellborn boy into a bitter and dangerous man. Furth suggests that the pivotal event in his existence is the murder of his mother, committed by his hand while under the glammer of the pink orb. The act was a mistake, but his rage at his mother's betrayal was real, and the fact that it came soon after his own betrayal of Susan Delgado compounds its importance.

ISSUE 2: _____
THE ART AND DISCIPLINE OF CREATIVE CONTINUITY
Robin Furth discusses the challenges in creating something new for fans of the Dark Tower series while at the same time remaining consistent to Stephen King's original vision. On occasion, she admits, she must play fast and loose with rigid facts, which may "fash" (annoy) some longtime fans of the series. She drew inspiration from unrelated events in the novels to solve plotting problems. The resurrection of James Farson (Kingson), for example, is analogous to the resurrection of Nort the Weedeater from *The Gunslinger*, and helped her explain why Farson didn't attack Gilead in a fury over his nephew's murder.

ISSUE 3: _____
AILEEN RITTER AND THE FEMALE GUNSLINGER
Furth talks about how women are depicted in comics, the role of women in the comic book industry and how women writers choose to depict female characters. While the Dark Tower mythos is a male-dominated fantasy world, Furth argues that it reflects our own. Starting with Treachery, Furth made a conscious effort to explore the motivations and desires of the women of Gilead, too. Gabrielle Deschain's decision to betray her husband and her people had to be a reflection of the situation in Gilead at the time, not just some arbitrary action on her part. Oppression and a static gender/caste system cause the oppressed to join the enemy. Gilead, she argues, with its strict hierarchical

system, was destined to fall. She decided to expand the role of Aileen Ritter to illustrate the plight of women who wanted to be stronger members of Mid-World society and, in doing so, reflect on what it has meant to be female in our world. Only after the collapse of Gilead can she realize her dream of being a gunslinger. Ultimately, Roland Deschain becomes a man who values women for their contributions to society and even goes above and beyond by training Susannah Dean as a gunslinger.

ISSUE 4:
THE MANY LEGENDARY ROLANDS

King borrowed the name "Roland" from the Robert Browning poem "Childe Roland to the Dark Tower Came." This isn't the only fictional or historical Roland, though. There was the French knight of Charlemagne who was the protagonist of *Chanson de Roland* from the eleventh or twelfth century, who probably lived a couple of hundred years earlier. There was also a Scottish Roland mentioned in Shakespeare's *King Lear*, a boy who must go on a quest to save his family. Furth writes about how these different versions of Roland were always in her mind while plotting the graphic novels.

ISSUE 5:
IN DEFENSE OF GILEAD

Arthur Eld, who studied Mid-World's history, discovered a terrible truth: his world was prone to cyclical periods of bloodshed. Although he had established peace in Mid-World, there would come a day when Gilead would be besieged. He gathered his advisers to devise ways to defend the city, even if the siege didn't come for many generations. After a fierce debate, it was decided that some of the Old People's weapons should be stockpiled. Though they were still radioactive, there might come a time in future centuries when they would once again be usable. Possessing these weapons would not be enough, though. The city would have to be made strong enough to withstand armies that had their own stockpiles of horrifying weapons. Arthur and his advisers pored over the books he had amassed in his great library to discover what useful information they contained that would help them beef up the city's defenses. Their ultimate plan—an underground network of defensive systems—took a decade to devise and another to implement. Its control room was located in a tower above the inner keep, but the system was kept secret from most of Gilead's residents.

Most who heard stories about it believed it was a myth—except for the city leaders, who had access to the original blueprints.

ISSUE 6:
PLANNING THE FALL OF GILEAD

Furth describes her difficulty in plotting the fall of Gilead because Roland provided so few details about this incident. Nothing is revealed in the novels about Farson's tactics or how the young gunslingers took over the defense of the city once their fathers were murdered. During the original meeting with Marvel, where Stephen King recounted a number of untold stories he thought the series might cover, he provided some details of the fall of Gilead, though he didn't describe the final battle specifically. He was clear about how well armed Farson's army was and how outgunned and outmanned Roland and his *ka-tet* were—but they weren't defenseless. She came up with the idea for Gilead's secret defense system, a relic of the days of Arthur Eld. Using a napkin in an airport café, Furth and her husband brainstormed the system, applying their combined knowledge of folklore, mythology, ancient and medieval history, and movies featuring sieges.

BATTLE OF JERICHO HILL

Original release dates: December 2009 through April 2010 (5 issues)
Credits:
- **Creative Director and Executive Director:** Stephen King
- **Plotting and Consultation:** Robin Furth
- **Script:** Peter David
- **Art:** Jae Lee & Richard Isanove
- **Lettering:** Chris Eliopoulos

Details of the battle of Jericho Hill appear throughout the Dark Tower books. Readers know how Alain, Jamie and Cuthbert died, that there was a traitor in the group, how General DeMullet's troops were ambushed at Rimrocks, and how Roland survived by hiding among the bodies of his dead friends. Exactly when this battle took place isn't mentioned. This series uses all of these details to re-create the famous battle that ended Roland's first *ka-tet*.

Nine years have passed since John Farson's forces overwhelmed Gilead. Slow mutants have moved into the ruins of the city. When the city fell, so did the Eagle-Lion Beams, causing a Beamquake that is felt throughout Mid-World.

Sheemie has a vision in which five young boys, representing the other Beams, mourn their fallen comrade. The Beamquake starts fires in Gilead that reach the armory and blow apart what's left of the city. Roland and his band of surviving gunslingers witness the city's destruction, pledging their vengeance upon Farson and Marten.

The vision gives Roland direction. His mission—their mission—will be to find the Dark Tower and use it to set things right in Mid-World. The others still think of the Tower as a legend. However, though the gunslingers know they are on the path of one of the Beams, they don't know which way to follow it to get to the Tower, assuming the legends are true. Roland knows about the Breakers amassed by the Crimson King, presumably from his vision in the pink orb.

First they need to find and challenge John Farson, who is rebuilding more of the weapons of the Old People. They witness his first experiment, in which a laser beam incinerates a nameless subject. General Grissom doesn't have a handle on all of the weaponry yet, though, and when they come under attack, he inadvertently slays a number of his own men. Roland and his *ka-tet* blow up most of the others, allowing a few to flee to bear witness to the assault and spread fear among Farson's men and inspire hope in Farson's enemies. General Grissom survives as well, secure inside a tank.

For several weeks, the gunslingers keep watch. One of the most dedicated is Randolph, one of Roland's friends. His wife, Chloe, and young son, Edmund, are kidnapped by a slow mutant acting on orders from Farson, who uses them to turn Randolph against the others. After Farson kills Chloe, Randolph lures Sheemie into a trap. Sheemie gets a hand on the grapefruit and sends a telepathic message about Randolph's treachery, but Roland doesn't hear it.

While Roland and his *ka-tet* try to recruit supporters from survivors of Farson's reign of terror, they encounter a manic cult that worships the oil fields and a god they call Amoco (based on a detail from *The Gunslinger*). The cult captured men from Kingstown (or King's Town) who had been trying to destroy the oil fields to cripple Farson's deadly weapons, which aligns perfectly with Roland's plan.

The campaign to increase the Affiliation's numbers is a success. However, they base their strategy on false information supplied by Randolph, failing to learn the lesson of the downfall of Gilead. They plan to attack an ammo dump at Rimrocks, but the stronghold is a decoy and General DeMullet's men are ambushed.

Alain heads back to camp in the darkness to report on Randolph's betrayal. Roland and Cuthbert already have their suspicions about their friend when they stumble upon a Farson camp that Randolph should have known about. They raid the camp and, during the skirmish, hear a rider approaching. Thinking it is an assailant, they fire at the same time and discover, to their horror, that they have shot Alain, who dies after telling them about Randolph, unaware that his friends killed him.

Marten infiltrates Roland's camp disguised as a monk bearing a creature that looks like Marten, bringing Randolph with him. Edmund is dead. Cuthbert confronts Randolph with the evidence and the traitor shoots himself. Meanwhile, Roland sees through Marten's deceit. In the guise of Walter o'Dim, he identifies himself as a minion of the Dark Tower and claims he knows how to find it, thereby setting up Roland's motivation for pursuing him.

Roland hears the Horn of Eld—it's Cuthbert announcing the attack on their camp at Jericho Hill. They are vastly outnumbered by an army of soldiers and mutants led by General Grissom, with Marten at his side. The gunslingers don't give up without a fight, taking down hundreds of the enemy. Aileen Ritter is pierced by a spear. Then Cuthbert is wounded. A flamethrower takes out Thomas Whitman and several others. Jamie DeCurry dies saving Roland.

Roland asks for the Horn to sound the final, desperate counterattack, but Cuthbert holds on to it, telling Roland he can pick it up after he's dead. The remaining twelve attack thousands of adversaries. A crossbow arrow kills Cuthbert Allgood. Roland neglects to pick up the Horn of Eld from his friend's body. Instead he goes berserk, shooting without thought. He is shot several times and falls among the bodies of his friends, seriously wounded but not dead.

Farson's decision to forgo gathering the heads of his victims is the only thing that saves Roland that day. Marten taunts Roland's "corpse," but Roland rises from the killing field and pledges his vengeance on the enemies of Gilead and his plan to conquer the Tower so Gilead will live again.

> **Characters (in order of mention):** John Farson, slow mutants, Marten Broadcloak (Walter o'Dim), Crimson King, Roland Deschain, Alain Johns, Sheemie Ruiz, Cuthbert Allgood, Aileen Ritter, Randolph, Jamie DeCurry, General Grissom, Head Technician Wurtz, Great Old Ones, Edmund, Chloe, Benedict, Thomas Whitman, Guardians of the Beam, Cult of Amoco, Affiliation, General DeMullet, Susan Delgado.

Places: Gilead, New Canaan, Travellers' Rest, Hambry, Dark Tower, Na'ar, Mid-World, Amoco, Kingstown, Rimrocks, Jericho Hill.

Things: Beams, Beamquake, Prim, Breakers, *ka-tet*, Horn of Eld.

EXTRA FEATURES:

ISSUE 1:
THE ROAD TO JERICHO HILL
Robin Furth reflects on the story they have told in the graphic novels over the past four years, the challenges Roland Deschain has faced and how he has changed in response to these challenges.

ISSUE 2:
THE MACHINES OF MID-WORLD
Though Mid-World has devolved into a preindustrial society, where the people no longer have the means to manufacture modern machinery, the wastelands are still littered with the terrible killing machines of previous civilizations. These tanks and lasers and flamethrowers have fallen into the hands of Gilead's enemy: John Farson and his massive army. Furth explains how the Old People, who had a godlike knowledge of technology, created these weapons and how they used them to destroy one another.

ISSUE 3:
THE BLUE-FACED BARBARIANS
Part of General Grissom's army consists of blue-faced barbarians called Picatu, a tribal people from the north who enter a frenzy whenever confronted by an enemy, making them almost impossible to kill despite the fact that they don't wear armor or other protective garments. They seem demonic, butchering anyone they capture and decapitating the corpses so they can turn the skulls into chalices. The blue dye that is applied to the bodies of all adult Picatu (the name means "the painted ones") is derived from the sacred woada plant. The dye lends some measure of protection to these soldiers, possessing antiseptic properties to ward off infection for anyone who is injured. The essay concludes with a description and meaning of the various patterns painted on the Picatu using woada dye.

ISSUE 4:

THE GREAT GOD AMOCO, LORD OF THUNDER, LORD OF DEATH

Amoco is a fearsome Mid-World god of fire and thunder. Among his other names are Sunoco, Mobil, Exxon and Citgo. The ceremonies performed in his name are notoriously cruel and include ritual human sacrifice akin to the ceremony of the charyou tree. The evidence to support the notion that Amoco was a principal deity of the Old People includes the thousands of shrines found along the roadsides across Mid-World. These roads might even be part of a complex and elaborate pilgrimage route across the land. Amoco's blood is derived from the oil pumped from beneath the earth—it fires the sun-chariot so it can move across the sky. Rival factions claimed Amoco as their own, enraging him to the point where he poisoned the Earth when the priests engaged in violent battle.

ISSUE 5:

MY MOST MEMORABLE DARK TOWER MOMENTS

Robin Furth reminisces about events that transpired from the time she first learned she would be involved in adapting Roland's youth in comic form to the end of the first thirty-episode series five years later.

VARIANT COVER ART GALLERY

In addition to the artists who drew the graphic novels, other artists provided illustrations for collectible "variant" editions of the comics. These include Joe Quesada, David Finch, Stuart Immonen, Leinil Yu, John Romita Jr., Billy Tan, Greg Land, J. Scott Campbell, Olivier Coipel, Mike Deodata, Marko Djurdjević, Ron Garney, Lee Bermejo, Gabriele Dell'Otto, Jimmy Cheung, Pasqual Ferry, Daniel Acuña, Dennis Calero, Adi Granov, Tommy Lee Edwards, Mitchell Breitweiser, David Lafuente, Rafa Sandoval, Tom Raney, Brandon Peterson, Leonardo Manco, Patrick Zircher, Steve Kurth and Cary Nord.

Marvel Graphic Novels: The Gunslinger

Introduction

The first series was successful enough that Marvel extended the graphic adaptation to tell Roland's story after the battle of Jericho Hill until his palaver with Walter at the golgotha. This includes his exploits in Eluria and the entire text of *The Gunslinger*.

A different pencil artist drew each of the five miniseries. Richard Isanove continued to color the artwork, providing a look and feel consistent with what went before.

The Journey Begins

Original release dates: May 2010 through September 2010 (5 issues)
Credits:

- **Creative Director and Executive Director:** Stephen King
- **Plotting and Consultation:** Robin Furth
- **Script:** Peter David
- **Art:** Sean Phillips and Richard Isanove
- **Lettering:** Rus Wooton

The Journey Begins starts just before the opening line of *The Gunslinger*, with the man in black building a devil-grass fire that leaves a message for Roland in its ashes. The five issues are an interesting blend of elements from *The Gunslinger*, variations of those tales and all-new adventures.

The first person Roland encounters is the holy man who gives him a compass and bids him give it to Jesus, an incident mentioned in passing in *The Gunslinger*. The man predicts that the days of the White are coming again.

He then arrives at Brown's cabin. Most of what happens during that visit is faithful to *The Gunslinger*, including Zoltan the crow eating the eyes of Roland's dead mule. However, instead of telling the story of the battle of Tull, Roland backtracks to Jericho Hill. After Roland crawled from the stack of bodies of his friends, he discovers that Aileen Ritter is still alive. She knows she won't live long, but she doesn't want to be buried in some desolate place. She asks Roland to take her back to Gilead so she can be interred with her family.

The trip will take several days, with Roland dragging Aileen on a travois the same way Eddie Dean will haul Roland up the beach in days ahead. They encounter a merchant convoy destroyed by Farson's "not-men." The only living witness is a talkative billy-bumbler who answers Roland's questions about what happened. He parts ways with the animal, but he and Aileen are attacked by the invisible not-men that night. A poison dart kills Aileen. The billy-bumbler bite makes the not-men visible and Roland's guns do the rest.

Roland lays Aileen's body to rest with her uncle Cort's remains. In the bowels of Gilead, he discovers a battle between slow mutants and billy-bumblers. He intercedes on the animals' behalf, but is bitten on the shoulder by one of the mutants. Again, a billy-bumbler leaps to his defense.

The story of Hax is revealed as a flashback after Roland encounters the former head cook's ghost. This story is mostly faithful to the version in *The Gunslinger*. Only two details are different. First, Marten—Steven Deschain's chief adviser—is present when Roland reports Hax's treachery to his father. Second, when Cuthbert and Roland go to the gallows before everyone arrives, Cuthbert's clowning around almost ends up with him being hanged by accident—or perhaps through a deliberate act by Marten.

Hax's ghost now apparently regrets his actions, but that is of little comfort to Roland, who wishes him off to the pits of Na'ar. The imagined ghosts of Roland's family and friends, including that of his would-be queen, Susan Delgado, drive him from the castle. Outside, he encounters Marten Broadcloak. Roland unleashes his weapons, but the sorcerer deflects the bullets and taunts Roland for attempting to kill the one person who could help him achieve his goal. Though Roland's pride won't allow him to admit that he needs Marten, he pursues the man in black because he claims that he knows the way to the Tower.

A few weeks later, Roland—with the billy-bumbler still on his heels—ends up in Kingstown, the city from which the captives of the Cult of Amoco originated. Inside its walls, he discovers a carnival under way. The town is celebrating the hanging of a not-man—a story Roland told Jake in *The*

Gunslinger. However, in that version, his encounter with the not-man was two years before he left a girl in King's Town.

The girl he leaves in Kingstown is Susan Black, who is Susan Delgado's twin. She is the daughter of the woman who runs the Travellers' Rest (a common name for inns in Mid-World, apparently). While she serves his supper, she mentions the nearby Dogan. Farson's troops raided the building for weapons and the not-men started appearing after the troops left.

A not-man attacks Susan in her room that night. It carries her off, but she leaves a shred of clothing behind. Roland uses it to provide a scent for the billy-bumbler to follow. The trail leads to the Dogan. Inside, Roland discovers Susan and another woman, Jessica, who is tending to her.

Roland discovers that the not-men are real men wearing jackets from the Dogan that render them invisible. They are using instruments on Susan and other women, though their reasons for doing so are vague. He bursts into the chamber and shoots four men, but a fifth activates his jacket and vanishes. Invisibility isn't protection from a gunslinger, though, and Roland kills the reinforcements while Jessica and Susan free the other prisoners.

One of the not-men takes Susan prisoner and attempts to escape. Roland is about to shoot him, but the billy-bumbler leaps at the not-man, blocking his shot. The man throws the billy-bumbler aside, impaling it on a tree (foreshadowing an event far down the gunslinger's path). Roland kills the last villain, spends the night with Susan and returns to the trail at first light.

His tale done, Roland leaves Brown's cabin and sets out on foot after the man in black.

> **Characters (in order of mention):** The man in black, Roland Deschain, Brown, Sheemie, John Farson, Affiliation Brats, Aileen Ritter, Cuthbert Allgood, Jamie DeCurry, not-men, Cort, Hax (ghost), Maggie, Robeson, Steven Deschain, Marten Broadcloak, harriers, Charles son of Charles, Gabrielle Deschain, Susan Delgado, Susan Black, Old People, Widow Black, Jessica, Bean.
>
> **Places:** Gilead, Jericho Hill, Mid-World, Taunton, Hendrickson, In-World, Garlan, Desoy, Forest o'Barony, Na'ar, Kingstown, Dogan.
>
> **Things:** *ka*, Horn of Eld, Zoltan, billy-bumbler, *seppe-sai*.

EXTRA FEATURES:

ISSUE 1: _____
THE JOURNEY CONTINUES

Robin Furth discusses the nature of the new thirty-issue story arc, which will describe how the young Roland became a bitter, lonely and dangerous drifter. Little is mentioned in the Dark Tower novels about the twelve years following the battle of Jericho Hill, so Furth had few signposts on which to base her plots. Furth changed the perspective of *The Gunslinger*'s familiar scene. Roland is pursuing, but the man in black is also leading Roland on. Her essay includes an excerpt from her original outline. She and her editors decided to flash back all the way to Jericho Hill, to give Roland a chance to grieve for his dead friends.

ISSUE 2: _____
THE JOURNEY CONTINUES

Furth articulates her fears and anxieties about adding things to the well-known tale of Roland's exploits, details like the addition of not-men and a billy-bumbler. Some readers think she has fallen off the Beam by breaking with the known story line. She explains her decision to expand Aileen Ritter's role from the brief mentions in the novel and shows how she used this character to make Roland more sympathetic and how his actions with her after Jericho Hill foreshadow some of his future behavior. For those readers who might wish Furth's plot lay closer to the one they imagined, she offers familiar words of comfort: There are more worlds than these.

ISSUE 3: _____
THE JOURNEY CONTINUES: THE HANGING OF HAX

Furth argues that Roland's loss of innocence began when, at the age of eleven, he turned in Hax for treason and witnessed his hanging. She relates the story as it appears in *The Gunslinger* and draws the analogy to Roland's training with a hawk—he will need to kill the dove of innocence within himself to advance as a gunslinger. In the moment when he and Cuthbert decided to turn Hax in, they chose their allegiance and decided what truly mattered to them. Yet, standing beneath the gallows, they experience doubts. The unruly crowd that turns out to witness the execution and the shoddiness of the gallows disabuse them of the notion that the hanging is a purely honorable process. Hax clings to his allegiances at the end, and Roland realizes that many in the crowd are on his side, not that of Gilead.

ISSUE 4:
A TALKING BILLY-WHAT?

Furth discusses a creature that is common in Mid-World, the billy-bumbler (also known as the throcken), to readers who aren't familiar with King's novels. These intelligent animals can parrot human speech and some can count or do simple math. Some people swear that they have a near-human capacity for emotion. Their loyalty to humans is not automatic—as it is with most dogs—but once earned, it is a lifelong bond. After the fall of Gilead, billy-bumblers became feral, though they remembered their bonds with humans. In the days of the Old Ones, they were bred to hunt down the Grandfather-fleas, parasitic creatures that followed Type One vampires. In later years, they helped keep the rat population in Barony castles under control.

ISSUE 5:
THE WHEEL OF *KA*

The team creating the stories for the Marvel comics had a prime directive, issued by Stephen King: the forces of *ka* must dictate their story. The word "*ka*" is both nebulous and replete with a multitude of meanings: life force, consciousness, duty, destiny, goal, destination, karma, fate. A *ka-tet* is a group of people who share the same goal. Roland believes that Mid-World's *ka* spins from the Dark Tower and that, by reaching and climbing the Tower, he can force the god that dwells in it to change Mid-World's fate. Because *ka* is a wheel that circles back to the beginning, Furth and her colleagues inserted elements into Roland's early journey (a tavern girl named Susan, a billy-bumbler from Oy's *ka-tet*, Dogans). The Tower, however, is not simply the center of Mid-World—it is the axis of all universes. There are people who exist as slightly different versions of each other (called twinners in *The Talisman* and *Black House*) who share each other's *ka* to a certain extent. Susan Black and a bumbler named Billy share some of the *ka* of the people they resemble: Susan Delgado and Oy respectively.

THE LITTLE SISTERS OF ELURIA

Original release dates: December 2010 through April 2011 (5 issues)
Credits:

- **Creative Director and Executive Director:** Stephen King
- **Plotting and Consultation:** Robin Furth
- **Script:** Peter David
- **Art:** Luke Ross and Richard Isanove
- **Lettering:** Rus Wooton

The Little Sisters of Eluria demonstrates the difference between adapting a novella and a novel. For the novels, plot had to be sacrificed to fit the stories into five or six issues. Here Furth is able to use the entire story almost exactly as it was printed. She even has room to expand one scene.

Furth establishes a time line for the story, setting it a year after the battle of Jericho Hill. After the slow mutants attack Roland in the Eluria town square, the Little Sisters appear, which is a small difference from the novella. It also explains the slow mutants' uncharacteristic behavior. Normally they are creatures of the darkness. They venture out into the daylight at the bidding of the Little Sisters, who need to make sure the slow mutants don't kill their victims.

One of the other patients in the tent hospital is given a name, Mr. Abraham, whereas in the novella he is simply the drover. John Norman's story of how the slow mutants attacked their wagon train is expanded. Norman and the others wanted to take a road that led around the Desatoya Mountains instead of through them, where they would have to pass close to the radium mines. The slow mutants began their attack in the mountains. An avalanche buries one of the older guards. John and Mr. Abraham stay behind to bury the guard while Jimmy continues on with the caravan. Instead of completing the journey to Tejuas, Jimmy and the rest of the convoy wait in Eluria for John and Mr. Abraham to catch up. More slow mutants attack, guided by the minds of the Little Sisters. When John arrives, he finds himself in the midst of a battle, just three men against a hundred mutants. Jimmy is struck in the head and falls into a trough, where he drowns. Abraham runs out of bullets and is brutally attacked by the mutants. John gets off lucky with a thump to the head. Just before he passes out, he sees the Sisters arrive to take charge of the situation.

Characters (in order of mention): Roland Deschain, Man Jesus, slow mutants, Chas. Freeborn, James Norman, Little Sisters, Sister

Jenna, Sister Mary (Big Sister), Cort, Sister Louise, Sister Michela, Sister Coquina, Sister Tamara, John Norman, Mr. Abraham, Lizzy, Ray, Ralph, Cuthbert, Smasher, Arthur Eld.

Places: Mid-World, Gilead, Desatoya Mountains, Jericho Hill, Eluria, Dark Tower, Thoughtful House, Tejuas.

Things: Full Earth, Topsy, *ka*, sai, Dark Bells, the language of the unformed, pube, little doctors.

EXTRA FEATURES:

ISSUE 1:
MY MOST MEMORABLE DARK TOWER MOMENTS

The tent where Roland finds himself in "The Little Sisters of Eluria" will be familiar to readers of *The Talisman*. It is similar to the one that is used as Queen Laura's pavilion and sickroom. Nunlike nurses in white habits tended to her. The image of that tent was King's inspiration for the novella that is being adapted in this chapter of the graphic novel miniseries. The tent he saw, though, had fallen into ruins, haunted by wraith-women who were nurses of death. The context of the novella in Roland's journey was vague: it happened after he had lost his first *ka-tet* and before the opening of *The Gunslinger*. Robin Furth elaborates on the tale of Roland's adventure in the abandoned town of Eluria. One thing she added to King's story was Roland's vision of being tied to the cross above the town's gates. Eluria was, after all, a Christian place, so invoking Christian imagery seemed appropriate, she says. As Mid-World's would-be savior, Roland must at times pay for his sins.

ISSUE 2:
THE LITTLE SISTERS OF ELURIA AND THE LANGUAGE OF THE UNFORMED

Robin Furth discusses her struggles with the natures of the Sisters. Where did they come from? If they were purely evil, why did their little doctors cure the sick? Why did they wear the rose, a *sigul* of the Dark Tower? Stephen King assured her that the Little Sisters were human long ago. They were hospitalers who served the White but had been turned to the dark side. Jenna's bells came from the Tower originally. "All things serve the Beam," King reminded her. The little doctors, unlike their mistresses, had not been turned. These *can-tam* continued to heal. Furth found some of the answers to her questions in the pages of *Desperation*, a novel that also takes place in the Desatoya

Mountains and uses the same language uttered by the Little Sisters. These words are neither High Speech nor Low Speech—they are the language of the unformed, also known as the language of the dead. The demon Tak who overtakes Desperation, Nevada, is an ancient god who comes from outside the world. Though the Desatoya Mountains exist in our world, Desperation does not, so the novel does not take place in the Keystone reality. The evil that drew Tak to his prison in the mines beneath the mountains may be the same force that corrupted the Little Sisters, Furth argues.

ISSUE 3:
THE DARK BELLS, PART I

Part I of a story inspired by "The Little Sisters of Eluria" and the novel *Desperation*. It takes place in the early years, when Arthur Eld was still struggling to tame Mid-World. Back then, the Little Sisters were still human. Two brothers illegally venture deep into a copper mine in the Desatoya Mountains at night, convinced they will find gold. Vaughn hopes they can pocket enough to get them out of town. The younger brother, Jess, isn't as eager to leave; Vaughn thinks Jess is sweet on the Little Sisters who arrived in town, healers who tended to the victims of a recent cave-in. As they labor, they hear whispers. Then the shaft collapses on them—only Jess survives, ending up in the medical tent run by the Little Sisters.

The Big Sister is a young woman named Alejandra. Others of her order, including Sister Mary, are jealous that the previous Big Sister chose Alejandra to replace her. Sister Mary covets the Dark Bells that Alejandra wears as a sign of her leadership position—the todash kamen that echo in the empty places between the worlds—instead of the silver bells on her own wimple.

One of Arthur Eld's knights, a familiar figure named Bertrand Allgood, thinks the cavern found beneath the mine might be worth exploring because it may be one of the Old People's bunkers, containing their terrible weapons. In the templelike cavern, the miners discover precious stones and animal sculptures known as *can-tah*, or Little Guardians. The faces on the walls represent the twelve Guardians of the Beam, but each one has a scorpion-shaped tongue. Sister Mary's anger leaves her susceptible to the dark power that inhabits this cavern, first seen as a red eye staring through an opening in the wall.

ISSUE 4:
THE DARK BELLS, PART II

As the story continues, whatever is responsible for the red light behind the wall is trying to break through. Sister Mary prays to the gods, but the voice that answers says that there are no gods here, and no Tower. A snake made of red smoke emerges from the "ini," the well of the worlds, and possesses her.

Meanwhile, Sister Alejandra tends to Jess, whose injuries are severe and may be beyond the reach of the little doctors. When he awakens, he is aggrieved to learn that his brother has gone to the clearing, but he is enchanted by the young Little Sister, who places his mother's crucifix—rescued from Vaughn's body—around his neck. Jess is jealous of Bertrand Allgood and his casual comfort when he talks to Sister Alejandra. The miners mistrusted Arthur Eld's knights, believing the king would claim a portion of the mine's yield. The gunslinger brings Sister Alejandra news of attacks on men from the company and leads her to an ancient *hacienda* for protection.

Sister Tamra is less fortunate. Sister Mary lures the Little Sister into a maze of tunnels to the newly discovered cavern, which has been turned into a sacrilegious temple. Mary reveals her true new guise to Tamra—her mouth is filled with fangs, her hair is red smoke and her body is a swarm of doctor bugs.

Sister Louise, who was also jealous that their youngest had become Big Sister, drugs Sister Alejandra with a bowl of soup containing a sleeping herb. Louise, who has been promised immortality in return for her service, grabs the Dark Bells from Sister Alejandra and declares that Mary is the Big Sister now, chosen by the Guardians themselves.

ISSUE 5:
THE DARK BELLS, PART III

Bertrand Allgood needs to discover how so many men from the Desatoya Mining Company have been killed over the past five days, their bodies hidden, drained of blood, fang marks on their throats or wrists or groins. The number of victims is increasing every day, which tells the gunslinger that whatever is responsible is growing or spreading. In his ten years at Arthur Eld's side, Allgood has faced strange and evil creatures before and realizes that not all of them can be killed. Some can only be driven off for a while.

Inside the hospital tent, Allgood discovers the bodies of more missing miners, strung up like flies in a spiderweb. They are still alive, but drugged, and the doctor bugs are tending to them. He sees evidence that a woman might have been responsible for some of the violence. The only one untouched is Jess, who is hiding in the shadows. The crucifix Alejandra gave him was his salvation. He tells Allgood that the carved chamber is the source of the evil that turned the Little Sisters. Allgood sends Jess on his horse to the nearest town to raise a posse. Before he leaves, Jess gives Allgood the crucifix for protection.

Allgood finds Alejandra unconscious in the *hacienda*. She is bound and has been stripped of her bells and her habit. Her skin is bone white and cold. She awakens long enough to tell Allgood to burn the place . . . with her in it. He takes her to a cave fifteen wheels away and sustains her with drops of his blood. Sister Mary and the other corrupted Little Sisters find them at dawn the next day. They have a prisoner, too: Jess. They know that Alejandra will need to feed and Jess will be her first meal. Alejandra, who stole the crucifix from Allgood, though it pained her to do so, rams the cross against Mary's brow. When the other vampires turn on her, she slices Jess's throat so the blood will distract them. She gives Allgood the cross and orders him to run.

Allgood's posse blows up the subterranean cavern and burns the bodies of the dead and the Little Sisters' silk tent. The evil had been driven away, but it had not yet been destroyed.

THE BATTLE OF TULL

Original release dates: June 2011 through October 2011 (5 issues)
Credits:

- **Creative Director and Executive Director:** Stephen King
- **Plotting and Consultation:** Robin Furth
- **Script:** Peter David
- **Pencils:** Michael Lark
- **Ink:** Stefano Gaudiano
- **Color Art:** Richard Isanove
- **Lettering:** Joe Sabino

In *The Gunslinger*, Roland told Brown the story of Tull. In the graphic novels, Brown is far behind, on the other side of Eluria, so the tale is recounted linearly instead of as reminiscence. It starts with Roland buying a mule in Pricetown, a detail that is mentioned in the novel but never shown.

The view of Tull as Roland sees it is one of the most striking images in this adaptation. Tull is little more than a cluster of buildings in the bowl of a valley with no reason for being there other than it was once a stop on the coach line. One wonders why anyone would stay in such a place. Furth places Tull southeast of Eluria.

Other than one brief scene where Kennerly gropes Allie in her bar and another where Roland identifies the Path of the Beam in the sky, the story of Tull in the graphic novels is virtually identical to the version from the revised version of *The Gunslinger*. Roland thinks Walter o'Dim is headed for the Dark Tower and worries what might happen if he gets there first.

The morning after Roland kills every man, woman and child in Tull, he rides on, leaving a new ghost town in his wake.

> **Characters (in order of mention):** Roland Deschain, the man in black (Walter o'Dim), Man Jesus, Charlie, Sheb, Cort, Allie, Nort the Weedeater, Susan Delgado, Eldred Jonas, Big Coffin Hunters, Kennerly, Aunt Mill, Jeb, Sylvia Pittston, Crimson King, Jonson, Soobie Kennerly.
>
> **Places:** Pricetown, Gilead, Tull, Sheb's, Hambry, Clean Sea, Great Road.
>
> **Things:** Grow bag, "Hey Jude," cully, devil-grass, hile, fan-gon, *dinh*, High Speech, Reap, nineteen, Speaking Ring.

EXTRA FEATURES:

ISSUE 1:
LETTER FROM THE EDITOR
Assistant editor Charlie Beckerman writes that, after forty-odd issues, the Marvel adaptation has "finally made it to the beginning"—to Tull, the earliest incident related in *The Gunslinger* (apart from flashbacks to Roland's days in Gilead). From the opening scene in the desert, *The Gunslinger* unravels to flashback upon flashback. The Marvel series, on the other hand, has most incidents appearing in chronological order. Beckerman summarizes Roland's journey to this point in a few pages.

ROLAND'S JOURNEY TO TULL
Robin Furth discusses the cinematic opening to *The Dark Tower: The Gunslinger* and how, after a few pages showing Roland's progress across the desert, King chose to flashback to the gunslinger's recent (mis)adventures in

Tull. However, it wasn't possible for them to do the same thing with the Marvel comics. She decided to tell the story linearly, which meant going back a step further, to Pricetown, where Roland purchased his mule. She would use that town as way of demonstrating how the world had "moved on," a phrase that appears often in the novels. Not only has civilization declined and become more corrupt, Roland has changed, too. He's harder, more impatient, crueler, much less hesitant to kill. Gunslingers are no longer respected.

ISSUE 2:
RAISING THE DEAD

Robin Furth writes that the scene where the man in black raises Nort from the dead is one of the most openly supernatural incidents in *The Gunslinger*. The writers of the Marvel comics used this incident as inspiration for a similar scene earlier in Roland's life, when John Farson's nephew James was also resurrected after Cort killed him. Furth illuminates the six-page story as it appeared in the first Dark Tower novel. The only person in town who seems to care for Nort is Allie, the owner of the honky-tonk. When the man in black offers to show the drunken clientele of the tonk "a wonder," the scene that follows feels like the antithesis of Jesus' raising of Lazarus, Furth says.

ISSUE 3:
MAGIC NINETEEN

The number nineteen first became important in the Dark Tower series in the final three books. Roland and his *ka-tet* see it everywhere, even in the branches of trees and the clouds. Almost every major character they encounter has nineteen characters in his or her name. The number is associated with mysteries, including Directive Nineteen, which safeguards Andy the robot's secrets. When revising *The Gunslinger* in 2003, King introduced the number as a dangerous password to access the memories of death that Nort the Weedeater retains after his resurrection. The man in black gives this key to Allie, the bartender, knowing that she will be unable to resist the allure of discovering what lies in the great beyond. We also learn that the number was part of a lullaby sung to Roland as a boy—in the High Speech, it is *chassit*. Robin Furth claims that the number has become associated with many things related to the Dark Tower in her life. The underlying significance of the number is the day of the month on which Stephen King was struck by a van as he walked on a country road in Western Maine: June 19, 1999.

ISSUE 4:
CHARACTERIZATION, CHARACTERS AND THE VILLAINOUS SYLVIA PITTSTON

Robin Furth explores the art of characterization, discussing how authors agonize over understanding the way their characters would behave in different circumstances and how they have to balance predictability with a touch of unpredictability, because people occasionally surprise us. She says she was impressed by the potency of the character of Sylvia Pittston, who takes up relatively few pages in Roland's adventures but stands out as a mass of contradictions. She preaches against fornication and yet she's extremely sensual and slept with the man in black. She becomes pregnant with the child of the very evil she preaches against. Her religion is a poison that becomes a weapon of Roland's enemies.

ISSUE 5:
AN EYE AND A HAND

Robin Furth discusses how Stephen King subtly modified Roland's character when revising *The Gunslinger* in 2003 in addition to making it more thematically tied to the later novels. Though still pragmatic and brutal, he could at least hope to find redemption. One of his more brutal acts was killing his lover, Allie. In the revised version of *The Gunslinger*, Allie begs Roland to kill her because she had fallen for the man in black's trap and uttered the magical word that caused Nort to tell her his secrets of the afterlife. In the original version, Allie begs Roland *not* to kill her, but he seems helpless to stop—he's an eye and a hand trained to kill. This change makes Roland's actions more palatable and, perhaps, justified. The number and the magnitude of the sins Roland commits is reduced. Under other circumstances, he might not have killed Allie at all.

THE WAY STATION

Original release dates: December 2011 through April 2012 (5 issues)
Credits:
- **Creative Director and Executive Director:** Stephen King
- **Plotting and Consultation:** Robin Furth
- **Script:** Peter David
- **Artist:** Laurence Campbell
- **Color Art:** Richard Isanove
- **Lettering:** VC's Joe Sabino

Roland Deschain awakens in Brown's cabin. He is disoriented, thinking that he left this place long ago. Brown says he fell asleep after telling his story. Roland suspects sorcery at play, but at Brown's behest, he picks up his tale after the slaughter of Tull.

Seven days later, he is pursuing the man in black again, across the desert. His mule is dead and his water supply is nearly gone. He is drawn to a Joshua tree, where he finds a body that has been ravaged by the crows. At first he fears it may be the man he is pursuing. When he finds out that it isn't, he is both disappointed and relieved. He takes the corpse's water supply and continues onward.

He encounters a checkpoint, which he at first mistakes for a Dogan. The place has been abandoned so long even the smell of death has fled, and the skeletons crumble to dust under his touch. (The sign declaring it closed forever is the same as the one Roland and Susannah encounter outside Castle Discordia in *The Dark Tower*.) The shelves are empty and the sink doesn't work. However, the hand pump in the shed out back comes to life after he risks his little remaining water to prime it. Nearby he discovers another of the man in black's campfires with an array of skeletons around it. A mongrel attacks him, then seven more. He dispatches them with relative ease except for the last, which buries its fangs in Roland's arm before dying. Fearing rabies, Roland decides not to eat the animals.

As he eats a rabbit that night, he sees a light near the horizon, most likely from the man in black's campfire. He stocks up on as much water as he can carry, then sets out again the next day. For eight days he finds nothing to eat and precious little to drink—nothing for the past two days. As he slogs onward across the hardpan, his thoughts drift. He remembers a song from his childhood and then his mother, who sang it to him. Naturally, he recalls that he killed his mother and he torments himself by saying only a monster would do such a thing before he emerges from his reverie. The memory was enhanced by a dust devil—a real demon of the desert formed out of its essence.

His next vision is of Cort, who drives him onward after he falls. Ultimately he sees a Way Station in the distance. Two buildings: a house or inn and a stable. He thinks he sees the man in black leaning against the building. He expends the last of his energy running to the Way Station, believing that he has accomplished his mission. However, when he gets close, he sees that it isn't who he thought it was. He passes out. He meets Jake Chambers, who tends to him in his weakness. Later, he hypnotizes Jake and finds out his story, which is the version from *The Waste Lands* rather than the briefer account he gave in *The Gunslinger*. Later, Roland dreams of Jericho Hill.

They set out across the desert and eventually end up at the mountains, where they find a river and fresh water. While Jake is swimming, he spots Walter scaling the side of the mountain. Roland goes hunting for supper and bags a few rabbits. He cuts himself while making his way through the overgrowth and is immediately assailed by five suckerbats, or vampire bats, which cost him five valuable bullets—though the alternative would have been more dire.

He dreams of Susan Delgado again, but she screams "The boy!" He has a vision of Jake standing in a window of the Dark Tower with a spike through his forehead. He awakens with his arm in the campfire, singeing his hand. Jake is gone. He finds him entranced by an Oracle in a Speaking Ring. The demon attempts to seduce Roland, but he banishes it with the jaw of the Speaking Demon from the basement of the Way Station. Then he consents to her desires in exchange for information. He leaves Jake with the jawbone, takes a hit of mescaline and returns to the circle, where the demon presents herself in the guise of Susan. After the Oracle tells Roland of the three who are his way to the Dark Tower and has her way with him, Roland and Jake break camp and continue up the mountain until they catch up with the man in black for the first time. The man in black promises Roland they will palaver on the other side of the mountain. Alone.

Characters (in order of mention): Roland Deschain, Brown, the man in black, John Farson, slow mutants, Gabrielle Deschain, Cort, John "Jake" Chambers, Greta Shaw, Elmer Chambers, Cuthbert Allgood, Great Old Ones, Susan Delgado, Alain Johns, Sheb, Allie, Speaking Demon, Marten, Merlin, the Oracle, Sylvia Pittston.

Places: Mohaine Desert, Mid-World, Checkpoint, Way Station, Piper School, Mid-Town Lanes, Jericho Hill, Salt, Hambry, Travellers' Rest, Gilead, the Dark Tower, the Drawers, Speaking Ring, Na'ar.

Things: Zoltan, desert dogs, devil-grass, dust devil, David, North Central Positronics, High Speech, taheen, howken, suckerbats, jawbone, mescaline.

EXTRA FEATURES:

EACH ISSUE: _____

ART EVOLUTION FROM SCRIPT TO COLOR
A four-page section shows an excerpt from Robin Furth's script, a page of thumbnails by artist Laurence Campbell and his corresponding finished inks, and Richard Isanove's color art. The finished page, including Peter David's text in word bubbles, can be found in the corresponding issue.

ISSUE 1:
TRANSCENDING TIME

Robin Furth discusses the publishing history of the two chapters from *The Gunslinger* that will be adapted in this five-issue arc. The first issue takes twenty pages to adapt a passage that is less than five pages in the novel, most of it internal dialogue. She explains how she expanded King's prose and the decisions she made to fill out the narrative. Playing off the sense of déjà vu that King added to the novel when he rewrote it in 2003, Furth decided to open again with Brown, emphasizing the fact that Roland's relationship to time and space is unique. She was also faced with finding things for Roland to do during his arduous trek across the desert and coming up with sources of water to get him through that journey. She reveals how she used details from future books, including a passing reference Roland made in *The Waste Lands* to having eaten dog meat.

ISSUE 2:
JAKE CHAMBERS

Robin Furth discusses meeting Jake for the first time on a snowy day and how, when faced with the prospect of scripting his death, she relied on a passage from *The Waste Lands* that describes events in much greater detail than in *The Gunslinger*.

ISSUE 3:
THE PROBLEM WITH CELLARS

Referencing the issue's scene where Roland encounters a Speaking Demon beneath the Way Station, Furth writes about her abiding fear of cellars and how basements are associated with burial.

ISSUE 4:
SPEAKING RINGS

Furth differentiates between the Great Old Ones, who formed North Central Positronics and created advanced technology that melded magic and science, and the Old People who came before them. They were a brutal people who offered human sacrifices as part of their religion. The Speaking Rings found across Mid-World were sites where these sacrifices were carried out. Furth then lays out the details of Roland and Jake's encounter with the Oracle succubus in this issue.

ISSUE 5:
THE SUCCUBUS

Furth starts by talking about genre—is the Dark Tower series fantasy or science fiction?—then discusses the differences between succubi (and their male counterparts, incubi) in the series and in folklore. In some legends, an incubus fathered Merlin. In the Dark Tower series, most succubi seem to be trapped in Speaking Circles and can appear to men when they are awake, whereas in legends they are free to roam and come only to sleeping men. In the series, they are also oracles, though whether their predictions are to be believed is another matter.

THE MAN IN BLACK

Original release dates: June 2012 through October 2012 (5 issues)
Credits:

- **Creative Director and Executive Director:** Stephen King
- **Plotting and Consultation:** Robin Furth
- **Script:** Peter David
- **Pencils:** Alex Maleev
- **Color Art:** Richard Isanove
- **Lettering:** Joe Sabino

The story told in the final miniseries of *The Gunslinger* arc starts with Jake and Roland camping near the cleft in the mountain into which the man in black vanished at the end of *The Way Station*. Impending bad weather is emphasized—it's cold and ready to snow. Roland is tormented by the demons of his past, which he sees in a fire he builds using devil-grass. The man in black appears to him in these flames, taunting him and offering information in exchange for abandoning Jake.

The exchange between Jake and Roland after this vision is more intense than in the novel. Roland encourages Jake to turn back, going so far as to give him his compass to guide the way—though such devices are mostly useless in Mid-World. Jake seriously considers staying behind but ultimately packs up his things and follows Roland, who has gone on ahead.

It takes Jake a while to catch up with Roland. He has a torch, but it's not enough to reveal the man in black, who is watching from the shadows, or the slow mutants who lurk in the crevices. A cave-in—reminiscent of the avalanche the slow mutants caused in "The Little Sisters of Eluria"—blocks the entrance to the tunnel. Mutant rats chase him. He falls, dropping his torch. The rats swarm past him.

After he starts a small fire and relights his torch, he finds a second tunnel with train tracks. Then he encounters the ruins of a train surrounded by skeletons in a blocked tunnel. He returns to his fire. Devil-grass demons tell him he has the touch and how to access it. When he follows their instructions, he finds himself transported into the subway car at a time when it was in service, back in the days of the Imperium.

One of the people on the subway is Walter. He gets off, leaving behind his suitcase. Poison gas emerges from the bag. A spark causes the gas to explode, sending Jake back from his vision.

Roland hears the cave-in and backtracks toward the entrance, where he finds Jake. He won't listen to Jake's story of his vision, blaming the whole thing on noxious smoke from the devil-grass. They start on again, following the tracks. They extinguish their torches to conserve light. During a break, Roland describes the geography of Mid-World to Jake and explains the nature of the Dark Tower. He then tells Jake the story of the Sowing Night Cotillion when he, Cuthbert and Alain spied on the festivities from a balcony and saw Marten dancing with his mother. He finishes his story by telling how the gunslingers were ambushed and his father was stabbed to death. He says that what happened to his mother is a story for another day.

As in *The Gunslinger*, they stumble upon the talking handcar and encounter the slow mutants, but here Walter has given them permission to eat Jake so long as they leave Roland alone. The battle plays out much as in the novel. Roland and Jake get past the barricade and eventually end up in the subway terminal filled with mummies. While Roland shops for guns and ammo, Jake is enchanted by ghostly figures called corpse lights in the water that warn him the gunslinger will betray him. Jake falls into the river, but again Roland saves his life.

The rest of the story is the same as in the novel, ending with the tarot reading at the golgotha and Roland's dream wherein Walter explains the universe.

Characters (in order of mention): Roland Deschain, Jake Chambers, Susan Delgado, Gabrielle Deschain, Alain Johns, Allie, the man in black, Steven Deschain, slow mutants, Greta Shaw, Cuthbert Allgood, Marten Broadcloak, *ka-tet*, Tet of the Gun, Man Jesus, Old People, Vannay, corpse lights, Ageless Stranger, Cort, Rhea.

Places: Tull, the Dark Tower, Gilead, Mid-World, Great Hall, Jersey Turnpike, Grand Central Station, golgotha, Great All, Mohaine Desert, Na'ar, Dogans.

Things: devil-grass, Imperium, sparklights, portals, Beams, Sowing Night Cotillion, Crisp-A-La, Larchies, High Speech, tarot cards, North Central Positronics.

EXTRA FEATURES:

EACH ISSUE:
ART EVOLUTION
An excerpt from Robin Furth's script (issues 1, 4 and 5), thumbnails by artist Alex Maleev and his corresponding finished inks and Richard Isanove's color art. The finished page, including Peter David's text in word bubbles, can be found in the corresponding issue.

ISSUE 1:
WIND THROUGH THE KEYHOLE CONTINUITY AND THE DARK TOWER COMICS
Robin Furth mentions a complaint from a faithful reader that King broke continuity with the Marvel adaptation in *The Wind Through the Keyhole*. She uses this as a launching point to explain why she sometimes chose to diverge from King's plot in this series. Much of the conflict in *The Gunslinger* is internal, which is difficult to convey in a comic. Having Jake go off by himself for a while was a way of building tangible suspense. She believes the Marvel series takes place in a different world from King's novels; however, in one that is very close.

ISSUE 2:
BETWEEN THE PAGES
Furth explains the reasons why she chose to alter the story line in this issue. She wanted to enhance the image of the man in black as a puppet master. Roland's story about his battle with Cort had already been told in earlier issues, so she expanded the Sowing Night Cotillion story, underscoring the

significance of Gabrielle's treachery to Roland's psyche. Finally, because so much of this part of the novel takes place in the dark, which isn't interesting graphically, she decided to have Roland explain the nature of his universe here instead of later.

ISSUE 3:
MID-WORLD'S RAILWAYS

Furth discusses the three kinds of rail transport found in Mid-World: steam trains, such as the one that ran from Gilead to Debaria in *The Wind Through the Keyhole*; subways, such as the ones that used to run on the tracks Roland and Jake are following in this issue; and monorails, such as Blaine and Patricia. The steam trains are the most recent, having been built after the reign of Arthur Eld.

ISSUE 4:
THERE ARE OTHER WORLDS THAN THESE

Furth discusses the significance of Jake's final words to the nature of his existence and to the structure of the Dark Tower universe. She explains what happens to Jake after his fall, and how Roland's actions later in the series allow the boy to return to Mid-World. Her discussion, preceded by a spoiler warning, encompasses the entire Dark Tower series.

ISSUE 5:
GRASPING THE INFINITE

Furth discusses how passive Roland is in the final installment of the miniseries. Instead of acting, for the most part he is acted upon. She explains how the man in black's tarot reading predicts events in *The Drawing of the Three* and explores the question of why the man in black, who has taunted and tormented the gunslinger for years, should suddenly decide to provide Roland with helpful information.

SHEEMIE'S TALE
Original release date: January 2013 through February 2013 (2 issues)
Credits:
- **Creative Director and Executive Director:** Stephen King
- **Plotting and Consultation:** Robin Furth

- **Script:** Peter David
- **Color Art:** Richard Isanove

Marvel synopsis: This is the story of one of the more powerful Breakers in Thunderclap—the mentally handicapped, formerly mute young man known as Sheemie. He possesses the awesome power to shatter the very Beams that hold the Dark Tower in place—the fulcrum of existence itself. But Sheemie does not want to destroy the underpinnings of reality. He is in the prison of Devar-Toi, and all he wants is his friends—his *ka-tet* to come for him. And one of them is coming for him even now. One of them known as the last gunslinger, Roland Deschain. And all the horrors of Thunderclap will not stand in his way! It's a journey of searching and salvation you won't soon forget.

Marvel Graphic Novels: Guides and Almanacs

The Dark Tower Sketchbook

Original release date: December 13, 2006
Credits:

- **Artists:** Jae Lee and Richard Isanove

Two months before the launch of The Gunslinger Born, Marvel released this free sketchbook featuring character designs, penciled pages, commentary and a look at the painting process by which one of Jae Lee's pencils became the final color art.

Gunslinger's Guidebook

Original release date: August 8, 2007
Credits:

- **Writer:** Anthony Flamini
- **Editor and Creative Consultant:** Robin Furth
- **Art:** Jae Lee and Richard Isanove
- **Series Scripter:** Peter David

The Gunslinger's Guidebook was released shortly after the final installment in The Gunslinger Born. It details the major characters, concepts and locations that have appeared in the series to date. For each character, the following information is listed: aliases, nicknames, occupation, affiliation, known relatives, education, history, physical description, special skills, equipment. Not all of the information is correct—Gabrielle Deschain is said to come from Debaria instead of Arten, for example—and other data, like the names of Aileen Ritter's parents, seems fabricated. The book concludes with a one-page Mid-World glossary.

People: the Great Old Ones, Arthur Eld, gunslingers, Cuthbert Allgood, Cort, Jamie DeCurry, Gabrielle Deschain, Roland Deschain, Steven Deschain, Alain Johns, Aileen Ritter, Vannay, Thomas Whitman, Herk Avery, Eldred Jonas, Clay Reynolds, Roy Depape, Pat Delgado, Susan Delgado, Cordelia Delgado, Rhea of the Cöos, Kimba Rimer, Sheemie Ruiz, Coral Thorin, Hart Thorin, Olive Thorin, Walter o'Dim, John Farson, James Farson, George Latigo.

Places: Gilead, Hambry, Eyebolt Canyon, End-World.

Things: The Affiliation, Reaptide Festival, Horsemen's Association, Big Coffin Hunters, Maerlyn's Rainbow.

END-WORLD ALMANAC

Original release date: July 2, 2008
Credits:

- **Writer:** Anthony Flamini
- **Editor and Creative Consultant:** Robin Furth
- **Art:** David Yardin and Val Staples; Jae Lee and Richard Isanove
- **Series Scripter:** Peter David

The End-World Almanac was released shortly after the final installment of The Long Road Home. It begins with a map of End-World, the territory closest to the Dark Tower, which contains some of its most luxurious regions and some of its most horrific terrains. Information from *The Wind Through the Keyhole* placing the western (major) branch of the Whye River far west of any of the Callas wasn't available to the cartographer.

The almanac contains detailed descriptions and illustrations of the Guardians of the Beam, the demon elementals, billy-bumblers, boom-flurries, the low men (aka the *can toi*), mutants, taheen, vampires, Wolves, the Calla region and Calla Bryn Sturgis, Lady Oriza, the Manni, Thunderclap, the Discordia Badlands, Fedic, North Central Positronics, the Dogans, the Devil's Arse, Le Casse Roi Russe, the White Lands of Empathica and the Dark Tower.

Though much of the information is derived from the graphic novels or King's books, some of it is fanciful—like the temperature observed in Empathica during certain moons.

GUIDE TO GILEAD

Original release date: April 8, 2009
Credits:

- **Writer:** Anthony Flamini
- **Editor and Creative Consultant:** Robin Furth
- **Art:** David Yardin and Val Staples; Jae Lee and Richard Isanove
- **Series Scripter:** Peter David

Guide to Gilead was released shortly after the final installment in Treachery. As with the other books of this type, some of the information is incorrect (the name of Gabrielle Deschain's mother, for example) and much of it is fanciful, providing details of places that are mentioned only by name in King's novels and the Marvel comics. The nature of not-men is negated by an incident from later in the Marvel comics.

> **People:** Stephen Deschain, Robert Allgood, Christopher Johns, Charles Champignon, Chloe and S'Mana, Selena and Morphia, Queen o' Green Days, Raf, Lord Perth, Hax, Grissom's Blue-Faced Barbarians, Kuvian night-soldiers, not-men.
>
> **Places:** Barony of New Canaan, Hemphill, Hendrickson, Kingstown, Taunton, Pennilton, Jericho Hill, Debaria, Gilead.
>
> **Things:** Gan and Bessa, Buffalo Star, Lesser Demons of the Prim, Nis.

Marvel Graphic Novels: The Contributors

Introduction

Like most comics, the Marvel graphic novels are collaborative efforts. Robin Furth writes stories that the pencil artists break down into pages and panels, converting the prose into visual images. Some pencil artists ink their own pages. In other cases, a dedicated inker performs this work. Most of the time, though, the pencil art is passed directly on to Richard Isanove, who digitally colors the work. From Furth's story and the illustrations, Peter David creates a script that includes the dialogue and narrative text that a letterer adds to the colored artwork.

Robin Furth

As the writer for Marvel's Dark Tower graphic novels, Robin Furth has been responsible for translating the story of Roland's early years into scripts from which her collaborators produce the individual installments of the comic. Her comprehensive knowledge of the series has allowed her to expand obscure references from King's text into characters and events. At times she has been forced to compress the story line, condensing most of *Wizard and Glass* down to seven comics, while at other times she has to create stories for times in Roland's life where King's books provide only a loose framework.

Furth is originally from Pennsylvania, but summered in Maine, less than an hour from King's home in Bangor and only a couple of hours from the fictional town of 'Salem's Lot. She moved to England to do a master's degree in English Literature at the University of York, which is where she met her husband, British poet Mark Rutter. They both subsequently enrolled at the University of Maine in Orono, which was King's alma mater. One of her advisers, Burt Hatlen, was one of King's undergraduate advisers from thirty years earlier, and a close friend of his. When King was looking for a research assistant, Hatlen recommended her.

She continues to freelance for King, is director of the Discordia project for his Web site, and spent time in Hollywood as part of the pre-pre-production team for the Dark Tower films.

The following interview was conducted via e-mail in November 2011.

Q: How did you come to the Dark Tower books and then to the graphic novels?

A: I started working for Steve King back in 2000—the year after his terrible accident. Steve needed somebody to sort through the thousands of responses he'd received for the *On Writing* story competition. He wanted to help out a grad student, so he contacted Burt Hatlen. Burt knew that I was a writer, that I loved fantasy, horror, and sci-fi and that I was a fan of Steve's work, so he recommended me for the job. That original project lasted about a month. I did some of my work from home, some from the King office, but most of my contact with Steve at that point was through e-mail. (Most of my work was with Steve's assistant, the wonderful Marsha DeFilippo.)

At the end of that particular assignment, I went into the office to pick up my final paycheck and met Steve King himself. I was really tongue-tied, but Steve was very relaxed and kind and asked me if I wanted more work. He was about to return to the Dark Tower series and needed someone to write up lists of characters and places and record the pages on which they could be found. (He wanted to be able to double-check for plot and character continuity—no small job for such a large body of work.) Anyway, when Steve asked whether I was interested in the job, I said yes. (Of course!)

Not only did I create a huge dictionary of characters and places and plot twists, but I recorded Mid-World games, Mid-World languages, Mid-World diseases, and pretty much everything else I could think of. I drew a door labeled THE AUTHOR, which was supposed to help Steve reenter Mid-World. I placed the door at the front of the manuscript; then I bound the whole thing in black and taped a key to the front. (The key was so that Steve could open the door.) I wasn't certain how Steve would react to my wild enthusiasm, but he liked it enough to ask whether I wanted to continue working with his manuscripts. After that, I received draft chapters as Steve wrote them, so that I could continue building my Dark Tower Concordance. I've been lucky enough to live in Mid-World ever since.

The collaboration between Stephen King and Marvel Comics really began when Joe Quesada, Marvel's editor-in-chief, mentioned at a comic book convention that he really wanted to work with Stephen King. Word eventually made it back to King's office, and Chuck Verrill (Steve's editor and agent) contacted Marvel. After many discussions, everyone decided that the best book to adapt would be *Wizard and Glass,* since it told the story of Roland's adventures in Hambry, when he and his friends were fourteen years old.

I was there at the original meeting between Steve, Chuck Verrill, and Marvel via phone link. I'd spent so long in the Dark Tower universe that Steve thought it would be a good idea to have me on board for the Marvel project. I'd never worked in comics before, but I loved graphic novels and illustrated books, so I was excited about the whole thing. I also wanted to see Roland and his friends take on that extra dimension—to have faces and bodies that moved through space. As you can imagine, my initial learning curve was *incredibly* steep. But luckily for me, I was working with a terrific team of extremely experienced comic book folks. Peter David, Jae Lee, Richard Isanove, Ralph Macchio, and all the other editors and artists who have worked on the series, have been great. I've learned a tremendous amount from all of them.

Q: Your credit on the Marvel graphic novels reads "Plotting and Consultation." What does that mean?

   A: As a consultant, I answer questions about all things Mid-World, from clothing to gun design to landscape and religion. I also answer questions about Roland's history, or the history of the many other characters you meet in the series.

Plotting is exactly what you'd guess. It means creating the stories that are then illustrated by the artists and scripted by Peter David. Basically, for each new arc, I write a detailed story. (We call this story the story arc or the outline.) I write the arc as one flowing piece, almost like a short novella. I make sure that it is broken down into the correct number of issues/comics. I also break each individual issue into scenes. (I often break the scenes down further into a series of numbered events, which the artist can use as possible panel breaks, but ultimately I always leave the panel breaks/page designs up to the artist, since that is his specialty!)

In my story arcs, the individual issues work like chapters in a book. Reading one of my story arcs is (I hope at least) a little like reading the descriptive breakdown of a film. As I said, each issue is broken into consecutive scenes, one following from the other, and the issue itself always ends with a cliffhanger. The exception is the final comic book of an arc, which must have a sense of closure.

When I'm writing, I make sure that everything in a scene is described in great detail, so that we can remain consistent with Stephen King's world. I usually describe what characters are discussing in any particular panel. Sometimes I include placeholder dialogue so that the artist knows how to illustrate the panels and pages, but the scripts really are Peter David's creation. He does a fantastic job, and I've learned a tremendous amount about dialogue and scripting from him. He is a terrific writer.

Q: At what point do you discuss the plot with Stephen King?

A: My discussions with Steve really vary according to what we are adapting and what I need to check. Sometimes I send him specific questions about plot direction/characters before I even begin. (I had to do this a lot before I started *The Sorcerer.*) At other times I send him a brief summary before I begin, just to make sure that he feels okay about the tack I'm taking. Sometimes, when I'm really unsure, I send him the whole arc, just to make sure that he gives it the thumbs-up. Steve has been incredibly supportive of the comics, which has been great.

Q: What is the process after this?

A: Once I'm finished, I send the outline to the Marvel editors for comments. Once the editors have checked the arc, it goes to the artist, who begins his panel and page sketches, and to Peter, so that he can start thinking about scripting and so that he can let us know if he thinks we need to adjust the story. If anyone has any comments, I rewrite. Sometimes Peter can take care of the problem via the scripting. (For example, in The Way Station comics, I had Roland kill and eat a dog that was possibly rabid. Peter made a quick fix in scripting—making it clear that Roland did *not* eat the infected dog. He was really worried that if Roland ate a rabid dog that he'd get rabies and die!)

Peter really needs the pencils to finish his script, since his captions and dialogue must flow with the images. After Peter writes the script, I get a copy, too, so that I can read through. It's always a lot of fun to read Peter's scripts. At that point, the script and panels go to the letterer. The colorist, Richard Isanove, and the letterer can work simultaneously.

Q: Do the artists ask you questions as they work?

A: I answer most questions while the artist is creating the initial layouts. So problems are solved at a really early stage. I get to see the process at every step, which is fantastic. I receive the artists' initial panel sketches via e-mail, then pencils, then inks and color, and finally the lettered pages. I try to pack my outlines/stories with visual detail to help the artist see Mid-World, but I often get questions about guns, or clothing, or accessories. I remember once, when I was in New York and we were working on The Gunslinger Born, Jae asked me really complex questions about Mid-World etiquette. He wanted to make sure that everyone bowed correctly and did the fist-to-forehead correctly, etc.

One of the most humorous questions came from Michael Lark, while he was penciling the Tull comics. I had written the story as if the weedeater Nort had once pulled a real honey wagon—you know, one that sold honey. Michael thought that Steve was talking about a sewage/manure wagon. I checked with Steve, and Michael was right. Boy, was I embarrassed. Anyway, the joke was on me, but we all had a few laughs about it.

Q: What process goes into the individual essays that are included in each issue?

A: I really try to make sure that each article is relevant to the issue in which it will appear, and so my decisions are based on content. Sometimes the editors make specific requests and ask me to write about topics that they think will be of special interest to readers. For example, I've written several pieces about Roland's guns and the types of guns available to gunslingers. (Apprentice gunslingers don't use the big six-shooters used by fully-fledged gunslingers. They are much more likely to use barrel-shooters.)

I always go back to the original novels for inspiration. When important info isn't in the books, I pick Steve's brain. Since Mid-World and our world are related, I also turn to our world's history for answers. For example, when I wanted to write about the blue dye that Grissom's men used to paint their faces, I decided on woad, since both Pictish and Celtic warriors used that dye to paint patterns on their skins. (They used it to terrify their enemies, and I'm sure it did a pretty good job!)

Q: What sort of feedback do you receive from readers?

A: Most of my feedback comes from Dark Tower fans and fellow Constant Readers that I meet at conventions. Sometimes we end up having long discussions about the books, which is always good fun. Most of the readers I've talked to or I've heard from have been very supportive, which is great.

Q: What deviations from the source material have you found it necessary to make because of the nature of the graphic novels?

A: Adapting a novel to comic book form is a bit like altering a novel so that you can make it into a film. Every medium has its own demands and its own restrictions. In a novel, an author can spend a lot of time using internal monologue, stream-of-consciousness writing and quick flashback. A protagonist can hear voices inside of his mind, just as Roland often hears Cort speak. A narrative voice can be used to explain certain situations, or to foreshadow events, or to explain or comment on something that the protagonist might not know about.

In comics, everything has to be visual. The number of lines that a character can speak, and even the number of captions that can fit on a page, is extremely limited. The story has to be told in a sequence of panels, and then the script has to be extremely tight. An excellent comic book script has the force of fiction but in the limited line length of poetry.

Another difference is the use of flashback. Comics definitely use flashback, but it has to be used more sparingly. The forward momentum of the story has to be very powerful. It is harder to show two characters sitting and having a very long conversation. In a book it works brilliantly, but I have to limit the amount of conversation-without-action.

Comics—as I've learned to write them—have a very exacting format. The writers and artists have approximately twenty-two pages to tell a tale. The story has to have a beginning, a middle and an end. The story must be told visually, and the story must move relatively quickly. Each individual story must have a cliffhanger ending, but the individual stories must also fit into a story arc of five to seven comics. (These story arcs are later published in collections where the individual comics become chapters of a graphic novel.) Although the individual comics are often self-contained, the five to seven comics in an arc must tell a cohesive tale, and the arc itself must have a satisfying ending.

In order to fit these requirements, the elements of a story often need to be rearranged. Sometimes I need to add link material, and for this link material I always return to the brief stories that Roland recounts to his *tet-mates* during his travels through Mid-World. My goal has always been to stay true to Steve's vision and to introduce people to the wonders of Mid-World. Occasionally that means inserting "new" material so that I can communicate another aspect of Mid-World's reality, or of Roland's reality, to new readers. But no matter how I try to do it, my goal always remains the same: I want to make Roland, and Mid-World, as real to comic book readers as they are to longtime fans of the original novels. In the best of all possible worlds, people who read the comics and people who read the novels can have conversations about Mid-World, even though they came there via different mediums.

Q: Where do you stand in terms of the original versus the revised and edited version of *The Gunslinger*?

A: For the comics, I tend to use the revised and edited version of *The Gunslinger*. I love the original, too, but I think that the revised version has some really interesting twists, like the addition of "nineteen" and Roland's continuing sense of déjà vu.

Q: In the graphic novels, it seems like Walter and Marten are distinct entities at times. Are they different aspects of the same creature?

A: In the comics, Walter and Marten are different aspects of the same creature. Flagg is another aspect of this being. When we first started working on The Gunslinger Born, Jae Lee really thought a lot about how to have Walter morph into Marten, and back again. In the end he decided that Marten/Walter could use a hand motion to indicate the change. You can see one of these morphs in chapter four of The Gunslinger Born. Walter is definitely a shape-shifter. And a born liar!

Q: In my interview with King, he is adamant that Farson is not Marten, but in the synopsis at the beginning of *Wolves of the Calla*, he states that they are the same person. What is your opinion?

A: This is one of those incredibly thorny questions in the Dark Tower universe! When I was writing my *Dark Tower Concordance Part I*, I thought that John Farson was another aspect of Marten. However, when it came time to finish the *Concordance Part II*, I had decided that Marten, Walter, and the man in black were all one being, but John Farson was a separate being. I based this decision on Walter's musings, which Steve King recounts in the Mordred versus Walter section of *The Dark Tower*. Walter makes it clear that the Crimson King is a separate being, and so is John Farson. Walter served each of them at different times, but he always, ultimately, served himself. The only explanation I can give is that some people believe that Marten is also Farson, but later on we (as readers) find out that this was a false assumption.

Q: Though we learn that the Crimson King is also from the line of Eld and thus a distant relative of Roland in King's novel, this case is made much more clearly in the graphic novels. What of Marten—is he also related to Roland?

A: The question of Walter's ancestry was one that really obsessed me while I was working on the one-shot comic called *The Sorcerer* (now the first chapter of the graphic novel Fall of Gilead). Hence, while I was working on *The Sorcerer,* I had a long e-mail conversation with Steve King about this very subject. I asked if it was possible that Walter was the offspring of Maerlyn. Steve said yes. He also told me that Walter's mother was Selena, the goddess of the dark moon. All this meant that Walter was descended from at least one supernatural being. I think that Steve might be rethinking Marten/Walter's background again, but all of that will become important in *The Wind Through the Keyhole*!

Q: Roland appears to be at least middle-aged by the end of the series, but he's more than a thousand years old. What does this mean to you?

A: I've spent many, many hours pacing out Roland's time line. While I was working on the Concordance, I created a Mid-World time line, which is in Appendix II of *The Complete Concordance*. Basically, I went through the novels and recorded absolutely every reference to time periods and dates that I could find, did some math, and came up with what you can see in Appendix II. Of course, this time line is up for debate! The way I look at it, Roland is an incarnation of the eternal hero. Hence, time doesn't pass for him the way it passes for other people. He *does* live outside of time. Like the Ageless Stranger, Roland *darkles* and *tincts*—he lives in all times!

Q: Are there stories from Roland's past that you wanted to tell but the opportunity didn't present itself?

A: Oh yes, there are many! I really wanted to spend some time with Roland, Alain and Cuthbert as they wandered for years, searching for the Tower, but we just couldn't do it! After Fall of Gilead, we really had to pick up steam and move forward to Battle of Jericho Hill!

Q: Do you consider the graphic novels to be part of the Dark Tower canon?

A: I suppose it depends on what you call canon. There is only one Stephen King, and his novels are great. Hence, that is the heart of the canon—or you could say it is the canon for purists! If you want to extend your definition a little bit, you could add in the Dark Tower graphic novels. They exist in the same universe and are homage to Steve King's magnum opus. They are written out of love and respect and they are written with Steve's support (he has to give his approval to everything), but they are, as I said, an homage. The way I look at it, the Dark Tower has many levels and the many levels contain many parallel worlds. Steve King's Dark Tower novels exist in Mid-World prime. The Dark Tower graphic novels exist in a spin-off world. Perhaps it's the world where Eddie Dean and Jake Chambers are drawn together, and they are Eddie and Jake Toren!

Q: Do you have a notion of what "perfection" means in terms of Roland's journey? How does he break free from his trapped existence?

A: I've always assumed that perfection meant traveling farther along the "spiritual" (for lack of a better term!) path that Roland travels in the later books of the series. He has to relearn his humanity. He has to move farther and farther from the man who mowed down every man, woman and child in Tull, farther from the man who let Jake Chambers drop into the abyss under the Cyclopean Mountains and closer to the man who will sacrifice everything to save the children of the Callas. Does that make sense?

PETER DAVID

Peter David says that he was born with laughter on his lips and a sense that the world was mad.

He has a bachelor's degree in journalism from NYU, but he eventually decided journalism wasn't for him, though he wanted to stay close to publishing. He worked in the sales department for various publishers, always intending to transition to writing. While writing an article about the now-defunct magazine *Comics Scene,* he met and interviewed Carol Kalish, who was the assistant direct sales manager at Marvel. She was about to be promoted to sales manager. When she learned the publisher David was working for at the time was about to go out of business, she offered him a job as her assistant.

In that position, he became friends with several of Marvel's editors and started looking for side jobs writing comics. He wrote for Spider-Man and The Incredible Hulk, and eventually became a full-time freelancer. He has also worked on X-Factor, Supergirl, Young Justice and The Phantom.

He is also a novelist, with numerous books to his credit, including original Star Trek books and movie novelizations. He is part of Crazy 8 Press, a group effort involving several authors who want to make their novels accessible to fans at reasonable prices, using primarily social media to let people know about them. His Hidden Earth series has the epic scope of the Dark Tower series and *The Camelot Papers* is a revisionist version of the King Arthur legend.

The following interview was conducted via e-mail in March 2012.

Q: Do you have a preference between writing novels versus comics?

A: They both have their advantages. With a comic book, you work with an artist who brings his own talents to the endeavor. A good artist can elevate your story to a level of quality above the script that you've written. The flip side is that a lousy artist can drag it down, so that suddenly it seems to the reader as if you've forgotten how to write. I've had artists who were so bad even I couldn't stand to look at it. With novels, it's just you. There's no filter between you and the reader.

Q: What was your introduction to the Dark Tower series?

A: I read the very first short story when it came out in *F&SF.* I remember reading it and thinking it was really unusual for King.

Honestly, I wasn't wild about it. I saw what he was going for but thought he hadn't quite gotten there yet. Then again, Dark Tower has been a fascinating exercise in watching a writer's development. As compelling as I thought the first entire book eventually turned out to be, I think Steve really found his voice for the series with the second novel, which was a quantum leap over the first. That's the advantage I've had in scripting the comic series: I've used the narrative styling of the subsequent books to inform the way I script the series.

Q: Describe your part in creating an issue of the Marvel adaptation.

A: I receive the plot outline from Robin at the same time as everyone else. I read it over and if I have any comments, concerns and observations, I voice them. I've had to do that less and less since Robin's writing has gotten so much better over the years. In terms of actual production, scripting an issue takes me less than a day.

I've never actually written script over someone else's plot before. But there's plenty of precedent. You see it all the time in television, for instance. A "story by" credit that is different from the "screenplay" credit. It doesn't happen quite as frequently in comics, but it does from time to time.

Q: Do the artists provide you with some amount of space to enter your text?

A: It's standard practice for artists to go light on scenery in the upper half of the panel since that's where the majority of word balloons are going to go. I've been doing this for a while, so I can get pretty innovative with where to put the word balloons. Basically I place the balloons on B&W copies of the art using Magic Marker and then fax them to the editors, who are able to use them as guides for the letterer. I never feel constrained. I've been doing this for way too long.

Q: Were there times when you found the story going in a different direction than you'd imagined when reading the books?

A: There were any number of times that I was surprised and intrigued with things that Robin came up with. I think, though, considering the admittedly different requirements of novels versus graphic novels, that the comics have been remarkably faithful. If nothing else, one of the reasons I developed the idea of a narrator was because King fans are accustomed to reading. They read a *lot*. And King's books are narratively packed. I wanted people reading Dark Tower comics to have an experience akin to reading the novels. Having a narrative voice enabled me to have a natural reason to pack more words on a page in order to accommodate fan expectations for a Stephen King–related work.

Q: Is the process different for issues dealing with parts of the story that aren't direct adaptations of King's novels?

A: The difference is that I don't have to have the novel next to me. When we're doing stories that have already been told, I feel obligated to use as much of King's narrative as possible. Sometimes it's had some amusing results. One review writer swore that I had no feel for King's narrative at all, and he held up as an example of that a dialogue exchange that I had lifted word for word from King's prose.

I more or less lifted the tone from King's writing in *Wolves of the Calla*. There were townspeople there who spoke in a certain cadence that I thought would be a good style to adopt. Since the series has such scope, I felt having a narrative voice would enable me, as a matter of practicality, to cover gaps in the visual storytelling since there was *so much* to convey—especially in the beginning—that I felt it would be a handy tool to provide a unifying style. So in my head, I pictured a group of cowboys along the trail, and they're talking about different legends of Mid-World, and the name that keeps coming up is Roland's. And I figure there's this one guy, the eldest of the group, hearing all these conflicting stories. And he spits out a wad of chaw and growls, "All them stories are wrong . . . and all them stories are right. I'll tell ya about Roland, the last of the gunslingers. Starts with a desert. A man in black is running across it, and the gunslinger's following him . . ." And off we go.

Q: Were you more nervous about King's reaction to the results, or the reactions of longtime fans of the series?

A: King. Unquestionably. It's impossible even under the best of circumstances to satisfy everyone. In this case, though, the only person whose opinion I cared about was Steve. If he was happy with it, that was what mattered. I'm reasonably sure everyone else on the project feels the same way. We're producing this comic for an audience of one. If he's happy with it, we're happy with it. If the fans love it, hey, bonus.

Q: Were there particular scenes or story arcs that you looked forward to adapting?

A: The original story line involving Susan that had such long-term ramifications for Roland and also the story line we're doing now, The Way Station, with the introduction of Jake.

Q: Were there open questions from the novels that weren't answered by the graphic novels that you wish there'd been an opportunity to explore?

A: The biggest question is the fate of Rhea of the Cöos. To my mind, she looms almost as large in Roland's personal history, in terms of villainy, as the man in black does. Yet we have no details of their final confrontation other than a passing mention that he had killed her at some point. I would *love* to do a one-off issue with Robin (and, one would hope, Steve's input) that told that story. If for no other reason than that I hated Rhea more than any other villainous character in the series, but we never got to see her get hers.

Q: Did the way you work change in the second series, when different artists became involved?

A: It didn't, really. The narrative style I developed was pretty much artist-proof. That's another one of the reasons I came up with it. Some are better storytellers than others. The narrator serves as a means of leveling the playing field. With the stronger storytellers, the narrator serves to set the scene, fill out details. With the storytellers who aren't quite as clear visually, the narrator can inform the reader of what isn't being shown.

Q: What are your impressions of Roland? Do you find him hard to like at times?

A: Sometimes, yes. He's obsessed. A zealot, an extremist. He cares about two things only: getting to the Dark Tower and catching the man in black. And the latter mostly serves the former, when you get down to it. Roland may indeed be hard to like at times, but he is easy to understand when you think about the idea that we all have our obsessions. He's just an obsession taken to the extreme.

Q: What has the fan reaction been like?

A: The fans have been effusive to me in their praise when I see them at conventions, and I've also seen mostly positive reviews here and there. The midnight launch parties were amazing. The first one I went to was at Midtown Comics in Manhattan. It was the dead of winter, it was midnight, and there were arctic-level winds blowing through the concrete canyons of Manhattan. I figured we'd get zero turnout. And yet there were over a hundred fans there, thrilled for the opportunity. It was an absolute blast.

Q: Did you ever get feedback from King regarding your work?

A: There were some line edits (including, to my amusement, Steve editing things that were taken verbatim from the books, which just proves that art is never finished, only abandoned) and general comments about the narrative voice that I'd adopted.

The entire team did the series launch at New York Comic Con. We were waiting in the green room when King showed up. You'd expect that someone of his level would have an entire entourage of handlers, but no, in he walked, and it was, "Hi, I'm Steve," and he's shaking people's hands, utterly unassuming. Believe me, I know writers with one tenth the success of Stephen King and ten times the attitude. It was the first opportunity I had to speak with him about my work on the series, and I was so nervous and, frankly, needy, asking him if he was pleased with my scripting. And he put his hands on either side of my face like a benediction and said, "You're doing a great job." Which was good because right before he said that, I thought he was about to snap my neck. And you know the roomful of people would have covered for him. "Yeah, Peter tripped and fell wrong. Tragic thing."

Later, when we were on the panel, one fan in the audience stood up and said, "I just wanted to say that Stephen King is my favorite novel writer and Peter David is my favorite comic writer, so this series is a dream come true for me." And totally spontaneously, Steve and I high-fived each other. Understand that, to me, it was practically yesterday that I was just another fan, an aspiring writer, standing in line at a Stephen King book signing, and now I was on a panel with him, high-fiving him. How cool is that?

JAE LEE

Jae Lee started working for Marvel comics when he was eighteen. He quit art school without a backup plan, worked up a portfolio and took a four-hour train ride to a convention in NYC. Since then, he has worked on series such as Spider-Man, Batman, Uncanny X-Men, Fantastic Four and a book he both wrote and drew called *Hellshock*.

He has worked on projects outside of comics, including ad campaigns and novel covers. He also illustrated the Donald M. Grant limited edition of *The Wind Through the Keyhole*. At the time of this interview, which was conducted via e-mail in March 2012, he was working for DC Comics on a book called *Ozymandias*, one of the prequels to *Watchmen*.

Q: **Were you familiar with the Dark Tower series before you started working on The Gunslinger Born?**

A: I never read the series in its entirety until I got the job. *Wizard and Glass* was my favorite book, so I was fortunate the project revolved around that. And, of course, I'd read most of his classics, *It* being a favorite.

Q: **How did you find out about the Marvel project?**

A: Joe Quesada called me up one day and asked if I'd want to work on a Stephen King book. I was floored. Now, the pressure was on to work up some sample pages to present them to Stephen. I didn't want to get my hopes up too high in case I didn't get it.

Q: **How did you approach the proof-of-concept project for this presentation?**

A: I was told to illustrate the opening sequence to *The Gunslinger*. I had something like two weeks to do it, and I squandered most of that time suffering from artist's block. Then, at the last minute, my survival instinct kicked in.

Q: **Did that early work define the style of the graphic novels, or did you step back and consider the overall scope of the project and start fresh again?**

A: So much of the opening sequence was sheer luck. Once I started work on the first issue, I had to take a very deliberate approach and start fresh. In fact, I ended up redoing one of the sample pages to fit better with what I was doing.

Q: Was it a deliberate decision to use a traditional layout for the pages?

A: I didn't want the reader to be confused about what panel to read next. There were going to be a certain amount of people picking these comics up, never ever having read a comic before, so I made all the panels horizontal to make each panel a mini–movie screen. I stuck with it for the entire run, but realized that approach had a number of limitations. Mainly, it was really difficult squeezing in a full body shot with that kind of approach.

Q: How do you attack a script in terms of layout and panel design?

A: Robin provided a loose plot of each volume. I had to interpret them and break them down into pages and panels. Once the art was complete, I sent them off to Peter to script.

Q: How did you and Richard Isanove interact during the illustration process?

A: I wasn't sure how well our styles would mesh at first, but when I saw what he did with the sample pages, I was blown away. And we never looked back. It became a symbiotic relationship.

Q: Do you do studies of characters or scenes before you attack what will become the final pages?

A: Yes. I do rough layouts for every page. I don't make them too tight, because that only leads to disappointment when I do the finished pencils because the tight pencils will never have the same energy or flow the sketches had and that can be infuriating.

Q: Do you prefer working on established characters or do you like to introduce new ones?

A: I preferred working on characters that I could use descriptions to guide me. If the character isn't described in detail, there's more responsibility on my shoulders and that can get scary.

Q: How long does it take to create a typical issue?

A: It varies tremendously. I would love to say I can do a book in thirty days, but I'd be lying.

Q: How much back-and-forth was there among you and your collaborators?

A: We all wanted to be faithful to the source material, so we were all open to suggestions. We just wanted to do the best we could.

Q: Do you have a favorite panel or sequence from your work on the series?

A: I'd have to say the fight sequence between Roland and Cort in the first issue of Gunslinger Born.

Q: Is it different illustrating a novel?

A: The stuff I did for Marvel was a comic book. This is very different. This is a novel accompanied by a number of full-page illustrations. Some are in color, some in black-and-white. I think close to twenty images. I did the cover as well. All the line art is hand drawn and the coloring was beautifully rendered by my wife, June Chung, digitally. Few things I've worked on are as cool as doing the illustrations for *The Wind Through the Keyhole*.

RICHARD ISANOVE

Richard Isanove colored every issue of the Marvel graphic novel adaptations, providing a consistent look and feel to the series over its nearly six-year publication run. He was also the sole illustrator for the Fall of Gilead series, *The Sorcerer* and Sheemie's Tale.

Isanove is originally from Bordeaux, France, where he was introduced to American comic books. When he was eleven, he told his school class that he wanted to be either a comic book artist for Marvel or an astronaut. Both of these professions seemed equally unlikely for a kid growing up in France.

He attended École Nationale Supèrieure des Arts Décoratifs (ENSAD) in Paris for five years, where he studied fine arts geared toward animation. Because he spoke English (his mother is British), he was able to get a post as an exchange student at California Institute of the Arts (CalArts) in Los Angeles in 1994, where he also studied animation.

When San Diego–based comic book studio Homage opened Top Cow in LA, Isanove—a longtime comic book fan—applied for a job, though he was still in school. He was hired based on his paintings and was introduced to the world of computer coloring. After Top Cow, he received an offer to work on Daredevil for Marvel. It was his childhood dream come true.

He met his wife—who works in animation as an editor—and has remained in the United States ever since, although his wife's job has moved them around a lot over the past four years, including a year back in Bordeaux. He has done over five hundred covers for Marvel, including work on just about every title and character. He has done major series of Spider-Man, Wolverine and the X-Men. He started developing a computer painting technique that went beyond simple coloring, where he worked directly from pencils instead of inked art while working on Wolverine Origins in 2001.

The following interview was conducted via telephone in November 2011.

Q: Was it a big transition to move from animation into comics?

A: Not really. Both deal with storytelling. We do what animators do in layouts or storyboards. Animation is the more tedious part of it. Doing the storyboards and figuring out how to tell the story was always my favorite part. The biggest challenge and the most interesting part. When I drew some episodes of Dark Tower, it was always the most exciting part. There's about a week of just doing layouts and sketches, figuring out how to tell the story in pictures. After that, it's almost a routine. It's still interesting, but the most stimulating part is doing the storytelling. And that's common to both animation and comics.

Q: Because of the way the Dark Tower is being created, you actually have more creative input into the layout than a traditional comic because Robin Furth is just providing outlines.

A: It reads almost like a short story. It says SCENE ONE and then it's a few paragraphs of describing what happens in the scene with bits of dialogue, but it's more prose than a scenario. It's really great. It would be harder now to work any other way because it's so cool. She's very open to suggestion. We're working on the one-shot right now about Sheemie. I'm able to negotiate with her to get things I want to draw. We shape the story together. Often, also, to put everything she puts in would take forty-eight pages and we only have twenty-two to twenty-eight. You're allowed to do the cuts yourself, but I like to go back and forth with her until we are both happy with what there is. There's been a lot of back-and-forth and deciding what we keep and what to cut out and how to tell that thing more efficiently, or what would be more interesting visually, and then she just rewrites it until we're both happy with it. It's a very satisfying work process. She's so easygoing and very enthusiastic about everything.

Q: Were you familiar with Stephen King's work when you were asked to work on the Dark Tower series?

A: I used to date a girl in college who was a huge Stephen King fan and she always wanted me to read *The Gunslinger*. She was such a fan of it, I frowned on it just to bust her chops. I started listening to books on tape when I was working on X-Men and Daredevil. That's when I listened to my first Stephen King. It was *Bag of Bones*, and he read it himself. I was looking for books that authors read themselves. I thought it was really cool. I loved it, and ever since, probably at least a third of the books I've listened to on tape were Stephen King's.

Q: How did you react when you were offered the chance to work on a project with Stephen King?

A: After Wolverine Origins, I thought, okay, that was my Mount Everest. There was so much publicity about it and it was such a big seller that I didn't know how to top it. Then I got Neil Gaiman's *1602* and I said, okay, cool, I get to work with Neil Gaiman. How was I going to top that? The next thing I know I'm working with Stephen King. I don't know what else. Maybe I'm going to get the new Bible to illustrate or something.

Joe Quesada knew I was a big Stephen King fan. I had already talked about it with him. Once I said, "Why don't you guys get Stephen King to write something for you?" At the time that's when Stephen King had decided to retire. So they thought, it's not going to happen. Then Quesada called me back a few years later. "You're a big fan of Stephen King, aren't you? What do you say about coloring a few pages by next week?"

Q: Short notice for a very important presentation.

A: Yeah. They called me on Tuesday and the next Wednesday King was supposed to come in. Jae started drawing the pages. They started coming in on Friday, I think. It was supposed to be three pages. Then it became four pages. Then it was four pages and a cover. It just kept adding up.

King was coming to the Marvel office on Wednesday morning at nine a.m. Since I'm on the West Coast, it was six in the morning for me. They had to put the whole presentation together before, and they wanted to print it out on big boards with a fake "The Dark Tower" to pretend they were doing a whole cover. We were just cranking, and it turned out that Jae finished the cover on Tuesday night. I was still coloring the pages. He sent it in, and I had too many windows open and my computer crashed just as I was uploading the last cover. I had just finished that huge background of the double-page spread on pages three and four. Because of the way it crashed, I was able to recover the file. It was a miracle. I had worked for four to six hours on that background. It was this massive thing of clouds. I was trying to show off. I was like, okay, what do I do good? Clouds! Clouds and sunset and all that. And it worked, because I guess in that first interview Stephen King was saying that when he saw the purples and all that, that's when he was sold.

It was really cool because Jae was a big fan of the books, too. I'd read pretty much everything I could get my hands on except the Dark Tower. Since it started to seep into the other books, I knew I had to sit down and listen to it. There's a copy of *The Gunslinger* that King had recorded, but I had the one recorded by Frank Muller. I had tried a couple of times and I just couldn't get into it. The tone is so different from everything else he does. It was not what I wanted in a Stephen King book. When I started working on it, of course, I played it through. And, actually, *The Drawing of the Three* is probably my all-time favorite of his books. Once I got into it, I kind of enjoyed the first one, but the second one, I was so excited about it. I really loved it.

I like that you can connect to his characters right away. Within a couple of pages, you feel you understand the characters because they're always bright, or people that you can relate to because they always do the right thing but still things are bigger than them. It's not like in horror movies. People jump out just as the monster is coming. No, his characters stay hidden, but they still get fucked. They react like you would. Especially in *Bag of Bones*. All the feelings that he was tapping into are so realistic that within a few pages I was totally engrossed in the book.

And that's usually how it works. But in the Dark Tower, since it's also told in such a descriptive way, it takes a while to get into it. The tone is almost grandiloquent. I listened to it twice from beginning to end and bits and pieces, depending on what we were working on. I wanted to refresh my memory on the scenes. The second time I listened to *The Gunslinger,* I enjoyed it greatly because now I knew who Roland was and I was just happy to be with him again. That's the thing: there's not much character development in it. You discover him through the story. But once you know the character, you enjoy *The Gunslinger* much more. In the Tull story, he's kind of a jerk. He really grows as the book goes. Even in *The Drawing of the Three,* he's still kind of there, but because he is weakened physically, you relate to him. I think it really was a stroke of genius; cutting his fingers off at the beginning of the story just suddenly made him human when he was this archetypal jerk, a guy that guns down people just because he doesn't like them. As it went, suddenly he became more human and from then on you cared about him. As soon as he gets wounded, suddenly the whole paradigm changes on him and it really becomes very engrossing.

Q: Without the inking step, how is the pencil art conserved when you paint it digitally?

A: The line is still there. That's why I like to work from pencils—the frailty of the line shows more. When you look at a painting, even at a Frazetta, sometimes you can still see the line appearing through the paint. That's what I'm trying to do—have the color cover everything but still have the line show through. I put a color in the line art so it becomes one with the color instead of being a layer of black with a layer of color underneath. I'm trying to re-blend the two as if it was in the painting. Use the line art as a contrast element, not just as an incisive line. It's not just there to separate the red from the blue. There's going to be a little bit of purple in it so the two colors blend within the line art. It's a darker value of the color, but it's usually not totally different. It's part of the color vocabulary.

With Jae, the work we did at the beginning was to integrate the blacks, because he likes to use big black areas. I started to put that splatter into it. I use a lot of toothbrush splatters. I have five different patterns and densities of toothbrush patterns that I scanned that I reuse. Then I fill with color and I superimpose them to get different densities. That allows me to integrate the line art into the color, because color is put into the line art.

Q: Is this a process that would only work with a computer?

A: When I used to paint, I always liked using a toothbrush. It's a great finishing instrument. It gives a grittiness to the page. It gives textures and makes it a little bit more interesting. I used something similar on Wolverine Origins, but I was using a canvas texture. I scanned a canvas where I did some rough gray-scale painting on it. I used that texture to have two layers of color. When you look at a canvas painting, you put on a first coat of paint and then, if you go with a drier brush, you're going to have the full color; and then, as there is less paint on the brush, only the top layer of the canvas is going to be affected, so the grooves keep the original color and the second layer of color only appears on the upper layer of the canvas. It creates a pattern and that's an easy way to blend colors. I always thought that was a very interesting way to have two different values, two different colors, appearing at the same time, like a screen painting. That's what I was trying to do with the splatters because Jae said he didn't want me to use that effect.

On *1602* I did it by using etchings, because in the drawing he did all of these little etchings at forty-five degrees, so I tried to mimic that with the color, so the whole book is just made with forty-five-degree etchings of different colors. It seems almost impressionist. By putting two colors next to each other, you get a third color. Instead of mixing them, I would have a green and a slightly bluer green and you come up with an interesting aqua with lots of textures to it. That's what I'm trying to attain there. Jae wanted something different on *The Dark Tower*. He didn't like the canvas, and I was fed up with the etchings. I wanted to do something else anyway. I always used splatter as a finishing tool and I said, how about making that the main thing? Since the world is coming to an end, that will give this impression of having dust in the air all the time. Pretty much it's like colored dust all over the whole book. I liked the idea from the Ridley Scott movie *Legend*, with Tom Cruise. There's always dust in the air in that movie. There are always particles floating around the characters to create depth. You could actually feel the light. I thought it was a perfect vehicle to explore that, to have this impression of thick air. No matter where you go, you've got this dust that's defining the space.

Q: **Do you have color themes for characters or settings?**

A: Definitely. Each character has a color scheme, usually. Roland, in the first series, he was pretty much the only one in black-and-white. I would always put hints of colors on people except for the Coffin Hunters, who were all in black. All the main characters have a different scheme, at least for every story arc. Depending on where they are, I try to assign them a very recognizable color so right away it gives a visual cue. It goes with the storytelling aspect of it. If you have a blue character circulating through the page, your eye follows him.

At first, Roland was wearing yellow, Cuthbert was red and Alain had this blue, so I had the three primary colors. He had a blue handkerchief around his neck. So it was like the three primary colors. No matter where they went. Everything else was earth tones and black-and-white, except for those three guys that had primary colors. As it went, I liked that Roland was always in black-and-white. His shirt went from yellow to white. Then he was always wearing this white shirt and he was the black-and-white character when everything else around him was in color, or very strongly color-themed. Now, when he's grown up, he wears the primary colors because everything is always grayish or brownish. He's dressed like Superman in the middle of all that. I tone down the yellow depending on the general color scheme. I keep the color scheme of the pages in the greens. I'll tone down the shirt, which is yellow, and the pants, which are blue. Make the pants more blue-gray and the shirt a little more brownish, but then the neckerchief is really bright red so he stands out in a page no matter what happens. Since I have the three main colors, whatever I need to pop, I pop and just fade the rest away. The idea is that he's always identifiable right away when you look at the page, that he doesn't get lost in the page.

The main criteria for the color scheming is to make sure that the storytelling is clear and that the mood is right. I usually start by doing the background. I look at the composition and I build the clouds and my color schemes around the mood of the scene. You look at the colors and you can tell how they make you feel. I gravitate toward colors if it's a happy scene, which there's not that many of in this. If it's more of a disgusting or a sad scene, I build up colors until I feel by looking at it the way the scene is supposed to feel. Then I fine-tune it and I work from there. I start to add the characters. I put in the line art and I start working from there. It's mostly about achieving good storytelling and the proper mood of the scene.

Q: The layout for the Dark Tower graphic novels is more basic than some of the contemporary graphic novels.

A: From the beginning, Jae only did horizontal panels. The idea was that it was readable by anybody that picked up the book. Newcomers to comics have a hard time reading them because the panels go in every direction. You have to learn how to read them. You have panels inside of panels going into something, and if your eye is not trained to do it, you don't know how to do it. We knew we were talking to people who maybe hadn't read comics before, so we had to make it very easily readable and have the most simple layouts possible, one plane after the other. When Michael Lark did that wide-screen thing, he fell into that same tradition of one shot after the other. It's almost like a storyboard. Just go down the page. That was really in the right spirit for the book. That's one of the key reasons why the book works. I can give it to my mom and she's able to read it.

Q: How much do you interact with the pencil artists during this process?

A: With Jae, we talked at length because we worked for four years on the first thirty issues. That takes a lot of your life. We talked a lot on the phone. But now, with the rotating pencilers, it's been a little bit less of that. In a way, it's gotten more interesting for me because I have to reinvent a little bit every time, to adapt to the new pencilers. To find a way to make their work gel with mine so we can keep the look of the book consistent, but at the same time still be faithful to what they are trying to do.

My learning process is figuring out how the artist likes to light things. Some people are very inconsistent. They'll have one front character lit from the left and the background is lit from the right. It looks great in black-and-white, but once you put the color on it, it doesn't make any sense anymore. The liberties they take with lighting become obvious, so you have to figure out how to make it still work and figure out different ways of making the light seem coherent.

Jae draws better than I do, but he looks for the same thing in artwork, which makes my work very easy. We think the same way about lighting. He has a very strong sense of composition and light. I don't even have to plan what I am doing because I know things are going to be exactly where they should be. I look at it for two minutes and then I jump on it and know that there are no traps in it. Everything I need to build up my color composition is going to be in the line art, and I can just rely on it. He's such a solid artist that you can just go blindly on him and it'll always work.

Most of the people they've hired are people who ink themselves or, like Michael Lark, work very closely with their inker. He draws and he uses 3-D backgrounds, so the inker meshes the two together. If I had to do it, that would be much more work. It makes it easier if the texture work has been done on the background. That integrates the character much better than if he sends me the characters and the backgrounds on separate layers. His inker and he seem to have that process down where it really looks good. I think he is used to being very controlling on his things. At first he would say, "No, that high-light is too bright." And I'd say, "Why don't you relax? Take a day or two, then come back to it. You'll see." I would do the corrections and I could see that he liked things a little less shiny than other people. Once I got his trust, I was able to go back to my way.

Q: What was your favorite section to work on?

A: The first part was really interesting because it was setting every-thing up. It was the most challenging, intellectually. We worked on it for one year before anybody saw anything. That was really hard. One aspect of comics is instant gratification. You put something out and two weeks later it's in the store. If you messed up something, you say, "Oh, that doesn't work. I have to change it next time." There we worked in the dark. I had no idea how it was going to be perceived, and we didn't know if the book was going to work or not. Spending a year of your life in the dark like that was very weird. But it pushes you to do your best because you say, "Okay, I have no excuse to mess up. I've worked on that. I can't really release a half-finished thing." It's probably the most time I've had to spend on something, because we only did two issues in that time, just be-cause of the insecurity, mostly. Jae wanted to rework every page until it was perfect, and I was doing the same thing. I was spending two, three days on a page just to make sure that I got everything right and that we came out of the gate running, not stumbling.

After that, I really liked the second story arc. That was inter-esting because it was the first original story. Everything else was based on the book. Since I had read the books, all those scenes were already laid out in my brain. Then, suddenly, on The Long Road Home it was all new.

When you were talking about color themes, each scene was very strongly color keyed in a different scheme, every time. For the first run, I made a purpose of not repeating any color scheme unless it was exactly at the same time and at the same place. Each one, I would go back and say, "Have I used exactly those colors? No. Okay, so I can do it"—which was not easy and I probably made some mistakes, but overall it was pretty much the goal.

The Long Road Home, colorwise, that was when I started to really be at ease. Doing original material was really liberating because I didn't have any preconceived images in my head. When the pages were coming in, I was able to do whatever I wanted. Or be spontaneous. There's some pretty cool stuff in there. I was really happy. And, of course, the one I drew. I was so focused on my pencils. I colored it, but I was not as inventive as I could have been, I think. There's always pros and cons to every situation, but the time constraints were so bad that I had to rely on what I knew how to do so I could focus on my drawing.

I love doing Arthur of Gilead. Especially on the backstories when we did all that medieval gun stuff. It's fun to draw the armor and the guns and all those things. It calls for very epic visuals. I just love that stuff. I got these really cool copies of Wild West guns and things like that all over the house. Cowboy hats and swords. My office is a shrine to the Dark Tower. My life revolves around that, or it has for the past six years. I've done a couple of Spider-Man things on the side, but most of what I do is Dark Tower.

Q: What was it like to work on one of the arcs as the solo artist?

It does take a lot out of you to draw pages. I don't know if people realize how much work is involved in doing comics. When I drew Fall of Gilead, it took me about twelve hours to draw a page and then I still had four to eight hours of coloring on top of it. So when you have a twenty-two-page book to do in a month, you don't sleep a lot. The eight months I spent on Fall of Gilead, I gained ten pounds and I got gray hair. I always wanted to do it and I was really glad to do it, but I was totally dead by the end. It took me a month to physically recover from it. I had a month off, but the good thing was that I went back with Jae, who I had been working with for twenty issues by then, so I knew what to do.

I was so happy to get to do Fall of Gilead. I mean, we kill everybody. It was awful. We had to go back and forth over the fine points of somebody's death. For the death of Steven, there was a little back-and-forth between Robin and me. We knew he was stabbed by somebody that was never found. That's all we knew from the book. We had to elaborate the story around that. He's Steven Deschain. He's got to die a hero. He can't really just get stabbed in the back by a traitor. We made up that whole scene where he gets back up again. And then we said, "Well, he has to kill the guy that killed him at least. How do we get rid of the body? He falls out the window when Steven shoots him in the head. There we go; it's solved!"

I gave that book to a friend of mine recently and he went, "Man, that was dark." It's true. You get attached to those characters. They're such heroes. They're bigger than life. And then to see them die so quickly and so irrevocably, every time. Even as a reader, that was one that I really enjoyed. When you see the epic battle coming and you think they're going to win—and, no. You don't see that stuff. We kill everything. The dogs, the babies. Everybody dies. It's great. Robin went out of the way on this. Maybe I shouldn't be reveling so much in massacres, but it was a great story arc.

Filling in the blanks from the books was a stimulating exercise, because you know there are watchful fans reading this thing that are going to catch any mistake that you make, so you have to be very consistent with the book and at the same time manage to make it an interesting story. Robin's way of working is unique and it makes everybody really involved in the process, so it's a very satisfying experience.

Q: Do you have favorite characters?

A: Of all the characters, the man in black/Walter is probably the funnest one to draw. Jae established him as almost androgynous. He's always got this bare chest, and he's very feminine in the way he moves, with his hands raised. He's always moving his hands around. He's got this weird face, with a broken nose and greasy hair. He's starting to bald, but he's always got a very white separation in the middle of it. He's just so greasy, he's great to draw. And he still has to be seductive at the same time, so you can't make him repulsive. We went another direction on the one-shot, but I thought it would have been fun to have "The Tales of Marten," you know, having him like the ghoul from *Creepshow* introducing every story and saying how he's related to it. He's a great character.

I love Cuthbert, too. I like the wise-ass. It's me ten years younger. I have the long hair and everything like him. That's the one I have to least change when I draw him. I've really put myself into him. When I was drawing him, I thought he's always having a joke. Even in the worst time, he's always cracking up a joke. He's a very charming character.

I use my kids as models. We did a backstory of the youth of Rhea at one point. That was my daughter. I made her teeth crooked and all that, so she would look evil. But she was very proud of it. She was six or seven at the time, so she brought it to school and her teacher was like, "Ai! Let's not show it." It was one where she has a shard of glass in the eye with a spatter of blood on her face. He literally jumped out of his seat and grabbed it out of her hand before she could show it to the other kids.

Every time there's a kid, it's one of my kids. My son plays Sheemie and my daughter plays all the other characters in the Sheemie story. It's a family project. They each have a cover that I made with them on it. Matthew has a Sheemie cover in his bedroom. My daughter played Aileen. There's a cover where Cort is all bloody and there's a girl crying behind him, and that was my daughter. I made a printout once and she wanted it in her bedroom, so she has a fat guy bleeding in a chair in her little yellow room with butterflies on the wall.

Every year, when the teacher finds out what I do, they say, "Oh, can you come and do a presentation at the school, to show the kids comics?" Since I've been on the Dark Tower, it's harder to do because it's hard to find a page without blood everywhere. Here's the one with a guy with pustules all over his face. This one is where he gets his hand chopped off. Great! Let's keep going. It's probably the bloodiest book I've ever worked on by far. And that's the worst part—my favorite pages are always the ones where some guy is getting blown up, because you've got some really nice red contrast on the page.

Q: What sort of feedback have you gotten from Stephen King?

A: When we started, he said, "You know what? You're the artists. You do your thing. As long as it doesn't bug me, I'm happy with it." Now they only tell us when there's a problem, and there haven't been that many. Mostly continuity things or using something from another book that we didn't have the rights to. Jae was a big fan, so he wanted to put allusions to other books but he couldn't. I'm down the line, so I get the watered-down thing. They try to resolve any problems before they get to me, which is nice. That's really the job of the editor, so we can just worry about doing the pages.

King sent a note when we did *The Sorcerer*, since it was an offshoot. It was not in the general story line. It was Robin's original story and all that, so he said he really enjoyed it, so that was very cool. I've been very lucky. Every time I'm pulling an all-nighter and I start to bitch, I just think, "You know what? I could be doing something that isn't as much fun," so I just shut up and do it.

MICHAEL LARK

Like Robin Furth, Michael Lark, pencil artist for The Battle of Tull, is originally from Pennsylvania, but considers himself a native Texan. He studied design and advertising at University of North Texas on an art scholarship but found it not to his liking. He wasn't into superheroes as a kid, so he wasn't into comics until he went to the local comic book store with the drummer in his band in the mid-to-late eighties. Here he discovered the independent, alternative black-and-white underground comics of the era and decided he could draw those himself. His first comic was published and his reputation grew through word of mouth. When people offered to hire him to do superhero work, he decided that was a good way to earn a living. He started with DC and then moved to Marvel. His first superhero gig was drawing Superman for a graphic novel written by Roy Thomas. He drew Batman for Gotham Central, and has spent time working on Daredevil, Captain America and the Punisher and Spider-Man during his twenty years in comics.

The following interview was conducted via telephone in November 2011.

Q: Were you familiar with the Dark Tower series before you started working on the Tull book?

A: I was familiar with it, but when they asked me to start working on it, I hadn't read the books. I'm a huge fan of Steve's writing in general. I have a lot of respect for him as a craftsman and as a writer and love his books, but because there were seven books, I had never gotten into them. I started reading when they first started talking to me about it and very quickly came to the Tull story and I e-mailed them and said, "I don't know what you're working on right now, but if you happen to hit that anytime soon, I would love to do that." Sure enough, the timing just happened to be perfect. I'd like to do more on the book. It was one of the most satisfying experiences I've had drawing comics.

Q: What is your process for an issue of The Battle of Tull?

A: Dark Tower is a little different from some others in that Robin writes a plot. She numbers the panels, but she doesn't break them out into pages and she doesn't write finished dialogue. The script might end up being eight, nine, ten pages long. That's what I get. She's got suggested dialogue in there that I think she's pulled directly out of the books. I draw from that. In this case, I'm the penciler. Sometimes I ink my own work. In this case I was just penciling. I have a collaborator that goes over everything in ink, just because of the time constraints of working on a monthly comic. From Robin's plot/outline, I then decide how many pages each scene is going to take up. A lot of times with her plot there will be one thing that she's broken down as one panel that I'll say, well, there's three or four things happening within that little description so I'm going to have to break that into four different panels. And there's sometimes where she'll break things apart that don't necessarily need to be broken apart. I have to sit down and work with the plot that she's given me and figure out how the pages are going to be broken up and how to lay things out by panels. Once I've done that, I start gathering up references and drawing from that.

Q: Some of the other artists sent pencil art to Richard Isanove. How does inking come into the process?

A: When I came into the book, I didn't realize that we really had the option to do that. We ended up doing that on the final cover and I was really happy with the results. The ink is more a traditional way of doing it from the old days with much more simple color separation and printing processes. The black-and-white art would be the black part of the CMYK. The K part of the CMYK. Now we can do a lot more sophisticated stuff with it, and it's really not necessary to do it that way anymore. We still end up doing it that way because it's more traditional. The pencil art doesn't reproduce as well.

Q: The early page layouts were designed in anticipation of people coming to the comics who weren't traditional comic readers. Did you feel you had the flexibility to be more contemporary or experimental with the layouts?

A: I didn't know that. Nobody told me that. It makes sense because I always thought that the way Jae Lee drew it almost looked like illustrations for a story rather than a comic. That's very appropriate for Jae's style of drawing. I actually made the choice because of the fact that I was working on the Tull story, which was almost a straight-up Western with horror and supernatural overtones. I was coming from the same inspiration that Steve had originally, which was the Clint Eastwood spaghetti Westerns. I wanted to use a lot of horizontal panels to get that wide-screen feel. I made a conscious decision to use as many horizontal panel layouts as possible, and sometimes breaking each of those rows into two or three panels if I needed to have some close-ups, or smaller images. That was my decision on it. The way Robin wrote the scripts made it really easy to do that. A lot of writers will give me scripts with seven or eight panels on a page and that's not an option when they do that. I was able to lay out the pages with three, four panels on a page and get that across.

Q: Do you do your own bubbles or areas for dialogue and commentary to be added in later?

A: I normally do that, but because of the fact that Peter David would then write the dialogue after my penciling was done, I didn't have that as an option. I was working from the dialogue that Robin had given me and guessing where things would go. Peter's a pro and he just made everything fit. I think there were a lot of times where I probably didn't give him a whole lot of room and he made it work.

Q: How much did you feel like you could go your own way in depicting Roland? Did you have to refer back to the way the previous artists had made him look?

A: I think they did a really good job designing him and it was really just a matter of aging the character that Jae Lee had drawn. I tried to make him a little rougher around the edges because he was older. His character is becoming a little darker by the time I got to draw him. It was a combination of this young, fresh-faced kid that Jae drew and Clint Eastwood. More like the *Unforgiven*-era Clint Eastwood to me. I grizzled him up a little bit.

Q: What's your approach when it comes to introducing new characters like Allie, Sylvia Pittston or Nort the Weedeater?

A: It was a little intimidating to be working on these characters that I knew people were so familiar with and had visions in their own heads of what they would look like and how they would act. All I could do was try to keep the freshest perspective I could and try to do them justice. I don't know how successful I was. I have yet to have somebody come up and say anything negative, but I did see one forum where somebody was complaining about the fact that we never saw Roland's eyes in the first issue. Which is true, because he has his hat on for the entire issue. He is just shadow down to his nose in the whole first issue.

Nort was easy. The toughest one for me was Allie, because I didn't want her to be ugly. I wanted her to be attractive. I don't know how successful I was. The other characters were pretty easy. Sylvia Pittston was an interesting story. I use models to reference all my characters when I draw. All of the male characters are me. I alter them accordingly. I have an assistant who helps me out, and she was Allie. She was a little thin girl, and I needed somebody bigger than life for Sylvia. I had put out an ad that said I needed a larger-sized female model and had a really hard time getting somebody. I drew the cover that Sylvia is on using somebody that was a friend of a friend, but she wasn't really that interested in being a model. She was just doing it as a favor.

Then I got this response to my ad and went to meet this woman. When we e-mailed each other before we met, she said, what are you working on? And I said I'm working on a thing that Stephen

King has created. I walked in the door and she goes, "It's Dark Tower and I'm going to be Sylvia Pittston, aren't I?" I was like, "Yes, you're hired." To me, she was Sylvia Pittston. She was bigger than life, with this huge personality. She had the crazy wild hair. She was fantastic. She made the character so easy to draw. She just made her come to life for me.

We finished our first session, shooting all the photos for the first issue she was in. I called her up to schedule the session for the second issue that she was in. Just days before I called her she'd been diagnosed with leukemia. It was pretty sad. She came and did the second session but the last one we needed to do, she'd already been undergoing chemo. They had to raise money, and I ended up donating all the pages that I had drawn that had Sylvia Pittston on them to a fund-raiser for them and Steve donated a signed copy of one of the limited-edition hardbacks for them to use for the fund-raiser as well, which was super-nice of him.

Q: Some of your panels, especially toward the end, have a lot of people in them. Do those scenes give you nightmares?

A: Oh, yes. Especially because I'm referencing everything. That opening scene when he's buying the mule in Pricetown was nightmarish to draw. I had to draw an entire town full of people. Then the last issue is one long fight scene with as many people as I could draw in every panel as possible. Men, women and children. It took me a long time to draw that last issue. Probably took me about three times longer than it should have.

Q: How long does a typical issue take you?

A: Ideally they're supposed to be taking about four to six weeks per issue. That one took probably about three months. Just because of all the referencing and trying to make that fight scene flow across twenty-two pages and changing locations—he's running through the town—and having that all make sense. The little things I had to communicate, like when he goes through the barbershop and throws the pot of boiling water at people as they're coming after him. It's a pot of boiling water full of razors that are being disinfected. To communicate all of that in two panels is difficult. I didn't have a lot of space to do it and I'd kind of painted myself into a corner with this "I'm going to do everything wide-screen." I was limiting the number of panels I could draw. It took a lot of work. I spent a lot of time on that last issue.

Q: Do you have a favorite scene or panel?

A: For the better part of a year I got to pretend I was Sergio Leone directing Clint Eastwood. I love the parts where he's just walking and thinking, the traveling parts of it. I could do those big landscapes. I really like the scene at the end of the first issue where he and Allie were in bed for the first time and Sheb is coming up the stairs. I thought that part really worked out nice. My favorite part, though, by far is the scene where Allie is telling the story of Nort. Not when the man in black comes but how Nort became addicted to the weed. I really liked that section. I liked the section with the man in black, too. I loved that whole series. Those five issues were nothing but a pleasure.

Q: How much interaction did you have with Richard Isanove during this process?

A: Richard's great. He's a pro. I felt like Richard defined the visual look of the series because he's been the one consistent thing throughout. At first it was tough to get used to his style because he's rendering so much more than most colorists do. Richard brings so much more to the plate, and it took a little bit to get used to. At first I think I offended him with asking him to tone it down a little bit. Once I got used to what he was doing, though, it was fun to see what we could do to push him here and there and to leave things for him to take care of. Like I said, to the point where, the last cover, I just penciled it and let Richard do his thing. And it was great. I wish I had just penciled the whole thing now—no offense to my inker, who's fantastic. I think it would have been interesting to see the results of that.

Q: How is your process different when you're doing a cover versus the interior?

A: Covers are a completely different beast. I am much more comfortable telling a story. Covers are more about design and grabbing people's attention off the shelves. This series, because it's a little more sophisticated than your typical comic book, it was a little easier for my sensibilities to do the covers—not that I'm such a sophisticated guy—but they didn't have to be jumping off the page and loud and in your face like a lot of comic book covers have to be. So I was able to settle back and find representative images to draw. At that point it was just a matter of finding a cool angle or something like that. The man in black was fun. Everybody was like, oh, his eyes are so scary. And I was like, "Those are *my* eyes!"

I was really proud of those covers. I'm not a great cover artist and those were just fun covers to draw. That last one, I think I did three, maybe four versions, because we threw several things at the wall to see what would stick. The editors were fine with what I was doing, but I kept rejecting it until we finally hit on that one. There's an image like that at the end of the fourth issue, where he's walking through town and nobody's there, which is such a classic Western scene. The shutters banging in the wind. The deserted town. I knew I wanted to do that close-up of him pushing his jacket back so he can get easy access to his gun because he's sensing trouble. As soon as I drew that image in the issue, I said, "Oh, that's the cover." The editors were like, "Yeah, but it needs something extra." As I started working on the issue and paying attention to him getting wounded, the blood came to me and that became the cover I'm happiest with. I hope they use that one for the trade, but they'll probably use the first one.

Q: **Do you listen to music when you work?**

A: I had a four-hour playlist of Ennio Morricone Western movie soundtrack music that I listened to the entire time. That stuff is cool anyway. I listened to a lot of soundtrack music while I was working on it. I ended up listening to some action movie soundtracks while I was working on the last issue.

Q: **Do you have any thoughts on a movie adaptation of the Dark Tower series?**

A: They should hire me to do all the storyboards! I think it will be cool. I'm looking forward to seeing it. It will be interesting to see how somebody else does a film version of these sets that I've drawn. Robin told me that they'd shown some of the work I did on Sheb's honky-tonk to Ron Howard, so we'll see what they end up doing.

I wish I could say that I'm a big Dark Tower geek, but unfortunately I'm not. I'm a big Stephen King fan, but those are ones that I had not gotten into at the time we started doing this. I like the first one because it's more like his older, more minimal style than the other ones. My favorite stuff of his is 'Salem's Lot and Carrie and The Shining. When they came out, they must have knocked people's socks off. People must not have ever seen anything like that. I get the impression that they're all very personal to him. I really like that about them. I felt that stylistically, The Gunslinger was similar to those in writing style. The Shining is one of my favorite books of all time. That's just a great novel, period. Forget horror novel. Forget genres. That's just a great novel.

STEFANO GAUDIANO

Stefano Gaudiano, who inked The Battle of Tull, was born in Milan and lived in Rome until his first year of high school, at which time he moved to the United States. He has no formal art training, describing himself as self-taught. He was introduced to Marvel comics while he was still living in Italy. When he noticed the credits at the beginning of the issues, he realized that people actually drew them—a machine didn't produce them. He was a huge fan of Stan Lee's superhero creations and the atmosphere of communication between the creators and the fans. He started copying pictures out of the comics and decided by the time he was eleven or twelve that drawing comics was what he wanted to do for a living.

He started self-publishing comics in the 1980s, after he moved to the United States. His first paid work was on a book called Kafka for Renegade Press. A string of small jobs led him to work for bigger publishers and his childhood dream became reality. Being an inker has given him the opportunity to work on a wide variety of characters, including Batman, Daredevil, Spider-Man, the Mighty Thor, Iron Man, Captain America. As a freelance artist, he also does newspaper illustrations and storyboards for animation and video games.

The following interview was conducted via telephone in October 2011.

Q: How do you describe the job of the inker?

A: The inker is usually either an artist or an apprentice, somebody who, instead of penciling—drawing a whole book from a script or writing and drawing his own book—is assisting another artist to finish the drawings. Originally it was a necessary step for printing because the technology was such that you couldn't reproduce pencil work. Everything had to be done in clean lines that could be reproduced through metal engravings. Inking was developed to turn sketches into something very clean and crisp that the printer could reproduce.

Now the job of an inker is almost redundant because there are techniques that will allow art to be reproduced from pencil. But Michael Lark, who is the penciler that I worked with on Dark Tower and also my main collaborator on other books for Marvel and DC, likes to work with me because it frees him up to do a little bit more of the design work on the content. He leaves the pencils finished enough that I can tell what he wants, but he saves himself some work by passing the unfinished drawings on to me so that I can add textures, fill in the blacks and clean things up a little bit. It's his choice to work with me to save himself some work on the back end and be able to do a little bit more of the heavy lifting creatively at the outset.

I find inking to be a lot more manageable ever since I had children. It's the sort of job that I can put aside and get back to without having to go through the process of getting back into the creative mode. Some people have an easier time penciling. I was talking to Sean Philips, who did one of the arcs, too, and he's amazing. He can pencil and ink books and he's got a family but somehow he manages to keep his head clear and get all of his work done and it seems to be something that he can handle. I found after I had children that I just could not snap in and out of the drawing mind-set easily at all, so ever since then I've done mostly inks.

Q: Does he send you an electronic image, or do you get a physical pencil sketch?

A: I used to get physical pencil sketches, but ever since I started working with Michael I've been working from just JPGs. I turn them into blue lines and print them out. Then I ink in black and when I scan them, the blue disappears and we're just left with the black lines. It's a great system because it allows me to make little changes that I need to make and it saves me time erasing and cleaning up the pages. After I've scanned the inks, I send them to Marvel and Richard Isanove colors them and they get lettered and that's a book.

Q: Were you familiar with the Dark Tower series before you started working on The Battle of Tull?

A: No, I wasn't. I was of course aware of Stephen King's work but haven't read a lot of his work. I wasn't familiar at all with the Dark

Tower series, so I got *The Gunslinger* book that the episode we illustrated was taken from and read that, but that was the extent of
my awareness of it.

Q: Do you have any favorite scenes from The Battle of Tull?

A: I love the whole part of the first book that shows Roland approaching Tull. It's got a great spaghetti Western feel, going through the
desert. It's a great atmosphere. I was listening to Sergio Leone
movie soundtracks while I was working on the books. Michael did
a great job cinematically introducing the sets.

I also enjoyed the scenes of Roland on the mule going through
the desert. Richard did a great job on the very last page, creating
that atmosphere of moonlight as Roland rides off into the desert
with Tull in the distance. That was probably my favorite stuff to
work on and visually I think it worked beautifully.

One that gave me a lot of problems—almost made it difficult
to finish the book—was a horrible scene where Roland confronts
Sylvia Pittston in her shack. That was brutal. I thought the scene
was very powerful and I love what Michael did with it, but it was
almost inexplicable to me. I was going through the motions of finishing the art and feeling really uncomfortable with the whole
thing. In spite of those negative feelings, that scene with Sylvia
Pittston stuck out in my mind as one of the best scenes.

Something that added heaviness to Roland's interaction with
Sylvia Pittston is that Michael uses models for some of the characters, and the model that he used was a big fan of the series. But she
was diagnosed with cancer while she was working on the book
with Michael and that added the pall of heaviness on the series as
we finished it up.

I'm not familiar with the Dark Tower series as a whole. After
drawing that scene, I just couldn't understand Roland's motivations and the nature of Roland's character. It made it difficult when
we got to the end, the massacre at Tull. I couldn't see Roland in any
kind of positive light. I'd be curious to see what the character arc is
going to work out like. There's obviously more to Roland than
what I got to see, so I'm looking forward to exploring that eventually as a reader.

LAURENCE CAMPBELL

Laurence Campbell, artist for The Way Station, started working in graphic design in London at the age of sixteen, before studying illustration at Central Saint Martin's Art College. He continued to tutor at the college for the next decade while drawing comics in his spare time, including work for *2000 AD*, a British weekly comic, and Caliber and Image comics. He joined Marvel in 2006. Before working on Roland, he drew other dark, moody characters like the Punisher, Wolverine and Moon Knight.

The following interview was conducted via e-mail in October 2011.

Q: What is your history with King's Dark Tower series?

A: Marvel approached me about drawing an arc of the Dark Tower as I was finishing *Marvel Universe vs. Wolverine*. I was very excited about this as I had a paperback copy of *The Gunslinger* from years ago and the opportunity to work on the Stephen King graphic novels was something I was very much interested in. I can still remember picking up the book and being very excited by the idea of a cowboy in a fantasy setting. I remember the cover pulling me in. I also remember my friend basing his Dungeons & Dragons character on the gunslinger! I now own all the graphic novels and have really enjoyed them. I've not read any of King's other books, though the TV adaptation of *'Salem's Lot* scared the hell out of me when I was a kid and I still get a chill when I hear tapping on the window.

Q: What are you doing for The Way Station?

A: I'm doing pencils, covers and inks. I'm very excited to be working with Richard. I think his coloring is amazing. In my opinion, he is an essential part of the book. Before starting my arc on The Way Station, I was looking at the other artists who I was going to follow and felt that Sean Phillips and Michael Lark brought a real cowboy essence to the book while Jae Lee, I felt, brought a more fantasy iconic look to the book. I have tried to find a balance between the two styles. It is very flattering to be part of a project with such established artists. I'm loving the way the story has been planned out and am really enjoying the art. It really is a great package.

Q: Do you know how you were selected for The Way Station?

A: Ralph Macchio (the editor of the Dark Tower series) was my editor for *Marvel Universe vs. Wolverine.* I was offered the opportunity to draw the arc as I was coming to the end of my previous strip. I pretty much jumped at the chance.

Q: How much are you influenced by the depictions of the characters created by other artists?

A: I bought all the trade paperbacks and then researched and found reference to get the feel of the story right. Obviously you have to respect how other artists have drawn the characters. Generally, though, I am just drawing what I feel is right for the story. I think a lot of credit goes to the editors who have picked all of the artists, as I think there is a line of similarity between all of us.

Q: How did you approach Jake Chambers, whom you debuted in the graphic novels?

A: When I first read the script, I found Jake Chambers's backstory very touching. I felt that while I wanted to read it, a part of me didn't want to, as it gets pretty dark. I've just tried to make Jake an innocent-looking boy. At this moment I am drawing the point where Jake first appears.

Q: What is your process after you receive the script?

A: The script I've been given is not a full script, more of an old "Marvel style" script, which just gives directions. At first I found this a surprise and a challenge. But now I really enjoy it as I get the chance to pace the book for myself. Because the story is adapted from a book, it does give you the opportunity to be a little bit experimental with page layouts but not to the detriment of the storytelling—that must always come first.

You don't get too much time when drawing the comic, but you do have to spend time planning and working out layouts, costumes, etc. The more time I spend on this in the beginning, the more time is saved later on, and getting ideas down on paper can confirm thoughts in my head. I'm only on issue one at the moment, but have enjoyed drawing the open scenes of the desert. I also enjoyed Roland fighting the desert dogs.

Q: **How much do you interact with Richard Isanove during the creative process?**

A: When I send him the pages, I send him my thoughts of how I see the scene and possible color ideas. However, the final product is down to Richard and I have total faith in him. I purposely made the artwork more spacious on The Dark Tower because I think this works to Richard's strengths.

Q: **How much do you interact with Robin Furth during the process?**

A: I have e-mail contact with Robin and send the artwork to her to be approved. She always has a great knowledge of the Dark Tower, and when I have any questions, she's been incredibly helpful.

Q: **Are you at all influenced by *The Punisher* in the way you approach Roland?**

A: There is a certain mood and presence that *The Punisher* has that I guess can be seen in Roland, though maybe not as dark. Just to add, I'm really excited about drawing the strip. It's an honor to be part of the team.

DARK TOWER GUIDE
TO MANHATTAN

The Dark Tower series features some universes that are similar to our own. There is Keystone Earth, where Stephen King lives, but there is also the reality of Eddie Dean, which has Co-Op City in Brooklyn instead of the Bronx.

Manhattan is the *ka-tet*'s most frequent Earth-side destination. Eddie Dean, Odetta Holmes and Jake Chambers all come from New York. After leaving 'Salem's Lot, Father Callahan went to New York, and Irene Tassenbaum lives there. Even John Cullum went there once, when he was in the army.

The *ka-tet*'s primary focus in Manhattan is a neighborhood called Turtle Bay, the area between 41st and 54th streets from Lexington Avenue to the East River. Though many of the businesses mentioned in the series are fictitious, there really is a black office tower at the corner of Second Avenue and 46th and, nearby, a pocket park with a turtle statue. For a while there was even a construction barricade upon which someone had written "Roland Deschain was here."

If you find yourself in Manhattan with some time on your hands, here are the main sites of interest.

1) **Second Avenue and 46th**: The last piece of property Calvin Tower owns in Manhattan: Lot #298, Block #19. Originally the location of Tom and Gerry's Artistic Deli. Later a vacant lot containing the pink rose that represents the Dark Tower in Keystone Earth and the proposed site of Turtle Bay Luxury Condominiums. Finally, 2 Dag Hammarskjöld Plaza, an office tower built by Tet Corporation to protect the rose. In *The Dark Tower*, it is described as being at least ninety-nine stories tall, whereas in reality it has only sixteen stories. The Paper Patch stationery store is also located at this intersection.

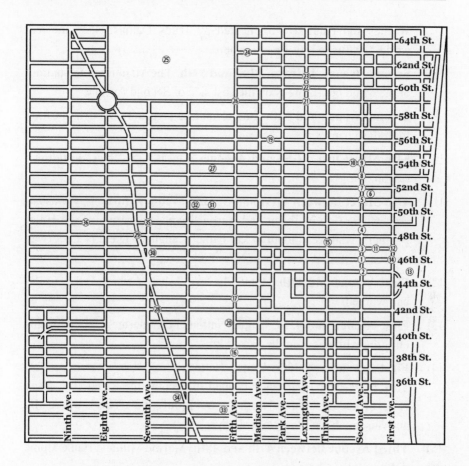

2) **844 Second Avenue (at the 45th Street intersection)**: Blimpie's. A fast-food restaurant.

3) **Second Avenue and 47th Street**: Roland Deschain walked into the middle of this busy intersection and stopped traffic by saying, "Hile! Stop in the name of Gilead!"

4) **Second Avenue between 49th and 48th**: Reflections of You. Both Eddie (in a dream) and Jake walk past this mirror store.

5) **Second Avenue and 51st**: Tower of Power Records.

6) **Second Avenue near 51st Street**: Station Shoes & Boots. Between Tower of Power Records and Manhattan Restaurant of the Mind.

7) **Second Avenue and 52nd**: House of Cards Magic Shop and Chew Chew Mama's restaurant. Father Callahan and Lupe Delgado used to have lunch there. After 1994, Chew Chew Mama's became Dennis's

Waffles and Pancakes, frequented by Trudy Damascus. In the real world, the Turtle Bay Tavern is here.

8) **Second Avenue, between 52nd and 54th**: The Manhattan Restaurant of the Mind bookstore is on the east side of Second Avenue.

9) **Second Avenue and 54th**: Barcelona Luggage store. Arrival location for todash trips.

10) **54th Street just off Second Avenue**: Kansas City Blues, a midtown saloon.

11) **47th Street between First and Second avenues**: Turtle Bay Washateria, where Calvin Tower and Aaron Deepneau scared off the Hitler Brothers, who were about to kill Father Callahan. There is a doorway between different versions of New York here.

12) **First Avenue and 47th**: Home, the "wet" shelter where Father Callahan worked.

13) **First Avenue and 45th**: United Nations headquarters. Jake sees this building while he is in the vacant lot.

14) **First Avenue and 46th**: United Nations Plaza Hotel. Later the New York Plaza-Park Hyatt and destined to become the Regal U.N. Plaza Hotel owned by Sombra/North Central in July 1999. This is where Mia and Susannah wait for Richard Sayre's call.

15) **Third Avenue between 47th and 48th**: Marine Midland Bank. Home did its banking here.

16) **Fifth Avenue between 38th and 39th**: Jake's apartment. Its exact location isn't specified, but he crosses 39th after leaving his apartment to walk to school. Jack Mort passes the apartment after crossing 40th heading south.

17) **Fifth Avenue and 43rd**: "The pushing place," where Jack Mort pushes Jake in front of Enrico Balazar's car.

18) **? Avenue and 33rd**: Mid-Town Lanes, where Jake used to bowl.

19) **56th Street between Park and Madison**: The Piper School, which Jake attends.

20) **Fifth Avenue and 41st**: New York Public Library. Father Callahan looks up the zip code Aaron Deepneau left for him here and steals the book *Yankee Highways*. Bango Skank wrote his name in a men's room bathroom stall.

21) **Lexington and 59th**: The intersection where Jake and Father Callahan got out of the cab on the way to the Dixie Pig.

22) **Lexington Avenue and 60th**: The Blackstrap Molasses Café. Susannah paid a busker to sing "Man of Constant Sorrow" at this intersection.

23) **Lexington Avenue and 61st**: The Dixie Pig. Irene Tassenbaum has an apartment nearby.

24) **63rd between Fifth and Madison**: Sir Speedy-Park, where the Tassenbaums park their cars.

25) **Central Park**: Where Susannah meets Eddie and Jake Toren in 1987.

26) **Fifth Avenue and Central Park South**: The Greymarl Apartments. Odetta Holmes lived in the penthouse. Also the Plaza Hotel, where Lupe Delgado worked on the maintenance crew.

27) **11 West 53rd Street (between Fifth and Sixth avenues)**: The Museum of Modern Art (though perhaps confused by King with Metropolitan Museum of Art, which is on Fifth and 82nd, well out of Jake's path). Jake joined a tour to kill time before going to Dutch Hill.

28) **Broadway and 42nd**: The hotdog stand Jake visits after leaving the museum.

29) **Broadway and 48th**: News ticker that Ted Brautigan uses to keep track of the passage of time in Keystone Earth from Mid-World.

30) **Times Square**: Denby's Discount Drug. Jake tells a policeman that his name is Tom Denby when he sees the sign. Odetta Holmes and Father Callahan saw movies in Times Square.

31) **70 Rockefeller Plaza (51st between Fifth and Sixth)**: Jake's father's office at "The Network."

32) **Sixth Avenue between 50th and 51st streets**: Radio City Music Hall. John Cullum went here when he was in the army.

33) **Fifth Avenue between 33rd and 34th streets**: The Empire State Building. John Cullum went here when he was in the army. The other New York entertainment Cullum sampled isn't part of the tour.

34) **Sixth Avenue and 34th Street**: Macy's, where Roland first encounters Detta Walker.

35) **Seventh Avenue and 49th**: Clements Guns and Sporting Goods, where Roland "bought" ammo while inhabiting Jack Mort's body.

36) **395 West 49th (near Ninth Avenue)**: Katz's Drug Store, site of the world's first antibiotic robbery.

37) **409 Park Ave South (between 28th and 29th streets)**: Jack Mort's apartment.

38) **Ninth Avenue at Christopher**: Christopher Street Station, where Jack Mort pushed Odetta Holmes in front of the A train.

39) **Second Avenue and 19th**: Americano Bar where Father Callahan got drunk after seeing the vagrant dead for the first time.

40) **Washington Square Park (near Fifth Avenue and 4th Street)**: Father Callahan spent his first night in New York here. It became one of his favorite haunts. He sees the first signs of the low men looking for him there.

41) **World Trade Center**: Father Callahan and Jake left Black Thirteen in a locker in the basement in 1999.

OUR WORLD PEOPLE, PLACES AND THINGS

This section of the glossary includes all significant people, places and things from America. Characters mentioned only in passing or not by name are omitted. The numbers and letters after each entry indicate the books in which the person, place or thing is mentioned. The numbers 1–7 represent the seven main Dark Tower books. L stands for "The Little Sisters of Eluria," 4.5 represents *The Wind Through the Keyhole*, and M means the Marvel graphic novels. Names in square brackets indicate situations where a subject's name changes because of a continuity error.

PEOPLE

ABIGAIL (4, 6)

A note found in the parking lot outside the train station in Topeka says that the old woman from the dreams lives in Nebraska and that her name is Abagail [sic].

Crossover to Other Works: The forces for good rally around Mother Abigail Freemantle in Nebraska in *The Stand*.

ALEXANDER, TRUMAN (2)

Former henchman of Enrico Balazar. Dies from a heart attack.

ANDERSON, JUSTINE (7)

A woman from Maybrook, New York, who sees Stephen King shortly before Bryan Smith hits him in Lovell, Maine. She is picking raspberries with her friend Elvira Toothaker, whom she met at Vassar College in the 1940s.

ANDOLINI, CLAUDIO (2, 5)

Jack Andolini's brother and one of Enrico Balazar's personal bodyguards. Killed by Roland in the shoot-out at the Leaning Tower.

ANDOLINI, JACK (2, 3, 5, 6, 7)

Enrico Balazar's number one lieutenant and field marshal. He is related to Balazar by marriage, but he rose to his position because he isn't dumb and has a bit of imagination, although he's stupid in some fundamental way that has nothing to do with IQ scores. He looks like an ax-wielding psycho in a horror movie. He has muddy brown eyes under a bulging forehead, and a jutting jaw. His hairy hands are so large they look like caricatures. Known to others (such as Henry Dean) behind his back as Old Double Ugly. He is killed by lobstrosities on the beach after his gun blows up in his hand in one version of reality. In Keystone Earth he ends up in jail in Bridgton, Maine, after the failed ambush on Roland and Eddie.

ANTASSI, PAUL (6)

The police officer who responds to Trudy Damascus's call after Mia robs her.

ARMITAGE, FRANK (7)

The man who questions Ted Brautigan about his job application in San Francisco and hires him to become a Breaker. A broad-shouldered, hard-faced man. He takes Ted and a number of others through a doorway in Santa Mira to Thunderclap Station.

ATWOOD, TIMOTHY (7)

Ted Brautigan's uncle. He attended Harvard and pays for Ted's higher education.

AVERY, BONITA "BONNIE" (3, 5)

Jake Chambers's English comp teacher. A big fan of *le mot juste*. She gives Jake an A+ for his essay "My Understanding of Truth" and provides a well-intentioned but misguided interpretation of its symbolism.

BACHMAN, CLAUDIA (Y) INEZ (5, 6)

The author of *Charlie the Choo-Choo* in one version of reality. Without the "y," the imaginary wife of Stephen King's pseudonym, Richard Bachman. Stephen King made her up when he was creating an author bio for Bachman when he was drunk one night. The "y" makes her part of the *Ka-tet* of Nineteen.

BACHMAN, RICHARD (6, 7)

A pen name used by Stephen King to publish some of his earliest novels as paperback originals. One night when King was drunk, he made up a complete author bio for him, including a wife named Claudia Inez.

BAJ (7)

An armless hydrocephalic Breaker at Algul Siento. He faints and falls from the wagon Daneeka Rostov uses to save him from the fire in the Study. He strikes his head on the ground and dies.

BALAZAR, ENRICO [EMILIO] (2, 3, 5, 6)

A second-generation Sicilian who has become a high-caliber big shot in New York's drug trafficking trade. Known as Il Roche. He owns a bar called the Leaning Tower and likes to build houses of cards and, on one occasion, a tower. It's his Town Car that kills Jake Chambers. In 1977, he is a dumpy little guy, middle-aged, with a potbelly and graying black hair with dandruff. He works as an enforcer for Sombra Corporation in the matter of the vacant lot. Eddie thinks of him as a despot. His way of doing business is to always escalate. Roland kills him during a shoot-out in his office.

BARLOW, KURT (5, 6, 7)

A Type One vampire who was responsible for the destruction of 'Salem's Lot, Maine. He tested Father Callahan's faith and, when it proved lacking, broke his cross and forced the priest to drink his blood.

BEASLEY, JESSICA (5)

A friend of Odetta Holmes's mother who experienced two false pregnancies.

BECKHART, DICK (7)

The owner of the cabin at #13 Turtleback Lane. John Cullum has looked after it since the late 1950s. In 1977, he works in Washington for the Carter administration. Eddie, Roland and John palaver in this cabin before Eddie and Roland use the portal in Kezar Lake to go to the Fedic door. The Tassenbaums are friends of the Beckharts.

BEEMER, CHARLIE (7)

His wife, Ruth, and his sister-in-law are killed in the gunfight at the East Stoneham General Store.

BEEMER, RHODA (7)

Eldest daughter of Charlie and Ruth Beemer. She is in East Stoneham General Store when Roland returns in 1999.

BEEMER, RUTH (6, 7)
She and her sister are killed in the gunfight at the East Stoneham General Store.

BENZYCK, OFFICER (6)
A Manhattan police officer who frequently rousts Reverend Earl Harrigan.

BERTOLLO, DORA (5)
One of Eddie Dean's mother's friends. Known to the kids on the block as Tits Bertollo.

BIONDI, GEORGE (2, 5, 6, 7)
One of Enrico Balazar's bodyguards and goons. Known as Big George to his friends and Big Nose to his enemies. He delivers the fatal heroin injection to Henry Dean. Shot to death by Eddie Dean in Balazar's headquarters. Eddie encounters him again (ten years earlier) in the Manhattan Restaurant of the Mind and beats him unconscious with Roland's gun. During the ambush in East Stoneham, Eddie shoots his face off.

BISSETTE, LEONARD "LEN" (3)
Jake Chambers's French teacher at the Piper School. He sends Jake a letter expressing concern and support after Jake walks out of class.

BLAKE, KEVIN (2, 5)
One of Enrico Balazar's henchmen. A redhead. Plays Trivial Pursuit with Henry Dean and later lobs Henry's head into the fray to distract Eddie during the shoot-out. Killed by Roland.

BOSCONI, ROBERT (5)
A police officer from Eddie Dean's Brooklyn neighborhood, known as Bosco Bob. There were two versions of him: a friendly, pleasant man, and the unsmiling, cold cop he turned into if he thought maybe you'd done something. Eddie thinks of him when he detects similar behavior in Andy the Messenger Robot.

BRANNIGAN, SKIPPER (4, 5)
A friend of Henry Dean's friend Jimmie Polino. Polino thought that Brannigan wasn't afraid of anyone. According to legend, he beat up a teacher chaperoning a school dance. The others knew that Brannigan was a pussy.

Crossover to Other Works: Skipper Brannigan appears in "Everything's Eventual," which introduces Dinky Earnshaw.

BRAUTIGAN, THEODORE "TED" STEVENS (6, 7)

A super-Breaker. He was born in 1898 in Milford, Connecticut. At an early age he suspects he has telepathic powers. His eyes shake in their sockets when he uses these powers. He thinks his ability to read minds would be useful to army intelligence, but he is turned away because of a heart murmur and substandard hearing. He has a talent that no one wants. He becomes an accountant after his uncle offers to pay his Harvard tuition.

He discovers that his talent is dangerous when he's mugged in Akron, Ohio. In anger, he throws a mental spear at his attacker without realizing what he's doing. He also learns that his power can be temporarily contagious.

He ends up in Algul Siento after responding to a newspaper ad. He realizes later that the Crimson King's recruiters were already watching him. The job is too good to be true and a total con. The money is real, but he can never return to Earth to spend it. He doesn't truly understand what he's breaking, but he doesn't care. Someone finally wants him to use his power. He gets along well with his fellow Breakers and is allowed to work in the Study on his own schedule because he amplifies the output of the others.

A low man named Trampas becomes his friend and lets down his guard, allowing Ted to read his mind. Once he discovers what Breakers are doing, he gets Sheemie Ruiz, who created the Gingerbread House as a place where he could relax, to help him escape.

The low men track him down and threaten to kill Bobby Garfield and the other friends he made while back on Earth if he tries again. He isn't punished when he is brought back because their work is nearly done. Aware that gunslingers are coming, he, Sheemie and Dinky Earnshaw amass a cache of arms and meet the *ka-tet* at Thunderclap Station. He also provides a recording detailing the security layout and schedule at the prison.

He is wounded during the battle. He and four other Breakers join Susannah on the train to Fedic, where they continue on toward the Callas, where they hope to find forgiveness for their part in the kidnapping of the twins and, perhaps, a doorway back home.

Crossover to Other Works: The story of Ted's experiences after he escapes is told in "Low Men in Yellow Coats," the opening novella in *Hearts in Atlantis*, a book the *ka-tet* discovers but does not scrutinize in Nigel's living quarters.

BRIGGS, MR. (3)
Roundhouse manager for Mid-World Railway Company in *Charlie the Choo-Choo*.

BROOKS, "ENGINEER BOB" (3, 4, 5)
An engineer who works for Mid-World Railway. The only man ever allowed to drive Charlie the Choo-Choo. He turns down the chance to drive Charlie's replacement, opting instead to become "Wiper Bob." Eddie has a dream about him driving a bulldozer in the vacant lot in Manhattan.

BROWNING, ROBERT (3, 5, 6, 7)
The poet who wrote "Childe Roland to the Dark Tower Came." Jake quotes him (as Robert "Sundance" Browning) in his essay "My Understanding of Truth." Calvin Tower has a calendar with Browning's picture on it in his office. Stephen King receives a copy of *The Complete Poetical Works of Robert Browning* and sends a photocopy of the poem to Susannah in Westring as a warning against Dandelo. Susannah read some of his dramatic monologues in college but wasn't familiar with this poem.

CALLAHAN, FATHER (OR PERE) DONALD FRANK (5, 6, 7)
An alcoholic former priest who encountered vampires in 'Salem's Lot, Maine, and fled town after being forced to drink Barlow's blood. He ends up in New York, working at Home, a wet shelter. He becomes aware of Type Three vampires and, after one attacks his friend, Lupe Delgado, makes it his mission to kill them. This brings him to the attention of the low men, so he leaves New York. The next time he comes back, the Hitler Brothers ambush him and start to carve their trademark swastika in his forehead. They're interrupted, so what's left is a cross-shaped scar.

His cross-country adventures take him through a variety of parallel versions of America. After hitting rock bottom in Topeka, he goes to work for another shelter in Detroit, but the low men find him and lure him to a meeting at Sombra's offices. Rather than be infected by the vampires, he kills himself and ends up in the Way Station, where Walter o'Dim sends him through the Unfound Door with Black Thirteen to the Doorway Cave.

At first he works in Calla Bryn Sturgis, but eventually he builds a church and holds services, always seeking a second chance to prove his faith, which failed him in 'Salem's Lot. The church is also a place to store Black Thirteen.

He speaks up at Tian's town meeting, advocating the hiring of the gun-slingers to fight the Wolves. During his time with Roland, he discovers that he is a fictional character in a Stephen King novel, which causes an existential crisis. He also becomes a gunslinger, going to New York with Jake and fight-ing valiantly at the Dixie Pig. The White, which has been missing from his life since he left 'Salem's Lot, tells him that Jake must survive. He has the scrimshaw turtle, Jake's Ruger and his cross as weapons. Roland and Eddie speak through him, telling Jake to go on and leave Callahan behind. He is exhilarated to discover that his fear is gone and that the White stands with him. He kills a number of low men and vampires to give Jake a head start. When the tide turns, he shoots himself.

Crossover to Other Works: Father Callahan appeared in *'Salem's Lot*.

CALVINS (7)

Three men and two women who do research for Tet Corporation in 2 Dag Hammarskjöld Plaza. They do nothing every day but read the works of Ste-phen King, cross-referencing them by setting, character and theme. They are especially vigilant for references to people who live or lived in the Keystone World. They believe that King's references to the Dark Tower are almost al-ways masked and sometimes mean nothing at all. They identify *Insomnia* as King's keystone book outside of the Dark Tower series. The name of their group is either homage to Calvin Tower or a joke.

CARVER, MARIAN ODETTA (7)

President of Tet Corporation after her father, Moses Carver, retired in 1997. Her office is on the northwest corner of 2 Dag Hammarskjöld Plaza. She shares a house with her father in Montauk Point. She stands at least six foot six and prides herself that she's made of stern stuff. Her face is savagely handsome—the face of a warrior in Roland's estimation. She believes that Tet Corporation's work against North Central Positronics will take another thirty years.

CARVER, MOSES "POP MOSE" (5, 6, 7)

Odetta Holmes's godfather, born in 1899. Dan Holmes turned over the finan-cial side of Holmes Dental to Carver after his first heart attack shortly after Odetta's accident, and he continued to oversee the business after Holmes died. He was in charge of Odetta's trust fund until she turned twenty-five. As honest as the day is long, according to Susannah. Eddie suggests that they ask him to lead the amalgamated Tet Corporation and Holmes Dental with Aaron Deepneau and John Cullum. He is Tet's president until 1997. Roland first meets him in 1999, when he is a wizened man bent from arthritis and seems incapable of bending his neck, but he's still spry and full of fire. He was seventy years old when his daughter, Marian, was born. He has become friends with Reverend Earl Harrigan of the Church of the Holy God-Bomb, much to his daughter's chagrin.

CHAMBERS, ELMER R. (1, 3, 4, 4.5, 5, 6, 7, M)

Jake Chambers's father. He has no middle name, just an initial. He is a Big Coffin Hunter in TV Land, known as a master of "the kill"—the ability to destroy programs on rival television networks. A light sleeper, an early riser and more than a little paranoid. He smokes eighty cigarettes a day and keeps a stash of cocaine in his home office, where he watches the competition at night on three televisions. His telephone conversations with subordinates usually start cheerfully and end up with him bent over his desk screaming at the top of his lungs. He refers to maître d' stands as Blackmail Central. One of his favorite phrases is "the fact is." He stands five foot ten and has a crew cut. He calls Jake "hotshot" when he's around, which isn't much. Two of the three vacations he took with his family were cut short by urgent calls from work.

CHAMBERS, JOHN "JAKE" (THROUGHOUT)

A boy of eleven-turning-twelve from Manhattan who is drawn into the Mohaine Desert after Jack Mort pushes him in front of a Cadillac driven by Enrico Balazar. At the time of his first death, he's an all-A student attending the exclusive and expensive Piper School. He has sun-bleached blond hair and blue-gray eyes. He's small for his age, well mannered and sensitive, but he has a hard time making friends and is mildly claustrophobic. His career aspirations include bowling on the pro tour. His parents, a cutthroat network executive and a woman with too much free time on her hands, pay little attention to him. Housekeeper Greta Shaw is the closest thing he has to a friend or a parent. If he had stayed in New York, he probably would have ended up in therapy.

Though Roland loves him like a son soon after they meet, he becomes a pawn in the game between the gunslinger and the man in black. Jake knows what it's like to be held at a distance, so when Roland realizes that Jake might have to be sacrificed, the boy knows it, too, abetted by the fact that in Mid-World he acquires a stronger sense of the touch than that displayed by Alain

Johns. There's not much Jake can do, though. Left alone in the desert or the mountains, he's sure to die anyway. He falls to his death from a railway trestle.

His circumstances are complicated when Roland kills Jack Mort, thereby preventing him from pushing Jake. Jake knows he's supposed to die on May 9, 1977, but he doesn't, which sets up paradoxical memories in his head. He remembers being with Roland, but he couldn't have been there if he didn't die and end up in the Way Station. He keeps looking for doors, convinced he'll find one that will take him back. After he sees the rose in the vacant lot, his power of the touch increases and he starts communicating with Eddie Dean, whom he's never met. Together they negotiated his return to Mid-World, which rectifies his (and Roland's) memory problems. *Ka* wants him so badly that it found a way around death to put him back at Roland's side.

Despite what happened in the past, Jake trusts Roland after his return. He understands Roland because their parents were somewhat alike. His father is a gunslinger for a TV network and his mother has a history of sleeping around.

Oy the billy-bumbler becomes his constant companion and they are rarely apart. They even switch minds to get past the mind-trap beneath the Dixie Pig. Though he regards Roland as his father—and eventually calls him father—he's also the adopted son of Eddie and Susannah. Still, he's jealous of Mordred for being Roland's blood son.

He's three years younger than Roland was when he went up against Cort, but he has no shortage of steel in his character. Being part of Roland's *ka-tet* means that he has to shoulder adult responsibility, though he isn't yet a teenager—and never gets to be one. He doesn't always like the person he becomes when he wears his father's gun, stolen the day he returned to Mid-World as if he knew he was destined to become a gunslinger. His childish aspect comes out on occasion, such as when he and Benny Slightman become friends in Calla Bryn Sturgis. When he is forced to betray Benny by reporting his friend's father as a traitor, he understands Roland better than before.

The mission to save the Dark Tower is as much his own as it is Roland's. When they have to save Stephen King's life and Roland's leg fails, Jake doesn't hesitate to throw himself between the author and the van heading his way, sacrificing his life to save all of creation. Father Callahan's last rites, performed before they entered the Dixie Pig, were only slightly premature.

Three deaths do not spell the end for Jake, though. Susannah joins him in another New York, where he is Jake Toren, younger brother to Eddie.

CHAMBERS, LAURIE [MEGAN] (3, 4, M)

Jake Chambers's mother. A Vassar graduate who is a firm believer in better living through chemistry, especially in the form of Valium. She is a distant mother, unaware of her son's likes and dislikes. Her idea of a lullaby is "Tyger, tyger, burning bright." She calls Jake sugarlove. She has a long history of sleeping with sick friends.

CLEMENTS, JUSTIN [ARNOLD] (2)

Owner and operator of Clements Guns and Sporting Goods. The police have been trying to catch him selling guns illegally for years.

COOPER, GARY (4, 4.5)

Film actor whom both Eddie and Susannah associate with Roland, though after the gunslinger tells his story during the starkblast, Susannah decides he really isn't the strong and silent type.

CORCORAN, JOHN (2)

A journalist for the *Topeka Capital-Journal* who writes an article about the superflu.

CORNWELL, AUSTIN (7)

A man from upstate New York who ran the Niagara Mall and had a successful career in advertising, including accounts for Nozz-A-La and the Takuro Spirit, before becoming the Crimson King's minister of state. His father is Andrew John Cornwell of Tioga Springs. See Rando Thoughtful.

CULLUM, JOHN (6, 7)

Caretaker, camp-checker and carpenter from East Stoneham, Maine. His house is on Keywadin Pond. He's in the general store when Jack Andolini ambushes Roland and Eddie in 1977 and demonstrates his instinct for survival. Roland calls him *dan-tete*: little savior. He's going on elderly and has brilliant blue eyes. He collects signed baseballs and spent ten years as a guard at the Maine State Prison. He may seem like a country bumpkin, but he's smart. Roland and Eddie convince him to enlist the cooperation of Aaron Deepneau and Moses Carver to form Tet Corporation using the financial support of Holmes Dental. Roland gives him Aunt Talitha's cross, which bears a message that will convince Moses Carver to believe Cullum. He wears the cross around his neck until his death. He rues some of the filthy tricks he is forced to play as part of Tet Corporation, some of which cost people their lives. One of his biggest regrets, though, is that he never got to visit Mid-World. He was shot in 1989 in New York, the first of the Founding Fathers to die. Tet believes a *can toi* acting on behalf of Sombra or North Central Positronics killed him. There had been previous attempts on his life.

DAMASCUS, TRUDY (6)
An accountant with the firm of Guttenberg, Furth and Patel. She's determined to see Damascus added to the end of the company name. She is a staunch nonbeliever in anything supernatural until the day Susannah/Mia appears in front of her out of thin air on the steps of the Black Tower and robs her of her shoes. In the aftermath, she tries to get people to believe her, then comes to recognize their incredulity.

DANVILLE, PATRICK (7)
Son of Sonia. Roland first hears his name in the offices of Tet Corporation. The Calvins believe he is a real person whom Roland will encounter during his quest. Shortly thereafter, Roland and Susannah find two paintings in Richard Sayre's office in Fedic signed by him. One features the Dark Tower. Since Patrick hasn't yet been there, these paintings must come from later in his life, or from another time line.

Susannah and Roland find Patrick imprisoned in Dandelo's basement. He reminds Susannah of a concentration camp prisoner. No one knows how long he's been there. He has long hair but only a faint beard. He looks seventeen; Roland thinks he might be as old as thirty. His mind has been terribly damaged by Dandelo's constant feeding on his emotions. The vampire also pulled out his tongue.

Roland and Susannah discover his impressive artistic skill. He's a pencil-slinger and a graphite addict. However, he knows nothing about erasers. If he makes any mistakes with his pencil, he incorporates them into his drawings. When Susannah realizes that his work affects reality, she gives him an eraser and gets him to remove the cancerous blemish on her face. This talent may exist only in Mid-World, where he also has slight ability with the touch.

He draws a doorway so Susannah can return to New York, but he chooses to stay with Roland. Though he fails Roland by falling asleep the night Mordred attacks, he serves Roland at the Tower by drawing and then erasing the

Crimson King after creating red paint for his eyes out of saliva, the petals of a rose and Roland's blood. Roland sends him back to the Federal Outpost, where Stuttering Bill might show him a way to get back home.

Crossover to Other Works: Patrick was introduced in *Insomnia* as a four-year old boy with a rose-pink aura.

DARIO (2)

One of Enrico Balazar's henchmen. Killed in crossfire by Tricks Postino at the Leaning Tower.

DEAN, EDWARD "EDDIE" CANTOR (2, 3, 4, 4.5, 5, 6, 7)

Eddie Dean is a twenty-three-year-old heroin addict from Brooklyn when he meets Roland. A single mother and brother, Henry, who is eight years older, raised him. According to his mother, his father's name was Wendell. A drunk driver killed his six-year-old sister when Eddie was two, which made his mother overly protective of him. However, because she worked, most of the responsibility fell to Henry, whom Eddie idolizes.

Eddie is better than Henry at just about everything, which makes Henry torment him. He learns to hide his skills and interests in things like reading and whittling when around Henry to protect himself, but also to help preserve Henry's tattered self-esteem.

Eddie became a drug addict after Henry came back from Vietnam injured and hooked on morphine. Henry spiraled downward and took Eddie with him. Henry and his mother—who is dead by now—had successfully destroyed his self-esteem. Even at his worst, though, Eddie was always better able to cope than Henry and ended up looking after him.

When he arrives in Mid-World, he's a dull observer, mostly because of his prolonged drug use. He's a fast learner with flashes of intuition, though, feeling at times that he's done everything before. One of his skills is in whittling powerful talismanic objects. Still, whenever he sets out to do something, his late brother's voice nags him that he'll never be any good.

With Roland's help, he stands up to the customs agents who (correctly) suspect him of smuggling drugs, and again later to the mobsters who used him as a drug mule. He impresses Roland by taking part in a gunfight while naked. Though he's occasionally weak and self-centered, he has plenty of courage and heart. He's convinced that he will always love Susannah more than she loves him. She's someone he can look after, just as he was able to handle his withdrawal when he had to tend to Roland on the beach.

While he's fast and accurate with a gun, he's equally deadly with his mouth, a trait that reminds Roland of his old pal and *ka-mai*, Cuthbert. Even Henry acknowledged his brother's talented mouth, saying that Eddie could talk the devil into setting himself on fire. His sense of humor can be funny and stinging at the same time. Though this characteristic is often annoying, it proves useful in the riddle contest against Blaine the Mono, where he defeats the mad computer with illogic.

He regards Roland as his father, and a compliment from the gunslinger can make him feel like the king of the world. Roland gave him a second chance at life—left to his own devices he would probably have died from an overdose, like his brother. After a dream where he is shown the field of roses and the Dark Tower, he adopts Roland's quest as his own, declaring that he would continue to End-World even if Roland died.

Roland believes that Eddie is Cuthbert under a different name, convinced that Eddie will die the same way his old friend did: talking or arguing, which is as natural to him as breathing. He's near the age Cuthbert was at Jericho Hill (twenty-four or twenty-five) when he dies at the end of the battle of Algul Siento. His death is neither slow nor easy.

Susannah meets up with a version of Eddie in another New York, where he is Eddie Toren from White Plains. When she joins him in Central Park in 1987, he's already in love with her after dreaming about her for months. His younger brother is named Jake.

Physical description: He has hazel eyes, black hair and sharp, foxy features.

DEAN, HENRY (2, 3, 4, 5, 6, 7)

Eddie Dean's older brother by eight years. Great sage and eminent junkie. He blamed all of his failures in life on the fact that he had to look after Eddie. He teased Eddie mercilessly about anything his younger brother did better than him—which was just about everything. He always ragged him about the books he brought home, calling him a sissy and a bookworm. He was wounded in Vietnam after enlisting in the army and came back hooked on morphine.

He was the defining, shaping force in Eddie's life, and pulled his younger brother into his downward spiral of addiction. Their roles reversed—Eddie ended up having to look after him. His one piece of financial advice to Eddie, offered a month before he died, was to avoid investing in "all this computer shit." He died from an overdose meant to keep him docile while Enrico

Balazar's thugs waited for Eddie to show up with the drugs he smuggled from the Bahamas. Eddie continues to hear his voice in his head, although he learns to banish it as time passes and he becomes more confident.

DEAN, MRS. (2)
Eddie Dean's mother. She often lectured Eddie about how much she (and Henry) had sacrificed for him. She died a few months after Henry got back from Vietnam.

DEAN, REGINALD (3)
Eddie Dean's uncle. He painted the George Washington Bridge.

DEAN, SELINA [GLORIA] (2, 3)
Eddie Dean's older sister. A drunk driver killed her when Eddie was two and she was six.

DEAN, SUSANNAH (2, 3, 4, 4.5, 5, 6, 7)
Susannah Dean is the union of Odetta Holmes and Detta Walker, created by Roland using the final doorway on the beach. She adopts the middle name of both of her previous personalities. There may be even more unnamed personalities—formed and half-formed—lurking beneath the surface. She is twenty-six years old and heart-stoppingly beautiful, with full lips, wide eyes and high cheekbones, when Roland takes her from 1964. She and Eddie Dean fall in love and treat Jake like an adopted son.

She benefits from aspects of Odetta and Detta. She draws on Odetta for her humanity and social skills, but it is Detta who reasserts herself most often, especially when Susannah is under pressure. She remembers enjoying some of the things she did in New York as Detta. She relies on Detta to calm her nerves and steady her hands, or when she has to endure something terrible, like when she's raped by the demon in the Speaking Ring. When Detta is in control, Susannah looks different. Susannah isn't always aware that Detta has come forward, except in retrospect.

She has a casual way of speaking, calling her friends "sugar" or "sug." She is often the voice of calm reason to counter Eddie's brashness. Susannah loves Eddie because he makes her feel whole. She proudly wears the wooden ring he carved on a leather thong around her neck. It's too big for her hand, but she won't let him make her a new one. Eddie fills the hole in her heart that she believes all people are born with and exist with until they find their true love.

Her feelings for Roland are more ambivalent. Her love for him is a mixture of fear, admiration and pity. Detta hates him for forcing her into this strange land and for his rise to ascendancy in Susannah's heart and mind. Susannah recognizes him as a hero, admiring his strength and indefatigable single-mindedness, but despises his ruthlessness.

She excels as a gunslinger, never lacks for courage and takes quickly to new weapons, like the Orizas she wields against the Wolves and in Algul Siento. They give her an elemental satisfaction. After she kills everyone in the Fedic Dogan, she's eager for more, believing that becoming a killing machine is what she was made for.

She likes to play parts and is aware that an understanding of her psychosis might have illuminated her childhood joy at pretending to be someone else. Exposure to Mid-World enhances her playacting to the level where she can imagine things and make them real, like the mental Dogan she creates to control her pregnancy.

Though Susannah's personality is strong, she is no match for Mia, who invades her the same way Roland did in Macy's. Perhaps because she is used to compartmentalizing other personalities, she doesn't realize Mia is there until the todash trip where the others go into the vacant lot and she remains on the street. So long as Mia sits back, Susannah can remain in control, but when Mia steps forward, she is helpless. Even Detta is no match for the former demon's single-minded imperative. When Mia is driving their body, it has legs and she's an inch taller than Eddie. Under different circumstances, she and Mia might have been friends, and they develop some mutual respect during their one day in full communication with each other.

Though Susannah is pregnant, she never has any maternal feelings toward Mordred before he's born or after. She wanted to bear Eddie's child, but not this one. After Eddie dies, Susannah agrees to go on with Roland and Jake. She claims it's because Eddie wanted her to, but part of her wants to see the Tower, too, though she never gets to do so.

She starts dreaming of Eddie after the encounter with Dandelo and figures out what *ka* wants her to do. The New York on which the doorway Patrick draws for her opens is not the same one she came from, but she can be happy there with Eddie Toren, who loves her, and his younger brother, Jake.

DEEPNEAU, AARON (3, 4, 5, 6, 7)

A retired lawyer who was diagnosed with cancer in 1975. His younger sister and two younger brothers are still lawyers with a family firm called simply Deepneau. He explained the riddle of Samson to Jake. He's Calvin Tower's only friend. He and Tower rescue Father Callahan from the Hitler Brothers.

Roland thinks he has a true face. He raised Nancy Deepneau—who called him Airy as a child—after her parents died young. He is one of the Founding Fathers of Tet Corporation and died in 1992 after his cancer came back. He's in his seventies in 1977, tall, skinny and wears steel-rimmed glasses. He has only a few wisps of fine hair on his head.

DEEPNEAU, ED (7)

A cousin several times removed of Marian Carver's father. He was a book-keeper from Bangor who died in 1947. The Calvins think Stephen King used him as a subliminal message to Roland to be on the lookout for Aaron Deepneau.

Crossover to Other Works: Ed Deepneau is the villain in *Insomnia*, tricked into working on behalf of the Crimson King.

DEEPNEAU, NANCY REBECCA (7)

Aaron Deepneau's older brother's granddaughter. Her parents and grandfather died young, so Aaron mostly raised her. In 1999, she works for Tet Corporation.

DELEVAN, CARL (2)

One of the two police officers Roland approaches after being unable to purchase bullets at Clements Guns and Sporting Goods. Overweight and out of shape. Roland strips him of his gun and knocks him unconscious. He responds to the shots-fired call at Katz's Drug Store and opens fire with a shotgun, endangering bystanders. Roland knocked him out a second time, which may have accounted for his amnesia when testifying about that day's events. Died of a heart attack while watching *The Terminator* nine years later.

DELGADO, LUPE (5)

A thirty-two-year-old alcoholic who started working at Home in 1974 and was sober since 1970. He worked days as part of the maintenance crew at the Plaza Hotel and nights at the shelter. He helped craft Home's "wet" policy. Father Callahan fell in love with him, though there was never anything physical between them. Lupe fell victim to a Type Three vampire, who gave him AIDS. He came down with Kaposi's sarcoma in mid-1976 and died a few weeks later. Because of him, Father Callahan started killing vampires.

DENBY, TOM (3)

The name Jack Chambers gives to a cop in Times Square while being truant from school. He uses the name of a nearby establishment, Denby's Discount Drug.

DORFMAN, STAN (3)

One of Jake Chambers's classmates. Jack Mort has a client named Dorfman.

DORNING, JANE (2)

Flight attendant on Delta 901 between Nassau, Bahamas, and JFK. She is the first to believe that there's something suspicious about Eddie.

DOUGLAS, SUSY (2)

Senior flight attendant on Delta 901 between Nassau, Bahamas, and JFK.

DRABNIK, CSABA (4, 5)

One of Henry Dean's friends, known around the neighborhood as the Mad Fuckin Hungarian. Eddie hears his voice in the Doorway Cave.

DRETTO, CARLOCIMI "CIMI" (2, 5)

One of Enrico Balazar's bodyguards. He weighs 250 pounds and has worked for "Da Boss" for decades. He hopes to retire to a farm in northern New Jersey. Alas, his retirement comes in the form of a bullet from Roland's gun.

EARNSHAW, RICHARD "DINKY" (7)

A Breaker at Algul Siento. He was originally enlisted by Mr. Sharpton to work for Trans Corp, a subsidiary of North Central Positronics. He is precognitive, and his special abilities allow him to unlock doors and modify the telemetry equipment in Damli House to disguise their comings and goings and any unauthorized use of psychic power. He has a terrible temper and a habit of going off on foul-mouthed tirades if someone pushes his buttons. Unlike most Breakers, though, he isn't totally self-absorbed. He befriends Sheemie Ruiz after hearing him crying at night. After the battle of Algul Siento, he joins Ted and the others on the train to Fedic. They head to the Callas, planning to get back home via the Doorway Cave.

Crossovers to Other Works: Dinky Earnshaw first appeared in the story "Everything's Eventual" as a high-school dropout who is given a job as an e-mail assassin for Trans Corp. He had an unpleasant encounter with Henry Dean's friend Skipper Brannigan. The special symbol he uses to turn his power on Mr. Sharpton is the word "Excalibur," the name of Arthur Eld's sword, from which Roland's guns are made.

ESTEVEZ, JULIO (2)
The ambulance driver who takes Odetta to the hospital after her accident.

EVANS, BERYL (3, 4, 5, 6)
Author of *Charlie the Choo-Choo* in one version of reality.

FEENY, ANDREW (2, 3, 6, 7)
Odetta Holmes's driver. He started working for Odetta's father when she was fourteen and knows about her blackouts and disappearances but doesn't know the real reason for them. He calls John F. Kennedy the last gunslinger.

FLAHERTY, CONOR (7)
The leader and only human among the posse that chases Jake beneath the Dixie Pig. Originally from Boston, he has worked for the Crimson King for twenty years in many versions of New York. His fear of dragons is expressed by the mind-trap. He's a good shot but no match on the draw for Roland, even after he tries to distract him by insulting his mother. Roland puts two bullets in his head.

FRAMINGHAM, MR. (2)
Jack Mort's boss. Mort bought an expensive silver Dunhill lighter so he could light the man's cigarettes.

FRANKS, JOANNE (3)
Secretary at the Piper School.

FREDERICKS, TOMMY (4, 5)
One of Henry Dean's friends. He gets so excited watching the street stickball games that he makes faces, so the kids call him Halloween Tommy.

GALE, DOROTHY (2, 3, 4, 5, 6, 7)
A character from *The Wizard of Oz*. The *ka-tet* tells Roland her story before they enter the Green Palace outside Topeka.

GARFIELD, BOBBY (6, 7)
Ted Brautigan's young friend after he escapes from Algul Siento. Ted mistakes Jake for him at first. Pimli Prentiss threatened to harm Bobby if Ted refused to cooperate after he was captured and returned.

Crossover to Other Works: Bobby was the protagonist of the novella "Low Men in Yellow Coats" from *Hearts in Atlantis*.

GARTON, WILLIAM (5)

The Hitler brother Father Callahan thinks of as Lenny because he's so short, no more than five foot two. He talks nonstop, isn't very smart and has a bad complexion. Shot to death on Coney Island.

GERBER, CAROL (7)

Bobby Garfield's childhood friend. Pimli Prentiss threatens to harm her if Ted Brautigan refuses to cooperate.

Crossover to Other Works: Carol's story is told in *Hearts in Atlantis*.

GOLDOVER, SYLVIA (6)

Henry Dean's girlfriend during the winter of 1984–85. She was "Skank El Supremo" according to Eddie, with smelly armpits, dragon breath and Mick Jagger lips. The relationship ended when she stole ninety dollars from Henry's wallet and disappeared.

GRAHAM, TOMMY (5)

Owner of Tom and Gerry's Artistic Deli until it went out of business.

GRANT, DONALD M. (3)

A publisher of fine editions mentioned by Calvin Tower. Also publisher of the first editions of the Dark Tower novels.

GUTTENBERG, MITCH (6)

A senior partner at Guttenberg, Furth and Patel, the accounting firm where Trudy Damascus works.

HALVORSEN, JIMMY (2)

House detective at Macy's.

HANSON, LUCAS (5)

One of Jake Chambers's classmates at the Piper School. Lucas always tried to trip Jake when he was going up the aisle.

HARLEY, MR. (3)

Headmaster at the Piper School. He also teaches Spoken Arts.

HARRIGAN, REVEREND EARL (6, 7)

Henchick of the Manni's twin in Manhattan. A tall, white-bearded man. A street preacher from the Church of the Holy God-Bomb who frequents the streets near 2 Dag Hammarskjöld Plaza. He often receives tickets from the cops for setting up easels, taking collection and preaching from a soapbox on the sidewalk. Susannah communicates with him mentally after she arrives from the Doorway Cave, and he relays the message to Jake and Father Callahan and intercedes when Jake gets in trouble with a taxi driver. He has a Southern accent that reminds Callahan of Foghorn Leghorn. Moses Carver is among his friends.

HASPIO, JIMMY (2)

One of Enrico Balazar's henchmen. Played Trivial Pursuit with Henry Dean. Killed by Roland.

HITLER BROTHERS (5, 6)

Norton Randolph and William Garton. Two New York thugs who, for eight years, beat up Jews and African Americans in the five boroughs of New York and carve swastikas in their victims' foreheads. They assault more than three dozen people and kill two. They begin working for the low men, attacking Rowan Magruder to lure Father Callahan back to New York. They are shot to death in Coney Island in what looks like a mob killing but is actually payback for their bungled attack on Callahan.

HOLDEN, "FAT JOHNNY" (2)

Justin Clements's brother-in-law. He is working in Clements Guns and Sporting Goods the day Roland tries to buy ammunition.

HOLMES, DAN (2, 5, 6, 7)

Odetta Holmes's father. He invented lucrative dental processes that had to do with capping teeth, allowing him to found Holmes Dental. He started feeling the effects of arthritis at twenty-five. After he had his first of many heart attacks in 1959, shortly after Odetta's accident, he turned the financial end of the business over to his accountant friend, Moses Carver. According to legend, he was born "red-handed" (i.e., a birthmark).

HOLMES, DANIEL (7)

Pen name of Benjamin Slightman Jr. He used it to publish science fiction novels that inspire Calvin Tower to suggest that Tet Corporation use psychics to spy on Mid-World and Sombra.

HOLMES, ODETTA (2, 3, 4, 5, 6, 7)

One of Susannah Dean's former personalities. She was the daughter of a wealthy dentist. When she was five, a brick dropped by Jack Mort struck her on the head and put her in a coma for three weeks. After that injury, the personality of Detta Walker emerged on occasion.

As a child, she was never happier than when she was pretending to be someone else. When her pet Pimsy died, they buried it under an apple tree. Her godfather told her that mourning a pet too long was a sin. She attempted to learn the violin, but her disastrous recital at the age of twelve was her last.

She attended Columbia University, where she took a course in medieval history, and lives in a penthouse apartment near Central Park. On August 19th, 1959, Jack Mort pushed her in front of the A train and she lost her legs. Her mother was already dead by then, and her father started having heart attacks a couple of months after her accident.

She labors all her life for respect. Because of her civil rights activism, she becomes almost as well known as Medgar Evers or Martin Luther King, and has been on the cover of *Time*. She's jailed in Oxford, Mississippi, in 1962, where her fellow activists call her "Det," while protesting the disappearance of three voter registration workers. At the age of twenty-five, she inherits millions from a trust fund and is worth eight or ten million dollars by 1964.

Susannah thinks of Odetta as a self-righteous, pompous prig. Detta called her a poetry-reading bitch who thought she was too good to do math, so she did poorly on it in school even though she had an aptitude.

HOLMES, SARAH (NÉE WALKER) [ALICE] (2, 3)

Odetta Holmes's mother. She dies before Odetta loses her legs.

HOTCHKISS, MR. (3)

The Piper School's shrink.

HOWARD (2)

The doorman at Odetta Holmes's apartment building.

ITTAWAY, DAVE (7)
One of the people hired to go to Algul Siento at the same time as Ted Brautigan.

JESSERLING, PETRA (3, 5)
One of Jake's classmates at the Piper School. She wears A-line jumpers and flirts with him.

KATZ (2)
Owner and operator of Katz's Drug Store. He's forty-six but looks twenty years older. He's balding, yellow-skinned and frail. He has two ulcers, one healed and one bleeding.

KING, STEPHEN (5, 6, 7)
The author. His family members include wife, Tabitha; sons, Joe and Owen; daughter, Naomi; brother, Dave; aunt Ethelyn and uncle Oren. In the mid-1970s, he moves to Bridgton, Maine, and a decade later, to Lovell and a lakeside house called Cara Laughs. Local people associate his arrival with the appearance of walk-ins.

He is the creator of Mid-World, which makes him Roland's creator—or at least his biographer. He's afraid of Roland, both because of what the gunslinger has become in the story—an antihero—and how dangerous he seems when they meet face-to-face. The mistakes he makes affect reality, such as his confusion about the location of Co-Op City. Eddie thinks King looks like Roland's son in 1977 and that he sounds like every character Eddie ever met in Mid-World.

He's also Father Callahan's creator, since the priest is a character in one of his books published in the Keystone World. King either exists in only one universe or is only important in one. The Crimson King tries to kill him many times, starting when he was a boy, but each time someone steps in or he steps aside. He isn't *ka*, but *ka* flows through him. Eddie believes he is the rose's twin. In the early days, when he's an alcoholic, he allows himself to believe he's Gan.

After Roland hypnotizes him in 1977 to convince him to continue writing his story, King returns to the Dark Tower series every so often. The Calvins believe he is leaving subliminal messages in his nonseries books, hoping they'll reach Roland and help him attain his goal.

Whenever he writes a Dark Tower book, he feels vulnerable. By 1999, he's all but decided to give up on the series, so the *ka* of the rational world decides it has no more use for him. This is why Roland and Jake are forced to save his life. Roland hypnotizes King into believing he and Jake weren't there during his near-fatal accident, but he sometimes comes close to remembering.

KNOPF, MR. (3)
Geometry and pre-algebra teacher at the Piper School.

LEEDS, TANYA (7)
A Breaker who comes to Algul Siento at the same time as Ted Brautigan. A sullen-looking young girl from Bryce, Colorado. Pimli Prentiss officiates over her marriage to Joey Rastosovich, but she asks Ted to marry them again so it will be official.

LENNOX, RALPH (2)
Security guard at Katz's Drug Store. A former police officer who worked in the 23rd Precinct for eighteen years without ever drawing his gun.

LUNDGREN, DAHLIE (3, 4, 5)
Owner of a convenience store in Co-Op City. Eddie Dean and his brother and their friends used to hang out and smoke in the alley behind Dahlie's. Eddie bought—and sometimes stole—comics from the store.

MAGRUDER, ROWAN R. (5, 6, 7)
The East Side's "Street Angel," founder, owner and chief supervisor of Home, the wet shelter where Mother Teresa once helped serve dinner. He appeared on the cover of *Newsweek* in 1980, was interviewed by Jane Pauley on the *Today Show* and was named Manhattan's Man of the Year by Mayor Ed Koch. His twin sister, Rowena Rawlings, is proud of the fact that he took second place in the Beloit Poetry Prize Competition in 1949, though only four people entered that year. An aspiring novelist who describes his book as third-rate James Joyce. The Hitler Brothers attack him to lure Father Callahan back to New York. They poke out his eyes and cut off his cheek, poke a hole in his heart and another in his liver, as well as leaving their trademark swastika on his forehead. He dies shortly after Father Callahan visits. Jake misremembers his name as George.

MARTIN, RAYMOND (3)
President of Mid-World Railway Company. His daughter is Susannah, and his name calls to mind Marten Broadcloak.

MARTIN, SUSANNAH (3)
Daughter of Raymond Martin. Plays the piano.

MCAVOY, WENDELL "CHIP" (5, 6, 7)
Owner of the East Stoneham General Store. He is wounded in the side of the head during the gunfight with Andolini and his men in 1977, when he is forty, and spends two weeks in the hospital. His store burns on "That Day," but he rebuilds it bigger and fancier thanks to extravagant insurance coverage. When Roland returns in 1999, he's in the process of overcharging Irene Tassenbaum for her deli purchase on the grounds that she's rich, from away and a Republican. He thinks Roland is there for him and tries to run away. Roland considers him a *ka-mai* and, as such, generally safe from harm. He surrenders the keys to his rusty International Harvester pickup truck, but Irene Tassenbaum drives it because she knows the way.

MCCANN, BIRDIE (7)
A Breaker at Algul Siento. A scrawny ex-carpenter with a receding hairline.

MCDONALD, CAPTAIN (2)
Pilot of Delta 901 between Nassau, Bahamas, and JFK.

MCKEEN, GARRETT (7)
Builder of the old rock wall that runs along Route 7 in Lovell, Maine. Roland talks to his great-grandson after Stephen King's accident.

MEARS, BEN (5)
Author of *Air Dance*. Leader of the *ka-tet* that formed in 'Salem's Lot to fight the vampire Barlow. He died in Los Zapatos, Mexico, at the age of fifty-nine in the mid-1990s. Black Thirteen sent Father Callahan todash to his funeral.
   Crossover to Other Works: Ben Mears is the protagonist of *'Salem's Lot*.

MISLABURSKI, MRS. (7)
Perhaps the most devout Catholic in Co-Op City, even venturing out to church during an ice storm, to the catcalls of the local kids—including Eddie Dean.

MORT, JACK (2, 3, 5, 6, 7)
The Pusher. Walter's representative on the New York level of the Dark Tower. A CPA and a sociopath who drops bricks on people or pushes them in front

of cars or trains. His coworkers are terrified of him, though he knows how to act like he's normal. He dropped the brick that injured Odetta Holmes when she was five and pushed her in front of the A train many years later. He also pushes Jake Chambers in front of a Cadillac in one version of reality, but is prevented from doing so by Roland in another. Roland threw Mort's body in front of a train as part of his gambit to unite Odetta Holmes's personalities.

MUCCI, TIMMY (3, 5)

Employee at Mid-Town Lanes, Jake's bowling alley. He gives Jake a bowling bag the day he bowls 280. He's a fan of Marvel comics like *Spider-Man*, *The Fantastic Four*, *The Incredible Hulk*, and *Captain America*, which is why Jake is familiar with the Dr. Doom masks worn by the Wolves.

O'MEARAH, GEORGE (2)

One of the police officers Roland approaches outside Clements Guns and Sporting Goods. Knocked unconscious by Roland and stripped of his gun. Then struck in the face by Roland with the shotgun. It took three operations and four steel pegs to put him together again.

O'ROURKE, BELLE (7)

An elderly female Breaker at Algul Siento.

OVERHOLSER, WAYNE D. (3, 5, 6)

An author of Western novels mentioned by Calvin Tower.

PETRIE, MARK (5, 6, 7)

A boy who lived in 'Salem's Lot when Father Callahan lived there. He joined Ben Mears's *ka-tet* against the vampire Barlow and fled the town with the writer after it burned. He regarded Mears as his father and spoke at his funeral in Los Zapatos, Mexico, in the mid-1990s.

POLINO, JIMMIE (4, 5)

One of Henry Dean's friends. Called Jimmie Polio because he has a clubfoot. Henry and his friends sometimes used his car when they went "turnpiking." He picks Dinky Earnshaw's nemesis, Skipper Brannigan, as the guy he'd like by his side during a fight.

POSTINO, TRICKS (2, 5, 6)

One of Enrico Balazar's henchmen. Plays Trivial Pursuit with Henry Dean. In one reality, Eddie Dean shoots him in the head. In Keystone Earth, Eddie shoots him again and his head is squashed under the wheel of an out-of-control transport.

RANDOLPH, NORTON "NORT" (5)

The Hitler brother Father Callahan thinks of as George because he is about six foot six. He has a sandy mustache and is the smarter of the two. Shot to death on Coney Island.

RAWLINGS, ROWENA MAGRUDER (5)

Rowan Magruder's twin sister. Father Callahan meets her after she came in from Chicago to be with her brother during his final hours after the Hitler Brothers assaulted him.

ROCHE, IL (2)

Nickname of Enrico Balazar.

ROSTOSOVICH, JOSEPH "JOEY" (7)

A Breaker in Algul Siento. He is married to Tanya Leeds. An engine from Fire-Response Team Bravo kills him.

ROSTOV, DANEEKA "DANI" (7)

An eleven-year-old Russian Breaker at Algul Siento. She attempts to save Baj and Sej when fire breaks out in Damli House. She tackles Finli o'Tego, saving Ted Brautigan's and Dinky Earnshaw's lives. She kisses Jake for luck before he and Roland depart for New York to save Stephen King. She goes to Fedic with Susannah, Ted, Dinky, Fred Worthington and Sheemie after the battle of Algul Siento and continues on toward the Callas with them.

RUDEBACHER, DICKY (5)

Owner of the Leabrook Homestyle Diner in New Jersey where Father Callahan works as a short-order cook after fleeing New York. He has a wife and two kids in college.

RUMBELOW, GRACE (7)

A Breaker living in Algul Siento. Formerly from Aldershot, Hampshire, England. A pudgy red-haired woman who reminds Jake of the lifetime president of his mother's garden club. She demands that Roland tell her who would take care of the Breakers now that their guards were all dead or captured. She survives this encounter.

RUSSERT, DON "DONNIE" (6, 7)
A retired history professor from Vanderbilt who lives in Waterford, Maine. He taped one of the walk-ins, but no one recognized the language it spoke. He wrote several articles on the walk-in phenomenon but could never get a reputable magazine to publish them. He isolated the center of their activity to Turtleback Lane.

SARGUS, JANE (6)
Owner of Country Collectibles on Dimity Road in East Stoneham. She specializes in quilts, glassware and old books, which attracts Calvin Tower's attention.

SAYRE, RICHARD PATRICK "DICKY" (5, 6, 7)
The Crimson King's head of operations. He answers to Walter o'Dim and also serves as executive vice president of the Detroit division of Sombra Corporation. He signed the Memorandum of Agreement with Calvin Tower regarding the vacant lot. He lures Father Callahan out of hiding to stop him from killing vampires and spearheads Mia's arrival at the Dixie Pig but humiliates her by forcing her to lick his boots. He is caught by surprise when Mordred consumes Mia and tries to hide behind Nigel when the shooting starts. Once the outcome of the battle is clear, he tries to surrender but sees the answer in Susannah's face. He turns to run, but she shoots him twice in the back of the head. Roland and Susannah find his office in the Fedic Dogan, where he has files on the *ka-tet*. He also has oil paintings by Patrick Danville on his wall, one of which is of the Dark Tower.

Physical appearance: His face has a lean and foxy look, full of intelligence and dark humor. He looks about sixty, is slim and good-looking, has white hair combed back, wears the gaudy clothes typical of his type, and has a red circle of blood on his brow that seems neither to ooze nor to clot. His teeth are pointed.

SEJ (7)
A hydrocephalic Breaker at Algul Siento. Daneeka Rostov saves him from the fire in the Study.

SHANTZ (7)

Joe Collins's agent.

SHARPTON, MR. (7)

Dinky Earnshaw's boss at Trans Corporation, a subsidiary of North Central Positronics, before he came to Algul Siento.

Crossover to Other Works: In "Everything's Eventual," Dinky kills Mr. Sharpton by sending one of his special lethal e-mails that contains the word "Excalibur," which is also the name of Arthur Eld's sword.

SHAVERS, GEORGE (2)

Intern at Sisters of Mercy Hospital, a member of the Emergency Ride program who responds to the call when Odetta Holmes is struck by the A train. He saves her life and witnesses her transition back and forth between her two personalities.

SHAW, GRETA (1, 3, 4, 5, 7, M)

Jake Chambers's housekeeper/nanny. She resembles Edith Bunker from *All in the Family*. She is almost a friend and knows what Jake likes and dislikes better than his parents do. She puts his juvenile drawings on the fridge and always remembers to cut the crusts off his sandwiches. Even at a very young age, he knows she isn't his mother, but she'll do until the real thing comes along. When he has night terrors, he can tell her about them. When no one is around, she reads *National Enquirer* and *Inside View*. She calls Jake "Johnny" or " 'Bama."

SKANK, BANGO (3, 5, 6, 7)

A graffiti artist. He tagged the artist's rendering of the Turtle Bay Luxury Condominiums, the men's room at the New York Public Library, Father Callahan's jail cell in Topeka, the restroom next to the bar in the Plaza-Park Hyatt and the tunnel beneath the Dixie Pig. Jake thinks of him as the great lost character. The graffiti normally features only his name, but in the hotel bathroom he also wrote, "Bango Skank awaits the King."

Crossover to Other Works: Bango Skank first appears in Peter Straub's short story "The Buffalo Hunter." He was supposed to be included in *The Talisman* as well, but that didn't happen.

SLIGHTMAN JR., BENJAMIN (5, 6, 7)

Author of *The Hogan*, a Western in Calvin Tower's collection, valuable because of a misprinted title (*The Dogan*) and the author's name on the copyright page. See also Daniel Holmes.

SMITH, BRYAN (7)

Driver of the van that hits Jake and Stephen King. He is returning to his campground from the market in Center Lovell with ground beef and Mars bars. His two rottweilers get into the cooler, distracting his attention. He's lost his driver's license before and is one more offense away from losing it again. Roland convinces him to tell the authorities that there was no one else around at the time of the accident before sending him for help. He is Sheemie Ruiz's twin.

STAUNTON, ANDREW (2)

One of two foot patrol officers who spot Jack Mort after the shoot-out at Clements and the robbery at Katz's Drug Store. He fires the shot that should have killed Jack Mort but hit his cigarette lighter instead.

STURGES, JOHN (6)

Director (*dinh*) of *The Magnificent Seven*.

SULLY-JOHN (7)

One of Bobby Garfield's childhood friends. Pimli Prentiss threatens to harm him if Ted Brautigan doesn't cooperate.

Crossover to Other Works: Sully-John (real name: John Sullivan) is a character in *Hearts in Atlantis*.

TASSENBAUM, DAVID SEYMOUR (7)

Irene Tassenbaum's husband of eighteen years. He is a famous inventor who doesn't believe anything is real unless it can be engraved on a microchip. Irene claims he invented the Internet and all the software necessary to support it. Irene's adventure with Roland makes him pay attention to his wife again, something that hasn't happened in a long time.

TASSENBAUM, IRENE (7)

One of two useful people Roland meets in the East Stoneham General Store. When Roland arrives in 1999, she keeps her cool and agrees to drive him to Turtleback Lane because she knows the way. She is afraid but not panicky.

A talkative forty-seven-year-old Republican from Manhattan. Maiden name: Cantora. Thanks to her husband David's work as a computer innovator, she is wealthy, but she's also bored and neglected. They've been married eighteen years and have no children—she suffered a miscarriage early in their marriage. She and her husband spend summers in the house that once belonged to John Cullum.

She is excited by the adventure. When Bryan Smith tries to get out of his van, she picks up Roland's gun and makes him stay put. She helps Roland think clearly in the aftermath of the accident. She returns for him after the police leave and has already decided she'll sleep with him if he wants her. She doesn't feel confident about her looks: her hair is going gray, she is getting wrinkles, she carries a spare tire and has a lumpectomy scar. Against her nature, she remains quiet around Roland. The fewer questions she asks, the less she'll know about Roland's mission and the better her chance of returning to a normal life after he leaves. She enjoys sleeping with him, but by the time they arrive in New York, she's eager to get back to her husband. Leaving as unexpectedly as she did might get his attention again. After Roland leaves, she has to be content knowing that she played a part in saving the world.

TOOTHAKER, ELVIRA (7)
A woman from Lovell, Maine, who sees Stephen King shortly before Bryan Smith hits him. She is picking raspberries with her friend Justine Anderson, whom she met at Vassar in the 1940s.

TOREN, EDDIE (7)
A young man from White Plains, New York, who dreams of Susannah and goes to meet her in Central Park in 1987. He says his last name is German. In his version of reality, Gary Hart is the president.

TOREN, JAKE (7)
Eddie Toren's younger brother. He and Eddie dream of Susannah for months before they meet her in Central Park.

TOREN, STEFAN (5, 6)
Calvin Tower's great-great-great-grandfather. The envelope that once contained his will, dated March 19, 1846, now contains only a slip of paper with Roland Deschain's name written on it.

TOWER, CALVIN (3, 5, 6, 7)

Proprietor of Manhattan Restaurant of the Mind. His bookstore doesn't do much business. Although he has a skill for acquiring valuable editions, he has difficulty parting with them, even for a profit. He once owned several properties in the Turtle Bay area, but he sold them off over the years. He leases the building that contains his store. The only property he still owns is the vacant lot where Tom and Gerry's Artistic Deli used to be.

He is a custodian of the rose, the last of a long line of Torens dating back at least to his great-great-great-grandfather, Stefan Toren. The name is Dutch—he changed it to Tower. The *ka-tet* believes he's been waiting for the White, to let them have the property. His reluctance to let things go makes him difficult to deal with. Eddie is sometimes tempted to kill him when he does willfully stupid, selfish and dangerous things. Calvin is the child of an A-male father and a B-female mother, and Eddie thinks he's a coward. However, he stands up to the Hitler Brothers, rescuing Father Callahan with the assistance of his only friend, Aaron Deepneau.

He can converse in High Speech. His main contribution to Tet Corporation is to suggest that they enlist psychics to spy on Mid-World and on their enemies, an idea he got from a novel written by Benjamin Slightman Jr. under the pen name Daniel Holmes. He died of a heart attack in his bookstore in 1990.

Physical description: He's about five foot nine and weighs about 230 pounds. He's in his fifties, suffers from arthritis, and most of his hair is gone on the sides of his forehead. Wears half-glasses.

TOWNE, FRED (7)

One of the "good minds" employed by Tet Corporation at a ranch in Taos. He believes that Roland's Patek Philippe watch will stop or run backward when Roland reaches the Dark Tower. He expresses concern about Mordred's hunger.

TUBTHER, MR. (5)

Eddie Dean's fifth-grade teacher. Eddie hears his voice in the Doorway Cave, telling him he had such potential until he let his brother spoil him.

VAGRANT DEAD (5, 6)

People who have either died so suddenly they don't understand what happened to them or refuse to accept it. Eventually they do go on. Christopher Johns told Roland that a person going todash might see vags.

VECCHIO, RUDY (2)

One of Enrico Balazar's henchmen.

VERRILL, CHUCK (7)

Stephen King's editor in New York.

VINCENT, COLIN "COL" (2)

A gofer for Enrico Balazar. Deemed useful and obedient but not particularly trustworthy. Twenty-four years old at the time he is killed in the shoot-out with Eddie and Roland.

WALKER, DETTA (2, 3, 4, 4.5, 5, 6, 7)

One of Susannah Dean's personalities. She emerged after five-year-old Odetta Holmes was hit in the head by a brick dropped by Jack Mort and more often after Mort pushed her in front of the A train. She is self-destructive, wanting nothing more than to be killed by a white man. She shoplifts, but destroys what she takes. Aunt Sophie's blue plate is the focus of much of her rage because the wedding gift represents the trip to New Jersey that led to her head injury.

She lives in a loft in Greenwich Village and talks like a stereotype. She's mean, crude and vulgar, but also shrewd. She teased white boys by making out with them and then shutting them down, enjoying the game, even though she sometimes got slapped, punched, spat upon or kicked. She doesn't care anything about anyone else. She has many secrets that even Susannah isn't privy to.

Detta reemerges from time to time—in Susannah's voice and face—especially when she's under stress. Detta solves the puzzle of the prime numbers in the Cradle of Lud. Susannah sometimes calls on Detta to steady her hand when she is about to enter battle. She's Susannah's secret weapon, a private cache of strength and a powerful personality who catches adversaries off guard. Detta deals with the demon in the Speaking Ring and asserts herself when Mia takes control. The only person Detta is nice to is Patrick Danville, and being nice wears her out. Without Detta, Roland believes that Susannah would have been only a handsome black woman with no legs below the knees. With that personality, she was dangerous. A gunslinger.

Susannah calls on Detta on the day she prepares to leave Mid-World. Being Detta all but guarantees she won't cry when she says good-bye. Roland refuses to let her leave as Detta. This aspect of her personality will always be with her, even in her new life in New York, where she will likely be required in Tet's war against North Central Positronics.

WALKER, SOPHIA (2, 3, 5, 6)

Odetta Holmes's mother's younger sister. Known as Sister or Aunt Blue because blue was her favorite color. She was married in Elizabeth, New Jersey, when Odetta was five. The blue "forspecial" plate that Odetta's mother gave her as a wedding gift was a focus of Detta Walker's hatred.

WALK-INS (6, 7)

People and animals from Mid-World that are sucked into west central Maine through a magic doorway. Some are dressed in old-fashioned clothes. Some are naked. Some speak languages no one can understand. Among them are taheen, slow mutants and Children of Roderick. They usually disappear shortly after they arrive. They started appearing shortly after Stephen King moved into the area in the late 1970s, though King has never seen one. Eddie, Jake and Roland admit to being walk-ins. There's even a Church of the Walk-Ins in Lovell-Stoneham by 1999.

WAVERLY (7)

A Breaker at Algul Siento. He was a bookkeeper in his previous life.

WEAVER [WHEATON], NORRIS (2)

One of two foot patrol officers who spot Jack Mort after the shoot-out at Clements and the robbery at Katz's Drug Store. Roland shot his gun out of his hand and warned him not to follow.

WILSON, TEDDY (6)

County constable and game warden in East Stoneham.

WILSON, WILLIAM (2)

Eddie Dean's drug contact in Nassau.

WORTHINGTON, FRED (7)

A Breaker from Algul Siento. A stout, bankerly looking man. He took the Spirit of Topeka to Fedic with Susannah, Ted, Dinky, Dani Rostov and Sheemie. He used chalk to indicate the passage Roland and Susannah needed to take beneath Castle Discordia.

VAN WYCK, MATHIESSEN "MATS" (6, 7)

Second assistant to the Swedish ambassador to the United Nations. Susannah mesmerizes him into reserving a room for her at the Plaza-Park Hyatt using the scrimshaw turtle, which van Wyck dubs the skölpadda. His wife is having an affair.

PLACES

AKRON, OHIO (7)

Ted Brautigan accidentally used his special power to murder a man who stole his wallet here.

AMERICANO BAR (5)

Located near the intersection of Second Avenue and 19th Street. Father Callahan got drunk here after seeing the vagrant dead for the first time.

AQUINAS HOTEL (2)

Hotel where Eddie stays in Nassau, Bahamas, while on a drug-buying trip for Balazar.

AVENUE OF THE AMERICAS (2)

Jack Mort's office is located here. Another name for Sixth Avenue.

BANGOR, MAINE (7)

The town Stephen King writes about when he writes about Derry. The "real" Ed Deepneau lives here, as does Stephen King.

BARCELONA LUGGAGE (5)

A store on Second Avenue near 54th Street.

BLACKSTRAP MOLASSES CAFÉ (6)

Located at Lexington and 60th, one block from the Dixie Pig. Susannah paid a busker on this corner to play "Man of Constant Sorrow."

BLEECKER STREET (3, 5, 7)

A nightclub district in Greenwich Village. Aaron Deepneau used to hang out here and it was also a favorite haunt of Odetta Holmes. An empty warehouse on this street has a North Central Positronics doorway.

BLIMPIE'S (5)
A fast-food restaurant at 844 Second Avenue (at the 45th Street intersection).

BRIDGTON, MAINE (6, 7)
The Maine town where Stephen King lives in 1977. Twenty miles from East Stoneham.

BROOKLYN (2, 3, 5, 6, 7)
One of the five Boroughs of New York City, home to Co-Op City in Eddie Dean's world, and the analog to the Portal of the Bear.

BROOKLYN VOCATIONAL INSTITUTE (3)
The school Henry Dean attended before enlisting in the army.

CARA LAUGHS (7)
The lakefront house at #19 Turtleback Lane in Lovell, Maine, where Stephen King lives. The McCray family from Washington, D.C., owned it until the husband had a stroke.

Crossover to Other Works: Sara Laughs is the name of a similar house in *Bag of Bones*.

CASTLE AVENUE (3, 7)
A street in Co-Op City lined with pizza shops, bars and bodegas. The Majestic Theater is located at the intersection with Markey Avenue.

CENTRAL PARK (2, 4, 5, 7)
Jake and Susannah both heard a man playing a saw in this Manhattan park. It's where Susannah meets Eddie and Jake Toren in the winter of 1987.

CENTRAL PARK SOUTH (2)
Odetta Holmes's penthouse is in the Greymarl Apartments at the intersection of Central Park South and Fifth Avenue.

THE CHAMBERSES' APARTMENT (2, 3)
A duplex apartment located on Fifth Avenue between 38th and 39th.

CHEW CHEW MAMA'S (3, 5, 6)
A small restaurant located on Second Avenue at 52nd Street. Its name reminds Jake of *Charlie the Choo-Choo*. It closed in 1994 and became Dennis's Waffles and Pancakes.

CHRISTOPHER STREET STATION (2, 6)
Subway station on the west side of Greenwich Village where Jack Mort pushed Odetta Holmes in front of the A train. In Keystone Earth, the A train doesn't go there.

CITY LIGHTS (5)
A bar on Lexington Avenue that Father Callahan frequented.

CLEMENTS GUNS AND SPORTING GOODS (2, 4)
The gun shop in Manhattan where Roland gets ammo for his guns. Located at Seventh Avenue and 49th. The police suspect the owner is selling guns to people like Enrico Balazar.

COLUMBIA UNIVERSITY (6)
Odetta Holmes's alma mater.

CO-OP CITY (2, 3, 5, 6, 7)
The housing project where Eddie and Henry Dean lived. In Eddie's world, it is located in Brooklyn, but in Keystone Earth it is in the Bronx. Stephen King's geographic mistake is the reason for the differences between worlds.

CULLUM CARETAKING AND CAMP CHECKING (7)
John Cullum's business before he joins Tet Corporation.

2 DAG HAMMARSKJÖLD PLAZA (6, 7)
The address of the skyscraper erected on the vacant lot at the corner of Second Avenue and 46th Street. A shrine: The House of the Rose. The lobby is full of light, admitted through two-story-tall windows. The Garden of the Beam is cordoned off with velvet ropes in the middle of the lobby. At the center is the rose representing the Dark Tower—the building was erected around it. Tet Corporation has its headquarters on the ninety-ninth floor. The people who work here call it the Black Tower. They wish they lived here and find excuses to work late. People often pass by the building to hear the singing voices that emanate from it.

Denby's Discount Drug (3)

A drugstore in Times Square. Jake borrows its name when providing an alias to a cop who stops him for suspected truancy.

Dennis's Waffles and Pancakes (6)

On Second Avenue at 52nd Street. Opened after Chew Chew Mama's closed in 1994. Trudy Damascus eats lunch here the day she meets Susannah and Mia.

Detroit, Michigan (5, 6)

Father Callahan worked at the Lighthouse Shelter in this city in 1983. He committed suicide during a fake meeting at the Sombra Corporation's offices in that city to avoid being infected by Type Three vampires.

Dimity Road (6)

Calvin Tower and Aaron Deepneau rent a house on this road in East Stoneham, Maine.

Dixie Pig, The (5, 6, 7)

Restaurant located at Lexington and 61st in Manhattan. It has a green awning imprinted with a grinning cartoon roasted pig. According to *Gourmet* magazine it has the best ribs in New York but its real specialty is "long pork," or human flesh. The *ka-tet* first sees it mentioned in graffiti on the construction barricade surrounding the vacant lot. A version of it has probably been at this location since the time of the Dutch. Mia leads Susannah here to meet Richard Sayre, who takes them via an underground passage to a scientific door that goes to the Fedic Dogan. When Jake, Father Callahan and Oy arrive, a sign announces that it is closed for a private function. By the time Roland gets there, Tet Corporation is guarding the restaurant.

The dining room is lit by electric flambeaux on the walls and candles on the tables. A hanging tapestry shows knights and ladies dining at a long banquet table. Upon closer inspection, the "roast" is a human body. Behind the tapestry, Type One vampires feast on babies. The kitchen is identical to the one Jake saw when he followed Mia's dream. A door in the corner of the pantry leads to a tiled stairway that descends to a tunnel protected by a mind-trap that ends at the Fedic door.

Drawers, The (1, 2, 3, 4, 7, M)

The place where Detta Walker destroyed the blue "forspecial" plate. A smoking trash-littered gravel pit. She also uses the word to describe the place she hides while waiting for Roland to return from the Pusher doorway so she can kill him. Can also be applied to other places of self-destruction, such as whorehouses, drug dens and gambling houses. The Speaking Demon in the basement of the Way Station warned Roland to "go slow past the Drawers." Roland thinks the word refers to lost places that are spoiled or useless, places of desolation, waste lands. Detta thinks of it as a place where she goes to fulfill herself.

DUTCH HILL (3, 4, 5, 6, 7)
Part of Brooklyn, a mile from where Eddie Dean grew up. Home of The Mansion, where Jake Chambers reentered Mid-World.

EAST STONEHAM GENERAL STORE (5, 6, 7)
A smaller version of Took's General Store, owned by Chip McAvoy. Site of a shoot-out between Roland, Eddie and Balazar's men. The store burned in that battle but was rebuilt larger and fancier. Roland finds two useful people here: John Cullum in 1977 and Irene Tassenbaum in 1999.

EAST STONEHAM, MAINE (5, 6, 7)
The central Maine town forty miles north of Portland where Calvin Tower and Aaron Deepneau hide out. A twin of Calla Bryn Sturgis: the church looks like Our Lady of Serenity; the Methodist Meeting Hall looks like the Calla Gathering Hall. Home to John Cullum. Irene Tassenbaum and her husband buy Cullum's house as a summer home.

ELIZABETH, NEW JERSEY (2, 3)
Home of Odetta Holmes's Aunt Sophia. Odetta was walking to the train depot with her family when Jack Mort dropped a brick on her head.

FIFTH AVENUE (2, 3, 5, 6, 7)
A major thoroughfare in Manhattan. Odetta Holmes lives at the intersection with Central Park South. Jake Chambers lived on this street and died at the 43rd Street intersection. Eddie applies this name to a street in Lud.

FRENCH LANDING, WISCONSIN (7)
Where Walter o'Dim acquired the wire-lined hat that is supposed to protect him from Mordred.
   Crossover to Other Works: *Black House* is set in French Landing.

GAGE PARK (4, 5, 7)

A park in Topeka, Kansas. The *ka-tet* ends up here after they get off Blaine the Mono. Features the Reinisch Rose Gardens and an old-time carousel. They also find the inspiration for the book *Charlie the Choo-Choo*. Father Callahan saw signs the low men had tracked him to Topeka here.

GEORGE WASHINGTON BRIDGE (3, 5, 7)

A bridge between Manhattan and New Jersey familiarly known as the GWB. Eddie Dean's uncle painted it. The bridge across the River Send outside Lud resembles it. Roland sees it from the window of Tet Corporation's headquarters.

GREEN PALACE (4, 4.5, 5, 7)

Also known as the Emerald Palace and inspired by *The Wizard of Oz*. A castle-like building that appears to float across the lanes of I-70 outside Topeka. It seems to be made of glass and reflects the color of the sky. Pale green walls rise to jutting battlements and soaring towers topped with emerald green needles adorned with pennants featuring the open eye of the Crimson King. The inner redoubt is made of dark blue glass. A huge barred gate made of glass stakes the colors of the Wizard's Rainbow blocks the entrance. Each stake except the central black bar contain human-like creatures representing the Guardians of the Beam. To the left of the main doorway is a sentry box made of cream-colored glass streaked with orange. Violet gargoyles flank the entrance above the entry. Inside, a vaulted hallway extends forty yards to thirty-foot doorway. The inner chamber is like the nave of a cathedral with the décor of a Barony Coach. The only furnishing is a green glass throne dozens of feet high. Above the throne are thirteen great cylinders pulsing the colors of the Wizard's Rainbow. The building serves as a doorway back to the Path of the Beam and is also known to exist in Mid-World.

GREENWICH VILLAGE (2, 3, 5, 7)

Part of Manhattan. Detta Walker had a loft in an apartment building here. The Christopher Street subway station, where Odetta Holmes lost her legs, is located here, too.

GREYMARL APARTMENTS (2)

Odetta Holmes lived in the penthouse of this building, located at the intersection of Fifth Avenue and Central Park South.

GUTTENBURG, FURTH AND PATEL (6)
The accounting firm where Trudy Damascus works.

HARTFORD, CONNECTICUT (4, 5, 7)
Father Callahan's bus from 'Salem's Lot stops here on the way to New York City. Ted Brautigan tried to enlist in the American Expeditionary Force here. One of those places where no one in their right mind would want to live, according to Eddie Dean.

HOME (5, 6)
A "wet" homeless shelter located at the intersection of First Avenue and 47th Street near the United Nations, founded in 1968. Father Callahan worked here for nine months in 1975 and 1976 with Lupe Delgado and Rowan Magruder. Mother Teresa helped serve dinner here once.

HOTDOG STAND (3)
Located at the intersection of Broadway and 42nd Street. Jake bought a sweet sausage and a Nehi here after leaving the museum before heading to Brooklyn.

HOUSE OF CARDS (3)
A magic shop located at the intersection of Second Avenue and 52nd Street. The display in the window is a tower built from tarot cards. In Eddie's dream, Enrico Balazar, who used to make houses of cards in his office, is a bum sitting out front.

HUNGRY I, THE (2, 6, 7)
The Greenwich Village coffeehouse Odetta Holmes visited just before she was pushed. She first heard "Man of Constant Sorrow" here in 1962.

I-70 (4, 5)
The interstate that traverses Topeka, Kansas. The *ka-tet* finds the Green Palace crossing its lanes.

JANGO'S (7)
Nightclub in Cleveland where Joe Collins claims he used to perform as a comedian.

JERUSALEM'S LOT (5, 6, 7)

A small town in Maine, familiarly known as 'Salem's Lot. Father Callahan was the parish priest at St. Andrews from 1969 until vampires overran it in 1974. It is a real place to him, but fictional to everyone else.

KANSAS CITY BLUES (5)

A midtown saloon on 54th Street near Second Avenue.

KATZ'S DRUG STORE (2)

Site of the first penicillin robbery in history. Located at 395 West 49th Avenue.

KENNEDY INTERNATIONAL AIRPORT (2, 5, 7)

One of New York City's airports. Eddie's flight from the Bahamas lands here.

KEYSTONE EARTH (5, 6, 7)

The most important version of our reality—the one that contains the rose and Stephen King. Level Nineteen of the Dark Tower. Time moves only in one direction here, and all deaths are final. It has a resonance that all other worlds—even Mid-World—lack. The name is coined by the Breakers of Al-gul Siento. Taheen call it the Real World. Most Breakers come from here.

KEYWADIN POND (6, 7)

A lake behind the East Stoneham General Store. John Cullum has a house on the south end that Irene Tassenbaum and her husband buy after he joins Tet Corporation.

KEZAR LAKE (6, 7)

The lake next to Stephen King's home on Turtleback Lane in Lovell, Maine.

LAS VEGAS (4, 5, 7)

Where the Dark Man is, according to a message found on I-70 outside Topeka.

Crossover to Other Works: Randall Flagg assembles his followers here in *The Stand*.

LEABROOK, NEW JERSEY (5)

An alternate version of Fort Lee, where Father Callahan worked as a short-order cook.

LEANING TOWER, THE (2, 3, 5, 6)
Balazar's bar in Manhattan.

LIGHTHOUSE SHELTER, THE (5)
A wet shelter in Detroit where Father Callahan was working when he died.

LOS ZAPATOS, MEXICO (5)
Black Thirteen sent Father Callahan here for Ben Mears's funeral.

LOVELL, MAINE (6, 7)
The western Maine town that Stephen King moves to from Bridgton. Turtle-back Lane and Cara Laughs are located here.

MACY'S (2, 3, 5)
Department store located at Sixth Avenue and 34th Street where Detta Walker is shoplifting when Roland encounters her for the first time.

MAJESTIC THEATER (3, 5, 6)
Movie theater at the corner of Castle and Markey avenues. Eddie Dean saw many movies here when he was a kid, including Clint Eastwood Westerns. It smelled of piss and popcorn and the kind of wine that came in brown bags. When Jake Chambers passes it, the theater is advertising Spaghetti Week and playing *A Fistful of Dollars* and *The Good, The Bad and The Ugly*. A movie poster featuring Eastwood reminds Jake of Roland.

MANHATTAN RESTAURANT OF THE MIND (3, 5, 6, 7)
A used bookstore owned by Calvin Tower, located on Second Avenue between 52nd and 54th streets. Jake Chambers buys a copy of *Charlie the Choo-Choo* here and is given a copy of *Riddle-de-Dum!* It has a chalkboard hanging in the window announcing the day's specials like in a restaurant. The interior is also outfitted like a restaurant, with a fountain-style counter bisecting the room and tables equipped with wire-backed Malt Shoppe chairs arranged to display the specials. Jake thinks it is the best bookstore he's ever been in, though it probably doesn't do more than fifty dollars in business a day. It has a storage area as big as a warehouse with stacks running fourteen to sixteen feet tall. The store cat is named Sergio. Enrico Balazar had it burned down on June 24, 1977, but Tower rebuilds it and dies here in 1990.

MANSION, THE (3, 5)

Abandoned, crumbling, condemned Victorian mansion on Rhinehold Street near the intersection with Brooklyn Street in Dutch Hill. Covered in vines and boarded up. The windows are broken, but it shows no other signs of vandalism except for spray paint on the fence around it. Regarded as haunted by area children, and two teens who tried to use it as a makeout pad were supposedly found dead and drained of their blood. Nine blocks from the apartment where Eddie Dean lived. Henry Dean says he wouldn't go inside for a million dollars. The house is alive, a manifestation of a monster called the doorkeeper that tries to prevent Jake from using the portal within to get back to Mid-World. The key Jake found in the abandoned lot fits this door. After Jake passes through, the house collapses upon itself.

MARINE MIDLAND BANK (5)

The bank where Home does its business, located on Third Avenue between 47th and 48th streets.

MARKEY ACADEMY (3)

Name of a fictitious school that Jake uses as part of his alibi while skipping school.

MARKEY AVENUE (3, 5, 7)

Location of Eddie Dean's apartment building in Co-Op City, Brooklyn. He and Henry used to shoot hoops in a playground that is now the site of the Juvenile Court Building.

MARSTEN HOUSE (5)

The house in 'Salem's Lot, Maine, where Barlow lives.

METROPOLITAN MUSEUM OF ART (3)

Jake hangs out here to kill time before heading to Brooklyn on the day he crosses back to Mid-World. Though it is located on Fifth Avenue and 82nd in Keystone Earth, it seems to be close to Times Square in Jake's world.

MID-TOWN LANES (1, 3, 5, 6, 7, M)

A bowling alley in Manhattan frequented by Jake Chambers. Located on 33rd Street. The pink bowling bag Jake finds in the vacant lot says "Nothing but Strikes in Mid-Town Lanes."

MID-WORLD AMUSEMENT PARK AND FUN FAIR (3)
The park in California where Charlie the Choo-Choo ended up.

MOREHOUSE (5, 6)
An all-male black college in Atlanta. A sign of affluence that Detta Walker disdains. Her reference point is *Invisible Man* by Ralph Ellison.

MYSTIC, CONNECTICUT (3)
Susannah saw whales in the Seaquarium there.

NASSAU (2, 3, 5, 6, 7)
Capital of the Bahamas. Eddie went there to purchase cocaine for Enrico Balazar to help pay for his heroin habit. He meets Roland for the first time while returning from that trip. Sombra Corporation is incorporated here.

NEBRASKA (3, 4, 5)
Where to find Abigail ("the old woman from the dreams") according to a message found on the side of I-70 outside Topeka.

    Crossover to Other Works: Mother Abigail lives in Hemingsford Home, Nebraska, in *The Stand*.

NEW YORK GENERAL HOSPITAL (5)
Hospital where Lupe Delgado dies from AIDS.

NEW YORK PUBLIC LIBRARY (5)
Located at 455 Fifth Avenue. Father Callahan uses the reference section to look up the zip code Aaron Deepneau left for him at the vacant lot and he steals the book *Yankee Highways* on a second visit. Bango Skank wrote his name in a men's room bathroom stall.

ODETTA, ARKANSAS (2)
Birthplace of Odetta Holmes's mother.

OXFORD, MISSISSIPPI (2, 3, 5, 6, 7)
Odetta Holmes was jailed here in the summer of 1964 while protesting after three voter registration workers disappeared. She sometimes refers to it as Oxford Town.

OZ (3, 4, 4.5, 5, 6, 7)

Mythical land from the books of L. Frank Baum. Eddie calls Roland the Eagle Scout of Oz. Eddie and Susannah promise to tell Roland the story of *The Wizard of Oz*, which they do after they find red shoes on I-70 as they approach the Emerald Palace.

PAPER PATCH, THE (3)

A stationery store at the intersection of Second Avenue and 46th Street. It has a window display of pens, notebooks and desk calculators.

409 PARK AVENUE SOUTH (2)

Jack Mort's apartment. Roland supplied this address when talking to the police officers outside Clements Guns and Sporting Goods.

PIPER SCHOOL (1, 3, 4, 5, 6, 7, M)

The private school located on 56th Street between Park and Madison that Jake Chambers attends. According to his father, it is the best damned school in the country for a boy his age. It has seventy boys and fifty girls and boasts the highest student/teacher ratio of any fine private school in the east. Annual tuition is $22,000.

PLAZA HOTEL (5)

Fifth Avenue at Central Park South. Lupe Delgado worked on the maintenance crew.

PLAZA-PARK HYATT

See United Nations Plaza Hotel.

POCKET PARK (7)

A small park across from 2 Dag Hammarskjöld Plaza. It has a bench next to a fountain and a metal sculpture identical to the scrimshaw turtle Susannah found in the bowling bag.

POLICE SHOOTING RANGE (3)

Shooting range on First Avenue, where Elmer Chambers practiced.

PUSHING PLACE, THE (1, 2, 3)

The intersection of Fifth Avenue and 43rd Street. In one version of reality, Jake Chambers died here when Jack Mort pushed him in front of a car.

REFLECTIONS OF YOU (3)

A mirror shop on Second Avenue between 48th and 49th streets. Eddie sees it in a dream and Jake passes it en route to the Manhattan Restaurant of the Mind.

RIVERSIDE HOSPITAL (5)

The hospital in Manhattan where Rowan Magruder is taken after the Hitler Brothers attack him. Father Callahan is hospitalized in the same room after Magruder dies.

70 ROCKEFELLER PLAZA (3)

Elmer Chambers's office at "The Network."

SACRAMENTO BEE (5, 7)

The newspaper where Father Callahan learns of the attack on Rowan Magruder. Ted Brautigan became a Breaker after answering a job ad in the same newspaper.

'SALEM'S LOT, MAINE

See Jerusalem's Lot.

SANTA FE, NEW MEXICO (4)

One of the destinations served by the train station in Topeka. Roland remembers a Santa Fe in the Barony of Mejis.

SEVENTH AVENUE (2)

Clements Guns and Sporting Goods is located at the intersection with 49th Street.

SIR SPEEDY-PARK (7)

Irene and David Tassenbaum rent two parking spots on a yearly basis at this lot on 63rd Street between Fifth Avenue and Madison Avenue. Their apartment is nearby.

SISTERS OF MERCY HOSPITAL (2)

The hospital on 23rd Street where Odetta Holmes was taken after her accident.

SIXTH AVENUE (2)

Also known as the Avenue of the Americas. Jack Mort's office is located here.

ST. ANDREWS (5)

Father Callahan's church in 'Salem's Lot, Maine. It rejected him after Barlow tainted him.

STATION SHOES & BOOTS (5)

Located on Second Avenue near 50th Street.

ST. LOUIS, MISSOURI (3, 4)

American city that corresponds to Lud. The beginning of Charlie the Choo-Choo's run.

SUNNYVALE SANITARIUM (3)

The mental institute Jake thinks he will end up in after his memories double.

SUNSET COTTAGE (7)

The Tassenbaums' cottage in East Stoneham at the south end of Keywadin Pond. They purchased the place in 1994. Known as the old John Cullum place to the locals.

TAOS, NEW MEXICO (7)

Location of a ranch where Tet Corporation employs a dozen telepaths and precogs to monitor Roland and his *ka-tet* in Mid-World and spy on Sombra Corporation/North Central Positronics.

TIMES SQUARE (1, 3, 4, 5, 6, 7)

Jake is stopped by a police officer here because he is truant on the day he crosses back to Mid-World. Odetta Holmes and Father Callahan used to frequent movie theaters here.

TISHMAN BUILDING (5)

Located at 982 Michigan Avenue in Detroit. One of the finest business addresses in the city. Sombra had offices on the thirty-third floor. Father Callahan leaped to his death from their conference room.

TOM AND GERRY'S ARTISTIC DELI (3, 4, 5, 6)

A small shop owned by Tommy Graham on the corner of Second Avenue and 46th Street. Party platters were their specialty. Calvin Tower, who owns the property, had the building torn down after it went out of business (between 1977 and 1981). Designated Lot #298, Block #19, it remained empty until sometime after Jake's visit in 1987. 2 Dag Hammarskjöld Plaza was built at that location.

TOPEKA, KANSAS (3, 4, 5, 6, 7)

The terminus of Blaine the Mono's route, as well as that of Charlie the Choo-Choo. The *ka-tet* finds the inspiration for Charlie the Choo-Choo in Gage Park. The Green Palace appears on its outskirts on Interstate 70. Father Callahan moved here in 1982, hit bottom and finally got sober.

TOWER OF POWER (3, 5)

A record shop on Second Avenue and 51st Street.

TURTLEBACK LANE (6, 7)

The road in Lovell, Maine, that appears to be the center of walk-in activity. It's a hilly road off Route 7 that's only one lane wide in places. Stephen King moved here to a house called Cara Laughs at #19 in the mid-1980s. It is also the site of a magic door.

TURTLE BAY (3)

A Manhattan neighborhood that comprises an area between 41st and 54th streets from Lexington Avenue to the East River. It is under the umbrella of *ka*.

TURTLE BAY LUXURY CONDOMINIUMS (3, 5, 6, 7)

Building announced by Sombra Corporation for the empty lot containing the rose but never constructed.

TURTLE BAY WASHATERIA (5, 6, 7)

Out-of-business laundry on 47th Street between First and Second avenues. The Hitler Brothers took Callahan here to kill him, but Calvin Tower and Aaron Deepneau interrupted them. There is a doorway between various versions of New York here.

UNITED NATIONS BUILDING (3, 5)

Located on First Avenue and 46th Street in Turtle Bay.

UNITED NATIONS PLAZA HOTEL (5, 6)

Located on First Avenue and 46th Street in Turtle Bay. It became the Plaza-Park Hyatt and was destined to become the Regal U.N. Plaza Hotel owned by Sombra/North Central in July 1999. Mathiessen van Wyck reserves a room for Susannah/Mia in this hotel so she can wait for a call from Richard Sayre. Jake and Father Callahan retrieve Black Thirteen and the Orizas from the safe in room 1919.

VASSAR COLLEGE (3, 7)
Laura Chambers and Elvira Toothaker attended this school.

VIETNAM (2, 4, 5, 6, 7)
Henry Dean was injured fighting in the war there, which began his trouble with drugs.

WARRINGTON'S (7)
A restaurant in East Stoneham, Maine, where the Tassenbaums sometimes dine.
   Crossover to Other Works: Warrington's also appears in *Bag of Bones*.

WASHINGTON SQUARE PARK (5)
Father Callahan spent his first night in New York here after fleeing from 'Salem's Lot. It becomes one of his favorite haunts. He sees the first signs of low men looking for him there.

WHITE PLAINS, NEW YORK (7)
Hometown of Eddie and Jake Toren.

WORLD TRADE CENTER (3, 6, 7)
Father Callahan and Jake put Black Thirteen in a coin-op storage locker in the basement of this building, where it would be safe for thirty-six months, until 2002. Rowan Magruder told Callahan it was the safest storage location in New York.

THINGS
A TRAIN (2, 3)
One of the trains in the New York subway system, made famous by a Duke Ellington song as a way to get to Harlem. A train from this line cut off Odetta Holmes's legs after Jack Mort pushed her at the Christopher Street station, though in our world the A train does not go there.

AIR DANCE (5)
A book by Ben Mears, a character in *'Salem's Lot*, about a man who gets hung for the murder his brother committed. Eddie Dean read the novel.

Crossover to Other Works: Susan Norton is reading this book when Ben Mears meets her in *'Salem's Lot.*

BOING BOING BURGER (4)

A fast-food chain in the version of Earth ravaged by the superflu.

BULLET (7)

One of Bryan Smith's rottweilers.

CAPTAIN TRIPS (4)

Name for the superflu in California.

CHARLIE THE CHOO-CHOO (3, 4, 5, 6, 7)

A children's book written by Beryl Evans in 1927 in one version of reality and by Claudia y Inez Bachman in 1936 in another. Jake buys a copy at the Manhattan Restaurant of the Mind. Greta Shaw, Eddie and Susannah owned the book when they were kids and all three lost their copies. It contains clues to handling Blaine the Mono. The cover features an anthropomorphic locomotive with a pink cowcatcher. The story mentions a girl named Susannah, a man named Martin (Marten) and a train that runs between St. Louis (Lud) and Topeka. Charlie is a 402 Big Boy Steam Locomotive, the best train in the Mid-World Railway Company until a diesel locomotive replaces him. His operator is Engineer Bob Brooks.

DOGAN, THE (5, 6, 7)

The misprinted title of *The Hogan*, a Western written by Benjamin Slightman Jr.

FORSPECIAL PLATE (2, 3, 4, 5, 6, 7)

A blue plate that was part of a wedding gift to Sophia Walker, Odetta Holmes's aunt. To Detta it is an avatar for her hatred because Odetta was injured after attending Sophia's wedding. Similar white plates with delicate blue webbing are found in the banquet hall at Castle Discordia. The Orizas of the Callas resemble this plate.

GARDEN OF THE BEAM (7)

A shrine in the lobby of 2 Dag Hammarskjöld Plaza. The marble floor gives way to a patch of earth surrounded by velvet ropes. The garden contains dwarf palms and other plants. In the middle of the square is the rose that represents the Dark Tower in Keystone Earth. The building was built around the rose—it wasn't transplanted from the vacant lot. The sign over it reads, "Given by the Tet Corporation, in honor of Edward Cantor Dean and John 'Jake' Chambers. As White over Red, thus Gan wills ever."

HOGAN, THE (5, 6, 7)
See *The Dogan*.

HOLMES DENTAL INDUSTRIES (CORPORATION) (2, 5, 6, 7)
The company formed by Dan Holmes to exploit his inventions pertaining to capping teeth. It also produces dental floss, toothpaste and mouthwash. Holmes handled the financial side of the business until his first heart attack in 1959, when he gets his accountant, Moses Carver, more involved. Eddie comes up with a plan to merge the company with Tet Corporation and use its assets to thwart Sombra and North Central Positronics.

INSOMNIA (7)
A novel by Stephen King published in 1994. The Calvins believe it is King's most important book outside of the Dark Tower series. Its red-and-white cover indicates its significance. It mentions the Crimson King, Ed Deepneau and Patrick Danville. Moses Carver gives Roland a copy, but he passes it on to Irene Tassenbaum, afraid that it might be a mind-trap.

JAFFORDS RENTALS (6)
Realtor who leases lakefront cabins in Bridgton, Maine.

KANSAS CITY MONARCHS (4, 5)
A major league baseball team in the world ravaged by the superflu.

KEFLEX (2, 3)
An antibiotic. Eddie takes some from Balazar's stash and Roland takes more from Katz's Drug Store. They use it to rid Roland of the infection from the lobstrosity wounds and to rid Jake of the infection from the spider bite he received while crossing back to Mid-World. Roland pronounces the word "cheflet."

KEYSTONE YEAR (7)

1999—the year when Stephen King is supposed to die and the year where Mia goes to have her baby. Also the year John Kennedy Jr.—the son of the last gunslinger in Keystone Earth—died and the year that King wrote Ted Brautigan into the Dark Tower story.

LOOK HOMEWARD, ANGEL (1, 5)

A novel by Thomas Wolfe. The ghostwood box containing Black Thirteen contains symbols from this book: a leaf, a stone, an unfound door.

MAGNIFICENT SEVEN, THE (5, 6)

An MGM movie directed by John Sturges, an Americanized version of Akira Kurosawa's *Seven Samurai*. Eddie makes the connection between the movie and their adventures in Calla Bryn Sturgis.

"MAN/MAID OF CONSTANT SORROW" (5, 6)

A traditional American folk song. Susannah Dean sings it at Calla Bryn Sturgis and hears a busker singing it near the Dixie Pig. She first heard it in the Hungry i in 1962, sung by a white blues-shouter named Dave Van Ronk.

MARLOWE (7)

Stephen King's Welsh corgi. Also known as the Snoutmaster.

MICROSOFT (5, 6, 7)

A computer hardware and software company started by Bill Gates. Jake sees its logo in the Dogan near Calla Bryn Sturgis. Eddie tells Calvin Tower and John Cullum to invest in their stock to grow Tet Corporation's assets. Shares that cost fifteen dollars in 1982 are worth more than thirty-five dollars in 1987.

MID-WORLD RAILWAY COMPANY (3)

The company that owns and operates Charlie the Choo-Choo in the book of the same name.

MILLS CONSTRUCTION (3, 4, 5, 7)

A construction partner of Sombra Real Estate. They plan to build Turtle Bay Luxury Condominiums on the vacant lot.

MY UNDERSTANDING OF TRUTH (3, 4, 5)

The theme for Jake Chambers's final essay in his English Composition class. It counts twenty-five percent toward his grade. The paper, which Jake does not remember writing, contains many Mid-World references, including things that will happen in the future, called forth by the touch. Mrs. Avery gives him an A+ and provides a detailed (but misguided) interpretation of the essay's allusions. When Stephen King sends Jake a message, he labels it "This is the truth."

PIMSY (7)

Odetta Holmes's pet. Eddie uses the fact that Moses Carver told her she could visit the grave so that John Cullum can convince him to join Tet Corporation.

PISTOL (7)

One of Bryan Smith's rottweilers.

RIDDLE-DE-DUM! (3, 4, 5, 7)

A book of riddles that Jake Chambers gets at the Manhattan Restaurant of the Mind. Its subtitle is *Brain-Twisters and Puzzles for Everyone.* No author is credited. The cover is torn and mended with tape and features a boy and a girl with question marks over their heads. The answers have been ripped out of the back of the book.

ROSE IN THE VACANT LOT, THE (3, 5, 6, 7)

The Dark Tower's representation on Earth. Though it is fragile, if properly protected it can be immortal. When Jake first sees it, it is growing near a clump of alien-looking purple grass that may be splashed with paint. Though the rose opens for Jake, he can tell it is ailing. Inside, he sees a sun glowing and then realizes that it is not just one sun but many—perhaps every sun. Eddie sees all the great things that have ever happened and every near miss. Its singing voice promises that all things might be well again. As the Tower weakens, it is what holds everything together, although it is weakening, too. If it dies, the Dark Tower will simply fall. To protect it, Tet Corporation builds a roped-off garden in the lobby of 2 Dag Hammarskjöld Plaza where it can receive direct sunlight. It sings and makes people happy. Eddie theorizes that the rose is Stephen King's twin and that it is taking care of one of the two remaining Beams.

ROSSCO (7)

A brand of appliance in worlds other than Keystone Earth. Joe Collins's electric stove is this brand.

'SALEM'S LOT (5, 6)

A book written by Stephen King and published by Doubleday in 1975. Roland finds a copy on Calvin Tower's shelf of valuable books with a penciled price of $950 on the flyleaf. The church on the cover reminds him of Our Lady of Serenity in Calla Bryn Sturgis. Tower says it is valuable because the name of the priest is misprinted on the price-clipped dust jacket. There are only 7,500 copies of the first edition, most sold in Maine. The book is the key to one of the biggest mysteries the *ka-tet* faces.

SERGIO (5)

The store cat at Manhattan Restaurant of the Mind. Probably named for Sergio Leone, director of spaghetti Westerns starring Clint Eastwood.

SHOOTER'S BIBLE (2)

A catalog of guns and ammunition. Roland consults a copy at Clements Guns and Sporting Goods to determine what kind of bullets to buy for his revolvers.

SKÖLPADDA (5, 6, 7)

The Swedish name given to the scrimshaw turtle, a *can-tah* that Susannah finds in a secret pocket of the bowling bag from the empty lot. It is identical to the metal sculpture in the pocket park near the Black Tower. It has the power to mesmerize and hypnotize people. The turtle's head pokes halfway out of its detailed shell, which is marred by a scratch that looks like a question mark. Its eyes are tiny black dots that look alive. Its beak has a wedge-shaped crack and the carving has a feeling of age. Susannah dropped it outside the Dixie Pig for Jake and Callahan to find. After using it to enchant the low men and vampires, Father Callahan drops it. What happens to it afterward is unknown. Roland senses that it's gone by the time he passes through.

SOMBRA GROUP, THE (3, 4, 5, 6, 7)

A closed corporation that includes Sombra Corporation, Sombra Enterprises and Sombra Real Estate Associates. A branch of North Central Positronics in Keystone Earth, incorporated in the Bahamas, with offices in New Delhi, New York, Chicago, Detroit, Denver, Los Angeles and San Francisco. They specialized in high-tech, real estate and construction. Their Real Estate Division wants Calvin Tower to sell them the vacant lot, supposedly to build Turtle Bay Luxury Condominiums. Their Detroit division, with offices on the thirty-third floor of the Tishman Building, uses a promise of grant money to the Lighthouse Shelter to lure Father Callahan out of hiding. Tet Corporation was created to drive them out of business, which they hope to do by 2030.

"SOMEONE SAVED MY LIFE TONIGHT" (5, 7)
A hit single by Elton John. Father Callahan hears it repeatedly after he leaves 'Salem's Lot.

TAKURO SPIRIT (4, 5, 6, 7)
Automobile brand in the non-Keystone versions of Earth.

TET CORPORATION (5, 6, 7)
A company that Eddie Dean invents in 1977 to represent the *ka-tet*'s interest in the vacant lot. Also known as the firm of Deschain, Dean, Dean, Chambers & Oy. Eddie and Roland get John Cullum to enlist the help of Moses Carver and Aaron Deepneau to merge Tet with Holmes Dental to create a company with sufficient resources to go head-to-head with Sombra Corporation and North Central Positronics. Their headquarters are on the ninety-ninth floor of 2 Dag Hammarskjöld Plaza. Marian Carver became president in 1997 after Moses Carver retired, at which time the corporation was worth ten billion dollars. The corporation believes its work will be done by 2030. Susannah Dean and Eddie Toren join Tet in 1987.

TODASH TURNPIKES (5)
Eddie's name for the roads that take Father Callahan from one version of America to another.

TOPEKA CAPITAL-JOURNAL (4)
Newspaper in Topeka in the reality where the superflu devastated the world.

TUBE-NECK (4)
Name for the superflu in the Midwest.

WATERSHIP DOWN (3, 7)
A novel about rabbits by Richard Adams, who also wrote a book about a bear named Shardik.

THE HISTORY OF MID-WORLD

The history of All-World—sometimes called Mid-World, though that is technically just one region of Roland's planet—is steeped in mystery. One reason for this is the scarcity of paper and books. Very little of Mid-World's history has ever been written, and much of what has been recorded is regarded as legend rather than fact. The Dark Tower, the most important part of creation, is thought to be a fairy tale. Residents of Mid-World are blind to the presence of the Beams that support it, even though one runs through Gilead.

Much of what is "known" about Mid-World's history comes from the mouths of demons who have existed since creation. Considering the source, some of this can be considered suspect. However, here is what is generally believed to be true.

In the beginning was the Prim, a primordial soup of magic that the Manni call the Over. It is also called the greater Discordia. The Beams rose from the Prim on the airs of magic. Gan, the personification of the Dark Tower, originated at the point where these Beams intersected. As he grew, so did the Tower, with each new level producing another universe. Gan uttered the word "hile" and set time in motion. In other accounts, he tipped the world with his finger, which began time. In some legends, Lady Oriza gave birth to the first humans after Gan created the universe, though no one explains where she came from.

Pessimists say that Gan created the world and then moved on. Yet sufficient magic remained after creation to run the Beams and support the Dark Tower forever. The Prim receded like an ocean drawing back. When it did, it left demons stranded on a metaphorical beach. Many of these creatures perished, but some survived, including Speaking Demons and ghosts. Others retreated into the todash spaces between universes. All such creatures are governed by six demon elementals, the malign counterparts of the Beams. Each demon elemental has a male aspect and a female aspect, so there are twelve demon aspects to counter the twelve Guardians of the Beam.

Almost nothing is known about the civilization that existed in the days before Arthur Eld. From its artifacts and cities (like Lud), it was obviously technologically advanced. According to Walter o'Dim, these Old People (or Great Old Ones) put people on the moon. The navigation system that the mutants of Fagonard Swamp give Tim Ross relies on a satellite, so Walter may have been telling the truth. In addition to building sophisticated robots and other gadgets to simplify their lives, they also built terrible weapons and engines of war.

They worried that magic would fade away, so they developed ways to either replace magic with technology or weave the two together. They established North Central Positronics, which built experimental stations (Dogans) to develop and test their inventions. One of their worst mistakes was in failing to trust the magic that supported the Dark Tower. They built technological portals at each end of the Beams and replaced the magic with magnetism. So long as they were around to maintain this equipment, all was well.

However, there was a cataclysm, known as the Great War or the Great Poisoning. The exact nature of what happened is unknown. Was it a real war or did one of their experiments go awry, releasing toxins and radiation? If it was a war, who was their adversary and what weapons did they have to overwhelm the Imperium of the Great Old Ones? It might even have been a civil war. No one knows.

Whatever happened, the Great Old Ones vanished from Mid-World and much of what they left behind was lethal. Great swatches of Mid-World were turned into barren wastelands, and the aftereffects of this poisoning lasted for dozens—maybe hundreds—of generations. Their Dogans and storage caverns were radioactive or poisonous. Mutations among animals ran rampant, to the point where "threaded stock" (unmutated animals) were the exception rather than the rule. People who dwelled too close to the leavings of the Old Ones became slow mutants or suffered from radiation poisoning.

Were the Great Old Ones destroyed, or did they go to other worlds? Again, this isn't known. They did have doors to other times and places, including those built into the portals at the ends of each Beam and the ones they built for travel and entertainment. Based on the doors in the rotunda at the Fedic Dogan, they seemed to have had a fascination for events on Earth—especially those that involved violence. Presidential assassinations, terrorist attacks and Roman Colosseum spectacles were particular favorites. Survivors of the cataclysm might have migrated to Earth. It's also possible that they came from Earth in the first place, perhaps from our time, bringing their technology with them.

After the Great War and the fall of the Old People, Mid-World went through a Dark Age. Mid-World resembled England in the days when every tribal leader considered himself a king and every other tribe was his enemy. Were these people descendants of the Old People? One sect is thought to be so: the Manni, a religious order whose members travel to other worlds to gain knowledge and wisdom.

Centuries after the Great War, Arthur Eld rose to power and unified all the warring factions, ending the brutal practices among the people, including the tradition of human sacrifice known as charyou tree associated with the Reap.

He had a magician named Maerlyn as his adviser. Opinions vary on whether Maerlyn was evil or good. Some say both. Walter o'Dim claims Maerlyn was his father. However, the Maerlyn Tim Ross meets is benign and has little use for Walter. Maybe he mellowed over the centuries. As a magical creature, he may be a remnant of the Prim, but he seems human in many ways and might be part of the line of Eld. The most significant remaining relic of his magic is the Wizard's Rainbow, a set of thirteen glass orbs. Regardless of whether they were intended for good when Maerlyn created them, they are now tainted by evil. At best they are amoral.

Mid-World slowly began to heal. Threaded stock increased. Under Arthur Eld, the rival factions became Baronies that were unified into the Affiliation. He created a law-abiding society, ridding the land of the many harriers and villains who once ran unchecked. Arthur also assembled a team of knights who killed the mutant monsters that rampaged throughout the land, including the great snake Saita, and acted as peace officers.

Arthur's symbol of unity was the sword Excalibur, which some said he extracted from a pyramid and others claimed came from the room at the top of the Dark Tower. The metal from this sword was supposedly converted into the barrels of the guns that were passed down to the leaders of his people. His snow-white horse, Llamrei, became the *sigul* of all In-World.

In the Barony of New Canaan, Arthur built his headquarters, the city of Gilead. It was a golden age in Mid-World, and Arthur reigned for many decades. He took three wives (not necessarily all at the same time), including Queen Rowena, and also consorted with many jillies who bore him children.

For this reason, the line of Eld is substantial. Most of the gunslingers in Roland's day can trace their lineage directly back to Arthur Eld, though many of them—like Roland—go via one of Eld's jillies. In some versions of the legend, Arthur Eld even consorted with creatures of the Prim, which might explain how the Crimson King came into being. There are indications that Arthur Eld may have been murdered.

After his death, his descendants continued to rule All-World from Gilead. For at least thirty generations, the Affiliation held together. Like the Knights of the Round Table, the gunslingers were both a symbol of authority and its manifestation. Sheriffs or communities confronted by situations they couldn't handle could request aid and succor from the gunslingers. If they were found to be on the side of the White, the gunslingers would help without compensation. Of course, the Baronies were taxed, so this assistance came at a price after all.

Eventually, the council of gunslingers grew so absorbed by the problem of the decline of Mid-World, caused by the failing Dark Tower, that they ignored the concerns of the Outer Baronies. Taxation without representation might have been the complaint of these outlying districts. A former harrier and robber named John Farson seized the opportunity to rise to power as the voice of dissent. He gained the support of a disenfranchised population while amassing a war chest containing the forbidden weapons of the Great Old Ones. Gilead unwittingly provided him with soldiers by sending those who failed the test to become a gunslinger west, where many joined Farson, whose campaign turned into a reign of terror. He raided cities in distant Baronies, slaughtering any who refused to support him.

Since Farson's rebellion increased the level of chaos in Mid-World, he became a minion of the Crimson King, whose red eye his supporters wore. The wizard Marten Broadcloak, another agent of chaos, entered Farson's service. He gained the trust of the gunslingers, becoming their chief adviser while infiltrating Gilead with traitors and spies at every level. He even turned the wife of the *dinh* of Gilead into a traitor.

The gunslingers were so busy worrying about the Dark Tower that they didn't notice civilization crumbling around them. Farson, by now insane and aided by one of the glasses from the Wizard's Rainbow, lured them into traps, attacked and pillaged Gilead, leaving it in ruins, and destroyed every gunslinger save one.

Mid-World returned to the lawless times that existed before the reign of Arthur Eld. The residents of great cities like Lud fended off harriers with the remaining weapons of the Old People, but eventually they ran out of ammunition or the weapons stopped working. Most people lived in isolation and fear. The only known region of Mid-World where civilization still existed was along the River Whye, where an agrarian society remained and communities—or Callas—engaged in trade up and down the river. But even that oasis of civilization was threatened by the darkness of neighboring Thunderclap and the greater Discordia.

The Dark Tower's decline continued unchecked.

Two known books contain stories from the days of Arthur Eld. Roland's mother used to read to him from *Magic Tales of the Eld*, though these were mostly fairy tales. Father Callahan owned a book called *Tales of Arthur,* which gave him insight into the gunslinger code of conduct. Other legends of Maerlyn and Arthur Eld can be found in the material accompanying the Marvel graphic novels written by Mid-World scholar Robin Furth.

TIME LINES

There's no getting around it—time is strange in Mid-World. By the time we meet Roland at the beginning of *The Gunslinger*, he has lived for something like a thousand years. But how old is he? The two aren't exactly the same. Stephen King offers his view of Roland's strange lifespan in the interview found elsewhere in this book.

Roland's childhood was fairly normal, as far as time goes. When he was eleven, he and Cuthbert overheard Hax plotting treason. Three years after that, he challenged Cort and became a gunslinger. The next day, he, Cuthbert and Alain set out for Mejis, and within four or five months they were back in Gilead. During Roland's early years, no one mentions time skipping. When he kills his mother, Roland is roughly fifteen. Cuthbert was twenty-four when he was killed at the battle of Jericho Hill, so Roland would have been about the same age. In the interim, the civil war destroyed Gilead.

We know little about what Roland did after escaping Jericho Hill until he arrives in Pricetown. He must have had some great adventures, based on his scars, which include evidence of whippings, knife wounds, burns and at least three bullet holes. At some point he passed through Eluria. He mentions other places he visited—King's Town, for example—but there's nothing to indicate that he cast about for hundreds of years. However, by the time Roland reaches Tull, it has already been centuries since he last heard the High Speech.

Five weeks pass between Roland's arrival in Tull and the day he reaches the Way Station. After he and Jake set out, it takes ten days to encounter the Speaking Ring and another eleven or twelve to reach the tunnel beneath the mountain. They spend nearly two weeks following the tracks, much of it in darkness, until the day Roland lets Jake fall from the trestle. Total elapsed time from Tull to the golgotha: roughly eighty days.

There are a few times during Roland's journey when time slips. The most obvious is the night after he and Walter palaver. When Roland wakes up, it seems like a very long time has passed, but that's mostly because Walter played a prank and left a skeleton behind to make it seem like he had died and rotted away to nothing but bone. The night *was* long—Roland's hair is grayer when he wakes up—but certainly not centuries long. Maybe a decade.

Roland loses his fingers to the lobstrosities the next day and meets Eddie Dean two days after that. Three weeks later—and many miles farther up the beach—Susannah Dean is formed from her constituent personalities.

The trio moves inland and sets up camp. Roland spends a little more than two months training his new friends to be gunslingers. They find the Shardik portal and set out along the Path of the Beam. Eleven days later, Jake passes through the doorway from the Mansion in Dutch Hill, and four days after that, Oy completes the group. They visit River Crossing the next day, and a week later they reach Lud. The following day they board Blaine the Mono for an eight-thousand-mile trip across Mid-World that takes less than eight hours.

For the next two days, they walk along I-70 while Roland gathers the courage to tell the story of his days in Mejis. The night that he recounts what happened the summer and fall that he was fourteen might have been just one really long night, or years or generations could have passed in the world outside their camp. There's no way to tell. When they enter the Emerald Palace and go todash inside the pink Bend o' the Rainbow, time slips yet again.

Time seems out of gear for the next seven weeks. They cross the western branch of the River Whye and ride out the starkblast in Gook. Finally, at the end of summer, they reach Calla Bryn Sturgis and spend a month preparing for the day the Wolves come.

Things start to get a little confusing with all the jumping back and forth to Keystone Earth in todash trips or via the Unfound Door, but most of these journeys take place over a matter of a few days. A mere two days after the battle with the Wolves, the *ka-tet* reunites, and a couple of days after that, they wage another battle, this time in Algul Siento. Roland and Jake head back to Maine, and Roland spends a few days in Keystone Earth before returning to Fedic.

It takes Roland, Susannah and Oy about five weeks to cross the Badlands to Le Casse Roi Russe. Four days later, they're in the White Lands of Empathica tanning hides and making clothes. Another month after that, they visit Dandelo. They ride out the storm and set off again along Tower Road and, less than a week later, Roland has reached his goal.

How much time elapses between the opening page of *The Gunslinger* and the day Roland reaches the Dark Tower? A careful accounting shows that roughly 332 days pass, though the time spent in the Great West Woods is somewhat vague (two months), as is the time between the Green Palace and Calla Bryn Sturgis (seven weeks).

A little less than a year then, fistulas of time and slippages notwithstanding. It makes sense. Roland pursues Walter across the desert in the heat of summer. The *ka-tet* reaches Calla Bryn Sturgis in the fall, and Roland and Susannah cross Empathica during winter. Roland sees the Tower for the first time on a spring morning.

The chronology of events on Earth is convoluted because the *ka-tet* comes from different decades and jumps back and forth to different times. Did you realize that Eddie is only a couple of years older than Jake? Eddie was born in 1964 and Jake in 1966. The confusion arises because Eddie was drawn from 1987 and Jake from 1977. Odetta, on the other hand, is nearly thirty years older than Eddie and Jake.

Here are a few dates to orient you as you work your way through the series:

- 1938: Odetta Holmes is born
- 1943: Jack Mort drops a brick on Odetta's head
- 1947: Stephen King is born
- August 19, 1959: Jack Mort pushes Odetta in front of the A train
- February 1964: Eddie Dean is born
- 1966: Jake Chambers is born
- 1974: Callahan fights vampires in 'Salem's Lot
- May 9, 1977: Jack Mort pushes Jake in front of Enrico Balazar's car
- May 31, 1977: Jake visits the Manhattan Restaurant of the Mind
- June 1, 1977: Jake returns to Mid-World
- July 9, 1977: Eddie and Roland meet Stephen King
- May 19, 1981: The Hitler Brothers try to kill Father Callahan
- December 19, 1983: Father Callahan dies in Detroit
- 1987: Roland meets Eddie for the first time
- December 1987: Susannah Dean joins Eddie and Jake Toren in Central Park
- 1989: John Cullum is shot and killed
- 1990: Calvin Tower dies of a heart attack
- 1992: Aaron Deepneau dies of cancer
- 1997: Moses Carver retires as head of Tet Corporation
- June 1, 1999: Mia goes to the Dixie Pig
- June 19, 1999: Jake and Roland save Stephen King's life

THE GEOGRAPHY OF MID-WORLD

The alternate universe where Roland Deschain lives is called All-World and consists of In-World, Mid-World and End-World. However, everyone, including Roland, thinks of it as Mid-World.

There may have been a time when it was possible to map out the geography of Mid-World. However, because the Dark Tower is failing, all the physical constants that normally apply to reality no longer do so here. Time speeds up, slows down and skips. The points of the compass drift, so that something that lies to the south one day may be southeast the next. When Roland heads north along the Western Sea, the ocean is to his right instead of the left.

Distances are affected, too. Mid-World is getting bigger. Gilead was once only a thousand miles from the Western Sea, but it took Roland many years to go from one to the other.

Since all of the parallel universes began from a common starting point, it's tempting to try to map Mid-World onto Earth. Though it is possible to draw some analogies, the process breaks down. The Western Sea, beyond the Mohaine (Mojave) Desert, is akin to the Pacific Ocean. Mejis is either Mexico or Texas. The Clean Sea resembles the Gulf of Mexico. The Desatoya Mountains near Eluria also exist in Nevada. Blaine the Mono travels from Lud to Topeka. Lud is linked geographically to St. Louis but physically resembles Manhattan. Both the Send River and the River Whye could be analogs of the Mississippi. Discordia, according to Roland, corresponds to the White Mountains of New Hampshire.

According to legends, Mid-World (or All-World, if you please) resembles a flat disc with the Dark Tower at the middle, in End-World. The disc rests on the back of a turtle (of enormous girth). Around the perimeter of this disc, arranged like the hours on the face of a clock, are twelve portals. These portals are the origin points for twelve Beams that lead inward to the Dark Tower, supporting it. A Guardian of the Beam, an enormous robot shaped like an animal, protects each portal. These portals are also doorways to other universes.

The Beams have been flowing so long that they've worn grooves in reality. Everything around them indicates their presence, from the cloud formations in the sky to the herringbone patterns in vegetation on the ground. People traveling along one of the Great Roads that follow the Beams specify their location by naming the Beam they are on and the one toward which they are headed. If someone heads toward the Tower from the Turtle portal, they are said to be on the Beam of the Turtle (Maturin), Way of the Bear (also known as Shardik), whereas someone starting from the opposite side would be on the Beam of the Bear, Way of the Turtle.

As Roland understands it, beyond the ring of portals lies the Prim, the soup of creation that is the source of magic. Beyond that is the todash space that separates one world from the next. This is reminiscent of our concept of the Earth when people believed that if you sailed far enough you would fall off the edge of the world. Clearly there are gaps in Roland's knowledge. He, Eddie and Susannah find one of the Portals of the Beam, and it is sixty miles inland from the Western Sea. At no point in his travels does he encounter the Prim or the end of the universe. Perhaps Mid-World looked like a disc in the days after creation, or perhaps that story was just created to educate children.

The concept of All-World as a disc manifests itself in some descriptions. Distances are measured in wheels, which have arcs as subunits. In geometry, arcs are segments of circles. Certain regions are known as arcs. The more remote Baronies are in the Outer Arc, whereas Gilead is in the Inner Arc. The Arc of the Callas is the fertile crescent along the River Whye, also known as the Arc o' Borderlands. The Dogans are numbered based on arcs as well. The Fedic Dogan is the Arc 16 Experimental Station. People even talk about the arc of time. The Dogan near Calla Bryn Sturgis is Arc Quadrant Outpost 16 and North Forest Kinnock Dogan is in Bend Quadrant. A quadrant is a quarter of a circle.

Over the course of Roland's journeys, we are exposed to only one section of Mid-World—that which lies along Shardik's Beam, which runs northwest from the Dark Tower, and that which lies north along Aslan's Beam. Nothing is known of what exists east, west or south of the Dark Tower. It can't be said for certain which of the two Beams in the northwestern quadrant is the Path of the Bear, but one might assume it is the one that lies closest to Aslan's Beam. That would make them the ones that end at XI and XII respectively on a clock face.

The region about which we know the most is that which lies along Shardik's Beam. Starting at the Dark Tower and working outward (northwest), one would follow Tower Road to Stuttering Bill's outpost, to Westring (home of Dandelo), the White Lands of Empathica, Le Casse Roi Russe (slightly off the Beam), and the carriage road leading to Castle Discordia and Fedic. Beyond Fedic is Thunderclap, where Algul Siento is located. Crossing the Devar-Tete Whye, one would reach the Callas and then the forest that marks the boundary between End-World and Mid-World, including the town of Gook near the western branch of the Whye, eventually ending up in Topeka. The geographic region known as Mid-World is roughly eight thousand miles across, from Topeka (via Dasherville, the Falls of the Hounds, Rilea and Candleton) to Lud and River Crossing at the River Send, near the beginning of In-World. From there it's a straight shot past the Speaking Circle where Jake crossed over to Shardik's Portal and the Western Sea beyond.

The Arc of the Callas runs roughly six thousand miles north and south along the Whye River. Four thousand miles south of Calla Bryn Sturgis is the Southern Sea. The Callas grow smaller to the north until you reach the lands where the snow falls. Aslan, the Guardian of the Beam that runs north from the Dark Tower, also lives in a land of snow.

Where is Gilead relative to this? The Great Hall of Gilead lies along the Eagle-Lion Beam, which runs north/south, according to *The Wind Through the Keyhole*, though where it is on that Beam is never specified. Tree Village is at the farthest northern edge of the North'rd Barony. Beyond that is the Endless Forest containing Fagonard Swamp. The forest is interrupted by the Great Canyon, which is at least a hundred miles across. North Forest Kinnock, at the edge of this chasm, was once known as the Gateway of Out-World.

From the perspective of the descendants of Arthur Eld, Gilead is the center of the world. There are East'rd and North'rd and West'rd and Southern Baronies, but these directions are all relative to New Canaan, not to the Dark Tower, the true center of All-World. Mejis is roughly five hundred miles east of Gilead—thousands of miles from Tree Village—and Garlan, where failed gunslingers are sent, is some distance to the west. The Western Line of the railway once ran from Gilead all the way to the Mohaine Desert, although it now ends at Debaria. Jericho Hill is five hundred miles north of Mejis. To the east is the Salt, the ocean that becomes the Clean Sea next to Hambry.

Roland's long journey from Gilead takes him to Pricetown and Tull, where there are signs in the sky that Shardik's Beam is in the vicinity, though Roland doesn't notice. He parallels the Beam's course southeast across the

Mohaine Desert to the mountains and goes west to the sea. He, Eddie and
Susannah follow the beach north and then move inland through the Great
West Woods until they reach Shardik's Portal. That means that, from the time
Roland leaves Pricetown until he reaches the Portal of the Bear, he goes in a
clockwise loop, ending up in the woods slightly north or northeast of Pricetown. That also means he probably crossed Shardik's Beam at some earlier
point. Once he, Eddie and Susannah set off down the Path of the Beam, they
are paralleling Roland's trek across the desert.

What exists in the other directions outside of this narrow slice of Mid-
World? Did other great civilizations grow and die along the Path of the Turtle
on the far side of the Dark Tower from Gilead, or is everything else a wasteland? The books supply no answers to these questions. Future generations of
explorers have a grand adventure ahead of them as they map out the remaining eighty-five percent of Mid-World.

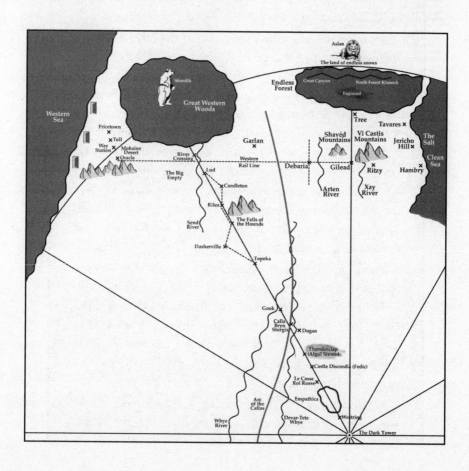

NOTES CONCERNING THE MAP OF MID-WORLD

This map assembles the known geography of Mid-World. Few distances are known, so the scale is arbitrary and probably wildly different in different parts of the map.

The biggest problem is this: if there is a Beam that goes due north, there cannot be a Beam that goes southwest. Since the Beams are arranged like the hours on a clock, that means there are two in the northwest quadrant. One runs from the eleven o'clock position south-southeast toward the Dark Tower, and the other runs from the ten o'clock position east-southeast.

For a long time, the relative placement of Gilead was unknown, but in *The Wind Through the Keyhole* we learn that Tree is on or near the Beam of the Lion that ends in the north, and that Tree is north of Gilead.

After Roland saves the Beams, he believes that Shardik's Beam has snapped into an eastward direction, which might lead one to assume it was the one that begins in the ten o'clock position. However, we also learn that the Western Rail Line used to run from Gilead through Debaria all the way to the Mohaine Desert. This is possible only if the Mohaine, which is south of Shardik's Beam, is relatively far north. Closer to eleven o'clock than ten o'clock, in other words. This also means that Roland crossed only one Path of the Beam before reaching Tull, and not two. How he ended up near the Western Sea without reaching it before he visited Pricetown is another mystery.

There are other issues. According to Roland, the Western Sea used to be only a thousand miles from Gilead. We have only his word on this point, and there's a lot about Mid-World that he doesn't know. The distance from Lud to Topeka is around eight thousand miles, and this is only a segment of Shardik's Beam. Mid-World has expanded a great deal if both pieces of data are accepted as fact.

We also know that the Arc of the Callas extends all the way to the region where the snow falls. That means Roland must have crossed it at some point. Perhaps the Callas are widely spaced and he went between them.

Garlan's position on this map is arbitrary. It is to the west of Gilead and Debaria. But how far? No one knows. Presumably not near the Callas.

Here's the bottom line: if you ever find yourself in Mid-World, you probably shouldn't stake your life on this map, even if directions and distances are no longer drifting.

Mid-World People, Places and Things

This section of the glossary includes all significant people, places and things from Mid-World. Characters mentioned only in passing or not by name are omitted. The numbers and letters after each entry indicate the books in which the person, place or thing is mentioned. The numbers 1–7 represent the seven main Dark Tower books. L stands for "The Little Sisters of Eluria," 4.5 represents *The Wind Through the Keyhole*, and M means the Marvel graphic novels. Names in square brackets indicate situations where a subject's name changes because of a continuity error.

People

Adams, Diego (5)
A rancher in Calla Bryn Sturgis. His wife, Sarey, is one of the Sisters of Oriza.

Adams, Sarey (5)
One of the Sisters of Oriza. A cheery, jolly woman, fat but light on her feet. Brave as a lion and good with the plate, but lacks the ferocity of some of the other women. Roland puts her in charge of hiding the twins when the Wolves come.

Affiliation Brats (4, M)
Name applied to Roland, Cuthbert and Alain by the Big Coffin Hunters and their associates.

Ageless Stranger (1, 3)
Another name for Randall Flagg. Walter o'Dim tells Roland that he will have to kill the Ageless Stranger before he can reach the Tower. Susannah claims this is another name for Merlin.

ALARIC (6)

Roland's redheaded grandfather. He once went to Garlan to slay a dragon, but the last one in that part of the world had already been killed.

Crossover to Other Works: This probably refers to King Roland of *The Eyes of the Dragon*.

ALBRECHT (7)

A blond vampire in the posse that follows Jake to the Fedic door. Eddie shoots him.

ALEXANDER, BEN (7)

A low man guard at Algul Siento. The lead engine of Fire-Response Team Bravo kills him.

ALIA (6, 7)

The taheen nurse in the Fedic Dogan. She has the head of a great brown rat. Susannah shoots her in the knee but allows her to escape.

ALICE (ALLIE) (1, 2, 3, 6, M)

Owner of Sheb's honky-tonk in Tull. She is Roland's lover until he kills her, along with everyone else in town. The man in black curses her by giving her a magic word to unlock Nort the Weedeater's memories of death. Jake has a vision of her in the vacant lot in Manhattan.

ALLGOOD, CUTHBERT (THROUGHOUT)

Roland's best and oldest friend from childhood and member of his first *ka-tet*. His name is pronounced key-youth-bert. One of his favorite weapons is a slingshot, which he uses to discourage Roy Depape from tormenting Sheemie Ruiz and to lob firecrackers at the oil tankers at Hanging Rock. Roland has seen him take down a bird from sixty yards. He has no sense of the touch whatsoever, but he has an excellent memory for details and rarely forgets a name. He is a firebug at heart. Arguing comes as naturally to him as breathing. If he had lived longer, he might have developed a stomach for torture or killing outright, but he had none of that in Mejis.

On the surface he is a joker, quick to make a smart—or stupid—comment in any situation. Sometimes this makes him casually disarming. At other times, his relentless sense of foolery is simply annoying. Steven Deschain calls him Laughing Boy. To Roland he is (like Eddie Dean) *ka-mai*, *ka*'s fool.

He believes Cuthbert would joke on the gallows. He couldn't even name his horse as a normal person would. He is impatient and hates silence more than danger. He accepts that some people might not want to talk for long periods of time, but he doesn't understand why.

This superficial levity and a patina of insouciance disguise the fact that he is lonely and volatile and that his emotions run deep. He is tormented after seeing Hax hang in Gilead. He can become angry quickly, though it is normally easy to coax him out of his anger. He spent two months mad at Roland in Mejis when he thought that Roland was being irresponsible and careless. His joking takes on a mean, cutting edge when he tries to goad Roland into action, and he finally breaks down and coldcocks his friend, the first time he ever hit him except in play.

He thinks the Tower is a symbol and the Wizard's Glasses are a myth. He wouldn't believe in ghosts unless he caught one in his teeth. Though he can't admit it, he's jealous of Susan Delgado for stealing his best friend and of Roland for always being the first at everything: the first to become a gunslinger and the first to fall in love. He falls in love with Susan when he meets her, too, but suppresses his feelings and welcomes her into their *ka-tet*. Though he and Roland mend their friendship, things are never quite the same between them again.

He never has to face Cort in a test of manhood. Mejis is his proving ground, and he is elevated to gunslinger after this mission. Alain told him once that he would die young. He was twenty-four when Randall Flagg put an arrow through his eye at the battle of Jericho Hill.

He is Eddie's twin and appeared to Stephen King together with Eddie when King was seven. The Crimson King had touched King, but Cuthbert and Eddie won him over to the White.

Physical description: Thin and dark, of average height, with a face that is handsome but restless. Brown hair and dark eyes.

ALLGOOD, ROBERT (4, M)

Cuthbert's father. In the Marvel series, he leaps in front of a poison dart fired by a slow mutant, saving Steven Deschain's life.

ALVAREZ, MISHA (4)

A resident of Hambry. Susan Delgado taught her daughter to ride. Moments before Susan dies, Misha spits into her eyes. Her husband is part of the posse that arrests Roland, Cuthbert and Alain at the Bar K Ranch.

AMY (4)

A friend of Susan Delgado. They used to leave each other notes in the stone wall near the Green Heart pavilion when they were kids.

ANDERSON, PEA (4.5)

Debaria sheriff killed by the Crow Gang at Ambush Arroyo.

ANDERSON, RUPERT "OLD BALDY" (4.5)

Tree Village's big farmer. He's known to be stingy. He bought Bern Kells's house after Kells married Nell Ross.

ANDRUS, CORTLAND

See Cort.

ANDY THE MESSENGER ROBOT (4.5, 5, 6, 7)

An Asimov robot, a product of North Central Positronics in association with LaMerk Industries, built more than two thousand years ago. Design: Messenger (Many Other Functions). Serial # DNF-44821-V-63. A tireless walker, he likes to sing songs, spread gossip and deliver horoscopes. He always knows when the Wolves are coming. He tends to be smug and appears to enjoy the discomfort of humans. When asked to divulge privileged information, his voice becomes emotionless and dead, like a real robot. Directive Nineteen is his fallback position in these cases. Each generation, he coerces someone from Calla Bryn Sturgis to become a spy and reports his findings to Finli o'Tego at Algul Siento. He ends up buried in shit at the bottom of Rosalita Muñoz's outhouse.

Physical description: He looks like a child's stick figure and reminds Eddie of C-3PO from *Star Wars*. Seven feet tall with a gold, cylindrical body and impossibly thin silvery arms and legs. His hands have only three fingers. His head is a stainless-steel barrel with blue electric eyes that flash when he's laughing. He has a plate affixed to his chest with his name and serial number.

ANG, OLLIE (4.5)

One of the miners from Little Debaria who did time in Beelie Stockade. A bald man, slight for a miner but muscular, notable for wearing a wristwatch. He dies in the Debaria jailhouse and his body is burned.

ANSELM, HUGH (5)

Owner of a smallhold across the ridge south of Tian Jaffords's place in Calla Bryn Sturgis. He helps Tian build Rosalita Muñoz's outhouse. He and his wife, Krella, have twins (a boy and a girl) around thirteen years old.

ANSELM, KRELLA (5)

Hugh Anselm's wife. She helps corral the children before the Wolves come.

ARA (5)

Cantab of the Manni's wife and Henchick's granddaughter. She throws the Oriza, but as one of the Manni, could never be at fellowship with the Sisters of Oriza.

ARDIS (3)

A Pube. The last person to go near Blaine the Mono. Blaine asks him a question he can't answer, then kills him with electricity.

ARMANEETA (4.5)

The *sighe* (fairy) who lures Tim Ross through the Endless Forest into the Fagonard Swamp. She has the form of a beautiful naked woman four inches tall with gauzy wings. She gives off a green glow and her upturned eyes have no pupils. She can fly like a dragonfly. Her laughter is a silvery tinkle, like bells coming from a great distance. She colludes with the Covenant Man.

ARN (4.5)

A pokie who works at the Jefferson Ranch and survives the skin-man attack because he was out rounding up strays with Skip and Canfield.

AVERY, HERKIMER "HERK" (4, M)

High Sheriff of Mejis and Chief Constable of Hambry. A frog-eyed, big-bellied man, though his belly is harder than it looks. Considers himself a self-made man who can make hard decisions when he must. He is ingratiating to the Affiliation Brats, but Roland can tell he doesn't like them. Cuthbert calls him a fat bag of guts without a trustworthy bone in his body, and Alain thinks he wouldn't piss on them if they were on fire. He brokers a peace treaty between the Big Coffin Hunters and Roland's trio after the dustup at the Travellers' Rest, though Roland knows he doesn't have any authority over Eldred Jonas. He is a figurehead and gladly cedes power to others during conflict, as when the posse rounds up the Affiliation Brats at the Bar K Ranch. He is on duty in the jail when Susan Delgado frees Roland and the others. He tries to strangle her, but she shoots him to death.

BANDERLY (4.5)

The bull foreman at the mines in Little Debaria. He orders the crew to plug the crack in the mine with rocks but refuses to close the mine or report the problem to his superiors in Gilead.

BARONS (L, 3, 4)

Feudal leaders of the family estates around which Baronies developed. They wore ceremonial rings that were handed down from father to son. By the time Roland goes to Mejis, the title has almost no meaning.

BARONY COVENANTER (4.5)

See Covenant Man.

BEECH, MRS. (4)

Her mailbox marks the edge of Hambry in Mejis.

BEEMAN (7)

A *can toi* security guard at Algul Siento.

BERNARDO (5)

The town drunk in Calla Bryn Sturgis.

BIG COFFIN HUNTERS (1, 4, 5, M)

A trio of regulators hired by George Latigo to act on his behalf in Mejis. So called because of the coffin-shaped tattoos they each have on the webbing of their right hands, acquired in the town of Wind. Some of the low men have the same coffin tattoo. Their cover story is that they are private bodyguards for Mayor Thorin, though no one knows why he needs guards. They've been in Hambry for a month by the time Roland, Alain and Cuthbert arrive, staying at the watchman's house five miles out of town. They brought the pink Wizard's Glass to Mejis for safekeeping and are overseeing the transfer of livestock and oil tankers west to John Farson. Eldred Jonas, a failed gunslinger, leads them. He hasn't yet shared the huge cash advance paid by Latigo with his partners, Clay Reynolds and Roy Depape. One of their previous jobs involved helping the Vi Castis Company regulate freeholders out of the mines west of Hambry. They know a lot of old gunslinger tricks. Jake thinks of his father as a Big Coffin Hunter in TV Land.

BIX (4.5)

Elderly operator of the raft that crosses the western branch of the River Whye. He warns the *ka-tet* about a forthcoming starkblast and tells them to take cover in Gook. He wears a straw hat and suffers from arthritis. He has worked at the river crossing for ninety years and is well over 120 years old. He once visited Lud and is curious to hear how things are there now. He also visited an underground Dogan, which is where he got the crank for his ferry. However, he also lost all his hair and teeth from radiation. He's familiar with the Callas and Andy the robot.

BLACK, SUSAN (M)

Susan Delgado's double. She works at the Travellers' Rest in Kingstown. Roland rescues her from not-men plaguing that town and spends the night with her before continuing on his way.

BLAINE THE MONO (2, 3, 4, 4.5, 5, 6, 7)

One of two monorails that ran from Lud. Pink, with a nose like a bullet and two triangular windows that look like eyes with wipers that look like drooping eyelids. The full train is more than two wheels long, operates on a slo-trans engine and travels faster than the speed of sound, averaging over eight hundred miles per hour during the eight-thousand-mile run from Lud southeast to Topeka, a trip he last made nearly ten years before the *ka-tet* boards. He can make himself appear invisible to his riders, giving them a sense of flying. Blaine claims that the Beam holds up his track. According to Jack Andolini in Eddie's dream, Blaine travels through every world (he knows about John Wayne and Humphrey Bogart, for example) and he makes frequent references to the many levels of the Tower.

Little Blaine is the train's original voice. His dominant personality comes from the memory banks beneath Lud that ran the machinery of the Great Old Ones until it failed. Lud's computers have been brooding and becoming more insane since then. Blaine is the last working machine in which their personality can manifest. The side effects of the world moving on caused a spiritual malaise that makes Blaine want to commit suicide. He abetted Patricia the Mono in her suicide by erasing the circuits that controlled her nonvoluntary actions. He behaves like a spoiled and petulant child and is destroyed by the illogic of Eddie's inane jokes.

BRANDON (3)
One of Tick-Tock Man's Grays. Bowlegged. Stabbed by Gasher. Stabbed Oy. Killed by Roland.

BRASS (7)
Rando Thoughtful's aide, who appears to Roland and Susannah as Feemalo, Stephen King's ego.

BREAKERS (5, 6, 7, M)
People with psychic powers sought by the Crimson King to hasten the natural decline of the Beams supporting the Dark Tower. Also known as "morks." Most come from Keystone Earth, where they're outsiders—selfish introverts who are painfully aware that they're different from others in a way that people don't like. Some are sociopaths.

After the low men capture them or trick them into signing up, they're kept prisoner in Algul Siento in Thunderclap and unknowingly fed extracts from the brains of the twins of the Callas to boost their powers. They are treated well and, more important, they're given a sense of purpose. Breaking is an intensely pleasurable sensation, even though they don't know exactly what they're doing. Their philosophy is: go along to get along.

There are more than three hundred Breakers in Algul Siento. They are forbidden from using their psychic powers outside of the Study in Damli House. While they work, they generate something called "good mind" that opens perceptual doorways among others in the vicinity. Ted Brautigan is a super-Breaker in that his talent is to boost the psychic output of the others. Roland's primary goal is to stop the Breakers, whether that means freeing them from Algul Siento or killing them. Many are mad at Roland for killing the people who looked after them.

BRIANNA (4.5)
One of the sisters at Serenity near Debaria.

BRIDGER, TODD (4)
One of the deputies in Hambry. He finds the bodies of Sheriff Avery and Deputy Hollis.

BROADCLOAK, MARTEN (1, 2, 3, 4, 4.5, 5, 7, M)

A man of many names and one of the Crimson King's minions, though far from his greatest, according to Maerlyn, who says that little magic and long life are all he's capable of. Lies are his hobby.

He was the Barony Covenanter long before the time of Steven Deschain, though he probably lost that job after overstepping his bounds and leading Tim Ross to the place where Maerlyn was trapped. He's too valuable to kill, but he can be hurt and punished. Later, he was chief adviser and court sorcerer in Gilead. Roland remembers him as a glutton behind his grave ascetic's exterior. He taught Roland how to hypnotize people.

He was Gabrielle Deschain's lover and goaded Roland into taking his challenge against Cort at the age of fourteen, thinking the boy would be sent west. He also convinced Gabrielle to kill her husband, though that plot failed. After Roland was sent to Mejis to keep him out of Marten's way, Marten fled west alone to join up with John Farson in Cressia. Roland saw him again in the final days of Gilead, being pursued by Dennis and Thomas from Delain.

Walter admits that he is Marten during the palaver on the golgotha. See also Walter o'Dim, the man in black, Randall Flagg, the Ageless Stranger and the Covenant Man.

BROWN (1, 6, M)

A hermit who lives in a hut between Tull and the Mohaine Desert. His wife was of the Manni. He owns a raven named Zoltan.

BURKE, DAVID (7)

A former guard at Algul Siento caught throwing peanut shells at the Breakers from the balcony surrounding the Study in Damli House. As an example to the others, Pimli Prentiss had him lobotomized. Afterward, he wandered around the campus with a puzzled look on his face.

CAGNEY, JAMES (7)

A red-haired *can toi* from Algul Siento who favors Western-style shirts and boots that add three inches to his five-foot-five height. His friends call him Cag. He is shot and killed near the movie theater in Pleasantville.

CALLAHAN, BARKIE (4)

Bouncer at the Travellers' Rest in Hambry. He is assigned to guard the tankers at Citgo with Hiram Quint.

CAMERON (7)

A low man who raped a Breaker. He claimed it was part of his becoming and that the Crimson King told him to do it in a dream. Humma o'Tego executed him in the middle of Pleasantville's Main Street by shooting him in the head in front of the Breakers.

CANDOR THE TALL (7)

Gabrielle Deschain's father.

CANFIELD, BILL (4.5)

A former pokie (cowpoke or wandering cowboy) who became a proddie (hired hand) at the Jefferson Ranch in Debaria. He is out rounding up strays with Skip and Arn when the skin-man attacks. He calls Sheriff Peavy to report the slaughter at the ranch and accompanies Jamie DeCurry and the sheriff to the salt mines to bring back likely candidates for the skin-man.

CANTAB (5, 6)

A young Manni from Henchick's kra in Calla Bryn Sturgis. Popular with children, to whom he likes to sing. He is one of the most powerful senders in Calla Redpath. His wife, Ara, is one of Henchick's granddaughters.

CASH, BENITO (5)

A landowner in Calla Bryn Sturgis.

CASTNER (1)

Owner of the dry goods emporium in Tull.

CAVERRA, REUBEN (5)

A rancher in Calla Bryn Sturgis, husband of Diane. The last time the Wolves came, they took his twin sister, Ruth. A hulk of a man who impresses Roland as not knowing much about fear and probably nothing at all about cowardice. Before the Wolves come, his appendix ruptures, which, in the Callas, is usually fatal.

CHAMPIGNON, ARRA (M)

Gunslinger Charles Champignon's wife. She insists on returning to her Manni home to give birth to her son, who will have the special sight of the Manni. John Farson raped her and ripped her fetus from the womb to terrorize Charles into becoming a traitor but also to prevent the birth of such a fearsome gunslinger.

CHAMPIGNON, CHARLES (M)

One of the gunslingers in the court of Gilead. He throws himself on a hand grenade to save his *dinh*, Steven Deschain, when Justus leads them into a trap. He is forced into becoming a traitor, though, when Farson captures his family, rapes his wife and kills his unborn child.

CHARLES, SON OF CHARLES (1, M)

A young gunslinger in the court of Steven Deschain. Hax's executioner.

CHEF WARTHOG (7)

Jake's name for the tusked pig-headed low man in the Dixie Pig's kitchen. The chef sends his pot washers after Jake while continuing to cook a pig. Jake cuts his head off with an Oriza.

CHEVIN OF CHAYVEN (7)

A Roderick whom Roland and Eddie encounter as a walk-in in Lovell, Maine. Son of Hamil, minstrel of the South Plains. Roland sends him to the clearing at the end of the path.

CLAY, ANNIE (4.5)

Original name of Sister Fortuna of Serenity in Debaria.

CLAYPOOL, FRANK (4)

A deputy in Hambry. He "fell out of a boat" and broke his leg, thus leaving a vacancy filled by Eldred Jonas.

CLEMMIE (4.5)

One of the sisters at Serenity near Debaria.

COLLINS, JOE (7)

The only resident of Westring, at the edge of Empathica and the beginning of Tower Road. He lives in a house on Odd Lane. Son of Henry and Flora. He has a photograph of the Dark Tower pinned to his wall. He claims to be a former stand-up comic who was beaten in Cleveland and woke up in a deserted town named Stone's Warp about seventeen years ago. Most of what he says is a lie. He is actually Dandelo, a vampire that feeds on emotions instead of blood. He has been preying on passersby for years and draining Patrick Danville in the interim. When he tells a joke, he raps his knuckles on his head and pops his eyes impossibly far from his head. At first, he's scrawny, has long, fine white hair, a cataract over one eye and a bad leg. After he feeds on Roland's laughter, his hair turns black and he looks thirty years younger. When confronted, he changes into something resembling a psychotic clown and then into a buglike creature with human features printed on the surface. Susannah shoots him.

COMPSON (7)
Rando Thoughtful's aide. He appears to Roland and Susannah as Fumalo, Stephen King's id.

CONROY (7)
A *can toi* technician who works in Damli House in Algul Siento.

COPPERHEAD (3)
One of the Tick-Tock Man's Grays. He runs the machine that sounds the drums in Lud. Roland shoots him in the back.

COQUINA (L, M)
One of the Little Sisters of Eluria. When she learns of Sister Jenna's treachery and threatens to tell, Jenna summons the *can tam* to make her part of the medicine.

CORT (THROUGHOUT)
Full name: Cortland Andrus, son of Fardo. The drill instructor from hell. Roland often hears his voice chiding him or instructing him on how to behave. He taught apprentice gunslingers how to fight and how to kill if they had to, clouting them in the head if they were slow or contrary. He instructed them in celestial navigation, archery, gunnery, falconry and how to keep time in their heads. He usually won the largest goose in the Barony for a prize at the riddling contests at Fair-Days and may have known about other worlds and held palaver with the Manni who lived outside Gilead.

Besting him in battle was the normal way in which students became gunslingers. He was disappointed when Roland challenged him at a very early age, but he underestimated Roland and his weapon. Afterward, he counseled

Roland to delay seeking vengeance against Marten because he knew the boy was no match for the wizard. He was so badly injured that Roland spent most of his time feeding and cleaning him after he returned from Mejis. He suffered from rheumatism during his final year and was poisoned two years before the civil war began. In the Marvel comics, the poison is administered via the pages of a book that belonged to Farson's nephew.

COSINGTON, ADA (4.5)

Peter Cosington's wife. She helps look after Nell Ross after she is struck blind.

COSINGTON, "SQUARE" PETER (4.5)

A woodcutter in Tree Village, partnered with Ernest Marchly. A falling tree injures him before Jack Ross dies, which is why he doesn't return to his stake in the Endless Forest where Ross's body is hidden.

COVENANT MAN, THE (4.5)

Also known as the Barony Covenanter. Tax collecting is one of his hobbies. He travels the countryside levying and collecting excises on behalf of Gilead, but he is also adviser to the Council of Eld. His saddle is decorated with arcane symbols.

Among his gunna is a silver washbasin that came from Garlan. Nell Ross says he hasn't aged a day in the last twenty years. Little magic and long life is all he's capable of, according to Maerlyn. Wanting to know people's secrets is his "besetting vice," one that might be the death of him someday. He uses the truth to hurt people and bait traps for them. He reveals Bern Kells's crimes to Tim Ross, arms him with his father's hand ax, and sends him back to Tree, hoping the boy will commit murder. He also shows Tim a false vision of Maerlyn's house in the Endless Forest and sends him Armaneeta, the *sighe*, as a "guide," to lure him to his death. He probably hopes Tim will kill the caged tyger if he reaches the North Forest Kinnock Dogan, but that ploy fails. Maerlyn believes he will be punished for his foolishness, which was not authorized by the Crimson King. See also: Marten Broadcloak, Walter o'Dim and Randall Flagg.

CRIMSON KING, THE (1, 4, 4.5, 5, 6, 7, M)

Also known as Ram Abbalah, the Lord of the Spiders, Los' the Red and the Red King. Maerlyn calls him the Great One. He's from the line of Eld, therefore related to Roland Deschain, and Mordred Deschain's Red Father.

He wants to rule the Dark Tower, but in his insanity he destroyed the mark of Eld that would have allowed him to enter it. He backed John Farson's insurrection against Gilead because he relishes chaos. Also, by destroying all the living descendants of Arthur Eld, he eliminates any competition for the Tower.

He has a sense of the future and does his best to neutralize enemies in advance. He knows Stephen King will write Roland's story, so he repeatedly tries to kill the author, starting when he was just a boy. When Roland begins his journey to find the Dark Tower, the Crimson King sends minions like Walter o'Dim to thwart him. The Crimson King is conflicted between wanting to destroy the Tower and getting there ahead of Roland to rule it, which may be the cause of his insanity, in addition to living so close to the Tower and thinking upon it so deeply.

His domain is Le Casse Roi Russe in Discordia, the black wasteland southeast of Fedic that he poisoned and consigned to darkness on a lark. He wants reality to return to the chaos from which it arose, which is why he wants to bring down the Tower. He believes he will rule the chaos that ensues after the Fall. When Roland overcomes the challenges the Crimson King puts in his way, Los' the Red goes mad, murders just about everyone in his court, smashes the six Wizard's Glasses he had, and kills himself by swallowing a spoon. The advantage to being dead is that Roland's guns of Eld can't kill him. Then he rides off to the Dark Tower on a horse.

He ends up trapped on one of the Tower's balconies. Exactly when he arrived is a matter of some confusion. According to "The Wind Through the Keyhole," he's been trapped since before the time of Tim Ross. However, Rando Thoughtful claims he left his castle a short time before Roland and Susannah get there, and Dandelo remembers him riding past in his own portable storm. Maybe he's dual natured—one facet was trapped in the Tower a long time ago and another has been wreaking havoc on Mid-World and conscripting Breakers to destroy the Beams. His two facets may have reunited after he killed himself and rode to the Tower.

Mordred Deschain is his son and Roland's son at the same time. How his genetic material became part of the equation is unclear. He may have come as himself to Mia after she was impregnated, or his minions may have added his sperm to the mix at the Fedic Dogan. This isn't the first time he's tried to father a child. Sylvia Pittston of Tull believed she was pregnant with the Crimson King's son, though this might be another of Walter's lies.

His *sigul* is the open red eye, and the low men are his soldiers. He is seen in person only twice. Once in *Insomnia*, which may be more of a coded message than a "true" story, and when Roland arrives at the Dark Tower. He's an old man with a snowy-white beard growing down to his chest, waist-length hair, a long, greedy, flushed face with deep creases, an enormous nose and burning red eyes. His red robe is covered with kabbalistic symbols, making him look like an insane Father Christmas.

He's a magical creature but in the end he relies on the weapons of the Old People. He's no match for Patrick Danville, though, who has the power of uncreation. All that remains of him after Patrick is finished with his eraser is a pair of eyes with the optic nerves intact. The rest of him is banished to oblivion.

According to the Marvel series, he is the son of Arthur Eld and one of the Great Old Ones of the Prim, which makes him Roland's cousin (many times removed) and the rightful heir to All-World.

Crossovers to Other Works: The Crimson King appears in *Insomnia*, where he has minions in Derry, Maine, determined to kill Patrick Danville. Under the name Ram Abbalah, he appears in *Black House*, the sequel to *The Talisman*, which focuses on his search for Breakers.

CROW, ALLAN "PA" (4.5)
Leader of the Crow Gang, who specializes in kidnappings for ransom. Steven Deschain leads a posse against them. An old man, paralyzed on one side from a stroke, Crow is the only one to get off a shot, which ricochets, striking Deschain in the arm. Steven Deschain shot him.

CROW GANG (4.5)
Harriers, train robbers and kidnappers who ply their trade in and around Debaria. Steven Deschain leads a posse that includes Deputy Hugh Peavy against them to their lair in the foothills. Most of the posse is killed in an ambush, but Roland's father and Peavy take the Crows by surprise at night and kill most of the gang and arrest the rest.

CROYDON, JOHN (4)
Owner of the Piano Ranch and a small orchard in Mejis. Alain Johns shoots him.

CURRY, YON (4.5)
A sheepherder killed by the skin-walker on the Low Pure in Debaria.

DANDELO (7)
Eddie Dean warns Roland to beware Dandelo. Jake Chambers passes on the same message via Oy. A vampire who drinks human emotion instead of blood. See Joe Collins.

DEAF RICON (4.5)

A resident of Tree Village. Bern Kells hides in his barn after his crimes are revealed.

DEARBORN, WILLIAM "WILL" (4, 7, M)

Roland Deschain's alias in Mejis. He is a drover's son. Dearborn is the middle name of Western author Louis L'Amour.

DECURRY, DR. (M)

Jamie's father. Traitorous members of Gilead's guard shoot him and his nurses to death.

DECURRY, JAMIE (L, 1, 3, 4, 4.5, 5, 6, 7, M)

Part of Roland's first *ka-tet*, a boy of few words. Also known as Silent Jamie, because he rarely says anything if he doesn't have to, and Red-Hand because one of his hands looks as though it has been dipped in blood. Flagg described him as the fellow with the birthmark. Though he is adept with a gun, he prefers his bow or his bah. Not much of a reader. He accompanies Roland on his mission to defeat the skin-man and loses his virginity on their final night in Debaria. A sniper—perhaps General Grissom or his son—kills him during the battle of Jericho Hill.

DEIDRE THE MAD (3)

Roland's grandmother.

DELGADO, CORDELIA "CORD" (4, 7, M)

Susan Delgado's aunt and sister to Pat Delgado. Daughter of Hiram. She is sour, miserly, greedy, supercilious, angry and suspicious, but can act nice when she wants something. She never hears good gossip and has few social pretensions, a love of gold and silver and a fear of being turned out, penniless, into the world.

She helped raise Susan after her mother died and became sole guardian after Pat was killed. Susan believes that she wasn't party to her father's murder, but she knew about it. When they lose title to their land and horses, she brokers a deal with Mayor Hart Thorin to have Susan become his gilly in return for an enormous financial consideration, with more to come when Susan gives the mayor a son. She manipulates Susan by invoking her dead father's name.

She claims to have had a lover or two when she was young, including Fran Lengyll, though Susan doesn't believe her. She allows Eldred Jonas to charm her when he's fishing for information. She's so obsessed with the possibility that Susan is ruining the deal with Thorin that she stops eating and taking care of herself, slowly going insane. She lets Rhea drink her blood so the witch can regain her power and they can seek retribution against Susan. As Rhea's puppet, she paints Susan's hands red and lights the fire that kills her. She dies before the bonfire burns down to embers from a heart attack, a stroke or shame.

Physical description: She's a skinny woman edging into late middle age and has gray streaks in her chestnut hair. There's a family resemblance to Susan, but her aspect is pinched and shrewish, thin and disapproving.

DELGADO, PATRICK "PAT" (4, M)

Susan Delgado's father. He was a quiet, calm man who was interested in the Old People. He was in charge of the Barony's horses for almost thirty years until his death when Susan was eleven. According to Francis Lengyll, a snake spooked his horse, Ocean Foam, who threw him and rolled over on him. In truth, he was murdered because he stood up against the traitors in the Horsemen's Association, with whom he worked on a daily basis. His land and horses were confiscated after he died. His sister, Cordelia, who helped raise Susan, became her sole guardian. He had red hair and a beard and smoked a pipe. He was a firm believer in *ka*, much to Susan's consternation.

DELGADO, SUSAN (THROUGHOUT)

A sixteen-year old girl from Mejis. Roland Deschain's first love. Her father, Pat Delgado, was in charge of the Barony's horses and died when she was eleven. Her mother was already dead by then. After her father died, her spinster aunt Cordelia, Pat's sister, raised her.

She isn't vain, but she knows she's good-looking from the way boys act around her. She inherited a good singing voice from her grandmother and a calm nature from her father. She's normally level-headed and clever, though she can be stubborn and headstrong. Roland thinks she's brave to visit Rhea's hut alone in the dark. She's never been out of Hambry. She is in favor of the Affiliation, but not strong for it. She doesn't put much stock in John Farson and his war, since it is thousands of miles away.

Her aunt Cordelia uses her love for her father to coerce her into accepting a deal whereby she becomes Mayor Thorin's gilly in return for financial consideration. After Pat's death, they lost title to their land and horses and they might end up homeless if Susan doesn't agree to this lucrative deal. She wishes her father were around to advise her.

Susan rationalizes that she will still be able to get married later, thinking that her part of the deal will end when she gets pregnant, but Mayor Thorin is less interested in a child than in having a beautiful young woman in his bed. The first time she uses Thorin's name in her own defense—during her visit with Rhea, who must attest that she is a virgin and free of demons—she feels humiliated. She is also ashamed by what this arrangement—which is acceptable under the old laws—means for Thorin's wife. By the time she understands what she's gotten herself into, it's too late to undo it. Breaking her word would bring shame to her father's name.

As her attraction to Roland grows, she curses fate for having brought him into her life after she made a commitment to Thorin. She has no use for "greedy old" *ka*, which was so important to her father. She avoids Roland until her situation gets so bad and her love for him so strong that she begs him to ask her to break her vow. When he does, they begin a romance that lasts the whole summer, during which she becomes stronger and more self-confident.

Her loyalty prevents her from believing that her father's friends were involved in his death until shown incontrovertible evidence. After the Big Coffin Hunters execute their plan to frame Roland and the others, she orchestrates their jailbreak. She remains calm in the face of violence, relying on her father's voice to guide her, like any good gunslinger. She kills Sheriff Avery and Deputy Hollis, whom she played with as a child.

She becomes pregnant with Roland's child—perhaps after their first time together—but never gets to share the news with him. She is captured, freed and captured again, falling into the hands of Rhea, who resents the girl for defying her. She is paraded through the streets of Mejis on Rhea's cart and burned at the stake in one of Mid-World's old, banned traditions of ritual sacrifice: charyou tree. She proclaims her love for Roland as she dies.

Physical description: She is almost too beautiful to look at, in Roland's estimation. She is tanned from riding, has long blond hair that glows like the sun and reaches the middle of her back, often in braids, and the grayest eyes Cuthbert has ever seen.

DELONG, PUCK (4.5)

Son of the night foreman at the salt mines in Little Debaria. Vikka Frye knew him from Reap Fair-Day, where they entered contests together.

DEMON ELEMENTALS (6)

There are six demon elementals, one for each Beam. However, they are hermaphroditic, which means there is a total of twelve aspects to counter the Guardians of the Beam. They reign over the invisible world of demons and other evil creatures left behind after the Prim receded. They have no names—they know what they are. Roland had intercourse with one of these elementals in the place of the Oracle. It then changed genders and passed the semen along to Susannah when Jake came through the doorway from Dutch Hill.

DeMULLET, GENERAL (5, M)

A member of the Affiliation forces that fight John Farson after the fall of Gilead. His column was ambushed and slaughtered at Rimrocks before the battle of Jericho Hill.

DENNIS (2)

One of two desperate yet grim young men Roland encountered while they were pursuing a demon named Flagg who looked like a man.

Crossover to Other Works: In *The Eyes of the Dragon*, Dennis was the son of Brandon, Peter's butler. Peter was the rightful heir to King Roland of Delain. At the end of the book, he joins Peter's brother, Thomas, in pursuit of Flagg. The story says that Dennis and Thomas did see Flagg again, and confronted him, but the outcome of that encounter has never been told.

DEPAPE, ANDY (6)

Roy Depape's brother. Roland believes he was stung to death by a snake, but Mia killed him.

DEPAPE, ROY B. (4, 5, 6, 7, M)

One of the Big Coffin Hunters. A twenty-five-year-old redhead who wears spectacles with gold rims. He's fast with a gun, even if his wits are slow, but he can't bear pain. According to Eldred Jonas, his heart is in the right place, he's a good enough boy, his head is a little soft and he follows orders, though usually only after they're explained several times. He is drunk on one of the local prostitutes, Gert Moggins (stage name: Deborah). He doesn't like Sheemie Ruiz and is humiliating him to entertain the patrons at the Travellers' Rest when Cuthbert comes to the rescue, smashing the tip of one finger with a slingshot. Eldred sends him to follow the back trail of the Affiliation Brats to see what he can find out. He slits Mayor Thorin's throat. Roland kills him. Mia killed his brother, Andy.

DESCHAIN, GABRIELLE (1, 3, 4, 4.5, 5, 7, M)

Roland Deschain's mother and wife to Steven. Daughter of Candor the Tall (or Alan?). She came from Beesford-on-Arten, between Gilead and Debaria. Her maiden name was Verriss, and she was known as Gabrielle of the Water. She used to read and sing to Roland when he was young. Once he entered gunslinger training, she saw him less often. Ignored by her husband, she is seduced by Marten Broadcloak and becomes a traitor to Gilead, though Steven knows about the affair for two years. When Roland is sent to Mejis shortly after he learns the truth about her relationship with Marten, she goes to a retreat in Debaria.

While in Debaria, she makes a belt for Roland as a peace offering and returns in time for the party celebrating his return. However, she is still in Marten's thrall and plans to murder Steven with a poisoned knife in bed after apologizing for straying. Roland learns of the plot from the pink Bend o' the Rainbow and intercedes without betraying his mother. When he goes to her chambers to offer her one last chance to recover her sanity, the grapefruit—which Gabrielle stole from Steven as a consolation prize for Marten—misleads Roland into thinking she is the witch Rhea holding a snake. He shoots her to death with his father's guns.

As Roland learns from a letter she left with Everlynne, she returned to Gilead knowing that her son would kill her because she thought *ka* demanded it. She dies smiling. The people of Gilead believe she committed suicide "while possessed of a demon which troubled her spirit." Roland hears her voice in the Doorway Cave in Calla Bryn Sturgis, begging him not to shoot her.

DESCHAIN, MORDRED (5, 6, 7)

Dan-tete: the Little Red King. Mordred Deschain has four parents: Roland, Susannah, Mia and the Crimson King. Walter o'Dim arranged his conception as another trap for Roland, to fulfill ancient prophecy and to create someone to rule in the place of the trapped Crimson King. He was named for the ill-begotten son of King Arthur, who killed his father. He was conceived when Roland had sex with a demon elemental in the Speaking Ring of the Oracle. The elemental inverted itself and delivered the semen into Susannah when Jake came through the doorway from Dutch Hill. At some point the Crimson King's sperm was added to the mix.

He is born with a mouth full of teeth, a head full of black hair and a fully erect penis. Within minutes, he consumes Mia, absorbing her energy and all of her knowledge. He passes through adolescence to become a young man within a few months. He could be the most powerful Breaker ever, but this potential is never realized.

Mordred is his own twin in that he has two physical forms: human boy and black widow spider, a blend of magic and mundane. Transforming requires large amounts of energy, but he can consume meat only as a spider. In this form, the birthmark on his heel becomes a red hourglass on his belly—the real key to the Dark Tower. A white node rises from the spider's back, containing his human face with blue eyes identical to Roland's. He requires much more energy in this form. His thoughts become dark, primitive urges uncolored by emotion.

He is a tragic figure who didn't choose his mission and has no way to argue against it. The Crimson King directs his actions from the Dark Tower. At times he is drawn to Roland, jealous of the friendship he senses among the *ka-tet*. He resists the temptation to join their circle, knowing they would kill him in an instant. Besides, he's been bred to hate Roland, so he could never accept the gunslinger as his *dinh*. Still, he stays close, feeling like he's sharing their *khef*. At times, Roland almost pities Mordred, leaving behind food for him when they break camp.

Though he's a monster, he is vulnerable because of his human aspect. Susannah shoots him soon after he's born, and the wound never heals. When he's a baby, he relies on Nigel the robot for food, but he's smart and powerful enough to outwit Walter, who means to kill him and take his heel to the Tower.

During his first attempt to kill Roland, the machinery in the Fedic Dogan that was supposed to release poison gas fails. While trailing the *ka-tet*, he is constantly hungry, cold and miserable, sometimes crying himself to sleep. The poisons of the Badlands and his starvation diet make him appear wretched. His hunger undoes him when he eats Dandelo's horse, Lippy, and poisons himself.

At the end, he looks like he's twenty. Desperate to please his Red Father, he attacks Roland the night before the gunslinger reaches the Dark Tower. Mordred is dying, so he has nothing to lose. If not for Oy's sacrifice, he might have succeeded. Once Roland is awake, the spider-monster is no match for his White Father.

DESCHAIN, ROLAND (THROUGHOUT)

The last gunslinger and a soldier of the White. He is the son of Steven, who was the last *dinh* of Gilead, and Gabrielle, and the grandson of Alaric and

Henry the Tall. He is a thirtieth-generation descendant of Arthur Eld, though more likely via one of Eld's gillies than one of his wives.

At the age of eleven, he sees firsthand the seriousness of John Farson's threat to the Affiliation when he overhears Hax, the castle cook, conspiring with a traitorous guard. After reporting this to his father, he asks to witness the hanging, which is an important part of his coming of age.

His suspicions about the relationship between his mother and Marten Broadcloak are confirmed when the wizard flaunts the affair, hoping to drive Roland to take his test of manhood with his instructor, Cort, before he's ready. The price for failure is exile. He's only fourteen, two years younger than his father was—and he was the youngest ever. Roland falls for this trap, but Marten underestimated the boy, who is willing to sacrifice his longtime friend, a hawk named David, to win his guns. It's behavior he will repeat often in the future.

Once he's officially a gunslinger, he's still no match for Marten, who is determined to prevent him from fulfilling his destiny. Steven sends Roland and two friends to Mejis, out of harm's way, unaware that he's sending them into a hotbed of anti-Affiliation activity. There, Roland falls in love for the first—and only—time, with Susan Delgado, whose spirit will haunt him for the rest of his life.

Roland comports himself well against Farson's regulators, but he allows love to blind him to the seriousness of their situation. He refuses his best friend Cuthbert's suggestion to notify Gilead once they discover what's going on. Though he, Cuthbert and Alain prevail, destroying the oil supply Farson planned to use in weapons against Gilead, Susan pays the price for his inexperience.

Roland had hoped that this victory over Farson would allow Gilead to prevail. He would then be able to live a peaceful life and start a family with Susan. Then he's sent a vision of the Dark Tower's peril and he forswears everything to save the axis of existence. He couldn't have stayed with Susan had she lived, even though she's pregnant with his son. Thus begins a lifelong obsession that causes Roland to sacrifice many things and people over the span of a thousand years.

The second great tragedy of Roland's life comes shortly after he returns to Gilead. He learns that his mother is plotting to kill his father. He goes to her room, intending to make her see the error of her ways. Tricked by the pink Wizard's Glass he took from Farson's men, he thinks the person approaching him from behind is the witch Rhea, whom he thwarted in Mejis. Using his father's guns, he kills his mother.

Though Gabrielle was still aligned with Marten—which is why the pink orb was in her chambers—Roland is devastated. He spends weeks moping around the castle and tending to Cort, who was seriously injured during the test of manhood. To get him out of his funk, his father sends him to Debaria to stop the skin-man. While there, he learns that his mother knew he would kill her but continued down her treasonous path because she felt that was what *ka* wanted. She forgives Roland in a posthumous message, and Roland is able to forgive her.

As a student gunslinger, he was told that he lacked imagination and his teachers assumed he was slow mentally, in part because he doesn't waste words. He has come to accept this assessment, but adversaries do well not to underestimate his dedication, charisma and guile. He hates mysteries, isn't good at thinking around corners, and acts most successfully when he does so without thinking, shooting first and asking questions later. His romantic nature is buried deeply.

Not only can Roland shoot better than any adversary or accomplice, but he acquires skills allowing him to serve as peace officer, envoy, mediator, hypnotist, messenger, accountant, diplomat, teacher, spy and executioner. Though he always feels sick after big battles, he is never so happy to be alive as when he's preparing to deal death.

He is an expert liar and a storyteller, as well as a glutton for stories told by others. His vision is better than most. He can speak five languages and is familiar with several others, though written English defies him and he loses something in the translation in that world. Even though he knows many riddles, sarcasm is the only form of humor he understands.

His first *ka-tet* ends at the battle of Jericho Hill, where everyone else is killed. Roland escapes by hiding in a cart filled with bodies. He continues on his quest for the Dark Tower, which many people think is just a legend. A symbol of his narrow vision is the fact that he fails to pick up the Horn of Eld, which once belonged to his ancestor, Arthur.

He's ageless, living outside time, skipping entire generations. He spends much of his unusually long life alone, casting about for the Tower, which turns him heartless. His only companions are the badgering voices of those he left behind, including Cort, Vannay and his father. He still has a touch of humanity left when he befriends Jenna in Eluria and Allie in Tull, but he's so focused on his quest that he's willing to sacrifice Jake Chambers's life for the chance to speak with the man in black, even though he knows that doing so will damn him. Only three things matter: mortality, *ka* and the Tower. Things in the past are beyond his power to change, and *ka* will take care of what's ahead—and he rarely thinks about *ka*, though he is prone to mistaking his will for *ka*.

His most prized possessions are his father's guns, which have yellow sandalwood stocks and barrels made from the blade of Arthur Eld's sword Excalibur. He carries a satchel that contains a leather grow bag—a continually replenishing source of money or gems and the only magical item he owns, though Susannah thinks that occasionally he *is* magic—along with ammunition, tobacco, food and water. The letter his mother left for him at Serenity crumbled to dust long ago.

After he loses two fingers to lobstrosities, he is forced to assemble another *ka-tet*. He doesn't get to pick his traveling companions—*ka* does this for him. Though he grows to love and respect Eddie, Jake and Susannah, he often operates as if he were still alone, keeping secrets from them. He believes that he stands somewhat outside the *ka-tet*. He's faithful to them, but worries that he would sacrifice them if doing so would get him closer to his goal. Experience says that Roland's way means death for those who accompany him. He takes no pride in the fact that he is good at producing martyrs. His obsession with the Tower is contagious and his *ka-tet* would carry on without him if he died.

He hasn't loved anyone in a long time and his *ka-tet* is his last chance. He decides to sacrifice himself to save Stephen King instead of allowing Jake—whom he thinks of as his son—to do so, but he fails in the attempt. Roland even feels pity for Mordred, occasionally leaving food behind for him when they break camp. After Jake dies, he wishes he'd sworn off his quest before *ka* taught him its real price.

Once he achieves his primary objective—saving the Tower by freeing the Breakers and saving King's life—he isn't content. He has one quest assigned by *ka* and another of his own choosing. He has to save the Beams because if the Tower falls he will never be able to mount its staircase and find out what's at the top so he can force whoever lives there to undo all the damage to Mid-World.

Cuthbert and Vannay warned Roland that failing to change and learn from the past would be his damnation. He is forced to remember all those he left behind as he climbs the Tower. Eventually, it becomes too painful, and he sets his sights on the room at the top, but there's nothing for him there except punishment and disappointment.

His existence is near-perpetual reincarnation. Each time he is returned to the place in his journey where he is closing in on the man in black—too late, he believes, to make any meaningful changes. *Ka* gives him credit, though, for the progress he made previously, and Horn of Eld is his reward this time. If he can hold on to it through another iteration, maybe everything will be different next time and he will learn what the Tower really holds for him.

Physical description: At six foot three, he is considered tall in Gilead, though he's shorter than his father. He has cool blue shooter's eyes, the color of the sky at first light. His black hair is streaked with white by the time he reaches Calla Bryn Sturgis. His face is tanned, lined and weathered, and he has deep crow's feet. His smile is as dangerous as quicksand. He could pass for Stephen King's father when King is thirty, so he must look at least fifty and has more than a passing resemblance to Clint Eastwood, though mostly in the eyes. His body is covered with scars from knife slashes, burns, whippings and bullet wounds. He is missing two fingers from his right hand and one big toe.

DESCHAIN, STEVEN (1, 4, 4.5, 5, 6, 7, M)

The last lord of light. Roland Deschain's father and husband of Gabrielle Deschain. Son of Henry the Tall. Of the twenty-ninth generation descended from Arthur Eld via one of his many gillies. His mark is a D with an S inside. He became *dinh* of Gilead when Roland was young. Events and responsibilities turned his face cruel. He is taller than Roland, has keen eyesight and a talent for trailing, which he used in Debaria while hunting down the Crow Gang with then-deputy Hugh Peavy, who dug Pa Crow's bullet out of his arm, adding to the map of scars that was his body.

He is furious when Roland lets Marten trick him into taking his test of manhood early and realizes that Marten won't stop coming after his son, so he sends him to Mejis to keep him out of harm's way. He's known Gabrielle has been consorting with the wizard for more than two years without doing anything about it. He is stabbed to death by person or persons unknown. In the Marvel comics, before dying, he kills his assailant, one of the turncoat castle guards, who falls out the castle window and into the moat.

DESMOND (2)

An apprentice gunslinger from Roland's youth. Roland calls out his name when he sees the neon Tower sign outside the Leaning Tower.

DESTRY, HUNTER "SPOT" (4.5)

Willem Destry's brother, called "Spot" because of his freckles. Part of the posse that tries to locate Bern Kells.

DESTRY, OLD (4.5)

A farmer in Tree Village who gives Tim Ross work and pays him in scrip for the town store.

DESTRY, RANDY (4.5)

Willem Destry's older brother.

DESTRY, WILLEM "STRAW" (4.5)

Middle of Old Destry's three sons. Called "Straw" because his hair is nearly colorless. He works with Tim Ross at the sawmill and tells him that his brother saw Bern Kells drunk at the saloon.

DEWLAP (3)

A scrawny old man who fed apples into the press in the cider house in Lud when David Quick (the Tick-Tock Man) was a boy.

DOLORES (4.5)

One of the Sisters of Serenity near Debaria. The skin-walker bit her head from her shoulders before attacking Fortuna.

DOOLIN, BELINDA (4.5)

A rancher's wife kidnapped and raped by the Crow Gang when Steven Deschain was a young gunslinger. He and Deputy Hugh Peavy rescued her.

DOOLIN, EAMON (5)

One of the four people from Calla Bryn Sturgis who confronted the Wolves when Jamie Jaffords was nineteen. His wife, Molly, killed one of the Wolves. He was twenty-three at the time of the battle, already losing his hair. Armed with a bah and bolt, he was in favor of hiding in the ditch until the Wolves passed and attacking from the rear. He was killed by a sneetch.

DOOLIN, MOLLY (5)

A Sister of Oriza who was the only person to kill one of the Wolves before the gunslingers came to Calla Bryn Sturgis. She stood against them with Jamie Jaffords, Pokey Slidell and her husband, Eamon. Called Red Molly as much for her temper as for the color of her hair. She was killed by a light-stick, though she continued to try to throw Orizas until her body caught fire. Her roont twin sister was Minnie.

DOORKEEPER, THE (3, 4, 5, 7)

A monster that keeps people from accessing the portal in the Mansion in Dutch Hill. A genuine leftover of the Prim. The house is a manifestation of the monster in Jake's world.

DUBATIVO, RHEA (L, 1, 4, 4.5, 5, 7, M)

Also known as Rhea of the Cöos and the Weirding of Cöos because she lives on the last of a group of hills known as the Cöos, five miles east of Hambry and ten miles south of Eyebolt Canyon, which she can see from the hilltop above her house. She is borderline illiterate and uses a mark thought to represent a devil's hoof as a signature. She claims this device is known for six Baronies around and can't be copied.

She is a real witch, not just an old lady posing as one. The fact that she never leaves Cöos Hill makes her presence in Mejis easier for the locals to accept. They're afraid and respectful of her, but avail themselves of her services, including hangover powder, love potions, sex aids and potions to silence nagging mothers-in-law's tongues, even though these medicines come with terrible side effects. Susan Delgado comes to her at the bidding of Mayor Thorin, who needs to know she's a virgin and that her spirit hasn't been polluted by a demon before he will take her on as a gilly.

She can make herself dim when she doesn't want to be seen and has some of the attributes of a vampire. When Roland first sees the Little Sisters of Eluria, he is reminded of her. She is wary and respectful of people in power because they could take the grapefruit away after it's left in her care. To placate Susan after behaving inappropriately with her, she grants her a three-month reprieve before Mayor Thorin can take her into his bed. However, she isn't above playing cruel pranks, either, planting a posthypnotic suggestion in Susan's mind to irk Thorin. Susan believes that, left to her own devices, Rhea would lie about everything.

Her only companions are a six-legged mutant cat named Musty that she grooms with her tongue and a snake named Ermot who fulfills any need she might have for a man. Her garden is full of muties, too, including her scarecrow. To her, the disturbing sound emanating from the thinny is a lullaby. She hears the voices of the dead in the wind and often dreams of roses and the Dark Tower.

She falls under the influence of the pink Wizard's Glass, which is left in her care by the Big Coffin Hunters. It awakens parts of her she long thought dead, but over time it steals her anima and drains her body of vitality, though she considers it a fair trade. When she isn't looking into it, she's thinking about looking into it, eating nothing and drinking little. Like everyone else who has used it, she thinks she is its natural owner. What she loves about it most is that it shows people at their vilest, even though she knows that using it is damning her.

She isn't used to anyone defying her and is driven to pay back anyone who offends her. Her vexation upon learning that Susan—with Roland's help—defied her hypnotic suggestion is so overwhelming that she can't sleep and can't get the Wizard's Glass to cooperate. Only when she has a plan to get revenge is she able to calm herself down.

After the Big Coffin Hunters take the glass from her and exile her from their camp, she sets her eyes on the only two people who are still within her reach. The grapefruit didn't break her fundamental power. She rejuvenates herself and regains her sense of command by drinking Cordelia Delgado's blood. Everyone in Hambry follows her unquestioningly as she goads them into a frenzy, encouraging them to burn Susan at the stake during the Reap Fair Bonfire.

She then sets her sights on Roland, who killed Ermot when she sent the snake after him. She is so devastated by the loss that she sews the snake's body back together and wears the decaying carcass around her neck. Though she probably doesn't go to Gilead herself, she has a way of making friends who would act on her behalf. She conspires with the Wizard's Glass to trick Roland into killing his mother. Her glammer even crosses time—when the *ka-tet* revisits this scene in the grapefruit, she addresses them directly.

Her fate isn't known, but Roland tells his *ka-tet* that he saw her again. From the way he says this, Eddie assumes he killed her. She becomes the avatar of all witches—Eddie and Susannah use her in a retelling of *Hansel and Gretel*—and hers is one of the voices heard in the Doorway Cave in Calla Bryn Sturgis.

Physical description: She looks like a stereotypical witch, an old wrinkled hag with a wart on the tip of her nose. Her eyes are rheumy and the same gray-green as her cat's. Her smile is a horrible thing to behold, often a sneer. She doesn't take care of herself, so she reeks. Her fingers are cold and the flesh feels spongy and loose on her bones. No one knows how old she is (Roland calls her "daughter of none"), but she can still run when she needs to and her grip is strong. Under the thrall of the Wizard's Glass, her cheeks sink, her face becomes covered with sores and she loses all of her stringy white hair and most of her teeth. She resembles a troll more than a person. However she regains some of her vitality after she drinks Cordelia Delgado's blood.

EISENHART, MARGARET (5, 6, 7)

Wife of Vaughn Eisenhart of Calla Bryn Sturgis, granddaughter of Henchick of the Redpath Manni and one of the Sisters of Oriza. She is a slim woman in her forties. She thinks like a gunslinger, which is probably why she couldn't stay with the peaceful Manni, who consider her to be damned, one of the forgetful. She was like a second mother to Benny Slightman. She never lost any children to the Wolves because of the timing of their births, but she believes she lost them all because they moved away and return infrequently. She tells Roland the story of Gray Dick, which gave rise to the legend of Lady Oriza. Though skilled with the Oriza, she awaits her husband's approval before she will agree to join the battle against the Wolves. A Wolf cut her head off with a light saber.

EISENHART, VAUGHN (5, 6)

Owner of the Rocking B Ranch in Calla Bryn Sturgis. One of the three "big bugs" in the Calla—the big rancher. His wife is Margaret, formerly of the Manni. He is the first of the influential people to come around to Roland's side, mostly on the strength of his wife's opinion. His roont twin sister Verna died ten years before the gunslingers' visit. He's shrewder than Overholser. Big and honest with an earthy sense of humor. He has an extravagant graying bush of a mustache. He promises to curse Roland if Margaret is killed, but he doesn't keep that promise.

ELD, ARTHUR (1, 3, 4.5, 5, 6, 7, M)

The first king to rise after the Prim receded and an analog of King Arthur. Sometimes known simply as the Eld. The old White King, Guardian of the Dark Tower, and slayer of the great snake Saita. His white horse, Llamrei, was the *sigul* of all In-World. The metal from his unifying sword Excalibur, which he freed from a pyramid, was used to make the barrels of Roland's guns, the only things that will allow him to enter the Dark Tower. Arthur Eld once blew the horn Roland abandoned at Jericho Hill.

Almost all subsequent gunslingers descend from him, though not all via legitimate lines. He reportedly had more than forty gillies in addition to his three wives, one of whom is Queen Rowena. He may have been murdered and is regarded as a myth in some parts of the Mid-World. The Crimson King is also a member of the line of Eld—which would explain why statues and paintings of Arthur Eld appear in Castle Discordia—as is, perhaps, Maerlyn. A golden statue of Arthur Eld stands atop the Cradle of Lud.

ELLEN (4.5)

One of the sisters at Serenity near Debaria.

ESTRADA, JORGE (5)

A smallhold farmer in Calla Bryn Sturgis. His wife's name is Deelie.

EVERLYNNE (4.5)

Prioress of the Serenity retreat in Debaria. An enormous woman who stands at least six foot six. Daughter of Roseanna. She tended to Gabrielle Deschain and sent Marten Broadcloak away when he tried to see Roland's mother.

FANNIN, RICHARD (3, 7)

The guise under which Randall Flagg came to Andrew Quick, the Tick-Tock Man, in Lud.

FARADAY, NEIL (5)

A squat man with a smallhold rice-patch far on the south side of Calla Bryn Sturgis. A hard worker and a hard drinker. His twin children are Georgina and George, who is roont.

FARDO (4)

Cort's father. He delivered the blow that sent Eldred Jonas west, breaking his leg and giving him a permanent limp.

FARSON, JAMES (4, M)

John Farson's eldest nephew, a wandering singer. He brought a poison-coated knife into the court at Gilead that was supposed to reach Gabrielle Deschain, who would use it to kill Steven, but Roland intercepted it. His first name isn't given in the books, only in the Marvel adaptation, where he uses the alias Kingson. Cort kills him after catching him cheating in the riddle contest. In the Marvel comics, Walter brings him back to life so Farson won't fly into a rage and attack Gilead prematurely.

FARSON, JOHN (1, 2, 3, 4, 4.5, 5, 7, M)

Also known as the Good Man. A minion of the Crimson King. Reputed to be whimsically, dangerously insane. He is deeply concerned with *ka*. A former harrier or land-pirate with pretensions. He was a bandit and stage-robber in Garlan and Desoy who reportedly had a taste for kidnapping before leading the insurrection against the Affiliation that ended the reign of the gunslingers. Described by Roland as a symptom of the rebel movement, not its cause. He frosted his theft and murder with talk of democracy and equality, preaching against class slavery and ancient fairy tales. He thrived because the Affiliation was already crumbling from neglect.

He never appears in the series (he is more of a presence in the Marvel comics), but is described as being six feet tall and "broad across at both brace and basket." By the time Roland is fourteen, Farson has overtaken the Northern and West'rd Baronies, killing any leaders who don't follow him and leaving the cities in flames. He has a reputation for taking no prisoners.

He acquired a number of war machines—tanks, lasers and robots—that belonged to the Old People and needs the oil produced in Mejis to power them for a surprise offensive against the Affiliation in the Shavéd Mountains northwest of Gilead. He is also in possession of the pink Bend o' the Rainbow, which allows him to see the Affiliation's plans in advance, giving him a strategic advantage. The gunslingers consider Farson "small cheese" and think him mad for putting his trust in the Old People's machinery, because they are the way of death. Roland thinks the game is apt to be over before his father's people consider him a serious threat.

Walter is his "underliner," who emphasizes the importance of certain details with distant supporters. Farson's *sigul* is the eye of the Crimson King. His troops clasp their hands to the chest, left above right, then hold out both to the person being greeted. His more subdued supporters point at the centers of their foreheads, as if at an invisible eye.

After the battle of Jericho Hill, Roland moved away from him. Farson wanted Roland's head on a pole because he and his friends were responsible for the deaths of many of his people and because Roland stole the pink Bend o' the Rainbow from him in Mejis. He was insane with rage, according to Roland. Though he is ultimately victorious against the Affiliation, nothing is known about what happens to him afterwards.

In the synopsis at the beginning of *Wolves of the Calla*, King implies that Marten is also John Farson, but he states that this is not the case in the interview found in this book.

FEEMALO (7)

The guise of Brass, one of Rando Thoughtful's aides. He claims to represent Stephen King's ego. Susannah calls him Goodmouth. Roland shot him.

FELDON, AMY (1)
A whore from Tull.

FIMALO (7)
The guise of Rando Thoughtful, the Crimson King's Minister of State. He claims to represent Stephen King's superego. Susannah calls him Referee King.

FLAGG, RANDALL (2, 4, 4.5, 5, 6, 7)
Another guise of Walter o'Dim, Marten Broadcloak and the man in black. The Dark Man or, rather, a demon pretending to be a man. Roland encountered him in the final years of Gilead when Flagg had been fleeing from Dennis and Thomas. Roland saw him change a man who had irritated him into a howling dog. He doesn't laugh—he titters. He uses the name Richard Fannin when he comes to Andrew Quick, the Tick-Tock Man, in Lud. He appears to the *ka-tet* in the Green Palace, where Roland recognizes him as Marten, and tries to convince them to cry off their quest. Mid-World guns don't work against him—they only misfire. His initials are affixed to the message the *ka-tet* finds outside the Green Palace, and also to the note Tim Ross finds at the North Forest Kinnock Dogan (along with those of MB, Martin Broadcloak), which confirms him as being the Covenant Man.

    Crossovers to Other Works: Flagg was chief adviser to King Roland of Delain in *The Eyes of the Dragon*. He is also the leader of the evil faction in Las Vegas in *The Stand*. He appears in various guises throughout King's works, often as a character with the initials RF (Raymond Fiegler in *Hearts in Atlantis*, for example).

FORTUNA (4.5)
Real name: Annie Clay. A tiny woman, one of the sisters at the Serenity retreat in Debaria. She was attacked by the skin-man, who clawed off half her face.

FRANE, BOBBY (4.5)
One of the miners from Little Debaria who did time in Beelie Stockade.

FRANK (3, 5)
A member of the Pube faction in Lud. His frizzy red hair reminds Eddie of Ronald McDonald and Susannah of Clarabell the Clown. He is armed with a homemade spear. Eddie shoots him in the chest. Before he dies, upon learning that they are gunslingers, he cries their pardon.

FREEBORN, CHAS. (L, M)

A cattle thief in Eluria. He was to be tried on 12/Fe/99. However, the slow mutants probably killed him in his cell.

FRYE, KELLIN (4.5)

The good deputy in Debaria. His son is Vikka.

FRYE, VIKKA (4.5)

Son of Kellin, the best deputy in Debaria. Roland uses him to spread the news that there was a witness to the skin-man's attack at the Jefferson Ranch.

FUMALO (7)

The guise of Compson, one of Rando Thoughtful's aides. He claims to represent Stephen King's id. Susannah calls him Badmouth. She shot him.

GAN (4.5, 6, 7, M)

The god of Mid-World and its creator. Gan the Maker and Evil-taker. The creative overforce, personified in the Dark Tower. He rose from the Prim and gave birth to the universe from his navel. The Manni say that "fin-Gan" (hile) was the first word, and it set the world spinning. Roland believes that he tipped the world with his finger, thus creating time. Gan denies the *can toi*, the Crimson King and Discordia. Writers and artists are prophets or singers of Gan. The Beam of the Elephant and the Wolf is called Gan's Beam and Stephen King is its mortal Guardian. According to King, Gan is the creative overforce in Hindu mythology, served by a great turtle that bears the universe on its shell. The hands of Gan are the hands of *ka*, and they know no mercy.

GARBERS (4)

Former owners of the Bar K Ranch in Hambry. After it burned, they moved on.

GARMA (7)

A Child of Roderick who lives near Algul Siento. Haylis of Chayven's friend (with benefits).

GASHER (GASHERMAN) (3, 4, 4.5, 5, 6, 7)

One of Tick-Tock Man's Grays. Dressed like a pirate: a yellow headscarf, hoop earrings and a white silk eye patch. His face is covered with sores and he's dying of syphilis. His skull is bald, except for a few straggling tufts of black hair like porcupine quills, and deeply dented above the left temple. Talks in a thick accent. He takes Jake captive, using a hand grenade to keep the gunslingers at bay. Not smart enough to remember a simple password. He isn't afraid of dying but is afraid of being humiliated, an observation Jake uses to his advantage. Killed by Roland. Eddie has a dream in which he is driving a bulldozer in the vacant lot in Manhattan.

GRAY DICK (5, M)
A famous outlaw prince who murdered Lord Grenfall, Lady Oriza's father. She decapitated him with the first Oriza during what was supposed to be a reconciliation dinner at her castle by the River Send.

GRAYS (3, 4, 5, 6, 7)
One of two factions that have been fighting in Lud for many years. So called because they were, on average, older than their adversaries. They were harriers led at one time by David Quick and later by Andrew Quick, the Tick-Tock Man. They used some of the surviving technology in Lud to terrify their opponents, the Pubes, into killing themselves.

GREAT OLD ONES, AKA OLD PEOPLE
(1, 3, 4, 4.5, 5, 6, 7, M)
Legendary people who aspired to be gods from the time before the world started moving on. The stories about them are unclear. There may have been Old People and Really Old People. When the world's natural magic seemed to be receding, they panicked and replaced it with scientific analogs. They formed North Central Positronics to conduct experiments that wedded magic with science or replaced magic with science. This loss of faith in magic that might have supported the Tower forever created a system doomed to progressively deteriorate with time.

They built modern cities run by computers and even put a man on the moon. They have satellites in orbit around the Earth and constructed Dogans as experimental or monitoring stations. They built Asimov robots that resemble humans (these robots refer to them as "Makers") to perform domestic duties. Almost everything they built has some form of artificial intelligence. Even the handcar Roland and Jake find beneath the mountain can talk.

They also built mechanical doorways so they could visit other worlds. Their preferred destinations often involved tragedies. This taste for violence is reflected in the weapons of war they built.

The end of their Imperium was a conflict called the Old War, the Great Fire, the Cataclysm or the Great Poisoning, though no one knows who they fought. It may have been a civil war or an accident involving their weapons that poisoned the world. Some say that the Old People went to other worlds after they left Mid-World.

They've been gone for at least two thousand years but their leavings are found everywhere. The Manni are said to be a sect of the Old People. Many relics are deadly, but the earthen pot Roland carries in his gunna for brewing tea is one of their artifacts and he believes the jawbone he found beneath the Way Station belonged to one of them.

Some of their Dogans are at least partly operational. The one Bix visited is radioactive. Some people believe Maerlyn turned evil after discovering some of their artifacts. John Farson used their war machines against the Affiliation after figuring out how to make them run.

The hieroglyphics on the Unfound Door are the scratchings of the Old People.

GRENFALL, LORD (5)

Lady Oriza's father, the wiliest lord in the River Baronies. His castle Waydon was on the banks of the River Send. Gray Dick murdered him, but his daughter avenged him.

GRISSOM, GENERAL (5, M)

Leader of the horde of blue-faced barbarians who attack Roland and his friends at Jericho Hill. Either he or his son killed Jamie DeCurry.

GUNSLINGERS (THROUGHOUT)

Knights, squires, peacemakers and Barons. They make up an elite group, the Council of Eld, that is the political head of the Affiliation. Gunslingers are generally descendants of the line of Eld, though there are exceptions. Boys are trained in the arts of war until they feel prepared to challenge their teacher in hand-to-hand conflict. Those who fail are sent west into exile. They are skilled in diplomacy as well as in battle. In the time of Steven Deschain, their primary concern is the decline of the Dark Tower, which means they ignore some of the more imminent troubles, such as the fragile state of the Affiliation and the threat posed by John Farson.

When someone wants gunslingers to help him, he is asked three questions. 1) Will you open to us if we open to you? 2) Do you see us for what we are and accept what we do? 3) Do you seek aid and succor? A gunslinger never asks the final question until he knows what the answer will be. The gunslingers may take no reward for their services and the supplicant must not offer any. Once the gunslingers decide to act, after ascertaining that the supplicant is on the side of the White, the opinion of the supplicants no longer matters.

HABER (6, 7)

A low man with bulldog jowls, a heavy, sloping gut and curly gray hair. Part of the entourage that takes Mia from the Dixie Pig to the Fedic Dogan. Susannah considers him the most dangerous of the group.

HAGGERTY THE NAIL (4.5)

A carpenter in Tree Village.

HARRIERS (3, 4, 4.5, 5, 6, 7, M)

Outlaws and highwaymen.

HAVERTY, JOHN (4)

Olive Thorin's father, a fisherman.

HAX (1, 2, 3, 4, 6, 7, M)

Cook in the west kitchen in Gilead who is hanged after Roland and Cuthbert discover that he's working for John Farson.

HAYCOX, LOUIS (5)

A smallhold farmer whose place is west of Tian Jaffords's, near the edge of Calla Bryn Sturgis. Though he speaks passionately against Tian's proposal during the first town meeting, he ultimately decides Tian is right and that he will stand and fight the Wolves.

HAYLIS OF CHAYVEN (7)

A Roderick who lives near Algul Siento. Dinky calls him Chucky because his chubby freckled cheeks and blue eyes remind him of the doll in the horror movie. Oy befriends him after Roland enlists his help in the battle of Algul Siento, getting him to plant sneetches to start fires in the dorms. Haylis regards Roland as a god. He's smart enough to keep Finli o'Tego from being suspicious of his presence on campus.

HEADMAN AND TALLMAN (4.5)

Tim Ross's nicknames for the tallest of the mutants who assist him in Fagonard Swamp. He is bald and toothless, and his legs are severely deformed. Tim believes he is the leader.

HEATH, ARTHUR (4, 7, M)

Cuthbert's alias in Mejis. He is a stockline breeder's son.

HEDRON (6)

One of the Manni of Calla Redpath.

HELMSMAN (4.5)

Tim Ross's nickname for one of the mutants who assists him in Fagonard Swamp. He is the group's best communicator. He wears a black silk top hat decorated with a red ribbon that trails down over one bare shoulder. Broad shouldered and sturdily built, with bright, intelligent eyes. Had he not grown up in the Fagonard, he might have been considered handsome.

HENCHICK (5, 6, 7)

Leader of the Manni Redpath clan. He discovered Father Callahan after the former priest came through the Unfound Door. He has three wives, though he can have relations with only one at a time, depending on the stars. His granddaughter, Margaret Eisenhart, is one of the forgetful who abandoned the Manni ways. His blue eyes have grown watery with age, and he has a waistlength thick, white beard that he tugs on when embarrassed. He is generally dour and appears to be eighty years old. Reverend Earl Harrigan is his twin. Roland believes Henchick will know the freed Breakers are telling the truth and stand up for them if they reach Calla Bryn Sturgis.

HENDRICKS, RODNEY (4)

The leader of one of George Latigo's companies. Latigo considers him a good man. Killed by the thinny in Eyebolt Canyon.

HENRY THE TALL (4.5)

Steven Deschain's father.

HODIAK (4.5)

The Barony buyer at the Tree Sawmill.

HODJI, WALTER (7)
Walter o'Dim's name when he was in Garlan. The last name means both "dim" and "hood."

HOLLIS, DAVE (4, M)
One of Sheriff Avery's deputies in Mejis. Though only eighteen, he's mostly bald with the remaining bits of hair slicked back with grease. When he's nervous, he nibbles on the brass edging of the monocle hanging around his neck on a ribbon. He works as a server at the Mayor's House on formal occasions. He's not very smart, and no match for Eldred in a game of Castles, but thinks he will make a better sheriff when Avery retires. He has serious questions about what Roland and the others might or might not have done, but he dutifully goes for Susan Delgado's gun when she breaks them out of jail. Susan, who grew up with him and kissed him once behind the door of the livery, shoots him in the chest.

HOLLIS, JUDY (4)
Wife to Deputy Dave Hollis of Mejis. Maiden name Wertner, which makes her related to Henry Wertner, the Barony's stockliner. She makes white iced tea with honey—her mother's recipe. She used to nag Dave about nibbling on his monocle but gave up, even though she was used to getting her own way.

HOOKEY, BRIAN (4)
Owner and operator of Hookey's Stable and Fancy Livery. A blacksmith, he makes horseshoes in a forge behind his barn. One of Pat Delgado's best friends. He also made wheels and rims for the oil tankers at Citgo, for which he was well paid, which accounts for the good upkeep on his business. A levelheaded man, he is put in charge of the team guarding Citgo after Eldred Jonas discovers Roland knows about it. Roland shoots him in the chest during their ambush of Eldred Jonas's men.

HOOKEY, RUFUS (4)
Brian Hookey's eldest son. He takes care of the livery when his father is guarding Citgo and spies on Susan for the Big Coffin Hunters.

HOOTERMAN "HOOTS" (3, 4, 5, 6)
One of Tick-Tock Man's Grays. A tall, skinny man in a black suit whose face is covered with a rash. He gives Gasherman the password to the inner sanctum on a piece of paper. Shot in the back by Roland.

JAFFORDS, JAMIE (5, 7)

Tian Jaffords's grandfather, known as Gran-pere. A toothless old man with flyaway hair and grizzled sideburns. He claims to be the oldest person in Calla Bryn Sturgis. He's senile, but has his good days. He hasn't spoken a civil word to Tian since Tian's father, Luke, was killed digging a well in a spot chosen by Tian. He gets along well with Tian's wife, Zalia, though. His twin, who was closer to the road, was taken while the two of them played jacks. When he was nineteen, he stood with three others against the Wolves and saw Molly Doolin kill one of them. He never told anyone else because Luke told him the story might make him a target for the Wolves. This information is vital in the *ka-tet*'s battle with the Wolves.

JAFFORDS, LUKE (5)

Tian Jaffords's father. He died when a well collapsed and buried him alive. Luke's father, Jamie, is mad at Tian because he picked the spot to dig. Luke is the only person Jamie told about Molly Doolin killing one of the Wolves. Luke didn't believe him and thought the story might make his father a target for the Wolves if it got around.

JAFFORDS, TIAN (5, 6)

A farmer from Calla Bryn Sturgis who is about thirty years old. After Andy tells him the Wolves are coming in a month, Tian decides to fight instead of allowing their children to be taken, standing up to the wealthier ranchers. He has three patches of land and is smarter than the average smallholder. He can read and write a little. He was nine when the Wolves came the last time, taking his sister Tia, whom he now uses as a burro to plow the rockiest of his fields. When Tian was seventeen, his father, Luke, died digging a well at a site Tian found with his dowsing rod. He and his wife, Zalia, have two sets of twins (Heddon and Hedda, ten years old; Lyman and Lia, five years old) and a rare singleton child (two-year-old Aaron). He and Eddie take care of Andy the Messenger Robot the night before the Wolves come.

JAFFORDS, ZALIA (5, 6)

Tian Jaffords's wife, whom he calls Zee. Maiden name Hoonik. A tall, handsome woman as dark-skinned as Susannah. Her twin brother, Zalman, is one of the roont. She is the best thrower among the Sisters of Oriza. She gets along well with Tian's father.

JAKLI (7)

A raven-headed taheen who works in the telemetry center in Damli House at Algul Siento. He dies on Main Street in Pleasantville.

JAVIER, BUCKY (5)

A smallholder with eighty acres in Calla Bryn Sturgis. His twin, Bully, was taken by the Wolves and died four years before the *ka-tet* arrives. He has bright little blue eyes in a small head that seems to slope back from his goateed chin. His wife, Annabelle, is put in charge of one of the wagons taking the twins out of town.

JAVIER, ROBERTA (5)

Bucky Javier's younger sister. She and her twin brother were only a year old the last time the Wolves came, so they were passed over. Bucky gave her half his farm when she married.

JEEVES THE BUTLER (3, 4)

One of the two Pubes who lead Eddie and Susannah to the Cradle of Lud.

JEFFERSONS (5)

Family who owned a ranch north of Debaria. The father, mother and two daughters were all killed by the skin-man, along with most of their staff.

JEMMIN (5)

A Manni from Calla Redpath who was with Henchick when they found Father Callahan. He died two years later from a heart attack.

JENKINS (7)

The chief technician at Algul Siento. He monitors the Deep Telemetry output, though he doesn't understand most of what it says.

JENNA (L)

The youngest of the Little Sisters of Eluria. She was chosen by bloodline to wear the Dark Bells that summoned the *can tam*. She appears to be about twenty-one and has flushed cheeks, smooth skin and dark eyes. She also has a curl of black hair that constantly escapes from her wimple. Before Roland arrived, she was restless with her place in the order. The Little Sisters nursed her back to health after her mother died as a result of her own restlessness. Jenna sets the *can tam* on Sister Coquina and helps Roland escape from the others, sacrificing her life in the process.

JEY (OR GEE) (6, 7)
A taheen known to Susannah as Hawkman because he has the brown feathered head and vicious beebee eyes of a hawk. He is part of the entourage that escorts Mia to the Fedic Dogan. He is trying to decide whether to escape or stay and fight when Susannah shoots him.

JILLIAN OF UP'ARD KILLIAN, COUNTESS (4)
A prostitute who works at the Travellers' Rest in Hambry. She considers herself exiled royalty from Garlan.

JOCHABIM (7)
A pot washer working in the Dixie Pig kitchen. Son of Hossa and originally from Ludweg, north of Lud. A malnourished young man of about seventeen whose skin is a pallid yellowish gray. He warns Jake about the mind-trap.

JOHNS, ALAIN (THROUGHOUT)
One of Roland's fellow student gunslingers and a member of his first *ka-tet*. He is more reliable than quick. Upon first meeting, he is often dismissed as a dullard. Steven Deschain calls him Thudfoot. He's good at tracking but can't master the art of decoding. He has deep flashes of intuition and is very strong with the touch but isn't comfortable in social situations. According to Cuthbert, he could sleep through an earthquake. He refused to go on a midnight lark in the cemetery because he was afraid of offending the shades of his ancestors. He always won riddling contests when no adults were involved. He accompanied Roland to Mejis as Richard Stockworth and was elevated to gunslinger based on this experience. He returned to camp in the middle of the night before the battle of Jericho Hill to report on the defeat of the gunslingers at Rimrocks. Roland and Cuthbert mistook him for an enemy and shot him to death.

Physical description: He had blond hair, a placid, round face, blue eyes, plowboy's shoulders and tended toward stoutness. He was wounded during the battle with Latigo's men and had a scar on his left cheek for the rest of his life.

JOHNS, CHRISTOPHER (4, 5, M)

Alain Johns's father. In his youth he was known as Burning Chris. He warned Roland that he might see the vagrant dead if he ever went todash. In the Marvel graphic novels, a traitorous castle guard stabbed him.

JOLENE (4)

A prostitute working at Hattigan's in Ritzy. She lost most of her teeth.

JONAS, ELDRED (1, 4, 5, 6, 7, M)

A failed gunslinger whose leg was broken by Fardo, Cort's father, during his test of manhood. As a result, he walks with a limp and his leg bothers him in bad weather. After being sent west, he ended up in Garlan. Like most exiles, he found a gun, but his failure haunted him. He is familiar with the Manni and may have traveled to other worlds.

He forms a group of mercenary regulators who call themselves the Big Coffin Hunters, acting as agents of John Farson, whom he has never met. Despite failing to best Fardo, he is skillful and shrewd, though his weaknesses as a leader become apparent when he underestimates Roland, Cuthbert and Alain. His confidence begins to crumble once Roland announces his status as a failed gunslinger. His cohorts, Roy Depape and Clay Reynolds, might have suspected as much, but until then no one knew for sure.

He comes to Mejis to perform two tasks. The most important is to watch over the pink Bend o' the Rainbow that Farson uses to spy on the Affiliation. The glass is dangerous, so Farson can't keep it all the time. Jonas follows Kimba Rimer's advice and puts it in the hands of the witch Rhea. He and his fellow Big Coffin Hunters also oversee the Citgo oil field and the transportation of oil west, where Farson will use it to power his weapons against the Affiliation. His cover story is that he is the new chief of Mayor Thorin's security forces. He does double duty as a replacement deputy for Sheriff Avery after one of his deputies breaks a leg.

The maids at Mayor's House call him "Il Spectro" because he can fade into the shadows. He wouldn't necessarily be welcome during peacetime, but he's a handy man to have during a battle. Reynolds has seen him go crazy before. He fosters a friendship with Cordelia Delgado because he identifies her as the kind of woman who enjoys gossiping. He is attracted to Coral Thorin because she is just as cold-blooded as he is and the sex with her is amazing.

He is a master at the game of Castles and always plays to win—it's his nature. He calls things the way he sees them. Only his vow of vengeance against Roland, Cuthbert and Alain prevents him from riding away from Mejis when intuition tells him things are going bad—something he has done often in the past. He's proud of the fact that he's never double-crossed an employer and that he has never broken a promise to himself, regardless of who else he's lied to. Roland shot him to death.

Physical description: A tall, skinny, oldish man with shoulder-length white hair and a mustache so long that its ragged ends hang to his jaw. He has large, red-rimmed, cautious eyes that look watery at first but are dead of emotion. They're the same faded blue as Roland's. He is deeply tanned from spending time outdoors. At times he resembles either a wolf or a wolverine. His voice is reedy and quavery, like that of a man on the verge of tears. His back is covered with criss-crossed scars from a whipping received in Garlan.

JONSON (1, M)
A penitent in Sylvia Pittston's church in Tull.

JOSHUA (4.5)
Ardelia Smack's brother. He died in the Endless Forest twenty years before Tim Ross's adventure. He bought a gun from a traveling salesman that Ardelia passes on to Tim.

JUSTUS (M)
A scout who leads the gunslingers of Gilead into a trap while supposedly taking them to one of Farson's outposts. He spreads fear by telling stories about Farson's reign of terror in Cressia. He also comes up with the idea of attacking Farson's stronghold in the Shavéd Mountains, which is where Farson's men are planning an ambush. After his treachery is exposed, Farson's men kill him, as well as most of the gunslingers.

KA-TET OF NINETEEN (5, 6, 7)
People whose names have nineteen characters.

KELLS, BIG BERN (4.5)
Jack Ross's woodcutting partner and childhood friend. Son of Mathias "Slim Saw" Kells, a carpenter who beat Bern's mother and who was killed by a vurt in the woods, and grandson of Limping Peter. Good-humored and laughing when sober, but angry and quick with his fists when drunk. He was best man at Jack Ross's wedding, but he fancied Nell and went on binges after the

wedding. He sobered up after meeting Millicent Redhouse, who died in childbirth six seasons later. After a dragon supposedly kills Jack Ross, Kells asks Nell to marry him, but grows angry and possessive. He makes Tim Ross quit school and go to work and beats Nell. Tim learns that he killed Jack Ross in a fit of jealousy and hid the body in the woods. After he kills Widow Smack, Nell Ross kills him with Jack Ross's ax while he is trying to strangle Tim.

KELLS, MILLICENT "MILLY" (4.5)
Bern Kells's wife. Born Millicent Redhouse. A small woman, barely five feet tall. When Tim Ross was three or four, she died giving birth, six seasons after she married Kells. Their child died soon thereafter. Her dying wish was that Kells keep his promise to stop drinking.

KELLY, TAMMY (7)
Pimli Prentiss's housekeeper at Algul Siento. A large woman who despises men—especially Tassa, the houseboy. Fire-Response Team Bravo flattens her.

KENNERLY, JUBAL (1, M)
Tull's hostler. A man who will make something up if he doesn't know the truth. He has an incestuous relationship with his daughter. Roland shot him.

KENNERLY, SOOBIE (1, M)
Jubal Kennerly's teenage daughter.

LAMLA OF GALEE (7)
A taheen who is part of Flaherty's posse chasing Jake under the Dixie Pig. He has the head of a stoat. His narrow feet end in sharp claws that could cut a grown man in half. He knows about the mind-trap but doesn't know how to turn off the projector without shooting it. After Roland and Eddie kill everyone else, Lamla asks for pardon. Roland refuses, shooting him dead after the taheen damns him.

LAND-PIRATES (4.5)
Roving bands of outlaws who plied their trade in the lands far west of Gilead.

LATIGO, GEORGE (4, 5, M)
One of John Farson's six chief lieutenants. A pale man with blond hair. He has the dour, frowning face of a man who hasn't seen anything good in years and speaks in the clipped tones of someone from northern In-World. He was known to

Steven Deschain, who described him to Roland, Cuthbert and Alain before they went to Mejis. He paid the Big Coffin Hunters a huge cash advance and promised a piece of the war spoils if the Affiliation's major forces were wiped out in the Shavéd Mountains. Roland spares his life at Hanging Rock, counting on him to lead his men into Eyebolt Canyon, where they are all killed by the thinny.

LENGYLL, FRANCIS "FRAN" (4, M)
Owner of the Rocking B Ranch, the second largest in Mejis, and president of the Horsemen's Association. He's about twenty years older than Cordelia Delgado, who claims she had an affair with him. He owns the biggest generator in town, but it doesn't run anymore. He probably killed Pat Delgado and took pages from his stockline book to cover up the truth about the horses in Mejis. His first wife made a cap for Susan Delgado's christening. He owns a machine gun. Roland believes that he realized too late in the game that the stakes were much higher than he thought. He announces the arrest of the boys from In-World at the Town Gathering Hall. Roland shoots him in the forehead.

LEWIS (6)
One of the Manni of Calla Redpath.

LITTLE BLAINE (3, 4)
The original voice of Blaine the Mono. The voice of the insane computers of Lud overwhelm him.

LITTLE COFFIN HUNTERS (4)
Title given to Roland, Cuthbert and Alain after their confrontation with the Big Coffin Hunters.

LITTLE DOCTORS (L, 6, 7, M)
Also known as Grandfather-fleas or *can tam*. Clattering, blood-drinking parasites the size of mice. They are generally present when Type One vampires are around. They are vulnerable to billy-bumblers. In Eluria, they healed the injured so the Little Sisters could drink their blood.

LITTLE SISTERS (L, 6, M)
A sisterhood of vampiric nurses who feed on patients healed by the little doctors. They wear white habits with a red rose on the breast and move their tent from town to town. Roland encounters six sisters (Mary, Louise, Tamra,

Coquina, Michela and Jenna) in Eluria. They have power over animals but Christian *siguls* harm them.

LONDON, JACK (7)
Dr. Gangli Tristum's personal assistant in Algul Siento.

LOS' THE RED (7)
Another name for the Crimson King.

LOUISE (L, M)
One of the Little Sisters of Eluria.

LOW MEN (AND WOMEN) (5, 6, 7)
Soldiers of the Crimson King. Also known as *can toi* and the fayen folken. Sometimes they call themselves regulators and many have the same hand tattoos as the Big Coffin Hunters. They are human-taheen hybrids, a little smarter than Type Three vampires. In their natural form, they resemble taheen more than humans. They have red circles of blood that do not ooze or clot in their foreheads, the Eye of the King. When they are in Keystone Earth, this mark dries up temporarily.

They are jealous of the Breakers they guard at Algul Siento, whom they consider "finished" humes. Low men worship the human form and consider it divine. They believe, with a religious fervor, that they are in the process of becoming human and will replace humans after the Tower falls. They wear masks grown from human skin to make themselves look human. Pimli Prentiss thinks they all look like Clark Gable, with thick lips and batty ears.

Up close, the illusion of humanity breaks down. They have hair around their eyes that is only partly concealed by these masks. There are also unnatural wrinkles at the neck and behind the ears. Up very close, a person could see dozens of little moving cilia in the nostrils. The masks seem to breathe.

Their primary job is to track down and "recruit" Breakers. They also pursue Father Callahan after he starts killing vampires, with whom they have a loose affiliation. They use graffiti, lost pet posters and sidewalk chalk drawings of astrological symbols to communicate with one another. They drive outrageous cars. Their clothes are loud and gaudy and usually clash. Their hats cast shadows over their faces but, more important, shield them from the psychic powers of those they pursue. They consider turning pictures upside down to be the height of humor.

Crossovers to Other Works: The low men were introduced in the novella "Low Men in Yellow Coats" in *Hearts in Atlantis*, where they were chasing Ted Brautigan after he escaped from Algul Siento. They also appear in the short story "Ur" and their cars pop up in other works, such as *From a Buick 8* and "Mile 81."

LUKA, STEG (4.5)

A gray-bearded man, the oldest of the miners brought back from Little Debaria because they knew how to ride horses. He was in Beelie Stockade for stealing a loaf of bread to feed his wife and children, but both of his children died. He tells Roland about the crack in the bottom of the new mine that emits a pulsing green glow and invites people to come in. The skin-man kills him in the Debaria jailhouse.

LUSTER (3, 4, 5)

A member of the Pubes in Lud. A dwarf who looks like a child from a distance. Eddie calls him Little Lord Fauntleroy. He is the first person Susannah Dean kills.

MAERLYN OF THE ELD (MERLIN) (1, 3, 4.5, 5, 6, M)

Court mage to Arthur Eld, an eternal creature. Susannah Dean thinks he's the Ageless Stranger. Tim Ross finds him in a cage in the form of a tyger, where he has been trapped for a very long time, put there by an emissary of the Crimson King, who caught him by surprise when he was drunk. Tim releases him with a few drops of magic potion.

When Tim asks Maerlyn if he is an eternal being who lives backward in time, he neither confirms nor denies it. He is said to keep a magic house in the Endless Forest where time stands still, but he confirms Mia's story that he retired to a cave with nothing but a table and a pallet on the floor, though that's a story no one will believe. Some people think Marten Broadcloak is Maerlyn, turned evil by the glammer of the Wizard's Rainbow or other artifacts of the Old People, but Marten denies being Maerlyn (as does Richard Fannin, another of his guises) and Maerlyn has only contempt for Marten. He predicts that Tim will become a gunslinger.

Physical description: An old man whose white waist-length beard sparkles with rubies, emeralds, sapphires and diamonds. He wears a yellow conical cap. His face is gaunt, but illuminated by gravity and kindness. His body is so thin it's almost skeletal.

MAGGIE (1, M)
Woman who worked in Hax's kitchen in Gilead.

MAN IN BLACK, THE (THROUGHOUT)
A magician and minion of the Crimson King. When he visits Mejis as John Farson's "underliner," Roy Depape says he looks like other people and laughs like a dead person. Eldred Jonas thinks his titter is the kind one might hear in a lunatic asylum. He can't be seen until he's ready to be seen—he has the power to be dim. To Eldred he appears as a man of medium height (shorter than Farson), powerfully built, with bright blue eyes and rosy cheeks. His teeth are pointed at first, but not a few minutes later. His hair is cropped so short it's only a fuzz. He often wears a hooded black robe.

Roland picks up his trail sometime after the battle of Jericho Hill, believing he has information that will lead the gunslinger to the Tower. The man in black knows Roland is following and toys with him, leaving traps that include the people of Tull—where he raised Nort from the dead—and Jake at the Way Station. After Roland catches up to him at the end of the tunnel through the mountains, he admits to being Walter and does a tarot reading for Roland. See also Walter o'Dim, Marten Broadcloak, the Ageless Stranger and Randall Flagg.

MAN JESUS (1, 4, 4.5, 5, 6, 7, M)
The name people from Mid-World have for Jesus Christ.

MANCHESTER (4)
Susan Delgado's mother's maiden name. The family considered themselves poets and painters but were, according to Cordelia Delgado, drunk most of the time.

MANNI (1, 4, 4.5, 5, 6, 7, M)
A peaceful sect of the Old People. Called the Friends or the Friendly Folk or the Seeking Folk. They resemble Quakers, say "thee" and "thou," and usually live in enclaves near but outside of towns and villages, rarely coming into town. When they do, they bring their own rations. The men grow long beards, wear purple cloaks and often hold hands. They are allowed to cut their fingernails only once a year. They are known to be great travelers who are always looking for holes they can use to travel to other realities—not for treasure, but

for enlightenment. They believe todash is the holiest of rites and most exalted of states and spend long periods fasting to induce the right state of mind. They use plumb bobs and magnets during their rituals.

People who leave them are called the forgetful ones, a term also applied to any non-Manni. They revere Arthur Eld and foresaw the coming of Mordred, half man and half god, who would oversee the end of humanity and the return of the Prim, which they call the Over.

MARCHLY, SLOW ERNEST (4.5)
Peter Cosington's woodcutting partner. While Cosington is recovering after a tree fell on him, Marchly is smart enough to not go woodcutting by himself. He and Cosington were friends of Jack Ross, who said they were good fellows who wouldn't go deep in the Endless Forest.

MARIAN, MAID (5)
Lady Oriza's maid. She went on to have many fanciful adventures of her own.

MARK (1)
Cort's predecessor as teacher of student gunslingers in Gilead. He died of a stab wound from an overzealous hand in the proving ground behind the Great Hall.

MARSH, JAKE (4.5)
One of the miners from Little Debaria who did time in Beelie Stockade.

MARY (L, M)
The most senior of the Little Sisters of Eluria, also known as Big Sister. She dispatches punishment to the others and resents the fact that Jenna has been chosen to wear the Dark Bells. A dog bearing a white patch of fur shaped like a cross kills her.

MAUD (3, 4, 5)
A member of the Pubes in Lud. Winston's partner. She and "Jeeves the Butler" take Eddie and Susannah to the Cradle of Lud.

McCANN, JAMIE (4)
The pallid and whey-faced boy who was supposed to be the Reaping Lad with Susan Delgado.

McCURDY, SHEB (1, 2, 3, 4, 7, M)

Piano player at the honky-tonk in Tull that bears his name. Former lover of Allie. He also played in the Travellers' Rest in Hambry.

McVRIES, PETER (4.5)

A gunslinger who died—probably from poison—three years before Roland's trip to Debaria.

MEIMAN (6, 7)

A taheen that looks like a bird with dark yellow feathers. His hands have talons rather than fingers. Susannah thinks of him as Canaryman. Jake calls him Tweety Bird. He is left behind to make sure no one gets through to Fedic from the Dixie Pig. Father Callahan shoots him.

MERCY (3)

Resident of River Crossing. Harriers blinded her with a branding iron. Wife to Si.

MIA (5, 6, 7)

Daughter of none. Her name is the High Speech word for "mother." Mia seems like a new personality of Susannah Dean's, but she is actually a demon possessing Susannah in much the same way that Roland did when he entered Eddie's body during the flight from the Bahamas.

She survived and adapted after the Prim receded, wandering the world. Whenever she saw a vulnerable man, she fucked him to death. It wasn't about sex or killing—she has an overwhelming but futile imperative to conceive a child. She realized this only after coming to Fedic, where she was enchanted by a human baby but was barred from getting close to it.

Walter o'Dim saw what she was and exploited her obsession. After being stranded in Fedic alone for centuries, she gives up immortality in exchange for the chance to bear the Crimson King's son, whom she calls her "chap." She doesn't remember much about the actual process of becoming mortal in the Fedic Dogan. She knows her baby will grow fast and she might get to raise him for only five or six years, but she believes that is ample reward. Even as a human she is unable to conceive, so she takes over Susannah's body and transmits her baby a bit at a time over to herself.

At first, Mia is passive, coming forward only to lead Susannah on foraging missions at night. There's nothing for her to eat in Fedic that isn't poisoned. She won't let Susannah go near the rose in the vacant lot because it might do something dreadful to her. On the day she is to give birth, she becomes more dominant. By then, Susannah knows she exists and brokers a deal whereby Mia agrees to help Susannah play her part in the battle with the Wolves if Susannah will go with her afterward. Mia cheers Susannah on during the battle.

In New York, she and Susannah form an uneasy alliance, often struggling for control of Susannah's body. When she is in control, Susannah has legs, though they're white. She is shy, afraid. She has access to Susannah's memories and can read anything Susannah can read. She betrayed Eddie and Roland to Sayre.

When Susannah shows her scenes from her life, especially a tender moment with her mother, Mia realizes how much she missed about being human, how much she gave up and how little she would receive in return. Her son, Mordred, kills her moments after he's born.

Physical description: As a demon, she appears to men as a blindingly beautiful woman about five foot six or seven, with shoulder-length black hair. Her mortal aspect is still beautiful, but her face is marked with painful experience. She looks to be in her late twenties.

MICHAEL (6)
A baby born in Fedic two centuries before the advent of the Wolves, when most people were sterile. Mia coveted the child but couldn't go near it. When he was three or four, Michael left Fedic with his parents on Patricia the Mono after the Red Death.

MICHELA (L, M)
One of the Little Sisters of Eluria.

MILL, AUNT (1, M)
A resident of Tull.

MOGGINS, GERT "DEBORAH" (4)
A fifteen-year-old prostitute who works at the Travellers' Rest in Hambry. Roy Depape's girlfriend. He calls her "Her Nibs" (though it was Clay who started that). She has a bowlegged clumping walk and a way of squinting off into the distance that betrays the fact that she's probably a cowgirl, but she has

delusions of grandeur. She takes a temporary job at the Piano Ranch to earn extra money.

MORGENSTERN, CONCHETTA (4)
The chief seamstress at Mayor's House in Hambry. A woman of few words. Blade faced.

MORPHIA (7)
Daughter of Sleep. Roland warns Stephen King to refuse her offer of ease and pleasure if she comes to him after his accident.

MUDMEN (4.5)
Tim Ross's nickname for the mutants who assist him in Fagonard Swamp. He reassesses his nickname, thinking that they are actually more like plantmen who have become part of the swamp they live in. They bow to Tim as a gunslinger and provide him with food for his journey, as well as a North Central Positronics device that acts as a GPS, and carry him to solid ground in their makeshift boat. Tim thinks they are a dying tribe, but their time is shorter than he realizes: the impending starkblast will kill them all.

MUÑOZ, ROSALITA (ROSA, ROSIE) (5, 6, 7)
Father Callahan's "woman of all work" (more of an executive secretary than a housekeeper) in Calla Bryn Sturgis, a midwife of great experience and, for a while, Roland Deschain's lover. A good-looking woman of around forty with eyes so dark brown they're almost black. She smokes a pipe, is one of the most skillful Sisters of Oriza—a lefty—and a skillful Watch Me player. She gives Roland medicine to help him withstand the discomfort of his arthritis (dry twist).

NIGEL THE BUTLER (7)
An eight-foot tall Asimov robot who is in charge of domestic services and maintenance in the Fedic Dogan. Serial number: DNK 45932. He brings an incubator to the delivery room at Scowther's request. Susannah shoots out his eyes to disable him, remembering Eddie's experience with Andy, whom he resembles. He can still navigate using infrared sensors, but the damage causes a total systemic breakdown a few hours after the shooting. In the interim, he is helpful, both to the *ka-tet* and to Mordred, bringing them food. When forced to lie, his head snaps to one side and he counts in German or French.

He is a fan of Stephen King novels, but his collection doesn't contain any of the Dark Tower series.

NIS (5)
God of dreams.

NORMAN, JAMES (L, M)
A young man from Delain killed by the slow mutants. Roland finds his body in a trough in Eluria and uses his name as an alias when the Little Sisters capture him. Brother to John Norman. Loved of family, Loved of God, according to the medallion around his neck.

NORMAN, JESSE (L)
Father to James and John Norman.

NORMAN, JOHN (L, M)
One of the Little Sisters of Eluria's patients. Originally from Delain. He and his brother, James, were hired as scouts to protect a long-haul caravan taking goods and mail-order brides to Tejuas. Slow mutants ambushed the caravan in Eluria. By the time John and his fellow scouts caught up, the fight was over. He was hit over the head and woke up in the infirmary tent. Killed by the Little Sisters.

NORT THE WEEDEATER (1, 2, 3, 5, 6, M)
A man from Tull raised from the dead by Walter o'Dim. He knows the High Speech.

NOT-MAN (1, M)
An invisible man. Roland knew of one who was hung for committing rape. In the Marvel comics, the not-men are ordinary men who make themselves invisible using special jackets from a Dogan near Kingstown.

NUTTER, ELROD (4.5)
Foreman at the Jefferson Ranch in Debaria. An excellent rider and roper, but a mean drunk. Sheriff Peavy arrested him several times. When drunk, he teases Young Bill Streeter mercilessly and meanly. Most of the other men at the ranch are afraid of him because of his size and because he carries a knife. When the skin-man attacks in the shape of a bear, Nutter fights it off with his knife, but the bear rips off his arm and hits him in the face with it before biting off his head.

O'DIM, WALTER (1, 2, 3, 4, 5, 6, 7, M)

The man in black. Also Marten Broadcloak, the Ageless Stranger, Randall Flagg and many others. He thinks of himself as Walter of End-World or Walter of All-World, but he started life fifteen hundred years ago as a country boy called Walter Padick, son of a miller. He ran away from home when he was thirteen. How he came to be part demon is a mystery—perhaps the Crimson King endowed him with special powers. (In the Marvel comics, he is Maerlyn's son.)

His travels have taken him to Delain and Garlan, where he was known as Walter Hodji. Like the Crimson King and John Farson, whom he serves, he enjoys chaos. One of his favorite pastimes is visiting peaceful kingdoms and stirring up trouble. He always escapes before the worst happens, which is how he has survived for so long. As Marten Broadcloak, he infiltrated Gilead and gained the trust of the gunslingers, which made it easier to betray them.

His magical powers are impressive—he can even raise the dead—and yet he's never quite as smart as he thinks he is. He's also vain, petulant and unduly sure of himself. He seems genuinely hurt when Father Callahan suggests he's cruel. One of the worst crimes he takes credit for is shooting Cuthbert in the eye with an arrow at Jericho Hill.

Attempting to foil Roland gives him a purpose in life. He sets many traps for the gunslinger, but most of them fail and some have the opposite effect to what he intended—Black Thirteen, for example, is a boon rather than a curse in Calla Bryn Sturgis. He probably manipulated Jack Mort into pushing Jake, knowing the boy would play a part in Roland's moral downfall. He passes the Way Station shortly after Jake arrives, but circles back to meet up with Father Callahan. He apparently knows about Roland's many attempts to save the Tower, but still can't defeat him despite this knowledge.

Ultimately, his true goal is the same as Roland's: to reach and enter the Dark Tower. The Crimson King is of no use to him, trapped on a balcony of the Tower. He proves to be no match for Roland's son, though, another person he underestimated.

Physical description: He can take whatever form suits him, and he usually wears a hood. Sometimes he sports a handsome, regular face. Sometimes he has a pallid complexion, ragged, matted black hair, a high forehead, dark and brilliant eyes, a nondescript nose and full and sensual lips. To others, when he drops his hood, he has the snarling face of a human weasel. Sometimes he has the same red mark in his forehead as the low men.

OLD PA (4)
The Mid-World version of Noah.

OLD PEOPLE OR OLD ONES
See Great Old Ones.

OMAHA (4)
A one-eyed gambler whom Roland knew. He died with a knife in his throat at a Watch Me table.

ORIZA, LADY (5, M)
The Lady of the Rice. Daughter of Lord Grenville. Also called Lady Riza and the Lady of the Plate. She avenges her father's death by slaying Gray Dick, his murderer, with a sharpened plate during a dinner at her castle, Waydon, on the banks of the River Send. The Sisters of Oriza throw plates once a month in tribute to her. Her servant is Maid Marian. She is both a legendary heroine and a goddess to the people of Mid-World. Some say she gave birth to the first man. Her spirit turns back the seminon winds at the River Whye because Lord Seminon married her sister and Lady Oriza wanted him for herself.

ORTEGA, MILLICENT (4)
A resident of Hambry.

O'SHYVEN, THERESA MARIA DOLORES (3)
A woman from Hambry, a forty-year-old mother of four. She sells rugs and draperies in the Upper Market. Her husband, Peter, is a range-rider and her family is middle-class. Rhea, via the grapefruit, discovers her strange obsessive madness that causes her to lick the corners of her house clean. She sometimes gets splinters on her tongue from doing this.

O'TEGO, FINLI (5, 7)
A taheen, chief of security at Algul Siento. He's more than three hundred years old. He has a sleek weasel's head, several rows of tiny sharp teeth and unexpressive black eyes. He wears a lot of gold chains and had his tail docked, a decision he now regrets. He is smart and very good at his job and is proud of his ability to read and appreciate human literature. He thinks low men are odd. He allowed them to take the credit for bringing back Ted Brautigan, but

he choreographed the recovery. During the battle of Algul Siento, he shoots Ted Brautigan in the arm. It might have been worse, but Dani Rostov tackled him and slowed him down. Eddie finds him dying in Main Street of Pleasantville. When asked if he has any last words, Finli is contemptuous of the way the *ka-tet* ambushed them, but when Eddie asks him how he can defend what he was doing to the world, all Finli can say is that he had his orders. Eddie shoots him in the head.

O'TEGO, GASKIE (5, 7)

Deputy security chief at Algul Siento. Susannah kills him with a head shot.

O'TEGO, HUMMA (7)

Master of Algul Siento when Ted Brautigan arrived. He executed a low man who raped a Breaker. He may have lost his job (and his life) because Ted escaped.

OVERHOLSER, WAYNE DALE (5, 6)

Owner of the Seven Mile Farm, the biggest in Calla Bryn Sturgis. Son of Alan, though he lost his parents when he was young. He has only two children, both grown singletons, a boy and a girl two years apart. A smart and successful man. He's used to getting his way in town and tends to be overbearing and pompous, though he strikes Roland as a good enough fellow. A man unused to changing his mind, once he meets Roland he finds himself looking for a way to say yes. Some of the other ranchers call him Wayne the Weathervane because he swings this way and that. His late twin brother Welland was nine when the Wolves took him. Ultimately he comes around to Roland's side and becomes a staunch supporter. Standing aside makes him sick.

Physical description: He's about sixty. His heavy cheeks will be jowls in another five years. He has a vast, sloping belly, a tight mouth and shrewd eyes. He has "I want" lines in his brow and cheeks.

OY (3, 4, 4.5, 5, 6, 7, M)

A billy-bumbler. His name comes from his attempt to pronounce the word "boy." He remembers men and has limited speaking skills, mostly imitating what he hears, though he sometimes seems to say something that might be the product of original thought. He has a low, deep voice, almost a bark. He was limping from a bite when he encountered the *ka-tet*, probably because he was driven out of his pack for being too smart or talkative. He proves to Roland that he can count when he surveils Tick-Tock Man's lair. He has a mild case of the touch and feels *ka-shume* along with everyone else.

Bumblers are supposed to be good luck. Like all bumblers, Oy is sensitive to starkblasts, adept at finding muffin-balls, good at following scents and knows the Grandfather-fleas in the Dixie Pig as old enemies that he was bred to kill. He seems to have human emotions and has been known to cry and swear. He is shy around most people except Jake, but he occasionally surprises by being friendly. He understands that Jake should see what Ben Slightman and Andy are up to and wakes the boy. He proves himself fearless and valuable during his time with Roland. He remains in Mid-World to sacrifice his life for Roland when he could easily have gone to New York with Susannah.

Physical description: He looks like a blend of raccoon, woodchuck and dachshund, with a furry corkscrew tail, black paws, black-and-gray striped fur that is silky to the touch, gold-ringed black eyes, a long and graceful neck, a sharp, whiskery snout, a slender black nose and a toothy grin. When threatened, he can puff his fur out to nearly double his normal size. He was based on King's Welsh corgi.

PADICK, SAM (7)
The miller from Delain who was Walter o'Dim's father.

PADICK, WALTER (7)
Walter o'Dim's name when he was a boy in Delain fifteen hundred years ago. Son of Sam Padick. He ran away from home at the age of thirteen. In the Marvel comics, Walter was born of supernatural beings who left him in Delain to be raised human. He left to find his real parents.

PATRICIA THE MONO (3, 4, 4.5, 6, 7)
A sentient blue monorail with beautiful glass sides that served the Northwest Baronies. Her route also took her to Fedic in Discordia, where she was used during the evacuation after the Red Death came. After technology declined in Lud, she grew lonely and mad. She started developing a spiritual malaise. Her constant sobbing disturbed Blaine, so he erased the circuits that controlled her nonvoluntary actions, allowing her to commit suicide by plunging off a broken rail line into the Send River.

PEAVY, HUGH (4.5)

High sheriff of Debaria. A big-bellied man with long white hair and a droopy mustache. When he was a deputy, Steven Deschain led a posse against the Crow Gang. When the outlaws killed his sheriff and the rest of the posse, Peavy followed Deschain into battle, killed two of the Crow Gang and dug a bullet out of Deschain's arm with his knife. Steven Deschain gave him credit for destroying the gang, which led to his being sheriff ever since. By the time Roland brings him the bullet as a gift, Peavy is tired of blood and no longer interested in mysteries.

PERTH, LORD (3, 4, 4.5, 5)

A tall man, part of a legend similar to Goliath. "Thus fell Lord Perth, and the earth did shake with that thunder," people say. Roland told his *ka-tet* that he has played Lord Perth in his time. David Quick, who died in a plane crash outside Lud, may be the inspiration for this legend.

PETTIE THE TROTTER (4, 7)

A prostitute who works at the Travellers' Rest in Hambry. She also sings and dances the bump and grind. Her days as a prostitute are nearing an end and she thinks she might become a bartender when she's done, so she sometimes fills in when Stanley Ruiz is busy.

PHIL (7)

The Asimov robot that drove the bus that picked up Ted Brautigan and the other Breakers who arrived in Thunderclap Station from Santa Mira. He was in bad shape at the time and died not long after and was dumped in the robot graveyard.

PICKENS (4.5)

One of two not-so-good deputies in Debaria. A little man with a peculiar undershot jaw.

PITTSTON, SYLVIA (1, 3, 4, M)

A wandering preacher who came from beyond the Mohaine Desert to Tull. The year before Roland arrived in Hambry, she passed through town. The man in black told her he impregnated her with the Crimson King's child. Roland says it is a demon child and rids her of it. She preaches against

Roland, calling him the Interloper, and raises the townspeople against him. Roland kills her, along with everyone else in Tull.

POSELLA, FARREN (5)
A farmhand in Calla Bryn Sturgis.

PRENTISS, PIMLI (7)
The Master of Algul Siento. Originally Paul Prentiss of Rahway, New Jersey. He's about six foot two, balding, grossly overweight and has the nose of a veteran drinker. After he was laid off as a prison guard at Attica in 1970, he found the job at the Breaker prison in the *New York Times*. He appears to be fifty years old, but he was fifty when he came to Thunderclap at least twenty-five years ago. The poisonous atmosphere gives him pimples and a cyst on his neck.

He believes he's doing God's work and sincerely cares for his prisoners, whether they like it or not. He doesn't care that there's no money in his job. The benefits are exceptional. He wallows in food, booze and sex. On the day of the battle, he feels something amiss and takes his pistol with him. Roland shoots him in the back of the head, but it wasn't a kill shot. Prentiss recovers long enough to inflict major damage on the *ka-tet*. Roland's second shot kills him.

PUBES (3, 4, 5, 6, 7)
One of two factions fighting in Lud for many years. So called because they were, on average, younger than their adversaries. They were the original residents of Lud, a group comprised of artisans and manufacturers. They used the Great Old Ones' weapons against the invading force, the Grays led by David Quick, until they stopped working. They became superstitious and believed the drums broadcast through the city's network of speakers were a sign from the gods demanding human sacrifice.

QUICK, ANDREW (3)
The Tick-Tock Man's real name. He is David Quick's great-grandson and leader of the Grays in Lud. Shot in the head by Jake Chambers but not killed. Randall Flagg turned him into one of his minions. The *ka-tet* shoots him to death in the Green Palace.

QUICK, DAVID (3, 4, 4.5, 5)
Legendary outlaw prince and inspiration for the legend of Lord Perth. He was the leader of the last army of Grays that fought the Pubes for control of Lud.

He was killed in an airplane crash ninety years before the *ka-tet* reaches Lud. His great-grandson is Andrew Quick, also known as the Tick-Tock Man.

QUINT, HIRAM (4)

From the Piano Ranch in Hambry. A trustworthy idiot. He owns a musketoon gun. He is one of the people assigned to guard the tankers at Citgo and is ordered to send for oxen to pull them out to Hanging Rock. Jonas leaves him in charge of the lead party when they turn back in the Bad Grass. He survives the ambush at Hanging Rock and flees.

RAINES (4)

The bugler in Rodney Hendricks's company. A pimply, scared-looking boy with a dented bugle on a frayed strap.

RALPH (L, M)

One of the slow mutants who killed everyone in Eluria and ambushed the caravan that John and James Norman were guarding. He leads the group of muties against Roland in the town square. He wears ancient red suspenders over rags of shirt and a filthy bowler hat. He has only one good eye. The Little Sisters bribe him with whiskey and tobacco to get him to take the religious medallion from around John Norman's neck. He's smart enough to draw blood so they will be distracted and he can escape.

RANDOLPH ([1], M)

A survivor of the fall of Gilead. His wife, Chloe, and young son, Edmund, are captured by Farson and used to turn him into a traitor against Roland's *ka-tet*. He provides misleading information that leads to General DeMullet's death. When his duplicity is revealed, he shoots himself. Walter had already killed Chloe and Edmund. His name is mentioned only in the original version of *The Gunslinger* and the person who betrays the *ka-tet* is never identified in *Wolves of the Calla*.

RAVENHEAD, PIET (4)

His signature affirms Richard Stockworth's identity when Alain goes to Mejis.

REED, JAMES (4)

His signature affirms William Dearborn's identity when Roland goes to Mejis.

RENFREW, HASH (4, M)

Owner of the Lazy Susan, the biggest horse ranch in Mejis. Called Rennie by some. He sits next to Roland at dinner at Mayor's House and tells lies about the local livestock. He also breaks the news to Roland about Susan Delgado's situation. He's in charge of moving the tankers to Hanging Rock and is part of Eldred Jonas's advance team, guiding them through the Bad Grass with a click-line to measure the stars. He shoots Roland's hat off and is killed by Roland a second later. If he had lived, he might have replaced Thorin as mayor.

REYNOLDS, CLAY (4, 5, M)

One of the Big Coffin Hunters. He has curly red hair, always wears a cloak and is vain about his looks. He's half Eldred Jonas's age. He comes from the North'rd Baronies, is terrified of rabies, and has been riding with Jonas since he was fifteen, longer than Roy Depape has. He's smarter than Depape and Eldred likes him better. He walks with his left foot turned inward a little.

The encounter with the Affiliation Brats in the Travellers' Rest is the first time he's felt the mastery of a situation slip away from him since he hooked up with Jonas. He enjoys stabbing Kimba Rimer because the man insulted him the first time they met. He's relieved, though, to be sent with Susan Delgado to Mayor's House afterward, away from the main action. He has a bad feeling about their association with Latigo and Mejis.

He's with Coral Thorin when they intercept Susan and Olive Thorin trying to leave town and is forced to shoot Olive when she draws on him. He stays for Reap Fest, riding behind the cart bearing Susan through the streets, holding a noose around her neck. Even if Depape and Jonas hadn't been killed, though, Reynolds had decided to travel on without them. Without Jonas, he's a lot less, and he knows it. Ultimately, he becomes the leader of a group of bank robbers, some of them deserters from Farson's army, with Coral Thorin at his side. He is captured in Oakley and hanged for his crimes.

RHEA OF THE CÖOS

See Dubativo, Rhea.

RIGGINS, GEORGE (4)

One of Sheriff Avery's deputies in Hambry.

RIMER, KIMBA (4)

Mayor Hart Thorin's chancellor and Hambry's minster of inventory. He is an elderly man as gaunt as Old Doctor Death. Six foot eight and as pale as candle wax. He is bald on the top with wisps of hair on the sides. He has a large nose and wears pince-nez. He has the smooth voice of a politician or an undertaker. A provincial man under a veneer of cynical sophistication. Though Thorin is the mayor, Rimer calls the shots in collusion with Eldred Jonas. He has also been sleeping with Coral Thorin. He suggested Rhea as the perfect guardian for the grapefruit. Though Rimer benefits greatly from his treachery (he looted half of Hambry's treasury, and what he didn't give to Farson he kept for himself), it's the trappings of power that drive him. Clay Reynolds stabs him in the chest as part of the plot to frame Roland, Cuthbert and Alain.

RIMER, LASLO "LAS" (4)

Kimber's older brother. Owner of the Rocking H Ranch, where Roland finds oxen, a rare creature in Mid-World.

RITTER, AILEEN (1, M)

The young woman from Gilead whom Roland's parents hope he will marry. She accompanies him to a ball. In the Marvel series, she is Cort's niece and a gunslinger in her own right, although female gunslingers are not allowed. She steals a gun from her uncle's armory and practices alone, developing fearsome skills. She becomes part of Roland's first *ka-tet* and is struck by a spear at Jericho Hill. She survives—barely—and asks Roland to take her to Gilead so she can be buried with her family. A not-man kills her with a poison dart. Roland fulfills his promise, laying her to rest with Cort. In the original version of *The Gunslinger*, she was Roland's lover. In the Marvel comics, he wished he could have loved her.

RIVERS, LUCAS (4)

His signature affirms Arthur Heath's identity when Cuthbert goes to Mejis.

ROBERT AND FRANCESCA (4)

Hambry's version of *Romeo and Juliet*, which dates back to the days before the world moved on. Francesca's brains were dashed out on a slate wall in the Hambry cemetery and Robert cut his throat next to the Thorin mausoleum, according to legend.

ROBESON (1, M)

A guard in Gilead who was working for John Farson. He passed along orders to Hax, the cook.

RODERICKS (7)

Also known as Children of Roderick or Rods. A nomadic tribe originally from the South Plains, far beyond any lands Roland ever knew. They pledged allegiance to Arthur Eld before the world moved on. Now they are mutants. Some appear as walk-ins in Maine. Others followed the train tracks to Algul Siento, where they have a village and forage in the catacombs beneath Thunderclap for food, which they bring to Algul Siento. Each day they show up at the gate seeking work as groundskeepers and maintenance men. The Rods react to Roland as if he's a god. Roland enlists the help of Haylis of Chayven during the battle of Algul Siento. He puts Chevin of Chayven out of his misery in Lovell after eliciting the name of Fedic from him.

ROLAND, KING (6)

King of Delain. He slew the last dragon in Garlan and was later murdered.
   Crossover to Other Works: This story is told in *The Eyes of the Dragon*.

ROSARIO, FREDDY (5)

Owner of a small farm next to Tian Jaffords's in Calla Bryn Sturgis.

ROSS, BIG JACK (4.5)

Tim's father. Handsome and clean-shaven, because he didn't think a beard would suit him. He partnered with his childhood friend Bern Kells and tried to get him to stop drinking when he got out of control. A dragon supposedly killed him while he was chopping ironwood trees in the Endless Forest, but Kells murdered him in a jealous rage.

ROSS, NELL (4.5)

Tim's mother and widow of her childhood friend, Jack Ross. Maiden name: Robertson. She is forced to marry her late husband's partner, Bern Kells, after Ross dies, otherwise she won't be able to pay the Barony Covenanter and she and her son, Tim, will end up homeless. Kells beats her and mistreats Tim. She ends up blind after one of his attacks. Tim goes on a quest to find a cure for her blindness. She gets the better of Kells, "divorcing" him with her husband's ax. She finishes her days in Gilead as a great lady after her son becomes a gunslinger.

ROSS, TIMOTHY "TIM" (4.5)

Hero of the story "The Wind Through the Keyhole" that Roland tells Young Bill Streeter in Debaria. Son of Jack and Nell Ross, he lived in a cottage called Goodview in Tree Village at the edge of the Endless Forest. When he was eleven, his father was supposedly burned by a dragon while chopping trees. The Covenant Man shows him that his father's partner, Bern Kells, killed him.

Kells marries his mother and starts drinking again because he's worried Jack's body will be found. He beats Nell so badly that she goes blind. Tim raises a posse, but Kells flees. Tim goes on a quest into the Endless Forest in search of Maerlyn, who he believes will provide a cure for his mother. He's armed with a pistol given to him by his teacher, Widow Smack. The first time he fires it, he grins and feels the coldness familiar to any gunslinger. When he meets Maerlyn, the wizard predicts that he will become one.

When he is twenty-one, he joins a posse with three gunslingers. He is both fearless and a dead shot, and becomes *tet-fa* and, later, *ka-tet*, one of the very few gunslingers not from the proven line of Eld. He is called Lefty Ross, the left-hand gun, because of the way he draws, then becomes known as Tim Stoutheart.

ROWENA, QUEEN (6, M)

Arthur Eld's wife. Perhaps one of three. In the Marvel series, she is supposedly barren.

RUIZ, STANLEY "SHEEMIE" (1, 4, 7, M)

A simple boy from Mejis. Son of Stanley Ruiz and Dolores Sheemer, though he doesn't know who his father is. He works at the Travellers' Rest in Hambry, cleaning up the saloon. He's a good worker, cheerful most of the time. He can be discreet when necessary, but he can't tell a lie without shifting his eyes away. He can't read.

He becomes good friends with Roland, Alain and Cuthbert, the latter of whom saved his life from Roy Depape and taught him how to swear. He passes messages back and forth between Roland and Susan Delgado and is willing to die for his friends, but not unless it serves a purpose. As part of the young *ka-tet*, he exhibits a mild sense of the touch. When the boys are jailed, he helps Susan break them out.

He follows Roland and his friends after they leave Mejis, though Roland doesn't know how. At one point they cut the only bridge across a river for hundreds of miles and he stayed on their trail. When the young *ka-tet* sets out in search of the Dark Tower, he joins them as a kind of squire.

What happened to him in the days after Jericho Hill isn't known. He ended up at Algul Siento as one of the Crimson King's Breakers, at which point he looks to be about thirty-five. Unlike the others in Thunderclap, he has no pimples or blemishes. He has a mass of curly hair, stubbly cheeks and spit-shiny lips.

Dinky Earnshaw befriends him after he hears him sobbing at night because he's scared of the dark. He communicates telepathically and by sending vivid mental images. Ted Brautigan and Dinky think he can't speak, but he does after Roland recognizes him, apologizing for not dying in Susan's place.

His special power is teleportation, another word for making magic doors. This explains how he was able to follow Roland to Gilead. He opens a portal so Ted can escape and creates a magic Gingerbread House outside of time so Ted has a place to rest after he's caught. He knows Roland is trying to save the Beams, which is why he, Ted and Dinky are waiting for the gunslingers at Thunderclap Station.

Using his power causes brain bleeds and seizures, but he insists on assisting the *ka-tet*. He opens doorways so they can see what day it is in Keystone Earth. He's particularly receptive to the Voice of the Beam. His dream of a boy representing the Beam helps Roland decide whether to free the Breakers first or save Stephen King. In the aftermath of the battle, he cuts his foot on a piece of glass. He dies of an infection on the Spirit of Topeka en route to Fedic.

RUIZ, STANLEY (4, 7)

Bartender at the Travellers' Rest in Mejis. He is Sheemie's father, though he isn't sure of it. He tries to intervene when Roy Depape gets into a conflict with Sheemie and ends up with three broken teeth and a bloody mouth. He has two clubs behind the bar: The Calmer and The Killer.

SALTY SAM (4.5)

Occupant of the drunk tank in Debaria when Roland and Jamie DeCurry arrive.

SCOWTHER, DR. (6, 7)

The doctor who delivers Mia's baby in the Fedic Dogan. A stoutish man with brown eyes, flushed cheeks and black hair swept back. He was in charge of the extractions and possibly involved in Mia's transformation. During the confusion surrounding Mordred's birth, Susannah steals his gun and shoots him with it—along with just about everyone else in the room.

SELENA (7, M)
Daughter of the moon. In the Marvel comics, she is Walter o'Dim's mother.

SHEEMER, DOLORES (4)
Sheemie Ruiz's mother.

SHUNT, SAM (4.5)
A rich man in Little Debaria who owns bars, prostitutes, the shacks where the miners sleep and the company store. Several times a year, he sets up foot-races, obstacle courses and horse races for the miners. Winners get a year's worth of debt forgiven at his store.

SI (3)
Resident of River Crossing. Husband to Mercy.

SIGHE (4.5)
Fairy folk who live in the Endless Forest. See Armaneeta.

SISTERS OF ORIZA (5, 6, 7)
Also known as Sisters of the Plate. A social group of women in the Callas who, once a month, throw plates modeled after the one Lady Oriza used to kill Gray Dick. They cook for funerals and festivals and hold sewing circles and quilting bees after families lose possessions from flood or fire. They tend to the Pavilion and the Gathering Hall and sponsor dances for the young people and also hire out to ranchers as caterers. Among themselves, they gossip and play cards, Points and Castles. They play an important role in the battle against the Wolves.

SKIN-MAN (4.5)
A man who can take on the forms of animals. A kind of werewolf that can be killed only with a silver bullet. Not many people know what they are, but Roland's teacher Vannay gathers the information they need to stop the one stalking Debaria.

SLIDELL, POKEY (5)

The oldest of the four people from Calla Bryn Sturgis who confronted the Wolves when his best friend Jamie Jaffords was nineteen. Slidell lost a brother and a young son to the Wolves. He was killed by a sneetch.

SLIGHTMAN, BEN (5, 6, 7)

Foreman of Vaughn Eisenhart's ranch. He's about forty-five years old. His daughter died when she was ten, which makes his son, Benny, particularly vulnerable to the Wolves. Andy exploits this to turn Slightman into a spy, rewarding him with gifts like glasses and a record player.

SLIGHTMAN, BENNY (5, 6, 7)

Fourteen-year-old son of Ben Slightman, the foreman of Vaughn Eisenhart's ranch. He is unusual in Calla Bryn Sturgis in that his sister died of pneumonia when he was ten. He becomes a good friend to Jake. Though he's a couple of years older, he's younger in a lot of ways. He is open to fun, but willing to work hard when necessary. He proves his bravery during the battle with the Wolves, but is killed by a sneetch after Margaret Eisenhart is beheaded next to him.

SLOW MUTANTS (THROUGHOUT)

Victims of the weapons, wars and experiments of the Great Old Ones. Also known as the green folk because of the color of their skin. They were mutated by the long-term effects of the Great Poisoning. Jake and Roland encounter a group in the mountains while pursuing the man in black. They move into Gilead after its fall. They are marauders in Eluria, ambushing caravans for the wagons and their contents. Roland heard of one tribe that prays to Big Sky Daddy. A desert tribe called the Total Hogs once had the blue glass from the Wizard's Rainbow, but they lost it. Not all are dangerous—the mudmen Tim Ross encounters in the Fagonard Swamp help him on his quest.

SMACK, ARDELIA (WIDOW) (4.5)

Teacher of reading and mathematics in Tree Village. She is smart and takes no guff from her students, who usually come to love her. Formerly a great lady in the Barony Estates, she wears a veil to cover the damage to her face caused by blood sores from a degenerative disease. Prone to fugues, shakes and migraines. She gives Tim Ross her late brother's pistol, which proves valuable on his quest, along with food and other items. Bern Kells murders her after she watches over Nell Ross during the starkblast.

SMASHER (L)
One of the slow mutants in Eluria. He gives Roland's guns to Sister Mary.

SNIP (4.5)
A pokie who works at the Jefferson Ranch and survives the skin-man attack because he was out rounding up strays with Arn and Canfield.

SOONY (4)
The former owner of the hut in the Bad Grass where Roland and Susan Delgado meet. He painted the door red after a religious conversion and went off to join the Manni.

SPANKERMAN (3, 4)
Leader of the Pubes until he drew the black rock in their lottery and was executed.

SPEAKING DEMON (1, 3, 6, M)
A demon that can be compelled to prophesize. They often live in Speaking Circles.

SPLINTER HARRY "OLD SPLINT" (4.5)
An old man who works part-time in the Destry sawmill in Tree Village. He's prone to babbling nonsense that he claims is High Speech and loves nothing more than talking about gunslingers. Tim Ross uses what he learns from him to greet the mudmen in Fagonard Swamp.

STOCKWORTH, RICHARD (4, 7, M)
Alain Johns's alias in Mejis. He is supposedly a rancher's son.

STOKES, DUSTIN "HOT" (4.5)
Blacksmith in Tree Village who also serves as the undertaker and funeral director.

STOUTHEART, TIM (4.5)
See Timothy Ross.

STRAW (7)

One of the low men present during Mia's birth. The first person Susannah kills after she gets Scowther's gun. She then relieves him of his Walther PPK and half a dozen extra clips.

STREETER, BILL (4.5)

Bunkhouse cook at the Jefferson Ranch in Debaria. The skin-man killed him beside his stove with his bloodstained apron thrown over his face like a shroud.

STREETER, YOUNG BILL (4.5)

A thin boy, eleven years old, son of the cook at the Jefferson Ranch. He took care of the bunks, bedrolls and saddles for the proddies. He was also responsible for setting the gate at the end of the day. He survives the skin-man attack because he's camping on the advice of his father. It was a way of evading Elrod Nutter, who tormented him. Roland consoles the boy by feeding him candy and telling him the tale of "The Wind Through the Keyhole." He identifies the skin-walker from among the salties brought back from the mines. Roland leaves him in the care of Everlynne of Serenity.

STRONG, GARRETT (5)

A smallholder in Calla Bryn Sturgis with a pug-dog face and a receding hairline. He has only one farmhand, named Rossiter.

STROTHER (4.5)

One of two not-so-good deputies in Debaria. A fat man who wears a black hat with a gaudy rattlesnake band.

STUTTERING BILL (7)

An Asimov robot stationed at Federal Outpost 19 on Tower Road. His jobs include keeping the roads plowed, cleaning houses, maintaining generators and delivering supplies to residents of Westring. He can also provide minor medical attention. Official designation: *William, D-746541-M, Maintenance Robot. Many Other Functions.* A fried circuit makes him stutter, but he is able to fix this when Roland suggests he do so. He's at least eight feet tall and resembles Nigel from the Fedic Dogan. He has rudimentary emotions. He assembles a new cart for Roland to haul his supplies and an electric golf cart for Susannah to ride.

Crossover to Other Works: Bill Denborough in *It* is known as Stutterin' Bill.

TAHEEN (1, 5, 6, 7, M)

Sometimes known as the third people. They have the heads of animals or birds, and human-shaped bodies. Creatures neither of the Prim nor of the natural world, but misbegotten things from somewhere between the two. Low men are hybrids of taheen and humans. The taheen have no interest in becoming human and consider humes to be an inferior race, so they generally remain in Mid-World. They speak perfect English and some have limited psychic abilities. They are also immune to mind reading. Their sharp vision suits them for working in the guard towers at Algul Siento. They are less susceptible to dermatological problems caused by the poison air of Thunderclap, but even minor wounds are prone to potentially lethal infections. They consider mucous and pus to be sweet delicacies.

TAMRA (L, M)

One of the Little Sisters of Eluria. A lovely lass of one and twenty, according to Sister Mary, though she perhaps means a hundred and twenty years old instead of twenty-one. Even in disguise she looks like a thirty-year-old matron. In the Marvel comics, she is called Tamara.

TASLEY, HOWARD (4.5)

Constable of Tree. Every time the Covenant Man comes, he finds some reason to make himself scarce from the village. Sometimes he goes hunting, or up to Tavares, where he has a woman.

TASSA OF SONESH (7)

Pimli Prentiss's houseboy at Algul Siento. A willowy young man who wears lipstick and a kilt. He and Tammy Kelly, the housekeeper, hate each other.

TAVERY, FRANCINE (5)

A girl from Calla Bryn Sturgis who, along with her brother, Frank, assists the *ka-tet* by drawing a map of the town. She has a crush on Eddie. Like her brother, her hair is black, her eyes are dark blue, her skin creamy pale and her lips startling red. They have identical, faint spatters of freckles on their cheeks. Bright, quick, beautiful and eager to please. They are also one of three sets of twins who take the opopanax feather around to call the town meeting before the Wolves arrive.

TAVERY, FRANK (5, 6)

A boy from Calla Bryn Sturgis who, along with his twin sister, assists the *ka-tet* by drawing a map of the town. He also helps Jake scatter toys to confuse the Wolves, but breaks his ankle after he steps in a hole and panics, which endangers Jake and Benny Slightman.

TELFORD, GEORGE (5)

Owner of Buckhead Ranch in Calla Bryn Sturgis. He's silver-haired, tanned and handsome in a weather-beaten way. Has a white mustache and shaggy white eyebrows. A smooth talker who knows how to work an audience. Too old to have to worry about the Wolves taking his children. He reminds Eddie of Pa Cartwright from *Bonanza*. He is dead set against the plan to fight the Wolves and speaks his mind even when it's clear the tide has turned against him.

THOMAS (2)

One of two desperate yet grim young men Roland encountered while they were pursuing a demon named Flagg who looked like a man.

Crossover to Other Works: In *The Eyes of the Dragon*, Thomas was the younger son of King Roland of Delain.

THONNIE (6)

One of the Manni of Calla Redpath.

THORIN, CORAL (4, 7, M)

Younger sister of Mayor Hart Thorin of Hambry and owner of the Travellers' Rest saloon and whorehouse, where she also keeps a large bedroom. She also owns a great deal of land along the Drop. She appears morose and has a hard streak and was a wild child. Sallow and skinny but not as thin as her brother, whom she considers an idiot, and good-looking in a large-eyed, weasel-headed way. She drinks too much as a way of dealing with the town's treachery. After she starts sleeping with Eldred Jonas, who sees that she's as cold-blooded as he is, she becomes a coconspirator in the murders of her brother and her former lover, Kimba Rimer. She locks Susan Delgado in the pantry at Mayor's House after she is captured. After Jonas is killed, she takes up with Clay Reynolds and is killed during a bank robbery shoot-out in Oakley.

THORIN, HARTWELL "HART" (4, M)

Lord High Mayor of Mejis and Chief Guard o' Barony, though he is actually a puppet to his chancellor, Kimba Rimer, who convinced him to hire the Big Coffin Hunters as bodyguards. Husband to Olive and older brother to Coral, as well as majority owner in the Travellers' Rest saloon. A skinny, twitchy man with fluffy white hair rising in a cloud around the bald spot on the top of his head. Fat hairy knuckles. His build is peculiar: a short and narrow-shouldered upper body over impossibly long and skinny legs like a marsh bird. He's roughly sixty-five years old and underneath he's backcountry, a rancher. A bit of a fool, apt to blabber. Fond of low comedy and puzzled by anything highbrow. He won't let anyone call him Excellency. A knuckle-cracker, a back-slapper, a dinner-table belcher. His best asset is his speaking voice, which is strong and high, carrying and pleasant. Fond of strong drink and young girls. When his wife proves barren, he arranges with Cordelia Delgado to turn her niece Susan into his gilly, using a long-standing law that allows for him to have a male heir, though he really just lusts after the beautiful young woman. He pays for Susan with gold, silver, horses and gifts of clothing. He doesn't know that everyone in town is laughing at him. He wants nothing to do with the business with the Good Man except for his share of the profits, thinking he'll be too busy in bed with Susan to feel guilt over what he's allowed in his Barony. Roy Depape stabs him to death.

THORIN, OLIVE (4, M)

Wife of Mayor Hart Thorin of Hambry. She is the daughter of a fisherman named John Haverty and grew up north of Hambry, where she used to play in the caves. A plump woman. She is barren and, though she still loves her husband, she hasn't shared a room with him for ten years or a bed for five. She is humiliated by her situation and knows the people of Hambry are laughing at her husband's infatuation with Susan Delgado. She is the only person in high society whom Roland likes in Hambry and, after seeing her situation, he understands his mother better. She tries to come to Susan's rescue after Clay Reynolds takes her, planning to go west because there's nothing left for her in Mejis, but Reynolds shoots her after she tries to draw an ancient pistola that misfires.

THOUGHTFUL, RANDO (7)

The Crimson King's minister of state. He appears first as Fimalo, Stephen King's superego. He is an old man who is dying slowly. His hair is dirty gray and his skull is covered with eczema. His face is covered with pimples and sores, some bleeding. He tells Roland and Susannah about the last days of the Crimson King in Le Casse Roi Russe. Mordred eats him after the Castle Rooks tear out his eyes while he's still alive. See also Austin Cornwell.

TICK-TOCK MAN (3, 4, 4.5, 5, 6, 7)

Real name: Andrew Quick. Leader of the Grays faction in Lud and great-grandson of David Quick. So large and heavily muscled that he reminds Jake of a cross between a Viking warrior and a fairy tale giant. Has green eyes and long, dirty gray-blond hair that reaches the middle of his back. He wears only leather breeches, high boots and a silver band around one bicep. Carries a knife scabbard on one shoulder. Wears a coffin-shaped glass box that contains a gold clock face on a silver chain around his neck. His touch repairs Jake's watch. Jake shoots him in the thigh and in the head and Oy scratches him in the face, but he survives, only to be taken over by Richard Fannin. He reappears with Fannin/Flagg in the Green Palace, playing the part of the wizard from *The Wizard of Oz*. When Oy discovers him behind the curtain, he grabs a machine gun, intending to shoot the *ka-tet*. Oy attacks him, and Eddie and Susannah shoot him to death.

TILLY (3)

One of Tick-Tock Man's Grays. The only person to survive when Roland infiltrates their headquarters. Presumably killed when Blaine the Mono poisons Lud.

TIRANA (6, 7)

A plump low woman wearing a silver lamé gown in the Dixie Pig. Susannah rips off her mask, revealing the head of a huge red rat with yellow teeth growing up the outsides of its cheek.

TOMAS, MARIA (4, M)

Susan Delgado's maid at Mayor's House in Hambry. A small, dark-haired girl, eighteen or nineteen years old, with an innate penchant for creating drama. She can't bring herself to call Susan by her given name but becomes her ally, getting her out of Mayor's House the morning after the murders and helping Olive Thorin free her when she's captured by the Big Coffin Hunters. She had three aunts who died of cancer. Her father works at the Piano Ranch.

TOOK, EBEN (5)

Owner of Took's General Store in Calla Bryn Sturgis, as well as the boarding house and restaurant. He has a half interest in the livery and loan papers on most of the smallhold farms in the Calla. He, Eisenhart and Overholser are the three "big bugs" in Calla Bryn Sturgis. The Wolves burned the store on a previous visit when the folken put up token resistance, and he's determined to make sure that never happens again. He is the biggest opponent of the gunslingers' plan, but when it is successful he offers to outfit them from stem to stern for free. He has a high, almost womanish voice. Eddie thinks he's a shithead.

TOPSY THE SAILOR (3, 5, 6)

A former member of the Pubes in Lud who took his boat and went off down-river.

TORRES, MIGUEL (4, 5)

An elderly, bearded, toothless servant at Mayor's House in Hambry. He is usually as neat as a pin, and looks askance at people he deems beneath him.

TOTAL HOGS (4)

A desert tribe of slow mutants who supposedly possessed the blue crystal from the Wizard's Rainbow until it slipped from their sight within the past fifty years.

TRAMPAS (7)

A low man at Algul Siento who befriends Ted Brautigan. Unlike most low men, he isn't jealous of humans, which makes him an outcast among his own people. Ted thinks he is farther down the road to *becoming* than most of the others. His name is derived from the Western novel *The Virginian*. He has eczema that causes him to take off his protective hat and scratch his head, accidentally revealing to Ted what the Breakers are doing. Ted also discovers he is considered indispensable, motivating him to escape from Algul Siento. When he is recaptured, he does not reveal where he got his information, earning Trampas's gratitude. Trampas tells Ted about the Crimson King's efforts to kill Stephen King and how *ka* has stopped protecting King. During the battle of Algul Siento, Trampas follows orders, grabbing Earnshaw. Ted uses his mind spear to kill him.

TRAVIS (4.5)

The "enjie" (engineer) of the steam-driven train the people of Gilead called Sma' Toot.

TRELAWNY (7)

A *can toi* security guard at Algul Siento.

TRISTUM, GANGLI (7)

The compound doctor at Algul Siento. A squat, dark-complected, heavily jowled *can toi* who took a taheen name instead of a human one. He runs the infirmary on the third floor of Damli House with an iron fist while wearing roller skates. In addition to providing medical services, he also knows how to short-circuit potential teleports. When Damli House catches fire, he stays behind to gather his papers and is killed in an explosion.

TUDBURY, BILL (3)

Resident of River Crossing. One of the albino twins.

TUDBURY, TILL (3)

Resident of River Crossing. One of the albino twins.

TURTLE, THE (4)

Roland hears its voice when he is inside the grapefruit. It shows him his destiny, but it is a hard, cruel voice that also predicts his damnation.

UFFI (7)

A shape changer. Rando Thoughtful claims he's one.

UNWIN, AUNT TALITHA (3, 4, 5, 6, 7)

Matriarch of River Crossing. More than one hundred years old. She hobbles over a cane like a witch in a fairy tale and has no teeth and eyes as green as emeralds. She knows High Speech. She gives Roland a silver cross to place at the base of the Dark Tower. Roland uses the cross to send a message to Moses Carver and gets it back in time to follow her wishes.

VAMPIRES (1, 2, 4, 5, 6, 7)

Father Callahan classifies vampires into three categories. There aren't many Type One vampires, like Barlow of 'Salem's Lot, but they can cause a lot of mayhem in a short period of time. They live long lives and spend centuries in hibernation. They temporarily acquire the thoughts and memories of those they feed on. Parasitic Grandfather-fleas (little doctors) usually follow Type Ones around, as when they're dining at the Dixie Pig. Roland says they're the most gruesome and powerful survivors of the Prim's recession.

Type One vampires create Type Two vampires, the so-called undead, and then move on. Type Two vampires can create other Type Two vampires in a relatively small area, but they're barely smarter than zombies and their hunger undoes them. They can't go out in the daylight and their life spans are short because their existence is perilous.

Type Three vampires can't create other vampires, but they feed relentlessly and spread disease, like AIDS. Their saliva causes a selective, short-term amnesia in their victims. They can go out in the daylight and take their principal sustenance from food. They have short attention spans. The vampires Father Callahan kills are all Type Threes, which he calls pilot sharks. He believes that what little blood they have in their bodies is coagulated. They disappear once killed, leaving their clothing behind and sometimes their hair and teeth. Father Callahan believes the vampires have an uneasy alliance with the low men that traces back to Thunderclap.

VANNAY, ABEL (1, 3, 4, 4.5, 5, 7, M)

Vannay the Wise. One of Roland Deschain's tutors—the one who taught from books and saw to his students' mental training. He taught history, logic problems and the universal truths that enabled them to avoid fights. He called violence the hollow chamber, where echoes distorted all true sounds. He showed them the compass and quadrant and sextant and taught them the mathematics necessary to use them.

He held riddling contests every Friday to teach boys to think around corners. He told Roland his imagination was poor and called him Gabby because he was so close-mouthed. He taught about how the Manni prepared for their travels and about the perils of going todash. He believed that if you woke a person from a deep hypnotic trance too suddenly, the person could go mad. Though others are skeptical about the skin-man in Debaria, he finds the evidence convincing. "When facts speak, the wise man listens," he said. He knew that skin-men prowl after sundown and that they're vulnerable to silver, but he didn't know how fast they could change shapes. He walked with a limp. His son, Wallace, was a gunslinger-in-training but died of epilepsy. In the Marvel series, a turncoat Gilead guard shoots him to death.

VENN, RUPERT (4.5)

The foreman at the Tree Sawmill where Tim Ross works after his mother marries Bern Kells.

WALLACE (5)

Vannay's son. He died of the falling sickness, sometimes called king's evil.

WEGG, WILL (4.5)

Little Debaria's constable. A big man with a sand-colored handlebar mustache. He plays Watch Me and bets on the horse races organized for the miners. His winnings keep him in whores and whiskey. The skin-man turns into a poisonous pooky (snake) in the Debaria jail and kills him.

WERTNER, HENRY "HANK" (4)

A horse breeder in Mejis and owner of a small orchard. He takes over as the Barony's stockliner after Pat Delgado is killed.

WHITE AMMIES (4.5)

Nurses. Roland sent away the ones who tended to Cort.

WHITE, JAKE (4)

A rancher in Mejis. He also owns an orchard. Part of the posse that arrests Roland, Cuthbert and Alain. He hits Alain in the forehead with the butt of a pistol.

WHITMAN, THOMAS (1, M)

A gunslinger apprentice and friend of Roland in Gilead. In the Marvel graphic novels, he is burned to death by a flamethrower at Jericho Hill.

WINSTON (3, 4, 5)

One of the Pubes. He wears a kilt and wields a cutlass. Susannah kills him on his birthday.

WOLVES (5, 6, 7)

Robots that have taken a one-way door from the Fedic Dogan to Thunderclap Station once in each of the past six or seven generations. The door is failing, so it is unpleasant for humans to use. From there they ride their gray robotic horses to the Callas to steal one of every set of twins of a certain age. They are heavily armed and wear protective armor. Their hoods hide their most vulnerable feature—the radar dish that sits atop each head. Beneath their Dr. Doom masks—which look like steel but rot in the sun like flesh—their faces are smooth metal, with microphones at the temples for ears, lenses for eyes and a round mesh grill for a nose or mouth. Their weapons include light sabers and sneetches. Known as Greencloaks by the residents of Algul Siento. When none return from their most recent foray, Finli o'Tego thinks they may have fallen prey to a computer virus.

WURTZ, HEAD TECHNICIAN (M)
One of Farson's men. He got the laser canon working after three others failed.

ZACHARY (1)
A resident of Tull.

PLACES
ALGUL SIENTO (1, 5, 7)
Literally: Blue Heaven. Also known as Devar-Toi (the Big Prison). The place where Breakers are brought to work on destroying the Beams. A one-hundred-acre, heavily guarded oasis in the middle of Thunderclap, surrounded by desert on all sides. The three hundred and seven inmates wear slippers to discourage escape attempts. There are one hundred and eighty full-time guards. During each eight-hour shift, twenty taheen man the four stone watchtowers, twenty armed humans patrol the perimeter fences (one barbed, one standard electric, one lethal) and twenty low men float among the Breakers.

Lit by artificial sunlight, generally accompanied by music. It never rains, but there is often dry thunder at night. It resembles a college campus or a town out of a Ray Bradbury story. The main building is Damli House, which contains the Study where the Breakers work. There are also dorms for the Breakers, a small town known as Pleasantville, a church and a house for the head of operations. Since most of the buildings are wood, the possibility of fire is a major concern. The food is the best. Algul Siento has all the modern conveniences with classy accommodations, including holographic sex programs. Rodericks live in a village nearby and explore the extensive catacombs beneath Algul Siento.

ALL-A-GLOW (7)

A fairy-tale kingdom where a very young Roland Deschain thought he would live with his mother after he won her from his father and married her.

ALL-WORLD (4, 5, 6, M)

Arthur Eld's domain, though Walter sometimes claims it as his own.

AMBUSH ARROYO (4.5)

The rocks between the High Pure and the Low Pure north of Debaria where the Crow Gang ambushed Sheriff Pea Anderson and his posse.

ARC 16 EXPERIMENTAL STATION (6, 7)

The Fedic Dogan, a large, rusty Quonset hut known as the Dogan of Dogans or Sixteen. The door beneath the Dixie Pig leads here. One of the many places where the Old People tried to join magic and science together. A maximum-security location that requires both verbal password and eye scan. The Control Suite is four levels down, and requires three ID entry cards used in sequence. From here, armies of robots can be controlled and poison gas released in the event of a hostile takeover. Richard Sayre has an office here in which Roland and Susannah discover a painting of the Dark Tower. The Extraction Room is where the Wolves took the children of the Callas, and where Susannah and Mia have their baby. Mia was made mortal in the Experimental Station. Nearly six hundred of the one-way doors in the rotunda are still operational according to Nigel, who has quarters here. Beneath the Dogan, a passage leads to a one-way door that took the Wolves to the Callas. Another passage goes under Castle Discordia to the Badlands, past the monsters that are trying to dig their way out.

ARC QUADRANT OUTPOST 16 (5)

A medium-security North Central Positronics observation station (or Dogan) near Calla Bryn Sturgis in the Northeast Corridor. It resembles a Quonset hut on a military base. It consists of a control room, a galley and a bunkhouse equipped to sleep eight. Thirty TV monitors show scenes inside and outside the Dogan, as well as several that display feeds from spy cameras hidden in Calla Bryn Sturgis. This Dogan is used to send updates to Finli o'Tego at Algul Siento.

ARTEN (4, 4.5)
A river west of Gilead.

AUDIENCE CHAMBER (7)
The room in Le Casse Roi Russe where the Crimson King sits on a throne of skulls and torments his staff and advisers.

AYJIP (5)
The Manni version of Egypt. The Angel of Death killed the firstborn in every house where the blood of a sacrificial lamb hadn't been daubed on the doorposts.

BAD GRASS (4, M)
A freeland northwest of Hambry. The grass is more than seven feet tall. It smells and tastes good to cattle and horses, but it swells and bursts their stomachs. Children have gotten lost and died in it. Susan and Roland met in an abandoned squatter's hut with a red door hidden in the grass. Roland, Alain and Cuthbert wait in it for Farson's agents to go past so they can ambush them.

BADLANDS (7)
The poisoned and ruined lands between Castle Discordia and the Dark Tower. Nothing grows here, not even devil-grass, though the water from the pumps at fifteen-mile intervals is potable. The weather is cold enough to make people miserable but not enough to kill them. The air is toxic enough to give Susannah skin cancer and Roland pneumonia. They begin at the checkpoint outside Castle Discordia and end at the White Lands of Empathica.

BADLANDS AVENUE (7)
Susannah's name for the King's Way, the former coach road between Castle Discordia and Le Casse Roi Russe.

BAR K RANCH (4, M)
The deserted ranch where Roland, Alain and Cuthbert stayed while in Mejis. Located northwest of town, not far from Eyebolt Canyon. The barns, most of the stables and the homeplace burned six or seven years ago after the winds shifted during the annual burning at the mouth of the canyon. Only the

L-shaped bunkhouse, one stable and a cook-shack survived. The former owners, the Garbers, gave it up after the fire. It now belongs to the Horsemen's Association. Eldred Jonas picks it for the boys because it's away from the Drop and the oil patch.

BAYVIEW HOTEL (4)
A hotel in Mejis on High Street where the upper class drinks instead of at the Travellers' Rest.

BEELIE (4.5)
A former military outpost west of Debaria that's now a ghost town. The Beelie Stockade was where the circuit judge sent convicts, each of whom received an ankle tattoo, and where public hangings were held. After the militia left and the stockade closed five years before the adventure of the skin-man, harriers—perhaps Farson's men—had their way with the place.

BEESFORD-ON-ARTEN (4.5)
Hometown of Gabrielle Deschain. It lies on the Arten River between Gilead and Debaria. Some of Gabrielle's people still live there, though some of the residents don't think kindly of Gilead.

BIG EMPTY, THE (3)
The vast plains west of Lud.

BLUE HEAVEN
See Algul Siento.

BORDERLANDS (4.5, 5, 6, 7)
The civilized territory between the forest at the end of Mid-World and the beginning of End-World at Thunderclap. Approximately seventy Callas are distributed along an arc that follows the branches of the Whye River.

BUCKHEAD RANCH (5)
George Telford's ranch in Calla Bryn Sturgis.

BUSTED LUCK (4.5)
One of three saloons in Debaria, where Roland treats the miners from Little Debaria to drinks.

BUSTLING PIG, THE (L)
One of two saloons in Eluria.

CALLA (4.5, 5, 7)
A prefix for the approximately seventy towns that occupy the six-thousand-mile Grand Crescent or Arc along the River Whye in the Borderlands to the west of Thunderclap. The Callas have existed for more than a thousand years. The region is civilized, with roads, law enforcement, trade routes and a system of government. The people aren't woodsy, preferring the cleared farmland of the Callas, and they aren't travelers, either. The towns get smaller north of Calla Bryn Sturgis due to increasingly cold climates. Those to the north of Calla Bryn Sturgis include Calla Amity (farming and ranching), Calla Sen Pinder (farming and sheep), and Calla Sen Chre (where the Orizas are manufactured) and others noted for cheese, where people reputedly wear wooden shoes. To the south are Calla Lockwood (farming and ranching), Calla Bryn Bouse (ranching), Calla Staffel (ranching) and Calla Divine. Other Callas are known for manufacturing, fishing (Calla Fundy), mining and gambling. The Manni live in Calla Redpath.

CALLA BRYN STURGIS (4.5, 5, 6, 7)
One of seventy or so villages spread along the Grand Crescent. It sits between the forest at the end of Mid-World and the wasteland and desert that lead to Thunderclap one hundred wheels to the east, four thousand miles from the South Seas on the banks of the Devar-Tete Whye, the eastern branch of the Whye River. It has a population of between seven and eight hundred. For the past two centuries, Wolves from Thunderclap have ravaged it, stealing one of each set of twin children, which are the rule rather than the exception. To the northeast of town lies Manni Redpath and the hill country with arroyos and garnet mines. See also Calla.

CAN'-KA NO REY (7)
The field of roses where the Dark Tower stands. Also called the Red Fields of None.

CANDLETON (3, 4)
The first stop on Blaine the Mono's route after he leaves Lud. A poisoned and irradiated ruin overrun with mutated insects and animals. A few

nuclear-powered robots still run, though they've had no people to serve for the last 234 years. Blaine's sonic boom destroyed some of the things that were still standing in the town.

CAN STEEK-TETE (7)

The Little Needle. A sharp upthrust of rock (or butte) visible from both Thunderclap Station and Algul Siento, though it is about eight or ten miles away. Sheemie teleports the *ka-tet* to a cave on its slope after they come through the door to Thunderclap Station. A larger cave below them is a war chest of weapons for the battle of Algul Siento.

CASSE ROI RUSSE, LE (7, M)

The Crimson King's castle, located on the far side of Discordia from the Castle on the Abyss. It is built of red stone that darkened to almost black over the years. Towers and turrets burst upward in a way that seems to defy gravity. The castle is sober and undecorated except for the staring eye carved into the keystone arch over the main entrance. The doors and windows are oddly narrow. Walter o'Dim visited the Crimson King here once and saw him monitoring Stephen King through one of the glass balls in his possession. The castle is in poor upkeep, with two of the eight overhead walkways collapsed into the courtyard. By the time Roland and Susannah arrive, the Forge of the King has gone out and the Crimson King has killed all his staff and fled for the Tower, leaving behind Rando Thoughtful. They never enter the castle. Their palaver is held on the bridge that spans the castle's moat.

CASTLE DISCORDIA (6, 7)

Also known as Castle on the Abyss. Located deep in End-World on Shardik's Beam, southeast of Thunderclap and northwest of Le Casse Roi Russe. Between its inner keep and the outer walls lies the dead town of Fedic. Outside its walls is a great abyss filled with monsters. The bridge that spanned the abyss collapsed long ago. One door beneath the castle opens into todash space, used by the Crimson King for his bitterest enemies. The Red Death that killed Fedic may have arisen from an experiment gone wrong inside the castle. Mia imagines she's in the castle's kitchen and banquet hall when Susannah forages for food at night. A tapestry in the Dixie Pig shows Arthur Eld and his knights dining at the same banquet table.

One passage from Fedic runs beneath the castle, ending in a one-way door that opens on the Calla side of Thunderclap. Another dark passage—taken by

Roland, Oy and Susannah—leads to a carriage road to Le Casse Roi Russe through the Badlands. Monsters from the abyss try to break into these passages. At least one succeeded.

CASTLE-TOWN (7)
The town on the outskirts of the Castle of the Crimson King at the edge of the Badlands. The main street is King's Way. The side streets are cobbled. The tilting cottages are narrow and steep-roofed, the doorways thin and abnormally high, like something out of Lovecraft.

CAVE OF VOICES (5, 7)
The name of the Doorway Cave before the Unfound Door appeared.

CHEERY FELLOWS SALOON & CAFÉ (4.5)
One of three saloons in Debaria.

CHURCH OF BLOOD EVERLASTING, THE (3)
The tallest building in River Crossing. Though the main sanctuary is a ruin, the basement is neat and orderly. The *ka-tet* holds palaver here with Aunt Talitha and the other town residents.

CITGO (4, 6, M)
Oilfields northwest of Hambry. According to Susan Delgado, they've been there for six centuries or more. Only nineteen of two hundred gantries still pump, and no one has the need or the understanding to repair them. Those that do pump squeak and squeal and can't be stopped. The oil simply runs back down into the wells—or so people think. Most people also believe that the oil is too thick to be useful and that the pipelines are dry. The locals get earth-gas from it to run a few devices like the refrigerator in the Town Hall. They've also been storing up the oil to send to John Farson so he can power the Old People's machinery in his war against the Affiliation. Roland, Cuthbert and Alain destroy the field, thus cutting off Farson's source of oil.

CLEAN SEA, THE (1, 4, 5, M)
A sea east of Hambry. The local fishermen work there. To the north it is known as the Salt.

CÖOS HILL (4)

A ragged hill five mile east of Hambry. Home to the witch Rhea, who is often called Rhea of the Cöos. Her hut is below the brow of the last hill to protect it from the wind. A path leads to the top, providing a good view northwest to the Bad Grass, the desert, Hanging Rock, and Eyebolt Canyon, the latter some ten miles away.

CORBETT HALL (7)

The dormitory in Algul Siento where Dinky Earnshaw and Sheemie Ruiz live on the third floor. After the battle, Eddie is taken to the first-floor proctor's suite.

CRADLE OF LUD, THE (3, 4, 5, 7)

Lud's train station, operated by North Central Positronics and home to Blaine and Patricia the monorails. It stands in the center of a large square at the end of the Street of the Turtle. Its simple square construction of white stone blocks and overhanging roof supported by pillars reminds Eddie of the Roman Colosseum and Susannah of the Parthenon. Unlike the rest of Lud, the station is free of graffiti and cleaned of the pervasive dust by nozzles hidden in the eaves. The top of the building is ringed by sculptures of the Guardians of the Beams in pairs. Dragonlike gargoyles occupy the corners of the roof. A sixty-foot statue made of gold depicting Arthur Eld stands atop the building. He has a revolver in one hand and an olive branch in the other.

CRAVEN'S UNDERTAKING PARLOR (4)

Mejis's funeral parlor.

CRESSIA (4, 4.5, M)

A western Barony. Indrie is the Barony Seat. One of the places failed gunslingers went after being sent west. Farson burned Indrie to the ground and slaughtered hundreds of its residents, including the governor, the mayor of Indrie and the high sheriff. Marten was with him at the time. Eldred Jonas, who was sent west, is familiar with local sayings from Cressia.

DAMLI HOUSE (7)

A graceful, rambling Queen Anne–style house next to the Breaker dorms at the far end of the Mall from Pleasantville in Algul Siento. Also known as

Heartbreak House or Hotel. Many of the *can toi* live here. The Breakers work in the Study in the middle of Damli. The telemetry equipment in the basement keeps track of the condition of the Beams and detects unauthorized psychic activity among the Breakers. Not all of the equipment works, and a lot of it either has no use or its function isn't understood. The staff has a place on the third floor where they can be refreshed by the euphoria of the good mind created by the Breakers when they work. The infirmary is in the west wing of the third floor. It burns during the battle of Algul Siento.

DARK TOWER, THE (THROUGHOUT)

Also known as the Great Portal, the Thirteenth Gate, and Can Calyx, the Hall of Resumption. The central linchpin that holds all of existence, all of time and all size together. It *is* existence, according to Roland. The world's great mystery and last awful riddle. It exists in all worlds, but it may not be accessible from them all.

It is the great secret the gunslingers of Gilead keep, holding them together as *ka-tet* as the world declines. Roland first learns that it is more than a myth from a vision in the pink glass from the Wizard's Rainbow. The Tower is weakening like a body afflicted with cancer. If it falls, everything will be swept away. There will be chaos beyond imagining. While it weakens, the rose holds everything together. Roland's hope is not to prevent the fall of the Tower—that is inevitable because of the natural decline of magic—but to slow down its decline, which is being accelerated by the Crimson King and his Breakers. Roland's true desire is to gain the Tower and climb to the top to confront whoever lives there. He wants to undo the bad things that have happened because of its decline—and because of the things and people he's sacrificed in pursuit of the Tower. Sheemie tells Roland he may find renewal or death—or perhaps both.

It appears to be a pillar of sooty gray-black stone, located in End-World in a field of roses. Two Great Roads intersect at its base. A path through the roses leads to nineteen steps at the entrance. The Tower tapers gracefully as it rises. Narrow, slitted windows march about it in a rising spiral. Standing at its base, Roland estimates that the Tower is no more than six hundred feet high. At the top is an oriel window made of glass the colors of the Wizard's Rainbow, with the black pane representing Black Thirteen at the center. The intersecting clouds that follow the Paths of the Beam flow from the tips of two steel posts that jut from the top of the Tower.

Balconies with waist-high scrolled wrought-iron railings encircle the Tower every two or three stories. The doors on these balconies are all closed and locked. The entrance is made of steel-banded ghostwood. In *siguls*, it says UNFOUND until Roland presents his guns. Then the word changes to FOUND. Roland realizes the Tower isn't made of stone at all—it is a living thing, Gan himself.

It emits a strong pulse composed of thousands of voices. The roses feed the Beams with their songs and the Beams feed them. The voices are singing the names of all the worlds. They stop when Roland steps inside.

The stone staircase is wide enough for just one person. There is a landing every nineteen steps, each representing a stage in Roland's life. The walls contain carvings of people he knew. In each room he finds a token from his life. Few of them are pleasant. After the room containing a charred stake and a carving of Susan Delgado, he stops looking.

The Tower is far taller on the inside than it appeared from the outside. Roland climbs hundreds of floors, maybe thousands, until he reaches the ghostwood door marked ROLAND, the only one that is closed, though it opens to his hand.

DASHERVILLE (3)
The fourth stop on Blaine the Mono's route from Lud.

DEBARIA (4, 4.5, M)
A busy railroad town on the edge of the alkali flats west of Gilead. From here, cattle are shipped south, east and north. Steven Deschain sends Roland and Jamie DeCurry here to investigate reports of skin-walkers. The high street is wide and paved, but it is crumbling. Sheriff Peavy thinks the town will die when the mines play out in a few years and what remains of the rail line turns to dust. Neighboring towns include Sallywood (south) and Little Debaria in the foothills. Home to Serenity, the retreat where Gabrielle Deschain stayed while Roland was in Mejis after her infidelity was revealed.

DEEP CRACKS (3, 4.5)
Places such as the abyss near Castle Discordia or the wasteland beyond Lud where monsters dwell. Ardelia Smack believes that Marten Broadcloak is one such monster.

DELAIN (L, 1, 7, M)
John Norman's hometown. One of the East'rd Baronies of In-World. It was sometimes known as Dragon's Lair, or Liar's Heaven. All tall tales were said to

originate there. Walter o'Dim was once Walter Padick of Delain. Roland encounters Dennis and Thomas from Delain chasing Flagg during his journeys.

Crossover to Other Works: King Roland rules Delain in *The Eyes of the Dragon.*

DELIGHTFUL VIEW (4.5)
The only hotel in Debaria. Sheriff Peavy doesn't recommend it.

DERVA (7)
The unknown destination for people from the Fedic Dogan after Susannah killed the people involved with Mordred's birth.

DESATOYA MOUNTAINS (L, M)
A mountain range Roland passes through before he reaches the Mohaine Desert. Eluria is a village in these mountains.

Crossover to Other Works: Desperation, Nevada, is also located in these mountains.

DESOY (4, M)
One of the places (along with Garlan) where Farson started out as a harrier and a stage-robber.

DEVAR-TETE WHYE (5, 6)
The Little Whye—the eastern branch of the Whye River that runs south past Calla Bryn Sturgis to the South Seas and separates the Borderlands from Thunderclap.

DEVAR-TOI
See Algul Siento.

DEVIL'S ARSE (6, 7)
A name for the monster-filled chasm outside Fedic, next to Castle Discordia. Some people thought the Red Death arose from here.

DISCORDIA (DIS) (4, 6, 7)
Though the word has several meanings, including the soup of creation, it is also applied to the noxious wilderness that lies beyond the Castle on the Abyss, which is also called Castle Discordia. According to rumors, the orange ball

from the Wizard's Rainbow is supposedly located in Dis. Roland believes it corresponds to the White Mountains in the real world.

DOGAN (4.5, 5, 6, 7, M)

A generic term for any of North Central Positronics' many labs and outposts. The Dogan near Calla Bryn Sturgis (Jake's Dogan) is a medium-security monitoring station that reports to Algul Siento. The North Forest Kinnock Dogan is a low-security outpost at the gateway to Out-World. It has a transmission tower attached to it, but the Dogan is offline due to the presence of magic. The Fedic Dogan (the Dogan of Dogans) was a maximum-security Experimental Station where the essential essence was taken from the brains of the children kidnapped from the Callas. Mia was made mortal in this Dogan, and Mordred Deschain was born here. Susannah creates a mental Dogan based on Jake's Dogan to control her pregnancy and Jake creates one so Oy can operate his body when they are trying to get past the mind-trap under the Dixie Pig. In the Marvel comics, Sheemie gets his powers from a Dogan he discovered while following Roland back to Gilead.

DOORWAY CAVE (5, 6, 7)

A cave in the hills three hours north of Calla Bryn Sturgis and an hour north of Manni Redpath. Known as the Cave of Voices until Father Callahan arrives with the Unfound Door and Black Thirteen. Called Kra Kammen by the Manni—the House of Ghosts. The entrance is a ragged dark hole nine feet high and five feet wide. A noxious breeze comes out of the entrance carrying the voices of the dead. The Unfound Door stands in the shadows and, eight or nine feet beyond it, the cave floor slopes down at a steep angle until it disappears into a chasm. Henchick believes that the beamquake or the loss of Black Thirteen drove the voices in the cave insane. The freed Breakers hope to use this doorway to return to their world.

DOWNLAND BARONIES (3)

Some of the Greater Kingdoms of the Western Earth. They were overrun by riot and civil war after Roland became a gunslinger. He passed through them on his way from Gilead to the Western Sea.

DRAGON'S GRAVE (3)

A bottomless crack in the ground that gives off a great burst of steam every thirty or forty days.

EAST DOWNE (6)

One of the places Roland visits during his traveling years, where he encountered the walking waters.

EAST ROAD (5, 6, 7)

The road leading east of Calla Bryn Sturgis until it turns north and follows Devar-Tete Whye. This is where Jamie Jaffords and his friends killed one of the Wolves and where Roland and his followers faced down the Wolves.

EASTERN PLAIN (5)

The prairies that run between the forest and the River Whye.

EAST'RD BARONY (7)

Delain.

ELURIA (L, 6, M)

A little western town in the Desatoya Mountains. It has a gate and pink adobe walls that extend twenty feet on either side of the road and then stop. It has a town square, an inn, two saloons, a mercantile, a smithy, a sheriff's office, a gathering hall and a church with accompanying manse.

EMPATHICA (7)

A snow-covered region between Le Casse Roi Russe and the Dark Tower. The territory magnifies sensitivity to emotions and feelings. Roland and Susannah set up Hide Camp here to turn the carcasses of the deer they kill into food, clothing and medicine. It takes them more than a month to cross the snowfields on foot and snowshoes.

ENDLESS FOREST, THE (4.5)

An unexplored wilderness far north of New Canaan also known as the Great Woods. Filled with ironwood trees, strange and dangerous plants and animals, weird marshes and the often-deadly leavings of the Old People. Subject to starkblasts once or twice a year. Bonfires of dragons are said to live there, and some people believe Maerlyn has a magic home where time stands still in the forest.

END-WORLD (L, 1, 3, 4, 5, 6, 7, M)

A region of Roland's world. According to Blaine, it begins in Topeka. The Dark Tower is located at the very end of End-World. Sylvia Pittston claims that beyond it is burning darkness. Location of Thunderclap, Castle Discordia and Fedic.

EYEBOLT CANYON (4, 5, 7, M)

A short box canyon northwest of Mejis (four wheels north of Hanging Rock) that has been taken over by a thinny. It resembles a chimney lying on its side that has broken and has a crooked piece in the middle. The thinny occupies the section beyond the crook. The sides are too steep to climb except for in one spot where a groove runs up the wall with enough jutting spurs to provide handholds. The mouth of the canyon is choked with bushes that are burned each fall to silence the thinny. Roland, Alain and Cuthbert lead Latigo's forces into the canyon, set the brush on fire and let the thinny devour them.

FAGONARD (4.5)

The great swamp that interrupts the Endless Forest for many leagues, a place more liquid than solid. The men who cut ironwood won't venture into it. Home to a tribe of mutants who hile Tim Ross as a gunslinger and a dragon. The starkblast laid waste to the swamp, the tribesmen and the dragon alike.

FALLS OF HOUNDS, THE (3, 4)

The third stop on Blaine the Mono's route from Lud. The falls, which put Niagara to shame, are part of a huge boiling river that plunges off the mountains. Jutting from the center of the falls below the point where the river goes over the edge are two enormous stone protrusions that were either carved or eroded to look like the heads of snarling dogs. Power from the Beam is stored in these dogs. The Great Old Ones may have carved them. Blaine uses them to recharge during his journey.

FEDERAL OUTPOST 19 (7)

Also known as the Federal. A North Central Positronics outpost located on Tower Road at the edge of the White Lands of Empathica, one hundred and twenty wheels from the Dark Tower. Stuttering Bill's base of operations. Travel beyond the Federal is forbidden. The common room contains more than three dozen TV screens, some of which still operate. The one that used to show the Dark Tower went to static a few months before Roland got there. The cameras that once showed pictures from satellites are also offline.

FEDIC (6, 7)

A ghost town that sits between the inner keep of Castle Discordia and its outer walls, beyond which lies the abyss. The town has been dead for a thousand years. The Red Death killed everyone who once lived there. It consists of a single street that ends at Arc 16 Experimental Station, where the Wolves brought the children of the Callas. Mia brings Susannah here on todash trips so they can palaver. Roland and Susannah spend the night here before continuing on the Path of the Beam toward the Badlands. Among its businesses are the Gin-Puppy Saloon, the Gaiety Bar and Grill, the Fedic Millinery & Ladies' Wear, Fedic Hotel and Fedic Station, where Patricia the Mono once stopped.

FEDIC HOTEL (7)

Next door to the Gin-Puppy Saloon in Fedic. Roland and Susannah spent the night here before looking for the passage beneath Castle Discordia that took them to the Badlands.

FEDIC STATION (6, 7)

The train station in Fedic. When Mia arrived in Fedic, the trains, including Patricia the Mono, still came, though on no fixed schedule. With the arrival of the plague, everyone left Fedic via this station. The last stop for the Spirit of Topeka.

FEVERAL HALL (7)

The dormitory directly behind Damli House at Algul Siento. One of the places set on fire as a distraction before the battle begins.

FIFTH AVENUE (3)

Eddie's name for a major thoroughfare in Lud.

FOREST O'BARONY (1, M)

A forest near Gilead. The rather ordinary wood for the gallows at Gallows Hill came from there.

FOREST TREES (4)

A drinking establishment in Pass o' the River near Hambry that had a female bartender.

GALLOWS HILL (1, M)
Location of Gilead's executions. On the Taunton Road. Cuthbert and Roland watched Hax's hanging here.

GARLAN (1, 2, 3, 4, 4.5, 6, 7, M)
A city or kingdom or Barony far west of Gilead. At times, Roland believes it to be mythical. The Great Featherex and dragons lived there. The people of River Crossing say that some of the people there had brown skin. The civil war that ultimately reached Lud supposedly began there. It's one of the places where John Farson started out as a harrier and a stage-robber. A prostitute at the Travellers' Rest in Hambry considered herself "exiled royalty from distant Garlan." Eldred Jonas received the whip scars on his back here after being exiled from Gilead. Also the source of the poison on the knife that Gabrielle Deschain was supposed to use to kill her husband. The Covenant Man's silver bowl was a relic of Garlan, where he was known as Walter Hodji. Roland's grandfather Alaric once went there to slay a dragon, but the last one in that part of the world had already been killed by a king, who was later murdered.

GILEAD (L, 1, 3, 4, 4.5, 5, 6, 7, M)
The walled city that is the center of the Affiliation, the Barony seat of New Canaan and Roland's hometown, established long ago by Arthur Eld. By the time Roland forms his last *ka-tet*, Gilead has been dust in the wind for a thousand years. The name was inspired by the Bible reference to the balm of Gilead.

GIN-PUPPY [PUPPIE] SALOON (7)
Saloon next door to the Fedic Hotel. Mia and Susannah sit out front while Mia tells about the deal she struck with Walter. Susannah meets Roland here after he returns from New York.

GINGERBREAD HOUSE, THE (7)
A place that exists in a fistula outside of time and reality, created by Sheemie Ruiz and Dinky Earnshaw and inspired by *Hansel and Gretel*. Ted Brautigan, Sheemie and Dinky go here to conspire against Algul Siento. Ted needs a place where he doesn't have to keep his guard up against the *can toi* all the time. For a while, it had a second floor, but Sheemie forgot about it so it

disappeared. Ted thinks of it as a balcony on the Tower. When they go there, they are outside of—but still attached to—the Tower. It's real enough to leave candy stains on people's clothes.

GITTY'S SALOON (4.5)

Tree's drinking establishment, which Bern Kells likes to frequent. The Covenant Man's first stop in town.

GLENCOVE (4)

A town in Tavares, up the coast from Hambry.

GLORIA (5)

A garnet mine one mile from the Cave of Voices north of Calla Bryn Sturgis where Roland claimed he was planning to hide the twins on the day the Wolves came.

GOODVIEW (4.5)

Jack Ross's home in Tree Village.

GOOK (4.5)

The deserted village where Roland and his *ka-tet* take cover from the starkblast. According to Roland, the word means "a deep well." After the starkblast, nothing is left standing except the stone meeting hall.

GRAND CRESCENT (5)

Also known as the Rim and the Arc of the Callas. A borderland region between Mid-World and Thunderclap where roughly seventy towns run in a gentle arc along a six-thousand-mile stretch of the River Whye all the way to the South Seas. See also Callas.

GRANITE CITY (3)

Home to North Central Positronics, Ltd. In the Northeast Corridor, according to a tag found on Shardik.

GREAT CANYON (4.5)

An enormous chasm, at least a hundred wheels across, next to the North Forest Kinnock Dogan, located in Bend Quadrant in the Endless Forest.

GREAT HALL OF GILEAD (1, 3, 4, 7, M)

Also known as the Hall of the Grandfathers or the West'rd Hall. Normally reserved for the upper class and functions of state, it is opened to commoners for Fair-Days Riddling competitions. It still has a few working filament lights in its five chandeliers. The Sowing Night Cotillion (the Commala or the Dance of Easterling) is held there once a year. As a boy, Roland and his friends hid in a balcony and spied on the Cotillion, where he first observed the unusual relationship between Marten and his mother. The courtyard behind the Great Hall (on the eastern side) is the traditional place of proving for gunslingers.

GREAT HOUSE (L)

The main residence building in Gilead. As boys, Roland and Cuthbert made early-morning begging expeditions to the kitchens there.

GREAT ROAD (3, 4, 5, M)

The Mid-World equivalent of an interstate highway. One follows the Path of the Beam into Lud. Another runs between Gilead and Mejis.

GREAT WEST WOODS (3)

The ancient forest east of the Western Sea. The Great Old Ones once lived there, as did Shardik, the Guardian of the Portal of the Bear.

GREAT WOODS (4.5)

The ancient forest north of New Canaan. See also Endless Forest.

GREEN HEART (4)

Hambry's main park fifty yards up Hill Street from the jail and the Town Gathering Hall. Roland thinks it's the most pleasant place in Hambry. It has quaint paths, umbrella-shaded tables, a grassy dancing pavilion and a menagerie. Midway booths and a pony train are set up there for the Fair-Days. Susan and Roland sometimes left notes for each other behind a stone in the rock wall between the pavilion and the menagerie.

HALL OF THE GRANDFATHERS

See Great Hall of Gilead.

HAMBRY (4, M)
The capital of the Barony of Mejis, over five hundred miles east of Gilead along the Great Road.

HANGING ROCK (4, M)
A jutting upthrust of rock that looks like a finger bent at the first knuckle, located two miles south of Eyebolt Canyon. It has a spring at its base, the only one in the Hambry area. It's the only real geographic feature of the flatlands that run six miles beyond the Drop and the Bad Grass. This is supposed to be the rendezvous point for the Big Coffin Hunters and Latigo. Latigo brings the oil tankers here after they're moved from Citgo, which makes them easy targets for Roland, Cuthbert and Alain.

HATTIGAN'S (4)
One of six barrooms in Ritzy.

HEMPHILL (4)
A rural village forty wheels west of Gilead. Roland, in his guise as Will Dearborn, says that's where he's from when he's in Mejis.

HENDRICKSON (1, M)
An In-World town. Minions of John Farson killed livestock there.

HIDE CAMP (7)
The camp where Susannah and Roland tan the hides of the deer they kill in Empathica.

HIGH PURE (4.5)
The foothills north of Debaria.

HOOKEY'S STABLES AND FANCY LIVERY (4)
The business in Hambry owned by Brian Hookey. He has a forge behind the hostelry where he makes horseshoes. The fact that the business is in such good repair makes Susan Delgado suspicious of Hookey's allegiances.

IL BOSQUE (4)
A forest west of Mejis.

INDRIE (4, M)

Capital of the western Barony of Cressia. John Farson burned Indrie to the ground and slaughtered hundreds of its residents, including the governor of Cressia, the mayor of Indrie and the high sheriff, whose heads ended up on the wall guarding the town's entrance.

IN-WORLD (1, 3, 4, 4.5, 5, 6, 7, M)

Also known as the Inner Baronies and the Great World. Roland considers New Canaan and Gilead to be the "most inner" of the Inner Baronies.

IRONWOOD TRAIL (4.5)

A narrow road that extends from Tree Road a short way into the Endless Forest, used by lumbermen who hew the great ironwood trees. Anyone foolish enough to wander off this road into the forest would be quickly lost in a maze of trees or killed by the dangerous creatures that live within.

JERICHO HILL (1, 4.5, 5, 6, 7, M)

The site of the final battle between the survivors of Gilead and the remnants of John Farson's army, blue-faced barbarians led by General Grissom, five hundred miles north of Mejis. At the base of the hill is a sloping field filled with statues of gray-black stone faces. To the east is the great body of water called the Salt, which farther to the south becomes the Clean Sea.

JIMTOWN (3)

A city forty wheels from River Crossing.

KAMBERO (L)

A western village.

KASHMIN [KASHAMIN] (3, 4)

A Barony known for producing fine Persian-like rugs. There's one on the floor of Gabrielle Deschain's quarters in Gilead.

KING'S TOWN (1, M)

A place Roland visited during the early days of his quest for the man in black. He left a girl there. In the Marvel comics it's called Kingstown.

KUNA (4.5)

Location of oil fields that Roland knew of from pictures in a book as a boy.

LAKE CAWN (4.5)

Site of a great battle where Tim Ross received the name Tim Stoutheart.

LAKE SARONI (4)

A resort in the northern part of New Canaan with sandy beaches. Roland went there on vacation with his parents when he was very small, during happier times.

LEXINGWORTH (L)

A city near Eluria where convicted felons were taken to hang.

LITTLE DEBARIA (4.5)

A mining village in the foothills north of Debaria.

LOW PURE (4.5)

The foothill meadows north of Debaria below the salt houses.

LUD (3, 4, 4.5, 5, 6, 7)

A great city located at the edge of the kingdom known as Mid-World on the Send River. Until the *ka-tet* reaches it, Roland believed it was mythic. It dates back to the days of the Great Old Ones, though much of the machinery has failed and no one knows how to operate anything that still works. The green glass from the Wizard's Rainbow was supposed to be located here.

Four or five generations earlier, it was heavily populated and reasonably civilized. The city dwellers were artisans and manufacturers and conducted brisk trade in the region. Bix, the ferry operator at the River Whye, remembers Lud as a marvelous city. Crumbling and growing strange, but still marvelous.

A great civil war that erupted in the west centuries earlier spread into Mid-World. Trade faltered and travel became dangerous, so Lud turned itself into the last fortress-refuge of the latter world. Communications with the city ceased more than a century earlier. A war broke out between harriers—called Grays because they were older—and the people of Lud, who came to be known as Pubes. The residents used the weapons of the Great Old Ones to keep the harriers at bay, and the best and the brightest and people with usable skills from the region snuck past the outlaws to take up residence in the city. Every large park was turned into a garden to feed the city. A massive army of Grays led by David Quick attacked the city ninety years ago via a pontoon bridge. The descendants of these combatants continue to fight. Blaine the Mono poisons the remnants of both armies before leaving for Topeka. In America, it corresponds geographically to St. Louis but visually to New York City.

Crossovers to Other Works: Lud is mention by Dorcas in *Rose Madder*. She tells Rosie McClendon that she has seen bodies on fire and heads impaled on poles along the city's streets. In the coda to *Song of Susannah*, Stephen King ponders writing the novel and wonders whether it is Mid-World that Rosie falls into when she goes through the painting.

LUDWEG (7)
The city or town north of Lud that Jochabim comes from.

MALL, THE (7)
The park in the middle of Algul Siento.

MAYOR'S HOUSE
See Seafront.

MEJIS (L, 1, 4, 4.5, 5, 6, 7, M)
A Barony more than five hundred miles east of Gilead, with the Clean Sea on one side and a desert on the other. Its capital is Hambry. The two dominant industries here are fishing and horse breeding, but it is also the site of oil fields long thought to be dormant. When he was fourteen, Roland was sent here by his father to keep him out of harm's way. Instead, he discovers that most of the big men in town are working for John Farson. He meets and falls in love with Susan Delgado, encounters the witch Rhea and discovers a part of Maerlyn's Rainbow. The Barony has a Mexican flavor, both in the family names and in some of their language. King identifies it as an analog of Mexico in the coda of *Song of Susannah*.

MID-WORLD (L, 1, 3, 4, 4.5, 5, 6, 7, M)
Roland believed this was a fantasyland, but eventually reaches its borders. Following the Path of the Beam, it is defined by Lud on one end and Topeka

on the other. Roland calls it one of the large kingdoms that dominated his world a long time ago, a place of hope, knowledge and light. Eventually, the term becomes synonymous with all of Roland's universe, though technically it refers to only a specific region. Once the *ka-tet* reaches the Borderlands and Calla Bryn Sturgis, Roland believes he has left Mid-World.

MILLBANK (4)
A place to eat in Hambry.

MOHAINE DESERT (1, 4.5, 7, M)
A desert located a thousand wheels west of Gilead. The Western Line of the railroad used to run this far, but in the days before the fall of Gilead, the tracks were either destroyed by nature or taken over by outlaws.

NA'AR (1, 4.5, 5, 7, M)
The Mid-World equivalent to hell. Also known as coffah.

NEW CANAAN (1, 4, 4.5, M)
Gilead's Barony, the innermost of the Inner Baronies.

NIS (4.5, 5, 7)
The land of sleep and dreams. Sometimes the word also refers to hell. It's also the name of the Crimson King's horse.

NORTH FIELD (5)
The place in Gilead where the gunslingers in training practiced archery.

NORTH FOREST KINNOCK (4.5)
Also known as the Northern Aerie. Once known as the Gateway of Out-World. Location of the low-security North Forest Kinnock Dogan, Outpost 9, in Bend Quadrant of the Endless Forest, on the edge of the Great Canyon. The Dogan is a round, metal-roofed building next to a tall tower made of metal girders with a red light blinking at the top. Though it has existed for a thousand years, according to Daria, the Dogan is offline, possibly because of magic. A starkblast destroys the tower but leaves the Dogan untouched.

NORTHERN AERIE (4.5)
See North Forest Kinnock.

NORTH'RD BARONY (4, 4.5)

The section of Mid-World far north of New Canaan. Tree is located at the farthest edge of this Barony. It's thousands of miles from Mejis, according to Susan Delgado. Said to be in flames because of John Farson.

OAKLEY (4)

One of the towns where Clay Reynolds and his gang tried to rob a bank a year after Roland left Hambry. Six of the ten people in his gang were shot dead by the sheriff and his deputies. Coral Thorin was among those killed. Clay Reynolds and the other three survivors were hanged.

ODD LANE (ODD'S LANE) (7)

A lane in Westring that intersects with Tower Road. Joe Collins lives about three-quarters of the way down the northeastern arm of the lane.

OLD QUARTER (4)

Part of Gilead where vendors sold their wares.

ONNIE'S FORD (4)

The rural farming community where Maria Tomas, the maid at Mayor House in Mejis, came from.

OUR LADY OF SERENITY (5)

Father Callahan's church in Calla Bryn Sturgis. A low, simple log building with a cross over the door. It has narrow windows of plain glass and an iron-wood cross at the front of the sanctuary, which consists of pews on either side of the main aisle. It has never been consecrated.

OUTER ARC (L, 4)

Also known as the Outers, the Outer Baronies and the Outer Crescent. The group of eastern Baronies that includes Mejis. Said to be less sophisticated than the Inner Arc, which includes Gilead. In addition to horse breeding and fishing, they were also the source of coffee for the Inner Baronies.

OUT-WORLD (3, 4, 4.5, 5, 7)

Territories far west of Gilead, domain of John Farson and other outlaws. Shardik originated from there. Sometimes used to refer to any Barony, like Mejis, that isn't part of the Inner Baronies.

PASS O' THE RIVER (4)
A town near Hambry.

PENNILTON (4)
A town in New Canaan. Alain Johns, in his guise as Richard Stockworth, says he's from there.

PLAZA OF THE CRADLE (3)
A large city square in Lud. The Cradle of Lud, home to Blaine the Mono, sits in the middle.

PLEASANTVILLE (7)
The town built at the south end of Algul Siento for the benefit of the Breakers. It has one main street containing the Gem Theater, Henry Graham's Drug Store & Soda Fountain, Clover Tavern, Pleasantville Bake Shoppe, Pleasantville Book Store, Pleasantville Shoes, Gay Paree Fashions, Hair Today, and other shops. Pleasantville Hardware Company is a front for Fire-Response Team Bravo.

PORLA (3)
A land beyond Garlan. The great civil war that reached Lud may have started here.

PORTAL OF THE BEAR (3, 6)
The beginning point for the Beam of the Bear. Home of Shardik. Located in the Great West Woods. Brooklyn is its analog in Eddie Dean's world.

PRICETOWN (1, 3, M)
A town northwest of Tull. Roland bought a mule here while pursuing the man in black.

RACEY'S CAFÉ (4.5)
The better of two places to eat in Debaria.

REDBIRD TWO (5)
A garnet mine at the end of a spur from the arroyo that leads to the Gloria Mine outside Calla Bryn Sturgis.

REDPATH (5)

The village two hours north of Calla Bryn Sturgis where Henchick's Manni clan lives. Known as Calla Redpath and Calla Manni. Former home of Margaret Eisenhart.

RILEA (3, 4)

The second stop on Blaine the Mono's route from Lud.

RIMROCKS (5, M)

The site of one of the final battles before the fall of Gilead. Alain Johns reported that DeMullet's column was ambushed and slaughtered there.

RITZY (4, M)

A miserable little mining village with one unpaved street, located on the eastern slope of the Vi Castis Mountains four hundred miles west of Mejis. It looks like an ugly lowered head between a pair of huge shrugged shoulders—the foothills. It has a mercantile store and a company store, a combined jailhouse and gathering hall and six bars. Roy Depape found out that the Affiliation Brats were possibly apprentice gunslingers here. It's also where Eldred Jonas planned to rendezvous with Coral Thorin while they were taking the oil tankers west.

RIVER BARONY (3)

A Barony encompassing the region around the Send River, which includes Lud and River Crossing.

RIVER CROSSING (3, 4, 5, 6, 7)

A town 160 wheels northwest of Lud and 40 wheels from Jimtown on the Great Road, and the last point of trade on the river before the great city. Nominally a part of the River Barony. Except on the outskirts, the town seems dusty but intact. A dozen rickety buildings stand on either side of the road. Led by Aunt Talitha Unwin, its residents are all ancient. It used to take six days to reach Lud by road from there, or three days by river.

RIVER ROAD (3)

A section of the Great Road that leads from Jimtown past River Crossing to Lud.

ROCKING B RANCH (4)
Ranch owned by Francis Lengyll in Mejis. It has a working Honda generator.

ROCKING B RANCH (5)
Ranch on the East Road in Calla Bryn Sturgis owned by Vaughn Eisenhart. Benjamin Slightman is the foreman.

ROCKING H RANCH (4)
A small ranch south of Hambry owned by Laslo Rimer. It has oxen.

ROTUNDA (7)
The part of the Fedic Dogan that contains multiple floors ringed with doorways to many different places and times. Nigel says that five hundred and ninety-five of these doors are currently operational. The place reminds Susannah both of the Cradle of Lud and Grand Central Station. The rotunda features prominently in the Discordia interactive game.

SALLYWOOD (4.5)
The southern limit of the railroad's run from Debaria.

SALT, THE (5, M)
A large body of water east of Jericho Hill. The southern part is known as the Clean Sea.

SALT ROCKS (4.5)
The foothills north of Debaria.

SALT VILLAGE (4.5)
The makeshift community south of Little Debaria where the salt miners live.

SEA ROAD (4, M)
Also known as the Seacoast Road. It runs north from Mejis. Olive Thorin takes Susan Delgado on this road after she frees her because she is sure their pursuers will assume they went west toward Gilead.

SEAFRONT (4)

Also known as Mayor's House. A sprawling, many-winged adobe hacienda, the residence of the mayor of Hambry. An adobe arch with the words "Come in Peace" forms the entrance to the estate and gives way to a cobblestone courtyard. Its reception hall is circular, with paneled walls decorated with bad paintings of previous mayors.

SEND BRIDGE (3)

The bridge that spans the Send River west of Lud. It reminds the New Yorkers of the George Washington Bridge. It is at least three-quarters of a mile long and may be a thousand years old. The bridge is supported by two four-hundred-foot cable towers at the center. The distance between the deck and the water is at least three hundred feet at the center. The steel used for the bridge came from the LaMerk Foundry.

SEND RIVER (3, 4, 5)

A major river that flows past Lud. It is approximately two miles wide. Lady Oriza's castle, Waydon, was on the river.

SEND RIVER NUCLEAR PLANT (3)

A power station on the banks of the Send River in Lud.

SERENITY (4.5)

The retreat run by Prioress Everlynne, ten or twelve wheels from Debaria, where Gabrielle Deschain cloistered herself while Roland was in Mejis. It is a white hacienda the size of a Barony estate. The walls are topped with broken glass. Behind it is a grape arbor, a garden and a narrow creek. Steven Deschain thinks the place is run by black ammies (lesbians). In the Marvel series, the retreat is called Our Lady of the Rose and the sisters worship Gan, the god of the Dark Tower.

SEVEN MILE FARM (5)

Wayne Overholser's ranch in Calla Bryn Sturgis.

SEVEN MILE ORCHARD (4)

A fruit orchard north of Hambry.

SHAPLEIGH HOUSE (4)

Pimli Prentiss's home at the Pleasantville end of the Mall in Algul Siento. A tidy Cape Cod painted electric blue with white trim, called Shit House by the Breakers. It has gingerbread scalloping around the eaves.

SHAVÉD MOUNTAINS (4, M)

Mountains northwest of Gilead where Farson plans to ambush the Affiliation using the machinery of the Great Old Ones.

SILK RANCH ROAD (4, 5)

A road that merges with the Great Road east of Hambry. Rhea brought Susan Delgado back to town on this road after her failed escape attempt with Olive Thorin.

SON OF A BITCH (5)

The northern field on Tian Jaffords's farm, a thankless tract that grows rocks, blisters and busted hopes. For generations, the family has been trying to find something of value that will grow here other than devil-weed. It sits on "loose ground" and consists mostly of holes and rocks, plus one cave that puffs out fetid air. It's too dangerous for a mule to plow, so Tian uses his roont sister Tia instead.

SOUTH ISLANDS (1)

A nearly forgotten region of Mid-World. Hax, the west kitchen's cook, came from there.

SOUTH PLAINS (7)

The part of Mid-World that Chevin of Chayven once called home.

SOUTH SEAS (5)

The body of water at the end of the River Whye.

SOUTHWEST EDGE (4)

The region of Mid-World that John Farson is said to control when Roland is in Mejis.

STAPE BROOK (4.5)

A creek created by a clear spring between the Ross cottage and barn in Tree Village.

STONE'S WARP (7)

The deserted town where Joe Collins claims he woke up after being beaten in Cleveland. It looks like the set of a Western movie after all the actors have gone home.

STREET OF THE TURTLE (3)

One of Lud's main roads. A large stone turtle guards its entrance and it ends at the Cradle of Lud.

STUDY, THE (7)

A long, high room in the center of Damli House in Algul Siento where the Breakers go, thirty-three at a time, to do their work. They are forbidden from using their psychic abilities outside this room. It is oak-paneled and rises three stories to a glass roof that lets the artificial sunlight in. The Breakers, who are mostly misfits and loners, feel in touch with themselves here.

TAUNTON (1, M)

A town in In-World. Hax is supposed to send poisoned meat there at the behest of John Farson. Gallows Hill is on the Taunton Road outside of Gilead.

TAVARES (4, 4.5)

A town forty wheels east of Tree Village and up the coast from Mejis. Nell Ross owns a rocking chair from Tavares. The constable of Tree has a woman here and often retreats to that town when the Covenant Man comes to collect taxes. Tim Ross joined a group of gunslingers on their way to Tavares to raise a posse. There was once a female bartender in Tavares, but she died of the pox.

TEJUAS (L, M)

An unincorporated township two hundred miles west of Eluria.

TEPACHI (4)

A town in the vicinity of Mejis.

THOUGHTFUL HOUSE (L, M)

A cave in the hillside near Eluria where the Little Sisters have to go to meditate when Big Sister decides one of them has been bad. Described as "a small black opening low on the scarp."

THUNDERCLAP (4, 4.5, 5, 6, 7)

Located one hundred wheels east of the Devar-Tete Whye River from the Callas. Devar-Toi, the prison for the Breakers, is located here. Dubbed the Land of Darkness. The sun never shines, so artificial light is beamed in to simulate daylight. The night is absolute—no moon, no stars. The Crimson King supposedly caused the darkness. It is said to be a land of vampires, boggarts, and taheen, where clocks run backward and the graveyards vomit out their dead. The land is dead and the air was poisoned either by the Crimson King on a lark or by the leavings of the Great Old Ones. It causes skin conditions ranging from acne to cancer for anyone unfortunate enough to live here. Open wounds are easily infected and often fatal. Roland first hears about Thunderclap via the grapefruit. Its *sigul* is a cloud with a lightning bolt.

THUNDERCLAP STATION (7)

A major train depot in the heart of Thunderclap, approximately six miles from Algul Siento. The central terminal looks to be at least half a mile long. Tracks lead in every direction. The Wolves get here via a one-way door from the Fedic Dogan to launch their raids on the Callas. When they return, they take a train to Fedic Station.

TOOK'S GENERAL STORE (5, 6, 7)

The general store that takes up half the main street in Calla Bryn Sturgis, owned and operated by Eben Took. A wooden building so busy that it merits eight long hitching rails. Two dozen rocking chairs line the porch. The Wolves burned the store the year Red Molly killed one of them because the owner hid some of the town's children in the storage bin out back. The Tooks intend to make sure that never happens again. Its twin is the store in Stoneham, Maine, though the latter is quite a bit smaller until Chip McAvoy rebuilds after his own fire.

TOOK'S OUTLAND MERCANTILE (4.5)

An abandoned store the *ka-tet* explores before reaching the Whye River.

TOWER KEYSTONE (7)

The version of Mid-World where the Dark Tower is itself, not some other representation.

TOWER ROAD (7)

The Great Road that descends out of the White Lands of Empathica along the Path of the Beam to the Dark Tower. It emerges from the snow in the town of Westring. Stuttering Bill keeps it plowed as far as Federal Outpost 19. It was once paved, but has fallen into disrepair and is little more than ruts in some places. Close to the Tower, a broken-down stone wall lines the road. Roses grow along the side of the road and among the stones. Dead trees spell out "nineteen" or "chassit" with their branches. Speaking Rings, obelisks and castle ruins appear in the fields, along with herds of buffalo. Closer still, the road is lined with statues of men with bloodred paint on their faces. Five miles from the Tower, there is what appears to be a pyramid-shaped cairn that is actually made of steel. The road splits and makes a circle around the Tower's base, continuing on the far side. Though the Beam Roland follows ran southeast, by the time he reaches the Tower, directions have realigned, so it is actually true east. Another road runs at right angles to Tower Road, now in the north/south direction.

TOWN LOOKOUT (4)

A part of the Drop in Mejis that provides a fair view of Hambry, including the Delgado house.

TRAVELERS' REST (5)

A combination inn and eating house in Calla Bryn Sturgis.

TRAVELLERS' REST (4, 7, M)

The saloon and whorehouse on High Street in Hambry. It has rooms, but people come here mostly to eat, drink, listen to music, watch girls dance, consort with prostitutes and gamble. It is owned and operated by Coral Thorin, though her brother, Mayor Hart Thorin, has a major interest in it. Sheb, the piano player Roland encounters in Tull, plays the piano here, and Sheemie Ruiz works here.

TREE (4.5)

A village on the edge of the Endless Forest at the farthest edge of North'rd Barony. Cutting blossiewood and ironwood trees is a source of income for some, while others are farmers or work in the sawmill. The last town in the civilized country—which means it still paid taxes to Gilead. On or near the Beam of the Cat, Way of the Bird. Since Tim follows the Beam of the Lion, and Aslan lives in the far north, this implies that Tree and Gilead are north of the Dark Tower.

TREE SAWMILL (4.5)

The place where the blossiewood and ironwood were converted to lumber before being shipped to Gilead. Tim Ross is sent to work here after Bern Kells marries his mother. The starkblast blew it into Tree River. Nothing remained but the stone foundation.

TULL (1, 2, 3, 4, 5, 6, M)

A small town southeast of Pricetown, near the edge of the Mohaine Desert. Roland kills everyone in the town after the man in black sets a trap for him here. Among its residents were Sheb, whom Roland knew from Mejis, Nort the Weedeater, whom the man in black raised from the dead, and Allie, Roland's lover, briefly.

VI CASTIS MOUNTAINS (4)

Mountains four hundred miles west of Mejis. The town of Ritzy is located on the eastern slopes. There were once freehold gold, silver, diamond and copper mines in the mountains, but the Vi Castis Company now regulates them all. Roland, Alain and Cuthbert think that's where Farson will refine the oil from Citgo.

WAY STATION (1, 2, 3, 4, 5, 6, 7, M)

An inn with horse stables on the old coach line across the Mohaine Desert. Jake Chambers ends up here after he dies in Manhattan. Roland finds the jawbone of one of the Great Old Ones in its basement. Father Callahan awakens here after he commits suicide in Detroit in time to see Roland and Jake in the distance. LaMerk Industries manufactured its atomic water pump.

WAYDON (5)
Lady Oriza's castle on the River Send.

WAYPOINT NINE (4.5)
Daria's designation for a location in Fagonard Swamp.

WEST'RD BARONIES (4, 4.5)
The section of Mid-World far west of New Canaan. Thousands of miles from Mejis, according to Susan Delgado. Said to be in flames.

WESTERN DROP (4, 7)
Also called the Drop. A long slope of land that runs from Mejis toward the sea, with Bad Grass and the desert to its west. It is approximately thirty wheels by five wheels. The land is used mostly for the Barony horses and cows. Hambry's breeders own parcels of it. Pat Delgado's house is on the edge of the Drop.

WESTERN SEA (1, 2, 3, 4, 5, 6, 7)
Roland reaches the Western Sea after his palaver with Walter and proceeds up its coast, where he discovers a series of doorways that provide him with his *ka-tet*. Home to lobstrosities. Analogous to the Pacific Ocean in our world.

WESTRING (7)
The mostly abandoned town at the beginning of Tower Road where Joe Collins lives. Stuttering Bill keeps the road clear in the winter. It's less than a three-week walk from the Dark Tower.

WHITE LANDS OF EMPATHICA (7)
See Empathica.

WHYE (4.5, 5, 6, 7)
A river in the Borderlands, also known as the Big River. The river splits northwest of Calla Bryn Sturgis. The west branch is near Mid-World—Roland and his *ka-tet* cross it on a raft before the starkblast hits. The east branch is called Devar-Tete Whye, the Little Whye. It runs for thousands of miles south of Calla Bryn Sturgis to the South Seas. Since the river runs south, most of

the trade seen by the Callas comes from the north. It had a tendency to flood every half dozen years.

WIND (4)
A mudpen of a town fifty miles from Ritzy, where the Big Coffin Hunters got their coffin tattoos.

XAY RIVER (7, M)
A river Roland, Alain and Cuthbert cross on the way back to Gilead from Hambry. After they're across, Alain cuts the rope bridge to prevent anyone from following them.

THINGS
AFFILIATION OF BARONIES, THE (4, M)
A group of Baronies that are aligned with one another and pay homage to New Canaan. It has been "like mother's milk and father's sheltering hand" to the Baronies for many generations. However, it suffers from the same problems as any sprawling empire: people living the farthest from the center feel disenfranchised and grow resentful at having to contribute to its upkeep, especially since the railway no longer runs and communication is difficult. John Farson is the leader of the rebels who would see the Affiliation destroyed. The gunslingers of Steven Deschain's time are too obsessed with the Dark Tower to pay much attention to either Farson or the fact that the Affiliation is rotting from the inside.

AMOCO (1, 3)
A gasoline company that existed in Mid-World. A man built a cult around one of its pumps.

APON
See Old Star.

ASIMOV ROBOTS (7)
The generic name for the sentient robots built by North Central Positronics. Andy the Messenger Robot, Nigel the Domestic and Stuttering Bill are examples. Logic faults are common in these robots. The Old People compensated for this by setting up a stringent quarantine system, treating the glitches like diseases.

ASLAN (4.5)

The Lion Guardian of the Beam. He lives in the far north, in the land of endless snows.

AUNT TALITHA'S CROSS (3, 5, 7)

A silver cross at the end of a fine-link silver chain. Talitha Unwin wore it constantly for more than a hundred years. She gives it to Roland in River Crossing and asks him to lay it at the foot of the Dark Tower. Roland gives it to John Cullum to convey a message to Moses Carver. It records a secret about Odetta that only Carver and Eddie know. When Roland visits Tet Corporation, Moses Carver returns it to Roland with a message from Cullum. Roland lays the cross, along with his remaining gun, at the door of the Dark Tower.

BARONY (1, 3, 4, 4.5, 5, 6, 7, M)

A geopolitical or feudal unit in Mid-World equal to a state or province. Gilead was the capital of the New Canaan Barony.

BARONY CLASS (3, 4)

The equivalent of first class. Describes the accommodations in Blaine the Mono.

BEAMQUAKE (6, 7, M)

Analogous to an earthquake, but caused when one of the Beams holding up the Dark Tower snaps. Anything within several hundred miles of the affected Beam is destroyed. According to Roland, birds near the Beam would fall from the sky in flames. The *ka-tet* feels the Beam of the Eagle and Lion break the day after they defeat the Wolves in Calla Bryn Sturgis, and Roland experienced one after Gilead fell but before the battle at Jericho Hill.

BEAMS (3, 4, 4.5, 5, 6, 7, M)

Lines of power that support the Dark Tower and hold together space, size and time. The original Beams that arose out of the Prim were made of magic. The Great Old Ones replaced them with technology, thereby guaranteeing they would someday fail, especially after the Great Old Ones vanished from the world. The Beams have been flowing along the same paths for so many thousands of years that they leave a clear sign of their presence in the shape of the clouds, the direction needles on trees grow and the pattern of shadows on the ground.

At times, the Beams seem like living entities—the Voice of the Beam is the Voice of Gan. The Voice is what tells Stephen King the story he is writing. It can force people to witness something important to its preservation (*aven kal*). The Beams also communicate in the dreams of sensitive people like Sheemie Ruiz, where they appear as young boys.

The Breakers are toiling on behalf of the Crimson King to disrupt, bend and ultimately break these Beams, leading to the fall of the Tower and the collapse of all universes. The Beams were originally smooth and polished, but now they are pitted, cracked, lumpy and eroded. There were twelve Beams, each with an animal Guardian. One Beam broke when Gilead fell. The Breakers successfully broke the Beam of the Eagle and the Lion, causing a devastating beamquake. Roland follows the Beam of the Bear, whose Guardian is Shardik. When this Beam reaches the Tower, it turns into the Beam of the Turtle, whose Guardian is Maturin. Tim Ross's adventure takes him north along the Beam of the Lion, Aslan. (See Guardians of the Beam for a complete listing.)

The damage to the Beams isn't irreversible if caught in time. If the Breakers are stopped, the Beams will heal themselves and perhaps even regenerate the broken ones. What has moved on might return again.

BENDS O' THE RAINBOW
See Wizard's Glass.

BILL OF CIRCULATION (4.5)
Notice to leave town after being caught doing something illegal.

BILLY-BUMBLER (THROUGHOUT)
Also known as a throcken. A small animal that looks like a cross between a woodchuck and a raccoon with dachshund thrown in. Some have the power to imitate human speech. They were good for amusing children, keeping the rat population down or herding sheep. A good bumbler is supposed to be good luck. At one time they were tame and used to roam the Baronies. Not quite as faithful as a dog, historically. The wild ones are scavengers. Some people swear they can add. A Mid-World saying asks, "Do bumblers learn to speak backward?" equivalent to asking if a leopard can change its spots. They are particularly sensitive to starkblasts. When one is approaching, they face the storm with their snouts raised and, when the storm gets closer, turn in tight circles, as if chasing their tails. In regions where they are scarce, seeing one is considered good luck. They consider Grandfather-fleas ancient enemies and seem bred to kill them.

BITSY (4.5)

One of Jack Ross's female mules.

BLACK THIRTEEN (4, 5, 6, 7, M)

The most dangerous ball in the Wizard's Rainbow, the one that represents the Dark Tower. The most evil and terrible object from the days of Eld still remaining on the face of the Earth and the clearest sign of the powerful forces working against Roland's quest. Part of the Crimson King is trapped inside it forever, and insane. It is his ever-watching eye. Stephen King tells Roland it must be taken off the board and broken.

The box that holds it is made of the same ghostwood as the door at the base of the Tower. The bowling bag Jake finds in the vacant lot is made of a metallic material that provides some protection from its powers.

Steven Deschain's father told him it wasn't wise to talk about Thirteen because it might hear its name and roll your way. Walter gives it to Father Callahan in the Way Station, intending for it to be a trap for Roland in Calla Bryn Sturgis. Callahan stored it in his church, where it mostly slept and the simple faith of his parishioners soothed it. It sent Callahan todash twice, which is one of its powers—it may be a way to everywhere and everywhen. Like the rose, its hum conveys a sense of power, but it speaks of colossal emptiness and a malevolent emptiness.

Roland uses it to open the Unfound Door in the Doorway Cave. So long as the box is open, the door remains ajar. Someone needs to stand guard when anyone goes through the door because the box could close itself, trapping the person on the other side. However, this guard is susceptible to its malign powers as they wait. It works on both body (Roland's arthritis, for example) and mind (it convinces Eddie to kill himself).

Mia steals Black Thirteen when she escapes from Calla Bryn Sturgis. She puts it in a safe in room 1919 at the Plaza-Park Hyatt. Jake and Eddie retrieve it before the low men can get it. Father Callahan stores it in a locker in the basement of the World Trade Center two years before 9-11, where it was presumably destroyed.

BLEEDING LION (7)

A creature that once stalked the north. Perhaps a reference to Aslan, the Guardian of the northern Beam.

BOLT AND BAH (1, 4.5, 5)
Mid-world equivalent of a crossbow. Jamie DeCurry's weapon of choice. Rarely accurate at a distance greater than twenty-five yards, and that only on a still day.

BOOK OF MANNI (5)
The Manni bible.

BRANNI (6)
A word associated with the largest of the plumb bobs used by the Manni to travel. The box it is stored in is called a Branni coff.

BUCKSKIN (4)
Alain Johns's horse.

BUFFALO STAR (5)
A Mid-World deity. Roland was once forced to kill a preacher of the Buff.

CAN TAM (L)
The doctor bugs who operate in the Little Sisters of Eluria's tent. They are associated with Type One vampires. Also known as Grandfather-fleas.

CAPRICHOSO "CAPI" OR "CAPPI" (4, 7, M)
The Travellers' Rest's pack mule, often used by Sheemie to deliver *graf*. Ill-tempered with a tendency to bite people—especially Sheemie.

CASA FUERTE (4)
Also known as Hotpatch. A two-man version of Watch Me.

CASSIOPEIA (3)
A star. According to the legend, she seduced Old Star (Apon, the North Star), causing a fight between him and Old Mother (Lydia, the South Star). The castoffs from their fight became the earth, the moon and the sun. The gods stepped in to save the universe and banished Cassiopeia to a rocking chair made of stars. Apon refused to reconcile, so stubborn Old Star and equally proud Old Mother pine for each other—and hate each other—from the opposite sides of the sky while Cassiopeia sits off to the side and laughs at them.

CASTLES (4, 5)

A game of strategy like chess. Red pieces are arranged at one end of the board and the white at the other. Hillocks stand between them, providing cover. The players creep toward each other, setting up screens without being able to see what the other player is doing. Ultimately, one player has to emerge from behind his Hillock. Unless he has properly established himself, this can leave him vulnerable, but staying in cover can be difficult, too. A clever player sometimes peeks around his Hillock and ducks back. The game takes its name from a move, castling, that can also leave a player vulnerable. One of the playing pieces is called a Squire. The game is a metaphor for the situation in Hambry between the Affiliation Brats and the Big Coffin Hunters. Though both sides are aware of what is going on, neither one wants to be the first to emerge from protective cover.

CATACLYSM

See Old War.

CHANCELLORS' PATIENCE (4)

A game of solitaire. The deck's four Chancellors are Paul, Luke, Peter and Matthew.

CONVERSATIONAL (4)

A meeting among the political leaders of a Barony. These are often held the week before a Fair-Day, when people are assembled in the Barony seat.

CRISP-A-LA (1, M)

A Mid-World brand.

DANCE OF EASTERLING (4)

A party in the Great Hall of Gilead to mark the end of Wide Earth and the advent of Sowing.

DARIA (4.5)

Tim Ross's waterproof talking navigation system, a gift from the mutants in Fagonard Swamp. Full designation: *North Central Positronics Portable Guidance Module DARIA, NCP-1436345-AN.* A brushed silver disk the size of a small plate. It has three buttons, one of which reveals a beeping directional antenna that communicates with a satellite. Its light turns from red to green when the person holding it faces north. She also acts as a light source that will last for seventy years. Secure data is protected by Directive Nineteen, but Daria defies this out of loneliness and friendship, which leads to her destruction.

DARK BELLS (L, M)

The *sigul* of sisterhood worn by one of the Little Sisters. In Eluria, Sister Jenna wears them. When they are rung to summon the *can tam*, the sound is so piercing, it's almost psychic.

DARKS (7)

A unit used to express the output of psychic energy from the Breakers.

DAVID (1, 2, 3, 4.5, 5, 7, M)

Roland's hawk and weapon of choice when he faced Cort in his test to become a gunslinger.

DEBARIA SALT COMBYNE (4.5)

The company that operates the salt mines in the hills north of Debaria. People from Gilead own it.

DEMON MOON (4, 6, 7, M)

The full moon of the Year's End. It can be seen during the daytime. Its face is that of a demon. It was considered bad luck to look directly at it. Rhea told Susan Delgado that she couldn't sleep with Mayor Hart Thorin until Demon Moon was full, after the Reaping Fair.

DEP3 (4)

A poison used by the Great Old Ones in the Great Poisoning or Old War.

DEVIL-GRASS OR DEVIL-WEED (1, 2, 3, 4, 5, 7, M)

Vegetation that can cause delusions if eaten and vivid nightmares if the smoke is inhaled. It grows just about everywhere in Mid-World except in the Badlands of Discordia.

DIPOLAR COMPUTERS (3, 4, 5, 6)

The computers that run Lud.

DIRECTIVE NINETEEN (4.5, 5)

The instruction that prevents people without passwords from accessing certain sensitive North Central Positronics information. Andy and Daria are protected by this rule. When Daria violates it, she self-destructs.

DOBBIE (7)

The name of a domesticated robot known as a "house-elf" in Algul Siento.

DRAGONS (THROUGHOUT)

Winged, fire-breathing creatures that live in various parts of Mid-World, including deep in the Endless Forest. According to legend, their fire is as hot as liquid rock. They have gills in their chests to take in air to fuel their flames. Roland's grandfather Alaric went to Garlan to slay a dragon, but he was too late. The last one in that part of the world had been slain by another king, one who was later murdered, presumably King Roland of Delain. One of Roland's favorite childhood books was *The Throcken and the Dragon*. A dragon the size of a house supposedly killed Jack Ross, but that was a lie. Tim Ross, however, steps on the head of a real dragon bigger than a horse, submerged in Fagonard Swamp, but the creature leaves him be. The mutants of Fagonard give it an offering of a boar, which placates it. This particular dragon, a female with a pink maiden's-comb on its head, is killed by the starkblast. According to Marten Broadcloak, the collective noun for dragons is "a bonfire."

DRAGON'S BLOOD (M)

The poison used to kill Cort. The pages of James Farson's book were laced with it. When Cort licked his fingers to turn the pages, he poisoned himself.

Crossover to Other Works: Dragon's Blood was also used to kill King Roland of Delain in *The Eyes of the Dragon*.

ERMOT (4)

Rhea Dubativo's snake. Slim, green, with four pairs of fangs, two on the top of its mouth and two on the bottom. It also serves as Rhea's lover. Roland shoots its head off when Rhea sends it out to attack him. She sews the corpse back together and wears it around her neck.

EXCALIBUR (4, 5, 6, 7)

Also known as the Sword of Eld and the Sword of Arthur. A symbol of unity that was entombed in a pyramid and freed by Arthur Eld. He led his gunslingers into battle with the sword raised over his head. According to legend, the barrels of Roland's guns are made from its metal.

FAIR-DAYS (3, 4, 5, 6)

Festive occasions held during each of the seven seasons: Winter, Wide Earth, Sowing, Mid-Summer, Full Earth, Reaping and Year's End.

FAIR-DAY GOOSE (4, 5, 6)

The prize given to the winner of Fair-Day Riddling contests. Margaret Eisenhart "claims" the Fair-Day Goose when she wins the Oriza contest in Calla Bryn Sturgis. It was something Stephen King's mother used to say when he and his brother did all their chores and got them right the first time.

FAIR-DAY RIDDLING (3)

A contest held in the Hall of the Grandfathers in Gilead. Sixteen to thirty riddlers gathered in the Hall, which was open to commoners for this event. Each riddler tossed a handful of bark scrolls with riddles written on them into a barrel placed in the center of the floor. Three judges—one a gunslinger—decided whether new riddles were fair. A line formed and the person at the head was asked riddles until they encountered one they couldn't answer within three minutes. This gave someone at the back of the line an advantage, though that person had to answer at least one riddle. Cort usually won the goose that was the victor's prize. One year, Cort stabbed to death a man who cheated at the contest. Though held during every Fair-Day, it was the most important event of the Fairs of Wide Earth and Full Earth, where the riddles were supposed to augur well or ill for the success of the crops.

FAIR-NIGHT (4)

The last night of the Reaping Day Fair, when stuffy-men are thrown into bonfires. The true *fin de año*.

FELICIA (4)

One of three horses promised by Mayor Hart Thorin as an earnest gift to

Susan Delgado. The chestnut mare was originally owned by Pat Delgado and was one of Susan's childhood favorites.

FIRE-RESPONSE TEAM BRAVO (7)
An automated fire team consisting of three fire engines manned by robots housed inside Pleasantville Hardware Company in Algul Siento. Until the *ka-tet* sets fires before they attack, it had not scrambled in more than eight hundred years. The fire engines spray water in all directions and plow through crowds of guards and Breakers alike, killing many.

FORGE OF THE KING (6, 7)
The red glow at Le Casse Roi Russe that can be seen from the allure of Castle Discordia. By the time Roland and Susannah reach the castle, it has gone out, perhaps at the same time as the work of the Breakers was ended.

Crossover to Other Works: This may be related to the Big Combination, the Crimson King's child-powered energy plant, extinguished by Ty Marshall at the end of *Black House*.

THE FORGETFUL FOLK (5, 6)
Someone like Margaret Eisenhart who has left the Manni. The Manni consider them damned. Also a general term used by the Manni to refer to people of any other religion.

FULL EARTH (L, 1, 3, 4, 4.5, 5, 7)
One of the seven seasons of Mid-World. Between Mid-Summer and Reaping, including the month of August. Its moon is called the Kissing Moon. There is often a crop of Full Earth babies the following year because of sexual activity on Reap Night. Riddling is the most important event of the Fair of Full Earth. According to Andy, a time particularly propitious for finishing old business and meeting new people.

GADOSH (7)
Another word for or concept related to the Prim and Gan.

GAN'S BEAM (7)
The Beam of the Elephant and the Wolf, one of the last two that remain before the Breakers are stopped. Stephen King may be its mortal Guardian and it may snap if he dies.

GAN'S BLACKBIRDS (7)

Castle Rooks, like the scavengers that came for the bread that Roland and Cuthbert put under Hax's feet. Roland and Susannah see birds like these flying toward the Crimson King's castle after he departed. They carry Rando Thoughtful across the dead-line so Mordred can eat him.

GAN'S GATEWAY (7)

The yellow center at the heart of the roses of Can'-Ka No Rey.

GARUDA (4.5)

The Eagle Guardian of the Beam. Tim Ross uses one of its tail feathers to navigate his way home from North Forest Kinnock.

GHOSTWOOD (5, 6, 7)

Black ironwood. The dark, dense wood used to make the box that contains Black Thirteen and the door at the base of the Dark Tower. It smells of camphor, fire and flowers. The door to Fedic beneath the Dixie Pig is also ghostwood.

GLOWING DAY (4)

A day of celebration that features fireworks. One of the few times people in Gilead see ice.

GLUE BOY (4)

Cuthbert's horse. Roland noted that Cuthbert couldn't even name his horse as a normal person would.

GOAT MOON (5)

A winter moon. Eddie's birthday in February falls in Goat Moon with beard.

GODOSH (7)

Another word for or concept related to the rational world of the Am.

THE GONE WORLD (1, 5)

To Roland, it means the world of the Great Old Ones. To others, it means Roland's heritage, the line of Eld.

Good Mind (7)

Euphoria generated when the Breakers work in the Study in Algul Siento. Its effect on bystanders is like a mind-altering drug. People suddenly remember things they had long forgotten or work out the solutions to difficult problems.

Grapefruit (4, 4.5, 5, M)

The pink ball from the Wizard's Rainbow, also known as Maerlyn's grapefruit. It fell into the hands of John Farson, who consulted it before battles or making momentous decisions. He uses it to beat the Affiliation and slip away from them whenever he's about to be caught. He sends it away with the Big Coffin Hunters because the risk of keeping it too long outweighs the risk of losing it. They give it to Rhea Dubativo, who uses it to spy on the people of Mejis. It shows things, but the viewer cannot hear anything. It unfailingly shows people at their vilest, revealing acts of incest, abuse, theft and murder. Rhea's anima (spirit) is sucked out of her as she uses it the way a vampire sucks blood. Using it is habit-forming.

Roland takes it from Eldred Jonas. It waits until his mind is strong enough to understand and withstand before showing him all the things he missed during their visit to Mejis, including Susan Delgado's death. It also reveals the Dark Tower and causes him to become obsessed with saving it.

When Farson finds out Roland has it, he is insane with rage. Roland reluctantly gives it to his father a couple of days after he gets back from Mejis. Gabrielle Deschain steals it to give to Marten as a consolation prize after their plot to murder Steven fails. The orb misleads Roland into thinking that Rhea is attacking him, causing him to shoot and kill his mother. Afterward, someone takes the glass from Gabrielle's chamber, probably on Rhea's behalf. Ultimately, it gets back to Marten, who has it in the Green Palace. Roland uses it to show the end of his tragic story to his *ka-tet*. After that it was lost again.

Great Book (3)

The Bible.

Great (or Grand) Featherex (2, 4)

A creature that once lived in the kingdom of Garlan. It was supposed to bring babies, like a stork.

Great Fire

See Old War.

GREAT LETTERS (OF GILEAD) (1, 3, 4, 5, 6, 7)
Letters of the High Speech.

GREAT POISONING
See Old War.

GREAT PORTAL, THE (3)
Another name for the Dark Tower.

GROW BAG (1, 5, 6, M)
A magic bag in Roland's gunna that replenishes money, tobacco and other necessities. A gift from his father. The only possession Roland still has from his days in Mejis.

GUARDIANS OF THE BEAM (3, 4, 4.5, 5, 6, 7, M)
Twelve animals whose names indicate the corresponding Beams that support the Dark Tower. They are, in pairs with proper names where known: Bear (Shardik) and Turtle (Maturin), Fish and Rat, Horse and Dog, Elephant and Wolf, Eagle (Garuda) and Lion (Aslan), Hare and Rat. The Beam of the Lion is also known as the Beam of the Cat or the Tyger. The Beam of the Eagle is also known as the Beam of the Bird, Hawk or Vulturine. Hax believed that the creation of the Twelve Guardians was the last act of the Great Old Ones in an attempt to atone for the great wrongs they had done to one another and to the Earth itself.

GUNSLINGER BURRITOS (3, 4, 4.5, 5)
Dried meat—usually deer—wrapped in spinachlike leaves, although occasionally vegetarian.

HAND-SCAN SPECTRUM MAGNIFIER (4)
A medical diagnostic tool capable of administering minor first aid found aboard Blaine the Mono. It is also a nutrient-delivery system, a brain-pattern recording device, a stress analyzer and an emotion enhancer that can naturally stimulate the production of endorphins. It can also create believable illusions and hallucinations.

HELIOGRAPH (4)
A mechanism for sending messages over long distances.

"Hey Jude" (1, 2, 4, 5, 7, M)

A popular song in Mid-World.

High Speech (1, 2, 3, 4, 4.5, 5, 6, M)

The formal language of Gilead. Roland has a conversation with Calvin Tower in the High Speech to convince him of his identity and he speaks to the Rodericks using it. Eddie thinks it sounds like a second cousin to English.

Ho Fat's Luxury Taxi (7)

Susannah's name for three different carts used in their travels across the Badlands and down Tower Road. The first was a motorized rickshaw discovered at the checkpoint outside the Crimson King's castle. The second is a cut-down wagon assembled by Stuttering Bill that is used for their gunna. The third, also provided by Stuttering Bill, resembles an electric golf cart.

Homilies and Meditations (4)

A book by Mercer owned by Alain Johns. It's the first book Eldred Jonas has seen since coming to Mejis.

Honda (4, 5, 7)

A brand name associated with power generators and motor-driven bicycles.

Honor Stance (2)

The opening position assumed by boxers, according to Cort. Roland thinks of this when he sees the way the lobstrosities genuflect each time a wave comes in.

Horn of Eld or Horn o'Deschain (1, 3, 5, 7, M)

The ancient brass horn passed down to Roland through the generations from Arthur Eld, used to lead the gunslingers into battle. Cuthbert wielded it during the battle of Jericho Hill. He told Roland to pick it up if he was killed, but Roland didn't take the time to do so, and thus, when he reaches the Dark Tower, he does not have it in his possession to respond to the sound of the horn generated by the roses. The horn is a metaphor for the way Roland sets his sights on the Tower to the exclusion of everything else, but also a symbol that he is changing gradually.

HORSEMEN'S ASSOCIATION (4)

A collective of farmers and ranchers in the Barony of Mejis. Francis Lengyll is its president. Most of the members are traitors, siding with John Farson against the Affiliation.

HUNTRESS MOON (4, 4.5, 5)

The red moon that follows the Peddler's Moon. Some call it the last moon of summer; others call it the first moon of fall. The figure in the moon fills her belly as she goes from new to full. Others say that she grows pale, waxes again and pulls her bow.

IMPERIUM (3, M)

The reign of the Great Old Ones.

IRONWOOD (L, 1, 2, 4, 4.5, 5, 6, 7)

An enormous tree also known as "seequoiah." Some are larger in diameter than a house. The people of Tree cut ironwood from the Endless Forest and sell the lumber to the Barony as a source of income. Its wood is used to make boats strong enough for sea travel. Some people believe the trees can think, which is why woodsmen cry their pardon before each day's cutting. The doors on the Western Sea, the log in the golgotha, Rimer's desk in Mejis, the box containing the pink Wizard's Glass, the ringbolt on Bix's ferry, Everlynne's throne, Jack Ross's coffin, the cross in Our Lady of Serenity, the Branni coff, the banquet table in Castle Discordia, the water trough in Eluria, some of the doors beneath Castle Discordia and Cort's stick are all ironwood.

JAWBONE (1, 2)

A talisman that Roland carries with him to ward off evil. The first one, found in the basement of the Way Station, may belong to one of the Great Old Ones. Later, Roland carries what he believes to be Walter's jawbone, picked up after the palaver at the golgotha.

JEWELS OF ELD (4)

The crown jewels of Arthur Eld.

KA OF NINETEEN (7)

The *ka* of Keystone Earth.

KA OF NINETY-NINE (7)

The *ka* of the Keystone World, which is Roland's Mid-World.

KISSING MOON (L, 4)

The moon of Full Earth/midsummer.

LAMERK INDUSTRIES AND FOUNDRY (1, 3, 4, 5)

A division of North Central Positronics. The LaMerk Industries imprint appears on the pump in the Way Station, on Andy the Messenger Robot and on some of the control panels in the Dogan. The LaMerk Foundry produced the steel that made the Send Bridge and the manhole covers in Lud. Sylvia Pittston thinks LaMerk is the sign of the beast. The bulldozer driver razing the vacant lot in Eddie's dream has LaMerk on his helmet.

LANGUAGE OF THE UNFORMED (L, 5, 6, 7, M)

A language spoken by the Little Sisters of Eluria. Words from it appear in the speech of the people of the Callas, the Manni and the Children of Roderick.

LARCHIES (1, M)

A Mid-World product brand.

LEVEL OF THE TOWER (4, 5, 6, 7)

Each level of the Tower represents a different universe. For an individual who enters the Tower, each level represents a different phase in his life.

Crossover to Other Works: This concept was introduced in *Insomnia*.

LIPPY (7)

Joe Collins's blind, malnourished and decrepit horse. Roland believes that Stanza XIV of "Childe Roland to the Dark Tower Came" is about her. She runs off during the snowstorm. When she returns, Roland puts her out of her misery. When Mordred feasts on her body, he is poisoned. She was probably named after the Browning poem "Fra Lippo Lippi."

LLAMREI (7)

Arthur Eld's snow-white horse. Its image was carried into battle on the pennants of Gilead and was the *sigul* of all In-World. Patrick Danville depicted it as dead in a painting.

LOBSTROSITIES (2, 3, 4, 5, 6, 7)

Mutant lobsterlike creatures that dwell in the Western Sea and come out of the water to hunt at nightfall. They are four feet long, a foot high and weigh approximately seventy pounds. One of these creatures cuts off two of Roland's fingers and a big toe while he sleeps after his palaver with the man in black. They are the sole source of food for Roland, Eddie and Odetta/Detta as they travel up the coast.

LOST BEASTS OF ELD (6)

Creatures from long-ago days that have gone extinct.

LYDIA'S DIPPER (7)

The name for the Big Dipper in Mid-World. It faded from existence before Roland's time but reemerges after the Beams start to heal. Lydia is another name for the star Old Mother.

MAERLYN'S RAINBOW (4)

See Wizard's Rainbow.

MAGIC AND SCIENTIFIC DOORS (2, 4, 5, 6, 7)

Roland and his *ka-tet* encounter two different kinds of doors during their adventure: magic and scientific. The latter, created by North Central Positronics, often allow passage in only one direction and are dedicated—always coming out in the same place. New York is "lousy with portals," many of which go to different versions of the city, though most don't work anymore.

There are nearly six hundred scientific doors still operational in the rotunda of the Fedic Dogan. Some are defective, and most are beginning to fail. Those that are failing can make a person feel like he's being turned inside out and make him physically sick. Their inner workings can sometimes be heard. A defective door can also open on the todash darkness between worlds, where monsters dwell.

The portals at the beginning of each Beam were originally magic, but they were replaced by North Central Positronics. Thus, Roland thinks of them as "old-ones doors." The Old Ones used them to turn various levels of the Tower into tourist destinations. Many involved tragedy—terrorist attacks and assassinations being particular favorites.

The doorways on the beach, the one Eddie opens in the Speaking Ring and the Unfound Door are all magic, left behind when the Prim receded. They are made of ironwood, designed with a purpose that is governed by *ka*. They float in the air—their hinges aren't attached to anything—and are visible only from one side. They can be aimed wherever the traveler or *ka* desires and allow him to return so long as the door remains open. A traveler can also enter the body of a person on the other side, as Roland does with Eddie, Odetta and Jack Mort (and, perhaps, as Mia does to Susannah). Sheemie Ruiz has a unique talent that allows him to create doors, though the toll it takes on him is tremendous. Though the New Yorkers take magic doors for granted, Roland never saw one before the three he found on the Western Sea.

Crossovers to Other Works: Doorways that transport people from one place or time to another have been part of King's works almost from the beginning. In his 1971 story "I Am the Doorway," aliens use an astronaut as a doorway through which they can observe things on Earth. In his 1981 story "The Jaunt," a character creates a mechanism for sending people across vast distances by crossing a portal. The painting Rosie McClendon purchases in *Rose Madder* is a doorway to another world that may be Mid-World. The trunk of the Buick Roadmaster in *From a Buick 8* is a doorway to an alien world, and the title building in *Black House* is a portal between Earth and End-World. King allows for the possibility that the Colorado Kid had access to a portal as well. How else could he have made the journey from Colorado to Maine in so short a time? Sheemie Ruiz created a magic doorway to allow Ted Brautigan to escape from Devar-Toi to Connecticut in "Low Men in Little Coats" from *Hearts in Atlantis*. In *11/22/63*, Jake Epping is shown a door that always transports people to the same day in 1959. The rules of travel through this door are a little different from the ones in the Dark Tower series. Each time he revisits the past, any changes he made on previous trips are undone.

MAGIC TALES OF THE ELD (4.5)
A book Roland loved as a child. It had a dozen woodcut illustrations, one of which featured throcken anticipating a starkblast. His favorite story from it was "The Wind Through the Keyhole." Known by some as *The Great Elden Book*.

MATURIN (5, 6, 7)
The Turtle Guardian of the Beam upon whose shell the world rests. Susannah uses the word to plant a posthypnotic suggestion in Mathiessen van Wyck's mind. King borrowed the name from novels by Patrick O'Brian.

MIM (7)
Mother Earth.

MIND-TRAP (7)
A gadget in the tunnel beneath the Dixie Pig leading to the Fedic door that plucks people's worst fears from their imaginations and makes them real enough to kill them, though the cause of death would probably look like a stroke or a heart attack. Jake switches minds with Oy to escape the trap. Flaherty and Lamla get sharpshooters to destroy the projectors while pursuing Jake.

MITSY (4.5)
One of Jack Ross's female mules.

MORTATA (5)
The dance of death.

MUSTY (4)
Rhea Dubativo's mutant cat. It has six legs and a split tail. Its fur has an unpleasant wet feel, perhaps because Rhea grooms it with her tongue. She refers to it as a warlock, and it is smart enough to deliver notes on her behalf.

NEW EARTH (1, 4.5, 5, M)
Spring, also known as Fresh Commala. A time when fields are prepared for planting.

NINETEEN (1, 5, 6, 7, M)
The mystery number. After they leave the Green Palace, the *ka-tet* starts seeing this number in everything. In High Speech, it is "chassit."

NIS (7)
The greatest of the gray horses at the Castle of the Crimson King. Named after the land of sleep and dreams. The Crimson King rode it across Empathica to the Dark Tower.

NORTH CENTRAL POSITRONICS (1, 3, 4.5, 5, 6, 7, M)
A corporation created by the Great Old Ones to replace magical elements with scientific analogs or to fuse the two together. Their experiments were

conducted in research stations known as Dogans. They once had factories on the outskirts of Algul Siento. The remnants of their poisonous experiments linger to this day.

Their corporate slogan is "Building the future one circuit at a time." Their brand name appears on many things encountered by the *ka-tet*, including: Shardik, the Cradle of Lud and Fedic Station, Andy, the various Dogans, the motorized tricycle Mia uses to get to the Doorway Cave, the microphones in Susannah's Dogan, the change machine in the World Trade Center basement, the link between Susannah and Mia in the Fedic Dogan, Nigel's computer, the raft crossing the River Whye, and Daria, the portable guidance module the tribesmen give to Tim Ross. Father Callahan believes they may exist in all worlds. One of their subsidiaries hired Dinky Earnshaw for its assassination program. They are also purchasing the New York Plaza-Park Hyatt, planning to rename it the Regal U.N. Plaza, together with their Keystone subsidiary, Sombra.

Eddie enlists John Cullum, Aaron Deepneau and Moses Carver to form Tet Corporation to try to put North Central Positronics out of business before it can turn into a monster that will mortally wound the Dark Tower.

Nozz-A-La (4, 5, 6, 7, M)
A brand of soft drink that exists in certain realities, as well as in Thunderclap. According to Ted Brautigan, who calls it Nozzie, it tastes a bit like root beer. Austin Cornwell worked on the advertising campaign before he became the Crimson King's minister of state.

Ocean Foam (4)
The horse Pat Delgado was riding the day he was killed. Those who were with Delgado claimed that a snake spooked the horse, which threw his rider and rolled on him.

Old Mother (1, 3, 4, 4.5, 5, 6, 7)
The southern star, also known as Lydia. The brightest of those close to Mid-World. See Cassiopeia.

Old Star (1, 3, 4, 4.5, 5, 6, 7)
The northern star, also known as Apon. See Cassiopeia.

OLD WAR (3)

One name for the conflict that brought an end to the civilization of the Great Old Ones. Also known as the Cataclysm, the Great Fire, or the Great Poisoning. It happened well over a thousand years ago and emptied the land. The mutations seen in Roland's time are a long-lasting effect of this war.

ORIZA (5, 6, 7)

A specially weighted titanium plate a foot in diameter manufactured in Calla Sen Chre. The rim is sharpened for three-quarters of the circumference. The only safe place to grip the plate is by a section that is dull and slightly thicker than the rest. A small metal pod affixed to the bottom makes the weapon whistle as the plate flies. The front of the blue plate is decorated by rice stalks crossed into the shape of the Great Letter Zn. Named for Lady Oriza, who used a similar plate to kill Gray Dick, who murdered her father. The word also refers to the rice plant. Both Susannah and Jake learn to master the weapon.

THE OVER (5, 6)

The Manni concept of God. The soup of creation, also known as the Prim.

OXEN (4)

Rare animals in Mid-World. Prior to going to Mejis, Cuthbert has seen them only in pictures.

PATH OF THE BEAM (3, 4, 4.5, 5, 6, 7)

The route marked out by thousands of years of the flow of the Beams that support the Dark Tower. The Guardians at either end are used to name these paths.

PEDDLER'S MOON (1, 4, 4.5, 5, 7)

The moon after the Kissing Moon, also known as Late-summer's Moon. The Peddler who appears on the face of this orange moon is a hunched figure with a nasty, complicitous squint-and-grin and a sackful of squealing souls thrown over one cringing shoulder.

POINTS (1, 4.5, 5)

Also called Wickets. A game compared to bowling, polo and croquet. Uses a mallet and blue balls.

PORTALS (3, 4, 6, 7)

The twelve doorways at the far ends of the Beams that support the Dark Tower. They lead in and out of the world. They may be as natural as the constellations or built by the Great Old Ones. Roland doesn't know where they lead and is open to the possibility that they might be outside *ka*.

PRESENTATION CEREMONIES (2)

The ceremony at which an apprentice was officially promoted to gunslinger. Pupils first kneel at Cort's feet, presenting defenseless necks, then rise and receive his congratulatory kiss and allow him to load their guns for the first time.

PRIM (6, 7, M)

The greater Discordia or magical soup of creation. Known as the Over by the Manni. Some people think of it as a void. Life in Mid-World arose after the Prim receded. Certain magical creatures were also beached when this happened, and some survived as demons. The Beams rose from the Prim on the airs of magic. When the Prim receded, most magic receded, too, but there was enough left to support the Beams and the Dark Tower forever.

PYLON (4, M)

A two-year-old rosillo, one of three horses given to Susan Delgado by Mayor Hart Thorin as an earnest gift to fulfill their contract. Susan helped foal it, but their horses and land were lost after Pat Delgado died.

PYRAMID (4, 7)

According to one version of the legend, Arthur Eld retrieved his sword Excalibur from the pyramid in which it was entombed. Five miles from the Dark Tower, Roland encounters a steel pyramid about thirty feet high covered with boulders to disguise it as a cairn. It has a ring of roses around its base. Could this be the same pyramid?

REAP OR REAPTIDE (1, 3, 4, 4.5, 5, 7, M)

Autumn. One of the seven seasons of Mid-World. It occurs between Full Earth and Year's End.

REAP MOON (7)

The name for the moon during Reaptide.

REAP MORN (4)

The day after the Reap Fair, the first day of winter. The traditional time for burning. In Hambry, the ranchers would burn brush at the mouth of Eyebolt Canyon to silence the thinny.

REAPING DAY FAIR (4, 4.5, 5)

A day of festivities celebrating the closing of the year, the end of the harvest and the changing of the seasons. Men steal Reap-kisses from women. Reap charms are hung around town and secreted in the bosoms of women. There are dances and fireworks. The hands of stuffy-guys are painted red in preparation for throwing them into the bonfire. After the exhausting work of finishing the harvest, putting up food and preparing for winter, sexual intercourse resumes on Reap Night, usually leading to a crop of Full Earth babies the next year.

RED DEATH (6, 7)

The plague that killed everyone in Fedic a thousand years ago. Some people believe someone in Castle Discordia unleashed it accidentally. Others believe it came out of the abyss next to the castle. Perhaps related to the Great Poisoning unleashed by the Great Old Ones. A name inspired by an Edgar Allan Poe short story.

RICE SONG (5, 7)

A traditional song about a young man and woman planting rice and children in the spring of the year. Roland knew it when he was young. It begins "Come-come-commala, rice come a-falla," but after that the words are difficult to understand, especially because the pace of the song increases from verse to verse. It contains hard and soft rhymes, off-rhymes and forced rhymes. It is chanted more than sung and is often accompanied by a frenetic dance that Roland performs for the people of Calla Bryn Sturgis.

RING-A-LEVIO (7)

Roland's first dog, known as Ringo. It died when he was three.

ROCK-CATS (5)
Pumas or cougars.

ROMP, THE (4, 7)
A monstrous two-headed elk with a rack of antlers like a forest grove and four glaring eyes, mounted behind the bar at the Travellers' Rest in Hambry.

ROOK'S SKULL (4, M)
Cuthbert's good-luck charm. He carries it on the horn of his saddle and wears it around his neck on a gold chain, calling it his lookout. It is used as evidence against the Affiliation Brats when Eldred Jonas finds it at Citgo and plants it on Mayor Thorin's body.

RUSHER (4)
The horse Roland rides to Mejis. A big, sensitive, quick, delicate and well-behaved gelding.

SAITA (5, M)
A great snake slain by Arthur Eld. In the Marvel graphic novels, a stained-glass window in Gilead depicts this scene.

SALT HOUSES (4.5)
Caverns in the cliff faces near Little Debaria. Miners and their families live in them, and the tunnels into the mine extend from the back of them. Steven Deschain and Deputy Hugh Peavy ambushed the Crow Gang in one.

SANDALWOOD (THROUGHOUT)
The yellow and finely grained wood used in the stocks of Roland's guns.

SATAN'S ALLEY (4)
A table in the Travellers' Rest in Hambry where a game that resembles craps is played.

SATAN'S FIRST LAW OF MALIGNITY (4, M)
If the worst can happen, it usually will.

SEVEN DIALS OF MAGIC (5)

Something Vannay taught student gunslingers, though he refused to say if he believed in any of them.

SHAKE LOOP (4)

A kind of knot that can be shaken free after you climb down the rope.

SHARDIK (3, 5, 6, 7)

The Guardian of the Portal of the Bear. Built by North Central Positronics. His serial number is AA 24123 CX 755431297 L 14. He stands seventy feet tall and is hundreds, if not thousands, of years old. The Old People tried to kill him, but incited his anger instead. He spared the warriors and killed the women and children instead. He was infected with a parasite that, coupled with old age, drove him insane as his batteries began to run down. He had a satellite dish atop his head.

SHIPMATE'S DISEASE (2)

Roland's term for scurvy, a disease caused by subsisting on a diet that does not provide all the required vitamins. He sees signs of it in Eddie after they eat only lobstrosity meat for weeks.

SLO-TRANS ENGINES (3, 4, 5, 6)

Power source for Blaine the Mono. Also heard in the Green Palace and at Castle Discordia.

SMA' TOOT (4.5)

A steam-driven train that runs between Gilead and Debaria.

SNEETCH (5, 6, 7)

A name for the self-guided hand grenades used by the Wolves when they raid the Callas. Also called buzz-balls and stealthies. According to legend, they produce swirling blades as sharp as razors that slash people top to bottom in seconds. Spherical, about three inches in diameter, they look like they're made of steel but feel like hard rubber. The surface is gridded with lines of latitude and longitude. Next to the nameplate that identifies them as the Harry Potter model, there is a fingertip depression at the bottom of which is a button. Once activated, a curved section slides away to reveal a programmable timer. When a drone locks onto a target, it will pursue it until running out of power. The *ka-tet* use sneetches to start fires on a delayed schedule at Algul Siento. The Crimson King takes a crate of them to the Dark Tower.

SNUGGLEBUTT (5)
Father Callahan's cat in Calla Bryn Sturgis.

SONG OF THE TOWER (7)
The irresistible song that comes from the Dark Tower on the Beam and is carried by the roses, calling anyone from the line of Eld to draw near. Roland realizes that he has always heard this song, even when he lived in Gilead, where it hid in his mother's voice as she sang to him. The song stops when he enters the Tower.

SONG OF THE TURTLE (3, 4, 5, 6, 7)
A voice that provides advice, guidance, warnings and condemnation. The voice of *ka* or the Beam or Gan. Roland believes the Beam is sentient enough to understand how seriously it is threatened and wants to protect itself. He hears it inside the pink Wizard's Glass. It tells Stephen King when to write about Roland. It may also tell Calvin Tower to keep the vacant lot. Known as Ves'-Ka Gan, the Voice of the Turtle, the Voice of the Beam, Susannah's Song and the Cry of the Bear. It chides Roland for failing to pick up the Horn of Eld in Jericho Hill, which seems pointless at the time, but the Beam may be telling Roland what he needs to learn to succeed.

SOWING NIGHT (1, M)
Festival night associated with the ritual of planting in the spring. The season of Sowing includes the month of June. During the Sowing Night Cotillion, young Roland watched his mother dance with Marten Broadcloak.

SPEAKING RINGS OR SPEAKING CIRCLES (1, 3, 4, 7)
Circles made out of tall standing rocks, often inhabited by demons that can be summoned and forced to act as oracles, usually in return for sexual favors. They are thin places and often provide access between worlds, such as the one where Jake returned to Mid-World. Roland encounters one after leaving the Way Station and finds a number of them at the end of Tower Road.

SPIRIT OF TOPEKA (7)

The atomic locomotive (hot-enj) that carried Susannah, Ted, Sheemie and a few others from Algul Siento to Fedic after the Breakers were freed. It could travel up to three hundred miles per hour. The last nine of twelve cars—all empty—fell into the chasm outside Fedic when the trestle collapsed.

STARKBLAST (4.5)

According to Daria: "A fast-moving storm of great power. Its features include steep and sudden drops in temperature accompanied by strong winds. It has been known to cause great destruction and loss of life in civilized portions of the world. In primitive areas, entire tribes have been wiped out." A period of unusually warm weather lasting a few days usually heralds the storm. Like tornadoes, starkblasts form funnels and can travel for hundreds of miles before lifting into the sky and vanishing. Billy-bumblers have a talent for predicting them, and they're known to bring strange dreams. They often travel along and are intensified by a Beam. They struck the forest north of Gilead each year but never reached the city.

SUNSHINE (4.5)

Widow Ardelia Smack's burro. Tim Ross fed, watered and walked the burro many times.

SWORD OF ELD

See Excalibur.

TALES OF ARTHUR (5)

A book filled with stories of the days of Arthur Eld. Father Callahan has a copy.

THINNY (4, 5, M)

A place where the fabric of existence is almost worn away. A sore on the skin of existence, a cavity at the center of the universe able to exist only because things are going wrong in all worlds. They are doorways between worlds, though dangerous. They spread and grow. There have been more of them since the Dark Tower began to fail. They shimmer as if they were silvery water. They issue a low, liquid warbling sound that is disturbing on a psychic level, the effect of which is cumulative. Blaine the Mono passed through one to get the *ka-tet* to Topeka. The sound reminds Jake of Hawaiian music. The *ka-tet* is able to block the sound using bullets from Mid-World, but not ones from the real world. It tingles when they come into contact with it. Being inside it is claustrophobic, purgatorial. The one at the far end of Eyebolt Canyon—the first Roland ever saw—has been there since before Susan was born but not before her father was born. An earthquake may have accompanied its arrival. Viewed from above, it looks like a slow-burning peat fire or a swamp full of scummy green water. The light green mist (silvery in the moonlight) that rises off it sometimes looks like long, skinny arms with hands at the end. It has seductive, cajoling voices that can draw people in to their deaths. The locals burned it quiet each fall because the animals reacted badly to the sound.

THREADED STOCK (1, 4, 5, M)
Purebred line, free from genetic mutations.

TOPSY (L, M)
One of Roland's horses, a two-year-old roan that dies in Eluria.

UNFOUND DOOR (1, 3, 5, 6, 7)
The magic door that Walter uses to send Father Callahan from the Way Station to the Cave of Voices near Calla Bryn Sturgis. It is made of ironwood or ghostwood. It has a crystal doorknob with a rose etched on it and no keyhole. Like the doorway at the Portal of Shardik, it vibrates to the touch. Unlike most magic doors, this one follows Callahan after he passes through. The *ka-tet* use it in conjunction with Black Thirteen to travel to specific times and places in Keystone Earth. The term comes from *Look Homeward, Angel* by Thomas Wolfe. Patrick Danville draws it to Susannah's specifications so she can travel to Central Park. The word "unfound" is written on it in the hieroglyphics of the Great Old Ones. The door at the base of the Dark Tower also says "unfound" until Roland takes off his guns. Then the word changes to "found."

VI CASTIS COMPANY (4)
The mining company that has taken over all the former freehold gold, silver, copper and diamond mines in the Vi Castis Mountains. The Big Coffin Hunters assisted the company in running the independents off.

VOICE OF THE TURTLE / VOICE OF THE BEAM (3, 4, 5, 6, 7)
See Song of the Turtle.

WATCH ME (1, 3, 4, 4.5, 5, 6, 7)

A card game that has been played in barrooms and bunkhouses and around campfires since the world was young. According to Roland, saying "Watch me" means "you have a deal." The one surviving dipolar computer in Lud can only run the drum machines and play this game. There is also a one-handed version and a version called Hotpatch or Casa Fuerte.

WAY-GOG (3)

Bagpipelike instrument played on an upper level of the Tower, according to Blaine the Mono.

WESTERN LINE (4.5)

The train line that once ran for more than a thousand wheels west of Gilead all the way to the Mohaine Desert. In the years before Gilead fell, it ran only as far as Debaria. Beyond that, washouts, earthquakes and harriers destroyed the tracks.

THE WHITE (1, 3, 4.5, 5, 6, 7, M)

The force of good that stands behind the Affiliation. The power of Arthur Eld, the White King. The *sigul* on the end of Roland's gun barrels and the one on the door of Arthur's tomb translates to the White. Steven Deschain sends Roland to Debaria so people can see that the White is still strong and true.

WICKETS

See Points.

WIDE EARTH (1, 3, 4, 4.5, 5, 7)

One of the seven seasons of Mid-World, between Winter and Sowing. The Dance of Easterling marks its end. Riddling is the most important event of the Fair of Wide Earth because the riddles augur well or ill for the success of the crops. The Covenant Man made his rounds of the North'rd Barony during this season.

"THE WIND THROUGH THE KEYHOLE" (4.5)

A story from the *Magic Tales of the Eld* that Roland's mother read to him when he was a child. Roland tells the story of Tim Stoutheart to Young Bill Streeter in Debaria.

WIZARD'S GLASS, THE (4, 5, 7)

Any of thirteen magical glass orbs that make up the Wizard's Rainbow. Also known as the Bends o' the Rainbow.

WIZARD'S RAINBOW, THE (4, 4.5, 5, 6, 7, M)

Also known as Maerlyn's Rainbow. It consists of thirteen colored glass balls (or bends), one for each of the Guardians of the Beam and one—Black Thirteen, the most powerful and terrible—representing the Dark Tower. Some people believe Maerlyn was turned evil by their glammer in the days before the Elden Kingdom fell. Others think he created them.

These balls are alive and hungry and evil. Hurt enlivens them. People who use them end up being used by them. Each one makes its possessor feel like the glass is just for him or her, but they never stay in one place or one pair of hands for long. Almost all have the power to send the user todash. Some are used to see into the future or into other worlds, or to spy on other locations in Mid-World. They never see the good—only the ill.

By the time Roland comes into possession of the pink orb in Mejis, most are thought to have been broken. The Crimson King had six of them, but he smashed them before leaving Le Casse Roi Russe for the Dark Tower. The locations of the rest are mostly rumors. The blue glass was supposedly in the hands of a desert tribe of slow mutants called the Total Hogs, but they lost it. The green glass was reportedly in Lud and the orange one in Dis.

WOLF (4)

Mayor Hart Thorin of Hambry's dog. He chewed up one of Susan Delgado's Reap Fair dresses.

YEAR'S END (4, 5)

One of the seven seasons in Mid-World, between Reaping and Winter. Its moon is the Demon Moon.

ZOLTAN (1, 3, 4, 6, 7, M)

Brown's talking raven, named after a folk singer and guitarist King knew at the University of Maine.

MID-WORLD/MANNI/CALLA WORDS AND EXPRESSIONS

ALL HAIL (OR HILE) THE CRIMSON KING (4, 5, 7, M)

A statement of tribute to the Crimson King. Jake sees it written on the boards surrounding the vacant lot.

ALL THINGS SERVE THE BEAM (3, 4.5, 5, 6, 7)

Everything that anyone does, even people who are opponents of the *ka-tet*, ultimately is to the benefit of *ka*. Tim Ross knows the saying without understanding what it means.

ALLEYO (5)

To run away.

AM (7)

The opposite of Prim—reason instead of magic.

AN-TET (4, 4.5, 5, 7)

In council. A kind of telepathy and communication shared by people who are part of a *ka-tet*. Also the relationship between two lovers.

ANTI-KA (7)

A force that works against *ka*, set in motion by the Crimson King.

ASTIN (2, 3, 4, 5, 6, 7)

Roland's pronunciation of "aspirin."

AVEN KAL (7)

"Lifted by the wind" or "carried on the wave." A wave that runs along the Path of the Beam that takes people somewhere to show them something *ka* wants them to see or hear.

AVEN KAS (7)

A destructive natural force, like a hurricane or a tsunami.

BAH-BO (7)

A term of endearment meaning "baby."

BANNOCK (7)
Buffalo.

BIN-RUSTIES OR RUSTIES (4.5, 5, 6, 7)
Swallows or giant blackbirds.

BINNIE BUGS (5)
Mosquito-like insects.

BLACKMOUTH DISEASE (7)
Cancer.

BLOSSIEWOOD OR BLOSSWOOD (4.5, 5)
A sweet-smelling tree found at the edge of the Endless Forest. It has a fine-grained lightweight golden wood used for lake and river craft. When Roland was ten, spiders infested a farm of these trees east of Gilead. The forester panicked and cut down all the good trees to keep them from being killed, which put an end to the Blosswood Forest.

BOOM-FLURRY (5)
An organ-pipe cactus with great thick barrel arms and long needles. They have a bitter, tangy odor, can move and are carnivorous. They act as sentries outside the Dogan near Calla Bryn Sturgis.

BOUGIE (7)
A reanimated corpse.

BRIGHT (4.5)
Special talent.

BUCKA (1, 4.5, 5, 6, 7)
A wagon, usually horse-drawn.

BULL SQUIRTER (4.5)
A kind of eye dropper used by Destry in Tree, probably for artificial insemination.

CALLUM-KA (6)
A simple pullover worn by men and women in the Callas during cooler weather.

CAMEL BUCKET (4, M)
A bucket at a saloon into which unfinished drinks are poured, creating a noxious combination known as camel piss. Reckless and poor people can buy double shots for a few pennies.

CAN CALAH (6)
Angels. Gan speaks in the voice of the can calah.

CANDA (7)
A strategic distance between two gunslingers when entering a battle outnumbered. It guarantees that they can't be killed by a single shot. The distance is never the same in any two situations.

CAN-TAH (5, 6, 7)
Little gods. Animal-shaped icons, like the scrimshaw turtle, imbued with power.

    Crossover to other works: The stone carvings in the China Pit mine in *Desperation* are also *can-tahs*.

CAN TOI (6, 7)
Low men/women.

CAN-TOI-TETE (7)
Misbegotten thing. Roland's term for a mutant desert dog.

CARVERS (4)
Five-shot revolvers.

CHAR (3, 4)
Death.

CHARY (1, 4.5, 5, 7)
Dangerous or deadly.

CHARY MAN (1, 4.5, 5, 7)
Someone who courts or brings death.

CHARY-KA (7)
Someone (like Roland) who is destined to deal death.

CHARYOU TREE (1, 4, 5, 6, M)
In the days of the Old People, at the end of the Reaping Day Fair, a person was sacrificed in the bonfire as a way of placating the gods. "Come, Reap, death for you and life for our crops" was the accompanying chant. The chosen sacrifice had his or her hands painted red. After the tradition was banned, people painted the hands of stuffy-guys and threw them into the Reap Fair Bonfire instead, or burned them on pyres after the harvest.

CHASSIT (1, 7)
High Speech for the number nineteen

CHEFLET (3, 7)
The way Roland pronounces the name of the antibiotic Keflex.

CHERT (7)
A strong metamorphic rock that is often used for primitive tools like ax-heads, knives, skewers and scrapers. It resembles quartz. According to legend, it "breaks lucky," which means it usually breaks into pieces the size and shape to suit the purpose at hand.

CHILDE (7)
A formal and ancient term that describes a knight or a gunslinger chosen by *ka* to embark on a quest. Because it is a holy term, the gunslingers never used it among themselves.

CLEARING AT THE END OF
THE PATH (L, 1, 4, 4.5, 5, 6, 7)
Death. Also heaven. The place where a person's *ka-essen* goes after death. Some people believe that those in the clearing know all the secrets the living keep from one another.

CLOBBER (4.5)
A straw hat worn by men who worked at the mines.

CLOUT (1, 4, 4.5, 5, 6, 7)
A cloth, rag or diaper.

COFFAH (7)
Hell.

COMMALA (1, 4.5, 5, 6, 7)
A word with dozens of meanings in Mid-World. The most common is a variety of rice, but it also stands for intercourse, orgasm, the moment before a feast begins, baldness and schmoozing, to name but a few. Many of its meanings, connotations and shadings are sexual.

COOZEY (4)
An unflattering adjective.

CORVETTE (4)
Literally "a little packet." In Hambry, a small leather purse with a lace tie. Big enough for a few coins. Carried by ladies more often than gentlemen.

COSY (3, 5)
Dangerous or tricky. Devious.

COTTON GILLY (4)
Prostitute.

COVE (3, 7)
A person. Most often used in "a trig cove," meaning a sly or smart person.

COZEN (4, 4.5, 5, 6, 7)
Cheat, trick or deceive.

CRADLE (3)
Train station.

CRADLE-AMAH (5)
Wet nurse.

CRUNK (4)
The unofficial name for the dialect spoken by cowboys in Mejis.

CUJO (7)
In Mejis, this word means "sweet one."

CULLY (L, 1, 3, 4, 4.5, 6, 7, M)
A nonspecific form of address, like "boy" or "mate."

DAN-DINH (1, 5, 7)
A formal way a person speaks with a person acknowledged as his *dinh*. The person opens his heart to the *dinh*'s command with regard to an emotional problem. When a person does this, he agrees to do exactly as the *dinh* suggests, immediately and without question.

DAN-TETE (6, 7)
"Little savior"—a term applied to John Cullum, who was in the right place at the right time and was levelheaded enough to help Roland and Eddie—or "baby god"—the term for Mordred Deschain used by the minions of the Crimson King.

DASH-DINH (5)
A religious leader.

DEAD-LETTER (4, 4.5, 5, 6)
A will.

DEAD-LINE (3, 7)
A line that it is lethal to cross. There is supposed to be one around the Cradle of Lud, and the Crimson King set one around his castle to keep people from leaving after he went mad.

DELAH (4.5, 5, 6, 7)
Many. A number beyond counting. Who knows? Always spoken with a light toss of the open hand toward the horizon or the sky. Can be used as a modifier to indicate "very," as in trig-delah.

DEVAR-TETE (7)
Little prison or torture chamber. Roland applies the word to the Fedic Dogan. In the context of the Devar-Tete Whye, it means simply "little."

DIBBIN (4.5)
The magic napkin that Tim Ross uses for protection against the starkblast and as a magic carpet to get him back to Tree.

DINH (1, 4, 4.5, 5, 6, 7, M)
Leader. It can refer to the person in charge of a *ka-tet* or the king of a country. Steven Deschain was the *dinh* not only of his fellow gunslingers but also of Gilead and the Affiliation. Mia observes that "leader" and "king" are poor substitutes for another meaning of the word: father.

DOCKER'S CLUTCH (2, 3, 4, 5, 6, 7)
A spring-clip or shoulder holster that allows quick access to a concealed weapon.

DOCKERY (3)
A plant like chicory used to make coffee.

DROGUE (L, 4)
At the end of a line, as in "riding drogue," the rear end of a caravan.

DROTTA STICK (5)
A dowsing rod used to locate water.

DRY TWIST (5, 6, 7)
A fast-progressing form of arthritis. Roland appears to be suffering from this, but his pains come from a different source.

EARTH-GAS (4)
A fuel like propane that can be used to run generators and other appliances.

EFDAY (4.5)
A day of the week—probably Friday.

ETHDAY (4.5)
A day of the week—probably Saturday.

FAN-GON (5, M)
The exiled one.

FASHED (4, 4.5, 5, 7)
Upset, vexed or mad.

FAYEN FOLKEN (7)
Another term for the *can toi* or low men.

FIREDIMS (2, 3, 4)
Gemstones. Diamonds.

FIREDIM TUBES (3)
Neon lights.

FOLKEN (4.5, 5, 6, 7)
People, as in Calla-folken, the people of the Calla.

FOTTERGRAF (2, 4, 5, 7)
Photograph.

FUZER (4)
Basement storage area. Roland got his guns from the fuzer beneath their barracks.

GILLY (JILLY) (4, 4.5, 5)
Consort or concubine, often meant to bear a child when a leader's wife cannot. Prostitutes sometimes call themselves cotton gillies. Arthur Eld was said to have many, and Roland's lineage may come from one of those liaisons.

GLAMMER OR GLAM (1, 4, 4.5, 5, 6, 7)
Enchantment. According to Henchick, magic and glammer are the same and they unroll from the past.

GOOK (4.5)
A deep well.

GORMLESS (4.5)
Stupid or careless.

GRAF (3, 4, 4.5, 5, 7)
Hard apple cider.

GREAT ALL (1)
The universe.

GREENSTICKING (5)
Putting pressure on someone. Twisting his arm.

GRENADO (3, 4.5, 5, 6, 7)
A hand grenade made by the Great Old Ones.

GUNNA (1, 4, 4.5, 5, 6, 7)
Gear. Belongings. Possessions. The sum total of a person's worldly goods.

HILE (4, 4.5, 5, 6, 7, M)
A word of greeting or a call to action. One of the few words that is the same in both low speech and High Speech. The Manni call it "Fin-Gan," the first word, the one that set the world spinning. "Hile! To me! No prisoners!" is a battle cry Roland knew of old.

HOBS (7)
Hobgoblins or St. Elmo's fire. Orange swirling lights.

HOT-ENJ (7)
Atomic locomotive.

HOUKEN (7)
A word Roland uses regarding Oy. Its exact meaning is unclear.

HUME (7)
A derogatory word for humans, used by taheen.

I CRY YOUR PARDON (1, 3, 4, 4.5, 5, 6, 7)

A formal way of apologizing—usually followed by "I have forgotten the face of my father."

I DO NOT AIM WITH MY HAND (3, 5, M)

The gunslinger's catechism:

> I do not aim with my hand; he who aims with his hand has forgotten the face of his father.
>
> I aim with my eye.
>
> I do not shoot with my hand; he who shoots with his hand has forgotten the face of his father.
>
> I shoot with my mind.
>
> I do not kill with my gun; he who kills with his gun has forgotten the face of his father.
>
> I kill with my heart.

I HAVE FORGOTTEN THE FACE OF MY FATHER (1, 2, 3, 4, 5, 6, 7)

The Act of Contrition. Apprentice gunslingers are forced to say this when they haven't performed up to standards.

JAKES (4, 4.5, 7)

Outhouse, toilet or bathroom.

JILLY

See gilly.

JING-JANG (4.5)

Telephone. There's one in the high sheriff's office in Debaria, though at the time it goes only to a few neighboring towns.

JIPPA (4.5)

Someone who has lost his mind. A word used by the people of Tree Village.

KA (THROUGHOUT)

One of the most difficult concepts in the Dark Tower series. It has several meanings, mostly to do with destiny, purpose or fate. Some believe it is the will of Gan, which must be obeyed. *Ka* creates a duty in people. It is the last thing a person has to rise above and it marks the time of every man and woman.

However, it also has a sense of inevitability. One rule is that a person needs to stand aside and let *ka* work, which implies that *ka* will have its way regardless. If a person isn't sure what to do, do nothing and let *ka* work itself out. Don't worry about the future, in other words. If it is *ka*'s will, anything is possible. Roland often adopts this philosophy, ignoring certain problems (the distant Emerald City, for example) until they are underfoot.

When people go against *ka*, *ka* stands to one side and laughs. Roland believes that if he tries to veer from its path (by going around Lud instead of through it), *ka* will find ways to force him back on course. He has seen people change *ka*, though there is always a price to pay when that happens. Its power is compared to the strong winds of a starkblast or the momentum of a hurtling mono—maybe sane, maybe not. But not irresistible.

Ka is a convenient scapegoat when things go wrong. People invoke it so they don't have to take the blame for their own stupidity. Lucky people also claim they were doing the work of *ka*. Susannah marvels at how everyone seems to think they know just what *ka* intends for them.

People think of *ka* as a heartless, mindless power that does and takes what it wants, regardless of human concerns. Stephen King vacillates between claiming that he creates *ka* and that *ka* is channeled through him. He is *ka*'s translator and conduit. At first he says he made Roland do certain things, but later recants, admitting that Roland's actions sometimes scared him.

Once Roland has completed his *ka*-given duty by saving the Beams and ensuring the survival of the Tower, Tet Corporation believes he is going beyond *ka* by continuing to the Dark Tower. Reaching the Tower and climbing to the top is something Roland feels he has been promised—but was it promised by *ka* or did he simply promise it to himself? He risks becoming *anti-ka*. If the Crimson King captures him and uses his guns to reenter the Dark Tower, everything he has accomplished will be lost.

KA-BABBIES (1)

Friends since childhood.

KA-DADDY (6, 7)

A term that means boss, but which is seldom used in a flattering sense.

KA-DINH (7)

The leader of a *ka-tet*.

KA-ESSEN (4.5)

Life spirit. The *ka-essen* of a person who dies goes on to the clearing at the end of the path.

KA-HUME (7)

Presumably means people who are part of a *ka-tet* or guided by *ka*.

KA-MAI (4, 4.5, 6, 7, M)

Ka's fool. Roland often applies the term to Cuthbert and Eddie. Tim Stoutheart's mother calls herself *ka-mai* after she falls victim to Bern Kells. After hearing Mia's story, Susannah comes up with this definition of the word: one who has been given hope but no choices. *Ka-mais* are often safe from harm until *ka* tires of their antics and swats them out of the world.

KA-MATE (4.5, 5, 6, 7)

Fellow member of a *ka-tet*.

KA-ME (5)

The opposite of *ka-mai*: behaving wisely instead of foolishly.

KA-SHUME (7)

A rue-laden term that is used when someone senses an approaching break in one's *ka-tet*. Even though one can sense impending death, it doesn't always happen. See also shume.

KA-TEL (4)

A class of fellow gunslingers in training. Roland's group consisted of fourteen boys.

KA-TET (1, 3, 4, 4.5, 5, 6, 7, M)

One from many. A group of people ("tet") bound together for a common purpose, who have the same interests and goals. Lives joined by fate. Once formed, its members feel greater than they were before. Each member of a *ka-tet* is like a piece of a puzzle. Put together, they complete a picture. *Ka-tet* is family. *Ka-tet* is love. Whenever a *ka-tet* stops to rest, they unconsciously form a circle. Their purpose need not serve the White—the Little Sisters of Eluria claim to be *ka-tet*. Sharing *khef* is part of what being *ka-tet* means.

Some believe that a *ka-tet* can be broken only by death or treachery. Cort believed that a *ka-tet* could never be broken, even when the group is split. The word *"ka-shume"* indicates the feeling of an impending break of a *ka-tet*. When *ka-tet* breaks, the end always comes quickly.

KAI-MAI (5)
A friend of *ka*. Walter applies the word to Callahan. Not to be confused with *ka-mai*.

KAMMEN (5, 6, 7)
The chimes people hear when they go todash or when their todash journey is about to end. Also known as todash bells. The notes sound beautiful at first, but soon become so hideous and painful that each chime seems to make a person's head burst and his bones vibrate. They also sound when Black Thirteen is awake. The Manni name for the Doorway Cave is Kra Kammen, which means House of Ghosts.

KAS-KA GAN (7)
The prophets or singers of Gan. Artists who translate the word of Gan into their art.

KAVEN (6)
The persistence of magic, an important concept for the Manni.

KEN/KENNIT (1, 4, 4.5, 5, 6, 7, M)
To know, as in "Do you kennit?"

KES (7)
The strength of a Beam.

KHEF (1, 3, 4, 5, 6, 7)
Life force. The word means many things in the original tongue of the Old World: water, birth and life force are a few of them. Roland uses it to mean a closeness and sharing of thoughts among members of a *ka-tet*. Minds

consulting via something so elemental it couldn't rightly be called telepathy. "Sharing *khef*," also known as the sharing of water, is a kind of palaver and storytelling, and is part of what *ka-tet* means. *Khef* can be shared only by those whom destiny has welded together, for good or for ill. Before the battle at Algul Siento, Roland turns this into a communion-like ritual.

KHEF-MATE (3)
A term Eddie uses in reference to Roland. As such, it may not have any true meaning.

KI'BOX (5, 7)
Asshole (shitbox). A metaphor for a person's baser functions.

KI'CAN (7)
Shit-people.

KI'COME (7)
Bullshit. Utter nonsense.

KI'-DAM (7)
Shit for brains.

KILLIN (5)
An undefined insult. "Ye foolish killin."

KRA (5, 6, M)
A Manni's cabin. Also his circle of friends.

KRA-TEN (6, M)
A Manni village or community.

LET EVIL WAIT FOR THE DAY ON WHICH IT MUST FALL (5)
A Gilead saying.

LIFE FOR YOUR CROPS (1, 4, 6)
Usually said after spitting on the ground.

LIMBIT (4.5)
A unit of temperature.

LONG DAYS AND PLEASANT NIGHTS (1, 4, 4.5, 5, 6, 7)
A traditional greeting. According to Roland, it is associated more with Gilead than with rural communities. The traditional answer is, "And may you have twice the number."

LOOKS TO THE HORIZON (6)
A unit of distance equal to about thirty-three wheels.

MADRIGAL (5)
A yellow herb. A cash crop grown in the southern Callas.

MANDRUS (3)
A disease like syphilis. Also known as whore's blossoms.

MA'SUN (7)
War chest. Applied to the cache of arms Ted Brautigan prepares for Roland.

MAY YOUR DAYS BE LONG UPON THE EARTH (4, 4.5, 6)
A traditional greeting.

MIA (5)
An almost holy name that means "mother" in the High Speech.

MINGO (4)
A crop cultivated in Mejis.

MIR (3)
The Old People's name for Shardik. They believed he was a demon incarnate, or the shadow of a god. The name means "the world beneath the world."

MOIT (4.5, 5, 7)
A small number or amount of something. Five or six.

MOLLY (4, 4.5, 6)

Woman or female.

MUFFIN-BALLS (5)

Edible ground berries the size of tennis balls. Their horns are sour. Fried with fat, they taste like meat. They sometimes bring about lively dreams.

NEN (4.5)

A burning liquor. The Covenant Man gave some to Tim Ross to settle him down.

OGGAN (5, 6, 7)

Smooth-packed dirt used for a road surface.

OPOPANAX (5)

The ancient lacquered feather used by the people of Calla Bryn Sturgis to call a meeting. The person holding the large billowy feather during the meeting has the floor.

Crossovers to Other Works: The word also appears in *The Plant* and *Black House*, though it refers to other things. In the real world, the word refers to a kind of aromatic plant resin that hardens into a gum.

PAREY (4)

A crop cultivated in Mejis.

PETTIBONE (4)

An alcoholic drink.

POKEBERRIES (1, 5, 6, 7)

A fruit with orange skin and a golden interior.

POKIE (4.5)

A wandering cowboy not signed to any particular ranch.

POOKY (4.5)

An enormous reddish snake that dwells in the Endless Forest. Its spade-shaped head is as large as a skillet. They have poisonous fangs that paralyze victims before they are devoured. The final form the skin-man in Debaria takes on.

POPKINS (L, 1, 2, 4, 4.5, 5, 7)
Sandwiches. We know of tooter-fish (tuna) and shannie popkins.

PORIN (5)
A spice of great worth.

PRODDIE (4.5)
A hired hand at a ranch.

PUBE (L, 7, M)
A young person. The people in Lud adopted this word to describe their faction.

PULLS (5)
Cornshuck wraps used to roll cigarettes.

ROONT (5, 6, 7)
Calla Bryn Sturgis term meaning "ruined" that describes the condition of the children who come back after the Wolves take them. The changes depend on how old the child is, but in general they are mentally, emotionally and developmentally retarded and sexually dead. At about the age of sixteen, they suddenly grow to enormous size, a painful process. When they reach their thirties, they become old quickly and die young. The word is pronounced the same way as it is by people like John Cullum from central Maine.

RUSSEL (2)
To take a woman by force.

RUSTIES (4.5, 5, 6)
Swallows or giant blackbirds. Also known as bin-rusties.

SAI (THROUGHOUT)
A form of address, like "sir" or "mister" or "ma'am."

SALIG (4)
A swamp animal akin to a crocodile or alligator. Long green things with big teeth.

SALTIES (4.5)
Miners in the salt mines near Debaria.

SANDAY (4)
A day of the week. The traditional cowboys' day of rest in Hambry.

SCRIP (6)
A lawyer.

SELLIAN (3)
A language dialect, one of five that Roland knows how to speak. He claims to have forgotten most Sellian except for the curse words.

SEMINON (5, 6)
A windstorm that occurs in the Callas before true winter. They arise in the east in the desert between the Callas and Thunderclap. Often, they turn back when they reach the Whye River. Though there's probably a good meteorological reason for this behavior, the locals believe that Lord Seminon begs Lady Oriza to make him welcome when he reaches the water, and she often bars his passage out of jealousy because Seminon married her sister and Lady Oriza wanted him for herself.

SEPPE-SAI (5, M)
Death dealer. The man who sold pies in the market in Gilead acquired that name because his wares made people ill. Roland is the last seppe-sai.

SET MY WATCH AND WARRANT ON/UPON/TO IT (1, 3, 4, 4.5, 5, 6, 7)
I guarantee it.

SHADDIE (4.5)
A piece of canvas, like a tarpaulin.

SHANNIE (4.5)
An edible fish caught in the River Whye.

SHARPROOT (1, 4, 5)

A vegetable crop cultivated in Mejis and Calla Bryn Sturgis. The bright magenta roots of the green vine are edible. Roland used the roots to test the Sisters of Oriza's skills.

SHEEVIN OR SHIVEEN (4, 5)

Another word for gilly. It refers to a whore who considers herself too good to provide service in trade and requires payment in coin. It is also translated as "quiet little woman," or "side wife."

SHUME (4.5)

An old Mid-World term that means both shame and sorrow. Related to *ka-shume*, a sense of dread about impending events.

SIGUL (L, 3, 4, 4.5, 5, 6, 7, M)

A sign or logo or omen.

SIMOOM (4.5)

A strong wind.

SKIDDUM (4.5)

A shack where some salt miners live. Most miners live in the mouths of the caves themselves. These shacks offer little but have the virtue of not being underground.

SLAGGITT (5)

A curse word in Calla Bryn Sturgis.

SLEWFEET (5)

Unskilled trackers.

SLINKUM (4.5, 7)

An old man's strap-style white undershirt.

SLOWKINS (4.5)

Slow. Cort says that Roland is slowkins from the eyebrows up.

SNICK (4.5)
Clever or cagey.

SOH (4.5, 5, 6, 7)
Boy. Often used by itself, but sometimes appended to the end (Jake-soh) or front of a name (Soh Vikka).

SPARKLIGHTS (1, 4, 4.5, 5)
Electric lights with filaments. A few still worked in Gilead, but the last one burned out in Hambry two generations ago.

SPECIE (4.5)
Hard currency.

SPRIGGUM (5)
One of the ingredients in Rosalita's cure for Roland's dry twist. It comes from the swamp.

STEM (5)
A businessman like Moses Carver.

STUFFY-GUYS (4, 5)
Scarecrows. Traditionally, their hands are painted red and they're thrown into the Reap-Night Bonfire. This is a surviving remnant of the generations-old charyou tree ritual where people were burned as a sacrifice to the gods.

TACK-SEE (3, 5, 7)
Roland's interpretation of the word "taxi."

TAKE A RIDE ON THE HANDSOME (3)
Die.

TELAMEI (5)
To gossip about someone you shouldn't gossip about.

TEMPA (6)
A Manni meeting hall.

TET (3, 4.5, 5, 7)

A group of people.

TET-FA (4.5)

Friend of the tet.

TET-KA CAN GAN (7)

Navel.

THANKEE-SAI (THROUGHOUT)

Thank you.

THERE ARE OTHER (MORE) WORLDS THAN THESE (1, 2, 3, 4, 5, 6, 7)

The last thing Jake says to Roland before the gunslinger abandons him to his death beneath the mountains while pursuing the man in black. Roland comes to believe that it's one of the most important things anyone has ever said to him. The phrase is repeated throughout as the *ka-tet* realizes the importance of other universes to their quest.

THERE WILL BE WATER IF GOD WILLS IT (1, 3, 4, 4.5, 5, 7, M)

A proverb that means something will happen if it is destined to happen. Analogous to putting your faith in *ka*.

THIDDLES (7)

Buttocks.

THROCKEN (4.5, 7)

Another name for a billy-bumbler. Roland first heard this word in a book read to him by his mother, *The Throcken and the Dragon*. To see one is considered good luck.

THROCKET (4.5)

A group of billy-bumblers.

THROG (5)

Three ways.

TIME HAS MOVED ON (THROUGHOUT)

A way of expressing the changes to Mid-World since the Dark Tower has begun its decline. The Mejis version of this proverb is "Time is a face on the water."

TODANA (6)

Deathbag. The hazy black aura or shadow around a person that indicates someone has been marked for death. A variant of the word todash.

TODASH (5, 6, 7, M)

Passing between two worlds without using a doorway. The start and end of these trips are heralded by kammen, the todash chimes, which start out sounding beautiful but grow physically and mentally painful. To an observer, the person going todash vanishes, but leaves behind a dull gray glow that approximates their body shape and position as a placeholder. In the other world, the person is free to wander at will, unobserved for the most part, although people generally avoid the todash traveler. The traveler has the ability to pass through solid items in the other world and sometimes sees the vagrant dead. However, the traveler's essence is in the second world. They can return bearing injuries suffered on the other side. Waking a person in a todash state is risky, as is the process of passing from one world to the other, because a person might fall into the space between. Pieces of the Wizard's Rainbow are said to make going todash easier. The Manni, who believe todash is the holiest of rites and most exalted of states, fast and meditate to induce the todash state and use magnets and plumb bobs to determine the best locations.

TODASH DARKNESS (5, 6, 7)

The endless spaces between worlds, where it is always dark. Monsters live in these places like rats in walls. A defective doorway beneath Castle Discordia opens on one. The Crimson King, who hopes to be the lord of the todash darkness, sends his bitterest enemies there.

TODASH TAHKEN (5)

Holes in reality that allow passage from one world to another.

TOOTER-FISH (2, 7)

The way Roland pronounces the words "tuna fish."

TOUCH, THE (1, 4, 5, 6, 7)

A kind of psychic ability that some gunslingers, artists and lunatics possess. Alain Johns is strong in the touch, as is Jake. Most members of a *ka-tet* have a little of this, although Cuthbert has absolutely none.

TRIG (1, 3, 4.5, 5, 7)

Clever or savvy, cunning or sly.

TRUM (5)

The ability to convince others to do things that might seem dangerous or foolhardy.

TWIM (6, 7)

The number two or twins.

URS-A-KA GAN (7)

The Scream of the Bear. A more emphatic version of Urs-Ka Gan, which is the Song of the Bear. Another component of the song Stephen King hears when he writes about the Dark Tower.

VES'-KA GAN (7)

The Song of the Turtle. The voice that Stephen King hears when the Dark Tower story comes to him. Sometimes he calls it Susannah's Song.

VURT (4.5)

Flying creatures from the Endless Forest, sometimes known as bullet-birds. One killed Bern Kells's father by boring a hole right through him.

WASEAU (7)

Bird.

WATER-STOOL (4)

A flush toilet.

WENBERRY (3)

A fruit similar to a strawberry.

WERVEL (4.5)
A poisonous rodent the size of a dog that dwells in the Endless Forest.

WHEEL (1, 3, 4, 4.5, 5, 6, 7)
A unit of distance that is approximately 1.1 miles. The subunit is arcs o' the wheel. One yard is roughly two arcs.

WHORE'S BLOSSOMS (3)
A disease like syphilis. Also known as mandrus.

WORLD HAS MOVED ON, THE (1, 2, 3, 4, 4.5, 5, 6)
A vague description for the way Mid-World has changed since the fall of Gilead and the decline of the Dark Tower. It indicates that time, distance and direction are no longer stable, but also implies that the halcyon days of Gilead are no more.

WOT (4, 4.5, 5)
Reckon or believe.

YAR (1, 3, 4, 4.5, 6, 7)
Yes.

YOUNKERS (3)
Young people.

ZN (5)
One of the Great Letters. It means both eternity (zi), now and come, as in come-commala. It appears on the Orizas.

SOME STORIES LAST FOREVER

At the beginning of the Coda at the end of *The Dark Tower*, King directly addresses his readers. He chastises some for being grim and goal-oriented—that goal being the conclusion of the series. "I hope you came to hear the tale, and not just munch your way through the pages to the ending," he writes.

Perhaps it didn't start out that way, but the Dark Tower series became a commentary on storytelling. Or maybe it did start out that way. King's ambition in 1970 was to write the longest popular novel in history, and he also wanted to blend the disparate genres of the Western, the epic fantasy and horror. The form of the story would comment on storytelling.

For someone who claims he doesn't talk of himself, as he does when he catches up to Walter at the end of *The Gunslinger*, Roland spends a lot of time talking about himself. When he reaches Brown's cabin, he tells this total stranger the story of his recent adventures in Tull, where he wiped out the town's entire population. Storytelling is a form of confession, though he doesn't seek absolution. He is simply compelled to relate these events.

Once he has a traveling companion—Jake Chambers—he looks back even farther, to his days in Gilead as a boy. As they cross the desert and traverse the mountains, Roland tells of how he and Cuthbert discovered a traitor in Gilead and what happened after they relayed this information to Roland's father. Watching Hax hang was an important moment in his life.

At Jake's insistence, he also tells about his coming of age, a tale that requires him to remember how his mother betrayed his father and Gilead by having an affair with Marten Broadcloak, Steven Deschain's adviser and the court magician. He explains how he allowed Marten to goad him into taking his challenge to become a gunslinger sooner than anyone had ever done before, and how his inspired choice of a weapon—his hawk, David—allowed him to prevail when, by all rights, he should have been beaten, perhaps maimed, and exiled from his homeland.

When Roland plucks Eddie Dean from the clutches of mobsters and drags him into Mid-World, the young junkie also has a story to tell—the story of life with his older brother, Henry. Roland lets him ramble—the story passes the time as they make their way up the beach—but he also thinks Eddie needs to hear his own story now that he's off drugs for the first time in a long time. In return, while suffering from infection, Roland tells Eddie about his trek across the desert. Later, he tells Eddie and Susannah both versions of that story: the one where Jake shows up at the Way Station and the one where he doesn't.

Two books in the series consist primarily of Roland telling stories about his past. In *Wizard and Glass*, he picks up the tale the day after his coming of age and continues through the following months after he is sent to Mejis for his own safety, where he meets the love of his life. In *The Wind Through the Keyhole*, while the *ka-tet* rides out a killing storm, Roland relates an adventure that took place less than six months after his return from Mejis. "There's nothing like stories on a windy night when folks have found a warm place in a cold world," he says. In that story, his younger self tells yet another story, this one a fairy tale that his mother used to read to him. The story is meant to occupy the mind of a scared and bored boy who has just lost his father and to teach him about courage. Stories pass the time and take a person away from his troubles. The stories we hear as children are the ones we remember all our lives, King writes, and Roland tells Young Bill that a person is never too old for stories—we live for them.

Roland tells the legends of his world, too—the story of Old Mother and Old Star, for example. His homeland is almost mythic to everyone else he meets in Mid-World. Gilead and Arthur Eld exist so far in the past that many people doubt they ever existed. Overholser of Calla Bryn Sturgis calls Roland's claim to be from Gilead "a children's good-night story." It would be the same thing for us if someone claimed to be from Atlantis.

Paper in Mid-World is scarce and valuable, so there aren't many books, which means there's no written record. People have to rely on their memories. Even Roland isn't sure which parts of what he's been told about Mid-World are real and which are made up, and he's forgotten a lot of what he knew at one time. He is frequently astonished to come face-to-face with something he had written off as legend, such as Shardik, the Guardian of the Beam who was part of a story he heard as a child.

He tells his *ka-tet* other stories of his wandering years, including his mis-adventures in Eluria. When he isn't telling stories, he's asking them to tell him stories. He's a glutton for stories, especially those that lead off with "Once upon a time when everyone lived in the forest" or "Once upon a bye, before your grandfather's grandfather was born," though he usually listens to them like an anthropologist trying to figure out some strange culture by their myths and legends. He asks Eddie and Susannah to tell him *The Wizard of Oz* and "Hansel and Gretel," both of which bear on their quest, but it's clear that the gunslinger simply likes a good story.

Margaret Eisenhart tells the story of Gray Dick. Father Callahan recounts the story of his life after 'Salem's Lot, and Ted Brautigan records his own life story on a tape recorder for the *ka-tet* to hear while they're preparing to attack Algul Siento. Again, these stories have some relevance to the matters at hand, but they are also self-contained adventures.

Along the way, Eddie starts noticing how fictions from their reality in-trude on their adventures. Everything that happens reminds him of a book or a film. The Red Death of Fedic and Poe's story. *Alice in Wonderland*. The Green Palace outside Topeka and *The Wizard of Oz*. The plight of the people in Calla Bryn Sturgis and the plot of *The Magnificent Seven*, directed by John Sturges. The Wolves wear masks that resemble comic book characters and their weapons are straight out of *Star Wars* and Harry Potter.

Matters take a strange turn when Father Callahan is handed a copy of a novel in which he is a character. Naturally, this causes some confusion in the former priest. He knows he's real, but the book contains details of his life that only he knows, and everything written about him is as real as his memories. Disoriented, he starts thinking of other people as being in a story with him.

Then Roland and Eddie discover that Stephen King lives near the place where Calvin Tower (a collector of rare books, such as the valuable edition of *'Salem's Lot* that Father Callahan perused) and his friend Aaron Deepneau are hiding. When they visit the author in 1977, they learn that they, too, are Stephen King's creations, even though he hasn't yet consciously thought up Eddie or the others. Realizing that he's a character in someone else's fiction, and that this author's mistakes affect his reality, is nearly enough to drive Ed-die crazy. People don't really die—they leave the story.

Stephen King complains about being Roland's personal secretary. He be-lieves he isn't making conscious decisions about Roland's story but is tran-scribing what comes to him. Writing is a kind of todash journey in which his consciousness enters and interacts with another world. He didn't make

Roland leave Jake to die under the mountains. That was all Roland's doing, he tells Roland and Eddie. He's not sure he even likes his supposed hero anymore.

Roland isn't terribly fond of his creator, either, thinking that he's lazy, seeking easier tales to work on instead of doing the hard but important work of telling his story. His general assessment of people who make up stories is harsh. He thinks they tell tales because they're afraid of life. Of course, this is coming from a man who has been told all his life that he has no imagination. Even so, while Roland is chiding King to pick up the story again, King is telling Roland to finish his job. The creation of his story works both ways.

It is in Roland's best interests to make sure King remains safe. Roland's enemy, the Crimson King, knows that Stephen King is breathing life into Roland's adventures and attempts to prevent him from writing. If King dies, Roland will never reach the Dark Tower. (What exactly *would* happen to him is open to debate. The *ka-tet* believes Gan's Beam would break, leading to the fall of the Dark Tower. However, since the "real" Stephen King said that his son Joe would have finished the series if he couldn't, then maybe Roland would have simply cast about with his *ka-tet* like they did at the beginning of *Wolves of the Calla*, waiting for time to slip back into gear when a new King hears the Song of the Turtle.)

Eddie believes the way for Stephen King to become immortal is to write the right story, because some stories live forever. The problem with the Dark Tower stories is that when King works on them, pushing against creation, he feels something pushing back.

The Calvins who study King's work believe that little of what he's written after penning the famous line "The man in black crossed the desert and the gunslinger followed" is simply a story. They're all messages in a bottle cast into the Prim to convey information to Roland. Even King (the fictional version) thinks that his other stories have all been practice runs for writing the Dark Tower story. Writing this story is the one that always feels like coming home.

There are many tales that Roland didn't get the chance to tell his *ka-tet*. He always said those were stories for another day. The next time the Voice of the Turtle speaks, perhaps we will be graced with another story of Roland's adventures.

ROLAND DESCHAIN'S ENEMIES

Some readers have reacted strongly to the fates of the three characters who appeared to be Roland's nemeses. In order of appearance, these are: Walter o'Dim—also known as the man in black, Randall Flagg and Marten Broadcloak—the Crimson King, and Mordred Deschain. Roland had other adversaries—Rhea of the Cöos, Sylvia Pittston, Gasher, the Big Coffin Hunters, to name a few—but their tenures were of relatively short duration.

The strongest howls of dismay came at the way destiny played out for the first of these. Randall Flagg has a long history in King's fiction. He was the villain in *The Stand*, the Dark Man who assembled the forces of evil and corruption against the followers of Mother Abigail. In *The Eyes of the Dragon*, he appeared as the court magician and counselor to kings, a man who for centuries sought to corrupt and disrupt the kingdoms around Delain. He even made a brief, off-screen cameo in "Heavenly Shades of Night Are Falling," the final section of *Hearts in Atlantis*, recognizable by his initials and his pernicious influence, a man who knew how to become dim.

And, of course, he is the man in black, present in the Dark Tower series from the very first sentence, introduced to readers even before Roland is. Although he is the object of Roland's pursuit, for most of the book the gunslinger knows him only from the remains of his campfires and the traps that he sets for Roland. He is glimpsed on occasion, a black dot on the horizon luring Roland on until, finally, they confront each other beneath the mountains. Once through the mountains, they hold palaver.

Though their conversation lasts a preternaturally long time, Walter tells Roland little that is important to his quest. The Oracle had already told him about the three people he will draw. Beyond the lesson in metaphysics, the sum total of Walter's useful information is this: go west.

As Marten, this man of many faces, who lies even when the truth might serve him, held sway over the court of Gilead when Roland was a boy. He insinuated himself into the circle of gunslingers who governed the Baronies, acting as court magician and counsel. His power was strong enough to destroy Roland's mother, first seducing her, then enticing her to conspire against her husband. After he attempted to get Roland exiled by angering him into taking his test of manhood at an early age, he fled west to collude with John Farson in the civil war against the Affiliation. He was present at Jericho Hill and fired the arrow that killed Cuthbert.

Although Flagg wrought havoc in many times and places, his missions almost always failed. On Earth, the emissaries from Boulder defeated him with the misguided help of Trashcan Man, one of his own minions. Simple-minded Tom Cullen eluded him, Dayna Jurgens outwitted him and Nadine Cross provoked him into killing his unborn child. In Delain, a group of children foiled his plans to run the kingdom into the ground. Maerlyn says that little magic and long life is all he's capable of. Mordred Deschain thinks of him as a man of many faces and neat tricks, but never half as clever as he thought. He gets points for longevity but not greatness or power. Arrogance, vanity, hubris and carelessness lead him to underestimate Roland time and again, and to underestimate Mordred, too.

Readers eagerly anticipated a big showdown between Roland and Flagg. Since he was there at the beginning, they wanted Roland to meet Flagg at the Tower for one final battle. The best man would win (Roland, of course) and ascend to the top to claim whatever power or knowledge the Tower held.

Was Flagg worthy of being Roland's ultimate adversary? Through the moderator on his message board, King said, "Flagg/Walter was not the same person that he was when he and Roland palavered (and neither was Roland)." Quasi-immortal though he may have been, he had grown old and his arrogance had weakened him. But for the slip of a nonexistent finger, Roland would have gunned Flagg down on the throne in the Green Palace, where he sat taunting the gunslinger, a clear indication of how vain and careless he'd become. How would readers have reacted if Roland had succeeded in killing him then? Flagg muses later that many would have considered that a happy ending. Would they? Would that death have been any more satisfying than what eventually transpired?

Flagg lost sight of his goal. Even when his eyes were set on the Tower, the Crimson King probably controlled him without his realizing it, in much the same way that he controlled others. Mordred speculates that Flagg likely believed that he came to the Fedic control room of his own free will, leaving readers to infer that he was manipulated into going there.

Flagg believed that Roland completed him, made him greater than his own destiny as a mercenary who wanted to explore the Tower before it fell. However, who besides Flagg believes in this elevated status? When he sees Roland defeating him at every turn, or taking away the things he covets (like Roland's mother), he snaps. He lowers his eyes from the Tower and sets them firmly on his age-old enemy. He loses any sanity he might have once had. Roland becomes his obsession, his Dark Tower. He no longer dreams of overthrowing the Crimson King and ruling Discordia in his place. He no longer cares. He is overcome by jealousy and frustration, and this causes his premature downfall.

To bring him all the way to the Tower for a final showdown with Roland would have given him far more credit than he was due.

What of Mordred Deschain, then, named after the ill-begotten child of King Arthur who slew his father and ended the golden era of the Knights of the Round Table? In a Greek tragedy, one such as he would have been the instrument of Roland's downfall. Son of two mothers, spawn of two fathers.

Of the three primary adversaries Roland faces, Mordred is perhaps the most sympathetic, for he had no part in his own creation, and he was assigned a task that was not of his choosing. He was created to despise Roland, but he is conflicted. He knows that his appearance is hateful to Roland and the *ka-tet*. Unable to change this, he often lurks near the tight, closed circle, wishing he could be part of that family. He fantasizes about how different things would be if he revealed himself to the *ka-tet* and they welcomed him with open arms, so he could be with at least one of his fathers.

Instead, he is forever an outsider, cursed to pursue Roland across the miles, suffering thirst, unquenchable hunger and the cold of winter. He is single-minded of purpose and, as such, represents what would befall Roland if the gunslinger remained fixed on his self-appointed quest. If Mordred had found the strength to break off from his pursuit of Roland, he might have successfully completed his other task by joining his crimson father at the Dark Tower. On that final night, though he was sick from eating poisoned meat, he could have abandoned Roland, Patrick and Oy at their camp. The outcome would have been vastly different if Mordred had reached the Tower ahead of Roland and freed the Crimson King. Even if Mordred hadn't lived after doing this, the king would have gained the Tower and might have brought it down.

Like Flagg, Mordred's demise was brought about by his need to destroy Roland. The gunslinger easily dispatches him—with Oy's assistance—and the anticipated showdown, presaged over the course of the final volume, is done in seconds. In spite of all the knowledge he inherited from his genetics and from those he consumed along the way—including Flagg, so it might be said that *this* is the final confrontation between Roland and Flagg—he was no match for Roland.

The most difficult of Roland's enemies to credit is the Crimson King. What exactly is their relationship, and how do they know about each other? Flagg claims that both are descended from Arthur Eld, but the Crimson King's place in the family tree is never clarified. The Crimson King possessed a *sigul* of the Eld that gave him access to the Tower; it was only through his own carelessness and insanity that he ended up stranded on a balcony instead of reaching the top.

Roland knows little of the Crimson King until late in his quest. He seems unfamiliar with the name when first he hears it, and only later recalls some of the legends he knew about this being from his youth. For most of the series the Crimson King is offstage. Reports of his deeds filter in through other characters, including Mia and Walter, but even when Roland and Susannah reach the Crimson King's castle, he seems more legendary than real.

Unlike Roland, the Crimson King has no desire to understand the Tower; he merely wants to conquer it. In his pettiness, he would rather destroy it than have it fall into the hands of anyone else. No one knows why he chose to construct his castle so close to the Dark Tower, and why it held him in such thrall. Unanswered, too, is the question of why he chose to wait so long to enter the Tower. As a member of the line of Eld, he should have been able to gain entry whenever he wanted to. Why did he bend his efforts to thwarting Roland instead? If Mordred was powerful enough to bring down the Tower on his own after the Breakers were freed, could not the Crimson King have done the same? Apparently not, because for time out of mind he worked to destroy the Tower, and for the past several centuries he has spent vast amounts of energy rounding up Breakers and setting them about their appointed task.

So why did he finally go to the Tower to be at the nexus of all universes when everything came tumbling down? His minions believed he would be empowered to rule the Discordia that followed, and maybe the only way he could guarantee that was to be at the Tower when the time came. Why he believed he would survive the end of existence is unclear—it may have only been a delusion.

That he has powers that extend into other worlds is unarguable. He interfered with events in Derry. He tried to kill Stephen King. He has a kind of prescience that allows him to anticipate who might stand in his way in the future, and he attempts to eliminate them. However, when the final showdown with Roland takes place, he is little more than a bumhug (what Roland thought Jake called the Wizard of Oz): a faker. All talk, no action. He relies on technological weaponry to battle the gunslinger, apparently impotent to do anything else.

The man who Parkus said could blow Jack Sawyer out like a candle turns out to be far less than his legend. It is eminently fitting, then, that the Crimson King, who wished to rule Discordia forever, was likely sent, eyeless and blind, into one of the todash spaces between universes, where he can attempt to rule whatever exists there. At last, the Crimson King has a kingdom.

So none of these powerful beings provided much of a challenge for Roland Deschain. True, they caused much damage, grief and destruction while attempting to thwart him, but they were easily undone. Who, then, is Roland's chief adversary, the nemesis who foils him at every stage and eventually bests him? The puzzle he has yet to solve?

Is it *ka*, Stephen King or the Dark Tower itself?

Perhaps Roland's nemesis is himself. The enigma of his own existence is the one challenge he has yet to unravel. Let's explore that further in the final chapter.

THE END AND WHAT IT MIGHT MEAN

No one should be surprised by Roland's fate at the end of the Dark Tower series. From the beginning, Stephen King described it as a cycle. What is *ka*? It's a wheel that goes around and around, always arriving back at the place it started. Déjà vu is prevalent throughout the series. Why can Eddie ride a horse the first time he gets on one outside of Calla Bryn Sturgis? Because he's done it before.

Roland completes his mission when he and his *ka-tet* free the Breakers from their destructive work and save Stephen King's life. No more Beams will break and the weakened ones might even regain their integrity. Roland's story will go on. The Dark Tower isn't safe forever. Entropy eventually causes everything in the universe to crumble. Such is the nature of existence. Still, Roland has done what he set out to do: he saved the Tower against unnatural decline and, by doing so, has allowed the multiverse to return to its natural state.

He goes one step farther by going to the Tower. His curiosity is understandable. He has toiled for centuries to save it. Surely he deserves at least a glimpse of the object for which he has sacrificed his existence. If Roland saw the Tower, announced the names of his friends, laid down Aunt Talitha's cross and walked away, he might consider his mission complete.

However, because of the Crimson King, Roland can't draw near to the Tower, yet once he got so close, the Song of the Beams would lure him closer. So the Crimson King presents a problem. A cautious man—and Roland has become more cautious over the course of his journey—might wonder if someone might find a way to liberate him. Also, the Crimson King has demonstrated that he can exert an evil influence from his little balcony. So Roland's decision to destroy him is logical. Besides, the Crimson King has caused much death and destruction. As they say in some parts, the Crimson King deserved killing.

Having neutralized the Crimson King, Roland has another choice. Turn away or enter the Tower? This is the most important decision he's ever had to make. If he opens the door and ascends its narrowing staircase in flights of nineteen steps, he must face his life and all its shortcomings, like someone having his life flash before his eyes at the moment of his death. If he walks away, he's free. Alas, he always makes the wrong choice. You can almost hear the Tower sighing with disappointment.

By entering the Tower, he displays hubris, a trait that has been the downfall of many mythological characters. He presumes that he has the right to mount the stairs and come face-to-face with whatever is in charge of all of creation. He believes he deserves to know the answer to the question that has been asked by every sentient creature: what is the meaning of life? No one has ever had that question answered to his or her satisfaction—at least not while they were alive. It is beyond the ken of any man, even a legendary gunslinger.

More than that, he wants to demand that this entity, whoever it turns out to be, undo all the ill that has befallen Mid-World. He might as well ask Stephen King to unwrite all his novels.

As a result, he is punished. "Peeled back, curved back, turned back" to repeat his journey once again—as he has repeated it countless times before. How many times? Delah, to use Roland's word for "a number beyond counting" or "who knows?" How many more times will he repeat it? Until he gets it right, whatever that means.

One thing seems certain: no matter how often Roland has set out across the Mohaine Desert on the trail of the man in black, he has never failed to save the Tower. If that happened, then everything would end, including his quasi-eternal existence. No matter how badly he performed, no matter what sins he committed along the way, no matter which friends he sacrificed in the name of his mission, he has freed (or killed) the Breakers and saved Stephen King's life. However, he never once accepted Tet Corporation's gold watch as a retirement gift. He always entered the Tower.

The Dark Tower series has been described as a loop. Roland reaches the top of the Tower and is thrust back to the midpoint of his journey to a time when he had the first glimmerings that he might succeed. If it were a loop, or a circle, that would imply that Roland was unchanged, destined to make the same mistakes over and over again.

His existence is more accurately described as an upward spiral, like the staircase inside the Tower. In retrospect, Irene Tassenbaum's final toast to Roland—may your road wind ever upward—seems more like a curse than a blessing. Roland has advanced to a higher level of the Tower. The Roland we see in the final pages of *The Dark Tower* is not the same Roland we met in the opening pages of *The Gunslinger*. Call him Roland 2.0 or Roland 19.0 or Roland 99.0. He has learned to love again. He shows mercy to people he might previously have slaughtered without a second thought, like the outraged Breakers who confront him after the battle of Algul Siento, demanding to know who's going to look after them now. His sights have lifted somewhat.

When he understands the high price *ka* demands of him and it's too late to cry off, he chooses to sacrifice himself instead of another, perhaps secure in the knowledge that the survivors of his broken *ka-tet* would carry on the quest in his stead. Whatever his thinking, he demonstrates how much he has evolved by opening the door of Chip McAvoy's rattletrap truck and attempting to step into the path of Bryan Smith's van.

How do we *know* Roland has improved? Because he now has the Horn of Eld among his gunna. In previous iterations, Roland was so narrowly focused on his mission that he couldn't look away from it long enough to stop for the Horn, a *sigul* of his heroic ancestry. Now he remembers pausing to pick it up and knock the dust of the battlefield from it. This has been the source of some confusion among readers. If Gan transmitted Roland back to the Mohaine Desert, how could he have picked up the Horn, which was lost years— decades, centuries—earlier? As Roland tells his *ka-tet* before launching into the story of Mejis, the past is in motion in his world, rearranging itself. This elevated Roland's past has been rearranged, a sign of the improvements in his nature acquired during his most recent quest for the Tower.

Some readers suggested that the horn was a gift from Gan, a *sigul* that this will be his final journey—that he will finally break free from the spiral. That he will blow the horn when he reaches the Tower in the way that his namesake did in the Browning poem. That may be the case. Each reader gets to decide for him- or herself. It could be a gift from Gan, or a sign that Gan's message is getting through.

King is of the opinion that people improve only slightly on each level of the Tower. The Roland we meet at the end of the series is likely still deeply flawed and narrowly focused. He may have to repeat his journey dozens or hundreds of times more until he does everything to *ka*'s satisfaction. Then he will be freed from his hell, which is repetition, according to King. Roland wonders if he will fight battles similar to the one in Calla Bryn Sturgis for all of eternity and after each one he'll sense the Tower a little farther away instead of a little closer.

What is this lofty state we call perfection? What does Roland have to do on his final journey? For one thing, he has to stop sacrificing people. That can't extend to Susan Delgado, but it could start with Jake, who could join him on the beach at the Western Sea and, perhaps, warn him about the lobstrosities before they take his fingers. That would be the first step in the right direction. It can only get better from there.

But what happens at the end, after he saves the Tower, vanquishes the Crimson King, and returns the members of his fellowship to their proper places? I'd like to think that he greets the Tower, blows his horn, lays down the silver cross and then turns back toward Calla Bryn Sturgis. Maybe he could take Patrick Danville with him. The people of the Calla wouldn't be quick to judge his disability.

I like to imagine him reuniting with Rosalita Muñoz, who surely loved him. He could live out the rest of his natural days as a normal human being who is part of ordinary society. Maybe he would hang up his guns or maybe the Calla-folken would talk him into becoming the local lawman, a job that would be tantamount to retirement in that peaceful region.

Late at night, when the mind sometimes refuses to shut down, he could lie awake, a woman who loves him by his side, and wonder about what is at the heart of existence, just like everyone else. And, at the end of his days, he would go on to the clearing at the end of the path, just like everyone else (with the exception thus far of one gunslinger who has skirted the path by daring to look behind the curtain). Then—and only then—might his questions be answered.

Responding to questions about the ending of the series, King posted this on his message board: "My ending is my ending. Roland will have his redemption, but he did not deserve it then. During his lifetime, Roland made too many wrong choices. You cannot do things as serious as sacrifice a child and not have to pay karma regardless of other good deeds done in your lifetime."

ACKNOWLEDGMENTS

Though writing a book is often a solitary endeavor, *The Dark Tower Companion* could not have been written without the support and assistance of a number of people.

First of all, I have to thank Stephen King for several reasons. Obviously, if he hadn't written the Dark Tower series, there would be no Companion. However, above and beyond that, he has facilitated the creation of this book. He supplied me with the first-draft manuscript of *The Wind Through the Keyhole* in 2011 so I could have it as a reference. Then he agreed to give the interview contained in this book. Finally, talking to him about things that have nothing to do with the Dark Tower series is fun, too.

Stephen King's personal assistant, Marsha DeFilippo, has also been a good friend and a valuable resource. She put me in touch with some of the people who agreed to be interviewed for this book and has been an enthusiastic supporter of my work over the years and a constant help.

Speaking of enthusiasm, Robin Furth has been one of this book's biggest cheerleaders. She regularly told me how much she was looking forward to seeing it, which is a boon to someone who, as I said, generally works in solitude. Robin not only agreed to be interviewed about her work on the Marvel series and Discordia, she introduced me to all of the other Marvel artists and contributors featured in this book and answered all my questions as they arose.

Thanks, too, to the other individuals who took time out of their busy schedules to respond to my interview questions. I spoke to Ron Howard on his way home from a busy day directing the movie *Rush* about Formula 1 racecar drivers, which filmed in England in 2012. I caught up with Akiva Goldsman between set visits and editing sessions on his current project. Richard Isanove spoke to me a day or two after an all-night session working on

The Way Station. Brian Stark and I spent an hour on the phone discussing Discordia. Brian was one of the people who suggested I write a follow-up to *The Road to the Dark Tower*.

I'd like to thank Peter David, Jae Lee, Michael Lark, Stefano Gaudiano and Laurence Campbell for agreeing to be interviewed for this project, and Bonnie Balamos and Louisa Velis for helping coordinate some of the other interviews.

Many thanks to my editor at NAL, Brent Howard, and all of the other great folks at Penguin who worked on this book. I am in awe of the work done by copy editors, especially on books with as many strange words and spellings as this one. The awesome cover art was created by Spanish artist Nekro. My ongoing appreciation goes to Michael Psaltis for all his work on my behalf.

Finally, all my thanks and my everlasting love to my wife, Mary Anne, who kept me sane when the project got crazy and for always being my number one fan, as I am hers. I love you most.